SWIMMERS GUIDE

DIRECTORY OF POOLS FOR FITNESS SWIMMERS

Bill Haverland

and

Tom Saunders

ALSA Publishing, Inc.
Stuart, Florida

Copyright © 1995 ALSA Publishing, Inc.
Second edition, first printing
Printed in the United States of America

1. **Publisher's Cataloging in Publication Data**
2. Haverland, Bill and Saunders, Tom
3. Swimmers Guide, Directory of Pools for Fitness Swimmers
4. 1, Swimming. 2, Travel.
5. 797.2'1
6. ISBN 0-9635960-1-2

ALSA Publishing, Inc.
P.O. Box 1064
Stuart, FL 34995
Phone & fax: (407) 288-3878

TABLE OF CONTENTS

ACKNOWLEDGMENTS

Finding pools, collecting information about them, and verifying the accuracy of our transcriptions required the assistance of thousands of public officials, association executives, pool operators, and individual swimmers. Without their assistance **Swimmers Guide** could not have been published. We thank them all for their help.

A few individuals made an extra effort to lend a hand, and we want to express special appreciation for their assistance —

- Laura K. Horn of Walnut Creek, California, sent us a long list of leads, several excellent suggestions on how to improve the book, and sports and health club reviews from a number of newspapers and magazines. Her leads resulted in 56 listings.

- John J. Harris of Columbia, Missouri, sent us several letters and at least a pound of photocopies of pool flyers that added 29 pools to the book.

- David Lewis of Juneau, Alaska, sent us pool names, addresses, and telephone numbers which resulted in 27 listings.

- Stephen R. Marian of Darien, Connecticut, sent us a letter, a book, magazine articles, and a YMCA brochure which gave us 19 listings.

- Masters swimmers Scott Rabalais of Baton Rouge, Louisiana, Betsy Owens of Albany, New York, and Jim Toedtman of Huntington, New York, were responsible for more than 30 pool and Masters listings.

Our sincere thanks to them and to the hundreds of other swimmers who took the time to help us make this the most complete directory of year-round pools ever compiled.

ABOUT SWIMMING

Swimming had its reputation as 'the perfect exercise' well before the fitness revolution of the '70s and '80s. And while thousands of books and videos have been sold promoting the health and fitness benefits of various forms of exercise, and billions of dollars have been spent on specialized exercise equipment, there is still no better way to get fit and to stay fit than to swim regularly.

Like any aerobic activity, swimming strengthens the heart, improves the blood's oxygen carrying capacity, promotes flexibility, and consumes calories at a prodigious rate.

But it is how swimming differs from other aerobic sports or exercise activities that makes it especially appealing:

- Swimming is a 'no impact' sport. It doesn't stress the bones, pound or twist the joints or damage the body.

- Swimming builds muscles. It broadens the shoulders and strengthens the abdomen, back, chest, arms, and legs.

- Swimming is usually done in safe, clean, regulated environments. There are no potholes, no pedestrian or automobile traffic, no traffic signals, no muggers, no rapists, no rain — and if you swim outdoors and it does rain, who cares?

- Interested in stress reduction? Swimming can bring you to a meditative state faster than anything short of hypnosis.

- Want to lose some weight? Body fat is buoyant in water, so an overweight person actually has an easier time taking up swimming than someone who's thin. And there's no stress on the ankles, knees, and hips, either!

- No reservations required. A quick swim can be squeezed into a busy schedule at just about any time of day.

- It can be competitive or contemplative.

- It can be learned at just about any stage of life and kept up well into old age.

- It can be safely continued into the late stages of pregnancy.

- It can be a social activity or a great way to get away from it all.

- It's inexpensive. All that's needed is a swim suit, goggles, and a pool. (You don't have to own the pool.)

- There's little gear to carry, and a swim suit doesn't have to be laundered after each use.

- And knowing that you'll be sharing a pool with some of the fittest and most attractive people around can be a real motivator for you to begin and maintain a healthy exercise routine.

From just about any point of view — physical and psychological benefits, cost, convenience, you name it — swimming is 'the perfect exercise'!

INTRODUCTION

Every day, in thousands of communities across the country, millions of Americans go to swimming pools to exercise and enjoy themselves. Some swim laps, some participate in aqua aerobics, water walking or water jogging. Others prepare for competitive Masters and triathlon events. Masters swimmers gather in groups to train together, adding a unique social dimension to what is usually seen as a highly individual activity.

But regardless of why they swim or how they go about it, swimmers have one thing in common — they need pools. They need them close to home, close to work, and they need to know where to find them when they travel.

Life-long lap swimmers and occasional travelers, we had long been aware of the difficulties swimmers encounter finding good pools, but it was not until we took an extended RV tour of the western United States in 1991, that we realized just how difficult finding a pool can be. And we decided to do something about it —

Armed with a couple of PCs, we set out to find a representative sample of year-round pools in several large communities. We wrote about 3,000 letters and came up with a list of nearly 1,200 facilities, which we published as the first edition of *Swimmers Guide* in 1993.

The first edition was a good start, but we knew there were many more pools that could have been included. We asked our readers to tell us about the pools where they swim. We sought leads from governmental authorities, parks and recreation associations, and Masters swimming groups. We gathered a collection of 31 hotel directories, and we requested the assistance of health club chains and affiliation groups. All told, we amassed a database of more than 7,400 addresses of places with pools.

We then mailed questionnaires to each of the 7,400 leads. About 700 replied, and Bally's Health & Tennis Corporation provided information on 200 of their locations. Those that responded, in combination with the 1,200 facilities in the first edition, would have made for a satisfactory second edition. But there were still more than 6,000 leads we had not heard from, and that was just not acceptable! So we picked up our telephones and started making calls. We spent two months on the phone and added 1,500 facilities.

Each facility added to the second edition of *Swimmers Guide* was then mailed a confirmation letter, which included a summary of the information we had about the pool and a request to be advised of any corrections that might be necessary. We also contacted each of the facilities listed in the first edition to confirm or update our information.

After mailing more than 10,000 letters and making nearly 5,000 telephone calls, we are proud to be able to present this compilation of information on more than 3,000 year-round swimming facilities in 1,700 communities in all 50 states and the District of Columbia.

LISTING CRITERIA:

Substantially all pools listed in *Swimmers Guide* meet the following criteria:

- Size:
  They are 20 or more yards long.

- Seasonality:
  They operate at least eight months of the year.

- Accessibility:
  They are accessible to the traveling public;

  or

  They are accessible to members of organizations likely to include large numbers of adult swimmers;

  or

  They have arrangements to admit guests registered at local hotels.

Swimmers traveling on business may find it difficult to go to a pool in a strange city after a busy day of meetings or sales calls, so we relaxed the length restriction to 50 feet for hotel pools. And if we found a club or a Y with an 18 meter (59 foot) pool, we threw it in too. But only 78 pools shorter than 20 yards have been included in the guide.

We inevitably found a few facilities that did not meet our accessibility criterion, many in areas where more accessible pools are likely to be crowded. Rather than keep the information to ourselves, we included 79 resident or member only facilities, with hopes that the information may be useful to a few swimmers.

None of the facilities listed in *Swimmers Guide* has paid any fee for inclusion in the directory. The decisions as to which pools to include or exclude from the guide and as to the content of each listing were made solely by the editors based on their perception of swimmers' needs.

HOW TO USE *SWIMMERS GUIDE*

ORGANIZATION:

Swimmers Guide listings are organized alphabetically by state; within each state, alphabetically by city; and within each city, numerically by ZIP code. Because there are so many listings in California, that state has been divided into two sections, California-Northern, and California-Southern.

Each section begins with a state map showing the names and locations of the cities where we found pools and the number of pools, if we found more than one. In areas near many major cities we found so many communities with pools that it was impossible to clearly label each one on the state maps. For those areas, the state maps include the name and number of pools only for the major city. Smaller scale area maps, with all communities labeled, follow the state maps.

Communities with more than ten listings have city maps near the beginning of the city's listings, with the general location of each pool marked by a numbered map point (dot). The dot numbers correspond to the numbers which precede the facilities' directory listings. In a few instances, two or more major cities located close to each other are shown in one map, which will be found at the beginning of the first city's listings.

Users should be aware that the placement of map points is by ZIP code, not by street address. The dots can be relied on only to give a general indication of the section or quadrant of the city in which the facilities are located. ZIP codes sometimes straddle the interstate highways and beltways which are shown on the maps as reference points; we know of several facilities whose dots appear on the wrong side of the nearby highway.

Before the first listing in each city is the name of the city followed by the telephone area code. New York City has been divided into its five boroughs. Los Angeles has been divided into two sections corresponding to its two telephone area codes.

LISTING INFORMATION:

A typical *Swimmers Guide* pool listing includes the following:

- The facility name and street address.

- One or more local telephone numbers for the facility or its operator. (Captioned 'Phone'.) For pools located in hotels, the hotel's toll free reservations phone number ('Reservations') is usually also provided.

- A description of the year-round swimming pool(s) at the facility. ('Pool' or 'Pool 1',

'Pool 2', if there is more than one qualifying pool at the location.)

- Single swim admission charges for unaccompanied, unaffiliated, non-member, adult visitors. ('Admission')

- Single swim charges for individuals entitled to use the facility at a reduced rate due to membership with an affiliated facility or organization. ('Affiliate')

- Single swim charges for hotel guests allowed to use the pool at a reduced rate. ('Hotel')

- Multiple swim pass rates for facilities which do not offer single swim admissions. ('Passes')

- Membership rates, also for facilities which do not offer single swim admissions. ('Memberships')

- The editors' observations on items of interest to swimmers which do not easily fall into any of the categories above. ('Notes')

- Directions to find the facility. ('To Find')

- Contact information for Masters swim groups which work out at the facility. ('Masters')

There are 126 Masters club listings which are formatted differently from the others. Seventy-seven of them are supplemental to an immediately preceding 'typical' listing. Masters listings include:

- The club name, the name of the pool where the club holds its workouts, and the pool's street address, if the pool is not separately listed.

- Telephone numbers for the pool ('Pool phone') and for the Masters club contact ('Masters').

- Single workout charges for unaffiliated visitors. ('Non-member participation')

- Single workout charges for members of affiliated groups. ('Affiliate')

- A description of the pool(s), if not described in an immediately preceding 'typical' listing. ('Pool')

- Workout schedules for a typical winter week, information about other facilities where the club works out, and anything else we thought might be helpful or interesting. ('Notes')

Irrespective of whether visiting non-Masters swimmers are permitted to join their workouts, most Masters clubs welcome local swimmers to participate in one or two sessions to see whether they would like to become members.

ADDITIONAL INFORMATION:
Following the last listing in the main directory, we have included a number of helpful appendices.

Appendix A is a table of pool length equivalents, lengths per mile, lengths per thousand yards, and lengths per thousand meters. The length of every listed pool has been converted from the measure in which it is shown in the listing to its equivalent length measured in feet, yards, or meters. The same chart also shows the number of lengths per mile, per thousand yards, and per thousand meters, both in 'precise' terms (to the 1/100th of a length) and in whole lengths.

Appendix B consists of fourteen cross-reference indices intended to help travelers locate particular types of listings. The indices are:

- Hotels with pools on-site. (251 listings in 190 cities in 41 states.)
- Non-hotel facilities which admit hotel guests at a discount. (445 listings in 362 cities in 49 states.)
- Cities with YMCAs which admit members of other YMCAs at a discount. (790 cities, at least one in each state.)
- Listings of interest to Masters swimmers. (562 listings in 447 cities in 49 states.)
- Clubs which admit members of International Health & Racquet Sportsclubs Association (IHRSA) affiliated clubs at a discount. (412 listings in 323 cities in 46 states.)
- Facilities which admit members of clubs operated by Bally's Health & Tennis Corp. or its subsidiaries (Bally's) at a discount. (186 listings in 160 cities in 27 states.)
- Cities with YWCAs and facilities which admit YWCA members at a discount. (151 listings in 147 cities in 35 states.)
- Clubs which admit members of International Physical Fitness Association (IPFA) affiliated clubs at a discount. (79 listings in 66 cities in 24 states.)
- U.S. Military facilities and facilities which admit members of the military at a discount. (49 listings in 47 cities in 20 states.)
- Jewish Community Centers (JCCs) and YM-YWHAs. (38 listings in 37 cities in 16 states.)

- Northwest Athletic Club Association (NACA) clubs and facilities which admit members of NACA clubs at a discount. (25 listings in 24 cities in 5 states.)
- Gold's Gyms and facilities which admit members of Gold's Gyms at a discount. (11 listings in 11 cities in 7 states.)
- Club Sports International (CSI) clubs and facilities which admit members of CSI clubs at a discount. (7 listings in 7 cities in 5 states.)
- Facilities which admit owners of the current edition of *Swimmers Guide* at a discount. (6 listings in 6 cities in 5 states.)

Appendix C is a list of the names and telephone numbers of some of the larger swimming supply mail order houses.

**LISTING CONTENTS
AND INTERPRETATIONS:**
Description:
To describe the pools, we attempted to collect data about the dimensions (length, width, and number of lap swimming lanes); whether the pool is indoors or outdoors; heated or unheated; and the water temperature or, for unheated pools, the range of water temperatures experienced over the course of a year.

Dimensions:
We define the length of a pool as the 'lap length', the longest distance that a swimmer can usually travel, in a straight line, without having to overcome any obstacles (ropes, partitions, etc.), and with vertical pool walls at either end (no staircase or 'beach type' entries across one end of the pool).

The 'standard' pool, if there is such a thing, is usually 25 yards long by 42 feet wide, with six lap lanes; our description of the dimensions of that pool would be '25y x 42f, 6 lanes'.

Many pools, particularly 50 meter by 25 yard pools, are routinely configured for 'long course' swimming (eight 50 meter lanes) in spring and summer, and short course swimming (as many as twenty-two 25 yard lanes) in fall and winter. We describe such a pool as '50m x 25y, 8 x 22 lanes'. If the same pool is always configured for short course swimming the description would be '25y x 50m, 22 lanes'.

A 50 meter pool that is 25 yards wide for part of its length and 25 meters for the rest, sometimes configured for 50 meter swimming and sometimes configured for 25 yard and 25 meter swimming, is described as '50m x 25y + 25m, 8 x 22 lanes'.

A 50 meter by 20 yard pool with a moveable bulkhead to divide the 50 meter length into two 25 yard by 20 yard sections is described '50m OR 25y + 25y x 20y, 8 OR 16 lanes'. A 50 meter by 20 yard pool permanently divided into two 25 meter sections would be described '25m + 25m x 20y, 16 lanes'.

Hotel pool dimension descriptions are usually limited to length and general shape, as an indication of the pools' suitability for your type of swimming workout.

Indoor v. Outdoor v. Indoor/outdoor:

'Indoor' and 'outdoor' are simple and descriptive terms. 'Indoor/outdoor' has a number of variations in meaning: Some have sliding walls; some have walls that retract to the ceiling; some have sliding roofs that can be opened or closed; and others have inflatable bubble covers that are erected or removed seasonally. We describe all of these simply as 'indoor/outdoor' pools.

Heated v. Unheated v. Temperature Controlled:

All of the indoor pools in **Swimmers Guide** are heated, and most indoor pool operators try to maintain a uniform temperature throughout the year. A wide range of temperatures for an indoor pool (more than 2° or 3°) may indicate that there are periodic temperature adjustments. (In one case, the temperature is adjusted daily to accommodate participants in that day's scheduled programs.)

Outdoor pools can be heated, unheated, temperature controlled (heated in winter, cooled in summer) or heated in winter but not in summer.

Some respondents were unable to tell us the range of temperatures experienced over the course of a year at their unheated pools. Living in Florida, we take a few of the replies of those who could with a grain of salt. The water in one Miami Beach pool where we used to swim would often drop to the low 60s for brief periods in winter, and by late May, would already be in the high 80s. (Winter water temperatures in Miami are usually in the mid-70s, or warmer; summer water temperatures rarely fall below 85°.)

Outdoor, heated pools are often heated only in winter. It's likely summer temperatures will be different from those reported here.

If water temperature is as important to you as it is to us, call before going to an outdoor pool in summer or to an indoor pool that reports a wide temperature variation.

Admission Policies and Rates:

Although conceived as a travel directory for adult swimmers, **Swimmers Guide** can be equally useful to those looking for good pools close to their homes and workplaces.

Because they often have less time available, however, we concentrated on collecting information that will enable traveling swimmers to narrow their search to facilities they are most likely to be able to use during a short visit.

Most of the facilities that charge an admission also have some form of membership available. Many offer passes (ticket books, punch cards, and the like) valid for a specific number of visits. To keep **Swimmers Guide** portable, we generally excluded membership and pass rates for facilities which had an 'Admission', 'Affiliate', or 'Hotel' rate, although exceptions were made for hotel and college facilities, and in a few other selected instances where we felt the information would be useful to local swimmers.

Admission:

We avoided describing admission rates as *general* admission because many of the private facilities (including community service organizations, such as YMCAs, YWCAs, and JCCs) permit out-of-town visitors single swim access, but require local residents to become members to use their pools.

Affiliate:

We asked every facility listed in **Swimmers Guide** for any special rates offered to members of affiliated facilities and groups, and have included that information, together with any applicable restrictions, under the affiliate caption.

Some facilities which have affiliate rates, but no 'Admission' entry, may have memberships available to out-of-town visitors for periods as short as three days.

Hotel:

More than 400 of the pools listed give preferential admission to guests registered at nearby hotels. If a pool offers a deal to hotel guests, we've included as much information about the arrangement as we could obtain.

Passes:

Multiple swim pass rates are shown for a very limited number of facilities. The usual format used to describe a pass arrangement is 'A swims [for] **$X**'. If passes are available for differing numbers of swims, you'll see '**A/B swims $X/$Y**', short for 'A swims for $X, B swims for $Y.'

Memberships:

Some private, membership-based facilities may require applicants to be sponsored by a current member and/or approved by a membership committee. The inclusion of information about private club memberships does not mean everyone willing to pay the necessary fees is automatically accepted.

The absence of a membership or pass rate in a **Swimmers Guide** listing should not be taken to mean that none is available.

Abbreviations and Conventions:

SC   indicates that the rate which follows is a Senior Citizen rate. The number in parenthesis following 'SC' is the minimum age to qualify for the rate.

NC   means there is no charge for admission.

Call   means that we were unable to determine the applicable rate. Swimmers should call.

I/S   is used for membership rates only and is short for 'initiation or sign-up' fees.

A reference to a particular number of admissions indicates a limit, for example, '3 visits per month NC' means that you will only be permitted to use the facility three times a month at no charge. Many of the facilities we contacted indicated a willingness to make special arrangements for visitors who may be staying in the area for a short time.

To Find:

The directions printed in **Swimmers Guide** were provided by the listed facilities and have been reproduced nearly verbatim from our respondents' directions. Some of them seem a bit unclear, but we were reluctant to make changes figuring they may be perfectly understandable to someone in the area. We recommend you clarify the directions when you call, before your first visit.

Masters:

In addition to the 126 Masters entries, more than 400 other listings include information on how to reach Masters groups which swim at their facilities. Many of the Masters contacts are volunteers who have been kind enough to permit us to publish their names and private home '(h)' or work '(w)' telephone numbers for your benefit. The staff at most of the pools in whose listings these names and numbers appear will be able to provide basic information on the groups' workouts and times. They may also be able to inform you of any changes in contact names and phone numbers. In order to minimize unnecessary interruptions of the contacts' work days or home lives, if the pool's phone number is included in a listing, please call the pool first.

If the pool can't help you out, by all means call the Masters contact, but be considerate when you do. Call a few days in advance, so your call can be returned, if necessary. Keep time zone differences in mind if you call long distance. If your call is answered by a spouse, a coworker, or an answering machine, leave a clear message and include your name, phone number (including the area code), and best times to reach you.

USEFUL INFORMATION

TRAVEL TIPS:

When planning a trip, refer to Appendix B to see if there's a hotel in your price range near your destination. Even if the hotel's pool is a bit smaller than you'd like or not just the right temperature, you'll be much more likely to be able to get in a swim when the pool is only an elevator ride away.

Also check the list of non-hotel facilities which offer preferred admission to local hotel guests. The pool will usually be close to the hotel, often within walking distance.

Some facilities, particularly municipal pools in large cities, may be located in areas you wouldn't knowingly go. Hotel staff, car rental agency personnel or other locals should be able to help you avoid areas where crime risk may be a factor in your pool selection decision.

Get yourself a nylon, competition style swim suit for travel. They're fast drying, light, and take almost no space. They're also usually cheaper and last longer than Lycra® suits. Since Lycra became popular, nylon suits have become harder to find, but are still available by mail order. See the list of mail order swimming suppliers in Appendix C.

Before you go:

Before you go to any facility listed in *Swimmers Guide*, **always call first**. Pools close, they change names, affiliations, admission policies, and rates. And just because a pool is listed in this guide doesn't mean it's open all day, every day, for just the type of swimming you want to do.

A 25¢ investment in a telephone call can save you a lot of time and aggravation.

When you go:

Many of the facilities listed in *Swimmers Guide* require visitors to present a photo ID at check-in. Even some municipal pools require all adult visitors to show a driver license or other proof of identity to get in.

If you expect to gain access to a pool on the basis of your membership in an affiliated facility or organization, you'll need to bring proof of your affiliation, too. We've included a few words about the affiliate admission requirements we are aware of in the Appendix, but we're not experts on the subject. Your home facility can give you better information about the general requirements of your affiliation group; specific requirements at the facility you'll be visiting should be confirmed when you call.

When you get there:

Before you jump in the water, check with the lifeguard to find out the best part of the pool to use for your workout, and ask about regulations covering the types of equipment you like to use. If you're a lap swimmer, inquire about swimming patterns and lane sharing requirements.

We've found that if you spend a moment with the guard, he or she may keep an eye out for you, shooing away playful kids and inconsiderate adults before they interrupt your workout.

PICKING A PLACE TO SWIM AT HOME:

If you travel a lot, your decision on where to swim at home may be influenced by the access your membership will give you to pools in the areas where you travel. Members of YMCAs and IHRSA clubs have access to the largest number of facilities listed in *Swimmers Guide*, but the geographical distribution of affiliated facilities may also be important. The lists in Appendix B will help make the decision that's best for you.

Some facilities offer a variety of levels of membership. The less expensive memberships often have restrictions on the times of the day or days of the week you can use the facility. If you're considering a limited access membership, be sure to find out whether this will impact your ability to visit affiliated facilities when you travel. The savings you make at home on a limited access membership can be more than eaten up by additional guest fees on the road.

POOL FINDING TIPS:

In the unlikely event that you find yourself in a community which doesn't have a pool listed in *Swimmers Guide* and you've checked the maps to be sure there are no listings nearby, ask the concierge or front desk manager at your hotel whether he or she knows of any good pools. Look in the local telephone book and call the nearest YMCA, YWCA or JCC. If they don't have a pool of their own, they may be able to tell you where to find one. In the government listings, call the county and city departments of parks and recreation. Also check the yellow pages under the listings for health clubs, gyms, and swimming instruction. In some areas, phone books have community interest sections which may aim you to a local municipal or public school pool. A nearby college or university may also have public access.

In your home town there may be a college or university pool you've tried to get into, only to be told that access is restricted to 'students, faculty, staff and alumni'. If you gave up because you didn't go to school there, get in touch with the alumni association. We found a few colleges that let members of the alumni association use the athletic facilities but don't require members to have graduated from (or even have attended) the school. An annual contribution to the association is all that's required.

PUBLICATIONS, PRODUCTS, AND ITEMS OF INTEREST:

The Complete Book of Swimming:

Swimmers Guide is intended to answer questions about where to swim; for the most up-to-date and readable book on the 'whys' and 'hows' of swimming, pick up a copy of Dr. Phillip Whitten's *The Complete Book of Swimming* (Random House, 1994).

If you learned to swim more than ten years ago and haven't kept up with the swimming world, Dr. Whitten's book will update you on developments over the past few years that have made swimming faster and and more efficient. It includes valuable tips for improving your strokes no matter what your level of swimming ability.

You'll be interested in the information he presents about swimming and health, swimming and longevity, and especially the chapter titled 'Swimming and Sexuality: How to Enhance Your Love Life.'

And if you're tired of reading health and fitness articles about body fat percentages which don't give you a clue how they're calculated, *The Complete Book of Swimming* not only tells you how to determine your own percentage of body fat, but has easy to use estimating charts based only on sex, weight, and waist size!

It's a good read with plenty of information you'll want to refer back to again and again.

SWIM Magazine:

A magazine targeted to adult swimmers is *SWIM Magazine*. Published bi-monthly, *SWIM* is the official publication of United States Masters Swimming and a subscription is included in the membership dues. As of January, 1995, a one year subscription for non-USMS members was $16.95 ($23.95 for non-U.S. subscriptions). For subscription orders call 800-345-7946 or 310-607-9956 Ext. 103.

Masters Swimming:

We've made several references to Masters swimming in the previous sections, without saying much about what it is. Masters programs are organized fitness swimming programs for adults.

Participants range in age from 19 to the 90s. Some are just interested in swimming for fitness, others are world class competitors and triathletes. There are Masters groups with professional swimming coaches who conduct structured and rigorous workouts, and there are groups that simply get together for lap swimming and mutual encouragement.

The YMCA operates a large Masters program. United States Masters Swimming (USMS) provides an administrative structure for more than 450 independent Masters Swim Clubs with nearly 30,000 members. Many YMCA Masters programs are also affiliated with USMS.

For information, call the Masters contact at the listing nearest you or write to: United States Masters Swimming Inc., 2 Peter Avenue, Rutland, Massachusetts 01543.

The 'Sports Chamois':

If you've ever watched a collegiate or Olympic competition, you probably noticed divers using what looks like a small rag to dry themselves. It's not a rag, it's a sports chamois, a highly absorbent, synthetic foam and fabric substitute for a towel. It's designed to be kept moist in its carrying tube, so you don't have to hang it out to dry every day, and it doesn't require frequent laundering either.

We've seen two types: 'The Sammy' (also available under a variety of other brand names) is 13" by 17" and comes in a tube 7" long and 3" in diameter. A larger version, called the 'Swimmers Towel', is 26" by 16.5", comes in a 9" long tube, and is sold in Champs Sports® sporting goods stores. The Sammy is available through most of the swimming mail order houses listed in Appendix C. For the address of the Champs Sports outlet nearest you, call 800-766-8272.

What we like best about the sports chamois is that you can roll up a wet men's competition style swim suit in it, stick it back in its tube, and pack it in your bag, briefcase or an overcoat pocket without getting anything else wet. Women will probably need the larger version, but men can use either. They're great for travel!

Getting The Water Out:

After a good swim, or even just a shower, a few drops of water in the ear canal can really be maddening. If not removed, bacterial growth can lead to that annoying infection called swimmers ear. Using a cotton swab to remove the water can aggravate the situation.

To solve the problem, pick up an 'ear wax removal system' from your local drug store. Use the small tear-drop shaped rubber bulb that comes as part of the system to send a little air into the ear canal. The air breaks the capillary action of the water, and what doesn't come out with the air will shake out easily.

Corrective Lens Goggles:

Bill wears Barracuda® goggles with corrective lenses fitted by Dr. Michael J.J. O'Brien, Jr., O.D., Inc., in San Pedro, California. (Phone 310-832-1348.) They're not cheap, but they're ground to prescription and they make swimming a lot more enjoyable.

vju® (pronounced 'view') goggles are sold with pre-ground corrective lenses ranging from -1.5 to -7.5 diopters, in 0.5 diopter increments. They can be purchased with different corrections for each eye. Call 800-647-0888 for information.

Speedo®, Arena®, and other manufacturers' pre-ground corrective lens goggles are available from some of the mail order suppliers in Appendix C.

USAmateur™:

USAmateur is a travel discount program. If you travel to amateur sporting events, meetings, camps or clinics, membership benefits can include significant airfare savings and in some cases equipment, e.g., a bicycle, flies free. Whether the travel is sports related or not, members get discounts on Alamo® car rentals and up to 50% off room rates at 2,400 hotels and resorts. For information, call 800-USA-1992.

Provincetown Swim for Life:

In our search for Masters groups to include in the guide, we wrote to the sponsors of a number of adult swimming events. One group wasn't able to help us find a listing, but did send us a nice note asking that we mention the event. So we will...

The Provincetown Swim for Life is a 1.4 mile, open water swim held annually on the Saturday after Labor Day in Provincetown, Massachusetts. The event is organized to raise funds for the Provincetown Positive People with AIDS Coalition and the AIDS Support Group. It is open to competitive and non-competitive swimmers. For information and pledge forms write: Provincetown Swim for Life, P.O. Box 819, Provincetown, MA, 02657; or call 508-487-3684. If you can't participate, send a check anyway.

HELP US HELP YOU

Tell us about any errors you find:

A lot of time and effort was expended to ensure that the information in *Swimmers Guide* is accurate. But we will inevitably have made errors, some serious, in preparing it. If we've printed an incorrect address or telephone number, included a facility that doesn't have a pool (that happened twice in the first edition), or given other seriously misleading information, we want to know about it, and we want to be able to alert our readers. But we can't do that unless you tell us about the 'screw-ups' you find, and let us know how to reach you.

If you find a mistake, a serious omission or if you become aware of a significant change other swimmers should know about, drop us a line and tell us about it.

Our address is:

Swimmers Guide
P.O. Box 1064
Stuart, Florida 34995

Or send a fax to:
407-288-3878

Or tell us by e-mail at:
swimmerg@aol.com

To be informed about errors, omissions, and significant changes to the listing data, send us your name and mailing address.

Help us improve the guide:

Readers of the the first edition of the guide were not shy about telling us what they liked and didn't like about it. Most of the suggestions they made have been incorporated into this edition. If you think *Swimmers Guide* can be improved, tell us how.

Help us find more pools:

Hundreds of the pools listed in this edition of *Swimmers Guide* came from swimmers who bought the first edition of the guide and took the trouble to send a card or a letter to tell us about the places where they swim. We'd like to hear from you.

We're particularly interested in improving the coverage of Alabama, Arkansas,

Georgia, Kentucky, Louisiana, Mississippi, New Jersey, Long Island (New York), Oklahoma, South Carolina, Tennessee, Texas, and West Virginia.

We'd also like to increase the number of listed hotels, colleges, independent private health clubs, and public pools, all of which are difficult to locate. But we'll gladly accept any kind of facility you tell us about, as long as it meets the criteria of size, accessibility, and length of operating season mentioned on page six.

Please do not tell us about condominium, home owners association, company fitness center or college facilities unless unaccompanied 'outsiders' are admitted on a regular basis, either as 'drop-ins' or for membership. And to keep the guide a manageable size, pools you tell us about should be open to the public more than just a day or two a week.

If you're the first to tell us about an unlisted facility that we include in the third edition, we'll send you a free copy of the new guide before it reaches the bookstores.

At a minimum, we need the name of the facility and its area code and telephone number. If possible, also include the street address, a description of the pool, and a contact name and title, so we can independently verify the information.

Spread the word:

Finding pools, collecting information about them, and publishing the results in *Swimmers Guide* has been a lot of fun. But it's also been expensive. The postage, stationery, long distance telephone, computer hardware and software, printing, and marketing and promotion expenses involved approach six figures. It has taken us three years of full-time work to gather and bring this information to you.

If you think *Swimmers Guide* is a worthwhile publication, please tell your friends about it. If you borrowed a copy from a friend, a library or a Masters club, go out and buy a copy for yourself.

If you can't find a copy at your local bookstore, see the last page for ordering information.

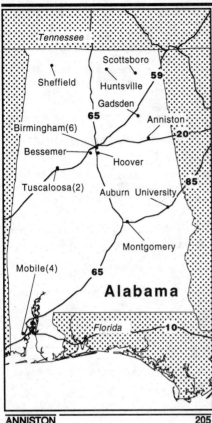

ANNISTON 205

CALHOUN COUNTY YMCA 29 W. 14th St.
Phone: 238-9622.
Pool: 25y x 30f, 4 lanes, indoors, heated, 85°.
Admission: $5.
Affiliate: Y AWAY 3 days NC, then $2.
Hotel: Ramada Inn (237-9777) & Victoria Inn (236-0503): NC with room key and a pass from the hotel.

AUBURN UNIVERSITY 334

JAMES E. MARTIN AQUATICS CENTER Auburn University, Biggio Dr.
Phone: 844-4182.
Pool 1: 77y x 25y, 8 x 22-28 lanes, usually configured as two 25y or 25m pools + diving well, indoors, heated, 80°.
Pool 2: 25y, 7 lanes, indoors, heated, 82°.
Admission: $2.
Memberships: $50/quarter.
Notes: The 25y pool is located in an attached building.
To find: One block southwest of the football stadium, next to the gymnasium.
Masters: The Auburn Masters. Contact Charlie Hendrix at 844-2688(w) or 821-0532(h).

BESSEMER 205

BESSEMER AREA YMCA 1501 - 4th Ave. S.W.
Phone: 426-1211.
Pool: 25y, 5 lanes, indoors, heated, 83°-85°.
Affiliate: YMCA 1 visit NC, then $3.

BIRMINGHAM 205

DOWNTOWN CENTER YMCA 321 N. 21st St.
Phone: 324-4563.
Pool: 25y x 36f, 6 lanes, indoors, heated, 82°-84°.
Admission: 3 visits per year $5 each.
Affiliate: Out-of-town YMCA 10 visits per year NC.
Hotel: All Birmingham area hotels $5 with room key.

SHADES VALLEY FAMILY YMCA 3551 Montgomery Hwy.
Phone: 871-7372.
Pool: 25y x 44f, 6 lanes, indoors, heated, 86°.
Admission: $7, photo ID required.
Affiliate: Y AWAY NC. YMCA $3.

FIVE POINTS SOUTH YMCA 1911 - 10th Ave. S.
Phone: 324-1643.
Pool: 25y x 30f, 4 lanes, indoors, heated, 85°.
Admission: $3.
Affiliate: Out-of-town YMCA 12 visits per year NC.
Hotel: Pickwick Hotel (933-9555) & University Inn (933-7700): NC with room key.

SPORTSLIFE - VESTAVIA 2086 Columbiana Rd.
Phone: 823-0144.
Pool: 25y, indoor/outdoor, heated, 86°.
Admission: Call.
Affiliate: IHRSA $5.

SPORTSLIFE - BIRMINGHAM 2401 - 20th Place S.
Phone: 870-0144.
Pool: 25y, indoor/outdoor, heated, 70°.
Admission: Call.
Affiliate: IHRSA Call.

SPORTSPLEX SOUTH 4766 Hwy. 280 S.
Phone: 980-1077.
Pool: 20m, indoor/outdoor, heated, 80°.
Admission: $5.

GADSDEN 205

GADSDEN-ETOWAH COUNTY YMCA 100 Walnut St.
Phone: 547-4947.
Pool: 25y x 39f, 5 lanes, indoors, heated, 84°.
Admission: $4.
Affiliate: Y AWAY NC. YMCA $2.
Masters: Alabama Star Swimming at Gadsden. Contact Lance Bezek at 547-4947.

HOOVER   205

SPORTSPLEX HOOVER 3447 Lorna Rd.
Phone: 822-8763.
Pool: 20m, indoor/outdoor, heated, 84°.
Affiliate: IHRSA $5.

HUNTSVILLE   205

BRAHAN SPRING NATATORIUM 2213 Drake Ave.
Phone: 883-3700.
Pool: 25y x 50m, 9 lanes, indoor/outdoor, heated, 83°.
Admission: $2, SC(65) & Disabled $1.
To find: Off Drake Ave., one mile west of Memorial Pkwy.

MOBILE   334

RAMADA INN CONFERENCE CENTER 600 S. Beltline Hwy.
Phone: 344-8030. **Reservations:** 800-752-0398.
Pool: 25m, rectangular, indoors, heated, 86°.
Admission: Registered guests only NC.

SPORTSPLEX MOBILE 6400 Piccadilly Square Dr.
Phone: 342-1777.
Pool: 25m, indoor/outdoor, heated, 80°-82°.
Admission: $10.
Affiliate: IHRSA $5.

CHANDLER BRANCH YMCA 951 Downtowner Blvd.
Phone: 344-4856.
Pool: 25m, 6 lanes, indoors, heated, 83°-86°.
Affiliate: YMCA NC.

MASTERS OF MOBILE at Pro Health, Mobile Infirmary Dr.
Masters: Contact Aquatics Coordinator Anne Marie Simms at 431-2010(w).
Pool: 25y x 51f, 3 lanes, indoors, heated, 86°.
Non-member participation: $6.
Notes: Workouts: Tu,Th: 6:30-7:30PM.

MONTGOMERY   334

MONTGOMERY EAST YMCA 3407 Pelzer Ave.
Phone: 272-3390.
Pool: 25y x 60f, 8 lanes, indoors, heated, 82°-86°.
Admission: 1 visit $5.
Affiliate: YMCA outside a 50 mile radius $2.

MONTGOMERY YMCA BARRACUDA MASTERS at Montgomery East YMCA
Pool phone: 272-3390. **Masters:** Contact Rick Harris at 263-3902(h) or 613-5383(w).
Non-member participation: Call.
Notes: Coached workouts: M,W: 7:05-8:05PM. Sa: 7-8AM. Uncoached workouts: M-F: 11:30AM-1PM.

SCOTTSBORO   205

SCOTTSBORO PARKS & RECREATION DEPT. 701 S. Houston St.
Phone: 259-0999.
Pool: 25y x 30f, 8 lanes, indoors, heated, 84°-86°.
Admission: $2, SC(62) $1.
To find: One block north of City Hall.

SHEFFIELD   205

SHEFFIELD INDOOR POOL 2901 - 19th Ave.
Phone: 386-5615.
Pool: 25m x 40f, 6 lanes, indoors, heated, 83°.
Admission: $1.50.
Notes: There is also a 35y, outdoor pool operated from Jun. through Aug.
To find: Across the Street from Sheffield High School.

TUSCALOOSA   205

YMCA OF TUSCALOOSA COUNTY 2405 Paul W. Bryant Dr.
Phone: 345-9622.
Pool: 25y, 4 lanes, indoors, heated, 82°-86°.
Admission: $7.
Affiliate: YMCA NC.

UNIVERSITY OF ALABAMA AQUATIC CENTER Hackberry Lane & Paul W. Bryant Dr.
Phone: 348-6156.
Pool 1: 25y x 50m, 17 x 8 lanes, indoors, heated, 82°.
Pool 2: 25y x 50f, 8 lanes, indoors, heated, 82°.
Memberships: $185/year. $70/semester.

BAMA MASTERS SWIM CLUB at the University of Alabama Aquatic Center
Masters: Contact Frances Bell or Garry Warren at 348-6155.
Affiliate: USMS $2, includes pool fees.
Notes: Coached workouts: M-F: Noon-1PM, 5:30-7PM. Sa: 10:30AM-Noon.

Alaska

Fairbanks(4)
North Pole
Nome
Anchorage(11)
Fort Richardson   Palmer(2)
Nikiski   Eagle River   Haines
Soldotna(2)
Juneau
Seward   Valdez   Hoonah   Petersburg
Naknek   Homer Cordova   Wrangell
Unalaska
Kodiak   Sitka(2)   Ketchikan

ANCHORAGE   907

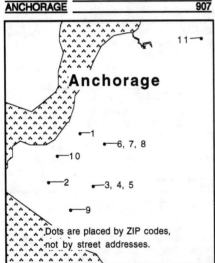

Anchorage

—1
—6, 7, 8
—10
—2   —3, 4, 5
—9
11—

Dots are placed by ZIP codes, not by street addresses.

1. HOTEL CAPTAIN COOK 5th at 'K' St.
Phone: 276-6000. **Reservations:** 800-323-7500.
Pool: 17y, indoors, heated, 84°.
Admission: Registered guests only NC.

2. DIMOND POOL 2909 W. 88th Ave.
Phone: Parks & Rec. Dept: 343-4293. Pool: 249-0355 after 5 PM.
Pool: 25y x 25y, 'L' shape, indoors, heated, 85°-86°.
Admission: $4.25, SC(62) & Disabled $2.75.
To find: In Dimond High School, between Jewel Lake Rd. and Arlene.

3. THE ALASKA CLUB 5201 E. Tudor Rd.
Phone: 337-9550.
Pool: 25y, 6 lanes, indoors, heated, 83°.
Affiliate: IHRSA $10.
To find: Near the intersection of Tudor Rd. and Boniface Pkwy.
Masters: The Alaska Club Masters. Contact Monte Lyons at 337-9550.

4. ANCHORAGE COMMUNITY YMCA 5353 Lake Otis Pkwy.
Phone: 563-3211 ext. 116.
Pool: 25m, 6 lanes, indoors, heated, 83°.
Admission: $8.
Affiliate: YMCA NC.
Masters: The Anchorage Community YMCA Masters. Contact Program Director David Alan Widick at 563-3211.

5. SERVICE POOL 5577 Abbott Rd.
Phone: Parks & Rec. Dept: 343-4293. Pool: 346-3040 after 5 PM.
Pool: 25m, 6 lanes, indoors, heated, 85°.
Admission: $4.25, SC(62) & Disabled $2.75.
To find: In Service High School.

6. MOSELEY SPORTS CENTER Alaska Pacific University, 4101 University Dr.
Phone: 564-8314.
Pool: 25y x 27f, 6 lanes, indoors, heated, 82°.
Admission: $3.25.
Memberships: $80/semester.
To find: East of Providence Hospital on Providence Dr. and University Dr.

7. UNIVERSITY OF ALASKA AT ANCHORAGE 3211 Providence Dr.

ANCHORAGE   CONTINUED

Phone: 786-1231.
Pool: 25y x 25m, 6 lanes, 'L' shape, indoors, heated, 80°-82°.
Admission: $4, SC(60) $2.50.
To find: Near Lake Otis Pkwy. and Providence Dr.

8. EAST POOL 4025 E. 24th Ave.
Phone: Parks & Rec. Dept: 343-4293. Pool: 278-9761 after 5 PM.
Pool: 25y x 25m, 'L' shape, indoors, heated, 86°.
Admission: $4.25, SC(62) & Disabled $2.75.
To find: In East High School, the parking lot is off Bragaw.

9. DIAMOND ATHLETIC CLUB 800 E. Diamond Blvd., Suite 3-030
Phone: 344-7788.
Pool: 20y x 24f 4in, indoors, heated, 82°-85°.
Admission: $10.

10. WEST POOL 1700 Hillcrest Dr.
Phone: Parks & Rec. Dept: 343-4293. Pool: 274-5161 after 5 PM.
Pool: 25y, 6 lanes, indoors, heated, 84°-85°.
Admission: $4.25, SC(62) & Disabled $2.75.
To find: In West High School, between Minnesota and Forrest Park Dr.

11. BARTLETT 50 METER SWIMMING POOL 25-500 Muldoon Rd.
Phone: Parks & Rec. Dept: 343-4293. Pool: 337-6375 after 5PM.
Pool: 50m OR 25y + 25y x 20y, 8 OR 16 lanes, indoors, heated, 85°.
Admission: $4.25, SC(62) & Disabled $2.75.
To find: North Muldoon Exit off the Glenn Hwy. Next to the Elmendorf Hospital.
Masters: The Bartlett Pool Competitive Swimming Club. Contact John Zell at 337-6375.

CORDOVA   907

BOB KORN MEMORIAL POOL Next to City Hall
Phone: 424-7200.
Pool: 25y, indoors, heated, 74°-75°.
Admission: Lap swimming $4.

EAGLE RIVER   907

CHUGIAK POOL S. Birchwood Loop
Phone: Parks & Rec. Dept: 343-4293. Pool: 696-2010 after 4PM.
Pool: 25y x 25m, 'L' shape, indoors, heated, 85°.
Admission: $4.25. Tu & Th $2.50. SC(62) & Disabled $2.75. SC Sep. to Jun: M-F 6-7AM NC.
To find: At Chugiak High School.

FAIRBANKS   907

FAIRBANKS ATHLETIC CLUB 747 Old Richards Hwy.

Phone: 452-6801.
Pool: 25y, 6 lanes, indoors, heated, 85°.
Affiliate: IHRSA $5.
Hotel: Sophies Station Hotel (479-3650) & WestMark Hotel (456-7722): Purchase passes for $8 at the hotel.
To find: East of downtown on the Old Richardson Hwy., near the Sunset Inn.

HAMME SWIMMING POOL 901 Airport Way
Phone: 459-1086.
Pool: 25m x 45f, 6 lanes, indoors, heated, 84°.
Admission: $3, SC(60) $1.
To find: Between Ryan Middle School and Lathrop High School.

MARY SIAH RECREATION CENTER 1025 - 14th Ave.
Phone: 459-1081.
Pool: 25y x 25f, 4 lanes, indoors, heated, 86°.
Admission: $3, SC(60) $1.
To find: Across the street from Lathrop High School.

PATTY GYM POOL Student Recreation Complex, University of Alaska at Fairbanks
Phone: 474-7205.
Pool: 25y x 45f, 6 lanes, indoors, heated, 82°.
Admission: $5.
Memberships: $900/year.
Notes: The pool closes in May for cleaning & repairs.

FORT RICHARDSON   907

BUCKNER PHYSICAL FITNESS CENTER SWIMMING POOL Bldg. #690 'D' St.
Phone: 384-1301/2.
Pool: 25y x 49f, 6.5 lanes, indoors, heated, 84°.
Affiliate: U.S. Military & family: NC.

HAINES   907

HAINES POOL 1/2 Mile Haines Hwy.
Phone: 766-2666.
Pool: 25y x 30f, 6 lanes, indoors, heated, 86°.
Admission: $3, SC(60) $1.50.
To find: The pool is attached to Haines High School.

HOMER   907

HOMER HIGH SCHOOL POOL 600 E. Fairview Ave.
Phone: 235-7416.
Pool: 25y, indoors, heated, 84°.
Passes: 10 swims $30.

HOONAH   907

HOONAH CITY SCHOOLS POOL Garteeni Hwy.
Phone: 945-3611 or 945-9911.
Pool: 25y x 45f, 5 lanes, indoors, heated, 86°.

Admission: $1.50, SC(65) NC.
To find: Beside the school, the driveway is located off Raven Dr.

JUNEAU 907

AUGUSTUS BROWN POOL 1619 Glacier Ave.
Phone: 586-5325.
Pool: 25y x 45f, 6 lanes, indoors, heated, 82°.
Admission: $3-$3.50, SC(65) $1.25-$1.75, based on duration of swim.
Notes: There is also a 45f x 35f, indoor, 90°, therapy pool.
To find: Next to Juneau-Douglas High School.
Masters: Contact Mike Williams at 586-5325.

KETCHIKAN 907

KAYHI POOL 2610 - 7th Ave.
Phone: 225-2010.
Pool: 25y x 45f, 6 lanes, indoors, heated, 81°.
Admission: $5, SC(55) $2.50.
Affiliate: U.S. Military, U.S. Coast Guard & families with ID: NC.
To find: Up the hill from the school.
Masters: The Ketchikan Master Swim Club. Contact Bev Zaugg at 225-2089(h).

KODIAK 907

KODIAK HIGH SCHOOL POOL Rezonoff St.
Phone: 486-8665 or 486-9263.
Pool: 25y, indoors, heated, 80°.
Admission: $2, SC(65) $1.

NAKNEK 907

KVIMARVIK POOL Alaska Peninsula Hwy.
Phone: 246-7665.
Pool: 25y x 30f, 4 lanes, indoors, heated, 83°.
Admission: Residents $3, non-residents $5. SC(60) NC.
To find: The pool is across the street from the public school and next to the health clinic.

NIKISKI 907

NIKISKI POOL Pool Side Ave. at Mile 23.4 on Spur Hwy.
Phone: 776-8800.
Pool: 25y, 6 lanes, indoors, heated, 84°.
Admission: Residents NC, non-residents $3.
To find: Spur Hwy. through Kenai to Captain Cook Park, about 12 miles.

NOME 907

NOME-BELTZ POOL Nome-Teller Rd.
Phone: 443-5717.
Pool: 25m, indoors, heated, 84°.
Admission: $4, SC(55) $2.50.

NORTH POLE 907

WESCOTT POOL 8th Ave.
Phone: Recording: 488-9401. Information: 488-9402.
Pool: 25y x 25m, indoors, heated, 83°.
Admission: $3.

PALMER 907

MAT-SU (MATANUSKA-SUSITNA) BOROUGH COMMUNITY POOL Arctic/Hemmer Rd.
Phone: Recorded schedule: 745-5091.
Information: 745-0207.
Pool: 100f, a bulkhead is set at 25y during lap swims, indoors, heated, 84°.
Admission: $4, SC(55) $2.75.
To find: From Glen Hwy., turn left onto Arctic, go one half mile to Palmer High School.

WASILLA POOL Bogard Rd.
Phone: 373-6897.
Pool: 25m, indoors, heated, 85°.
Admission: $4.
To find: The pool is connected to Wasilla High School on Bogard Rd. at Cruesey Rd.
Masters: The Mat-Su Masters. Contact Debby Jones at 376-7286(h).

PETERSBURG 907

MELVIN ROUNDTREE MEMORIAL POOL
Elementary School Building, Dolphin St.
Phone: 772-3304.
Pool: 25y x 45f, 6 lanes, indoors, heated, 84°.
Admission: $2.50.
To find: Behind the elementary school, three blocks from The Trading Union.

SEWARD 907

SEWARD JUNIOR / SENIOR HIGH SCHOOL POOL
Phone: 224-3900.
Pool: 25y x 43f, 6 lanes, indoors, heated, 84°.
Admission: $3, SC(60) $1.50.
To find: At the north end of the school parking lot.

SITKA 907

BLATCHLEY POOL 601 Halibut Point Rd.
Phone: 747-8670 or 747-5677.
Pool: 25y, indoors, heated, 82°.
Admission: $2.50.

AMES P.E. CENTER Sheldon Jackson College, 801 Lincoln St.
Phone: 747-5231 or 747-5221.
Pool: 25m, indoors, heated, water temperature not reported.
Admission: $3.

SOLDOTNA   907

SOLDOTNA HIGH SCHOOL POOL 425 Marydale Ave.
Phone: 262-7419.
Pool: 25y x 45f, 6 lanes, indoors, heated, 82°.
Admission: $2.50, SC(60) $1.50.

SKYVIEW HIGH SCHOOL SWIMMING POOL
32689 Sterling Hwy.
Phone: 262-3905.
Pool: 25y, 6 lanes, indoors, heated, 83°.
Admission: $2.50, SC(60) $1.50.
Masters: The Peninsula Masters. Contact Joanne Wainwright at 262-3905(w) or 262-5308(h).

UNALASKA   907

UNALASKA POOL Broadway
Phone: 581-1649.
Pool: 25y, 6 lanes, indoors, heated, 84°.
Admission: $3.

VALDEZ   907

VALDEZ POOL Robe River Dr.
Phone: 835-2531.
Pool: 25y, indoors, heated, 84°.
Admission: $2.
To find: The pool is connected to Valdez High School.

WRANGELL   907

WRANGELL POOL Church St.
Phone: 874-2444.
Pool: 25y, indoors, heated, 85°.
Admission: $1.50, SC(65) NC.
Hotel: RV campsite guests NC with deposit stub.
To find: The pool is connected to the public school on Church St.

ALWAYS CALL FIRST

Pools close, they change names, affiliations, admission policies, and rates. And just because a pool is listed in *Swimmers Guide* doesn't mean it's open all day, every day, for just the type of workout you want to do. Spend a quarter to save time and aggravation. . . always call first!

MASTERS

For information about Arizona Masters clubs not listed in *Swimmers Guide*, contact Judy Gillies, Arizona Masters' State Chairman, in Tucson, at (520) 623-8152(h).

CAREFREE 602

THE BOULDERS RESORT 34631 N. Tom Darlington Dr.
Phone: 488-9009. **Reservations:** 800-553-1717.
Pool: 22y, rectangular, outdoors, heated, 81°.
Admission: Registered guests only NC.

CHANDLER 602

L.A. FITNESS & SPORTS CLUB 3029 N. Alma School Rd. #122
Phone: 345-8944.
Pool: 20y x 25f, 6 lanes, indoors, heated, 83°.
Admission: $10.
Affiliate: IPFA NC.
Hotel: Sheraton San Marcos (963-6655), Dobson Ranch Inn (831-7000), Mesa Hilton Pavilion (833-5555), and seven other area hotels: NC with room key.

FLAGSTAFF 520

FLAGSTAFF ATHLETIC CLUB WEST 1200 W. Route 66

Phone: 779-4593.
Pool: 25y, 3 lanes, indoors, heated, 83°-84°.
Admission: $12.
Affiliate: IHRSA $9.
Hotel: Several local hotels. Call the club for information.
Masters: Contact Ken Kotalik at 779-4593.

NORTHERN ARIZONA UNIVERSITY NATATORIUM Building 21-A
Phone: 523-4508.
Pool: 25m x 50m, indoors, heated, 79°-81°.
Admission: $1.75.
Memberships: $35/semester.
To find: At the intersection of Franklin and San Francisco Sts.
Masters: Northern Arizona Aquatics. Contact Chuck Arabas at 523-6324(w) or William Cobb at 523-8010(w).

FOUNTAIN HILLS 602

CLUB MIRAGE 14815 Fountain Hills Blvd.
Phone: 837-8000.
Pool: 25m, outdoors, heated, 84°.
Admission: $6.

GLENDALE 602

BALLY'S U.S. SWIM & FITNESS 5720 W. Peoria Ave.

Phone: 486-8896.
Pool: 25y, indoors, heated, 82°-85°.
Admission: $10.
Affiliate: Bally's NC.

LAKE HAVASU CITY   520

**LAKE HAVASU CITY RECREATION / AQUATIC
FACILITY** 100 Park Ave.
Phone: 453-2687.
Pool: 25m, 6 lanes, indoors, heated, 84°-86°.
Admission: Lap swim sessions $1. Recreational
swimming* $6, SC(62) $5.
Notes: The facility opened in Oct., 1994.
*Recreational swimming rates include admission to
a wave pool, 257f water slide, and two therapy
pools.

LITCHFIELD PARK   602

**LITCHFIELD PARK RECREATION CENTER
POOL** 100 S. Litchfield Rd.
Phone: 935-9040.
Pool: 25y x 50f, 6 lanes, outdoors, heated, 79°-82°.
Admission: $3.
Notes: There is also an 11f x 19f therapy spa.
Masters: The Litchfield Park Masters. Contact
Mary Liotta at 935-9040.

THE WIGWAM RESORT 300 E. Indian School Rd.
Phone: 935-3811. **Reservations:** 800-327-0396.
Pool 1: 100f, 'tadpole' shape, outdoors, heated,
84°-86°.
Pool 2: 20y, outdoors, heated, 84°-86°.
Admission: Registered guests only NC.

MESA   602

MESA FAMILY YMCA 207 N. Mesa Dr.
Phone: 969-8166.
Pool: 25y, 6 lanes, outdoors, heated, 82°.
Admission: $6.
Affiliate: Out-of-state YMCA NC.

KINO JUNIOR HIGH SCHOOL 848 N. Horne
Phone: 644-2376.
Pool: 25y x 50m, 14 lanes, outdoors, heated, 78°.
Admission: $1.
Masters: The Mesa Aquatics Club. Contact Mark
Taylor at 827-1964(w).

GOLDEN'S HEALTH & RACQUET CLUB 931 S.
Gilbert Rd.
Phone: 497-0470.
Pool: 62f, indoors, heated, 82°.
Admission: $7.
Affiliate: IHRSA $5.

ARIZONA GOLF RESORT 425 S. Power Rd.
Phone: 832-3202. **Reservations:** 800-528-8282.
Pool: 20y, rectangular, outdoors, heated, 83°.
Admission: Registered guests only NC.

PHOENIX   602

Phoenix & Scottsdale

Dots are placed by ZIP codes,
not by street addresses.

1. DOWNTOWN YMCA 350 N. 1st Ave.
Phone: 253-6181.
Pool: 25y, indoors, heated, 84°.
Admission: $6.
Affiliate: YMCA 1 visit NC.

2. CENTRAL PARK SQUARE ATHLETIC CLUB
2020 N. Central Ave., Suite L100
Phone: 252-0092.
Pool: 20y, 4 lanes, indoors, heated, 87°-88° in winter, 84°-85° in summer.
Admission: $10.
Affiliate: IHRSA $5.

3. CITY SQUARE ATHLETIC CLUB 100 W.
Claredon
Phone: 285-2929.
Pool: 25y, outdoors, heated, 84°-85°.
Admission: $10.
Affiliate: IHRSA $8.
Hotel: Lexington Hotel (279-9811) NC.

4. FITNESS WEST 1505 E. Bethany Home Rd.
Phone: 248-8920.
Pool: 25m, indoors, heated, 83°-86°.
Admission: $10.
Affiliate: IHRSA NC.

5. CHRIS-TOWN YMCA 5517 N. 17th Ave.
Phone: 242-7717.
Pool: 25y, 6 lanes, outdoors, heated, 82°.
Admission: $6.
Affiliate: Y AWAY NC.
Masters: The Chris-Town YMCA Masters. Contact
Harry Liber or Elisa Hagins at 242-7717.

6. PHOENIX SWIM CLUB 2902 E. Campbell
Phone: 468-9088.
Pool 1: 50m, outdoors, heated, 81°.
Pool 2: 25m, outdoors, heated, 81°.
Affiliate: USMS $5.
Masters: The Phoenx Swim Club Masters. Call 468-9088.

7. THE VILLAGE RACQUET & HEALTH CLUB 4444 E. Camelback
Phone: 840-6412.
Pool: 25y x 35f, outdoors, heated, 82°.
Admission: $15.
Affiliate: IHRSA $7.

8. POINTE HILTON RESORT AT SQUAW PEAK 7677 N. 16th St.
Phone: 997-2626. **Reservations:** 800-876-4683 or 800-445-8667.
Pool: 27y, 3f deep, irregular 'L' shape, outdoors, heated, 82°.
Admission: Registered guests only NC.
Notes: The resort has ten pools, Jacuzzis, and a 'river'. The pool described above is called the 'Sports Pool'. There is also a 'Superpool' which averages 3.25 ft. in depth and covers 5,000 sq. ft., and an 890 ft., artificial river which flows at 1.36 m.p.h.

9. LA MANCHA ATHLETIC CLUB 8221 N. 23rd Ave.
Phone: 995-1234.
Pool: 25y, outdoors, heated, 80°-82°.
Admission: $10.

10. BALLY'S U.S. SWIM & FITNESS 12235 N. Cave Creek Rd.
Phone: 482-1151.
Pool: 25y, indoors, heated, 78°-82°.
Affiliate: Bally's NC.

11. BALLY'S U.S. SWIM & FITNESS 15401 N. 29th Ave.
Phone: 993-3366.
Pool: 25y, indoors, heated, 80°.
Admission: $10.
Affiliate: Bally's NC.

12. ARIZONA SPORTS RANCH 19232 N. 38th St.
Phone: 569-1457. **Reservations:** 800-TEL-SWIM.
Pool: 25y x 32f, 4 lanes, indoor/outdoor, heated, 80°.
Admission: $5. Registered guests* NC.
Notes: There is also a 50m x 25y, 8 lane, outdoor pool operated in the summer. *There are eight guest suites at the ranch, available from Aug. through May.
To find: One half mile north of Union Hills on 38th St., north edge of Phoenix - Scottsdale. Enter 38th St. from Union Hills.

13. WYNDHAM GARDEN HOTEL-NORTH PHOENIX 2641 W. Union Hills Dr.
Phone: 978-2222. **Reservations:** 800-WYND-HAM.
Pool: 58f, rectangular, outdoors, heated, 83°.
Admission: Registered guests only NC.

14. SCOTTSDALE YMCA 6869 E. Shea Blvd.
Phone: 951-9622.
Pool: 25y, outdoors, heated, 82°.
Affiliate: Y AWAY $3.

15. MARYVALE SAMARITAN HEALTH INSTITUTE 5260 W. Campbell Ave.
Phone: 846-8549.
Pool: 25y x 42f, 5 lanes, outdoors, heated, 89°.
Admission: $3.
Notes: The Institute offers exercise classes in an indoor heated therapy pool.
To find: At the intersection of 53rd and W. Campbell Aves. Parking is available in a lot north of the building.

16. THE SPORTS CLUB 777 S. Point Pkwy.
Phone: 431-6484.
Pool: 20m, outdoors, heated, 85°.
Admission: $10.
Hotel: The Pointe Hilton on South Mountain (438-9000) NC.

PRESCOTT   520

YAVAPAI COLLEGE POOL 1100 E. Sheldon
Phone: 776-2231 or 445-7300 ext. POOL.
Pool: 25y x 45f, 6 lanes, indoors, heated, 83°.
Admission: $1.50.

SCOTTSDALE   602

17. ELDORADO POOL 2301 N. Miller Rd.
Phone: 994-2484.
Pool: 25y x 75f - 90f, 7 lanes, outdoors, heated, 84°.
Admission: $1.
To find: One block south of Thomas and one block east of Scottsdale Rd., across the street from Coronado High School.

18. THE PHOENICIAN 6000 E. Camelback Rd.
Phone: 941-8200. **Reservations:** 800-888-8234.
Pool: 74f, oval shape, outdoors, heated, 85°.
Admission: Registered guests only NC.
Notes: The hotel's Public Relations Dept. advises '... our pools...are not designed for fitness swimmers...'

19. CLUB ULTRA SPORT 7303 E. Earll Dr.
Phone: 941-0800.
Pool: 20y, 3 lanes, outdoors, heated, 85°.
Admission: $10.
Affiliate: IHRSA $5 per day, $12.50 per week.

SCOTTSDALE   CONTINUED

20. RED LION LA POSADA RESORT 4949 E.
Lincoln Dr.
Phone: 952-0420. **Reservations:** 800-547-8010.
Pool: 100y, 'lagoon shape', outdoors, heated, 80°.
Admission: Registered guests only NC.
Notes: The resort says the pool covers more than a
half-acre, which would make it one of the largest
pools in the country.

**21. MARRIOTT'S MOUNTAIN SHADOWS
RESORT & GOLF CLUB** 5641 E. Lincoln Dr.
Phone: 948-7111. **Reservations:** 800-782-2123.
Pool: 70f, 'L' shape, outdoors, heated, 81°.
Admission: $6. Registered guests NC.
Memberships: $250/year.

22. RADISSON RESORT 7171 N. Scottsdale Rd.
Phone: 991-3800. **Reservations:** 800-333-3333.
Pool 1: 48y x 24y, free form, outdoors, unheated,
the range of water temperatures was not reported.
Pool 2: Two pools, both 54f x 24f, outdoors, heat-
ed, water temperature not reported.
Admission: Registered guests only NC.

**23. REGAL MCCORMICK RANCH RESORT &
VILLAS** 7401 N. Scottsdale Rd.
Phone: 948-5050. **Reservations:** 800-243-1332.
Pool: 54.5f, 'L' shape, outdoors, heated, 82°.
Admission: Registered guests only NC.

24. SCOTTSDALE PRINCESS 7575 E. Princess
Dr.
Phone: 585-4848. **Reservations:** 800-344-4758.
Pool: 25y, rectangular, outdoors, heated, 83°-86°.
Admission: Registered guests only NC.

25. SCOTTSDALE PIMA MOTEL 7330 N. Pima
Rd.
Phone: 948-3800. **Reservations:** 800-344-0262.
Pool: 76f, rectangular, outdoors, heated, 80°.
Admission: Registered guests NC.
Memberships: $25/month.

**26. CACTUS AQUATIC & FITNESS CENTER
POOL** 7202 E. Cactus Rd.
Phone: 994-7665.
Pool: 25y x 50m, 23 lanes, outdoors, heated, 82°.
Admission: $1.
To find: At the northeast corner of the intersection
of Scottsdale and Cactus Rds.

SEDONA   520

**SEDONA HEALTH SPA AT LOS ABRIGADOS
RESORT** 160 Portal Lane
Phone: 282-5108. **Reservations:** 800-521-3131.
Pool: 20y x 40f, irregularly shaped, indoors, heat-
ed, 84°-86° in winter, 80°-82° in summer.
Admission: $20. Registered guests NC.
Affiliate: IHRSA Call.
Notes: Measurements are approximations. We are

advised the pool may not be suitable for lap swimming.

POCO DIABLO RESORT 1752 S. Hwy, 179
Phone: 282-7333.
Pool: 52f x 30f, outdoors, heated, water tempera-
ture not reported.
Admission: Registered guests only NC.

SEDONA COMMUNITY POOL at the West Sedona
School off Posse Grounds Rd.
Phone: Pool: 282-0112. Parks Dept: 282-7098.
Pool: 25y, 4 lanes, outdoors, temperature con-
trolled, 78°-82°.
Admission: $2.50.

SHOW LOW   520

**SHOW LOW FAMILY AQUATIC FITNESS
CENTER** 1100 W. Deuce of Clubs
Phone: 537-2800.
Pool: 25y, indoors, heated, 82°-84°.
Admission: $2, SC(55) $1.50.

SIERRA VISTA   520

THUNDER MOUNTAIN INN 1631 S. Hwy. 92
Phone: 458-7900. **Reservations:** 800-222-5811.
Pool: 50f x 25f, rectangular, outdoors, unheated,
50°-75°.
Admission: Registered guests only NC.

TEMPE   602

**WESTERN RESERVE CLUB FAMILY SPORTS
CENTER** 2140 E. Broadway Rd.
Phone: 968-9231.
Pool: 25y, outdoors, heated, 78°-82°.
Admission: $15, SC(55) $5.
Affiliate: IHRSA outside a 50 mile radius $5.
Hotel: Fiesta Inn (833-5555) & Hilton Pavillion
(967-1441): $5 with room key.
To find: Just west of Price Rd.
Masters: The Western Reserve Club Family Sports
Center Masters. Contact Magnus Eriksson at 968-
9231.

ARIZONA MASTERS at Mona Plummer Aquatic
Complex, Arizona State Univ., 6th St. & College
Pool phone: 965-4040. **Masters:** Contact State
Chairman Judy Gillies, in Tucson, at (520) 623-
8152(h).
Pool: 50m x 25y, outdoors, temperature controlled,
80°.
Affiliate: USMS $1, includes pool fees*.
Notes: Lap swimming: M-F: 6-7:15AM, Noon-
1:30PM, 5:15-6:30PM. Sa,Su: Noon-4PM.
*Visitors must be accompanied by a local Masters
member.

TEMPE RIO SALADO MASTERS at McClintock
Swim Pool, 1830 E. del Rio

Pool phone: 491-4864. **Masters:** Contact Coach Mike Troy at 491-4864 or 491-1572.
Pool: 50m x 25y, 8 x 16 lanes, outdoors, heated, 80°-82°.
Affiliate: USMS $2, includes pool fees.
Notes: Workouts: M-Th: 5:30-7AM, 5-6:30PM. F: 5:30-7AM. Sa: 8-10AM.

KIWANIS PARK RECREATION CENTER 6111 S. All America Way
Phone: 350-5201. TDD: 350-5050.
Pool: 25y x 25y, 8 lanes, indoors, heated, 84°.
Admission: $2.25.

TEMPE YMCA 7070 S. Rural Rd.
Phone: 730-0240.
Pool: 25m x 48f, 6 lanes, outdoors, temperature controlled, 80°.
Admission: $6.
Affiliate: Y AWAY $3.
To find: On Rural Rd. between Guadalupe and Elliott.

TUCSON   **602**

Dots are placed by ZIP codes, not by street addresses.

27. RAMADA DOWNTOWN TUCSON 475 N. Granada
Phone: 622-3000. **Reservations:** 800-446-6589.
Pool: 25m, rectangular, outdoors, heated, 82°.
Admission: Registered guests only NC.

28. BALLY'S U.S. SWIM & FITNESS 4690 N. Oracle Rd.
Phone: 293-2330.
Pool: 20y, indoors, heated, 86°.
Admission: $10.
Affiliate: Bally's NC.

29. SUNNYSIDE POOL 1710 E. Bilby
Phone: 791-5167.
Pool: 25m x 25y, 8 x 9 lanes, outdoors, heated, 80°-83°.

Admission: Winter $1. Summer 50¢.
To find: At Sunnyside High School.

30. RESULTS SPORTS & FITNESS CENTER 6444 E. Broadway
Phone: 747-7400.
Pool: 25y, 5 lanes, outdoors, heated, 80°-82°.
Admission: Pool $5. Full facility $10.
Hotel: Embassy Suites (745-2700) & Viscount Suites: NC with a pass from the hotel.
To find: At the intersection of Broadway and Wilmot, directly behind the Buena Vista Movie Theatre.

31. OTT YMCA 401 S. Prudence Rd.
Phone: 885-2317.
Pool: 40y x 60f, 6 lanes, outdoors, heated, 80°-84°.
Admission: $5.
Affiliate: Y AWAY 3 visits per month NC, then $2. YMCA $2.

32. FT. LOWELL POOL Glenn & Craycroft
Phone: 791-2585.
Pool: 50m x 25y, 6 x 6 lanes, outdoors, heated, 80°-83°.
Admission: Winter $1. Summer 50¢.

33. ARCHER POOL 1665 S. LaCholla Blvd.
Phone: 791-5388.
Pool: 25m x 25y, 8 x 9 lanes, outdoors, heated, 81°-83°.
Admission: Winter $1. Summer 50¢.
To find: Next to Archer Center.

34. UDALL POOL 7200 E. Tanque Verde
Phone: 791-4004.
Pool: 25m x 75f, 9 lanes, outdoors, heated, 81°-83°.
Admission: Winter $1. Summer 50¢.

35. LOEWS VENTANA CANYON RESORT 7000 N. Resort Dr.
Phone: 299-2020. **Reservations:** 800-234-5117.
Pool: 50f, multi-cornered, outdoors, heated, 80°-86°.
Admission: Registered guests only NC.

36. CANYON RANCH 8600 E. Rock Cliff Rd.
Phone: 749-9655. **Reservations:** 800-726-9900.
Pool: 25y, outdoors, heated, 85°.
Admission: Registered guests only NC.
Notes: A four night minimum stay is required.

37. TUCSON RACQUET CLUB 4001 N. Country Club Dr.
Phone: 795-6960.
Pool: 25y x 45f, 6 lanes, outdoors, temperature controlled, 82°.
Admission: $10.
Notes: Uses an ionization water purification system that permits a reduction of the chlorine content by 70%.

TUCSON CONTINUED

To find: Country Club Dr. ends at the Racquet Club, just north of Prince Rd.

38. CATALINA POOL 3645 E. Pima
Phone: 791-4245.
Pool: 25m x 25y, 8 x 9 lanes, outdoors, heated, 80°-82°.
Admission: Winter $1. Summer 50¢.

39. HILLENBRAND AQUATIC CENTER University of Arizona, Enke Dr.
Phone: 621-4203.
Pool: 50m x 25y, 8 x 18 lanes, outdoors, heated, 80°.
Admission: $1.

HILLENBRAND AQUATIC MASTERS at the Hillenbrand Aquatic Center, University of Arizona
Masters: Contact Head Masters Coach Jim Stites at 621-4203.
Affiliate: USMS NC, includes pool fees.
Notes: Workouts: M-F: 6-7AM, Noon-1PM, 6:30-7:30PM. Sa: Call.

40. LAKESIDE SPORTSCLUB 8140 E. Golf Links Rd.
Phone: 886-2532.
Pool: 25y x 50f, 6 lanes, outdoors, heated, 82°.
Admission: $6.
Affiliate: IHRSA: 1/2 weeks $15/$25.

41. EL CONQUISTADOR RACQUET CLUB 10555 La Canada
Phone: 544-1900.
Pool: 25y, outdoors, heated, 82°.
Admission: $10.
Affiliate: IHRSA $7.
Hotel: Sheraton El Conquistador Resort (742-7000) $5. The Sheraton runs a shuttle to the Club.

42. TUCSON NATIONAL GOLF & CONFERENCE RESORT 2727 W. Club Dr.
Phone: 297-2271. **Reservations:** 800-528-4856.
Pool: 25y, oblong lap swimming area, outdoors, heated, 75°-80°.
Admission: Registered guests only NC.

YUMA 520

MARCUS POOL 5th St. & 5th Ave.
Phone: 343-8686.
Pool: 25y x 25m, outdoors, temperature controlled, 84°-88°.
Admission: $2.25.
Notes: The city also operates two seasonal pools. Although they're not open long enough to qualify for listing, the season in Yuma is longer than in most parts of the U.S. When you call, ask whether either of the other pools is open and might be more convenient.
Masters: The Southern Arizona Sand Sharks. Contact Kay Malone at 344-8386(w).

HELP MAKE THE NEXT *SWIMMERS GUIDE* EVEN BETTER

To receive a free copy of the next *Swimmers Guide* tell us about pools you know of that aren't in this edition. See page 14 for details.

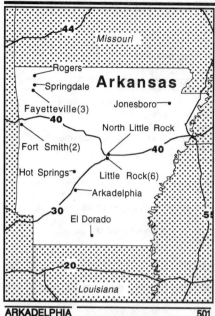

SUMMERHILL RACQUET CLUB 3480 Summerhill Dr.
Phone: 521-8241.
Pool: 25y, indoors, heated, 84°.
Admission: $5.

FORT SMITH   501

MARVIN ALTMAN FITNESS CENTER 810 Lexington
Phone: 441-5469.
Pool: 25y x 48f, 6 lanes, indoors, heated, 85.7°.
Admission: 1 visit NC, then $5.

FORT SMITH RACQUET CLUB 5400 Gary
Phone: 452-4031.
Pool: 25y, indoor/outdoor, heated, 82°.
Affiliate: IHRSA $8.

HOT SPRINGS   501

HOT SPRINGS FAMILY YMCA 130 Werner
Phone: 623-8803.
Pool: 25m x 25y, 8 x 10 lanes, indoors, heated, 85°.
Admission: $5.
To find: Next to St. Joseph's Hospital, one block off Central Ave. and 1.3 miles south of Oaklawn Race Track.

JONESBORO   501

JONESBORO YMCA AQUATIC CENTER 1421 W. Nettleton
Phone: 932-8482.
Pool: 25m x 75f, 10 lanes, indoor/outdoor, heated, 80°.
Admission: $4.
Affiliate: Y AWAY NC. USS NC for team practice.
Masters: Contact Aquatics Director Sam Kendricks at 932-8482.

LITTLE ROCK   501

DOWNTOWN YMCA 524 Broadway St.
Phone: 372-5421.
Pool: 20y, indoors, heated, 83°.
Admission: $9.
Affiliate: Y AWAY $2. YMCA $3. U.S. Military & Southwest Airlines: $5.
Hotel: Holiday Inn Little Rock City Center (376-2071) & Legacy Hotel (374-0100): NC with a pass from the hotel.
To find: From I-630 exit on Broadway north to 6th St. Park in the Holiday Inn City Center Parking Deck. The Y validates parking.

BESS CHISUM STEPHENS YWCA 1200 Cleveland St.
Phone: 664-4268.
Pool: 25m x 45f, 6 lanes, indoors, heated, 83°-84°.
Admission: $5.

ARKADELPHIA   501

WELLS H.P.E.R BUILDING Henderson State University, Hwy. 67 and Russell Dr.
Phone: 230-5000 ext. 2305206.
Pool: 25y x 57f, 8 lanes, indoors, heated, 83°.
Admission: NC if prior arrangements have been made for regular recreation hours.

EL DORADO   501

YWCA OF EL DORADO 410 E. Elm
Phone: 862-5442.
Pool: 25m x 25y, 10 lanes, indoors, heated, 85°.
Admission: Residents $5, non-residents $3.
To find: Three blocks east of the downtown square and courthouse.

FAYETTEVILLE   501

FAYETTEVILLE YOUTH CENTER 915 California Dr.
Phone: 442-9336.
Pool: 25y x 42f, 6 lanes, indoors, heated, 81°.
Admission: $2.
To find: Between the University of Arkansas Campus and the high school.

INTRAMURAL / RECREATIONAL SPORTS HPER Building, University of Arkansas
Phone: 575-4646.
Pool: 50m OR 25m + 25y x 25y, indoors, heated, 82°.
Memberships: $225/year. (Alumni Assn. $25 +$200 Building Membership).
Masters: The H₂OG Masters Swim Club. Contact Darren Fullerton at 575-6381(w).

LITTLE ROCK   CONTINUED

Affiliate: YWCA NC.
To find: Two blocks west of University.

WAR MEMORIAL FITNESS CENTER 300 S.
 Monroe
Phone: 664-6976.
Pool: 25y, 6 lanes, indoors, heated, 83°.
Admission: $4, SC(62) $2.50.
Notes: There are also outdoor recreation pools
open from Memorial Day to Labor Day.
To find: Between the Little Rock Zoo and War
Memorial Stadium.
Masters: The Arkansas Masters. Contact Aquatics
Specialist Kellie Stratton at 664-6976.

LITTLE ROCK RACQUET CLUB 1 Huntington Rd.
Phone: 227-7946.
Pool: 25y x 64f, 8 lanes, indoor/outdoor, heated,
82°.
Admission: $5.

WESTSIDE YMCA 4701 Sam Peck Rd.
Phone: 227-8343.
Pool: 25y, 4 lanes, indoors, heated, 86°.
Admission: $5, SC(55) $3.
Affiliate: YMCA NC.
Notes: There is also a 50m, outdoor pool operated
from Memorial Day to Labor Day.
To find: On Sam Peck Rd. off Cantrell (Hwy. 10)
about a mile west of I-430.

LITTLE ROCK ATHLETIC CLUB 4610 Sam Peck
 Rd.
Phone: 225-3600.
Pool: 25y, indoor/outdoor, heated, 82°-84°.
Affiliate: IHRSA $8.

NORTH LITTLE ROCK   501

NORTHSIDE FAMILY BRANCH YMCA 6101 John
 F. Kennedy Blvd.
Phone: 758-3170.
Pool: 25y, 8 lanes, indoor/outdoor, heated, 84°.
Admission: $3.
Affiliate: YMCA NC.

ROGERS   501

SUMMERHILL RACQUET CLUB 201 N. 37th
Phone: 636-8241.
Pool: 25y, indoors, heated, 81°-82°.
Admission: $4.

SPRINGDALE   501

NORTHWEST ATHLETIC CLUB Hwy. 71 S.
Phone: 756-6920.
Pool: 25y, 4 lanes, indoors, heated, 83°-85°.
Admission: $5.
Hotel: Executive Inn (756-6101) & Holiday Inn
Springdale (751-8300): NC with room key.
To find: Between Fayetteville and Springdale, one
mile north of Northwest Arkansas Mall.

ALWAYS CALL FIRST

Pools close, they change names, affiliations, admission policies, and rates. And
just because a pool is listed in *Swimmers Guide* doesn't mean it's open all day,
every day, for just the type of workout you want to do. Spend a quarter to save
time and aggravation. . . always call first!

Northern
California

Oregon

Crescent City

Arcata
Eureka
Redding

Nevada

Chico(2)
Paradise
Truckee
Fort Bragg
Citrus Heights(2)
Yuba City
Ukiah
Auburn
Sacramento(10)
Rocklin
South Lake Tahoe
Woodland
Roseville
Saint Helena
Davis(3)
Shingle Springs
Santa Rosa(7)
Napa
Fair Oaks
Cotati
Elk Grove
Carmichael
Gold River
Petaluma
Vacaville
Lodi(3)
Angels Camp
San Francisco(25)
Antioch
Stockton(2)
Oakland(10)
Livermore
Tracy
Modesto
Saratoga
Campbell
Merced(2)
Los Gatos(4)
Gilroy
Santa Cruz(2)
Watsonville(2)
Madera
Capitola Aptos
Salinas(4)
Fresno(4)
Clovis
Pebble Beach(2)
Seaside
Death Valley
Monterey
Coalinga
Big Sur
Tulare

ALAMEDA — 510

HARBOR BAY CLUB 200 Packet Landing Rd.
Phone: 521-5414.
Pool: 25m, outdoors, heated, 80°-81°.
Admission: Call.
Affiliate: IHRSA $6.

MARINER SQUARE ATHLETIC CLUB 2227
 Mariner Square Loop
Phone: 523-8011.
Pool: 25y x 45f, 6 lanes, indoors, heated, 80°.
Memberships: I/S $400 +$56/month.
Masters: The Mariner Square Aquatic Masters.
 Contact Coach Diane Sosnoski or Aquatic Director
 Richard Jarratt at 523-8011.

ALBANY — 510

ALBANY POOL 1311 Portland Ave.
Phone: 559-6640.
Pool: 100f x 40f, 6 lanes, indoors, heated, 84°-86°.
Admission: $3.50, SC(60) $3.
To find: Two blocks north of Solano Ave., between
 Albany High School and Memorial Park.

ANGELS CAMP — 209

VILLAGE SPA & COMMUNITY CENTER 1270
 Suzanne Dr.
Phone: 736-2400.
Pool: 25y, outdoors, heated, 80°.
Admission: $7.

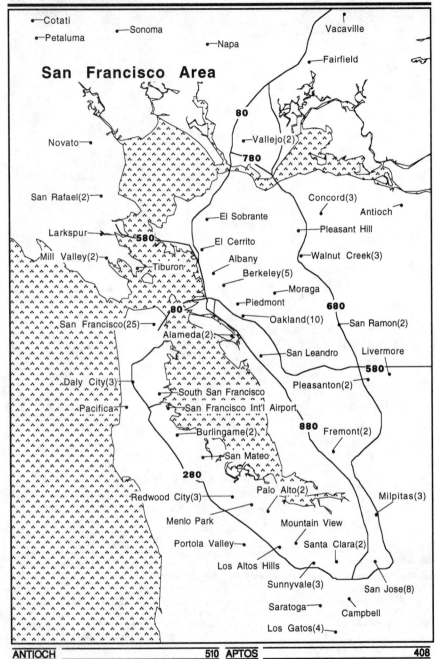

San Francisco Area

- Cotati
- Petaluma
- Sonoma
- Napa
- Vacaville
- Fairfield
- **80**
- Novato
- Vallejo(2)
- **780**
- San Rafael(2)
- El Sobrante
- Concord(3)
- Antioch
- Larkspur
- **580**
- El Cerrito
- Pleasant Hill
- Mill Valley(2)
- Albany
- Walnut Creek(3)
- Tiburon
- Berkeley(5)
- Moraga
- Piedmont
- **680**
- **80**
- San Francisco(25)
- Oakland(10)
- San Ramon(2)
- Alameda(2)
- San Leandro
- Livermore
- **580**
- Daly City(3)
- South San Francisco
- Pleasanton(2)
- Pacifica
- San Francisco Int'l Airport
- **880**
- Fremont(2)
- Burlingame(2)
- San Mateo
- **280**
- Redwood City(3)
- Palo Alto(2)
- Milpitas(3)
- Menlo Park
- Mountain View
- Portola Valley
- Santa Clara(2)
- Los Altos Hills
- Sunnyvale(3)
- San Jose(8)
- Saratoga
- Campbell
- Los Gatos(4)

ANTIOCH　　510

DELTA PARK ATHLETIC CLUB 1300 Vern
　Roberts Circle
Phone: 778-7070.
Pool: 25y, indoors, heated, 80°-85°.
Admission: Call.
Affiliate: IHRSA $10.

APTOS　　408

SEASCAPE SPORTS CLUB 1505 Seascape Blvd.
Phone: 688-1993.
Pool: 25y, outdoors, heated, 80°.
Affiliate: IHRSA: Weekdays $6. Weekends $10.

ARCATA   707

ARCATA COMMUNITY POOL 1150 - 16th Ave.
Phone: 822-6801.
Pool: 25y, indoors, heated, 82°.
Admission: $3.50.
Masters: Contact Steve Ludwig or Shawna
McLaughlin at 822-6801.

AUBURN   916

AUBURN COURT HOUSE & ATHLETIC CLUB
11558 'F' St.
Phone: 885-1964.
Pool: 100f x 50f, outdoors, heated, 78°.
Admission: $10.
Affiliate: IHRSA $5.

BERKELEY   510

BERKELEY YMCA 2001 Allston Way
Phone: 848-6800.
Pool: 20y, 3 lanes, indoors, heated, 80°-84°.
Affiliate: Y AWAY outside a 50 mile radius NC.

**STRAWBERRY CANYON RECREATION AREA
POOL** U. C. Berkeley Campus, 5 Haas Club
House
Phone: 643-3720.
Pool: 25y, 6 lanes, outdoors, heated, 80°.
Admission: $3.75.
Masters: Strawberry Canyon Aquatic Masters.
Contact Polly Upshaw by leaving a message at
642-9821.

HEARST GYM POOL U. C. Berkeley Campus,
Bancroft Way at Bowditch
Phone: Schedules: 643-7470. Information: 643-
7796.
Pool: 100f, 5 lanes, outdoors, heated, 80°-82°.
Admission: $8.
Memberships: 1/3/12 months $75/$175/$480.
Notes: Day passes and memberships are sold at
the Recreation Sports Facility at 2301 Bancroft
Way.

GOLDEN BEAR RECREATION CENTER U. C.
Berkeley - Clark Kerr Campus, 25 Sports Lane
Phone: Schedules: 643-7470. Information: 642-
9821.
Pool: 25y, 6 lanes, outdoors, heated, 80°.
Admission: $3.50.
Memberships: Oct.-Mar. $150*.
Passes: 15 swims $50.
Notes: *Also valid for the Strawberry Canyon
Recreation Area pool.

SPIEKER POOL U. C. Berkeley Campus, 2301
Bancroft Way
Phone: Schedules: 643-7470.
Pool: 25y x 50m, 20 lanes, outdoors, heated, 80°.
Admission: $8.
Memberships: 1/3/12 months $75/$175/$480.

BIG SUR   408

VENTANA INN Hwy. 1
Phone: 667-2331. **Reservations:** 800-628-6500.
Pool 1: 25y, outdoors, heated, 78°.
Pool 2: 25y, outdoors, heated, 78°.
Admission: Registered guests only NC.

BURLINGAME   415

ROYAL ATHLETIC CLUB 1718 Rollins Rd.
Phone: 692-3300.
Pool: 50m, outdoors, heated, 81°-82°.
Admission: Weekdays $15. Weekends $10.
Hotel: All local hotels $8.

PRIME TIME ATHLETIC CLUB 1730 Rollins Rd.
Phone: 697-7311.
Pool: 25y, outdoors, heated, 80°.
Affiliate: IHRSA $10.
Masters: Contact Athletic Director Ray Jungwirth at
697-7311.

CAMPBELL   408

CAMPBELL COMMUNITY CENTER POOL 1 W.
Campbell Ave.
Phone: 866-2105.
Pool: 25y, 8 lanes, outdoors, heated, 80°.
Admission: $3.

CAPITOLA   408

SPA FITNESS CENTER 1100 - 41st Ave.
Phone: 476-7373.
Pool: 25y x 28f, 4 lanes, outdoors, heated, 80°.
Admission: Out-of-town visitors $10.
Affiliate: IPFA & AHA: Call.

CARMICHAEL   916

SPORTS COURTS 6001 Fair Oak
Phone: 485-0714.
Pool: 25y, indoor/outdoor, heated, 80°-82°.
Affiliate: IHRSA $7.
Masters: Contact Club Manager Kurt Mellick at
485-0714.

CHICO   916

CHICO SPORTS CLUB 260 C Cohasset Rd.
Phone: 345-9427.
Pool: 25y x 40f, 5 lanes, outdoors, heated, 80°.
Admission: $10.
Affiliate: IHRSA $7.50.
Hotel: Holiday Inn Chico (345-2491), Heritage Inn
(894-8600), & EconoLodge (895-1323): NC.
To find: At the intersection of Cohasset and
Parmac, in the back of a large parking lot.
Masters: The Chico Swim Club. Contact Diana
Berexa at 345-9427.

CHICO   CONTINUED

KANGAROO KOURTS 1026 Skyway
Phone: 895-8666.
Pool: 25y, outdoors, heated, 78°-80°.
Admission: $12.50.
Affiliate: NACA NC. IHRSA $7.50.
Hotel: Oxford Suites — Call the club for information.
Masters: The Kangaroo Kourts Masters & Junior Masters. Contact Cara Jarrad at 895-8666.

CITRUS HEIGHTS   916

WILLOW CREEK RACQUET CLUB 5555 Mariposa Ave.
Phone: 961-6171.
Pool: 25y x 21f, 3 lanes, indoors, heated, 83°.
Admission: Owners of the current edition of *Swimmers Guide* $7. You must call in advance and show your copy of the book on check in.
Affiliate: IHRSA $7. Please call first.
Notes: There is also a 25y, outdoor, heated, 78°-82° pool operated from May to Oct.

24 HOUR NAUTILUS FITNESS CENTER at the corner of Greenback & San Juan
Phone: 722-7588.
Pool: 20y, indoors, heated, 82°.
Admission: $10.
To find: In the Pack 'n Save parking lot.

CLOVIS   209

CLOVIS ATHLETIC CLUB 781 W. Shaw
Phone: 297-8488.
Pool: 25m, outdoors, heated, 85°.
Admission: Weekdays $7.50. Weekends $5.

COALINGA   209

THE INN AT HARRIS RANCH I-5 & Hwy. 198, 2450 W. Dorris
Phone: 935-0717. **Reservations:** 800-942-2333.
Pool: 25m, 6 lanes, rectangular, outdoors, heated, 75°-85°.
Admission: Registered guests only NC.

CONCORD   510

CONCORD COMMUNITY POOL 3501 Cowell Rd.
Phone: 671-3480.
Pool: 50m x 25y, 6 x 9 lanes, outdoors, heated, 78°.
Admission: $2.25.
To find: One mile from the Concord BART Station.

BIG 'C' ATHLETIC CLUB 1381 Galaxy Way
Phone: 671-2110.
Pool: 25m, outdoors, heated, 78°-80°.
Affiliate: IHRSA $12.

CLAYTON VALLEY ATHLETIC CLUB 5294 Clayton Rd.

Phone: 682-1060.
Pool: 25y, outdoors, heated, 80°-84°.
Admission: $10.
Affiliate: IHRSA $5.

COTATI   707

24 HOUR CLUB 680 E. Cotati Ave.
Phone: 795-0400.
Pool: 20y, indoors, heated, 80°.
Admission: $15.
Affiliate: IHRSA $10.

CRESCENT CITY   707

FRED ENDERT MUNICIPAL SWIMMING POOL 1000 Play St.
Phone: 464-9503.
Pool: 25y, indoors, heated, 84°.
Admission: Lap swimming: $2.75, SC(60) $2.50. Recreation swimming: $2.25, SC $1.75.

DALY CITY   415

WHAT A RACQUET ATHLETIC CLUB 2945 Junipero Serra Blvd.
Phone: 994-9080.
Pool: 20m, 4 lanes, indoors, heated, 82°.
Affiliate: IHRSA $12.
To find: Five minutes from San Francisco, just off I-280 at the Mission St. and Eastmoor Exits. The sign is visible from the highway.

GIAMMONA WESTMOOR HIGH POOL 131 Westmoor Ave.
Phone: 991-8022.
Pool: 25y x 45f, indoors, heated, 85°.
Admission: $2, SC(55) $1.

24-HOUR NAUTILUS 373 Gellert Blvd.
Phone: 756-3303.
Pool: 22y, indoors, heated, 80°.
Admission: $10.
Affiliate: IHRSA $6.

DAVIS   916

CIVIC CENTER POOL 23 Russell Blvd.
Phone: Parks & Community Svcs. Dept: 757-5626.
Pool: 25y x 60f, 8 lanes, outdoors, heated, 78°-82°.
Admission: Lap swim sessions $1. Recreation swim sessions $1.25.
Notes: The city offers structured, additional fee 'Fitness Lap Swimming' classes featuring instructions on all strokes, turns, etc. The programs usually operate M-Th: 6:30-8PM for 2 week periods and rotate among the city's year-round and seasonal pools.
To find: At the corner of Russell Blvd. and 'B' St., next to the Civic Center Gym and City Hall Bldg.

DAVIS AQUATIC MASTERS at Civic Center Pool
Masters: Contact Barbara Paulson at 756-4234.

Affiliate: USMS Call.
Notes: Coached workouts: M-F: 6-8AM, 10AM-2PM, 6-8PM. Sa: 8:30-10AM. Su: 8:30-9:30AM. Uncoached workouts: Sa,Su: 11AM-2PM.

DAVIS ATHLETIC CLUB 1809 Picasso Ave.
Phone: 753-5282.
Pool: 25y x 60f, 6 lanes, indoor/outdoor, heated, 80°.
Admission: $6.
Hotel: Ramada Inn (753-3600) $3.
Notes: Masters swimmers are welcomed.

COMMUNITY POOL 203 E. 14th St.
Phone: Parks & Community Svcs. Dept: 757-5626.
Pool: 25y x 56f, 6 lanes, outdoors, heated, 78-82°.
Admission: Lap swim sessions $1. Recreation swim sessions $1.25.
Notes: See 'Notes' for Civic Center Pool, above.

DEATH VALLEY 619

FURNACE CREEK RANCH RESORT Hwy. 190
Phone: 786-2345.
Pool: 80f x 40f, rectangular, outdoors, heated, 80°.
Admission: Registered guests only NC.
Notes: The pool is free flowing, naturally spring fed, and unchlorinated. There is also a Furnace Creek Inn Resort (same address and phone), about a mile down the road, which has a 25 yard, outdoor, spring fed, 80° pool operated mid-Oct. to mid-May.

EL CERRITO 510

EL CERRITO SWIM CENTER 7007 Moeser Lane
Phone: Recorded schedule: 273-9096.
Information: 215-4375.
Pool: 25m x 25y, 6 x 6 lanes, 'L' shape, outdoors, heated, 79°-80°.
Admission: $5.
To find: At the intersection of Moeser Lane and Ashbury. The nearest large cross street is San Pablo Ave.
Masters: The El Cerrito Masters. Contact the Swim Center at 215-4375.

EL SOBRANTE 510

LAKERIDGE ATHLETIC CLUB 6350 San Pablo Dam Rd.
Phone: 222-2500.
Pool: 25y, 6 lanes, outdoors, heated, 80°.
Affiliate: IHRSA outside a 20 mile radius 4 visits per month $10 each, SC(60) $5.

ELK GROVE 916

LAGUNA CREEK RACQUET CLUB 9570 Racquet Court
Phone: 684-8855.
Pool: 25y, 8 lanes, outdoors, heated, 82°-84°.
Affiliate: IHRSA $8.

Masters: The Laguna Creek Seals. Contact Dr. Brett Lemire at 684-8855 or 392-3900(w).

EUREKA 707

COLLEGE OF THE REDWOODS 7351 Tompkins Hill Rd.
Phone: 445-6965.
Pool: 25y, indoors, heated, water temperature not reported.
Memberships: 5/10/30 day passes $8/$15/$40.

FAIR OAKS 916

ROLLINGWOOD RACQUET CLUB 9373 Winding Oak Dr.
Phone: 988-1727.
Pool: 25y x 24f, 3 lanes, indoors, heated, 83°.
Admission: Owners of the current edition of *Swimmers Guide* $7. You must call in advance and show your copy of the book on check in.
Affiliate: IHRSA $7. Please call first.
Notes: There is also a 25y, outdoor, heated, 78°-82° pool operated from May to Oct.
Masters: Contact Tip Vemphel at 988-1727.

FAIRFIELD 707

SOLANO ATHLETIC CLUB 3001 Dover Ave.
Phone: 422-2858.
Pool: 25y x 30f, 5 lanes, indoors, heated, 82°.
Admission: $10.

FORT BRAGG 707

MENDOCINO COAST RECREATION & PARK DISTRICT 213 E. Laurel St.
Phone: 964-2231.
Pool: 20y x 20f, 3 lanes, indoors, heated, 85°.
Admission: $2, SC(60) $1.50.
To find: On the corner of Franklin & Laurel Sts., one block east of Main St. and two blocks east of the Skunk Depot, across from the Sears store.
Masters: The Mendocino Coast Masters. Contact Tessie Branscomb at 964-2231.

FREMONT 510

SCHOEBER'S ATHLETIC CLUB 3411 Capitol Ave.
Phone: 791-6350.
Pool: 20y, outdoors, heated, 82°-84°.
Affiliate: IHRSA $10.
Hotel: Thunderbird Inn NC with a pass from the hotel.

CLUBSPORT 46650 Landing Pkwy.
Phone: 226-8500.
Pool: 25y x 48f, 6 lanes, outdoors, heated, 80°-82°.
Admission: Call.
Affiliate: IHRSA $10.
To find: Warm Springs Exit off Mission and I-880.

FRESNO   209

FIG GARDEN SWIM & RACQUET CLUB 4722 N.
Maroa
Phone: 222-4816.
Pool: 25m, outdoors, heated, 80°-82°.
Affiliate: IHRSA $10.

DOWNTOWN FITNESS CENTER YMCA 1408 'N'
St.
Phone: 233-5737.
Pool: 20y, 4 lanes, indoors, heated, 86°.
Admission: $6.
Affiliate: YMCA NC.

HOLIDAY INN - AIRPORT 5090 E. Clinton
Phone: 252-3611. **Reservations:** 800-HOLIDAY.
Pool: 50f, 'L' shape, indoors, heated, 72°.
Admission: Registered guests only NC.

FRESNO STATE UNIVERSITY 5305 N. Campus
Dr.
Phone: 278-2526.
Pool: 25y x 36f, 6 lanes, outdoors, heated, 80°.
Admission: $2, SC(60) $1.
To find: In the North Gym Building.

GILROY   408

PARKSIDE ATHLETIC CLUB 8542 Church
Phone: 848-1234.
Pool: 20y x 20f, indoor/outdoor, heated, 83°.
Admission: $8.
Affiliate: IHRSA $4.
Hotel: Local hotels $4 with room key.
Masters: Contact Dan Ordaz at 848-1234.

GOLD RIVER   916

GOLD RIVER RACQUET CLUB 2201 Goldrush Dr.
Phone: 638-7001.
Pool: 25y, outdoors, heated, 81°.
Admission: $8.
Affiliate: IHRSA Call.
Hotel: Sheraton (638-5803), Quality Suites (638-
4141), and most hotels on Folsom: $5.

LARKSPUR   415

REDWOOD HIGH SCHOOL POOL 395 Doherty
Dr.
Phone: 924-2048.
Pool: 25y, 8 lanes, outdoors, heated, 78°-82°.
Admission: $5.

LIVERMORE   510

LIVERMORE VALLEY TENNIS CLUB 2000 Arroyo
Rd.
Phone: 443-7700.
Pool: 25y, outdoors, heated, 81°-82°.
Affiliate: IHRSA $10.

LODI   209

**HUTCHINS STREET SQUARE / COMMUNITY
CENTER** 125 S. Hutchins St.
Phone: 369-2765.
Pool: 25y x 30f, 4 lanes, indoors, heated, 83°.
Admission: $3, SC(60) $2.

TWIN ARBORS ATHLETIC CLUB 2040 W.
Cochran Rd.
Phone: 334-2993.
Pool: 25y x 45f, 6 lanes, outdoors, heated, 80°.
Admission: $7.
Affiliate: IHRSA $5 to $7.

TWIN ARBORS ATHLETIC CLUB 1900 S.
Hutchins
Phone: 334-4897.
Pool: 25y, outdoors, unheated, the range of water
temperatures was not reported.
Affiliate: IHRSA $5.

LOS ALTOS HILLS   415

FOOTHILL COLLEGE POOL 12345 El Monte Rd.
Phone: 949-7327.
Pool: 25y x 25y, 6 x 8 lanes, 'T' shape, outdoors,
heated, 82°.
Admission: $2.
To find: Two blocks west of I-280.

LOS GATOS   408

COURTSIDE TENNIS CLUB 14675 Winchester
Blvd.
Phone: 395-7111.
Pool: 25m, outdoors, heated, 80°-81°.
Affiliate: IHRSA $6.
Masters: The Courtside Masters. Contact Lynn
Williams at 395-7111.

LOS GATOS SWIM & RACQUET CLUB 14700
Oka Rd.
Phone: 356-2136.
Pool: 100f x 25y, outdoors, heated, 81°.
Affiliate: IHRSA $7.
Masters: The Los Gatos Athletic Club Masters.
Contact Patrick Bitter at 354-5808.

**ADDISON PENZAC JEWISH COMMUNITY
CENTER** 14855 Oka Rd.
Phone: 358-3636.
Pool: 25y, 6 lanes, outdoors, heated, 82°.
Admission: $3.
Affiliate: JCC NC. USMS 1 week NC.
To find: Off Lark Rd., very close to Hwy. 17.
Masters: The JCC Masters. Contact Darin Higgins
at 358-3636.

LOS GATOS ATHLETIC CLUB 285 E. Main St.
Phone: 354-5808.
Pool: 25m, outdoors, heated, 80°.
Admission: $8.

Hotel: Toll House & Garden Inn: Contact the hotels for information.

MADERA   209

MADERA ATHLETIC CLUB 1803 Sunset
Phone: 673-3054.
Pool: 25y x 45f, 5 lanes, indoors, heated, 82°.
Admission: $10.
Affiliate: IHRSA $7.
Hotel: Madera Valley Inn (673-5164) NC with a pass from the Inn.
To find: Two blocks west of Thomas Jefferson Junior High School.

MENLO PARK   415

BURGESS MEMORIAL POOL 501 Laurel St.
Phone: 858-3486.
Pool: 100f x 50f, 6 lanes, outdoors, heated, 79°-82°.
Admission: $3, SC(62) $2.
Masters: The Menlo Park Masters. Contact Diane Lovell at 858-3486.

MERCED   209

MERCED SPORTS CLUB 350 E. Yosemite Ave.
Phone: 722-3988.
Pool: 25y, indoor/outdoor, heated, 81°.
Admission: $10.
Affiliate: IHRSA $8.

MERCED COLLEGE 3600 'M' St.
Phone: 384-6029.
Pool: 25y x 50m, 20 lanes, outdoors, heated, 78°.
Admission: From Jun. 1 to Aug. 15 $1.
Memberships: From Aug. 20 to May 31 $10/semester non-credit registration.

MILL VALLEY   415

HARBOR POINT RACQUET & BEACH CLUB 475 E. Strawberry Dr.
Phone: 383-3448.
Pool: 25y, outdoors, heated, 80°-82°.
Memberships: Swim memberships $750/year.

TAMALPAIS HIGH SCHOOL POOL Miller and Camion Alto
Phone: 388-0172 or 924-2048.
Pool: 50m, 6-8 lanes, outdoors, heated, 81°-82°.
Admission: $5.

MILPITAS   408

SHERATON SAN JOSE HOTEL 1801 Barber Lane
Phone: 943-0600. **Reservations:** 800-943-0660.
Pool: 20y, rectangular, outdoors, heated, 80°.
Admission: Registered guests only NC.

SOUTH BAY ATHLETIC CLUB 271 Houret Dr.
Phone: 946-0600.

Pool: 20y, outdoors, heated, 80°.
Affiliate: IHRSA $5.
Hotel: Beverly Heritage, Hyatt San Jose (993-1234), Homewood Suites, & Sheraton San Jose (943-0600): $5.

MILPITAS COMMUNITY SPORTS CENTER 1325 E. Calaveras Blvd.
Phone: 942-2493.
Pool 1: 25m, outdoors, heated, 82°.
Pool 2: 25y, outdoors, heated, 82°.
Admission: $4, SC(50) $3.
To find: Take the Calaveras Blvd. Exit from I-880 and/or I-680 and go east. Just after the intersection of Calaveras Blvd. and Park Victoria turn left into the Samual Ayer Adult Education Center and go straight to the back.

MODESTO   209

S.O.S. CLUB 819 Sunset
Phone: 578-5801.
Pool: 25m, outdoors, heated, 80°.
Affiliate: IHRSA $5.

MONTEREY   408

MONTEREY SPORTS CENTER 301 E. Franklin St.
Phone: 646-3700.
Pool 1: 30m x 25y, 9 x 12 lanes, indoors, heated, 82°.
Pool 2: 25y x 20f, indoors, heated, 90°.
Admission: Residents $4.50, SC(55) $3. Non-residents $5.50, SC $4.
Hotel: Doubletree Hotel at Fisherman's Wharf (649-4511), Monterey Marriott (649-4234), & Monterey Plaza: $1 off non-resident rates.
To find: Two blocks east of Alvarado, Monterey's main street.
Masters: The Monterey Sports Center (Masters). Contact Aquatics Director Brian Schonfeldt at 646-3700.

MORAGA   510

MORAGA TENNIS & SWIM CLUB 1161 Larch Ave.
Phone: 376-1622.
Pool: 25y, outdoors, heated, 81°.
Affiliate: IHRSA: Weekdays $4. Weekends $6.

MOUNTAIN VIEW   415

EL CAMINO YMCA 2400 Grant Rd.
Phone: 969-9622.
Pool: 25y x 36f, 6 lanes, outdoors, heated, 82°.
Admission: $10.
Affiliate: Y AWAY $3. YMCA $6.
Masters: The El Camino Masters. Contact David Buin at 969-9622.

NAPA   707

EXERTEC FITNESS CENTER 920 Yount, Suite A
Phone: 226-1842.
Pool: 25y, 5 lanes, indoors, heated, 83°-84°.
Admission: $7.
Affiliate: IHRSA $3.50.

NOVATO   415

ROLLING HILLS CLUB 351 San Andreas
Phone: 897-2185.
Pool: 25y, outdoors, heated, 80°-83°.
Affiliate: IHRSA $8.

OAKLAND   510

Dots are placed by ZIP codes, not by street addresses.

1. LIONS POOL 3860 Hanly Rd.
Phone: 238-2250.
Pool: 35y x 35f, outdoors, heated, 83°-85°.
Admission: $2, SC(50) $1.

2. COURTHOUSE ATHLETIC CLUB 2935
Telegraph Ave.
Phone: 834-5600.
Pool: 25y x 30f, 4 lanes, indoor/outdoor, heated,
80°.
Affiliate: IHRSA $8.
To find: At the intersection of 29th St. and
Telegraph Ave.

3. TEMESCAL POOL 371 - 45th St.
Phone: 238-2202 or 238-SWIM.
Pool: 100f x 50f, 6 lanes, outdoors, heated, 81°-
83°.
Admission: $2, SC(50) $1.
To find: Behind Oakland Technical High School.
The cross street is Lawton off 51st St.
Masters: The Temescal Masters. Contact Linda
Buchannan at 238-2202.

4. LIVE OAK MEMORIAL POOL 1055 MacArthur
Blvd.
Phone: 238-2292, 238-3494 or 238-SWIM.
Pool: 25y, outdoors, heated, 80°.
Admission: $2, SC(55) $1.

Affiliate: USS & USMS: Call.
Masters: The Oakland Aquatic Masters. Contact
Steve Haufler at 339-8013(w).

5. THE HILLS SWIM & TENNIS CLUB 2400
Manzanita Dr.
Phone: 339-0234.
Pool: 25y, outdoors, heated, 80°.
Affiliate: IHRSA: Weekdays $6. Weekends $10.

6. MONTCLAIR SWIM CLUB 1901 Woodhaven
Way
Phone: 339-2500.
Pool: 25y, outdoors, heated, 78°-80°.
Memberships: I/S $300 +$63/month.
Masters: The Montclair Swim Club Masters.
Contact Steve Haufler at 339-8013(w).

7. SPORTS CLUB AT CITY CENTER OAKLAND
1200 Clay St.
Phone: 835-2000.
Pool: 25y, outdoors, heated, 78°-82°.
Admission: $15.
Affiliate: IHRSA $10.
Hotel: Parc Oakland Hotel $10.

8. OAKLAND YMCA 2350 Broadway
Phone: 451-9622.
Pool: 25m, indoors, heated, 80°.
Affiliate: Y AWAY $5.

9. OAKLAND HILLS TENNIS CLUB 5475
Redwood Rd.
Phone: 531-3300.
Pool: 25y x 25f, outdoors, heated, 80°-81°.
Affiliate: IHRSA $10.

10. CLAREMONT RESORT, SPA & TENNIS CLUB
Ashby and Domingo St.
Phone: Club: 549-8517. Hotel: 843-3000.
Reservations: 800-323-7500.
Pool 1: 25m, rectangular, outdoors, heated, 80°.
Pool 2: 25m, rectangular, outdoors, heated, 80°.
Admission: Registered guests NC.
Memberships: Call.

PACIFICA   415

OCEANA POOL 401 Paloma Ave.
Phone: Pool: 355-3786. Rec. Dept: 738-7381.
Pool: 25y x 25m, 10 lanes, indoors, heated, 81°.
Admission: Lap swimming $3, SC(60) $2. Water
aerobics classes $3.
To find: About a quarter of a mile east of Hwy. 1.
From the north, use the Francisco/Paloma Exit,
from the south use the Oceana/Clarendon Exit.
Masters: Contact the pool staff at 355-3786.

PALO ALTO   415

RINCONADA POOL Newell & Embarcadero Rds.
Phone: 329-2351.

Pool: 25y x 100f, 13 lanes, outdoors, heated, 80°-82°.
Admission: $2, SC(62) $1.25.
Masters: The Rinconada Masters. Contact Cindy Baxter at 326-6630(h), or Carol MacPherson at 493-2930(h). USMS registration is required to participate in workouts.

ALBERT L. SCHULTZ JEWISH COMMUNITY CENTER 655 Arastradero Rd.
Phone: 493-9400.
Pool: 25m, outdoors, heated, 82°.
Admission: $7.

PARADISE   916

SPORTHAVEN HEALTH CLUB 6854 Pentz Rd.
Phone: 872-2232.
Pool: 25y x 30f, 4 lanes, indoor/outdoor, heated, 82°.
Admission: $8.
Affiliate: IHRSA $5.
Notes: There is also an indoor, heated, 86°, exercise pool.

PEBBLE BEACH   408

THE LODGE AT PEBBLE BEACH 17 Mile Dr.
Phone: 625-3811. **Reservations:** 800-654-9300.
Pool: 25m, rectangular, outdoors, heated, 82°.
Admission: Registered guests NC.
Hotel: The Inn at Spanish Bay (647-7500) NC.
Notes: Guests also have access to the facilities at the Inn at Spanish Bay, listed below.

THE INN AT SPANISH BAY 2700 - 17 Mile Dr.
Phone: 647-7500. **Reservations:** 800-654-9300.
Pool: 25y, rectangular, outdoors, heated, 81°-82°.
Admission: Registered guests NC.
Hotel: The Lodge at Pebble Beach (625-3811) NC.
Notes: Guests also have access to the facilities at the Lodge at Pebble Beach, listed above.

PETALUMA   707

RANCHO ARROYO RACQUET CLUB 85 Corona
Phone: 795-5461.
Pool: 20m, outdoors, heated, 80°.
Affiliate: IHRSA $8.

PIEDMONT   510

PIEDMONT SWIM CLUB 777 Magnolia Ave.
Phone: 655-5163.
Pool: 25y, outdoors, heated, 81°-82°.
Memberships: I/S (purchase/can be re-sold) $2,500 + $565/year.

PLEASANT HILL   510

MT. DIABLO YMCA 350 Civic Dr.
Phone: 687-8900.
Pool: 25y, outdoors, heated, 85°.

Admission: $10.
Affiliate: YMCA NC.

PLEASANTON   510

SCHOEBER'S ATHLETIC CLUB 5341 Owens Court
Phone: 463-0950.
Pool: 20y, indoors, heated, 81°.
Affiliate: IHRSA $10.
Hotel: Holiday Inn Pleasanton (847-6000) NC. Residence Inn (373-1800) $3.50. Sheraton (460-8800) & Doubletree (463-3330): $6. Super 8 (463-1300) $8.

CLUBSPORT 7090 Johnson Dr.
Phone: 463-2822.
Pool: 25y, outdoors, heated, 80°.
Admission: $10.

PORTOLA VALLEY   415

SOLO MASTERS SWIM CLUB at Ladera Oaks Swim & Tennis Club, 4139 Alpine Rd.
Masters: Contact Diane Campbell, Head Coach, at 851-9091.
Pool: 25y x 60f, 6 lanes, outdoors, heated, 80°.
Affiliate: USMS $5, includes pool fees.
Notes: Coached workouts: M,W,F: 5:45-7AM, 11:45AM-1PM.

REDDING   916

REDDING FITNESS CENTER 1740 Eureka Way
Phone: 244-6694.
Pool: 20y, indoors, heated, 86°.
Admission: $7.

REDWOOD CITY   415

SEQUOIA YMCA 1445 Hudson St.
Phone: 368-4168.
Pool: 25y x 30f, 4 lanes, indoors, heated, 84°.
Admission: $8.
Affiliate: Y AWAY 2 weeks NC. Neighboring YMCA $4.
Masters: The Sequoia YMCA Masters Swim Team. Contact Tim Meikle at 368-4168.

PENINSULA COVENANT COMMUNITY CENTER 3623 Jefferson Ave.
Phone: 364-6272.
Pool: 25m x 25y, 6 x 5 lanes, 'L' shape, outdoors, heated, 80°.
Affiliate: IHRSA 4 visits per month $6 each, SC $5.
To find: On the corner of Jefferson and Farm Hill Blvd.
Masters: Woodside Hills Aquatics. Contact Ron Chlasta at 364-6272.

PACIFIC ATHLETIC CLUB 200 Redwood Shores Pkwy.
Phone: 593-4900.

Pool: 25y, outdoors, heated, 82°.
Affiliate: IHRSA $15.

ROCKLIN   916

ROCKLIN AQUATICS MASTERS (RAMS) at Rocklin High School Pool, 5301 Victory Lane **Pool phone:** 765-8833. **Masters:** Contact Mrs. Nancy L. Kelley at 624-0715 or 632-2039 (before 8PM, please).
Pool: 25y x 75f, 8 lanes, outdoors, temperature controlled, 76°-78°.
Affiliate: USMS Call.
Notes: Coached workouts: M-Th: 6-7AM, 7:30-8:30PM. F: 6-7AM. Lap swimming: M-F: Noon-1PM. This is a new club in formation; visitor policies had not yet been established when we contacted them. The club also works out at the 25y x 45f, 6 lane, outdoor, heated, 80° Sierra College Pool (781-0577).
To find: At the corner of Stanford Ranch Rd. & Victory Lane.

ROSEVILLE   916

JOHNSON RANCH RACQUET CLUB 2501 Eureka Rd.
Phone: 782-2300.
Pool: 25y, outdoors, heated, 80°.
Affiliate: IHRSA $6.

SACRAMENTO   916

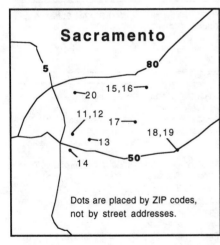

Dots are placed by ZIP codes, not by street addresses.

11. HYATT REGENCY SACRAMENTO 1209 'L' St.
Phone: 443-1234. **Reservations:** 800-233-1234.
Pool: 20y x 22f, rectangular, outdoors, heated, 82°-84°.
Admission: Registered guests only NC.
Notes: Guests also have access to the Capital Athletic Club, listed below.

---

12. CAPITAL ATHLETIC CLUB 1515 - 8th St.
Phone: 442-3927.
Pool: 25y, 4 lanes, outdoors, heated, 80°.
Affiliate: IHRSA $10.
Hotel: Hyatt Regency Sacramento (443-1234) $10.
To find: Downtown, at the intersection of 8th and 'P' Sts.
Masters: Contact Tamir Wardinay at 442-3927.

13. ALHAMBRA ATHLETIC CLUB 1671 Alhambra Blvd.
Phone: 457-9300.
Pool: 25m, indoors, heated, 80°.
Affiliate: $10 with valid membership card from any health club.

14. SACRAMENTO CENTRAL BRANCH YMCA 2021 'W' St.
Phone: 737-3181.
Pool: 25y x 46f, 6 lanes, indoors, heated, 82°.
Admission: $10.
Affiliate: Y AWAY 3 visits per month NC, then $5.

15. NORTHEAST YMCA 3127 Eastern Ave.
Phone: 483-6426.
Pool: 25y x 30f, 5 lanes, outdoors, heated, 82°.
Admission: $4.
Affiliate: Y AWAY 6 visits NC.

16. DEL NORTE SWIMMING & TENNIS CLUB 3040 Becerra Way
Phone: 483-5111.
Pool: 25y, indoors, heated, 85°.
Affiliate: IHRSA $5.

17. RIO DEL ORO RACQUET CLUB 119 Scripps Dr.
Phone: 488-8100.
Pool: 25y, 6 lanes, outdoors, heated, 80°.
Affiliate: IHRSA $8.

18. 24 HOUR WORKOUT 9574 Micron Ave.
Phone: 363-4382.
Pool: 20y, indoors, heated, 78°-82°.
Admission: $10.
Affiliate: IHRSA $5.

19. RANCHO ARROYO RACQUET CLUB 9880 Jackson Rd.
Phone: 362-3212.
Pool: 50m x 25y, indoors, heated, 77°-80°.
Admission: $10.

20. NATOMAS RACQUET CLUB 2450 Natomas Park Dr.
Phone: 649-0909.
Pool: 25y, indoor/outdoor, heated, 82°.
Affiliate: IHRSA Call.
Masters: The NRC Clams. Contact Heather Matwich at 649-0909.

SAINT HELENA   707

MEADOWOOD RESORT 900 Meadowood Lane
Phone: 963-3646. **Reservations:** 800-458-8080.
Pool: 25y, 3 lanes, outdoors, heated, 80°.
Admission: Registered guests only NC.

SALINAS   408

SALINAS YMCA 117 Clay St.
Phone: 758-3811.
Pool: 25y, outdoors, heated, 80°-82°.
Admission: $15.
Affiliate: YMCA 5 visits NC.
Notes: There is also an 18y, indoor, heated, 90°-
92° pool.

SALINAS ATHLETIC CLUB 20 E. San Joaquin St.
Phone: 757-8331.
Pool: 25y, indoors, heated, 80°-82°.
Admission: Call.

SALINAS MUNICIPAL POOL 920 N. Main
Phone: 758-7301.
Pool: 25y x 54f, 7 lanes, indoors, heated, 84°.
Admission: $1.50, SC(65) $1.
To find: Next to the Rodeo Grounds on N. Main St.

CHAMISAL TENNIS & FITNESS CLUB 185
Robley Rd.
Phone: 649-1135.
Pool: 25y x 18f, 3 lanes, outdoors, heated, 80°.
Admission: $15.
Affiliate: IHRSA $8.
To find: Two miles from the Laguna Seca
Raceway.

SAN FRANCISCO   415

**21. SWIMMING & FITNESS AT THE SHEEHAN
HOTEL** 620 Sutter St.
Phone: 775-6500. **Reservations:** 800-848-1529.
Pool: 21y x 30f, 4 lanes, indoors, heated, 79°-83°.
Admission: $4, SC $2.50. Regestered guests NC.
Hotel: The Fitzgerald Hotel (775-8100) NC.
Affiliate: YMCA & YWCA: $2.50.
Notes: Kickboards, pull buoys, hand paddles, &
Aqua Belts are available for use at no charge.
Admission includes use of the Fitness Gym.
To find: Two blocks west of the Powell St. Cable
Car.

22. CENTRAL YMCA 220 Golden Gate Ave.
Phone: 885-0460.
Pool: 25m x 10m, indoors, heated, 83°.
Admission: $13.
Affiliate: YMCA $3.
To find: Near the Civic Center and City Hall.

23. BERT'S CONDITIONING CLINIC 609 Sutter St.
Phone: 885-2918.
Pool: 25y x 25f, indoors, heated, 85°.
Admission: $10.

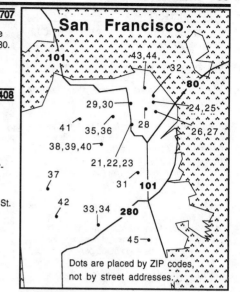

San Francisco

Dots are placed by ZIP codes,
not by street addresses.

24. PHYSIS 1 Post St.
Phone: 781-6400.
Pool: 20y, 3 lanes, indoors, heated, 78°-80°.
Admission: $10.
To find: In the McKesson Building courtyard.

25. CLUB ONE AT MUSEUM PARC 350 - 3rd St.
Phone: 512-1010.
Pool: 22y, outdoors, heated, 78°-80°.
Admission: $15.
Affiliate: IHRSA $10.

26. EMBARCADERO YMCA 169 Steuart St.
Phone: 957-9622.
Pool: 34m OR 25m x 35f, 5 lanes, indoors, heated,
83°.
Admission: $12.
Affiliate: YMCA $6.
Hotel: The Harbour Court Hotel (882-1300) NC.
Notes: The pool length is set at 25m M,W,F,Sa;
34m Tu,Th,Su.
To find: Two blocks south of the ferry building on
the Embarcadero.
Masters: Contact Barbara Barnes at 957-9622.

27. SHERATON PALACE HOTEL 2 New
Montgomery St.
Phone: 392-8600. **Reservations:** 800-325-3535.
Pool: 20y, rectangular, indoors, heated, 80°.
Admission: Registered guests only NC.

28. CHINATOWN YMCA 855 Sacramento St.
Phone: 982-4412.
Pool: 20y x 20f, 3 lanes, indoors, heated, 82°.
Admission: $12.
Affiliate: YMCA $3.
To find: Located between Stockton and Grant Sts.

SAN FRANCISCO   CONTINUED

29. CATHEDRAL HILL PLAZA ATHLETIC CLUB
1333 Gough St.
Phone: 346-3868.
Pool: 20y x 30f, 4 lanes, indoors, heated, 82°.
Admission: $10.
To find: At Geary & Gough, across the street from
St. Mary's Cathedral.

30. SAN FRANCISCO AQUATIC PARK at the
Dolphin Swim Club and the South End Rowing
Club, 500 & 502 Jefferson St.
Phone: 441-9329 or 776-7372.
Pool: 1/4 mile*, salt water, outdoors, unheated,
47°-63°.
Admission: $6.50.
Notes: *Year-round open water swimming in a pro-
tected area of San Francisco Bay, directly in front
of the National Maritime Museum. A buoy is
placed 1/4 mile from the clubs' dock; a swim
around the circumference of the park is 1 mile.
This is not for the faint-hearted, thin-blooded, or
timid. The two clubs accommodate swimmers on
alternating days.
To find: On the bay at Fisherman's Wharf.

31. GARFIELD POOL 26th & Harrison Sts.,
Mission
Phone: 695-5001.
Pool: 100f x 40f, 6 lanes, indoors, heated, 80°-82°.
Admission: $3.
Notes: Closes for one month each year for mainte-
nance. Call.
To find: Near Army St.

32. SAN FRANCISCO BAY CLUB 150 Greenwich
St.
Phone: 433-2550.
Pool 1: 20y x 45f, indoors, heated, 78°.
Pool 2: 20y x 45f, indoors, heated, 83°.
Memberships: I/S $1,100 + $110/month.
Notes: The club has squash, tennis, racquetball,
basketball, volleyball, etc. in an 80,000 sq. ft. facili-
ty.

33. BALBOA POOL San Jose Ave. & Havelock St.,
Ingleside
Phone: 337-4701.
Pool: 100f x 40f, 6 lanes, indoors, heated, 80°-82°.
Admission: $3.
Notes: Closes for one month each year for mainte-
nance. Call.

34. KING POOL 3rd St. & Carroll Ave.
Phone: 822-5707.
Pool: 25y, indoors, heated, 80°-82°.
Admission: $3.
Notes: Closes for one month each year for mainte-
nance. Call.

35. SAN FRANCISCO ATHLETIC CLUB 1755
O'Farrell St.

Phone: 776-2260.
Pool: 25y x 38f, 5 lanes, indoors, heated, 80°.
Admission: 3 visits per month $8-$12 each.
Affiliate: IHRSA $8.
To find: One block south of Japan Town, at the
intersection of O'Farrell and Fillmore.
Masters: Contact Katie Welch at 776-2260.

36. HAMILTON POOL Geary Blvd. & Steiner St.,
Western Addition
Phone: 292-2001.
Pool: 100f x 40f, 6 lanes, indoors, heated, 80°-82°.
Admission: $3.
Notes: Closes for one month each year for mainte-
nance. Call.
Masters: This facility hosts a Masters Group.

37. SAVA POOL 19th Ave. & Wawona St., Sunset
Phone: 753-7000.
Pool: 100f x 40f, 6 lanes, indoors, heated, 80°-82°.
Admission: $3.
Notes: Closes for one month each year for mainte-
nance. Call.
Masters: This facility hosts a Masters Group.

38. ROSSI POOL Arguello Blvd. & Anza St.,
Richmond
Phone: 666-7014.
Pool: 100f x 40f, 6 lanes, indoors, heated, 80°-82°.
Admission: $3.
Notes: Closes for one month each year for mainte-
nance. Call.

39. SAN FRANCISCO BOYS' & GIRLS' CLUB
Ernest Ingold Branch, 1950 Page St.
Phone: 221-6100.
Pool: 25y x 42f, 7 lanes, indoors, heated, 82°.
Admission: $2.
To find: Down from Kezar Pavillion on Stanyan St.

40. KORET HEALTH & RECREATION CENTER
University of San Francisco, 2130 Fulton St.
Phone: 666-6820.
Pool: 50m x 25y, indoors, heated, 81°.
Admission: $8, SC(55) $3.
Masters: Call 666-6821.

**41. SAN FRANCISCO JEWISH COMMUNITY
CENTER** 3200 California St.
Phone: 346-6040.
Pool: 20y x 27f, 3 lanes, indoors, heated, 84°.
Admission: $10, SC(55) $5.
Affiliate: Out-of-state JCC NC.
Hotel: Laurel Motor Inn $5 with room key.

42. STONESTOWN FAMILY BRANCH YMCA 333
Eucalyptus
Phone: 759-9622.
Pool: 25m, 4 lanes, indoors, heated, 81°-82°.
Affiliate: YMCA NC.

43. NORTH BEACH POOL at Lombard and Mason
Sts., North Beach

Phone: 274-0200.
Pool 1: 30y x 30f, 2 double lanes, indoors, heated, 80°-82°.
Pool 2: 30y x 30f, 2 double lanes, indoors, heated, 80°-82°.
Admission: $3.
Notes: Closes for one month each year for maintenance. Call.

44. HYATT AT FISHERMAN'S WHARF 555 N. Point St.
Phone: 563-1234. **Reservations:** 800-233-1234.
Pool: 50f x 20f, 3.5f deep, outdoors, heated, 82°-86°.
Admission: Registered guests only NC.

45. COFFMAN POOL Visitacion Ave. and Hahn St., Visitacion Valley
Phone: 337-4702.
Pool: 100f x 40f, 5-6 lanes, indoors, heated, 80°-82°.
Admission: $3.
Notes: Closes for one month each year for maintenance. Call.

SAN FRANCISCO INT'L AIRPORT 415

SAN FRANCISCO AIRPORT HILTON
Phone: 589-0770. **Reservations:** 800-HILTONS.
Pool: 76f x 35f 5in, outdoors, heated, 78°.
Admission: Registered guests only NC.
Notes: The hotel is two minutes from the airport baggage claim.

SAN JOSE 408

SAN JOSE ATHLETIC CLUB / CLUB WEST 196 N. 3rd St.
Phone: 292-1141.
Pool: 25y, outdoors, heated, 80°.
Admission: $10.

SCHOEBER'S ATHLETIC CLUB 7012 Realm Dr.
Phone: 629-3333.
Pool: 22y, 3 lanes, outdoors, heated, 78°-82°.
Affiliate: IHRSA $8.

SOUTH VALLEY FAMILY YMCA 5632 Santa Teresa Blvd.
Phone: 226-9622.
Pool: 25y, 6 lanes, outdoors, heated, 82°.
Admission: $8.
Affiliate: YMCA outside a 50 mile radius NC.
To find: Near Oak Ridge Mall, just off Blossom Hill Blvd., between Blossom Hill Blvd. and Coleman Ave.

ALMADEN VALLEY ATHLETIC CLUB 5400 Camden Ave.
Phone: 267-3700.
Pool: 25y, 5 lanes, outdoors, heated, 82°-86°.
Admission: $10.

CENTRAL YMCA 1717 The Alameda
Phone: 298-1717.
Pool: 25y x 35f, 5 lanes, indoors, heated, 85°.
Admission: $10.
Affiliate: YMCA outside a 50 mile radius NC, within 50 miles $5.

24-HOUR NAUTILUS 375A N. Capitol Ave.
Phone: 923-2639.
Pool: 25y, indoors, heated, 82°.
Admission: $10.
Affiliate: IHRSA $8.

SAN JOSE AQUATICS MASTERS at Gunderson High School, 622 Gaundabert Lane
Masters: Contact Coach Chris Carriere at 281-3517.
Pool 1: 50m x 25y, 9 lanes, outdoors, heated, 80°.
Pool 2: 25y, outdoors, heated, 80°.
Non-member participation: $3.
Notes: Masters workouts: M-Th: 5-7:30AM, 6-8PM. F: 5-7:30AM. Sa: 10AM-Noon.

SAN JOSE STATE UNIVERSITY AQUATIC CENTER at the corner of 8th and San Carlos Sts.
Phone: 924-6340/1.
Pool: 60m x 25y, 8 x 20 lanes, outdoors, heated, 80°.
Admission: $3.
Memberships: $25/month.
To find: At the end of the 8th St. parking lot off San Salvador St.

SAN LEANDRO 510

BOYS & GIRLS CLUB POOL 401 Marina Blvd.
Phone: Pool: 483-0832. Community Services Dept: 577-3462.
Pool: 25y, indoors, heated, 80°.
Admission: $3.50.

SAN MATEO 415

JOINVILLE SWIM CENTER 2111 Kehoe Ave.
Phone: 377-4717.
Pool: 25m x 44f, 6 lanes, outdoors, heated, 81°.
Admission: $3.50.
To find: Off U.S. 101, at the first exit north of Hwy. 92.

SAN MATEO MASTER MARILINS at Joinville Swim Center
Masters: Contact Community Services Supervisor Jim Kelly at 377-4717.
Non-member participation: $4.50.
Notes: Coached workouts: M-Th: 6-8AM, 11AM-1PM, 6:30-7:30PM. F: 6-8AM, 11AM-1PM. Sa: 8-10AM. Su: 9-10AM. All interested swimmers are invited to participate in Masters workouts, irrespective of USMS membership.

SAN RAFAEL   415

MARIN BRANCH YMCA 1500 Los Gamos Dr.
Phone: 492-9622.
Pool: 25y, indoors, heated, 82°-84°.
Affiliate: Y AWAY $3. YMCA $5.

MARIN JEWISH COMMUNITY CENTER 200 N.
San Pedro Rd.
Phone: 479-2000.
Pool 1: 25y, outdoors, heated, 82°.
Pool 2: 25y, indoors, heated, 88°.
Affiliate: JCC NC.

SAN RAMON   510

SAN RAMON OLYMPIC POOL 9870 Broadmoor
Dr.
Phone: 275-2340.
Pool: 25y x 50m, 21 lanes, outdoors, heated, 80°.
Admission: $2.
To find: Next to California High School.
Masters: The San Ramon Masters. Contact Stuart
Smith at 275-2345(w).

CLUBSPORT 350 Bollinger Canyon Lane
Phone: 735-8500.
Pool: 25y, 6 lanes, outdoors, heated, 81°.
Affiliate: IHRSA $10.
To find: Two miles east of I-680 on Bollinger
Canyon Lane.

SANTA CLARA   408

DECATHLON CLUB 3250 Central Expwy.
Phone: 738-2582.
Pool: 25y, 4 lanes, outdoors, heated, 80°.
Affiliate: IHRSA $15. Out-of-town USMS — Call.
Hotel: Residence Inn Silicon Valley I (720-1000),
Residence Inn Silicon Valley II (720-8893), &
Embassy Suites (496-6400): NC with a pass pur-
chased at the hotel.
Masters: Contact Maria Paris at 738-2582 ext. 137.

INTERNATIONAL SWIM CENTER 969 Kiely Blvd.
Phone: 243-7727.
Pool: 50m x 25y, 9 lanes, outdoors, heated, 80°.
Admission: $1.
Masters: The Santa Clara Swim Club. Contact Jay
Fitzgerald at 243-7727.

SANTA CRUZ   408

HARVEY WEST POOL Harvey West Park
Phone: 429-3770.
Pool: 25y, outdoors, heated, 80°.
Admission: $2.25, SC(60) $1.75.
Notes: The pool is closed for rebuilding until June,
1995. In the interim, pools at Harbor High School
and Santa Cruz High School are open to the pub-
lic. For information, call the Santa Cruz Parks &
Recreation Dept. at 429-3663.
Masters: Call 429-3770.

**UNIVERSITY OF CALIFORNIA AT SANTA CRUZ
POOL COMPLEX** 1156 High St.
Phone: 459-3372.
Pool: 50m x 25y, 8 x19 lanes, outdoors, heated,
81°.
Admission: $3.
Memberships: $35/month, SC $25.
To find: At the East Field House, at the top of the
hill going up Hager.

SANTA CRUZ MASTERS AQUATICS at the
University of California at Santa Cruz Pool
Complex
Masters: Contact Aquatics Manager Mickey
Wender at 459-3372 or Joel Wilson at 425-5762.
Non-member participation: $3, includes pool fees.
Notes: Coached workouts: M-F: 6-7:30AM, Noon-
1:30PM, 5:30-7PM*. Sa: 9-10:30AM. *Change to
6:30-8PM from mid-Jun. to mid-Sep.

SANTA ROSA   707

THE PARKPOINT CLUB 1200 N. Dutton Ave.
Phone: 578-1640.
Pool: 20y, 3 lanes, outdoors, heated, 80°.
Affiliate: IHRSA outside a 50 mile radius $10.
Preferred Clubs outside a 50 mile radius 4 visits
per month NC.
Hotel: All Santa Rosa hotels $10 with a voucher
from the hotel.

FINLEY AQUATICS COMPLEX 2060 W. College
Ave.
Phone: 543-3760.
Pool: 25m, 10 lanes, outdoors, heated, 82°-85°.
Admission: $1.75, SC(55) $1.50.

DOUBLETREE HOTEL 3555 Round Barn Blvd.
Phone: 523-7555. **Reservations:** 800-222-TREE.
Pool: 20y, rectangular, outdoors, heated, 82°.
Admission: Registered guests only NC.

SANTA ROSA SWIM CENTER 455 Ridgway Ave.
Phone: 543-3421.
Pool: 25m, 6 lanes, outdoors, heated, 82°.
Admission: $1.75, SC(55) $1.50.
Masters: Contact Nancy Breen at 543-3421.

SONOMA COUNTY FAMILY YMCA 1111 College
Ave.
Phone: 545-9622.
Pool: 25y, indoors, heated, 84°.
Admission: $10.
Affiliate: YMCA 5 visits per month NC, then $5.

**MONTECITO HEIGHTS HEALTH & RACQUET
CLUB** at the Flamingo Resort Hotel & Fitness
Center, 2777 - 4th St.
Phone: Club: 526-0529. Hotel: 545-8530.
Reservations: 800-848-8300.
Pool: 25m, 7 lanes, outdoors, heated, 80°.
Admission: Registered guests: Pool NC. Full
facility $10.

Affiliate: IHRSA outside a 50 mile radius $10.
To find: The club is on the Flamingo Hotel property, follow the driveway around back.

LA CANTERA RACQUET & SWIM CLUB 3737 Montgomery Dr.
Phone: 544-9494.
Pool: 25m, outdoors, heated, 80°.
Affiliate: IHRSA $5.

SARATOGA 408

SOUTHWEST YMCA 13500 Quito Rd.
Phone: 370-1877.
Pool: 25y x 35f, 5 lanes, indoors, heated, 84°.
Admission: $10.
Affiliate: Y AWAY NC.
Masters: Contact J. Kerklove at 370-1877.

SEASIDE 408

PATTULLO SWIM CENTER 1148 Wheeler St.
Phone: 899-6272.
Pool: 25y, 6 lanes, indoors, heated, 83°.
Admission: Lap swimming: Residents $2, SC(60) $1.50. Non-residents $2.50.

SHINGLE SPRINGS 916

SPORTS CLUB OF EL DORADO 4242 Sports Club Dr.
Phone: 677-5705.
Pool: 25y, outdoors, heated, 79°-82°.
Admission: $7.
Masters: A Masters program is in formation. Contact Terry Smith at 677-5705.

SONOMA 707

THE PARKPOINT CLUB 19111 Sonoma Hwy.
Phone: 996-3111.
Pool: 25y x 30f, 4 lanes, outdoors, heated, 80°.
Affiliate: IHRSA outside a 50 mile radius $10. Preferred Clubs outside a 50 mile radius 4 visits per month NC.

SOUTH LAKE TAHOE 916

CITY OF SOUTH LAKE TAHOE RECREATION & SWIM POOL COMPLEX 1180 Rufus Allen Blvd.
Phone: 542-6055.
Pool: 25y x 45f, 6 lanes, indoor/outdoor, heated, 83°.
Admission: $2.75, SC(55) & Disabled $1.75.
To find: Rufus Allen Blvd. is off Hwy. 50.

SOUTH SAN FRANCISCO 415

ORANGE POOL at the corner of Orange & Tennis
Phone: 877-8572.
Pool: 25y, 6 lanes, indoors, heated, 84°-86°.
Admission: $2.50.
Masters: Contact the pool staff at 877-8572.

STOCKTON 209

WEST LANE RACQUET CLUB 1074 E. Bianchi
Phone: 472-2100.
Pool: 25y, outdoors, unheated, the range of water temperatures was not reported.
Admission: $10.
Affiliate: IHRSA $5.

MARINA TENNIS & SWIM CLUB 6545 Embarcadero Dr.
Phone: 472-2110.
Pool: 30y, outdoors, heated, 80°.
Admission: $10.

SUNNYVALE 408

24-HOUR NAUTILUS 150 E. Fremont
Phone: 737-8600.
Pool: 20y, indoors, heated, 82°.
Admission: $10.
Affiliate: IHRSA $7.

SUNNYVALE MIDDLE SCHOOL POOL 1080 Mango Ave.
Phone: 730-7350.
Pool: 25y x 15m, 6 lanes, outdoors, heated, 82°.
Admission: Residents $2, non-residents $3.
To find: At the intersection of Mary and Remington. Mary connects with El Camino Real.

SHERATON INN SUNNYVALE 1100 N. Mathilda Ave.
Phone: 745-6000. **Reservations:** 800-836-8686.
Pool: 20y, rectangular, outdoors, heated, 82°.
Admission: Registered guests only NC.

TIBURON 415

TIBURON PENINSULA CLUB 1600 Mar West
Phone: 435-0968.
Pool: 25y, outdoors, heated, 82°.
Memberships: I/S $3,000 + $90/month.
Notes: As of Jul., 1994, there was a one year waiting list for membership. A $100 deposit is required to be placed on the list and is credited against the initiation fee when a membership becomes available.

TRACY 209

TRACY SPORTS CLUB 101 S. Tracy Blvd.
Phone: 836-2504.
Pool: 25y, 3 lanes, indoor/outdoor, heated, 82°.
Affiliate: IHRSA $7, 5 visits $25.

TRUCKEE 916

TRUCKEE-DONNER COMMUNITY POOL 11839 Donner Pass Rd.
Phone: 582-7725.
Pool: 25y x 45f, 6 lanes, indoors, heated, 82°-84°.
Admission: $2, SC(60) $1.

To find: Behind Tahoe-Truckee High School.
Masters: The Sierra Nevada Masters. Contact
Sally Dillon at 583-7439(h).

TULARE   209

TULARE FUN & FITNESS CENTER 1675 N. Gem
Phone: 685-9030.
Pool: 20y, indoor/outdoor, heated, 82°.
Admission: $8.

UKIAH   707

REDWOOD HEALTH CLUB 3101 S. State St.
Phone: 468-0441.
Pool 1: 25y x 60f, 4 lanes, outdoors, heated, 80°.
Pool 2: 20y x 40f, 2 lanes, indoors, heated, 90°.
Admission: $10, SC $6.
Affiliate: IHRSA $7.
Notes: Half of each pool is always open to lap
swimmers.
To find: At the south end of town, near the Hwy.
253 Exit.
Masters: The Ukiah Masters. Contact Rick
Mulvihill at 468-8942(h).

VACAVILLE   707

VACAVILLE COMMUNITY POOL 1100 Alamo Dr.
Phone: 449-5378.
Pool: 25y x 60f, 8 lanes, outdoors, heated, 82°.
Admission: $2.25.

VALLEJO   707

LAKERIDGE ATHLETIC CLUB 124 Frontage Rd.
Phone: 644-7788.
Pool: 25y, indoors, heated, 82°.
Affiliate: IHRSA $10.

CUNNINGHAM POOL 801 Heartwood
Phone: 648-4635.
Pool: 25y x 50m, outdoors, heated, 80°-84°.
Admission: $1.50.

WALNUT CREEK   510

WALNUT CREEK SPORTS & FITNESS CLUB
1908 Olympic Blvd.
Phone: 932-6400.
Pool: 20m, 3 lanes, outdoors, heated, 83°.
Affiliate: IHRSA $8.50.
Hotel: Holiday Inn (932-3332), Marriott (934-2000),
& Walnut Creek Inn: $8.50 with room key.
To find: In the downtown area, two blocks west of
Longs Drugs.

CLARKE MEMORIAL POOL Heather Farms Park,
1750 Heather Dr.
Phone: 943-5856.
Pool: 50m x 25y, 9 x 22 lanes, outdoors, heated,
81°.

Admission: $2.25.
Affiliate: USS NC with prior arrangement.
Hotel: Marriott Walnut Creek (934-2000) NC with
room key.

WALNUT CREEK MASTERS at Clarke Memorial
Pool
Masters: Contact Head Coach Kerry O'Brien at
943-5856.
Affiliate: USMS $2.25, includes pool fees.
Notes: Workouts: M,Tu,Th: 5:30-6:45AM, 10:30-
11:30AM, Noon-1:15PM, 7-8:15PM. W: 5:30-
6:45AM, Noon-1:15PM, 7-8:15PM. F: 5:30-
6:45AM, 10:30-11:30AM, Noon-1:15PM.

VALLEY VISTA TENNIS CLUB 3737 Valley Vista
Rd.
Phone: 934-4050.
Pool: 25y, outdoors, heated, 80°.
Admission: $12.
Affiliate: IHRSA NC.

WATSONVILLE   408

WATSONVILLE SPA FITNESS CENTER 25 Penny
Lane
Phone: 722-3895.
Pool: 25y x 36f, 5 lanes, outdoors, heated, 80°.
Admission: $10.
To find: Two miles north of Main St. on Green
Valley Rd.

WATSONVILLE YMCA 27 Sudden St.
Phone: 728-9622.
Pool: 25y, indoors, heated, 85°.
Admission: $10.
Affiliate: YMCA 3 visits NC.

WOODLAND   916

COUNTRY OAKS RACQUET CLUB 1341 E. Gum
Ave.
Phone: 666-2444.
Pool: 25y, outdoors, heated, 80°-85°.
Admission: $8.
Affiliate: IHRSA $6.

YUBA CITY   916

YUBA CITY RACQUET & HEALTH CLUB 825
Jones Rd.
Phone: 673-6900.
Pool: 25y x 28f, 4 lanes, indoors, heated, 82°.
Admission: $10.
Affiliate: IHRSA $5.
Notes: The club also has a 55f outdoor pool.
To find: Just off Hwy. 99. Go east on Jones Rd.
six blocks. The club is between Lincoln and
Richland Rds.
Masters: Contact Dottie Banta at 673-6900.

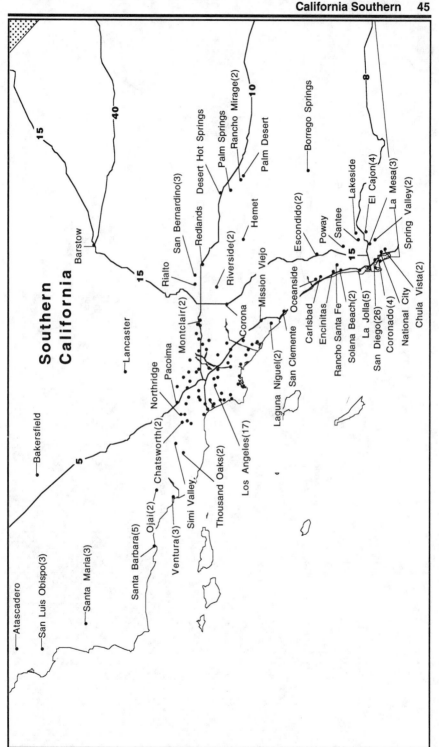

Southern California

Atascadero
San Luis Obispo(3)
Santa Maria(3)
Bakersfield
Lancaster
Barstow
Santa Barbara(5)
Ojai(2)
Chatsworth(2)
Ventura(3)
Simi Valley
Thousand Oaks(2)
Northridge
Pacoima
Montclair(2)
Los Angeles(17)
Laguna Niguel(2)
San Clemente
Corona
Mission Viejo
Rialto
San Bernardino(3)
Redlands
Desert Hot Springs
Palm Springs
Rancho Mirage(2)
Palm Desert
Riverside(2)
Hemet
Oceanside
Carlsbad
Encinitas
Rancho Santa Fe
Solana Beach(2)
La Jolla(5)
San Diego(26)
Coronado(4)
National City
Chula Vista(2)
Escondido(2)
Borrego Springs
Poway
Santee
Lakeside
El Cajon(4)
La Mesa(3)
Spring Valley(2)
Barstow
15
40
10
8
5

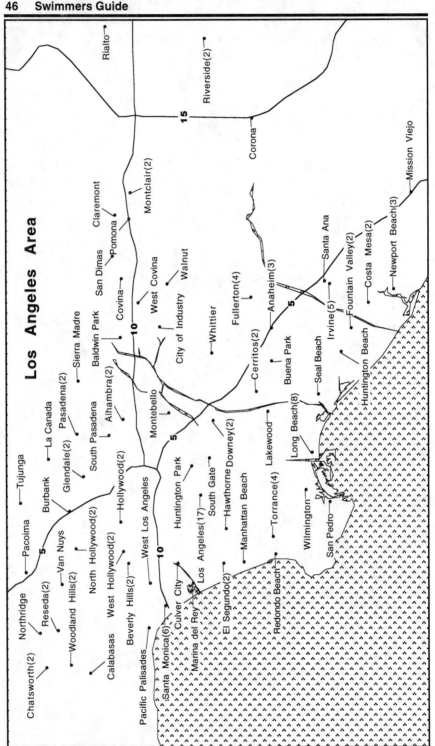

Los Angeles Area

ALHAMBRA   818

ALHAMBRA PARK POOL 500 N. Palm Ave.
Phone: 570-5051.
Pool: 25y x 25m, 8 lanes, outdoors, temperature controlled, 81°-82°.
Admission: $1.25.
Masters: The Alhambra Masters Swim Team. Contact Fabio Astudillo at 570-5051.

WEST SAN GABRIEL VALLEY YMCA 401 E. Corto St.
Phone: 576-0226 or (213) 283-7466.
Pool: 25y x 45f, 6 lanes, indoors, heated, 84°.
Admission: $8, SC(62) $7.
Affiliate: Y AWAY 3 visits per month NC, then $4, SC(62) $3.50.
To find: At the intersection of Chapel and Mission, next to Almansor Park. The building entrance faces Corto St.

ANAHEIM   714

ANAHEIM FAMILY YMCA 1515 W. North St.
Phone: 635-9622.
Pool: 25y x 38f, 6 lanes, indoors, heated, 86°.
Admission: $10.
Affiliate: YMCA $5.
To find: Directly behind the Anaheim Plaza on Euclid.

BALLY'S HOLIDAY SPA 310 S. Magnolia
Phone: 952-3101.
Pool: 20y, indoors, heated, 80°-88°.
Admission: 1 visit NC.
Affiliate: Bally's NC.

L.A. FITNESS 2560 E. Katelia
Phone: 634-1919.
Pool: 25m, outdoors, heated, 82°.
Admission: $10.

ATASCADERO   805

KENNEDY NAUTILUS CENTER 3534 El Camino Real
Phone: 466-6775.
Pool: 25y x 18f, 3 lanes, indoors, heated, 82°.
Admission: $10.
Affiliate: IHRSA $5.
Hotel: Best Western Colony Inn (466-4449) NC with a pass from the hotel.

BAKERSFIELD   805

HILLMAN AQUATIC CENTER California State University, 9001 Stockdale Hwy.
Phone: 664-2071.
Pool 1: 50m x 25y, 8 x 20 lanes, outdoors, heated, 80°.
Pool 2: 25y (3.5f deep), 6 lanes, outdoors, heated, water temperature not reported.
Admission: $3.

Memberships: $30/month.
Notes: The pool closes for school breaks.
To find: The CSUB Campus is on Stockdale Hwy., just west of Gasford Rd.

BALDWIN PARK   818

BALDWIN PARK POOL 4100 Baldwin Park Blvd.
Phone: 813-5245.
Pool: 25m, indoors, heated, 82°.
Admission: Residents 50¢, non-residents $1.50.
To find: At the intersection of Baldwin Park Blvd. and Ramona.

BARSTOW   619

AL VIGIL COMMUNITY SWIM CENTER 840 Barstow Rd.
Phone: 256-SWIM.
Pool: 25y x 25m, 8 lanes, indoors, heated, 84°.
Admission: $1.50.
Notes: The Park District also operates an outdoor pool in Foglesong Park from Memorial Day to Labor Day.
To find: One block north of the I-15/Barstow Rd. interchange.
Masters: The Barstow Swim Team Association. Contact Scott Lemming at 256-SWIM.

BEVERLY HILLS   310

THE BEVERLY HILTON 9876 Wilshire Blvd.
Phone: 274-7777. **Reservations:** 800-HILTONS.
Pool: 92f x 50f, 'rectangle at an angle', outdoors, heated, water temperature not reported.
Admission: Registered guests only NC.

THE PENINSULA BEVERLY HILLS 9882 Little Santa Monica Blvd.
Phone: 551-2888. **Reservations:** 800-462-7899.
Pool: 20y, rectangular, outdoors, heated, 68°.
Admission: Registered guests only NC.

BORREGO SPRINGS   619

LA CASA DEL ZORRO 3845 Yaqui Pass Rd.
Phone: 767-5323. **Reservations:** 800-824-1884.
Pool: 20y, outdoors, heated, 84°.
Admission: Registered guests only NC.

BUENA PARK   714

SEQUOIA ATHLETIC CLUB 7530 Orangethorpe Ave.
Phone: 739-4141.
Pool: 25m, indoors, heated, 80°.
Admission: $15.

BURBANK   818

BURBANK FAMILY YMCA 321 E. Magnolia Blvd.
Phone: 845-8551.
Pool: 20y, indoors, heated, 83°-87°.

Admission: M-F: 6AM-4PM $10.
Affiliate: Y AWAY 3 visits per month NC.

CALABASAS   818

CALABASAS PARK TENNIS & SWIM CENTER
23400 Park Sorrento
Phone: 222-2782.
Pool: 25y, outdoors, heated, 82°.
Admission: $2, SC(50) $1.

CARLSBAD   619

**CITY OF CARLSBAD COMMUNITY SWIM
COMPLEX** 3401 Monroe St.
Phone: 434-2860.
Pool: 25m x 25y, 10 x 8 lanes, outdoors, heated,
82°.
Admission: Residents $1.75, non-residents $2.75.
To find: From I-5 take the Carlsbad Village Dr. Exit,
proceed east seven tenths of a mile to Monroe St.
and turn right (south) onto Monroe. The Swim
Complex is three tenths of a mile down on the right
(west) side of the street, just north of Carlsbad
High School.

CARLSBAD MASTERS at the City of Carlsbad
Community Swim Complex
Masters: Contact Head Coach Jeff Pease at 943-
0810.
Non-member participation: $4.
Notes: Coached workouts: M-F: 6-7:30AM, Noon-
1:15PM, 1:15-2:30PM*. Sa: 7:30-8:45AM. *This
time block is seasonal.

CERRITOS   310

BALLY'S HOLIDAY SPA 11881 E. Del Amo Blvd.
Phone: 924-1514.
Pool: 20y, indoors, heated, 88°.
Admission: 1 visit NC.
Affiliate: Bally's NC.

CERRITOS OLYMPIC SWIM CENTER 13150 E.
166th St.
Phone: 926-7568.
Pool: 25y x 50m, 10 lanes, indoors, heated, 83°.
Admission: $1.50.
To find: Less than a mile off the 91 Frwy. at
Bloomfield. Ten minutes northeast of the Cerritos
Mall.

CHATSWORTH   818

BALLY'S HOLIDAY SPA 9143 De Soto Ave.
Phone: 882-5912.
Pool: 25y, outdoors, heated, 87°.
Affiliate: Bally's NC.

IRIS RYKER POOL 9825 Topanga Canyon Blvd.
Phone: 709-5588.
Pool: 50m, outdoors, heated, 84°.
Admission: $5.

CHULA VISTA   619

PARK WAY SWIM POOL 385 Park Way
Phone: 691-5088.
Pool: 25y, outdoors, heated, 80°-84°.
Admission: 75¢.

LOMA VERDE POOL 1420 Loma Lane
Phone: 691-5081.
Pool: 50m x 25y, 8 lanes, outdoors, heated, 82°.
Admission: 75¢.

CITY OF INDUSTRY   818

INDUSTRY HILLS SWIM STADIUM 1 Industry Hills
Pkwy.
Phone: 854-2364.
Pool 1: 25y x 50m, 26 lanes, outdoors, heated, 82°.
Pool 2: 25m x 25y, outdoors, heated, 82°.
Admission: $5.
Hotel: Sheraton Resort & Conference Center (965-
0861) NC.
To find: Just off the 60 Frwy. and Azusa Blvd.
Masters: Contact Michelle Stem, Head Coach, at
854-2364.

CLAREMONT   909

THE CLAREMONT CLUB 1777 Monte Vista Ave.
Phone: 625-6791.
Pool: 50m, outdoors, heated, 80°.
Affiliate: IHRSA $10.
Hotel: Griswold's Hotel (626-2411) & Red Lion
(983-0909): NC with room key.
Notes: There is also a 30f, outdoor, recreational /
therapy pool.
Masters: Contact John Ries at 625-6791.

CORONA   909

L.A. FITNESS 1750 W. 6th St.
Phone: 734-7850.
Pool: 20m, outdoors, heated, 81°.
Admission: $10.

CORONADO   619

CORONADO MUNICIPAL POOL 1845 Strand Way
Phone: 522-7803.
Pool 1: 50m x 25y, 10 lanes, outdoors, heated, 80°.
Pool 2: 25y diving pool, outdoors, heated, 83°.
Admission: Residents $1, SC(60) 75¢. Non-resi-
dents $3, SC $2.
Notes: The diving pool has one 3m and two 1m
boards.
To find: Approximately one half mile south of the
Hotel del Coronado, across the street from the
Shores Condominium, on the east (bay) side of
Strand Way.

CORONADO MASTERS ASSOCIATION at
Coronado Municipal Pool
Masters: Contact Bill Earley at 435-2953 or Alicia
Coleman at 423-9468(h).

Affiliate: USMS NC, includes pool fees. Visiting Masters are expected to attend social functions scheduled during their stay.
Notes: Uncoached workouts: M,W,F: 6-7:30PM.

HOTEL DEL CORONADO 1500 Orange Ave.
Phone: 435-6611. **Reservations:** 800-HOTELDEL.
Pool: 100f x 30f, rectangular, outdoors, heated, 70°.
Admission: Registered guests only NC.

LE MERIDIEN SAN DIEGO 2000 - 2nd St.
Phone: 435-3000. **Reservations:** 800-543-4300.
Pool: 25y, rectangular, outdoors, heated, 80°.
Admission: $15. Registered guests NC.
Memberships: 3 months $200.

LOEWS CORONADO BAY RESORT 4000 Coronado Bay Rd.
Phone: 424-4000. **Reservations:** 800-81-LOEWS.
Pool: 100f x 39.75f, 'T' shape, outdoors, heated, 76°.
Admission: Registered guests only NC.

COSTA MESA   714

THE WESTIN SOUTH COAST PLAZA 686 Anton Blvd.
Phone: 540-2500. **Reservations:** 800-228-3000.
Pool: 58f x 28f, rectangular, outdoors, heated, 80°.
Admission: Registered guests only NC.

BALLY'S SPORTS CONNECTION 555 W. 19th St.
Phone: 650-3600.
Pool: 20m, indoors, heated, 82°.
Admission: Call.
Affiliate: Bally's NC.

COVINA   818

EMBASSY SUITES 1211 E. Garvey
Phone: 915-3441. **Reservations:** 800-EMBASSY.
Pool: 61f x 29f, oval or kidney shape, outdoors, heated, 76°-78° in winter, 74°-78° in summer.
Admission: Registered guests only NC.

CULVER CITY   310

CULVER-PALMS FAMILY YMCA 4500 S. Sepulveda Blvd.
Phone: 390-3604.
Pool: 25y x 25f, 4 lanes, indoors, heated, 85°.
Admission: $5, SC(62) $3.
Affiliate: YMCA NC.
Masters: The Culver-Palms YMCA Masters.
Contact Program Director Liz Weiner at 390-3604.

DESERT HOT SPRINGS   619

DESERT HOT SPRINGS SPA HOTEL 10805 Palm Dr.

Phone: 329-6495. **Reservations:** 800-843-6053.
Pool: 30m, outdoors, unheated, 70°-75°.
Admission: $3-$6. Registered guests NC.

DOWNEY   310

DOWNEY FAMILY BRANCH YMCA 11531 Downey Ave.
Phone: 862-4201.
Pool: 25y, indoors, heated, 84°.
Admission: Weekdays before 4PM $7.
Affiliate: YMCA Call.

IMPERIAL SPA, INC. 9440 E. Imperial Hwy.
Phone: 803-4411.
Pool: 25y, outdoors, heated, 80°.
Affiliate: IPFA NC.

EL CAJON   619

MONTGOMERY MIDDLE SCHOOL POOL 1570 Melody Lane
Phone: 698-2502.
Pool: 25y x 25m, 10 lanes, outdoors, heated, 81°.
Admission: $2.

VALHALLA HIGH SCHOOL POOL 1725 Hillsdale Rd.
Phone: 698-2502.
Pool: 25y x 25m, 10 lanes, outdoors, heated, 81°.
Admission: $2.

GROSSMONT HIGH SCHOOL POOL 1100 Murray Dr.
Phone: 698-2502.
Pool: 25y x 25m, 10 lanes, outdoors, heated, 81°.
Admission: $2.
Masters: The Heartland Swim Association.
Contact Chuck Hay at 464-8680(h).

EL CAJON VALLEY HIGH SCHOOL POOL 1035 Madison Ave.
Phone: 698-2502.
Pool: 25y x 25m, 10 lanes, outdoors, heated, 81°.
Admission: $2.
Masters: The Heartland Swim Association.
Contact Pat Tope at 475-4741(h).

EL SEGUNDO   310

SPECTRUM CLUB - MANHATTAN BEACH 2250 Park Place
Phone: 643-6878.
Pool: 25y x 35f, 5 lanes, indoors, heated, 79°.
Admission: Call.
Affiliate: IHRSA $10.

DOUBLETREE CLUB HOTEL LAX 1985 E. Grand Ave.
Phone: 322-0999. **Reservations:** 800-222-8733.
Pool: 20y x 30f, rectangular, outdoors, heated, 80°.
Admission: Registered guests NC.

ENCINITAS 619

MAGDALENA ECKE FAMILY YMCA 200 Saxsony Rd.
Phone: 942-9622.
Pool: 25y x 45f, 5 lanes, indoors, heated, 82°.
Admission: $7.
Affiliate: Out-of-county Y AWAY NC, in-county $3.50.
Hotel: Radisson Hotel (942-7455) $3.50 with room key.
Notes: There is also a dive pool with 1m and 3m boards.
To find: Directly off I-5, the cross street is Encinitas Blvd.

ESCONDIDO 619

PALOMAR FAMILY YMCA 1050 N. Broadway
Phone: 745-7490.
Pool: 25m, 6 lanes, outdoors, heated, 82°.
Admission: $5.
Affiliate: Out-of-area YMCA NC, in-area $2.50.

ESCONDIDO ATHLETIC CLUB 130 W. Lincoln
Phone: 746-9300.
Pool: 25y, outdoors, heated, 80°.
Admission: $10.

FOUNTAIN VALLEY 714

SEQUOIA ATHLETIC CLUB / RACQUETBALL WORLD 10115 Talbert Ave.
Phone: 962-1374.
Pool: 20m, indoors, heated, 86°.
Admission: $10.

LOS CABALLEROS SPORTS CLUB 17272 Newhope St.
Phone: 546-8560.
Pool: 50m x 25y, outdoors, heated, 78°.
Admission: $10.

FULLERTON 714

SEQUOIA ATHLETIC CLUB / RACQUETBALL WORLD 1535 Deer Park Dr.
Phone: 961-0400.
Pool: 20m, indoors, heated, 82°.
Admission: $15.
Affiliate: IHRSA $5.

BALLY'S HOLIDAY SPA 246 E. Orangethorp Ave.
Phone: 879-6611.
Pool: 25m, indoors, heated, 82°-85°.
Admission: Call.
Affiliate: Bally's NC.

INDEPENDENCE PARK POOL 801 W. Valencia Dr.
Phone: 738-5369.
Pool: 25y + 33m x 50m, 18 x 8 lanes, outdoors, heated, 79°-80°.

Admission: $2, SC(55) $1.
Notes: There is also a 25y x 35y, outdoor, unheated, summer pool.
To find: At the intersection of Valencia Dr. and Euclid, next to the Fullerton Dept. of Motor Vehicles.
Masters: The Fullerton Aquatic Sports Team (FAST). Contact Coach Kevin Perry at 871-9616(h).

NORTH ORANGE BRANCH YMCA 2000 Youth Way
Phone: 879-9622.
Pool: 25y, indoors, heated, 83°.
Admission: $5.

GLENDALE 818

GLENDALE YMCA 140 N. Louise St.
Phone: 240-4130.
Pool: 25y x 40f, 6 lanes, indoors, heated, water temperature not reported.
Admission: $10.
Affiliate: Y AWAY NC.
To find: At the intersection of Louise St. and Wilson, two blocks east of Brand Blvd.

YWCA OF GLENDALE 735 E. Lexington Dr.
Phone: 242-4155.
Pool: 25y x 37f, 3 lanes, indoors, heated, 86°.
Admission: $2.50, SC(60) $1.
Affiliate: YWCA $1, SC 50¢.
To find: From I-210, take the Glendale Exit and go south about two blocks to Lexington Dr. The YWCA is a big white building marked 'YWCA', across the street from Albertson's.

HAWTHORNE 310

HAWTHORNE MUNICIPAL POOL 12501 Inglewood Ave.
Phone: 970-7228.
Pool: 40y x 60f, 8 lanes, outdoors, heated, 82°.
Admission: $3, SC $1.

HEMET 909

HEMET SPORT-N-FITNESS 630 W. Lathem
Phone: 652-4303.
Pool: 20y x 40f, indoors, heated, 86°.
Admission: $10.

HOLLYWOOD 213

HOLLYWOOD WILSHIRE YMCA 1553 N. Hudson Ave.
Phone: 467-4161.
Pool: 20y x 40f, 6 lanes, indoors, heated, 82°.
Affiliate: YMCA 3 visits per week NC.
To find: Five blocks west of Vine St., between Sunset and Hollywood Blvds.

BALLY'S HOLIDAY SPA 1628 El Centro Ave. off Grower
Phone: 461-0227.
Pool: 25y, indoors, heated, 80°-83°.
Admission: Call.
Affiliate: Bally's NC.

HUNTINGTON BEACH   714

BALLY'S HOLIDAY SPA 17091 Beach Blvd.
Phone: 848-1919.
Pool: 25m, indoors, heated, 80°-82°.
Affiliate: Bally's NC.

HUNTINGTON PARK   213

SOUTHEAST-RIO VISTA YMCA 6208 Seville Ave.
Phone: 588-2256.
Pool: 25y x 24f, 4 lanes, indoors, heated, 80°-85°.
Admission: Pool $1 per hour.
Affiliate: YMCA NC.

IRVINE   714

HERITAGE PARK AQUATICS COMPLEX 4601 Walnut Ave.
Phone: 559-0472.
Pool 1: 25y x 50m, 18 lanes, outdoors, heated, 79°.
Pool 2: 25y x 33m, 9 lanes, outdoors, heated, 79°.
Pool 3: 25y x 24y, 6 lanes, outdoors, heated, 79°.
Admission: $2, SC(55) $1.50.
To find: Next to Irvine High School.
Masters: The Irvine Novaquatics. Contact Dave Salo at 559-6682(w&h).

RADISSON PLAZA HOTEL ORANGE COUNTY AIRPORT 18800 MacArthur Blvd.
Phone: 833-9999. **Reservations:** 800-333-3333.
Pool: 85f, 'lazy 8' shape, outdoors, heated, 78°.
Admission: Registered guests only NC.

THE SPORTING CLUB 18007 Von Karman Ave.
Phone: 250-4422.
Pool: 25m, 8 lanes, outdoors, heated, 78°-80°.
Admission: $15.
Affiliate: IHRSA $11.

RACQUET CLUB OF IRVINE 5 Sandburg Way
Phone: 786-3000.
Pool: 25m, outdoors, heated, 82°.
Affiliate: IHRSA $4.

CRAWFORD HALL POOL University of California at Irvine, 1368 Crawford Hall
Phone: 856-6401.
Pool: 25y, 6 lanes, outdoors, heated, 78°-80°.
Admission: $3.
Memberships: 3 months $70.

LA CANADA   818

CRESCENTA-CANADA FAMILY YMCA 1930 Foothill Blvd.

Phone: 790-0123.
Pool: 25y, indoors, heated, 84°.
Admission: $11.
Affiliate: YMCA NC.

LA JOLLA   619

LAWRENCE FAMILY JEWISH COMMUNITY CENTER OF SAN DIEGO COUNTY 4126 Executive Dr.
Phone: 457-3030.
Pool: 50m x 35y + 25y, 8 x 5 + 10 lanes, outdoors, heated, 81°.
Admission: $5.
Affiliate: JCC NC.
Hotel: Marriott La Jolla (587-1414) NC with a pass from the hotel.
To find: The big white building on Executive Dr., between Regents and Genessee.
Masters: The Golden Triangle Masters. Contact Aquatics Director Randy Franke at 457-3030.

LA JOLLA YMCA 8355 Cliffridge Ave.
Phone: 453-3483.
Pool: 25y x 37.5f, 5 lanes, outdoors, heated, 83°.
Admission: $7.
Affiliate: Y AWAY NC.
Hotel: Residence Inn (587-1770) — Call the Residence Inn for information.

SHILEY SPORTS & HEALTH CENTER OF SCRIPPS CLINIC 10820 N. Torrey Pines Rd.
Phone: 554-3488.
Pool: 25y x 28f, 4 lanes, outdoors, heated, 81°.
Admission: $15.
Hotel: Sheraton Grande Torrey Pines Hotel (558-1500) $7.50.
To find: Between the Scripps Clinic and the Sheraton Grande Torrey Pines.
Masters: The Shiley Sports & Health Center Masters. Contact Terri Kolb at 554-9066.

RADISSON HOTEL LA JOLLA 3299 Holiday Court
Phone: 453-5500. **Reservations:** 800-345-9995.
Pool: 50f, 'L' shape, outdoors, heated, 75°.
Admission: Registered guests only NC.

CANYONVIEW POOL University of California - San Diego, 9500 Gilman Dr.
Phone: 534-6034.
Pool: 25y x 50m, 19 lanes, outdoors, heated, 80°.
Admission: $5.
Masters: U.C.S.D. Masters Swimming. Contact Ron Marcikic at 534-6034.

LA MESA   619

HELIX HIGH SCHOOL POOL 7323 University Ave.
Phone: 698-2502.
Pool: 25y x 25m, 10 lanes, outdoors, heated, 81°.
Admission: $2.

LA MESA ═══════════ CONTINUED

LA MESA MUNICIPAL POOL 5100 Memorial Dr.
Phone: 466-4178.
Pool: 25m x 25y, 6 x 5 lanes, outdoors, heated, 80°-82°.
Admission: $2, SC(55) $1.
To find: In McArthur Park, near downtown La Mesa. La Mesa Blvd. and University meet at Memorial Dr., there is a Little League Field on the corner. The pool is located at the end of Memorial Dr.
Masters: The La Mesa Masters. Contact Jill Lapp or Becky Jackman at 466-4178.

DAVIS / GROSSMONT YMCA 8881 Dallas St.
Phone: 464-1323.
Pool: 25y x 33f, 5 lanes, outdoors, heated, 82°.
Admission: $5.
Affiliate: Out-of-county YMCA NC, in-county $2.50.
To find: At La Mesita Park behind 125 N.

LAGUNA NIGUEL ═══════════ 714

CROWN VALLEY COMMUNITY POOL 29751 Crown Valley Pkwy.
Phone: 362-4351.
Pool: 25y x 99f, 9 lanes, outdoors, heated, 82°.
Admission: $2, SC(60) $1.

LAGUNA NIGUEL RACQUET CLUB 23500 Clubhouse Dr.
Phone: 496-4665.
Pool: 20y x 30f, outdoors, heated, 82°.
Admission: Call.
Affiliate: IHRSA $8.
Hotel: Some local hotels have arrangements. Call the club for information.

LAKESIDE ═══════════ 619

EL CAPITAN HIGH SCHOOL POOL 10410 Ashwood St.
Phone: 698-2502.
Pool: 25y x 25m, 10 lanes, outdoors, heated, 81°.
Admission: $2.

LAKEWOOD ═══════════ 310

LAKEWOOD FAMILY YMCA 5835 E. Carson St.
Phone: 425-7431.
Pool: 25m, outdoors, heated, 82°.
Admission: $5, SC(60) $3.
Affiliate: YMCA Call.

LANCASTER ═══════════ 805

EASTSIDE POOL - CITY OF LANCASTER 45045 N. 5th St. E.
Phone: 723-6255.
Pool: 25y x 25m, 8 x 8 lanes, indoors, heated, 81°.
Admission: $1.50, SC(55) 75¢.
To find: At the southwest corner of Ave. 'I' & 5th St. E., one half mile east of the Antelope Valley Fairgrounds.
Masters: Oasis Aquatics. Contact Coach Lisa Dahl at 723-2146(w).

LONG BEACH ═══════════ 310

BUFFUM-DOWNTOWN BRANCH YMCA 600 Long Beach Blvd.
Phone: 436-9622.
Pool: 25y, 8 lanes, outdoors, heated, 80°-81°.
Admission: $10.
Affiliate: YMCA 30 days NC.

BELMONT PLAZA OLYMPIC POOL 4000 Olympic Plaza
Phone: 438-1142.
Pool: 25m + 25m x 25y, 9 + 9 lanes, indoors, heated, 80°-82°.
Admission: $1.25.
Notes: Kickboards and pull buoys are available. Deep and shallow water aerobics classes are offered.
To find: At the intersection of Ocean & Termino. Termino ends at the parking lot and pool.

BALLY'S HOLIDAY SPA 4438 E. Pacific Hwy.
Phone: 494-1216.
Pool: 25m, indoors, heated, 82°.
Admission: Call.
Affiliate: Bally's NC.

FAIRFIELD FAMILY YMCA 4949 Atlantic Ave.
Phone: 423-0491.
Pool: 25y, 4 lanes, outdoors, heated, 84°.
Admission: $5.
Affiliate: YMCA NC.
To find: At the intersection of Delamo and Atlantic Ave.

BALLY'S SPORTS CONNECTION 3030 Bellflower Blvd.
Phone: 420-1444.
Pool: 20y, 4 lanes, indoors, heated, 80°.
Admission: Out-of-town visitors 1 week NC.
Affiliate: Bally's NC. IHRSA $10.

SILVERADO POOL 1540 W. 32nd
Phone: 570-1721.
Pool: 25m x 60f, 6 lanes, indoors, heated, 86°.
Admission: $1.25.
To find: Just off Santa Fe between Willow and Wardlow.

LONG BEACH AIRPORT MARRIOTT 4700 Airport Plaza Dr.
Phone: 425-5210. **Reservations:** 800-321-5642.
Pool: 25y, oval or kidney shape, indoors, heated, 80°-85°.
Admission: Registered guests only NC.

LOS ALTOS YMCA 1720 Bellflower Blvd.
Phone: 596-3394.
Pool: 25y, 4 lanes, outdoors, heated, 83°.

Admission: $5.
Affiliate: YMCA 3 visits per month NC, then $2.50.
To find: Just north of California State University at Long Beach.

LOS ANGELES   213

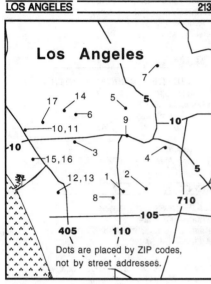

Los Angeles

7

17   14   5   5

6

9   10

10,11

-10

15,16   3   4

5

12,13   1   2

8   710

105

405   110

Dots are placed by ZIP codes, not by street addresses.

1. FREMONT POOL 7630 Towne Ave.
Phone: 847-3401.
Pool: 25y, indoors, heated, 84°.
Admission: $1.25, SC(65) 50¢.

2. LOS ANGELES ATHLETIC CLUB 431 W. 7th St.
Phone: 625-2211.
Pool: 25y, 5 lanes, indoors, heated, 82°.
Admission: Registered guests at the club's private hotel NC.
Memberships: Call for membership information.
Notes: An 'Executive Athletic Club', voted 'The Best Health Club Downtown' in The Downtown News, August, 1994. Members of the club have access to similarly prestigious facilities in many major U.S. cities.
Masters: Contact Nicholas Orazco at 625-2211.

3. RANCHOS CIENEGA POOL 5001 Rodeo Dr.
Phone: 847-3406.
Pool: 25m, 6 lanes, indoors, heated, 82°.
Admission: $1.25, SC(65) & Disabled 50¢.

4. WEINGART-EAST LOS ANGELES YMCA 2900 Whittier Blvd.
Phone: 260-7005.
Pool: 25y x 45f, 4.5f deep, indoors, heated, 82°-84°.
Admission: Lap swim $2. Day pass $7..

5. ECHO PARK POOL 1419 Colton St.
Phone: 481-2640.

Pool: 25y x 50y, 16 lanes, indoors, heated, 82°-83°.
Admission: $1.25.

SOUTHERN CALIFORNIA AQUATIC MASTERS (SCAQ) at Echo Park Pool
Masters: Contact Head Coach Clay Evans at (310) 451-6666.
Affiliate: USMS 3 workouts per year NC.
Notes: Coached workouts: M,W,F: 6-7AM.

6. WESTSIDE JEWISH COMMUNITY CENTER 5870 W. Olympic Blvd.
Phone: 938-2531 ext. 2245.
Pool: 25y x 30f, 5 lanes, indoors, heated, 83°.
Admission: $10.
Affiliate: JCC NC.

7. TAYLOR POOL Occidental College, 1600 Campus Rd.
Phone: 259-2608.
Pool: 25y, 6 lanes, outdoors, heated, 80°.
Memberships: $125/year.

8. WEINGART URBAN CENTER YMCA 9900 S. Vermont
Phone: 754-3191.
Pool: 25y, indoors, heated, 85°.
Admission: Call.

9. KETCHUM-DOWNTOWN YMCA 401 S. Hope St.
Phone: 624-2348.
Pool: 25y x 45f, 4 lanes, indoors, heated, 81°.
Admission: Weekdays $15. Weekends $10.
Affiliate: YMCA $5.
Hotel: Westin Bonaventure (624-1000) & Sheraton Grande Hotel (617-1133): NC with a pass obtained from the hotel concierge.
To find: At the intersection of 4th and Hope St., up the hill from the Bonaventure Hotel.
Masters: KDTY Masters. Contact Tara Shrinter at 624-2348 ext. 308.

LOS ANGELES   310

10. WESTSIDE FAMILY YMCA 1311 La Grange Ave.
Phone: 477-1511.
Pool: 25y, 6 lanes, indoors, heated, 82°.
Affiliate: Y AWAY 3 visits per month NC.

11. WESTWOOD RECREATIONAL COMPLEX 1350 Sepulveda Blvd. **Phone:** 478-7019 or 473-3610.
Pool: 25m x 25y, 10 x 10 lanes, indoors, heated, 82°-83°.
Admission: $1.25, SC(65) & Disabled 50¢.

SOUTHERN CALIFORNIA AQUATIC MASTERS (SCAQ) at Westwood Recreational Complex
Masters: Contact Head Coach Clay Evans at 451-6666.
Affiliate: USMS 3 workouts per year NC.

LOS ANGELES   CONTINUED

Notes: Coached workouts: M-F: 5:30-6:30AM, 6:30-7:30AM, Noon-1PM, 6:30-7:30PM.

12. WESTCHESTER YMCA 8015 S. Sepulveda Blvd.
Phone: 670-4316.
Pool: 25y x 30f, 5 lanes, indoors, heated, 84°.
Admission: $10.
Affiliate: YMCA outside a 10 mile radius 3 visits per month NC, then $5, within 10 miles $5.
To find: One half mile north of the Los Angeles Airport (LAX).

13. SPECTRUM CLUB AT HOWARD HUGHES CENTER 6833 Park Terrace
Phone: 216-3060.
Pool: 25m, indoors, heated, 78°-82°.
Admission: Out-of-town visitors $15.

14. FOUR SEASONS HOTEL AT BEVERLY HILLS 300 S. Doheny Dr.
Phone: 273-2222. **Reservations:** 800-332-3442.
Pool: 55f x 33.5f, rectangular, outdoors, heated, 79°-81°.
Admission: Registered guests only NC.

15. VENICE POOL 2490 Walgrove Ave.
Phone: 575-8260.
Pool: 25y x 18y, 7 lanes, indoors, heated, 81°-82°.
Admission: $1.25, SC(65) & Disabled 50¢.

SOUTHERN CALIFORNIA AQUATIC MASTERS (SCAQ) at Venice Pool
Masters: Contact Head Coach Clay Evans at 451-6666.
Affiliate: USMS 3 workouts per year NC.
Notes: Sep.-May: Coached workouts: M-F: 5:45AM-6:45AM, 6:45AM-7:45AM.

16. MARINA ATHLETIC CLUB 12980 Culver Blvd.
Phone: 301-2582.
Pool: 25m, outdoors, heated, 78°.
Admission: $10.
Affiliate: IHRSA $5.

17. CENTURY PLAZA HOTEL & TOWER 2025 Ave. of the Stars
Phone: 277-2000. **Reservations:** 800-228-3000.
Pool: 20y x 30f, outdoors, heated, 78°-81°.
Admission: Registered guests only NC.

MANHATTAN BEACH   310

RADISSON PLAZA HOTEL / LAX SOUTH 1400 Parkview
Phone: 546-7511. **Reservations:** 800-333-3333.
Pool: 20y, rectangular, outdoors, heated, 78°.
Admission: Registered guests only NC.

MARINA DEL REY   310

THE RITZ-CARLTON, MARINA DEL REY 4375 Admiralty Way
Phone: 823-1700.
Pool: 73f, outdoors, heated, 80°.
Admission: 2 visits per month $15 each. Registered guests NC.
Memberships: $75/week. $200/month.

MISSION VIEJO   714

MARGUERITE RECREATION CENTER 27341 Trabuco Circle
Phone: 380-2552.
Pool 1: 50m x 25y, outdoors, heated, 82°.
Pool 2: 25y, 5 lanes, outdoors, heated, 87°.
Pool 3: 25m x 25y, outdoors, heated, 82°.
Admission: $5.
To find: At Marguerite Pkwy. & Trabuco Rd.

MONTCLAIR   909

L.A. FITNESS 5515 Moreno St.
Phone: 985-2324.
Pool: 25m, outdoors, heated, 79°.
Affiliate: IHRSA NC.

BALLY'S HOLIDAY SPA 9385 Monte Vista
Phone: 625-2411.
Pool: 25m, indoors, heated, 80°-82°.
Admission: Call.
Affiliate: Bally's NC.

MONTEBELLO   213

BALLY'S HOLIDAY SPA 2222 W. Beverly Blvd.
Phone: 722-0994.
Pool: 27y, indoors, heated, 82°-85°.
Admission: Call.
Affiliate: Bally's NC.

NATIONAL CITY   619

NATIONAL CITY POOL 1800 E. 22nd St.
Phone: 336-4298.
Pool: 50m, outdoors, heated, 81°.
Admission: $1.

NEWPORT BEACH   714

NEWPORT-COSTA MESA YMCA 2300 University Dr.
Phone: 642-9990.
Pool: 25y, 6 lanes, indoor/outdoor, heated, 81°.
Admission: $10.
Affiliate: YMCA 3 visits per month NC, then $5.
To find: On the Back Bay, the major cross streets are University Dr. and Irvine Ave.

UNIVERSITY ATHLETIC CLUB 1701 Quail St.
Phone: 752-7903.
Pool: 25y x 25f, 4 lanes, outdoors, temperature

controlled, 78°-80°.
Affiliate: IHRSA & other reciprocal clubs:
Weekdays $12. Weekends $7.

MARIAN BURGESON AQUATIC COMPLEX at
Corona del Mar High School, 2102 Eastbluff Dr.
Phone: 644-3151.
Pool: 25y x 50m, 13± lanes, outdoors, heated, 80°.
Admission: $2.
To find: South on 73 to Jamboree, turn right onto
Eastbluff, the school is on the right.

NORTH HOLLYWOOD   213

EAST VALLEY YMCA 5142 Tijunga Ave.
Phone: 877-3881 or (818) 763-5126.
Pool: 25y, indoors, heated, 85°.
Admission: $5, SC $3.
Affiliate: YMCA 2 visits per month NC, then $3.

BALLY'S HOLIDAY SPA 13069 Victory Blvd.
Phone: 506-4208.
Pool: 25m, indoors, heated, 82°.
Admission: Call.
Affiliate: Bally's NC.

NORTHRIDGE   818

UNIVERSITY STUDENT UNION POOL California
State University, 18111 Nordhoff St.
Phone: 885-3604.
Pool: 24y+, 6 lanes, outdoors, heated, 82°.
Admission: $2.25.
Memberships: $65/semester.
Masters: Contact Richard Hadvina at 885-3604.

OCEANSIDE   619

BROOKS STREET SWIM CENTER 130 Brooks St.
Phone: 966-4537.
Pool: 100f x 50f, 7 lanes, outdoors, heated, 80°-
82°.
Admission: $1.
To find: One block east of I-5, two blocks south of
Mission Ave. Enter from the rear gate, parking to
the rear.

OJAI   805

OJAI VALLEY INN Country Club Rd.
Phone: 646-5511. **Reservations:** 800-422-6524.
Pool 1: 22y, rectangular, outdoors, heated, 79°-80°.
Pool 2: 22y, outdoors, heated, 87°.
Admission: Registered guests only NC.

OJAI VALLEY RACQUET CLUB 409 Fox St.
Phone: 646-7213.
Pool: 25m, outdoors, heated, 80°.
Affiliate: IHRSA: Weekdays $5. Weekends $6.50.

PACIFIC PALISADES   310

PALISADES-MALIBU YMCA POOL at 15601
Sunset Blvd.
Phone: 454-5591.
Pool: 25y, 6 lanes, outdoors, heated, 81°-83°.
Admission: $15, SC(65) $8.
Affiliate: YMCA 3 visits per month NC.
Notes: Other Y facilities are at a different location.
The address above is for the pool only.
Masters: The Palisades Malibu YMCA Masters.
Contact Gina Robbiano at 454-5591.

PACOIMA   818

HUBERT HUMPHREY POOL 12560 Filmore St.
Phone: 896-0067.
Pool: 25y x 100f, 6 lanes, 'L' shape, outdoors, heat-
ed, 80°.
Admission: $1.25, SC(65) 50¢.
To find: Three blocks south of the 118 Frwy.

PALM DESERT   619

PALM VALLEY SPA & RACQUET CLUB 76200
Country Club Dr.
Phone: 345-2747.
Pool: 25m, outdoors, heated, 78°-82°.
Affiliate: IHRSA $20.

PALM SPRINGS   619

PALM SPRINGS SWIM CENTER 405 S. Pavilion
Way
Phone: 323-8278.
Pool: 50m x 25y, 8 x 15 lanes, outdoors, tempera-
ture controlled, 80°-84°.
Admission: $3.
To find: In Sunrise Park, at the intersection of
Ramon and Sunrise.
Masters: The Palm Springs Piranhas. Contact
Tracy McFarlane at 322-1362.

PASADENA   818

AAF ROSE BOWL AQUATIC CENTER 36 N.
Arroyo Blvd.
Phone: 564-0330.
Pool 1: 50m x 25y, outdoors, heated, 79°.
Pool 2: 50m x 25y, outdoors, heated, 79°.
Admission: $5, SC(55) $3.75.

THE RITZ-CARLTON, HUNTINGTON HOTEL
1401 S. Oak Knoll Ave.
Phone: 568-3900. **Reservations:** 800-241-3333.
Pool: 70f x 24f, rectangular, outdoors, heated, 80°.
Admission: Registered guests only NC.

POMONA   909

POMONA YMCA 350 N. Garey Ave.
Phone: 623-6433.
Pool: 20y x 20f, 4 lanes, indoors, heated, 83°.

Admission: $6.
Affiliate: YMCA 3 visits per month NC.

POWAY   619

RANCHO ARBOLITOS SWIM & TENNIS CLUB
14343 Silverset St.
Phone: 486-3670.
Pool: 25y, outdoors, heated, 79°.
Memberships: I/S $268 + $40/month.

RANCHO MIRAGE   619

MARRIOTT'S RANCHO LAS PALMAS RESORT
41000 Bob Hope Dr.
Phone: 568-2727. **Reservations:** 800-458-8786.
Pool: 40y, oval or kidney shape, outdoors, heated,
72°.
Admission: Registered guests only NC.

THE RITZ-CARLTON, RANCHO MIRAGE 68-900
Frank Sinatra Dr.
Phone: 321-8282. **Reservations:** 800-241-3333.
Pool: 80f x 45f, multi-cornered, outdoors, tempera-
ture controlled, 81°.
Admission: $10. Registered guests NC.

RANCHO SANTA FE   619

THE INN AT RANCHO SANTA FE 5951 Linea del
Cielo
Phone: 756-1131. **Reservations:** 800-654-2928.
Pool: 50f, rectangular, outdoors, heated, 88°.
Admission: Registered guests only NC.
Notes: The Inn is located inland of Solana Beach
and has a cottage on the ocean for guests.

REDLANDS   909

REDLANDS SWIM & TENNIS CLUB 12626
Wabash Ave.
Phone: 794-3918.
Pool 1: 25y, outdoors, unheated, the range of water
temperatures was not reported.
Pool 2: 20y, outdoors, heated, 88°.
Affiliate: IHRSA $3.

REDONDO BEACH   310

EXECUTIVE GOLD'S GYM 200 N. Harbor Dr.
Phone: 374-5522.
Pool: 20m, outdoors, heated, 82°.
Admission: $10.
Affiliate: Gold's Gym — Call.

RESEDA   818

WEST VALLEY FAMILY YMCA 18810 Vanowen
St.
Phone: 345-7393.
Pool: 25y x 30f, 5 lanes, outdoors, heated, 82°.
Admission: $7.
Affiliate: YMCA 3 visits per month NC, then $3.50.

CLEVELAND POOL 8120 Vanalden Ave.
Phone: 756-9798.
Pool: 25y x 25m, 12 lanes, indoors, heated, 80°.
Admission: $1.25, SC(65) 50¢.
To find: Two Blocks south of Roscoe on Vanalden
Ave.
Masters: There is a Masters group in formation.
Contact Mike Shanto at 765-0284.

RIALTO   909

RIALTO RACQUET & FITNESS CENTER City of
Rialto, at the corner of Riverside and San
Bernardino
Phone: 820-2611.
Pool: 25y, 8 lanes, indoors, heated, 82°-85°.
Admission: Before 5PM: $4, SC(60) $2. 5-8PM:
$8, SC $4.
Masters: Contact Marcia Clure Lewis at 889-
9536(w).

RIVERSIDE   909

BALLY'S HOLIDAY SPA 3490 Madison Ave.
Phone: 687-2991.
Pool: 25m, indoors, heated, 80°-82°.
Admission: Call.
Affiliate: Bally's NC.

RIVERSIDE FAMILY YMCA 4020 Jefferson St.
Phone: 689-9622.
Pool: 25y x 75f, 6 lanes, indoors, heated, 86°.
Admission: $10.
Affiliate: Y AWAY NC. YMCA 3 visits per month
NC, then $5.
To find: Across from the Ramona High School foot-
ball field.

SAN BERNARDINO   909

DOWNTOWN YMCA 216 W. 6th St.
Phone: 885-3268.
Pool: 25y, 4 lanes, indoors, heated, 84°.
Admission: $7.
Affiliate: YMCA 3 visits per month NC, then $3.50.

UPTOWN YMCA OF SAN BERNARDINO 808 E.
21st St.
Phone: 886-4661.
Pool: 20y, 4 lanes, indoors, heated, 91°.
Admission: $3.
Affiliate: YMCA 3 visits per month NC, then $1.50.
Notes: There is also a 25y, 4 lane, outdoor,
unheated, 75°-85°, pool operated from Jun. to Oct.

YWCA OF SAN BERNARDINO 567 N. Sierra Way
Phone: 889-9536.
Pool: 25m, 6 lanes, indoors, heated, 83°.
Notes: The pool was closed in April of 1994, the
YWCA hopes to reopen it in the spring of 1995.
The Masters group is currently working out at
another location.
To find: At the intersection of 6th St. and Sierra

Way, at the entrance to the Seccomb Lake Recreation Area.
Masters: Contact Aquatics Director Marcia Clure Lewis at 889-9536.

SAN CLEMENTE   714

OLE HANSON BEACH CLUB City of San Clemente, 105 W. Pico
Phone: 361-8207.
Pool: 25y x 60f, 6 lanes, outdoors, heated, 81°.
Admission: $1.50.
Hotel: Best Western Casablanca Hotel/Inn (361-1644) 1 day NC.
To find: Next to the 7-11 Store on the north side of Pico.
Masters: The San Clemente Masters. Contact Pat Burch at 362-2934(h).

SAN DIEGO   619

San Diego

37
38→
39
36→
15
33,34   42
5 40,41
31,32→   29,30
—35
25,26,27   805
28   8
43→
23,24   —20
—22   —18,19
21
Dots are placed by ZIP codes, not by street addresses.

18. DOWNTOWN YMCA 500 W. Broadway
Phone: 232-7451.
Pool: 20y x 20f, 4 lanes, indoors, heated, 79°-80°.
Admission: $10.
Affiliate: Out-of-town YMCA NC. Local YMCA $5.
Hotel: All local hotels $5 with room key.
To find: One and a half blocks east of the San Diego Amtrak Station.

19. HYATT REGENCY SAN DIEGO 1 Market Place
Phone: 232-1234. **Reservations:** 800-233-6464.

Pool: 25y, rectangular, outdoors, heated, 80°-84°.
Admission: Registered guests only NC.

20. COPLEY FAMILY YMCA 3901 Landis St.
Phone: 283-2251.
Pool: 25y, 4 lanes, indoors, heated, 82°-84°.
Admission: $10.
Affiliate: Y AWAY 10 visits NC, then $2. YMCA $2.
To find: Two blocks south of University Ave. from 39th St.

21. HUMPHREY'S HALF MOON INN & SUITES 2303 Shelter Island Dr.
Phone: 224-3411. **Reservations:** 800-345-9995.
Pool: 79f, outdoors, heated, 80°.
Admission: Registered guests only NC.

22. PENINSULA FAMILY YMCA 4390 Valeta St.
Phone: 226-8888.
Pool: 25m, 6 lanes, outdoors, heated, 82°.
Admission: Pool: $2.50, SC(55) $2. Day pass $5.
Affiliate: YMCA 3 visits per month NC.
Masters: Contact Curt Werner or Sylvie Knutsen at 226-8888.

23. BALLY'S HOLIDAY SPA 405 Camino del Rio S.
Phone: 297-6062.
Pool: 20y, indoors, heated, 82°.
Admission: Call.
Affiliate: Bally's NC.

24. MISSION VALLEY HEALTH CLUB 901 Hotel Circle S.
Phone: 298-9321.
Pool: 25y, 3 lanes, outdoors, heated, 79°-81°.
Admission: $10.
Hotel: Mission Valley Inn (298-8281) NC.

25. MISSION BEACH PLUNGE 3115 Ocean Front Walk, Belmont Park, Mission Beach
Phone: 488-3110.
Pool: 20y x 174f, 10-13 lanes, indoors, heated, 83°.
Admission: $2.25, SC(55) $2.
To find: In Belmont Park next to the rollercoaster.
Masters: A Masters group is in formation. Call 488-3110.

26. SAN DIEGO PRINCESS RESORT 1404 W. Vacation Rd.
Phone: 274-4630. **Reservations:** 800-344-2626.
Pool: 25y, irregular shape with a rectangular, 2 lane lap swim area, outdoors, heated, 82°.
Admission: Registered guests only NC.
Notes: On the beach. There are four other outdoor pools, one heated, 82°, the other three are not heated.

27. DOUBLETREE HOTEL AT HORTON PLAZA 910 Broadway Circle
Phone: 239-2200. **Reservations:** 800-222-8733.

Pool: 20y, rectangular, outdoors, heated, 80°.
Admission: Registered guests only NC.

28. MISSION VALLEY YMCA 5505 Friars Rd.
Phone: 298-3576.
Pool: 25m, 6 lanes, outdoors, heated, 82°.
Admission: $10.
Affiliate: Y AWAY, San Diego area YMCAs excluded, frequency restrictions apply, NC.
Masters: An informal Masters group works out at this YMCA. Contact Jeanine Perkins or Barb Madsen at 298-3576.

29. RAMADA INN SAN DIEGO NORTH 5550 Kearney Mesa Rd.
Phone: 278-0800. **Reservations:** 800-447-2637.
Pool: 21.75y, oval or kidney shape, outdoors, heated, 77°.
Admission: Registered guests only NC.

30. FAMILY FITNESS CENTER 7620 Balboa Ave.
Phone: 292-5539.
Pool: 25m, 3 lanes, outdoors, heated, 80°.
Admission: $10.
Affiliate: IPFA NC.

31. CLAIREMONT COMMUNITY POOL 3605 Clairemont Dr.
Phone: 581-9923.
Pool: 25y x 25m, 8 lanes, outdoors, heated, 82°.
Admission: $2, SC(55) $1.50.
To find: Just south of Balboa Ave. off I-5, close to the beach areas.

32. CALIFORNIA HEALTH SPAS 3040 Clairemont Dr.
Phone: 276-3185.
Pool: 20y, outdoors, heated, 78°-80°.
Admission: $5.
Affiliate: IPFA NC.

33. SWANSON POOL 3585 Governor Dr.
Phone: 552-1653.
Pool: 25m x 25y, 4 x 6 lanes, outdoors, heated, 83°-84°.
Admission: $2, SC(62) $1.50.
Notes: The pool closes for the month of Dec.
To find: In Standley Park on Govenor Dr. at Mercer St.

34. SPORTING CLUB AT AVENTINE 8930 University Center Lane
Phone: 552-8000.
Pool: 25m, outdoors, heated, 80°.
Admission: $15.
Hotel: Hyatt La Jolla (552-1234) $7 or $9.

35. CENTER FOR SPORTS MEDICINE 8010 Frost St., Plaza Level
Phone: 569-0885.
Pool: 25y, outdoors, heated, 82°.

Admission: 1 visit NC, then $10.
Masters: The Sharp Attack. Contact Alan Voisard at 569-0885.

36. MIRA MESA RACQUET & SWIM CLUB 11347 Zapata Ave.
Phone: 566-1414.
Pool: 25y x 96f, 8 lanes, outdoors, heated, 80°.
Admission: $6.
To find: On Camino Ruiz, one mile north of Mira Mesa Blvd.

37. DOUBLETREE CLUB HOTEL RANCHO BERNARDO 11611 Bernardo Plaza Court
Phone: 485-9250. **Reservations:** 800-222-TREE.
Pool: 50f, rectangular, outdoors, heated, 80°.
Admission: Registered guests only NC.

38. MT. CARMEL HIGH SCHOOL 9550 Carmel Mountain Rd.
Phone: 484-2715.
Pool: 25y x 25m, 14 lanes, outdoors, heated, 82°.
Admission: $1.50.

39. SCRIPPS RANCH SWIM & RACQUET 9875 Aviary Dr.
Phone: 271-6222.
Pool: 25m, outdoors, heated, 80°.
Memberships: Scripps Ranch residents: I/S $825 + $58/month.

40. THE FIELD HOUSE POOL Building 3279, Naval Station San Diego
Phone: 556-8659.
Pool: 50m x 25y, outdoors, heated, 78°-82°.
Affiliate: U.S. Military NC.

41. NAVAL STATION INDOOR POOL Building 153, Naval Station San Diego
Phone: 556-2171.
Pool: 50m x 25y, 8 x 8 lanes, indoors, heated, 84°-85°.
Affiliate: U.S. Military NC.

42. BASE POOL Building 151, Naval Amphibious Base Coronado
Phone: 437-3065/6/7.
Pool: 50m x 25y, 10 lanes, outdoors, heated, 80°.
Affiliate: U.S. Military NC.

43. WILLIAM B. TERRY POOL Peterson Gym, San Diego State University
Phone: Recorded schedule: 594-5512.
Information: 594-6424.
Pool: 25y x 45f, 8 lanes, outdoors, heated, 78°.
Admission: $2.
Memberships: $35/semester or summer.
To find: On the campus of San Diego State University, at 55th St. and Montezuma.

SAN DIMAS   909

SAN DIMAS SWIM & RACQUET CLUB 990 W.
Covina Blvd.
Phone: 592-1430.
Pool: 25y x 25m, 8 lanes, outdoors, heated, 80°.
Admission: Residents $4, non-residents $4.50. All
SC(55) $1.50.
Notes: The pool is closed in Dec. and Jan.
To find: Off I-210, next to San Dimas High School.

SAN LUIS OBISPO   805

SAN LUIS OBISPO SWIM CENTER 900
Southwood Dr.
Phone: 781-7284.
Pool: 50m x 25y, 8 x 10+ lanes, outdoors, heated,
80°.
Admission: $1.25, SC(55) 75¢.

SAN LUIS AQUATIC MASTERS at San Luis
Obispo Swim Center
Pool phone: 781-7288. **Masters:** Call 543-9515.
Affiliate: USMS 5 visits per week $2 each, includes
pool fees.
Notes: Coached workouts: M-F: 8-9:30AM,
10:30AM-1:30PM, 6:20-8PM. Sa: 8-10AM.

CUESTA COLLEGE Hwy. 1
Phone: 546-3220.
Pool: 51m configured as 25m + 25y, 10+ lanes,
outdoors, heated, 86°.
Admission: $2.
Memberships: $65/semester.

AVILA HOT SPRINGS SPA & RV RESORT 250
Avila Beach Dr.
Phone: 595-2359.
Pool: 100f x 50f, outdoors, heated, 86°.
Admission: $7.50.
Hotel: Avila Hot Springs Spa & RV Resort (595-
2395) 40% discount.

SAN PEDRO   310

SAN PEDRO PENINSULA YMCA 301 S. Bandini
St.
Phone: 832-4211.
Pool: 25y x 45f, 6 lanes, indoors, heated, 83°.
Admission: $12.
Affiliate: YMCA 3 visits per month NC, then $6.
To find: Less than a mile from I-110, which ends in
San Pedro.

SANTA ANA   714

**SEQUOIA ATHLETIC CLUB / RACQUETBALL
WORLD** 1901 E. 1st
Phone: 972-2999.
Pool: 22y, 4 lanes, indoors, heated, 87°.
Admission: $15.
Affiliate: IHRSA Call.

SANTA BARBARA   805

LOS BANOS DEL MAR 401 Shoreline Dr.
Phone: 966-6110.
Pool: 50m, 7 lanes, 'L' shape, outdoors, heated,
80°-81°.
Admission: $2.
To find: At the intersection of Castillo and Cabrillo
Sts. One half mile west of the pier, on the ocean
side.

SANTA BARBARA SWIM CLUB at Los Banos del
Mar Pool
Masters: Contact Masters Coach Susan Ortwein at
966-6110.
Non-member participation: $2 per workout, limit
one half month, includes pool fees.
Notes: Coached workouts: M-F: 6-7:15AM, 5:30-
6:45PM.

SANTA BARBARA ATHLETIC CLUB 520 Castilla
Phone: 966-6147.
Pool: 25y, outdoors, heated, 80°.
Affiliate: IHRSA $10.
Hotel: Four Seasons Biltmore Resort (969-2261),
San Ysidro Ranch, Harbor View Inn, Eagle Inn, &
Villa Rosa Hotel: $10.

FESS PARKER'S RED LION RESORT 633 E.
Cabrillo Blvd.
Phone: 564-4333. **Reservations:** 800-879-2929.
Pool: 30y x 50f, oval shape, outdoors, heated, 78°.
Admission: Registered guests only NC.

SANTA BARBARA FAMILY YMCA 36 Hitchcock
Way
Phone: 687-7727.
Pool: 25y x 45f, 6 lanes, indoors, heated, 83°.
Admission: $15.
Affiliate: Y AWAY 6 visits per month NC.
Hotel: Sandeman Hotel & Peppertree Hotel: NC.
To find: Four blocks east of La Cumbre Plaza Mall.
Masters: The YMCA Masters. Contact Vic
Anderson at 687-7727.

MONTECITO FAMILY YMCA 591 Santa Rosa
Lane
Phone: 969-3288.
Pool: 25y x 60f, 5 lanes, outdoors, heated, 80.5°.
Admission: $15.
Affiliate: Y AWAY NC. YMCA 3 visits NC.

SANTA MARIA   805

PAUL NELSON POOL 516 S. McClelland
Phone: 925-0951 ext. 248.
Pool: 25y x 40y, 7 x 6 lanes, 'L' shape, outdoors,
heated, 80°.
Admission: $1.50, SC(65) $1.
To find: One block south of Town Center Shopping
Mall.

SANTA MARIA   CONTINUED

SANTA MARIA VALLEY YMCA 3400 Skyway Dr.
Phone: 937-8521.
Pool: 25y x 45f, 6 lanes, outdoors, heated, 85°.
Admission: $10.
Affiliate: Y AWAY NC.
Hotel: Santa Maria Hilton (928-8000) $3 with a
pass from the hotel.
To find: Across from the Airport Hilton.

SANTA MARIA AIRPORT HILTON 3455 Skyway
Dr.
Phone: 928-8000. **Reservations:** 800-HILTONS.
Pool: 50f x 27f, rectangular, outdoors, heated, 70°.
Admission: Registered guests only NC.

SANTA MONICA   310

SANTA MONICA FAMILY YMCA 1332 - 6th St.
Phone: 393-2721.
Pool: 25y x 36f, 6 lanes, indoors, heated, 80°.
Admission: $10.
Affiliate: YMCA 3 visits per month NC, then $5.
Hotel: Huntley Hotel & Miramar Sheraton (576-
7777): NC with a pass from the hotel.
To find: Sixth St. off Santa Monica Blvd.

LOEWS SANTA MONICA BEACH HOTEL 1700
Ocean Ave.
Phone: 458-6700. **Reservations:** 800-23-
LOEWS.
Pool: 73f x 18.5f, rectangular, indoor/outdoor, heat-
ed, 81°.
Admission: Registered guests only NC.

SOUTHERN CALIFORNIA AQUATIC MASTERS
(SCAQ) at Santa Monica High School Pool, 4th &
Pico Blvd.
Masters: Contact Head Coach Clay Evans at 451-
6666.
Pool: 25y, 10 lanes, indoors, heated, 80°.
Affiliate: USMS 3 workouts per year NC.
Notes: Coached workouts: M,W,F: 6-7PM, 7-8PM.

THE CLUB AT MGM PLAZA 2425 Colorado Ave.,
Suite 120
Phone: 829-2227.
Pool: 25y, 3 lanes, indoors, heated, 78°-82°.
Admission: $10. With 24 hrs. advance notice and
on Saturdays $5.
Affiliate: IHRSA Call.

BALLY'S SPORTS CONNECTION 2929 - 31st St.
Phone: 450-4464.
Pool: 30m, 3 lanes, indoors, heated, 82°.
Affiliate: Bally's NC.

SOUTHERN CALIFORNIA AQUATIC MASTERS
(SCAQ) at Santa Monica Municipal Pool, 1700
Pico Blvd.
Pool phone: 450-7578. **Masters:** Contact Head
Coach Clay Evans at 451-6666.

Pool: 25y x 50m, outdoors, temperature controlled,
80°.
Affiliate: USMS 3 workouts per year NC.
Notes: Coached workouts: Fall, winter, spring:
Tu,Th: 5:45-6:45AM, 6:30-7:30PM. Sa: 7-8AM, 8-
9AM, 4-5PM. Su: 11AM-12:30PM, 4-5PM.
Summer: M,W,F: 5:45-6:45AM, 6:45-7:45AM.
Tu,Th: 5:45-6:45AM, 6:45-7:45AM, 6:30-7:30PM.
Sa: 7-8AM, 8-9AM, 4-5PM. Su: 11AM-12:30PM.
4-5PM.

SANTEE   619

SANTANA HIGH SCHOOL 9915 N. Magnolia Ave.
Phone: 698-2502.
Pool: 25y x 25m, 10 lanes, outdoors, heated, 81°.
Admission: $2.

SEAL BEACH   310

SEAL BEACH POOL at McGaw Elementary
School, 1698 Bolsa Ave.
Phone: 430-9612.
Pool: 25y, outdoors, heated, 78°-82°.
Passes: 16 swims $20*.
Notes: *Passes are sold at City Hall, 211 - 8th St.,
Seal Beach.

SIERRA MADRE   818

CITY OF SIERRA MADRE MUNICIPAL POOL 611
E. Sierra Madre Blvd.
Phone: 355-2356.
Pool: 100f x 40f, 6 lanes, outdoors, heated, 81°.
Admission: Residents $1.50, SC(55) 50¢. Non-
residents $2, SC 75¢.
To find: One mile north of I-210, between Baldwin
& Santa Anita.

SIMI VALLEY   805

OAKRIDGE ATHLETIC CLUB 2655 Erringer Rd.
Phone: 522-5454.
Pool: 25y, outdoors, heated, 78°.
Affiliate: IHRSA $8.

SOLANA BEACH   619

SAN DIEGUITO BOYS & GIRLS CLUB 533 Lomas
Santa Fe Dr.
Phone: 755-4904.
Pool: 25y, outdoors, heated, 80°-83°.
Admission: Lap swim $3.50, SC(55) $2.50.
Masters workout $4.50.
Masters: The Solana Beach Masters. Contact Joe
Benjamin or Heather Bannan at 755-4904.

LOMAS SANTA FE COUNTRY CLUB 1505 Lomas
Santa Fe Dr.
Phone: 755-3372.
Pool: 25m x 13m, 6 lanes, outdoors, heated, 82°.
Memberships: Call.

SOUTH GATE   213

SOUTH GATE SPORTS CENTER POOL 9520
Hildreth Ave.
Phone: 563-5445/6.
Pool: 50m x 25y, indoors, heated, 84°.
Admission: $2.

SOUTH PASADENA   818

SOUTH PASADENA-SAN MARINO YMCA 1605
Garfield Ave.
Phone: 799-9119.
Pool: 25y x 24f, 4 lanes, indoors, heated, 85°.
Admission: Pool $5. Fitness Center $10.
Affiliate: Y AWAY 3 visits per month NC.
To find: Two blocks north of Huntington Dr. at the
intersection of Oak and Garfield Ave.

SPRING VALLEY   619

MOUNT MIGUEL HIGH SCHOOL POOL 1800
Sweetwater Rd.
Phone: 698-2502.
Pool: 25y x 25m, 10 lanes, outdoors, heated, 81°.
Admission: $2.

MONTE VISTA HIGH SCHOOL POOL 3230
Sweetwater Springs Blvd.
Phone: 698-2502.
Pool: 25y x 25m, 10 lanes, outdoors, heated, 81°.
Admission: $2.

THOUSAND OAKS   805

DALAND SWIM SCHOOL 135 E. Wilbur Rd.
Phone: 495-5210.
Pool: 25y x 45f, 6 lanes, indoor/outdoor, heated,
82°.
Admission: 10 visits per month $5 each.
To find: Across from AAA and down a long drive-
way. Look for the sign.

DALAND UNITED MASTERS at Daland Swim
School
Masters: Contact Coach Peter Daland at 495-5210.
Non-member participation: 5 workouts per month
$6 each, includes pool fees.
Notes: Coached workouts: M,W,F: 6-7:30PM.
Tu,Th: 6-7:30AM, 6-7:30PM.

THOUSAND OAKS RACQUET CLUB 645
Tuolumne Ave.
Phone: 495-0437.
Pool: 25y, indoors, heated, 80°.
Memberships: I/S $50 + $41/month.

TORRANCE   310

BALLY'S SPORTS CONNECTION 21345
Hawthorne Blvd.
Phone: 316-0173.
Pool: 20y, indoors, heated, 78°-80°.

Admission: $10.
Affiliate: Bally's NC.

WEST END RACQUET & HEALTH CLUB 4343
Spencer St.
Phone: 542-7373.
Pool: 25y, 3 lanes, outdoors, heated, 82°.
Admission: $10.

TORRANCE SOUTH BAY YMCA 2900 W.
Sepulveda Blvd.
Phone: 325-5885.
Pool: 25m x 36f, 6 lanes, indoors, heated, 83°.
Admission: Before 4PM $10.
Affiliate: Y AWAY NC.

SOUTH END RACQUET & HEALTH CLUB, INC.
2800 Skypark Dr.
Phone: 530-0630.
Pool 1: 25y, outdoors, heated, 78°-82°.
Pool 2: 25y, outdoors, heated, 78°-82°.
Affiliate: IHRSA $10.
Masters: The South End Aquatics Masters.
Contact Ken Taylor at 530-0630.

TUJUNGA   818

VERDUGO HILLS FAMILY YMCA 6840 Foothill
Blvd.
Phone: 352-3255.
Pool: 25y x 45f, 8 lanes, indoor/outdoor, heated,
84°.
Admission: $10.
Affiliate: YMCA NC.
To find: Take I-210 to Lowell, follow Lowell up the
hill to Foothill Blvd., turn left onto Foothill Blvd. and
go approximately six blocks.

VAN NUYS   818

MID VALLEY FAMILY YMCA 6901 Lennox Ave.
Phone: 989-3800.
Pool: 25y x 36f, 4 lanes, indoors, heated, 85°.
Admission: 3 visits NC, then $15.
Affiliate: Y AWAY from outside Los Angeles
County up to 2 weeks NC. Los Angeles County
YMCA 3 visits per month NC, then $7.50.
To find: One block east of Van Nuys Blvd.,
between Sherman Way and Vanowen St.

VENTURA   805

VENTURA FAMILY YMCA 3760 Telegraph Rd.
Phone: 642-2131.
Pool: 25y x 60f, 6 lanes, indoors, heated, 80°.
Admission: $15.
Affiliate: YMCA NC.
To find: Two blocks from Main St.

PIERPONT RACQUET CLUB 550 San Jon Rd.
Phone: 648-5161.
Pool: 25y, outdoors, heated, 82°-83°.
Hotel: Pierpont Inn (643-6144) $7.50.

VENTURA   CONTINUED

VENTURA COLLEGE 4667 Telegraph Rd.
Phone: 654-6352.
Pool: 25y + 20y x 50m, 8 + 8 x 8 lanes, outdoors,
heated, 80°.
Admission: $2.
Memberships: $25/month.

VENTURA AQUATIC CLUB at Ventura College
Pool phone: 654-6352. **Masters:** Contact Bob
Anderson at 654-6400 ext. 1345(w).
Non-member participation: $2, includes pool fees.
Notes: Workouts: M-F: 5-7PM.

WALNUT   909

MARIE MILLS POOL Mount San Antonio College,
1100 N. Grand
Phone: 594-5611 ext. 4735.
Pool: 25y x 50m, 20 lanes, outdoors, heated, 78°-
80°.
Admission: NC*.
Notes: *Lap swimming is operated as a no fee
adult education program. Swimmers sign up at the
beginning of each session, subject to space avail-
ability. There is no instruction or coaching.
To find: At the intersection of Temple and Grand.
Our respondent made a point of requesting that
swimmers observe the parking regulations in the
area.

WEST COVINA   818

BALLY'S HOLIDAY HEALTH SPA 441 N. Azusa
Phone: 966-7532.
Pool: 20y, indoors, heated, 82°-85°.
Affiliate: Bally's NC.

WEST HOLLYWOOD   310

CITY OF WEST HOLLYWOOD POOL 647 N. San
Vicente Blvd.
Phone: 659-3087.
Pool: 25y x 45f, 6 lanes, outdoors, heated, 82°-84°.
Admission: $2, SC(60) NC.
Masters: West Hollywood Aquatics. Contact the
club's office at 288-6555.

BALLY'S SPORTS CONNECTION 8612 Santa
Monica Blvd.
Phone: 652-7440.

Pool: 25y, 4 lanes, outdoors, heated, 78°-82°.
Affiliate: Bally's NC. IHRSA Call.

WEST LOS ANGELES   310

BALLY'S HOLIDAY SPA 1914 Bundy
Phone: 820-7571.
Pool: 20m, indoors, heated, 82°.
Affiliate: Bally's NC.

WHITTIER   310

EAST WHITTIER CENTER BRANCH YMCA
15740 Starbuck
Phone: 943-7241.
Pool: 25y, indoors, heated, 83°-86°.
Admission: $10.
Affiliate: YMCA Call.

WILMINGTON   310

BANNING POOL 1450 N. Avalon Blvd.
Phone: 548-7420.
Pool: 20y x 25y, 8 lanes, outdoors, heated, 84°.
Admission: $1.25, SC(65) & Disabled 50¢.

WOODLAND HILLS   818

WARNER CENTER CLUB 6336 Canoga Ave.
Phone: 884-1100.
Pool: 25m, outdoors, heated, 82°.
Admission: $10.
Affiliate: IHRSA $5.
Hotel: Warner Center Hilton & Towers (595-1000)
NC for pool.

LOS ANGELES PIERCE COLLEGE 6201
Winnetka Ave.
Phone: 347-0551 ext. 343.
Pool: 25y x 25m, 10 lanes, outdoors, heated, 81°.
Admission: Noon-1PM $2.
Memberships: $30/month, SC $25.
To find: One half mile north of the Ventura Frwy.

SOUTHWEST AQUATIC MASTERS at Los Angeles
Pierce College
Pool phone: 347-0551. **Masters:** Contact Steve
Schofield at 992-1820.
Non-member participation: $2, includes pool fees.
Notes: Workouts: M-F: 5-6PM or 7-8PM.

HELP MAKE THE NEXT *SWIMMERS GUIDE* EVEN BETTER

To receive a free copy of the next **Swimmers Guide** tell us about pools you
know of that aren't in this edition. See page 14 for details.

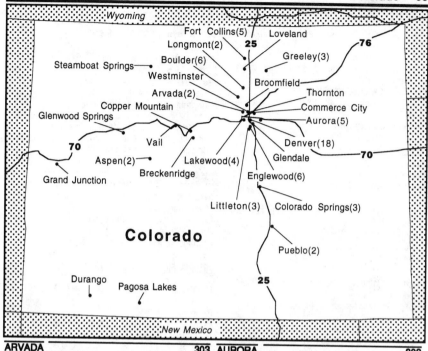

Wyoming

Fort Collins(5) · Loveland
Longmont(2) · **25**
· **76**
Boulder(6) · Greeley(3)
Steamboat Springs
Westminster · Broomfield
Arvada(2) · Thornton
Copper Mountain · Commerce City
Glenwood Springs · Aurora(5)
Vail · Denver(18)
70
Aspen(2) · Lakewood(4) · Glendale · **70**
Breckenridge · Englewood(6)
Grand Junction
Littleton(3) · Colorado Springs(3)

Colorado

Pueblo(2)

Durango · Pagosa Lakes · **25**

New Mexico

ARVADA   303

GEORGE MEYERS POOL 7900 Carr Dr.
Phone: 420-2838.
Pool: 25y x 50m, 20 lanes, indoors, heated, 82°.
Admission: $2.25, SC(62) $1.
Masters: The North Jeffco Masters. Contact Lani
Lesoing at 420-2838.

BALLY'S HOLIDAY HEALTH & FITNESS CENTER
7635 W. 88th Ave.
Phone: 425-6966.
Pool: 25m, indoors, heated, 78°.
Affiliate: Bally's NC.

ASPEN   970

ASPEN ATHLETIC CLUB 720 E. Hyman
Phone: 925-2531.
Pool: 20y, indoors, heated, 80°.
Admission: $20.

JAMES E. MOORE POOL 895 Maroon Creek
Road
Phone: 920-5145.
Pool: 25y x 40f, 6 lanes, indoors, heated, 84°.
Admission: $3, SC(65) NC (donations appreciated).
To find: Across from Aspen High School.
Masters: The Aspen Masters. Contact Barb Van
Horn at 920-5145.

AURORA   303

BECK POOL 800 Telluride
Phone: 361-0877.
Pool: 25y, 6 lanes, indoors, heated, 86°.
Admission: $2, SC(62) $1.50.

BALLY'S HOLIDAY HEALTH & FITNESS CENTER
13801 E. Exposition Ave.
Phone: 363-6060.
Pool: 25m, indoors, heated, 78°.
Admission: Out-of-state visitors NC.
Affiliate: Bally's NC.

UTAH PARK POOL 1800 S. Peoria St.
Phone: 696-4303.
Pool: 25m x 60f, 8 lanes, indoors, heated, 83°.
Admission: $2, SC(62) $1.50.
To find: One half mile north of Iliff & Peoria.

HEARTWOOD ATHLETIC CLUB 15528 E.
Hampden Circle
Phone: 693-3550.
Pool: 25y, 6 lanes, indoors, heated, 82°.
Affiliate: IHRSA $5.18.

INTERNATIONAL ATHLETIC CLUB 3191 S.
Vaughn Way
Phone: 696-9313.
Pool: 25y, outdoors, heated, 82°.
Admission: $12.
Affiliate: IHRSA $7.50.

BOULDER   303

YMCA OF BOULDER VALLEY 2850 Mapleton Ave.
Phone: 442-2778.
Pool: 25y x 25f, 4 lanes, indoors, heated, 82°.
Admission: $7.
Affiliate: Y AWAY NC. YMCA $3.50.
Hotel: Residence Inn (449-5545) NC with a pass from the hotel.
Masters: Contact Dave Snow at 447-2277(h).

RALLY SPORT 2727 - 29th St.
Phone: 449-4800.
Pool: 25y, indoors, heated, 78°-84°.
Affiliate: IHRSA $8.

SOUTH BOULDER RECREATION CENTER 1360 Gillaspie Dr.
Phone: 441-3448.
Pool: 25y, indoors, heated, 82°.
Admission: $3.50, SC(60) $1.50.

BOULDER AQUATIC MASTERS at South Boulder Recreation Center
Pool phone: 441-3448. **Masters:** Contact Liz Teichler at 666-5417(h).
Non-member participation: Pool fees only.
Notes: Coached workouts: Tu,Th: 5:15-6:30PM. Su: 8-9:30AM, 9:30-11AM. In the summer, this schedule is moved to the 25y, 8 lane, outdoor, heated, 78°-82° Spruce Pool at 2102 Spruce St. (441-3426).

FLATIRON ATHLETIC CLUB 505 Thunderbird Dr.
Phone: 499-6590.
Pool: 20m, indoors, heated, 80°.
Admission: $8.
Affiliate: IHRSA $5.

EAST BOULDER COMMUNITY CENTER 5660 Sioux Dr.
Phone: 441-4400.
Pool 1: 25y, indoors, heated, 80°.
Pool 2: 25y, indoors, heated, 88°.
Admission: $3.50, SC(60) $1.50.

BOULDER AQUATIC MASTERS at East Boulder Community Center
Pool phone: 441-4400. **Masters:** Contact Liz Teichler at 666-5417(h).
Non-member participation: Pool fees only.
Notes: Coached workouts: M-F: 5:45-7AM, 7-8:15AM, Noon-1PM. Sa: 7:45-9AM. In the summer, all but the noon workouts are moved to the 50m, 6 lane, outdoor, heated, 80°-82°, Scott Carpenter Pool at 30th & Arapaho (441-3427). Noon workouts continue at East Boulder Recreation Center year-round.

NORTH BOULDER RECREATION CENTER 3170 N. Broadway

Phone: 441-3444.
Pool: 25m, indoors, heated, 83°.
Admission: $3.50, SC(60) $1.50.

BOULDER AQUATIC MASTERS at North Boulder Recreation Center
Pool phone: 441-3444. **Masters:** Contact Liz Teichler at 666-5417(h).
Non-member participation: Pool fees only.
Notes: Coached workouts: M,W,F: 6:30-7:45PM. Sa: 5-6:15PM. In the summer, this schedule is moved to the 25y, 8 lane, outdoor, heated, 78°-82° Spruce Pool at 2102 Spruce St. (441-3426).

BRECKENRIDGE   970

BRECKENRIDGE BEACH CLUB at the Village of Breckenridge Resort, 605 S. Park
Phone: 453-2000. **Reservations:** 800-800-7829.
Pool: 25y, rectangular, outdoors, heated, 89°.
Admission: Registered guests only NC.

BROOMFIELD   303

BROOMFIELD RECREATION CENTER 300 Community Park Dr.
Phone: 469-5351.
Pool: 25y x 45f, 6 lanes, indoors, heated, 84°.
Admission: $2.75, SC(50) $1.50.
To find: Take Main St. to 3rd, go east on 3rd to the Recreation Center.

COLORADO SPRINGS   719

PIKES PEAK YMCA - DOWNTOWN BRANCH 207 N. Nevada Ave.
Phone: 471-9790.
Pool: 25y, 6 lanes, indoors, heated, 82°-83°.
Admission: $7.
Affiliate: Y AWAY NC.
Notes: There is also a 16f x 33f, 3f deep, indoor, heated, 86°-88° pool.
To find: Across the street from Acacia Park, at the intersection of Bijou and Nevada Ave.

BALLY'S U.S. SWIM & FITNESS 2410 S. Academy Blvd.
Phone: 390-7700.
Pool: 27m, indoors, heated, 78°-81°.
Affiliate: Bally's NC.

GARDEN RANCH YMCA 2380 Montebello Dr. W.
Phone: 593-9622.
Pool: 25y x 45f, 6 lanes, indoors, heated, 84°.
Admission: $7, SC(65) $3.50.
Affiliate: Y AWAY NC. YMCA 1 month NC.

COMMERCE CITY   303

COMMERCE CITY PARKS & RECREATION POOL 6060 Parkway Dr.
Phone: 289-3765.
Pool: 25y, indoors, heated, 84°.

Admission: $5. With 'Recreation ID'*: Residents $2.50, non-residents $3.50, all SC(55) NC.
Notes: *'Recreation ID': Residents & non-residents under 55 $4/year. Resident SC $6/year. Non-resident SC $12/year.

COPPER MOUNTAIN 970

COPPER MOUNTAIN RACQUET & ATHLETIC CLUB at Copper Mountain Resort, 0509 Copper Rd.
Phone: 968-2826.
Pool: 25y, 4 lanes, indoors, heated, 82°.
Admission: $12.
Affiliate: Any other athletic club $8.
Hotel: Hotel guests & condo renters booked through Copper Mountain Lodging Services (800-458-8386): NC.
To find: Near the tennis bubble.

DENVER 303

Denver

76
270
70
13
7
8,9,10
1,2,3,4
5,6
25
17
11
14
12
15,16
18
Dots are placed by ZIP codes, not by street addresses.
225

1. EXECUTIVE TOWER INN 1405 Curtis St.
Phone: 571-0300. **Reservations:** 800-525-6651.
Pool: 23y, rectangular, indoors, heated, 78°-83°.
Admission: $5. Registered guests NC.
Memberships: $30/month.

2. CENTRAL BRANCH YMCA 25 E. 16th St.
Phone: 861-8300.
Pool: 25y, 5 lanes, indoors, heated, 80°.
Admission: $10.
Affiliate: Y AWAY Call.
To find: At the intersection of 16th and Lincoln.
Masters: Contact Judy Saxe at 861-8300.

3. ATHLETIC CLUB AT DENVER PLACE 1849 Curtis St.
Phone: 294-9494.
Pool: 25m x 21f, 3 lanes, indoors, heated, 81°-82°.
Admission: $10.
Affiliate: IHRSA $9.

Masters: The ACDP Masters. Contact Charles Hugo at 294-9494.

4. 20TH STREET SWIMMING POOL 1011 - 20th St.
Phone: 295-4430.
Pool: 20y, indoors, heated, 84°.
Admission: $2. With recreation card* $1.
Notes: *Recreation cards: Residents $5, non-residents $20.

5. DENVER ATHLETIC CLUB 1325 Glenarm Place
Phone: 534-1211.
Pool: 25m, 8 lanes, indoors, heated, 82°.
Memberships: I/S $750 + $148.50/month.
Notes: This is an 'Executive Athletic Club', with restaurants, tavern, child care, masseur, barber, etc. It has reciprocal arrangements with more than 100 similarly prestigious facilities.
Masters: The DAC Masters. Contact Aquatics Director Dana Dutcher May at 534-7331 ext. 1151.

6. RUDE RECREATION CENTER 2855 W. Holden Place
Phone: 572-4795.
Pool: 25m x 20m, 6 lanes, indoors, heated, 84°.
Admission: Residents $3, SC(64) $2.50. Non-residents $5, SC $2.50.
To find: Four blocks south of Mile High Stadium on Federal Blvd.

7. GLENARM SWIMMING POOL 2800 Glenarm St.
Phone: 295-4475.
Pool: 25y, indoors, heated, 80°-85°.
Admission: With recreation card* $1.
Notes: *Recreation cards: Residents $5, non-residents $20.

8. SHERATON INN DENVER AIRPORT 3535 Quebec St.
Phone: 333-7711. **Reservations:** 800-328-2268.
Pool: 58f, rectangular, indoors, heated, 85°.
Admission: Registered guests only NC.

9. M.L. KING SWIMMING POOL 3880 Newport St.
Phone: 331-4034.
Pool: 25m, indoors, heated, 87°.
Admission: $4. With recreation card* $1.
Notes: *Recreation cards: Residents $5, non-residents $20.

10. SKYLAND SWIMMING POOL 3334 Holly St.
Phone: 331-4037.
Pool: 25m, indoors, heated, 83°.
Admission: With recreation card* $1, SC(65) 50¢.
Notes: *Recreation cards: Residents $5, non-residents $20.

11. WASHINGTON PARK 701 S. Franklin St.
Phone: 698-4960.
Pool: 25m x 13m, 6 lanes, indoors, heated, 84°.
Admission: Residents $2, SC(65) $1. Non-residents $4.

DENVER   CONTINUED

12. SCHLESSMAN FAMILY BRANCH YMCA 3901
E. Yale Ave.
Phone: 757-8484.
Pool: 25y x 28f, 5 lanes, indoors, heated, 83°.
Admission: $10.
Affiliate: YMCA 12 visits per year NC.
To find: Three traffic lights south of I-25 on
Colorado Blvd. turn right.

13. BERKELEY RECREATION CENTER W. 46th
Ave. & Sheridan Blvd.
Phone: 458-4898.
Pool: 25y, indoors, heated, 85°.
Admission: With recreation card* $1, SC(65) 50¢.
Notes: *Recreation cards: Residents $5, non-residents $20.

14. ATHMAR POOL 2680 W. Mexico Ave.
Phone: 937-4600.
Pool: 25y x 45f, 5 lanes, indoors, heated, 86°.
Admission: Residents $3, SC(65) $2.50. Non-residents $5, SC $4.50.
To find: In southwest Denver, four blocks east of
Federal Blvd. and four blocks north of Evans Ave.

15. ATHLETIC CLUB AT MONACO 2695 S.
Monaco Pkwy.
Phone: 758-7080.
Pool: 25m x 10m, 4 lanes, indoors, heated, 81°.
Admission: $10.
Affiliate: IHRSA $6.
Hotel: Quality Inn South (758-2211) — Call the club
for details.
Notes: There is also a 25m, outdoor, summer pool.
To find: At the intersection of Monaco and Yale.

**16. AEROBIC & SPORTS CONDITIONING
CENTER** 600 S. Holly
Phone: 377-0800.
Pool: 20m, indoors, heated, 80°-82°.
Affiliate: CSI NC. IHRSA $5.

17. LA FAMILIA SWIMMING POOL 65 S. Elati St.
Phone: 698-4995.
Pool: 25y, indoors, heated, 86°.
Admission: With recreation card* $1.
Notes: *Recreation cards: Residents $5, non-residents $20.

18. SOUTHWEST YMCA 5181 W. Kenyon Ave.
Phone: 761-7530.
Pool: 25y x 36f, 6 lanes, indoors, heated, 84°.
Admission: $10.
Affiliate: YMCA NC.

DURANGO   970

FITNESS WORKS AT THE DAYS INN-DURANGO
1700 County Rd. 203
Phone: Pool: 259-1519. Hotel: 259-1430.
Reservations: 800-325-2525.

Pool: 25y x 45f, 4 lap lanes, 2 open lanes, indoors,
heated, 83°-84°.
Admission: Registered guests NC.
Passes: 10 swims $49, SC(60) $35. Punch cards
can be shared, but are limited to two punches per
visit.
Memberships: 1/3/6/12 months $45/$120/$180/
$300, SC $40.50/$108/$162/$270.
To find: One and a half miles north of Durango on
Hwy. 550.
Masters: The Durango Masters. Contact John
Stevens at 247-2128(h).

ENGLEWOOD   303

ENGLEWOOD RECREATION CENTER 1155 W.
Oxford
Phone: 762-1168.
Pool: 25m, 8 lanes, indoors, heated, 84°.
Admission: Residents $2, non-residents $2.50.
To find: Two blocks east of Santa Fe Dr. on
Oxford.

GREENWOOD ATHLETIC CLUB 5801 S. Quebec
Phone: 770-2582.
Pool: 25m, indoors, heated, 82°.
Affiliate: IHRSA $10.

THE SCANTICON HOTEL & RESORT 200
Inverness Dr. W.
Phone: 799-5800. **Reservations:** 800-346-4891.
Pool: 18.5m, rectangular, indoors, heated, 78°-82°.
Admission: Registered guests NC.
Memberships: $30/month.
Notes: There is also a 25m, outdoor pool operated
from May 15 to Sep. 15. Guests also have access
to the Athletic Club at Inverness, see listing below.

ATHLETIC CLUB AT INVERNESS 374 Inverness
Dr. S.
Phone: 790-7777.
Pool: 25m, indoors, heated, 81°.
Affiliate: IHRSA $11.
Hotel: The Scanticon Hotel & Resort (799-
5800)[listed above], Hyatt Regency Tech Center
(779-1234), & Radisson Hotel Denver South (799-
6200): $12.

AMERICAN FITNESS, INC. 9650 E. Arapahoe Rd.
Phone: 799-6767.
Pool: 20m, indoors, heated, 84±°.
Admission: $8.
Affiliate: IPFA NC.
Hotel: Residence Inn (740-7177) & Hampton Inn
(792-9999): Call the club for information.

THE SPORTING CLUB 5151 DTC Pkwy.
Phone: 779-0700.
Pool: 25y, indoors, heated, 80°.
Admission: $8.
Affiliate: IHRSA $5.

FORT COLLINS　　　　　970

MULBERRY POOL 424 W. Mulberry
Phone: 221-6657.
Pool: 25y, indoors, heated, 81°-83°.
Admission: $2, SC(60) $1.80, SC(70) $1.70,
SC(80) $1.60.

FITNESS PLUS 201 Racquet Dr.
Phone: 482-5117.
Pool: 25y, indoors, heated, 84°.
Admission: 1 visit NC, then $4.

FORT COLLINS CLUB 1307 E. Prospect Rd.
Phone: 224-2582.
Pool: 25m, 4 lanes, indoors, heated, 82°-84°.
Hotel: Marriott (226-5200) & Holiday Inn (482-2626): $6.
Memberships: I/S $35 + $57/month.

EDORA POOL & ICE CENTER (EPIC) 1801
Riverside
Phone: 221-6683.
Pool: 50m OR 25y, 6 lanes + rec. swim area + dive
well, indoors, heated, 81°-83°.
Admission: $2, SC(60) $1.80, SC(70) $1.70,
SC(80) $1.60.
Masters: The Ft. Collins Area Swim Team Masters.
Contact Tom Johnson at 498-9202.

**FORT COLLINS PULSE AEROBIC & FITNESS
CENTER** 2555 S. Shields St.
Phone: 490-1300.
Pool: 25m, 4 lanes, indoors, heated, 83°.
Admission: Out-of-area visitors $7.
Affiliate: IHRSA $5.
Hotel: Empire Hotel, Ft. Collins Marriott (226-5200),
Holiday Inn Ft. Collins (482-2626), & Helmshire
Inn: $5.

GLENDALE　　　　　303

CHERRY CREEK SPORTING CLUB 500 S. Cherry
St.
Phone: 399-3050.
Pool: 20m x 15m, 5 lanes, indoors, heated, 82°.
Admission: $15.
Affiliate: IHRSA $10.
Hotel: Loews Giorgio Hotel (782-9300) & Cherry
Creek Inn (757-3341): $5 with room key.
To find: Two blocks east of Colorado Blvd., at the
intersection of Virginia and Cherry St.

GLENWOOD SPRINGS　　　　　970

HOT SPRINGS POOL 401 River Rd.
Phone: 945-6571.
Pool: 100f*, irregularly shaped, outdoors, spring fed
and naturally temperature controlled, 90°-92°.
Admission: Pool: $6.25. Athletic Club and Pool:
$11.50
Notes: *The pool is 100f wide at its widest point.

GRAND JUNCTION　　　　　970

ORCHARD MESA COMMUNITY CENTER POOL
2736 'C' Rd.
Phone: 244-3866.
Pool: 25m, indoors, heated, 84°.
Admission: $3.25.

GREELEY　　　　　970

GREELEY RECREATION CENTER 651 - 10th
Ave.
Phone: 350-9400.
Pool: 25y x 60f, 8 lanes, indoors, heated, 84°.
Admission: $3, SC(60) $2.
Notes: There is also a 35f x 25f x 12f diving well
with two 1m boards.
Masters: A Masters swim club is in formation.
Contact Recreation Supervisor Eldon Lampson at
350-9415.

THE CONDITIONING SPA 2640 - 11th Ave.
Phone: 352-0974.
Pool: 25m, indoors, heated, 80°-83°.
Admission: $8.

GREELEY WORK OUT WEST 5699 W. 20th St.
Phone: 330-9691.
Pool: 25y, indoors, heated, 82°.
Admission: $10.
Affiliate: IHRSA $6.

LAKEWOOD　　　　　303

JEFFCO FAMILY YMCA 11050 W. 20th Ave.
Phone: 233-8877.
Pool: 25y x 30f, 5 lanes, indoors, heated, 85°.
Admission: $10.
Affiliate: YMCA NC.
Masters: The Jeffco Family YMCA Masters.
Contact John Lallott or Vickie Sund at 233-8877.

FOOTHILLS RECREATION POOL Kepling Rd.
Phone: 985-3694.
Pool: 25m x 53m, indoors, heated, 83°.
Admission: Residents $2.75, non-residents $4.

LAKEWOOD ATHLETIC CLUB 3333 S.
Wadsworth
Phone: 989-5545.
Pool: 20m x 16f, 4 lanes, indoors, heated, 83°.
Admission: $15.
Affiliate: IHRSA & Colorado Association of Quality
Athletic Clubs: $7.50.
Hotel: Holiday Inn-Lakewood (980-9200) &
Hampton Inn (989-6900): $7.50 with room key.
To find: One block north of the intersection of
Wadsworth and Hwy. 285. One half mile north of
the Holiday Inn - Lakewood.

GREEN MOUNTAIN RECREATION CENTER
13198 W. Green Mountain Dr.

Phone: 987-7830.
Pool: 25m, 6 lanes, indoors, heated, 82°-84°.
Admission: $2.25.
Masters: The Green Mountain Dawgs. Contact Doug Graham at 745-8954(h).

LITTLETON   303

LITTLETON YMCA 2233 W. Shepperd Ave.
Phone: 794-2694.
Pool: 20y x 30f, 4 lanes, indoors, heated, 84°.
Admission: $7.
Affiliate: Y AWAY NC.
To find: Behind A.C.C. on S. Santa Fe Dr.

GOODSON RECREATION CENTER & POOL
6315 S. University Blvd.
Phone: 798-2476.
Pool: 25m x 42f, 6 lanes, indoors, heated, 84°.
Admission: Residents $3.50, non-residents $4.50.
To find: Five blocks north of the intersection of University and Arapahoe Rd. The center shares a parking lot and entrance with St. Andrew's Church.
Masters: The South Suburban Finnaddicts. Contact Melanie Dullea at 798-2476 ext. 144.

BALLY'S SOUTHWEST 8996 W. Bowles
Phone: 971-0140.
Pool: 25m, indoors, heated, 80°.
Admission: Call.
Affiliate: Bally's NC.

LONGMONT   303

LONGMONT ATHLETIC CLUB 10 Mountain View Ave.
Phone: 447-9919.
Pool: 25m, indoors, heated, 82°-84°.
Admission: $6.
Affiliate: IHRSA $5.

CENTENNIAL POOL 1201 Alpine St.
Phone: 651-8406.
Pool: 25m x 42y, 6 lanes, indoors, heated, 83°.
Admission: $2, SC(55) $1.25.
To find: At the intersection of Mountain View Ave. and Alpine St., across from Skyline High School.
Masters: The Longmasters. Contact Lynn Miller at 651-8406.

LOVELAND   970

ORCHARD'S ATHLETIC CLUB 289 E. 29th St.
Phone: 667-3800.
Pool: 76f x 20f, 4 lanes, indoors, heated, 84°.
Admission: $6.
To find: At the intersection of 29th St. and Hwy. 287, on the southeast corner of Orchards Shopping Center.

PAGOSA LAKES   970

PAGOSA LAKES RECREATION CENTER 45 Eagles Loft Circle
Phone: 731-2051.
Pool: 25y, 4 lanes, indoors, heated, 83°.
Admission: Out-of-town visitors $4. Please call in advance.

PUEBLO   719

SAM JONES SWIMMING POOL University of Southern Colorado, 2200 Bonforte Blvd.
Phone: 549-2012.
Pool: 25y, 6 lanes, indoors, heated, 83°.
Admission: $1.
Hotel: Hampton Inn (544-4700) 1 visit NC with a pass from the hotel.
To find: In the Massari Gymnasium on campus.

PUEBLO YMCA 700 Albany Ave.
Phone: 543-5151.
Pool: 25m, indoors, heated, 82°-84°.
Admission: $6.
Affiliate: YMCA NC.
Hotel: Best Western Town House Motor Hotel (543-6530) NC with a voucher from the hotel.

STEAMBOAT SPRINGS   970

STEAMBOAT SPRINGS RECREATION CENTER
On Hwy. 40 at 3rd St.
Phone: 879-1828.
Pool: 25y, outdoors, heated, 82°.
Admission: $5.

THORNTON   303

HURON PLAZA ATHLETIC CLUB 720 W. 84th Ave.
Phone: 426-6161.
Pool: 20m, indoors, heated, 84°.
Admission: $7.

VAIL   970

VAIL ATHLETIC CLUB 352 E. Meadow Dr.
Phone: 476-7960. **Reservations:** 800-822-4754.
Pool: 20m, indoors, heated, 82°.
Admission: $15. Registered guests NC.
Affiliate: Western Association of Clubs $6. IHRSA $10.

WESTMINSTER   303

CITY PARK RECREATION CENTER 4800 W. 92nd Ave.
Phone: 460-9690.
Pool: 25y, indoors, heated, 86°.
Admission: Residents $2.25, non-residents $3.50.

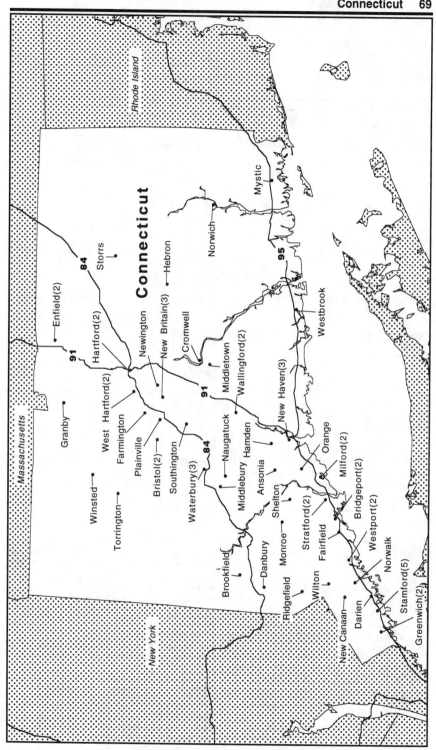

Connecticut

Massachusetts

Rhode Island

New York

Enfield(2)
91
Granby
Winsted
Torrington
Hartford(2)
West Hartford(2)
Farmington
Plainville
Bristol(2)
Southington
Waterbury(3)
Middlebury
Ansonia
Brookfield
Danbury
Ridgefield
Wilton
New Canaan
84
Storrs
Newington
New Britain(3)
Cromwell
91
Naugatuck
Hamden
84
Shelton
Monroe
Stratford(2)
Fairfield
Darien
Greenwich(2)
Stamford(5)
Norwalk
Westport(2)
Bridgeport(2)
Milford(2)
Orange
New Haven(3)
Wallingford(2)
Middletown
Hebron
Norwich
95
Mystic
Westbrook

ANSONIA   203

VALLEY YMCA 12 State St.
Phone: 736-9975.
Pool: 25y, 6 lanes, indoors, heated, 84°.
Affiliate: Out-of-state YMCA NC, in-state $5.

BRIDGEPORT   203

BRIDGEPORT YMCA 651 State St.
Phone: 334-5551.
Pool: 20y x 22f, 4 lanes, indoors, heated, 85°.
Affiliate: YMCA $8.
To find: At the intersection of State St. and Park
Ave.

**ITALIAN COMMUNITY CENTER OF GREATER
BRIDGEPORT** 4000 Park Ave.
Phone: 374-9231.
Pool: 25y x 32f, indoors, heated, 82°-83°.
Admission: $15.

BRISTOL   203

NEW ENGLAND HEALTH & RACQUET CLUB
842 Clark Ave.
Phone: 583-1843.
Pool: 20y x 42f, 4 lanes, indoors, heated, 82°.
Admission: $14.
Affiliate: IHRSA $7.

THE FAMILY CENTER FOR GIRLS & BOYS 47
Upson St.
Phone: 583-1679.
Pool: 25y, 5 lanes, indoors, heated, 82°.
Admission: $3.

BROOKFIELD   203

**REGIONAL YMCA OF WESTERN CONNECTICUT
- GREENKNOLL BRANCH** 2 Huckelberry Hill Rd.
Phone: 775-4444.
Pool: 25y x 42f, 6 lanes, indoors, heated, 82°.
Affiliate: YMCA Call.

CROMWELL   203

TRI-TOWN SPORTS 6 Progress Dr.
Phone: 632-1226.
Pool: 25y x 40f, 6 lanes, indoors, heated, 81°.
Admission: $10.
Affiliate: IHRSA NC.
Hotel: Holiday Inn Cromwell (635-1001) NC.
To find: Exit 21 Route 91 one half mile north on
Sebethe.

DANBURY   203

**REGIONAL YMCA OF WESTERN CONNECTICUT
- BOUGHTON ST. BRANCH** 12 Boughton St.
Phone: 744-1000.
Pool: 20y x 25f, 5 lanes, indoors, heated, 84°.
Affiliate: YMCA $2.50.

To find: Boughton St. is the first right after the
police station on Main St.

DARIEN   203

DARIEN YMCA 2420 Post Rd.
Phone: 655-8228.
Pool: 25y, indoors, heated, 78°.
Affiliate: YMCA $5.

ENFIELD   203

NEW ENGLAND HEALTH & RACQUET CLUB 3
Weymouth Rd.
Phone: 745-2408.
Pool: 20y x 20f, indoors, heated, 80°.
Admission: $15.
Affiliate: IHRSA $8.
Hotel: Most local hotels $8. Call the club for
details.
To find: From I-91, Exit 46 turn left onto King
St./Route 5, and turn left at the light onto
Weymouth Rd.

THE CLUB AT BIGELOW COMMONS 55 Main St.
Phone: 741-5549.
Pool: 20y x 20f, 3 lanes, indoors, heated, 80°.
Admission: $10.
Affiliate: IHRSA $5.

FAIRFIELD   203

FAIRFIELD BRANCH YMCA 841 Old Post Rd.
Phone: 255-2834.
Pool: 25y, indoors, heated, 82°-86°.
Admission: $10.
Affiliate: YMCA $5.

FARMINGTON   203

FARMINGTON FARMS RACQUET CLUB 94
Brickyard
Phone: 677-2489.
Pool: 25y, indoors, heated, 84°.
Affiliate: IHRSA $10.

GRANBY   203

SWIM CENTER ONE 97 Salmon Brook St.
Phone: 653-5524.
Pool 1: 25y x 60f, 8 lanes, indoors, heated, 79°.
Pool 2: 20y, 3 lanes, indoors, heated, 84°.
Admission: Call.
Affiliate: IHRSA $5.
To find: On Routes 10 and 202, one mile north of
the Simsbury/Granby town line.

GREENWICH   203

GREENWICH YWCA 259 E. Putnam Ave. (U.S. 1)
Phone: 869-6501.
Pool: 25y x 30f, 4 lanes, indoors, heated, 83°.
Admission: $5.25, SC(62) $3.25.

Affiliate: YWCA $3.25.
Notes: The pool closes for the last two weeks of Aug.

GREENWICH MASTERS at the Greenwich YWCA
Masters: Contact Peter Crumbine at 961-7290(w).
Non-member participation: Call.
Notes: Workouts: M-F: 6-7:30AM.

GREENWICH YMCA 50 E. Putnam Ave.
Phone: 869-1630.
Pool: 20y x 20f, 6 lanes, indoors, heated, 84°.
Admission: $10.
Affiliate: YMCA outside a 50 mile radius NC.
To find: One block east of Greenwich Ave., the side street is Mason.

HAMDEN   203

HAMDEN-NORTH HAVEN YMCA 1605 Sherman Ave.
Phone: 248-6361.
Pool: 25y x 30f, 4 lanes, indoors, heated, 82°-83°.
Admission: $7.
Affiliate: Y AWAY $3.50.
Notes: There is also a seasonal, outdoor pool about 5 miles west of the main facility.
To find: Approximately three quarters of a mile north of the Anderson Little Store on Shepard Ave.

HARTFORD   203

HARTFORD PARKS & RECREATION
Phone: 722-6505.
The city operates several year-round pools, but the pools that are open change from season to season. Call for information.

DOWNTOWN HARTFORD YMCA 160 Jewell St.
Phone: 522-4183 ext. 355.
Pool: 25y, 7 lanes, indoors, heated, water temperature not reported.
Admission: Out-of-area visitors $5.
Affiliate: YMCA $3.

HARTFORD REGION YWCA 135 Broad St.
Phone: 525-1163.
Pool: 25y x 35f, 5 lanes, indoors, heated, 81°.
Admission: $8, SC(55) $5.
Affiliate: YWCA $5.
To find: At the convergence of Broad, Farmington, and Asylum Sts.

HARTFORD REGION YWCA MASTERS at the Hartford Region YWCA
Masters: Contact Fitness Center Coordinator Donna Peloquin at 525-1163 ext. 214.
Non-member participation: $8, includes pool fees.
Notes: Coached workouts: Tu: 5:30-7PM. F: 6-7PM.

HEBRON   203

HEMLOCK RECREATION CENTER 147 Jones St.
Phone: 228-9496.
Pool: 20y, indoors, heated, 86°.
Admission: $4, SC $3.
Notes: Lap swimming is available from Sep. through May.

MIDDLEBURY   203

BALLY'S HOLIDAY MATRIX FITNESS 930 Straight Tpk.
Phone: 598-0833.
Pool: 25y, indoors, heated, 80°.
Affiliate: Bally's NC.

MIDDLETOWN   203

NORTHERN MIDDLESEX YMCA 99 Union St.
Phone: 347-6907.
Pool: 25y, 6 lanes, indoors, heated, 79°-81°.
Admission: $10.
Affiliate: Y AWAY $2.

MILFORD   203

THE MILFORD ACADEMY 150 Gulf St.
Phone: 878-8432.
Pool: 25y x 45f, 6 lanes, indoors, heated, 80°.
Admission: $3.

MILFORD-ORANGE YMCA 631 Orange Ave.
Phone: 878-6501.
Pool: 25y, indoor/outdoor, heated, 83°-84°.
Admission: $7, SC(65) $4.
Affiliate: YMCA NC.
Masters: The Halibuts. Contact Mike Kravit at 878-6501.

MONROE   203

MASUK HIGH SCHOOL 1014 Monroe Tpk.
Phone: 268-9836.
Pool: 25y, 6 lanes, indoors, heated, 81°.
Admission: $6.
Notes: The pool closes for the month of Sep.
To find: North of Monroe Green 1.2 miles.

MYSTIC   203

MYSTIC COMMUNITY CENTER Harry Austin Dr.
Phone: 536-3575.
Pool: 25y x 45f, 6 lanes, indoors, heated, 83°.
Admission: $8.
Hotel: Mystic Hilton (572-0731) & Inn at Mystic (536-9604): NC with room key.
To find: From Route 1 take Mason's Island Rd. south, cross the bridge and take the first right onto Harry Austin Rd. The center is on the right.

NAUGATUCK   203

NAUGATUCK YMCA 284 Church St.
Phone: 729-8239.
Pool: 25y, 6 lanes, indoors, heated, 84°.
Admission: $5.
Affiliate: Y AWAY $2.50.
To find: One block north of the Naugatuck Town Green.

NEW BRITAIN   203

BOYS CLUB 150 Washington St.
Phone: 229-2865.
Pool: 25y, indoors, heated, 76°.
Admission: $2.

YWCA OF NEW BRITAIN 22 Glen St.
Phone: 225-4681.
Pool: 25y x 33f, 5 lanes, indoors, heated, 86°.
Admission: $5, SC(60) $3.
Affiliate: YWCA $3, SC $2.50.
Notes: This YWCA offers shallow & deep water walking, arthritic, back care, & aqua aerobics programs.

NEW BRITAIN-BERLIN YMCA 50 High St.
Phone: 229-3787.
Pool: 25y, indoors, heated, 83°-86°.
Admission: $8.
Affiliate: Out-of-state YMCA & U.S. Military: NC. In-state YMCA $4.
Hotel: Ramada Inn (224-9161) NC with room key.

NEW CANAAN   203

NEW CANAAN YMCA 564 South Ave.
Phone: 966-4528.
Pool: 40m, indoors, heated, 78°.
Admission: $7.
Affiliate: YMCA $3.

NEW HAVEN   203

WILBUR CROSS SENIOR HIGH SCHOOL 181 Mitchell Dr.
Phone: 787-8731.
Pool: 25y, indoors, heated, 82°.
Admission: NC.

HILLHOUSE SENIOR HIGH SCHOOL 480 Sherman Ave.
Phone: 787-8579.
Pool: 25y, indoors, heated, 82°.
Admission: NC.

YWCA OF GREATER NEW HAVEN 48 Howe St.
Phone: 865-5171.
Pool: 25y x 25f, 7 lanes, indoors, heated, 85°.
Admission: $3.
To find: At the corner of Crown and Howe St.

NEWINGTON   203

NEW ENGLAND HEALTH & RACQUET CLUB 375 E. Cedar
Phone: 666-8451.
Pool: 20y, 4 lanes, indoor/outdoor, heated, 81°.
Admission: $14. Before 5PM $7.
Affiliate: IHRSA Call.

NORWALK   203

NORWALK YMCA 370 West Ave.
Phone: 866-4425.
Pool: 25y, 6 lanes, indoors, heated, 80°-82°.
Affiliate: Out-of-state YMCA NC, in-state $5.

NORWICH   203

CENTRAL YMCA 337 Main St.
Phone: 889-7349.
Pool: 25y, indoors, heated, 80°-82°.
Admission: $6.
Affiliate: YMCA $2.

ORANGE   203

ORANGE TOWN POOL High Plains Community Center, 525 Orange Center Rd.
Phone: 795-4119.
Pool: 25y x 60f, 8 lanes, indoors, heated, 81°-84°.
Admission: Residents $3, SC(60) NC. Non-residents $5.
Affiliate: USMS $3.
Masters: The Orange Masters. Contact Stephen Bergethon at 795-0801.

PLAINVILLE   203

WHEELER REGIONAL FAMILY YMCA 149 Farmington Ave., Route 10
Phone: 293-2274.
Pool: 25y, indoors, heated, 82°.
Admission: 3 visits $5 each.
Affiliate: Y AWAY Call.
Hotel: Howard Johnsons Hotel (747-6876) 5 visits NC.

RIDGEFIELD   203

RIDGEFIELD PARKS & RECREATION DEPT. POOL 115 Barlow Mountain Rd.
Phone: 431-2755.
Pool: 25m x 42f, 6 lanes, indoors, heated, 83°.
Admission: Recreation swims $5.
To find: Adjacent to and shares a parking lot with Scotland Elementary School.
Masters: The Ridgefield Aquatics Masters. Contact Coach David Palumbo at 431-4613(w).

SHELTON   203

SHELTON COMMUNITY CENTER 41 Church St.
Phone: 925-8422.
Pool: 25y x 60f, 8 lanes, indoors, heated, 82°-84°.

Admission: $4.
Hotel: Marriott Residence Inn (926-9000) NC with pass from the hotel.
To find: Diagonally across from the Huntington Green and directly across from the Huntington Firehouse.

SOUTHINGTON   203

SOUTHINGTON YMCA 29 High St.
Phone: 628-5597.
Pool: 25y, indoors, heated, 84°.
Admission: $7.
Affiliate: Y AWAY NC.

STAMFORD   203

STAMFORD YMCA 909 Washington Blvd.
Phone: 357-7000.
Pool: 25y x 36f, 6 lanes, indoors, heated, 82°.
Affiliate: YMCA & U.S. Military: $3.
Hotel: Ramada Plaza Hotel (358-8400) $6 with a pass from the hotel.

SPORTSPLEX 49 Brownhouse Rd.
Phone: 358-0066.
Pool: 25y, 3 lanes, indoors, heated, 80°-82°.
Affiliate: IHRSA $12.

STAMFORD ITALIAN CENTER 1620 Newfield Ave.
Phone: 322-6941.
Pool: 25y, 6 lanes, indoors, heated, 81°.
Admission: Winter $5. Summer $10.
Notes: There is also a 25m, outdoor, unheated, summer pool.

THE STAMFORD ATHLETIC CLUB 75 - 3rd St.
Phone: 357-7555.
Pool: 25y x 25f, 5 lanes, indoors, heated, 82°-83°.
Admission: $10.
Affiliate: IHRSA outside a 75 mile radius 4 visits per month $8 each.
To find: At the intersection of 3rd St. and Bedford, behind a church.

STAMFORD JCC 1035 Newfield Ave.
Phone: 322-7900.
Pool: 25m x 15m, 6 lanes, indoors, heated, 84°.
Affiliate: JCC 4 visits per month NC.
To find: At the intersection of Newfield Ave. and Vine Rd.

STORRS   203

UNIVERSITY OF CONNECTICUT MASTERS SWIM CLUB at Wolf- Zackin Natatorium
Masters: Contact Janit Romayko at 429-3317(w).
Pool: 50m OR 25y + 25y, 6 OR 12 lanes, indoors, heated, 80°.
Affiliate: USMS 1 workout per week NC.
Notes: Coached workouts: Tu,Th: 8-9:30PM. Su: 4-6PM.

STRATFORD   203

STRATFORD CLUB 140 Watson Blvd.
Phone: 378-2211.
Pool: 20y, indoors, heated, 82°.
Affiliate: IHRSA $8.
Hotel: Ramada Inn (375-8866) $10.

STRATFORD BRANCH YMCA 3045 Main St.
Phone: 375-5844.
Pool: 25y, indoors, heated, 84°.
Admission: $5.
Affiliate: YMCA $2.

TORRINGTON   203

NORTHWEST YMCA 259 Prospect St.
Phone: 489-3133.
Pool: 25y, 6 lanes, indoors, heated, water temperature not reported.
Admission: $8.
Affiliate: Y AWAY NC.

WALLINGFORD   203

HEALTHWORKS 100 Neal Rd.
Phone: 265-2861.
Pool: 20y x 32f, 4 lanes, indoors, heated, 86°.
Admission: $15.
Affiliate: Association of Hospital Fitness Centers NC. IHRSA $5.
Hotel: Hampton Inn (235-5154) & Courtyards by Marriott (284-9400): $10 with a pass from the hotel.
To find: One quarter of a mile north of the Yankee Silversmith Restaurant on Route 5.

WALLINGFORD FAMILY YMCA 81 S. Elm St.
Phone: 269-4497.
Pool: 25y, indoors, heated, 82°.
Admission: $10.
Affiliate: Out-of-state YMCA NC.

WATERBURY   203

YMCA OF GREATER WATERBURY 136 W. Main St.
Phone: 754-2181.
Pool: 25y, 6 lanes, indoors, heated, 80°.
Admission: $5.
Affiliate: YMCA 3 visits NC.

YWCA OF WATERBURY 80 Prospect St.
Phone: 754-5136.
Pool: 25y, 5 lanes, indoors, heated, 84°-86°.
Admission: $3.
Notes: Swim caps are required at all times, and are available for purchase or rental at the YWCA.

BOYS CLUB OF WATERBURY 1037 E. Main St.
Phone: 756-8104.
Pool: 25y, 5 lanes, indoors, heated, 80°-83°.
Admission: $2.

WEST HARTFORD   203

CORNERSTONE AQUATICS CENTER 55 Buena
Vista Rd.
Phone: 521-3242.
Pool 1: 25y x 25m, 11 lanes, indoors, heated, 79°.
Pool 2: 25y x 45f, 6 lanes, indoors, heated, 85°.
Admission: Call.
Affiliate: IHRSA $7.

**GREATER HARTFORD JEWISH COMMUNITY
CENTER** 335 Bloomfield Ave.
Phone: 236-4571.
Pool: 25y, 6 lanes, indoors, heated, 82°.
Affiliate: JCC NC.

WESTBROOK   203

VALLEY SHORE YMCA Spencer Plains Rd.
Phone: 399-9622.
Pool: 25y, 6 lanes, indoors, heated, 83°.
Admission: $5.
Affiliate: Y AWAY NC. YMCA Call.
Masters: The Valley Shore YMCA Masters.
Contact Patrick Callahan at 399-9622.

WESTPORT   203

WESTPORT YMCA 59 Post Rd. E.
Phone: 226-8981.
Pool: 25y x 37f, 6 lanes, indoors, heated, 82°.
Admission: $10.

Affiliate: Out-of-county YMCA NC.
To find: Downtown, at the intersection of Main St.
and Post Rd.

STAPLES HIGH SCHOOL North Ave.
Phone: 226-8311. Ask for the Recreation
Commission.
Pool: 25m, indoors, heated, water temperature not
reported.
Affiliate: Residents $3.
Notes: The facility is not operated in the summer.

WILTON   203

WILTON FAMILY Y 404 Danbury Rd.
Phone: 762-8384.
Pool 1: 50m x 44f, 6 lanes, indoor/outdoor, heated,
80°.
Pool 2: 25y, 6 lanes, indoors, heated, 82°.
Admission: $8, SC(62) $4.
Affiliate: Y AWAY NC. YMCA & U.S. Military:
Call.
To find: Across from Wilton High School.

WINSTED   203

NORTHWEST YMCA 480 Main St.
Phone: 379-0708.
Pool: 25m, indoors, heated, 82°-84°.
Admission: $8.
Affiliate: Y AWAY 2 weeks NC.

ALWAYS CALL FIRST

Pools close, they change names, affiliations, admission policies, and rates. And
just because a pool is listed in *Swimmers Guide* doesn't mean it's open all day,
every day, for just the type of workout you want to do. Spend a quarter to save
time and aggravation. . . always call first!

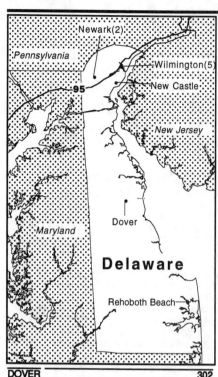

Newark(2)

Pennsylvania

Wilmington(5)

New Castle

95

New Jersey

Maryland

Dover

Delaware

Rehoboth Beach

WESTERN YMCA 2600 Kirkwood Hwy.
Phone: 453-1482.
Pool: 25y, indoors, heated, 80°-84°.
Affiliate: YMCA NC.

REHOBOTH BEACH   302

SUSSEX FAMILY YMCA 105 Church St.
Phone: 227-8018.
Pool: 25y, 6 lanes, indoors, heated, 84°.
Admission: 4 visits $8 each.
Affiliate: Y AWAY $5.
To find: Off Route 1 at the Rehoboth Ave. Exit.
Take the first right onto Church St.

WILMINGTON   302

CENTRAL YMCA 501 W. 11th St.
Phone: 571-6900.
Pool: 25y x 45f, 7 lanes, indoors, heated, 84°.
Admission: $10.
Affiliate: YMCA NC.
Hotel: Several local hotels NC with a pass from the
hotel. Call the Y for details.
To find: At the intersection of 11th St. and
Washington St., across from the Marriott.
Masters: The Central Masters. Contact Chuck
Ohline at 571-6900.

WALNUT STREET YMCA 1000A Walnut St.
Phone: 571-6935.
Pool: 20y x 36f, 3 lanes, indoors, heated, 84°.
Admission: $5.
Affiliate: YMCA Call.
To find: At the intersection of Walnut and 10th Sts.

WILLIAM ANDERSON COMMUNITY CENTER
501 N. Madison St.
Phone: 571-4266.
Pool: 25y, indoors, heated, water temperature not
reported.
Admission: NC.

PIKE CREEK FITNESS CLUB 4905 Mermaid Blvd.
Phone: 239-6688.
Pool: 25y x 54f, 6 lanes, indoors, heated, 82°.
Affiliate: IHRSA $8.
To find: Near Goldey Beacom College and the Pike
Creek Shopping Center.
Masters: A Masters group is in formation. Contact
Kris Knutsen at 239-6688.

BRANDYWINE YMCA 3 Mt. Lebanon Rd.
Phone: 478-8303.
Pool: 25y x 20f, 4 lanes, indoors, heated, 86°.
Affiliate: YMCA outside a 75 mile radius NC.

DOVER   302

CENTRAL DELAWARE YMCA 1137 S. State St.
Phone: 674-3000.
Pool: 25y x 25f, 4 lanes, indoors, heated, 86°.
Admission: $7.50.
Affiliate: Y AWAY NC.

NEW CASTLE   302

DELAWARE SWIM & FITNESS CENTER 2150
New Castle Ave.
Phone: 658-4372.
Pool 1: 25y x 60f, 8 lanes, indoors, heated, 82°.
Pool 2: 20y, 2 lanes, indoors, heated, 96°.
Admission: $4 - $6, depending on season.
Affiliate: IHRSA Call.
Hotel: TraveLodge (654-5544) NC with a pass from
the hotel.
To find: From I-295, two exits south of the
Delaware Memorial Bridge (Route 9 South).
Masters: Contact Coach Chris Collier at 658-4372.

NEWARK   302

DELAWARE AQUATIC MASTERS at Harry
Rawstrom Pool, University of Delaware
Masters: Contact Dr. Art Mayer at 368-5176(w).
Pool: 25y, 8 lanes, indoors, heated, 78°-80°.
Notes: Workouts: M-Sa: 5:30-7:30AM. Due to
pool space and time limitations, new members are
admitted only as openings occur.

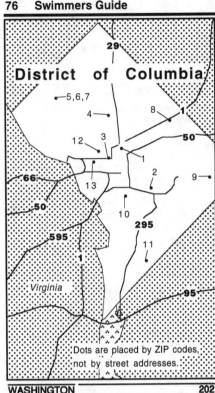

District of Columbia

Virginia

Dots are placed by ZIP codes, not by street addresses.

WASHINGTON ━━━━━━━━━━ **202**

1. YWCA FITNESS CENTER AT GALLERY PLACE 624 - 9th St. N.W.
Phone: 626-0710.
Pool: 25y x 45f, 4 lanes, indoors, heated, 83°.
Admission: $10.
Affiliate: YWCA $8.
To find: Near the Gallery Place Metro Station. At the intersection of 9th and 'G' Sts. N.W.
Masters: The YWCA DC Masters. Contact Ralph Laughlin at 387-6096(h).

2. CAPITOL EAST NATATORIUM 635 North Carolina Ave. S.E.
Phone: Pool: 724-4495. Parks & Rec. Dept: 576-6436.
Pool: 20y x 75f, 10 lanes, indoors, heated, 80°.
Admission: NC.

3. DUNBAR SENIOR HIGH SCHOOL POOL 1301 New Jersey Ave. N.W.
Phone: Pool: 673-7744. Parks & Rec. Dept: 576-6436.
Pool: 25m x 20m, 2 or 3 lanes, indoors, heated, 80°.
Admission: NC.

4. MARIE H. REED LEARNING CENTER 2200 Champlain St. N.W.

Phone: Pool: 673-7771. Parks & Rec. Dept: 576-6436.
Pool: 25y x 60f, 8 lanes, indoors, heated, 78°.
Admission: NC.

DISTRICT OF COLUMBIA AQUATICS CLUB at Marie H. Reed Learning Center
Masters: Contact Glenn Mlaker at (703) 553-9040
Affiliate: USMS NC.
Notes: Coached workouts M,W: 8-9PM. Also Su: 10-11:30AM at Washington-Lee Swimming Pool. See that listing under Arlington, VA.

5. WOODROW WILSON HIGH SCHOOL POOL 3950 Nebraska Ave. N.W.
Phone: Pool: 282-2216. Parks & Rec. Dept: 576-6436.
Pool: 25y x 60f, 4 lanes, indoors, heated, 78°.
Admission: NC.
To find: Between Albemarle St. & Brandywine.

DCRP MASTERS SWIM TEAM at Woodrow Wilson High School Pool
Masters: Contact Colleen Morgan at 232-7949(h).
Affiliate: USMS NC.
Notes: Coached workouts: Tu,Th: 6-7:30PM. In summer, the club holds workouts M-F evenings at the 50m, 8 lane, outdoor, unheated, 77°-82° Haines Point Pool in E. Potomac Park (727-6523).

6. ST. ALBAN'S LAWRENCE POOL 3551 Garfield St. N.W.
Phone: 537-6462 or 537-5594.
Pool: 25y, 6 lanes, indoors, heated, 79°-80°.
Memberships: $550/year for early morning access. $450/year for evening and weekend access.
Masters: The Capitol Sea Devils. Contact Mark Lewis at 537-6462.

7. TENLEY SPORT & HEALTH CLUB 4000 Wisconsin Ave. N. W.
Phone: 362-8000.
Pool: 25m, indoors, heated, 80°.
Affiliate: IHRSA $10.

8. FT. LINCOLN JUNIOR HIGH SCHOOL POOL 31st St. & Ft. Lincoln Dr. N.E.
Phone: Pool: 576-6135. Parks & Rec. Dept: 576-6436.
Pool: 25y x 48f, indoors, heated, 80°.
Admission: NC.
Notes: There is also a 25y, outdoor, summer pool.

9. H.D. WOODSON SENIOR HIGH SCHOOL POOL 55th & Eads Sts. N.W.
Phone: Pool: 724-4499. Parks & Rec. Dept: 576-6436.
Pool: 25y x 60f, 3 lanes, indoors, heated, 80°.
Admission: NC.
Notes: The pool is closed for the 1994-1995 school year, plans for the future are uncertain. When open, the pool operates from Sep. to early Jun.

10. LOEWS L'ENFANT PLAZA HOTEL 480 L'enfant Plaza S.W.
Phone: 484-1000. **Reservations:** 800-23-LOEWS.
Pool: 20y x 30f, indoor/outdoor, heated, water temperature not reported.
Admission: $10. Registered guests NC.

11. WASHINGTON HIGHLANDS POOL at Ferebee Hope Elementary School, 8th & Yuma Sts. S.E.
Phone: Pool: 767-7449. Parks & Rec. Dept: 576-6436.
Pool: 25y x 60f, 4 lanes, indoors, heated, 80°.
Admission: NC.

12. NATIONAL CAPITAL YMCA 1711 Rhode Island Ave. N.W.
Phone: 862-9622.
Pool: 25m x 20m, 6 lanes, indoors, heated, 81°.

Affiliate: Y AWAY $5. YMCA: $5. Peak hours $10.
Hotel: Radisson Park Terrace Hotel (232-7000) NC with room key.
To find: Near the White House, adjacent to St. Mathews Cathedral.

13. ANA HOTEL, WASHINGTON, D.C. 2401 'M' St. N.W.
Phone: 429-2400. **Reservations:** 800-228-3000.
Pool: 50f, rectangular, indoors, heated, 82°.
Admission: Registered guests NC.
Hotel: Guests at neighboring hotels $20 with room key.
Affiliate: The Fitness Company Clubs — 4 visits per month $7.50 each. IHRSA outside a 50 mile radius $15.

HELP MAKE THE NEXT *SWIMMERS GUIDE* EVEN BETTER

To receive a free copy of the next ***Swimmers Guide*** tell us about pools you know of that aren't in this edition. See page 14 for details.

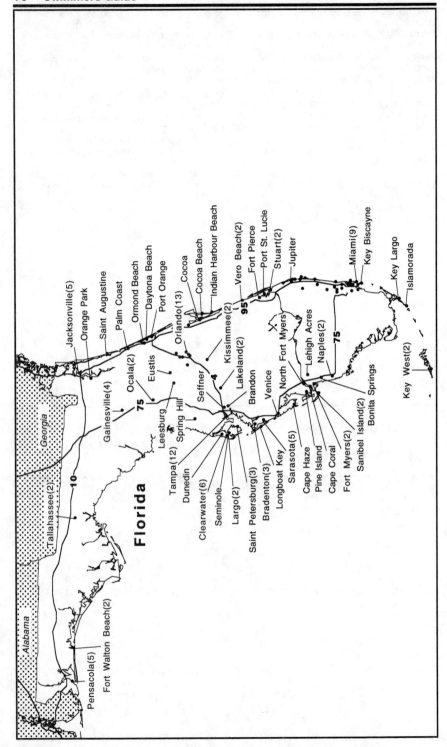

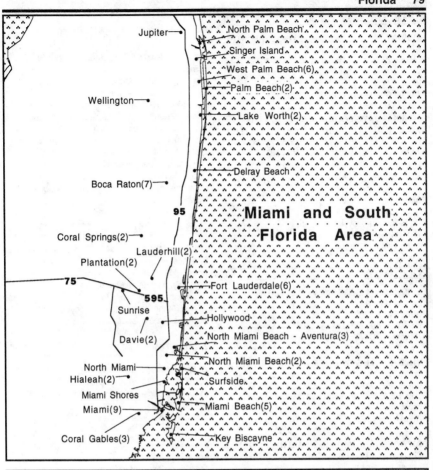

Jupiter
North Palm Beach
Singer Island
West Palm Beach(6)
Palm Beach(2)
Wellington
Lake Worth(2)

Delray Beach
Boca Raton(7)

95

Miami and South Florida Area

Coral Springs(2)
Lauderhill(2)
Plantation(2)

75
595
Fort Lauderdale(6)
Sunrise
Hollywood
Davie(2)
North Miami Beach - Aventura(3)
North Miami
North Miami Beach(2)
Hialeah(2)
Miami Shores
Surfside
Miami(9)
Miami Beach(5)
Coral Gables(3)
Key Biscayne

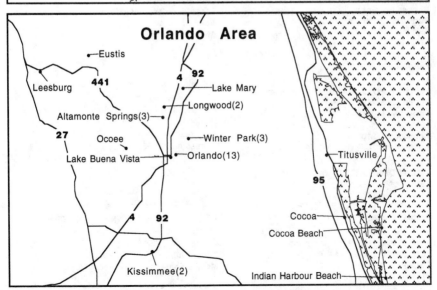

Orlando Area

Eustis
Leesburg
441
4 92
Lake Mary
Longwood(2)
Altamonte Springs(3)
27
Ocoee
Winter Park(3)
Lake Buena Vista
Orlando(13)
Titusville

95

Cocoa
Cocoa Beach

4 92

Kissimmee(2)
Indian Harbour Beach

ALTAMONTE SPRINGS   407

**HOLIDAY INN ORLANDO NORTH-ALTAMONTE
SPRINGS** 230 W. Hwy. 436
Phone: 862-4455. **Reservations:** 800-226-4544.
Pool: 24y, rectangular, outdoors, unheated, 60°-
90°.
Admission: Registered guests only NC.

DAYS INN DAYS LODGE 450 Douglas Ave.
Phone: 862-7111. **Reservations:** 800-327-2221.
Pool: 64f x 40f, rectangular, outdoors, heated, 80°.
Admission: Registered guests only NC.

BALLY'S HEALTH & RACQUET CLUB 733 W.
State Rd. 436
Phone: 869-9858.
Pool: 25y, indoors, heated, 80°.
Admission: 1 visit NC.
Affiliate: Bally's NC.
Hotel: Hilton Hotel (830-1985) NC.

BOCA RATON   407

LEVIS JEWISH COMMUNITY CENTER 9801
Donna Klein Blvd.
Phone: 852-3200.
Pool: 25y, outdoors, heated, 84°.
Affiliate: JCC NC.

ATHLETIC CLUB OF BOCA RATON 1499 Yamato
Rd.
Phone: 241-5088.
Pool: 25m, indoors, heated, 81°-83°.
Admission: $17.
Affiliate: IHRSA $14.

**BALLY'S SCANDIANVIAN HEALTH & FITNESS
CENTER** 21069 Military Trail
Phone: 368-6441.
Pool: 25y, outdoors, heated, 78°-84°.
Admission: 1 visit NC.
Affiliate: Bally's NC.
Hotel: Marriott (392-4600), Holiday Inn (368-5200),
& Embassy Suites (994-8200): NC.

YMCA OF BOCA RATON 6631 Palmetto Circle S.
Phone: 395-9622.
Pool: 25y x 45f, 6 lanes, indoor/outdoor, heated,
86°.
Admission: $10.
Affiliate: YMCA 6 visits NC.

BOCA POINTE ATHLETIC CENTER 22971 Via De
Sunrisa N.
Phone: 394-3000.
Pool: 25m, outdoors, temperature controlled, 82°.
Admission: $6.

**ATHLETIC CENTER AT BOCA POINTE
COUNTRY CLUB** 7144 Boca Pointe Dr.
Phone: 391-5100.
Pool: 25m, 5 lanes, outdoors, temperature con-
trolled, 80°-84°.
Memberships: I/S $300 + $249/6 months.

MEADOWS PARK POOL 1300 N.W. 8th St.
Phone: 393-7851.
Pool: 25y x 25m, 8 lanes, outdoors, heated, 80° fall
through spring, 85°-88° in summer.
Admission: Residents $2.25, non-residents $3.25.
To find: From I-95 take Palmetto Pk. Rd. east to
N.W. 12th Ave., go north (left) to N.W. 8th St. (the
1st light), go west (left) to the end; the pool is on
the right, in Meadows Park.
Masters: The Boca Raton Masters. Call 393-7851.
Visiting Masters are invited to join team practices.
No special rates apply, but you must bring your
USMS card to participate.

BONITA SPRINGS   813

BONITA SPRINGS COMMUNITY POOL 26890
Pine Ave.
Phone: 947-1948.
Pool: 25y, 3 lanes, outdoors, heated, 80°-90°.
Admission: $2, SC(55) $1.
To find: At the intersection of Pine Ave. and Terry
Rd., next to the public library.

BRADENTON   813

HOLIDAY INN RIVERFRONT 100 Riverfront Dr. W.
Phone: 747-3727. **Reservations:** 800-HOLIDAY.
Pool: 52f, elongated hexagon shape, outdoors,
heated, 78°-80°.
Admission: Registered guests only NC.

MANATEE FAMILY YMCA 3805 - 59th St. W.
Phone: 792-7484.
Pool: 25y x 70f, 8 lanes, indoors, heated, 85°.
Admission: $6.
Affiliate: YMCA $2.
To find: A quarter of a mile from Cortez Rd., two
miles from Manatee Ave.

G.T. BRAY PARK AQUATICS CENTER 5502 -
33rd Ave. Dr. W.
Phone: 749-7188.
Pool: 25y x 50m, outdoors, temperature controlled,
78°-82°.
Admission: $2.25, SC(55) $1.25.
To find: In G.T. Bray Park on 59th St., between
Manatee Ave. & Cortez Rd.

BRANDON   813

BRANDON SWIM & TENNIS CLUB 405 Beverly
Blvd.
Phone: 689-0908.
Pool: 50m, outdoors, heated, 82°.
Memberships: Call.

CAPE CORAL 813

CAPE CORAL YACHT CLUB POOL Cape Coral Parks & Recreation Dept., 5819 Driftwood Pkwy.
Phone: 542-3903.
Pool: 25m, 6 lanes, outdoors, heated, 80°-85°.
Admission: Residents $2, non-residents $3.50.
Hotel: Live-aboards docked at the Yacht Club (574-0806) $2 with a letter from the Harbor Master.

CAPE HAZE 813

PALM ISLAND RESORT 7092 Placida Rd.
Phone: 697-4800. **Reservations:** 800-824-5412.
Pool: 20y, rectangular, outdoors, heated, 75°.
Admission: Registered guests only NC.

CLEARWATER 813

CLEARWATER YMCA 1005 S. Highland Ave.
Phone: 461-9622.
Pool: 25y, indoors, heated, 82°.
Admission: $8.
Affiliate: YMCA $3.

ROSS NORTON POOL 1426 S. Greenwood Ave.
Phone: 462-6130.
Pool: 25y x 25m, 6 x 6 lanes, outdoors, heated, 80° in winter, 80°-90° in summer.
Admission: Apr. -Oct: Residents $1.25, non-residents $2.50. Nov.-Mar: Residents $1.75, non-residents $3.50.
Hotel: All hotels within city limits — Resident rates with proof of hotel registration (room key, receipt, etc.)
To find: On S. Greenwood between Lakeview and Bellair Rd.
Masters: The Clearwater Masters. Contact Jim Tynan at 462-6097.

BALLY'S HEALTH & RACQUET CENTER 28272 U.S. Hwy. 19 N.
Phone: 791-0008.
Pool: 25y, indoors, heated, 78°.
Admission: $10.
Affiliate: Bally's NC.

BALLY'S TOTAL FITNESS 13455 U.S. 19 S.
Phone: 539-7474.
Pool: 25m, indoors, heated, 78°-82°.
Admission: $10.
Affiliate: Bally's NC.
Hotel: Holiday Inn Express (577-9100), Days Inn (573-3334), & Ramada Inn (796-1234): NC.

QUADRANGLE ATHLETIC CLUB 2147 Pine Forest Dr.
Phone: 535-4901.
Pool: 25y, outdoors, heated, 85°.
Admission: $10.

LONG CENTER 1501 N. Belcher Rd.
Phone: 726-2181.

Pool 1: 50m x 25y, 10 x 20 lanes, indoors, heated, 81°.
Pool 2: 25y x 18f, 3 lanes, indoors, heated, 88°-90°.
Admission: $5.
Hotel: J.P. Hotel - Holiday Inn Central (797-8173) $1.
To find: On Belcher Rd., one mile north of Gulf-to-Bay (Route 60) between Drew St. and Sunset Point Rd.

CLEARWATER AQUATIC MASTERS at Long Center
Pool phone: 726-2181. **Masters:** Contact Coach Cashel Mack at 462-6097(w) or 736-2532(h).
Affiliate: USMS 2 weeks NC, includes pool fees.
Notes: Workouts: M,W,F: 5-8AM, 6-7:30PM. Tu,Th: 5-8AM. Sa: 8-10AM.

COCOA 407

BREVARD COMMUNITY COLLEGE POOL
Phone: 632-1111.
Pool: 25m x 50m, outdoors, temperature controlled, 80°-82°.
Admission: $2.
Memberships: $75/year.
To find: The campus is located on Clearlake Ave. The pool is in the center of the campus.

COCOA BEACH 407

COCOA BEACH MUNICIPAL POOL 4800 Tom Waringer Blvd.
Phone: 868-3240.
Pool: 50m x 25y, 8 lanes, outdoors, unheated, 60°-88°*.
Admission: Residents $1.50, non-residents $2.50.
Notes: *The pool plans to install a solar water heater in 1995.
To find: Recreation complex off Minuteman Causeway.

CORAL GABLES 305

VENETIAN POOL 2701 DeSoto Blvd.
Phone: 460-5356.
Pool: Irregular shape & size, outdoors, spring fed, unheated, 76°-82°.
Admission: Residents $3, non-residents $4.
Hotel: Biltmore Hotel (445-1926) $3 with a voucher from the hotel.
Notes: Although not well suited for lap swimming, there is an area of the pool on the left side as you enter that can be used in a pinch.
To find: Five blocks west of 'Miracle Mile' (Coral Way) & LeJune Rd. Going west on Coral Way, turn left (south) onto Granada Blvd. and go to the fountain. Parking is adjacent to the fountain and the pool is across the street.

THE BILTMORE HOTEL, WESTIN HOTELS & RESORTS 1200 Anastasia Ave.

CORAL GABLES — CONTINUED

Phone: 445-1926. **Reservations:** 800-727-1926.
Pool: 149f x 48f, rectangular lap swimming area, outdoors, unheated, 66°-92°.
Admission: Registered guests only NC.

STINGRAY AQUATIC CLUB at Gulliver Academy Pool, 12595 Red Rd.
Pool phone: 663-1543. **Masters:** Contact Head Coach Lou Manganiello at 235-5573.
Pool: 25y, 6 lanes, outdoors, temperature controlled, 82°.
Non-member participation: 4 workouts per week pool fees only.
Notes: Coached workouts: M,W,F: 5:30-7AM. Sa: Call for times.

CORAL SPRINGS   305

MULLINS PARK POOL 10180 N.W. 29th St.
Phone: 345-2170.
Pool: 25y x 42f, 6 lanes, outdoors, heated, 82°.
Admission: $2.25, SC(55) $1.25.
To find: Off Coral Springs Dr. in Mullins Park, across from the public library.

CORAL SPRINGS AQUATIC COMPLEX 12441 Royal Palm Blvd.
Phone: 345-2121.
Pool: 50m x 25y, 8 x 18 lanes, outdoors, temperature controlled, 82°.
Admission: $2.50.

CORAL SPRINGS MASTERS SWIM PROGRAM at the Coral Springs Aquatic Complex
Pool phone: 345-2121. **Masters:** Contact Head Masters Coach Judy Bonning at 345-5370(w).
Affiliate: USMS (or candidate) 2 workouts per day $5 each, includes pool fees.
Notes: Workouts: M,W,F: 6-8AM, Noon-1:30PM, 7-8:30PM. Tu: Noon-1:30PM, 7-8:30PM. Th: 7-8:30PM. Sa: Noon-1:30PM. USMS membership is preferable for visitors, non-members are invited on a trial membership basis.

DAVIE   305

BALLY'S SCANDINAVIAN HEALTH & FITNESS CENTER 2701 S. University Dr.
Phone: 474-9801.
Pool: 25m, indoors, heated, 82°-85°.
Affiliate: Bally's NC.

JEWISH COMMUNITY CENTER 5850 Pine Island Rd.
Phone: 434-0499.
Pool: 25y, 5 lanes, outdoors, heated, 80°.
Affiliate: JCC 1 week NC.

DAYTONA BEACH   904

DAYTONA BEACH YMCA 825 Derbyshire Rd.

Phone: 253-5675.
Pool: 25y, 6 lanes, outdoors, heated, 81°.
Admission: Pool $4. Full facility $6.
Affiliate: Y AWAY $3.
To find: From U.S. 92, turn north onto White St. and proceed to the end. The Daytona Beach Community College and University of Central Florida are at the intersection of U.S. 92 and White St.

DELRAY BEACH   407

AQUA CREST POOL 2503 Seacrest Blvd.
Phone: 278-7174.
Pool: 25y + 25m x 50m, 16 lanes, outdoors, temperature controlled, 79°.
Admission: $1.50.
To find: Two miles south of Woolbright Rd. on Seacrest Blvd.
Masters: The Aqua Crest Masters. Call 278-7174.

DUNEDIN   813

HIGHLANDER POOL 903 Michigan Blvd.
Phone: 738-1904.
Pool: 25y x 75f, 8 lanes, indoor/outdoor, heated, 82°.
Admission: $2.50, SC(55) $2.
To find: Two blocks east of Alt. U.S. 19.

EUSTIS   904

EUSTIS AQUATIC CENTER 250 Ferran Park Dr.
Phone: Pool: 357-3264. Rec. Dept: 357-7969.
Pool: 25y, 6 lanes, outdoors, heated, 80°.
Admission: Summer $1.65. Winter $2.07.
Notes: There is also a 40f, outdoor, exercise and warm up/cool down pool heated to 85°.

FORT LAUDERDALE   305

DOWNTOWN YMCA 512 N.E. 5th St.
Phone: 764-6444.
Pool: 25y, 6 lanes, outdoors, heated, 82°.
Admission: $5.
Affiliate: YMCA 2 weeks NC.
To find: Five blocks north of Broward Blvd. and one block west of U.S.1.

SHERATON YANKEE TRADER BEACH RESORT 321 N. Atlantic Blvd.
Phone: 467-1111. **Reservations:** 800-325-3535.
Pool: 20y, rectangular, outdoors, heated, 80°-82°.
Admission: Registered guests only NC.
Notes: This hotel is three quarters of a mile north of the International Swimming Hall of Fame Complex, which is also listed in *Swimmers Guide*.

FT. LAUDERDALE HIGH SCHOOL POOL 1600 N.E. 4th Ave.
Phone: 761-5401.
Pool: 25y x 25m, 5 lap swimming lanes, outdoors, heated, 83°-85°.

Admission: $1.
Notes: Changing facilities are limited to the rest rooms, which are very small.
To find: The pool is located on the north side of the campus.

BALLY'S SCANDINAVIAN HEALTH & FITNESS CENTER 750 W. Sunrise Blvd.
Phone: 764-8666.
Pool: 20y, indoors, heated, 85°-87°.
Admission: 1 visit per 90 days NC.
Affiliate: Bally's NC.

INTERNATIONAL SWIMMING HALL OF FAME AQUATIC COMPLEX 501 Seabreeze Blvd.
Phone: 468-1580.
Pool 1: 50m x 25y, 10 lanes, outdoors, temperature controlled, 80°.
Pool 2: 25y x 50m, 20 lanes, outdoors, temperature controlled, 84°.
Admission: Residents $2, non-residents $3.
Notes: The pools are often closed for competitive events. Collegiate swim team training usually closes the facility from mid-Dec. to mid-Jan.
To find: One block south of Las Olas Blvd., one block west of A1A and the ocean.

FORT LAUDERDALE SWIM TEAM MASTERS at the International Swimming Hall of Fame Complex
Masters: Contact Head Coach Mark Davin at 764-4822.
Non-member participation: $5, includes pool fees.
Notes: Coached workouts: M-F: 6-8AM, 6-8PM. Sa: 9:30-11AM.

THE ATHLETIC CLUB AT WESTON 2300 Arvida Pkwy.
Phone: 384-2582.
Pool: 25y x 25m, outdoors, heated, 83°.
Affiliate: IHRSA $10.

FORT MYERS 813

RADISSON INN SANIBEL GATEWAY 20091 Summerlin Rd.
Phone: 466-1200. Reservations: 800-333-3333.
Pool: 70f, rectangular, outdoors, heated, 80°.
Admission: Registered guests only NC.

SAN CARLOS COMMUNITY POOL 8208 Sanibel Blvd.
Phone: 267-6002.
Pool: 25y, outdoors, heated, 85°.
Admission: $2, SC(55) $1.

FORT PIERCE 407

INDIAN RIVER COMMUNITY COLLEGE 3209 Virginia Ave.
Phone: 462-4700 ext. Pool.
Pool 1: 50m x 25y, 8 x 20 lanes, outdoors, temperature controlled, 79°-82°.
Pool 2: 25y, outdoors, temperature controlled, 79°-82°.
Admission: NC*.
Notes: *Activities Card required, available from Student Services M-Th 7:30AM-5:30PM.

INDIAN RIVER COMMUNITY COLLEGE MASTER SWIM TEAM at Indian River Community College
Pool phone: 462-4700. Masters: Contact Coach Tom Harmon at 462-4751(w) or 465-8385(h).
Affiliate: USMS & YMCA: 8 workouts in a 2 week period NC, includes pool fees.
Notes: Coached workouts: M-F: 7-9AM. Lap swimming: M-F: Noon-2PM, 5-7PM. Sa,Su: Noon-4PM. Tom advises that theirs is a small club, but 'boasts many world class swimmers'.

FORT WALTON BEACH 904

RAMADA BEACH RESORT 1500 Miracle Strip Pkwy. S.E. (Hwy. 98)
Phone: 243-9161. Reservations: 800-874-8962.
Pool: 50f x 25f, rectangular, indoors, heated, 88°.
Admission: $5. Registered guests NC.

PLAYGROUND AREA YMCA 1127 Hospital Rd.
Phone: 863-9622.
Pool: 25y, indoors, heated, 82°.
Admission: 1 visit NC, then $5.
Affiliate: Y AWAY NC.

GAINESVILLE 904

FLORIDA AQUATIC MASTERS at O'Connell Center, University of Florida Campus
Masters: Contact Coach Heather O'Keefe at 375-4683.
Pool: 50m, 5 lanes, outdoors, temperature controlled, 78°.
Affiliate: USMS 3 workouts per week $10 per week, includes pool fees.
Notes: Coached workouts: M,W,F: 11:30AM-1PM, 7-8:30PM. Tu: 7-8:30PM. Th: 11:30AM-1PM.

NORTH CENTRAL FLORIDA YMCA 5201 N.W. 34th St.
Phone: 335-7298.
Pool: 25m x 25y, 6 lanes, 'L' shape, outdoors, heated, 78°.
Affiliate: Y AWAY NC. YMCA $10.
Notes: The pool is closed in Dec.
To find: From University Ave. go north on 34th St. The Y is on the right after the bend in 34th St.

300 CLUB INC. 3715 N.W. 12th Ave.
Phone: 378-2898.
Pool: 25y x 42f, 6 lanes, outdoors, heated, 82°.
Memberships: I/S $600 + $160/quarter.

F.A.S.T. MASTERS at the 300 Club, Inc.
Pool phone: 376-1163. Masters: Contact Meegan Wilson at 373-0023(h).
Affiliate: USMS $5, includes pool fees.
Notes: Coached workouts: M-F: 6-7:30PM.

GAINESVILLE   CONTINUED

GAINESVILLE HEALTH & FITNESS CENTER
3441 W. University Ave.
Phone: 377-4955.
Pool: 25y, 3 lanes, indoors, heated, 84°.
Admission: $10.
Affiliate: IHRSA $8.

HIALEAH   305

RAMADA INN MIAMI / HIALEAH 1950 W. 49th St.
Phone: 823-2000. **Reservations:** 800-228-2828.
Pool: 50f, rectangular, outdoors, unheated, 70°-80°.
Admission: Registered guests only NC.

MILANDER POOL 4800 Palm Ave.
Phone: 822-2931.
Pool: 50m x 25y, 9 lanes, outdoors, heated, 82°.
Admission: $1.

HIALEAH STORM at Milander Pool
Masters: Contact Head Coach Julie Sue Ingram at 822-2931.
Non-member participation: $1, includes pool fees.
Notes: Coached workouts: M-F: 5-7PM. Sa: 8AM-Noon. Lap swimming: M-F: 11AM-3PM.

HOLLYWOOD   305

GREATER HOLLYWOOD YMCA 3161 Taft St.
Phone: 989-9622.
Pool: 20y, 2 lanes, indoors, heated, 84°.
Admission: $7.
Affiliate: Y AWAY 10 visits NC.

INDIAN HARBOUR BEACH   407

INDIAN HARBOUR BEACH SWIMMING POOL
1233 Yacht Club Blvd.
Phone: 773-0552.
Pool: 25y x 44f, 6 lanes, outdoors, temperature controlled, 80°.
Admission: Residents $2, SC(55) $1. Non-residents $4, SC $2.
To find: One block from the Eau Gallie Causeway.
Masters: The Space Coast Masters. Contact Ben Ogilvie at 773-0552.

ISLAMORADA   305

CHEECA LODGE Mile Marker 82
Phone: 664-4651. **Reservations:** 800-327-2888.
Pool: 70f, 'L' shape, outdoors, heated, 82°.
Admission: Registered guests NC.
Memberships: $500/year.

JACKSONVILLE   904

CLAUDE J. YATES YMCA 221 Riverside Ave.
Phone: 355-1436.
Pool: 25y x 26f, 4 lanes, indoors, heated, 82°-84°.
Admission: $10.

Affiliate: YMCA NC.
To find: Between Blue Cross/Blue Shield and Haskell Company.

CHURCH OF THE GOOD SHEPARD POOL & EXERCISE CENTER 1100 Stockton St.
Phone: 387-4298.
Pool: 80f x 30f, 6 lanes, indoors, heated, 83°.
Admission: Call the Pool Director.
To find: Exit I-10 at Stockton St., go south to the intersection with Park St.

JACKSONVILLE NAVAL AIR STATION POOL
Building 614
Phone: 772-2930.
Pool: 50m x 25y, indoors, heated, 80°.
Affiliate: U.S. Military & Dept. of Defense: Call.

UNIVERSITY OF NORTH FLORIDA AQUATIC CENTER 4567 St. Johns Bluff Rd.
Phone: 646-2854.
Pool: 25y x 50m, 13 x 8 lanes, indoors, heated, 82.5°.
Admission: $3.20.
Memberships: 4/12 months $77/$182.
Masters: The Holmes LumberJax. Contact Jack McKeon at 772-6100(w).

DOUBLETREE CLUB HOTEL 4700 Salisbury Rd.
Phone: 281-9700. **Reservations:** 800-222-8733.
Pool: 50f x 20f, rectangular, outdoors, heated, 75°.
Admission: Registered guests only NC.

JUPITER   407

NORTH COUNTY AQUATIC COMPLEX 861 Toney Penna Dr.
Phone: 745-0243.
Pool: 50m x 25y + 25m, 8 x 14 + 8 lanes, outdoors, heated, 83°.
Admission: $1.50.
To find: One half mile west of Jupiter High School on the north side of Toney Penna Dr.

KEY BISCAYNE   305

SONESTA BEACH RESORT 350 Ocean Dr.
Phone: 361-2021. **Reservations:** 800-SONESTA.
Pool: 25m, rectangular, outdoors, heated, 78°.
Admission: Registered guests only NC.

KEY LARGO   305

SHERATON KEY LARGO RESORT at Mile Marker 97, 97000 S. Overseas Hwy.
Phone: 852-5553. **Reservations:** 800-826-1006.
Pool: 20y, kidney shape, outdoors, heated, 82°.
Admission: Registered guests NC.
Memberships: VIP Key Club $150/year.
Notes: There is also a 45f outdoor pool.

KEY WEST   305

DR. M.L. KING COMMUNITY POOL 300 Catherine St.
Phone: 292-8248.
Pool: 30y x 60f 'clipped football', 4 lanes, outdoors, unheated, 65°-95°.
Admission: NC.
To find: At the intersection of Thomas and Catherine Sts., one block west of Whitehead, just a few blocks from the Southernmost Point Monument.

HOLIDAY INN BEACHSIDE 3841 N. Roosevelt Blvd.
Phone: 294-2571. **Reservations:** 800-292-7706.
Pool: 70f, rectangular, outdoors, unheated, 75°-90°.
Admission: Registered guests only NC.
Notes: At the entrance to Key West, this hotel is well away from the hubbub of the 'Old Town' area.

KISSIMMEE   407

ORANGE LAKE RESORT & COUNTRY CLUB 8505 W. Irlo Bronson Memorial Hwy.
Phone: 239-0000. **Reservations:** 800-877-6522.
Pool: 50m, rectangular, outdoors, heated, 75°-80°.
Admission: Registered guests only NC.
Notes: Two new pools are planned for 1995.

HOLIDAY INN MAIN GATE EAST 5678 Irlo Bronson Memorial Hwy.
Phone: 396-4488. **Reservations:** 800-366-5437.
Pool 1: 70f, rectangular, outdoors, heated, 80°.
Pool 2: 70f, rectangular, outdoors, unheated, the range of water temperatures was not reported.
Admission: Registered guests only NC.

LAKE BUENA VISTA   407

WALT DISNEY WORLD DOLPHIN 1500 Epcot Resorts Blvd.
Phone: 934-4000. **Reservations:** 800-227-1500.
Pool: 100f, rectangular, outdoors, heated, 80°.
Admission: Registered guests only NC.
Notes: There is also a large, free form, outdoor, unheated, 70°-86°, 'grotto' pool.

LAKE MARY   407

SEMINOLE FAMILY YMCA 665 Longwood-Lake Mary Rd.
Phone: 321-8944.
Pool: 25y, 6 lanes, outdoors, heated, 80°.
Admission: $3.
Affiliate: Y AWAY 1 week NC.
To find: From I-4, take the Lake Mary Blvd. Exit. Go east to the third traffic light, turn right onto Longwood-Lake Mary Rd. and go two and a half miles. The Y is on the right.
Masters: The Y hopes to have a Masters program in place in Jan., 1995.

LAKE WORTH   407

CITY OF LAKE WORTH MUNICIPAL POOL 50 S. Ocean Blvd.
Phone: 533-7367.
Pool: 50m x 25y, outdoors, heated, 78°-80° mid-Dec. to mid-Jan., unheated, 70°-90° the rest of the year.
Admission: $2, SC(55) $1.
Notes: From mid-Dec. to mid-Jan., the pool is used by visiting college swim teams. During that period, all public lap swimming is long course (50m lengths).

LAKE WORTH RACQUET & SWIM CLUB 4090 Coconut Rd.
Phone: 967-3900.
Pool: 25y, outdoors, heated, 78°.
Admission: $6.

LAKELAND   813

HOLIDAY INN LAKESIDE 910 E. Memorial Blvd.
Phone: 682-0101. **Reservations:** 800-HOLIDAY.
Pool: 17y, rectangular, outdoors, unheated, the range of water temperatures was not reported.
Admission: Registered guests NC.

LAKELAND FAMILY YMCA 3620 Cleveland Heights Blvd.
Phone: 644-3528.
Pool: 25y, indoors, heated, 82°.
Affiliate: YMCA 5 visits NC, then $2.

LARGO   813

HIGHLAND RECREATION COMPLEX 400 Highland Ave.
Phone: 587-6752.
Pool: 25y x 25m, indoor/outdoor, temperature controlled, 85°.
Admission: $2.50.

BROADMOOR TENNIS & FITNESS CLUB 8000 Cumberland Rd.
Phone: 391-2205.
Pool: 25y, outdoors, unheated, 65°-90°.
Admission: $10.75.

LAUDERHILL   305

WOLK PARK POOL 1080 N.W. 42nd Way
Phone: Recording: 321-2465. Information: 321-2466.
Pool: 25m, outdoors, heated, 80°-81° in winter.
Admission: Non-residents $2.50.

VETERANS PARK POOL 7600 N.W. 50th St.
Phone: 730-2985.
Pool: 25m, outdoors, heated, 80° in winter.
Admission: Non-residents $2.50.
Notes: Of the two Lauderhill pools, we are advised this is the better one for lap swimming.

Masters: The Veterans Pool Masters. Contact Rick Zlotziver at 730-2985.

VENETIAN GARDENS POOL Dozier Circle
Phone: 787-8018.
Pool: 25y, 6 lanes, outdoors, heated, 78°.
Admission: $1.
To find: At the corner of Canal St. & Dixie Ave.
Masters: The Lake Masters. Call 728-9885.

LEHIGH ACRES COMMUNITY POOL 1400 W. 5th St.
Phone: 369-8277.
Pool: 25y, 8 lanes, outdoors, heated, 85°.
Admission: $2, SC(55) $1.
To find: Three blocks northeast of the 'Welcome to Lehigh' sign.

THE RESORT AT LONGBOAT KEY 301 Gulf of Mexico Dr.
Phone: 383-8821.
Pool: 74f x 54f, outdoors, heated, water temperature not reported.
Admission: Registered guests only NC.

LAKE BRANTLEY AQUATIC CENTER 1002 Palm Springs Rd.
Phone: 862-2207.
Pool: 50m x 25y, 8 x 24 lanes, outdoors, temperature controlled, 80°-82°.
Admission: $3.
Hotel: All Seminole County hotels $2 with the hotel business card.

TEAM ORLANDO MASTERS at Lake Brantley Aquatic Center
Masters: Contact Coach Larry Peck at 862-2207.
Affiliate: USMS $4, includes pool fees.
Notes: Coached workouts: M-Th: 7-8:30PM. Sa: 10:30AM-Noon. Lap swimming: M-F: 6:30AM-6PM, 7-8:30PM. Sa: 10:30AM-5PM. Su: Noon-5PM.

LONGWOOD AQUATIC CLUB 1655 E.E. Williamson Rd.
Phone: 862-3232.
Pool: 50m x 25y + 25m, 10 x 16 lanes, outdoors, heated, 79°.
Admission: $5.
Notes: Long course (50m) swimming Mar. 15 to Aug. 15 and Dec. 15 to Jan. 15 with one short course lane; short course swimming the rest of the year. There is also a 16f deep diving well.
To find: Two blocks west of I-4 on S.R. 434 to Markham Woods Rd. Take Markham Woods Rd.

for 1.5 miles to E.E. Williamson Rd., then go east for two blocks.
Masters: The Longwood Aquatic Wave (The LAW). Contact Daniel H. Dittmer at 862-3232.

JOSE MARTI POOL 351 S.W. 4th St.
Phone: 575-5265.
Pool: 25m, outdoors, heated, 84°.
Admission: 75¢, SC(62) & Disabled NC.
Notes: Hours are 11AM-5PM.

THE GRAND PRIX HOTEL 1717 N. Bayshore Dr.
Phone: 372-0313. **Reservations:** 800-872-PRIX.
Pool: 76f x 31f, outdoors, heated, water temperature not reported.
Admission: Registered guests only NC.

BALLY'S SCANDINAVIAN HEALTH & FITNESS CENTER Miracle Center, 3301 Coral Way
Phone: 445-7140.
Pool: 25m, outdoors, heated, 82°.
Affiliate: Bally's NC.
Hotel: Holiday Inn Coral Gables (443-2301) NC.

MIAMI OLYMPIAN SWIM TEAM (MOST) at the Miami Rowing Club, 3601 Rickenbacker Causeway, Virginia Key
Pool phone: 361-3225. **Masters:** Contact Coach Robert Strauss at 444-5968.
Pool: 25y x 45f, 6 lanes, outdoors, heated, 82° in winter, 84°-88° in summer.
Non-member participation: $7.50 for workouts, includes pool fees.
Notes: Coached workouts: M,W,F: 6-8AM, 3-7PM. Tu,Th: 6-8:30AM, 3-7PM. Sa: 7-10AM. The club is located on a large, calm Biscayne Bay inlet, sheltered on three sides. Open water swimming for a mile or more is possible there.
To find: The Miami Rowing Club is next to the Miami Marine Stadium, about a mile past the Rickenbacker Cswy. Bridge.

RANGE POOL 525 N.W. 62nd St., Liberty City
Phone: 759-1865.
Pool: 25m x 50m, outdoors, heated, 84°*.
Admission: 75¢, SC(62) & Disabled NC.
Notes: *The pool is temporarily closed for repairs. It is expected to reopen before the summer of 1995.
To find: Off I-95 at the northeast corner of the 62nd St. Exit, across from Miami Edison Senior High School, located in an inner city neighborhood.

SOUTHWEST YMCA 4300 S.W. 58th Ave.
Phone: 665-3513.
Pool: 20y x 45f, 3 lanes, outdoors, heated, 85°.
Admission: $10.
Affiliate: YMCA $5.
To find: Behind David Fairchild Elementary School.

TAMIAMI PARK POOL 11201 S.W. 24th St.
Phone: 223-7077.
Pool: 25y x 50m, 20 lanes, outdoors, heated, 79°.
Admission: $1.75.

MIAMI DADE COMMUNITY COLLEGE - KENDALL CAMPUS 11011 S.W. 104th St.
Phone: 237-2235.
Pool: 25y x 50m, 19 x 10 lanes, outdoors, temperature controlled, 80°-82°.
Admission: 50¢.
Notes: This is one of the nicest pools in Dade County and worth the (long) drive from downtown Miami. We used to swim here when we lived in the area. It usually closes for school breaks and three day holiday weekends, so always call first.
To find: The campus is east of the Don Shula Expwy. and a few blocks south of Kendall Dr. The pool is on the north side of the campus, just south of the playing fields and gymnasium, west of the tennis courts.

STINGRAY AQUATIC CLUB at Miami-Dade Community College - Kendall Campus
Pool phone: 237-2235. **Masters:** Contact Head Coach Lou Manganiello at 235-5573.
Non-member participation: 4 workouts per week pool fees only.
Notes: Coached workouts: M-F: 7-8PM. Sa: Call.

JEWISH COMMUNITY CENTER 11155 S.W. 112th Ave.
Phone: 271-9000.
Pool: 25y, outdoors, heated, 83°.
Affiliate: JCC Call.

MIAMI BEACH   305

FLAMINGO PARK POOL 11th St. & Jefferson Ave.
Phone: 673-7750.
Pool: 25y, 6 lanes, outdoors, unheated, 65°-90°.
Admission: Fall, winter, and spring: NC. Summer: $1.25, SC(65) 75¢.
To find: Between Alton Rd. & Meridian Ave. at 11th St. The pool is an above-ground structure north of the parking lot and west of the tennis courts.

THE RALEIGH HOTEL 1775 Collins Ave.
Phone: 534-6300. **Reservations:** 800-848-1775.
Pool: 25y, oblong with Morrocan curves, outdoors, unheated, 70°-80°.
Admission: Registered guests only NC.
Notes: This is a completely restored period hotel in Miami Beach's historic Art Deco District. The pool was called 'the most beautiful pool in Florida' by Life magazine in 1947.

THE SPA AT THE FONTAINEBLEAU HILTON RESORT 4441 Collins Ave.
Phone: Spa: 538-7600. Hotel: 538-2000.
Reservations: 800-HILTONS.
Pool: 25y x 25f, saltwater, outdoors, unheated, 65°-90°.

Admission: Registered guests NC.
Affiliate: IHRSA $12 per day or $50 per week.
Memberships: 1/3 months $150/$300.

SCOTT RAKOW YOUTH CENTER 2700 Sheridan Ave.
Phone: 673-7767.
Pool: 25y x 45f, 6 lanes, outdoors, temperature controlled, 80°.
Admission: Sundays $3.
Memberships: $50/quarter.
Notes: Adult lap swimming M,W,F: Noon-2PM, 6-8PM. Tu,Th: 6-8PM. Su: 1-6PM.
To find: A half mile north of the Miami Beach Convention Center, around the curve just past the fire station.

NORMANDY ISLE POOL 7030 Trouville Esplanade
Phone: 993-2021 or 993-2023.
Pool: 25y, 6 lanes, outdoors, heated, 78°.
Admission: Fall, winter, and spring: NC. Summer: $1.25, SC(65) 75¢.
To find: At the east end of Miami's 79th St. Causeway, in the 1700 block of Miami Beach's 71st St., between the east and west-bound lanes.

MIAMI SHORES   305

MIAMI SHORES VILLAGE AQUATIC CENTER 10000 Biscayne Blvd.
Phone: 758-8105.
Pool: 100f x 40f, 6 lanes, outdoors, heated, 84°.
Admission: Lap swimming: Residents $1.60, non-residents $3.20.
To find: At Biscayne Blvd. and 100th St., next to the Miami Shores Country Club.

NAPLES   813

YMCA OF COLLIER COUNTY 5450 YMCA Rd.
Phone: 597-3148.
Pool: 25y x 25m, 8 lanes, outdoors, heated, 83°.
Admission: $8.
Affiliate: Out-of-town YMCA NC. USS & USMS: Pool $5.
To find: West of I-75 (Exit 16) and east of Airport Rd. on Pine Ridge Rd.

SWIM FLORIDA MASTERS at the YMCA of Collier County
Pool phone: 597-3148. **Masters:** Contact Joan Gamso at 495-9639(h).
Non-member participation: $8, includes pool fees.
Affiliate: YMCA NC.
Notes: Coached fitness workouts: M,F: 6-7PM. Uncoached, structured workouts: Tu,Th: 5:30-7PM. Su 1-2:30PM.

THE RITZ-CARLTON, NAPLES 280 Vanderbilt Beach Rd.
Phone: 598-3300. **Reservations:** 800-241-3333.

Pool: 25y, free form, outdoors, heated, 84°.
Admission: Registered guests only NC.

NORTH FORT MYERS   813

NORTH FT. MYERS SENIOR CENTER POOL 960
Iris Dr.
Phone: 656-7763.
Pool: 25y, 8 lanes, outdoors, heated, 86°.
Admission: $2, SC(55) $1.

NORTH MIAMI   305

THOMAS SASSO POOL 12502 N.W. 11th Ave.
Phone: 681-0701.
Pool: 25y x 45f, 6 lanes, outdoors, unheated, 68°-
92°.
Admission: Residents: $1, SC(55) 75¢. Non-residents $2, SC $1.50.

NORTH MIAMI BEACH   305

ULETA POOL 16880 N.E. 4th Ave.
Phone: 652-6197.
Pool: 25y, 5 lanes, outdoors, heated, 82°-84°.
Admission: Residents $1, non-residents $3.10.
Noon lap swim is $1 for all.

VICTORY POOL 1980 N.E. 171st St.
Phone: 948-2926.
Pool: 50m x 19.75y, 8 x 15 lanes, outdoors, unheated, 73°-85°.
Admission: Residents $1, non-residents $3.10.
Noon lap swim is $1 for all.
Notes: There is a diving well with 1m and 3m boards, and 5m, 7m, and 10m platforms.
To find: Behind North Miami Beach City Hall, at 171st St. and 19th Ave.
Masters: The Victory Pool Masters. Call 948-2926.

NORTH MIAMI BEACH - AVENTURA   305

TURNBURRY ISLE RESORT & CLUB 19999 W.
Country Club Dr.
Phone: 932-6200. **Reservations:** 800-223-6800.
Pool: 65ft±, outdoors, heated, 87°-88°.
Admission: Registered guests only NC.

**BALLY'S SCANDINAVIAN HEALTH & FITNESS
CENTER** 3455 N.E. 207th St.
Phone: 931-3181.
Pool: 25m, indoors, heated, 78°-83°.
Affiliate: Bally's NC.

**MICHAEL ANN RUSSELL JEWISH COMMUNITY
CENTER** 18900 N.E. 25th Ave.
Phone: 932-4200.
Pool: 25y, 6 lanes, indoors, heated, 86°.
Affiliate: JCC Call.
Notes: There is also an unheated, outdoor pool which is cooler in the fall, winter, and spring.

NORTH PALM BEACH   407

NORTH PALM BEACH SWIM CLUB at North Palm Beach Country Club, 951 U.S. Hwy. 1
Masters: Contact Coach Dick Cavanah at 626-4346.
Pool: 50m x 25y, 6 x 6 lanes, 'L' shape, outdoors, temperature controlled, 80°-84°.
Non-member participation: $5 + pool fees.
Notes: Workouts: M: 6-7AM, 6:30-8PM. Tu,Th: 6:30-8PM. W,F: 6-7AM.

OCALA   904

LIFETIME FITNESS & REHABILITATION 1100 S.
W. 1st Ave.
Phone: 368-7099.
Pool: 25y, indoors, heated, 83°-86°.
Admission: $5.

OCALA MASTERS SWIM CLUB at Central Florida Community College Aquatic Center, 3001 S.W. College Rd.
Masters: Contact Head Coach Mark MacDonald at 237-2111 ext. 398.
Pool: 25y x 50m, 6 x 8 lanes, indoor/outdoor, temperature controlled, 82°.
Non-member participation: Call.
Notes: Coached workouts: M-Th: 7-8PM.
Uncoached workouts: M-F: Noon-3PM.

OCOEE   407

HOLIDAY INN-ORLANDO WEST 10945 W.
Colonial Dr.
Phone: 656-5050. **Reservations:** 800-327-5429.
Pool: 50f, rectangular, outdoors, unheated, 60°-80°.
Admission: Registered guests only NC.

ORANGE PARK   904

'Q' THE SPORTS CLUB 1731 Wells Rd.
Phone: 269-3222.
Pool: 25m x 45f, 4 lanes, indoors, heated, 85°-86°.
Affiliate: IHRSA NC.
Hotel: Holiday Inn (264-9513), Comfort Inn (264-3297), & Best Western Hotel (264-1211): 1 day NC.
To find: One half mile east of the Orange Park Mall, turning off Blanding headed south.

ORLANDO   407

1. DOWNTOWN YMCA 433 N. Mills Ave.
Phone: 896-6901.
Pool: 25y, 6 lanes, indoors, heated, 85°-86°.
Admission: $7.
Affiliate: YMCA 3 visits NC, then $3.50.

2. JOHN LONG POOL 1218 N. Ferncreek Ave.
Phone: 895-7279.
Pool: 25y, outdoors, heated, 84°-86°.
Admission: $3.

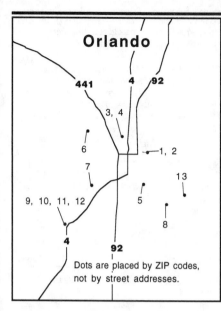

Orlando

441

4 92

3, 4

6 ——1, 2

7 13

9, 10, 11, 12 5

8

4

92

Dots are placed by ZIP codes, not by street addresses.

3. COLLEGE PARK POOL 2411 Elizabeth Ave.
Phone: 246-2706.
Pool: 25y, outdoors, heated, 84°-86°.
Admission: $3.

4. ORLANDO FITNESS & RACQUET CLUB 825 Courtland St.
Phone: 645-3550.
Pool: 25y, outdoors, heated, 82°.
Admission: $5.

5. WADEVIEW POOL 801 E. Grant St.
Phone: 246-2885.
Pool: 25y, outdoors, heated, 84°-86°.
Admission: $3.

6. BOYS & GIRLS CLUB OF CENTRAL FLORIDA 5211 Hernandes Dr.
Phone: 295-1100.
Pool: 25m, 4f deep, 8 lanes, indoors, heated, 80°-82°.
Admission: $1.

7. BALLY'S BAY HILL 4850 Lawling Lane
Phone: 297-8400.
Pool: 25m, indoors, heated, 78°.
Admission: $10.
Affiliate: Bally's NC.
Hotel: Several local hotels NC. Call the club for details.

8. DOVER SHORES POOL 1400 Gaston Foster Rd.
Phone: 381-2531.
Pool: 25y, outdoors, heated, 84°-86°.
Admission: $3.

9. INTERNATIONAL DRIVE YMCA & AQUATIC CENTER 8422 International Dr.
Phone: 363-1911.
Pool: 25y x 50m, 12+ lanes, indoors, heated, 79°.
Admission: $8.
Affiliate: Out-of-area YMCA 3 visits NC, then $4.
Hotel: Radisson Inn (345-0505) NC with a pass from the hotel.
To find: Across International Dr. from The Mercado Shopping Center.

TEAM ORLANDO MASTERS at the International Drive YMCA & Aquatic Center
Masters: Contact Dr. Lucky Meisenheimer or Sandee Crowther at 352-2444(w).
Non-member participation: $7, includes pool fees.
Affiliate: USMS $4, includes pool fees.
Notes: Coached workouts: M-Th: 6-7:15PM.

10. THE PEABODY 9801 International Dr.
Phone: 352-4000. **Reservations:** 800-PEABODY.
Pool: 50y, primarily rectangular, outdoors, heated, 80°.
Admission: Registered guests NC.
Memberships: $26.50/month, restricted hours. $40/month unrestricted access.

11. BEST WESTERN PLAZA INTERNATIONAL 8738 International Dr.
Phone: 345-8195. **Reservations:** 800-654-7160.
Pool: 20y, 'Y' shape, outdoors, heated, 78°.
Admission: Registered guests only NC.

12. DAYS INN LAKESIDE 7335 Sandlake Rd.
Phone: 351-1900. **Reservations:** 800-777-3297.
Pool: 18y x 24f, rectangular, outdoors, unheated, 68°-78°.
Admission: Registered guests only NC.
Notes: There are also two 15y x 24f pools; one is heated to 82°, the other is unheated.

13. BALLY'S SOUTH ORLANDO 4650 S. Semoran Blvd.
Phone: 277-1144.
Pool: 25y, indoors, heated, 78°-82°.
Affiliate: Bally's NC.
Hotel: Several local hotels NC with room key. Call the club for details.

ORMOND BEACH ============ **904**

ORMOND BEACH YMCA 51 N. Center St.
Phone: 673-9622.
Pool: 25y + 20y x 50m, outdoors, heated, 80°-82°.
Admission: $4.
Affiliate: YMCA $3.

PALM BEACH ============ **407**

THE BREAKERS 1 S. Country Rd.
Phone: 655-6611. **Reservations:** 800-833-3141.
Pool: 23m, 'L' shape, outdoors, heated, 84°.
Admission: Registered guests NC.

PALM BEACH _____ CONTINUED

Memberships: Call.
Notes: Awarded the national 'Top Water Fitness Program' (Hotel category) by the U.S. Water Fitness Association.

PALM BEACH HILTON OCEANFRONT RESORT 2842 S. Ocean Blvd.
Phone: 586-6542. **Reservations:** 800-433-1718.
Pool: 55f x 35f, rectangular, outdoors, heated, 80°.
Admission: $15*. Registered guests NC.
Notes: *Includes parking, pool, beach, beach chair, and soft drink or beer/wine.

PALM COAST _____ 904

BELLE TERRE SWIM & RACQUET CLUB 73 Patricia Dr.
Phone: 445-0838.
Pool: 25m, outdoors, heated, 82°.
Admission: $6.
Affiliate: IHRSA Call.

PENSACOLA _____ 904

DOWNTOWN YMCA 400 N. Palafox St.
Phone: 438-4406.
Pool: 20y, 4 lanes, indoors, heated, 83°.
Admission: $5.
Affiliate: YMCA NC.

GREATER PENSACOLA AQUATIC CLUB at Pensacola Junior College Pool, 1000 College Blvd.
Masters: Contact Head Coach Steve Panzram at 484-1312.
Pool: 25y x 30f, 6 lanes, indoors, heated, 82°.
Affiliate: USMS 5 workouts per week NC, includes pool fees.
Notes: Workouts: M-F: 6-7AM.

RAMADA INN NORTH 6550 Pensacola Blvd.
Phone: 477-0711.
Pool: 20y x 20f, rectangular, outdoors, unheated, 40°-85°.
Admission: Registered guests only NC.

PENSACOLA ATHLETIC CENTER 7700 Hwy. 98 W.
Phone: 453-1534.
Pool: 25y x 36f, 6 lanes, indoor/outdoor, heated, 82°.
Admission: $7.
To find: One mile west of Navy Hospital and a quarter of a mile east of Fairfield Dr.

UNIVERSITY OF WEST FLORIDA NATATORIUM 11000 University Pkwy.
Phone: 474-2497.
Pool: 50m x 25y, 8 x 14 lanes, indoors, heated, 80°-82°.
Admission: $2.
Memberships: 4 months $40, SC(60) $36.

To find: Park in the Water Tower Parking Lot, use the pedestrian crosswalk to cross the four lanes and follow signs to the Natatorium.

GREATER PENSACOLA AQUATIC CLUB at the University of West Florida Natatorium
Pool phone: 474-2497. **Masters:** Contact Head Coach Steve Panzram at 484-1312.
Affiliate: USMS 5 workouts per week NC, includes pool fees.
Notes: Workouts: M-F: 6-7AM. Sa: 9-10AM.

PINE ISLAND _____ 813

PHILLIPS PARK COMMUNITY POOL 5675 Sesame Dr.
Phone: 283-2220.
Pool: 25y, outdoors, heated, 86°.
Admission: $2, SC(55) $1.

PLANTATION _____ 305

SHERATON SUITES PLANTATION 311 N. University Dr.
Phone: 424-3300. **Reservations:** 800-325-3535.
Pool: 20y x 40f, rectangular, outdoors, heated, 80°-85°.
Admission: Registered guests only NC.

PLANTATION CENTRAL PARK POOL 9141 N.W. 2nd St.
Phone: 452-2525.
Pool: 50m x 25y, 9 x 14 lanes, outdoors, temperature controlled, 78°-82°.
Admission: Residents $1.25, non-residents $3.
To find: From I-595 exit at Pine Island; go north on Pine Island to Broward Blvd; go west (left) on Broward Blvd; go north (right) onto Central Park Dr. (the first light) and take the first right into the park.
Masters: The Plantation Swim Team. Contact June Woolger or Nicole Hahn at 452-2525.

PORT ORANGE _____ 904

PORT ORANGE YMCA 4701 City Center Pkwy.
Phone: 760-9622.
Pool: 50m x 25y, outdoors, temperature controlled, 82°-84°.
Admission: $4.
Affiliate: YMCA $2.

PORT SAINT LUCIE _____ 407

CLUB MED VILLAGE HOTEL at Sandpiper Village, 3500 Morningside Blvd.
Phone: 335-4400. **Reservations:** 800-CLUB MED.
Pool 1: 24y x 36f, 6 lanes, outdoors, heated from Nov. to Apr., water temperatures not reported.
Pool 2: 137f x 40f, outdoors, unheated, the range of water temperatures was not reported.
Admission: $56*. Registered guests NC.

Memberships: Pool/fitness membership $370/year + $44.40 food minimum.
Notes: *The daily rate includes two meals and access to water-skiing, tennis, sailing, etc. at no additional charge. There's also a smaller fitness pool, not suitable for lap swimming. Non-hotel guest hours are limited to 8:30AM-6PM.

SAINT AUGUSTINE   904

ANASTASIA ATHLETIC CLUB 1045 Anastasia Blvd.
Phone: 471-4300.
Pool: 20y, outdoors, heated, 80°.
Admission: Call.
Affiliate: IHRSA $6.

SAINT PETERSBURG   813

NORTH SHORE POOL 901 N. Shore Dr. N.E.
Phone: 893-7727.
Pool: 50m x 25y, 10 x 22 lanes, outdoors, heated, 80°.
Admission: $1.85, SC(55) $1.60.

ST. PETE MASTERS at North Shore Pool
Masters: Contact Coach George Bole at 893-7727.
Affiliate: USMS $2.45 per workout, includes pool fees.
Notes: Coached workouts: M,W,F: 5:30-8:30AM, 4:30-6:30PM. Tu,Th: 6-8:30AM, 4:30-6:30PM. Su: 9:30AM-12:30PM.

THE FITNESS CONNECTION at the St. Petersburg Hilton Hotel, 333 - 1st St. S.
Phone: Club: 823-2727. Hotel: 894-5000.
Reservations: 800-HILTONS.
Pool: 21y*, outdoors, heated, 80°.
Admission: $5.
Hotel: St. Petersburg Hilton (894-5000) NC.
Notes: *The club told us the pool is 23y long, the hotel told us 19y on one occasion and 21y the next.

ST. PETERSBURG FAMILY YMCA 116 - 5th St. S.
Phone: 895-9622.
Pool: 20y x 20f, 4 lanes, indoors, heated, 87°.
Admission: $5.
Affiliate: Y AWAY $3.
To find: At 5th St. and 2nd Ave. across from Florida Power and The St. Petersburg Times, by the Suncoast Dome off I-275.

SANIBEL ISLAND   813

SUNDIAL BEACH & TENNIS RESORT 1451 Middle Gulf Dr.
Phone: 472-4151. **Reservations:** 800-237-4184.
Pool: 24m, rectangular, outdoors, heated, 70°-80°.
Admission: Registered guests only NC.

SANIBEL RECREATION COMPLEX 3840 Sanibel-Captiva Rd.

Phone: 472-0345 or 472-0302.
Pool: 25y x 45f, 4 lap lanes, outdoors, heated, 84°.
Admission: NC, voluntary donations are accepted.

SARASOTA   813

SARASOTA FAMILY YMCA 1075 S. Euclid Ave.
Phone: 955-8194.
Pool: 25y, 4 lanes, indoors, heated, 80°.
Admission: 1 visit NC, then $10.
Affiliate: YMCA $5.

COUNTRY CLUB OF SARASOTA TENNIS CENTER 3600 Torrey Pines Blvd.
Phone: 922-1591.
Pool: 25m, outdoors, heated, 80°.
Memberships: I/S $300 + $300/year.

LIDO POOL 400 Ben Franklin Dr.
Phone: 388-3626.
Pool: 25m, 6 lane, outdoors, heated, 80°-82°.
Admission: $1.50, SC(55) $1.
Hotel: Tyler Apartments (388-3227) NC with room key.

ARLINGTON AQUATIC COMPLEX 2650 Waldemere St.
Phone: 364-4655.
Pool: 50m x 25y, 8 x 20 lanes, indoor/outdoor, temperature controlled, 80°-82°.
Admission: $1.50, SC(55) $1.
To find: Three blocks east of Route 41, near the hospital.

SUNCOAST MASTERS at Arlington Aquatic Complex
Pool phone: 364-4655. **Masters:** Contact Deb Walker at 923-3540(h).
Non-member participation: $1.50, includes pool fees.
Notes: Workouts: M-F: 5:30-7AM, Noon-1PM, 5:30-7PM.

RAMADA INN AIRPORT 8440 N. Tamiami Tr.
Phone: 355-7771.
Pool: 50f, oval or kidney shape, outdoors, heated, 78°.
Admission: Registered guests only NC.

SEFFNER   813

BRANDON FAMILY YMCA 3097 N. Kingsway Rd.
Phone: 685-5402.
Pool: 25y, 8 lanes, outdoors, temperature controlled, 82°.
Admission: 1 visit NC.
Affiliate: YMCA outside a 60 mile radius 30 days NC, within 60 miles $7.

SEMINOLE   813

BALLY'S TOTAL FITNESS 10761 Park Blvd.

Phone: 391-2639.
Pool: 20m, indoors, heated, 83°.
Affiliate: Bally's NC.

SINGER ISLAND   407

HOLIDAY INN PALM BEACH OCEANFRONT RESORT 3700 N. Ocean Dr.
Phone: 848-3888. **Reservations:** 800-443-4077.
Pool: 76f x 20f, rectangular, outdoors, heated, 82°.
Admission: Registered guests only NC.

SPRING HILL   904

SUNCOAST YMCA - HERNANDO COUNTY FAMILY YMCA 1300 Mariner Blvd.
Phone: 688-9622.
Pool: 25y, indoor/outdoor, heated, 86°.
Admission: $7.
Affiliate: YMCA $3.50.

STUART   407

MARTIN COUNTY COMMUNITY POOL at the Martin County High School Campus, 2801 S. Kanner Hwy.
Phone: 286-0133.
Pool: 25y x 25m, 9 x 7 lanes, outdoors, temperature controlled, 80°-82°.
Admission: $1.50.
To find: On the north side of the Martin County High School campus, a few blocks south of Monterey Rd. Kanner Hwy. is State Rd. 76.
Masters: The Martin County Masters. Call 286-0133.

FAMILY YMCA OF MARTIN COUNTY 1700 S.E. Monterey Rd.
Phone: 286-4444.
Pool: 25y, 8 lanes, outdoors, heated, 82°.
Admission: $6.
Affiliate: Y AWAY 2 weeks NC.

SUNRISE   305

MARKHAM PARK SWIMMING POOL 16001 W. State Rd. 84
Phone: 389-2026.
Pool: 55y, freeform shape, outdoors, unheated, 72°-89°.
Admission: $1.75.
Hotel: Markham Park RV Campground NC.
Notes: This pool is not well suited for lap swimming, but sounds fine for other types of water exercise.

SURFSIDE   305

SURFSIDE COMMUNITY CENTER 9301 Collins Ave.
Phone: 866-3635.
Pool: 25y, outdoors, heated, 82°-84° in winter.
Admission: Residents $1, non-residents $3.

TALLAHASSEE   904

WADE WEHUNT POOL 907 Myers Park Dr.
Phone: 891-3985.
Pool: 25y, 8 lanes, indoor/outdoor, heated, 80°-82°.
Admission: $1.50, SC(62) $1.
Masters: The Myers Lunch Bunch. Contact Gerry Norris at 891-3878(o).

N.B. STULTS AQUATIC CENTER Florida State University, Woodward Ave.
Phone: 644-1867.
Pool: 50m x 25y, 8 x 16 lanes, outdoors, heated, 82°.
Admission: $1.
Memberships: $48/semester.
To find: Next to the Student Union and the heating plant smoke stack.

TAMPA   813

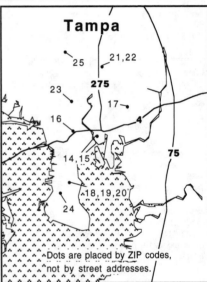

Tampa

Dots are placed by ZIP codes, not by street addresses.

14. CENTRAL CITY YMCA 110 E. Palm Ave.
Phone: 229-9622.
Pool: 25y, 8 lanes, outdoors, heated, 82°.
Admission: 1 visit NC.
Affiliate: YMCA NC.
Hotel: All local hotels 1 visit NC, then $7 per day.
Masters: Contact Bob Gilbertson at 224-9622.

15. HARBOUR ISLAND ATHLETIC CLUB 900 S. Harbor Island Blvd.
Phone: 229-5062.
Pool: 25m x 9.75m, 4 lanes, outdoors, temperature controlled, 80°.
Hotel: Wyndham Hotel (229-5000) $10.65 with a pass from the hotel.
Notes: There is also a smaller, youth/recreational pool.

16. TAMPA MARRIOTT WESTSHORE 1001 N.
Westshore Blvd.
Phone: 287-2555. **Reservations:** 800-228-9290.
Pool: 30y, figure 8 shape, indoor/outdoor, heated,
80°-85°.
Admission: $5. Registered guests NC.

17. CROWNE PLAZA AT SABAL PARK 10221
Princess Palm Ave.
Phone: 623-6363. **Reservations:** 800-866-
ROOM.
Pool: 25y, 2 lap lanes, outdoors, heated, 78°.
Admission: Registered guests only NC.

18. INTERBAY YMCA 4411 S. Himes Ave.
Phone: 839-0210.
Pool: 25y x 75f, 6 lanes, outdoors, heated, 82°-86°.
Admission: 1 visit NC.
Affiliate: YMCA 2 months NC.
To find: On Himes Ave. between Gandy and
Euclid.

19. CONN NATATORIUM 4002 S. Coolidge Ave.
Phone: 837-9857.
Pool: 25y, indoors, heated, 80°.
Admission: NC.

20. BALLY'S TOTAL FITNESS 4002 Gandy Blvd.
Phone: 831-5996.
Pool: 25m, indoors, heated, 80°.
Admission: $10.
Affiliate: Bally's NC.

21. COPELAND POOL 11001 N. 15th St.
Phone: 972-0827.
Pool: 25y, fan shape, outdoors, heated, 80°.
Admission: NC.

22. THE FOREST HILL AQUATIC CLUB at Danny
Del Rio Pool, 10208 North Blvd.
Masters: Contact Coach Milt Bedingfield at 949-
5398(h).
Pool: 25y, 7 lanes, outdoors, heated, 80°.
Affiliate: USMS Call.
Notes: Workouts: M,W: 6:30-7:30PM, 7:30-
8:30PM. Sa: 11AM-Noon, Noon-1PM.

23. BALLY'S TOTAL FITNESS 4340 W.
Hillsborough Ave.
Phone: 873-2010.
Pool: 25m, indoors, heated, 83°.
Admission: $10.
Affiliate: Bally's NC.
Hotel: Days Inn (877-6181) & two Holiday Inns
(876-1531 & 879-4800): NC.

24. BOBBY HICKS MEMORIAL SWIMMING POOL
4120 W. Mango
Phone: 832-1203.
Pool: 50m x 25y, outdoors, heated, 80°.
Admission: NC.

25. NORTHWEST YMCA 4029 Northdale Blvd.
Phone: 962-3220.
Pool: 25y, outdoors, heated, 80°.
Admission: Call.

TITUSVILLE 407

ROYAL OAK RESORT & GOLF CLUB 2150
Country Club Dr.
Phone: 269-4500. **Reservations:** 800-267-1384.
Pool: 25y, 6 lanes, outdoors, unheated, the range
of water temperatures was not reported.
Admission: $4. Registered guests NC.
Memberships: 3 months $350.

VENICE 813

SOUTH COUNTY YMCA 701 Center Rd.
Phone: 493-6130.
Pool: 25y, outdoors, heated, 80°.
Admission: Call.
Affiliate: YMCA $3.

VERO BEACH 407

JUNGLE CLUB 1060 - 6th Ave.
Phone: 567-1400.
Pool: 20y, outdoors, heated, 84°.
Admission: $10.70.

ST. EDWARD'S SCHOOL St. Edward's Dr. off A1A
Phone: 231-7048.
Pool: 25m x 25y, 6 x 8 lanes, 'L' shape, outdoors,
heated, 83°.
Admission: $5.
To find: Two and a half miles south of the south
bridge over the Indian River, on the west side of
A1A.
Masters: St. Edward's Vero Beach Masters.
Contact Don Sonia at 231-7048 or 778-5933(h).

WELLINGTON 407

PALM BEACH POLO & COUNTRY CLUB 13198
Forest Hills Blvd.
Phone: 798-7251.
Pool: 25y x 60f, 5 lanes, outdoors, temperature
controlled, 82°. .
Admission: Call.
Masters: Contact Aquatics Manager Shelly
Frandsen Johnson at 798-7251.

WEST PALM BEACH 407

YWCA OF PALM BEACH COUNTY 901 S. Olive
Ave.
Phone: 833-2439.
Pool: 62f x 30f, 4 lanes, outdoors, heated, 85°.
Admission: $5.
Affiliate: YWCA Call.

GAINES PARK POOL 1501 N. Australian Ave.
Phone: 835-7095.

WEST PALM BEACH   CONTINUED

Pool: 25y x 23m, 8 lanes, outdoors, heated in winter, 80°.
Admission: $1.50.
To find: From I-95 exit at Palm Beach Lakes Blvd., go east 1.5 miles to Australian Ave, turn north (left), the pool is 1,000 yards up on the west (left) side of the street.
Masters: Contact Sally Welsh-Franke at 835-7095.

YMCA OF THE PALM BEACHES, EDWIN W. BROWN BRANCH 2085 S. Congress Ave.
Phone: 967-3573.
Pool: 25y x 40f, 4 lanes, indoors, heated, 87°.
Admission: $6.
Affiliate: Y AWAY 2 weeks NC.
To find: One block south of Forest Hill.

LAKE LYTAL POOL 3645 Gun Club Rd.
Phone: 233-1426.
Pool: 50m x 25y, 8 x 20 lanes, outdoors, heated, 82°.
Admission: $1.50.
To find: One block south of Southern Blvd. between Kirk Rd. and Congress Ave.

JEWISH COMMUNITY CENTER OF THE PALM BEACHES 3151 N. Military Trail
Phone: 689-7700 ext. 307.
Pool: 25y x 38f, 6 lanes, outdoors, temperature controlled, 82°.
Affiliate: JCC & USMS: Call.
Masters: The JCC Sharks. Contact Aquatic Director Lois H. Schwartz at 689-7700 ext. 307.

BALLY'S SCANDINAVIAN HEALTH & FITNESS CENTER 501 Village Blvd.
Phone: 683-5800.

Pool: 25m, indoors, heated, 78°-84°.
Affiliate: Bally's NC.
Hotel: Best Western Palm Beach Lakes (683-8810), Omni (689-6400) & Comfort Inn (697-3388): NC.

WINTER PARK   407

BALLY'S HEALTH & RACQUET 1865 N. Semoran Blvd.
Phone: 678-1118.
Pool: 25y, indoors, heated, 75°-80°.
Admission: $10.
Affiliate: Bally's NC.

CADY WAY POOL 2525 Cady Way
Phone: 740-7946.
Pool: 50m x 25y, 6 x 6 lanes, 'L' shape, outdoors, temperature controlled, 82°.
Admission: Residents $1. Non-residents $2.50, SC(55) $1.
To find: One mile west of the intersection of State Rd. 436 and University Blvd.

TEAM ORLANDO MASTERS at Cady Way Pool
Masters: Contact Coach Larry Campbell at 657-6734(h).
Non-member participation: $4, includes pool fees.
Notes: Coached workouts: M,W: 7:15-8:30PM. Tu,F: 5:30-7AM. Th: 5:30-7AM, 7:15-8:30PM. Sa: 10:30-11:45AM.

WINTER PARK BRANCH YMCA 1201 N. Lakemont Ave.
Phone: 644-1509.
Pool: 25m, outdoors, heated, 78°-82°.
Admission: Call.
Affiliate: YMCA 1 week NC, then $4.

ALWAYS CALL FIRST

Pools close, they change names, affiliations, admission policies, and rates. And just because a pool is listed in *Swimmers Guide* doesn't mean it's open all day, every day, for just the type of workout you want to do. Spend a quarter to save time and aggravation. . . always call first!

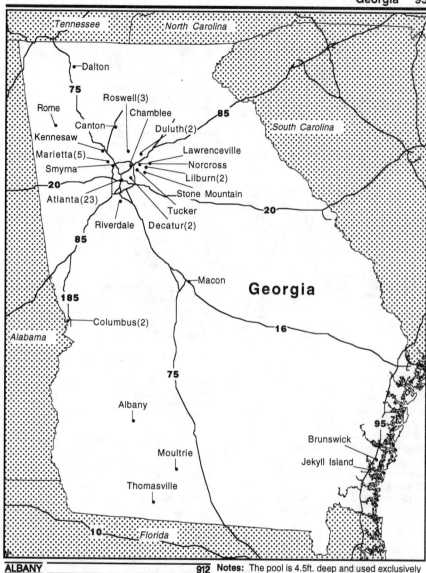

ALBANY YMCA 1701 Gillionville Rd.
Phone: 436-0531.
Pool: 25y x 42f, 6 lanes, indoors, heated, 84°.
Admission: $7. Visitors must call in advance.
Affiliate: YMCA NC.

1. CITY ATHLETIC CLUB 1 CNN Center - #211
Phone: 659-4097.
Pool: 20m, 4 lanes, indoors, heated, 79°.
Admission: $12. 3 days $29.
Hotel: Omni Hotel at CNN Center (659-0000) NC.

Notes: The pool is 4.5ft. deep and used exclusively for lap swimming.
To find: On the lower level of the CNN Center, by the entrance nearest the OMNI Coliseum.

2. ATLANTA MARRIOTT MARQUIS 265 Peachtree Ctr. Ave.
Phone: 521-0000. **Reservations:** 800-228-9290.
Pool: 20y, oval or kidney shape, indoor/outdoor, heated, 86°.
Admission: $10. Registered guests NC.

3. PEACHTREE CENTER ATHLETIC CLUB 227 Courtland St., 9th Floor

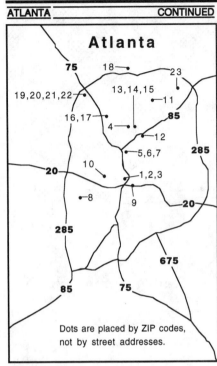

Atlanta

75   18   23
19,20,21,22   13,14,15
              11
16,17
              85
         4
              12
         5,6,7   285
20   10
              1,2,3
         8   9   20
285
                   675
85   75

Dots are placed by ZIP codes, not by street addresses.

Phone: 523-3833.
Pool: 25m, indoors, heated, 80°-82°.
Affiliate: IHRSA $8.
Hotel: Passes are available for purchase from the concierges at the downtown Marriott, Hilton, Hyatt, Ritz-Carlton, & Radisson hotels.
Masters: Contact Angela Singleton at 523-3833.

4. BUCKHEAD YMCA 3424 Roswell Rd.
Phone: 261-3111.
Pool: 25y x 28f, 4 lanes, indoors, heated, 82°-84°.
Affiliate: YMCA outside the greater Atlanta area NC.

5. WYNDHAM GARDEN HOTEL-MIDTOWN
Peachtree & 10th St.
Phone: 873-4800. **Reservations:** 800-WYND-HAM.
Pool: 18y, rectangular, indoors, heated, 74°.
Admission: Registered guests only NC.

6. JEWISH COMMUNITY CENTER 1745
Peachtree Rd. N.E.
Phone: 875-7881.
Pool: 25y, indoors, heated, 85°.
Affiliate: JCC NC.

7. SHEPHERD SPINAL CENTER 2020 Peachtree
Rd. N.W.
Phone: 352-2020.

Pool: 25y, 4 lanes, indoors, heated, 86°-88°.
Admission: 3 visits $5 each.

8. YMCA SOUTHWEST 2220 Campbellton Rd. S.W.
Phone: 753-4169.
Pool: 25m, indoors, heated, 83°-84°.
Admission: 1 visit NC.
Affiliate: YMCA NC.

9. MARTIN LUTHER KING (NORTH) NATATORIUM 70 Boulevard N.E.
Phone: 688-3791.
Pool: 25m, indoors, heated, 82°-84°.
Admission: $1.

10. JOHN F. KENNEDY NATATORIUM Kennedy Community Center / School, 255 James P. Brawley Dr.
Phone: 588-0839 or 522-5028.
Pool: 25m, 6 lanes, indoors, heated, 84°.
Admission: $1.

11. ASHFORD DUNWOODY YMCA 3692 Ashford Dunwoody Rd. N.E.
Phone: 451-9622.
Pool: 25y, 7 lanes, indoors, heated, 83°.
Affiliate: Y AWAY NC.

12. ATLANTA SPORTING CLUB 1515 Sheridan Rd. N. E.
Phone: 325-2700.
Pool: 25m, indoors, heated, 82°.
Admission: $10.
Notes: There is also a 25m, outdoor, summer pool.

13. THE RITZ-CARLTON, BUCKHEAD 3434 Peachtree Rd. N.E.
Phone: 237-2700. **Reservations:** 800-241-3333.
Pool: 20y, indoors, heated, 78°-80°.
Admission: Registered guests NC.
Memberships: 6 months $400.

14. SPORTSLIFE BUCKHEAD 3340 Peachtree Rd. N. E.
Phone: 262-2120.
Pool: 25y, indoors, heated, 80°-82°.
Admission: $10.
Affiliate: IHRSA Call.

15. BUCKHEAD ATHLETIC CLUB 3353 Peachtree Rd. N.E.
Phone: 364-2222.
Pool: 18m, 3 lanes, indoors, heated, 80°.
Admission: $10.

16. GEORGIA MASTERS KILLER WHALES at Pace Academy, 966 W. Paces Ferry Rd. N.W.
Masters: Contact Lisa Watson 497-1901(h) or Bill Lotz at 261-1906(h) or 705-9011(w).
Pool: 25y x 42f, 6 lanes, indoors, heated, 84°.
Affiliate: USMS NC, includes pool fees.

Notes: Uncoached Masters workouts: M-Th: 6:15-8PM. Sa: 9-10:30AM. Su*: 10-11:30AM, 5:30-7:PM. *From Jun.1 to Sep. 1, Sunday workouts are 9-10:30AM.

17. NORTHSIDE ATHLETIC CLUB 1160 Moore's Mill Rd.
Phone: 352-1919.
Pool: 25y, 5 lanes, indoor/outdoor, heated, 82°.
Admission: $10.
Hotel: Castlegate Hotel (351-6100), Biltmore Hotel (874-0824), & Regency Suites (876-5003): NC.
Notes: The pool is 3f deep at the shallow end.

18. CONCOURSE ATHLETIC CLUB 8 Concourse Pkwy. N.E.
Phone: 698-2000.
Pool: 25m, 5 lanes, indoors, heated, 82°.
Affiliate: IHRSA Call.
Hotel: Doubletree Hotel (395-3900) $5.
Masters: The Concourse Athletic Club Masters. Contact Diana Antonini at 698-2081.

19. THE SPORTING CLUB AT WINDY HILL 135 Interstate North Pkwy.
Phone: 953-1100.
Pool: 25m, 8 lanes, indoors, heated, 81°-83°.
Admission: $11.
Notes: There is also an outdoor, unheated, kidney shaped, recreation pool operated from Memorial Day to Labor Day.

20. THE VININGS CLUB 2859 Paces Ferry Rd. N. W., Club Level
Phone: 431-9166.
Pool: 25m, 3 lanes, indoors, heated, 82°.
Admission: $7.50.
Hotel: Wyndham Hotel (432-5555) & Hampton Inn (333-6066): $5 with room key.
To find: In the Overlook III Building in the Vinings area.
Masters: Contact Penny Purvis at 509-8586(w).

21. SPORTSLIFE COBB 1775 Water Place N.W.
Phone: 952-3200.
Pool: 25m, indoors, heated, 81°.
Admission: $10.
Affiliate: IHRSA Call.
Notes: There is also an outdoor pool.

22. CUMBERLAND CENTER II HEALTH CLUB at the Courtyard by Marriott, 3000 Cumberland Circle
Phone: Club: 951-1616. Hotel: 952-2555.
Reservations: 800-321-2211.
Pool: 50f, 3 lanes, rectangular, indoors, heated, 78°-82°.
Admission: $5. Registered guests NC.

23. THE COURT HOUSE AT MERCER in the Sheffield Phys. Ed. Bldg., Mercer University, 3001 Flowers Rd.
Phone: 986-3369.
Pool: 25y x 45f, 6 lanes, indoors, heated, 80°.

Admission: $5.
To find: One mile east of the Chamblee-Tucker Rd. Exit off I-85.

BRUNSWICK   912

YWCA OF BRUNSWICK 144 Scranton Connector
Phone: 265-4100.
Pool: 25y, 6 lanes, indoors, heated, 82°-84°.
Admission: $7.
Hotel: Glynn Mall Suites Hotel $4.
Masters: The Brunswick Y Barracudas. Contact Tom Wilson at 265-4100.

CANTON   404

CITY CLUB OF CANTON 700 Marietta Hwy.
Phone: 479-6777.
Pool: 20y x 30f, 2 lanes, indoor/outdoor, heated, 87°.
Admission: $10.

CHAMBLEE   404

DYNAMO SWIM CENTER 3119 Shallowford Rd.
Phone: 451-3272 or 458-9422.
Pool 1: 25y x 25m, 10 lanes, indoors, heated, water temperature not reported.
Pool 2: 25y, 5 lanes, indoors, heated, water temperature not reported.
Admission: $3, SC(55) $2.
Notes: There is also a 50m x 25y, 8 lane, seasonal, outdoor pool.
To find: From I-85 take Exit 33 (Shallowford Rd.) The Center is one mile inside the Perimeter.
Masters: The Georgia Killer Whales - Dynamo. Contact Steve Franklin at 457-7946(w).

COLUMBUS   706

COLUMBUS DOWNTOWN YMCA 118 E. 11th St.
Phone: 322-8269.
Pool: 25y, indoors, heated, 84°.
Admission: 2 visits NC.
Affiliate: YMCA Call.

D.A. TURNER YMCA 4384 Warm Springs Rd.
Phone: 563-7001.
Pool: 25y x 60f, 8 lanes, indoors, heated, 83°.
Admission: $4.
Affiliate: Y AWAY & USMS: NC. YMCA $1.

DALTON   706

BRADLEY WELLNESS CENTER 1225 Broadrick Dr.
Phone: 278-9355.
Pool: 25m, 5 lanes, indoors, heated, 87°.
Admission: Out-of-town visitors 1 visit NC, then $7.

DECATUR 404

DECATUR / DEKALB YMCA OF METRO ATLANTA 1100 Clairemont Ave.
Phone: 377-0241.
Pool: 25y x 24f, 4 lanes, indoors, heated, 85°.
Affiliate: Y AWAY NC, Metro Atlanta area YMCAs excluded.

SOUTH DEKALB YMCA 2565 Snapfinger Rd.
Phone: 987-3500.
Pool: 25y x 45f, 6 lanes, indoors, heated, 86°-87°.
Affiliate: YMCA NC.

DULUTH 404

WORKOUT AMERICA 122 Proctor Square
Phone: 497-0944.
Pool: 25m, indoors, heated, 82°-87°.
Admission: $10.
Affiliate: IPFA NC.

SPORTSLIFE GWINNETT 3540 Old Norcross Rd.
Phone: 497-2120.
Pool: 25m, indoors, heated, 80°.
Admission: $10.
Affiliate: IHRSA $5.

JEKYLL ISLAND 912

JEKYLL ISLAND CLUB HOTEL 371 Riverview Dr.
Phone: 635-2600. **Reservations:** 800-333-3333.
Pool: 20y, rectangular, outdoors, heated, water temperature not reported.
Admission: Registered guests only NC.

KENNESAW 404

WORKOUT AMERICA 425 Earnest Barrett Pkwy. F-1
Phone: 421-0402.
Pool: 25y, indoors, heated, 78°.
Admission: $10.
Affiliate: IPFA NC.

LAWRENCEVILLE 404

GWINETT COUNTY YMCA 750 Johnson Rd.
Phone: 963-1313.
Pool: 25m, indoors, heated, 82°.
Affiliate: YMCA NC.

LILBURN 404

MOUNTAIN PARK POOL 5050 Five Forks Trickum Rd.
Phone: 564-4650.
Pool: 50y x 25y, indoor/outdoor, heated, 84°-86°.
Admission: $2, SC(55) $1.

SWIM ATLANTA-GWINNETT 324 Holly Ridge Dr.
Phone: 381-7946.

Pool: 25y, indoors, heated, 82°.
Admission: $3, SC(60) $2.40.

MACON 912

YWCA OF MACON 775 - 2nd St.
Phone: 743-5468.
Pool: 25y, indoor/outdoor, heated, water temperature not reported.
Admission: $3.

MARIETTA 404

COBB AQUATIC CENTER 520 Fairground St. S.E.
Phone: 528-8465.
Pool: 25m, indoors, heated, 80°.
Admission: $3.

YMCA OF COBB COUNTY 1055 E. Piedmont Rd.
Phone: 977-5991.
Pool: 25y x 42f, 6 lanes, indoors, heated, 83°.
Affiliate: Y AWAY $2, Metro Atlanta YMCAs excluded.
Notes: The pool is 3f deep at the shallow end.
To find: One block off Roswell Rd. (Hwy. 120) on Piedmont Rd.

YWCA OF COBB COUNTY 48 Henderson St.
Phone: 427-2902.
Pool: 20y, indoors, heated, 87°-89°.
Admission: $3.

WILDWOOD ATHLETIC CLUB 2300 Windy Ridge Pkwy.
Phone: 953-2120.
Pool: 25y x 24f, 3 lanes, indoors, heated, 81°.
Admission: $7.50.
Notes: The pool is used exclusively for lap swimming.
To find: Directly behind T.G.I. Fridays on the 4th level of the Wildwood 2300 Building Parking Garage. Enter the garage at the entrance designated by the WAC sign.

MAIN EVENT FITNESS 2000 Powers Ferry Rd.
Phone: 951-2120.
Pool: 25y, 3 lanes, indoors, heated, 78°.
Admission: $6.
Affiliate: IHRSA $5.
Hotel: All local hotels $5.
To find: At the intersection of Windy Hill Rd. and Powers Ferry Rd., behind the office tower.

MOULTRIE 912

MOULTRIE YMCA 601 - 26th Ave. S.E.
Phone: 985-1154.
Pool: 25y x 60f, 8 lanes, indoors, heated, 84°.
Affiliate: Y AWAY NC. Colquitt County residents 1 visit $3.
To find: One mile south of the Square on Main St. One half mile north of the hospital on 5th St.

NORCROSS   404

BALLY'S HOLIDAY HEALTH CLUB 5050 Jimmy
Carter Blvd.
Phone: 449-8044.
Pool: 25y, indoors, heated, 85°.
Admission: Call.
Affiliate: Bally's NC.

RIVERDALE   404

WORKOUT AMERICA 691 Hwy. 138
Phone: 996-2120.
Pool: 25m, indoors, heated, 78°.
Admission: $5.
Affiliate: IPFA NC.

ROME   706

ROME-FLOYD COUNTY YMCA 810 E. 2nd Ave.
Phone: 232-2468.
Pool: 20y, indoors, heated, 84°-86°.
Admission: 1 visit NC, then $4.
Affiliate: YMCA NC.

ROSWELL   404

SPORTSLIFE 11060 Alpharetta Hwy.
Phone: 992-2120.
Pool: 25y, 5 lanes, indoors, heated, 81°.
Admission: $10.
Hotel: All local hotels $5.

BALLY'S HOLIDAY HEALTH CLUB 10701
Alpharetta Rd.
Phone: 993-8933.
Pool: 20m, indoors, heated, 78°-80°.
Admission: Out-of-state visitors NC.
Affiliate: Bally's NC.

SWIM ATLANTA LTD. 795 Old Roswell Rd.
Phone: 992-1778.
Pool: 25y, 6 lanes, indoors, heated, 82°.
Admission: $3.
To find: One half mile west of GA 400 off Holcomb
Bridge Rd.

SMYRNA   404

BALLY'S HOLIDAY HEALTH CLUB 2211 Cobb
Pkwy.
Phone: 988-0000.
Pool: 25m, indoors, heated, 82°.
Admission: Call.
Affiliate: Bally's NC.

STONE MOUNTAIN   404

SPORTSLIFE Stone Mountain Square Shopping
Center, 5370 Hwy. 78
Phone: 469-2120.
Pool: 25y, indoors, heated, 80°.
Admission: $10.

THOMASVILLE   912

FRANCIS F. WESTON BRANCH YMCA N.
Dawson St.
Phone: 226-2482.
Pool: 25y, indoors, heated, 82°.
Affiliate: Y AWAY NC.

TUCKER   404

BALLY'S NORTHLAKE 3993 La Vista Rd.
Phone: 938-9999.
Pool: 25m, indoors, heated, 70°-75°.
Admission: 1 visit NC.
Affiliate: Bally's NC.

HELP MAKE THE NEXT *SWIMMERS GUIDE* EVEN BETTER

To receive a free copy of the next *Swimmers Guide* tell us about pools you
know of that aren't in this edition. See page 14 for details.

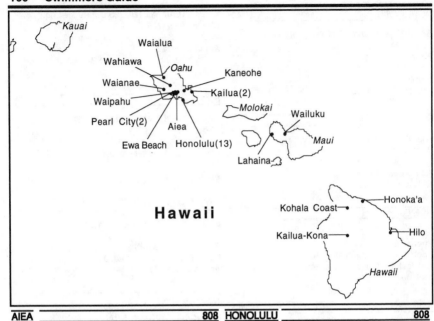

Hawaii

AIEA DISTRICT PARK SWIMMING POOL 99-350
 Aiea Heights Rd.
Phone: 483-7858.
Pool: 25y x 33f, outdoors, unheated, 70°-80°.
Admission: NC.

**MAKAKILO NEIGHBORHOOD PARK SWIMMING
 POOL** 92-665 Anipeahi St.
Phone: 672-3840.
Pool: 20y x 30f, outdoors, unheated, 70°-80°.
Admission: NC.

**CHARLES 'SPARKY' KAWAMOTO SWIM
 STADIUM** Kalanikoa St.
Phone: 935-8907.
Pool: 25y x 50m, 25 lanes, indoor/outdoor, unheat-
 ed, 70°-80°.
Admission: NC.
To find: Within walking distance from the Banyan
 Dr. hotels, around the block from Waiakea Triplex
 Theaters and McDonalds.

HONOKA'A SWIMMING COMPLEX 25 Aupuni St.
Phone: 775-0650.
Pool: 25y x 45f, 6 lanes, outdoors, unheated, 67°-
 78°.
Admission: NC.

Honolulu

8,9

1,2,3   10,11,12

4
13

5,6,7

Dots are placed by ZIP codes,
not by street addresses.

1. NUUANU YMCA 1441 Pali Hwy.
Phone: 536-3556.
Pool: 25y x 42f, 6 lanes, outdoors, heated, 80°-82°.
Admission: $10.
Affiliate: YMCA $5.
To find: Downtown, at the intersection of Pali Hwy.
 and Vineyard.

2. YWCA OF OAHU 1040 Richards St.
Phone: 538-7061.
Pool: 20y x 30f, outdoors, heated, water tempera-

ture not reported.
Admission: $3.50.

3. BOOTH DISTRICT PARK SWIMMING POOL
2331 Kanealii Ave.
Phone: 522-7037.
Pool: 25y x 33f, outdoors, unheated, 70°-80°.
Admission: NC.

4. CENTRAL BRANCH YMCA 401 Atkinson Dr.
Phone: 941-3344.
Pool: 25y x 30f, 5 lanes, outdoors, heated, 82°.
Admission: $10.
Affiliate: YMCA $5.
To find: Across the street from the Ala Moana Shopping Center.

5. KAIMUKI-WAIALAE BRANCH YMCA 4835 Kilauea Ave.
Phone: 737-5544.
Pool: 20m, outdoors, heated, 84°.
Memberships: $15/month for M,W,F early morning lap swimming.

6. PALOLO VALLEY DISTRICT PARK SWIMMING POOL 2007 Palolo Ave.
Phone: 733-7362.
Pool: 50m x 25y, outdoors, heated, 70°-80°.
Admission: NC.

7. KAPAOLONO POOL 701 - 11th Ave.
Phone: 733-7369.
Pool: 25y x 30f, 5 lanes, outdoors, unheated, 65°-82°.
Admission: NC.
To find: Two blocks 'mauka' (towards mountains) from Diamond Head.

8. KALIHI VALLEY DISTRICT PARK SWIMMING POOL 1911 Kamehameha IV Rd.
Phone: 832-7814.
Pool: 50m x 25y, outdoors, heated, 70°-80°.
Admission: NC.

9. MOANALUA COMMUNITY PARK SWIMMING POOL 1289 Mahiole St.
Phone: 831-7106.
Pool: 20y x 30f, outdoors, unheated, 70°-80°.
Admission: NC.

10. RAINBOW AQUATICS - MASTERS SWIMMING DIVISION at the Duke Kahanamoku Aquatic Complex - University of Hawaii, 1337 Lower Campus Rd.
Masters: Contact Head Coach Scott Hardman at 956-7510.
Pool: 25y x 50m, 22 lanes, outdoors, heated, 80°.
Non-member participation: $3.
Notes: Coached workouts: M-F: 6-7:15PM. M-Th: 7:15-8:30PM.
To find: About four miles east of downtown Honolulu, on the campus of the University of Hawaii - Manoa.

11. KANEWAI COMMUNITY PARK SWIMMING POOL 2695 Dole St.
Phone: 733-7365.
Pool: 25y x 33f, outdoors, unheated, 70°-80°.
Admission: NC.

12. MANOA VALLEY DISTRICT PARK POOL 2721 Kaaipu Ave.
Phone: 988-6868.
Pool: 50m x 20y, 8 lanes, outdoors, heated, 76°-84°.
Admission: NC.
To find: Two miles form the University of Hawaii.

13. MCCULLY DISTRICT PARK SWIMMING POOL 831 Pumehana St.
Phone: 973-7268.
Pool: 25y x 33f, outdoors, heated, 70°-80°.
Admission: NC.

KAILUA   808

KAILUA DISTRICT PARK SWIMMING POOL 21 S. Kainalu Dr.
Phone: 266-7661.
Pool: 50m x 25y, outdoors, heated, 70°-80°.
Admission: NC.

WINDWARD YMCA 1200 Kailua Rd.
Phone: 261-0808.
Pool: 25y, 6 lanes, outdoors, heated, 84°.
Admission: Pool $2. Full facility $5.
Affiliate: No reciprocity with other YMCAs.

KAILUA-KONA   808

KONA SURF RESORT & COUNTRY CLUB 78-128 Ehukai St.
Phone: 322-3411. **Reservations:** 800-367-8011.
Pool 1: 103f x 36f, salt water, kidney shape, outdoors, unheated, the range of water temperatures was not reported.
Pool 2: 73f x 25f, fresh water, outdoors, unheated, the range of water temperatures was not reported.
Admission: Registered guests only NC.

KANEOHE   808

KANEOHE DISTRICT PARK SWIMMING POOL 45-660 Keaahala Rd.
Phone: 233-7311.
Pool: 50m x 60f, 8 lanes, outdoors, temperature controlled, 78°.
Admission: NC.
To find: Next to Windward Community College, bottom of Like Like Tunnel, Kaneohe side.

KOHALA COAST   808

MAUNA LANI RACQUET CLUB
Phone: 885-7765.
Pool: 25m, outdoors, unheated, the range of water temperatures was not reported.

Affiliate: IHRSA Call.
Hotel: Mauna Lani Bay Hotel & Bungalows (885-6622) $10.

LAHAINA   808

LAHAINA AQUATIC CENTER 245 Shaw St.
Phone: 661-7611.
Pool: 50m x 25y, 8-10 lanes, outdoors, temperature controlled, 79°-82°.
Admission: NC.

MASTERS AT LAHAINA at Lahaina Aquatic Center
Masters: Contact Pool Manager Jack Spottswood at 661-7611 or Head Coach Janet Renner at 875-0623.
Non-member participation: $2.50*.
Affiliate: USMS $2.50.
Notes: *USMS registration or payment of $17.25 per year insurance is required for participation. Coached workouts: M,W,F: 6:30-8:30AM. Tu,Th: 6:30-8:30PM. Su: 4:30-6:30PM. Anyone 19 years or older who can swim unassisted freestyle for 50 meters is welcome to join workouts for fun and fitness.

PEARL CITY   808

PEARL CITY DISTRICT PARK SWIMMING POOL 785 Hoomaemae St.
Phone: 453-7552.
Pool: 25y x 33f, outdoors, unheated, 70°-80°.
Admission: NC.

MANANA SWIMMING POOL 1550 Kuahaka St.
Phone: 453-7556.
Pool: 25y x 33f, 5 lanes, outdoors, unheated, 69°-82°.
Admission: NC.

WAHIAWA   808

WAHIAWA DISTRICT PARK SWIMMING POOL 1139-A Kilani Ave.
Phone: 621-0857.
Pool: 25y x 33f, outdoors, heated, 70°-80°.
Admission: NC.

WAIALUA   808

WAIALUA DISTRICT PARK SWIMMING POOL 67-180 Goodale Ave.
Phone: 637-6061.
Pool: 25y x 33f, outdoors, unheated, 70°-80°.
Admission: NC.

WAIANAE   808

SHERATON MAKAHA RESORT & COUNTRY CLUB 84-626 Makaha Valley Rd.
Phone: 695-9511. **Reservations:** 800-325-3535.
Pool: 20y x 20y, outdoors, unheated, 68°-75°.
Admission: Registered guests only NC.

WAILUKU   808

WAR MEMORIAL POOL at Baldwin High School, 1850 Kaahumanu Ave.
Phone: 243-7394.
Pool: 50m, 8 lanes, outdoors, heated, 78°-79°.
Admission: NC.

MAUI OCEAN SWIM CLUB at War Memorial Pool
Masters: Contact Jim Krueger at 244-7444(w) or 572-1355(h).
Non-member participation: NC.
Notes: Uncoached Masters workouts: M-F: 6:30-8AM. Lap swimming: Sa: 9-11:45AM. Su: 12:45-4:30PM.

WAIPAHU   808

WAIPAHU DISTRICT PARK SWIMMING POOL 94-230 Paiwa St.
Phone: 677-4733.
Pool: 25y x 33f, outdoors, unheated, 70°-80°.
Admission: NC.

ALWAYS CALL FIRST

Pools close, they change names, affiliations, admission policies, and rates. And just because a pool is listed in *Swimmers Guide* doesn't mean it's open all day, every day, for just the type of workout you want to do. Spend a quarter to save time and aggravation. . . always call first!

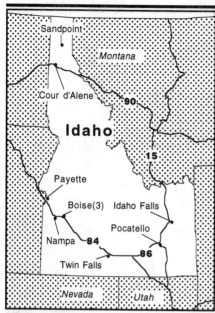

Idaho

IDAHO FALLS   208

IDAHO FALLS AQUATIC CENTER 149 - 7th St.
Phone: 528-5519.
Pool: 25y x 64f, 8 lanes, indoors, heated, 84°.
Admission: $2.25, SC(62) $1.75.
Masters: The Idaho Falls Masters. Contact Jim Smith at 522-4391(h).

NAMPA   208

NAMPA RECREATION CENTER 131 Constitution Way at 12th Ave.
Phone: 465-2288.
Pool: 25y x 25m, indoors, heated, 79°-80°.
Admission: $6.
Notes: There is also a recreation pool, a therapy pool, a diving well and a very large Jacuzzi, all indoors.
Masters: A Masters program is in formation. Contact Laurie Freshment at 465-2288.

PAYETTE   208

PAYETTE CITY POOL Kiwanis Park, 7th St. S.
Phone: 642-6030.
Pool: 25y, indoors, heated, 82°.
Admission: $2, SC(62) $1.50.
Notes: The indoor pool operates Sep. through May. In summer, a similar outdoor pool is opened.

POCATELLO   208

THE SWIM & GYM Pocatello Recreation & Parks Dept., 144 Wilson
Phone: 232-3901.
Pool: 25y, 6 lanes, indoors, heated, 86°.
Admission: $4.

SANDPOINT   208

SANDPOINT WEST ATHLETIC CLUB 1905 Pine St.
Phone: 263-6633.
Pool: 25m, indoors, heated, 84°.
Admission: $10.
Affiliate: NACA NC. IHRSA $5.

TWIN FALLS   208

MAGIC VALLEY YFCA 1751 Elizabeth Blvd.
Phone: 733-4384.
Pool: 25y, 4 lanes, indoors, heated, 84°.
Admission: $4.
Affiliate: YMCA NC.

BOISE   208

BOISE FAMILY YMCA 1050 W. State St.
Phone: 344-5501.
Pool: 25y, 6 lanes, indoors, heated, 84°.
Admission: $8.
Affiliate: YMCA NC.
Masters: The Sawtooth Masters. Contact Craig Faircloth at 344-5501.

PARK CENTER HEALTH & RACQUET CLUB 555 Park Center Blvd.
Phone: 343-2288.
Pool: 20y, indoors, heated, 86°.
Admission: $9.
Affiliate: IHRSA Call.

THE COURT HOUSE 7211 Colonial Dr.
Phone: 377-0040.
Pool: 22y x 22f, 4 lanes, indoor/outdoor, heated, 82°.
Admission: $10.
Affiliate: NACA NC. IHRSA $7.
Notes: A second pool, to be operated in the summer, is under construction.
To find: One block east and south of Cole and Franklin, near Towne Square Mall.

COUR D'ALENE   208

STA-FIT ATHLETIC CLUB 208 Cour d'Alene Ave.
Phone: 667-5010.
Pool: 25y, indoors, heated, 82°-83°.
Admission: $7.

Vernon Hills

Chicago
Area

Bannockburn Highland Park

Barrington Buffalo Grove Deerfield(2)

Palatine(4) Wheeling 94

Arlington Heights Northfield

Northbrook

90 294

Elgin Mount Prospect(3) Des Plaines Morton Grove Evanston(2)

Schaumburg(2) Niles Skokie(2)

Rosemont(2)

Elk Grove Village Park Ridge Lincolnwood

Wood Dale 90

Itasca

Glendale Heights

290

Carol Stream(2) 355 Melrose Park(3) Chicago(55)

Lombard Oak Park(2)

West Chicago Elmhurst(2) 290

Wheaton Oakbrook Terrace Berwyn

Glen Ellyn 88

Downers Grove(4) Countryside 55

294 La Grange 94

Aurora(2) Lisle

Willowbrook Oak Lawn 90

Naperville(2) Palos Hills

Alsip

ALSIP   708

HOLIDAY INN CHICAGO / ALSIP 5000 W. 127th St.
Phone: 371-7300. **Reservations:** 800-HOLIDAY.
Pool: 50f x 28f, rectangular, indoors, heated, 84°.
Admission: Registered guests only NC.

ALTON   618

NAUTILUS FITNESS / RACQUET CENTER 4425 Industrial Dr.
Phone: 466-9115.
Pool: 20y x 25f, 5 lanes, indoors, heated, 85°.
Admission: $10.
Affiliate: IHRSA $5.
Hotel: Holiday Inn Alton (462-1220), Ramada Inn (463-0800), & Super 8 Motel (465-8885): $5.
To find: Across the street from Alton Square.

YWCA OF ALTON 304 E. 3rd St.
Phone: 465-7774.

Pool: 20y, indoors, heated, 86°-88°.
Affiliate: YWCA $2.

ARLINGTON HEIGHTS   708

OLYMPIC SWIM CENTER 660 N. Ridge
Phone: 577-3025.
Pool: 25y, indoors, heated, 83°-84°.
Admission: $3.50.

AURORA   708

BALLY'S CHICAGO HEALTH CLUB 4220 W. Brook Dr.
Phone: 898-8700.
Pool: 25y, indoors, heated, 81°-82°.
Affiliate: Bally's NC.

AURORA YMCA 460 Garfield Ave.
Phone: 896-9782.

Pool: 25m, indoors, heated, 84°.
Affiliate: YMCA NC.

BANNOCKBURN   708

BANNOCKBURN BATH & TENNIS CLUB, INC.
2211 Waukegan Rd.
Phone: 945-4413.
Pool: 25y x 45f, 4 lanes, indoors, heated, 82°.
Admission: Out-of-town visitors $10.
Hotel: Hawthorne Suites (945-9300) & Deer Path
Inn (234-2280): $5 with room key.

BARRINGTON   708

BARRINGTON HIGH SCHOOL 616 W. Main St.
Phone: 842-3261.
Pool: 25y, 6 lanes, indoors, heated, 78°-80°.
Admission: $2.
Notes: The pool is closed in summer.
Masters: The Barrington Area Masters. Contact
Lee D. McCloud at 842-3261.

BELLEVILLE   618

BELLEVILLE YMCA 15 N. 1st St.
Phone: 233-1243.
Pool: 25y x 27f, 4 lanes, indoors, heated, 86°.
Affiliate: Y AWAY NC.
Hotel: Town House Inn NC.

BELLEVILLE FITNESS CENTER 1234 Centerville
Rd.
Phone: 235-2833.
Pool: 20y, indoors, heated, 80°.
Admission: $5.
Affiliate: IPFA NC.

BI-COUNTY YMCA 9100 Lebanon Rd.
Phone: 398-1745.
Pool: 25y x 25f, 4 lanes, indoors, heated, 86°.
Affiliate: Y AWAY NC. YMCA Call.
Hotel: Town House Inn NC.

BELVIDERE   815

BELVIDERE FAMILY YMCA 220 W. Locust St.
Phone: 547-5307.
Pool: 25y, indoors, heated, 84°.
Admission: $4.50.
Affiliate: YMCA $2.25.

BERWYN   708

BERWYN-CICERO YMCA 2947 Oak Park Ave.
Phone: 749-0606.
Pool: 25y, indoors, heated, 82°-83°.
Admission: $10.
Affiliate: YMCA NC.

BLOOMINGTON   309

BLOOMINGTON-NORMAL YMCA 602 S. Main St.
Phone: 827-6233.
Pool: 25y, 6 lanes, indoors, heated, 84°-86°.
Admission: $8.
Affiliate: YMCA 3 visits per year NC, then $4.

YWCA OF MCLEAN COUNTY 1201 Hershey Rd.
Phone: 662-0461.
Pool: 25y x 45f, 6 lanes, indoors, heated, 85°.
Admission: $4.
Affiliate: YWCA NC.
Hotel: Days Inn (663-1361) NC with a pass from
the hotel.
To find: Near the Bloomington Normal Airport and
Eastland Mall.

BUFFALO GROVE   708

BUFFALO GROVE AQUADOME 1100 W. Dundee
Rd.
Phone: 459-2310.
Pool: 25y x 42f, 6 lanes, indoors, heated, 80°.
Admission: Fall, winter, spring: Weekdays $1.50.
Weekends $2.50. Summer: Weekdays $2.50.
Weekends $3.50.
To find: The entrance is on Arlington Heights Rd.,
just north of Dundee Rd.

CALUMET CITY   708

BALLY'S CHICAGO HEALTH CLUB 1500
Torrence Ave.
Phone: 891-8800.
Pool: 25y, indoors, heated, 80°.
Affiliate: Bally's NC.
Hotel: Fairfield Inn (474-6900) NC.

CANTON   309

CANTON FAMILY YMCA 1325 E. Ash St.
Phone: 647-1616.
Pool: 25y, 4 lanes, indoors, heated, 84°.
Admission: $5.
Affiliate: YMCA NC.

CARBONDALE   618

LIFE COMMUNITY CENTER POOL 2500 Sunset
Dr.
Phone: 549-4222.
Pool: 25y x 36f, 6 lanes, indoors, heated, 85°.
Admission: Residents: $1.75, SC(55) 60¢. Non-
residents: $2.40.
To find: In a brick building surrounded by soccer
fields. There is a sign in front.

CAROL STREAM   708

SPORTSMED CENTER FOR FITNESS, LTD. 327
E. Gundersen Dr.
Phone: 668-8400.
Pool: 20y x 20f, 4 lanes, indoors, heated, 84°.

Admission: $8.
To find: Two blocks north of Geneva Rd. and two blocks west of Schmale Rd.

MICHAEL COLLINS POOL 391 Illini Dr.
Phone: 665-5615.
Pool: 25m, 6 lanes, indoors, heated, 83°.
Admission: $3, SC(55) $1.

CHAMPAIGN _____ **217**

MCKINLEY FAMILY YMCA 500 W. Church St.
Phone: 356-2597.
Pool 1: 25y x 54f, 6 lanes, indoors, heated, 83°.
Pool 2: 20y x 36f, 5 lanes, indoors, heated, 86°.
Admission: Basic $5. Fitness Center $8.
Affiliate: Y AWAY $2.
To find: On W. Church St., five blocks west of Neil St.

CHICAGO _____ **312**

1. THE RANDOLPH ATHLETIC CLUB 188 W. Randolph St., 27th Level
Phone: 269-5820.
Pool: 20y x 30f, 7 lanes, indoors, heated, 78°-82°.
Admission: $10.
Affiliate: IHRSA $6.
To find: At the intersection of Randolph and Wells, one block from the State of Illinois Building.

2. ATHLETIC CLUB AT ILLINOIS CENTER 211 N. Stetson
Phone: 616-9000.
Pool: 25y, 8 lanes, indoors, heated, 81°.
Affiliate: IHRSA Call.
Hotel: Fairmont Hotel (565-8000) & Park Hyatt Hotel (280-2222): $12. All other local hotels $15.

3. BALLY'S CHICAGO HEALTH CLUB 25 E. Washington St.
Phone: 372-7755.
Pool: 20m, indoors, heated, 79°-80°.
Admission: Call.

4. CHICAGO HILTON & TOWERS 720 S. Michigan Ave.
Phone: 922-4400. **Reservations:** 800-HILTONS.
Pool: 20y, rectangular, indoors, heated, 82°.
Admission: $10. Registered guests NC.
Memberships: $500/year.

5. BALLY'S CHICAGO HEALTH CLUB 230 W. Monroe
Phone: 263-4500.
Pool: 20m, indoors, heated, 80°.
Affiliate: Bally's NC.

6. SHERIDAN PARK POOL 910 S. Aberdeen St.
Phone: 294-4717.
Pool: 25y x 42f, 6 lanes, indoors, heated, 79°.
Admission: NC.

7. UNIVERSITY OF ILLINOIS AT CHICAGO POOL 750 S. Halsted
Phone: 413-5160.
Pool: 25y, 6 lanes, indoors, heated, 78°-80°.
Admission: $3, picture ID required.
Hotel: Quality Inn-Downtown (829-5000) & Inn at University Village (243-7200): $2.50 with a voucher from the hotel and room key or picture ID.
Memberships: 3/12 months $75/$190.
To find: On Halsted between Taylor & Harrison (on Polk St.), behind Jane Adam's Hull House. The pool is in the basement, under the bowling alley.
Masters: The Chicago Masters Swim Club. Contact Bill Muliken at (708) 594-0031(w).

8. BALLY'S HEALTH CLUB 800 S. Wells St.
Phone: 431-0100.
Pool: 25m, indoors, heated, 82°-85°.
Affiliate: Bally's NC.
Hotel: Hyatt Regency (565-1234) NC.

9. HARRISON PARK POOL 1824 S. Wood St.
Phone: 421-8542.
Pool: 25y x 42f, 6 lanes, indoor/outdoor, heated, 79°.
Admission: NC.

10. MCGUANE PARK POOL 2901 S. Poplar
Phone: 294-4692.
Pool: 25y x 42f, 6 lanes, indoors, heated, 79°.
Admission: NC.

11. BALLY'S CHICAGO HEALTH CLUB 300 N. State St.
Phone: 321-9600.
Pool: 25m, indoors, heated, 78°-80°.
Affiliate: Bally's NC.

12. STANTON PARK POOL 650 W. Scott St.
Phone: 294-4733.
Pool: 25y x 42f, 6 lanes, indoors, heated, 79°.
Admission: NC.

13. EAST BANK CLUB 500 N. Kingsbury
Phone: 527-5800.
Pool: 25y, 5 lanes, indoors, heated, 78°.
Affiliate: IHRSA $15.

14. COURTYARD BY MARRIOTT / CHICAGO DOWNTOWN 30 E. Hubbard St.
Phone: 329-2500. **Reservations:** 800-321-2211.
Pool: 20y, rectangular, indoors, heated, 80°.
Admission: Registered guests only NC.

15. DOWNTOWN SPORTS CLUB 441 N. Wabash Ave.
Phone: 644-4880.
Pool: 20y x 33f, 4 lanes, indoors, heated, 80°.
Affiliate: IHRSA $10.
Hotel: All local hotels $10 with room key.
To find: One block west of Michigan Ave. at the intersection of Wabash and Hubbard.

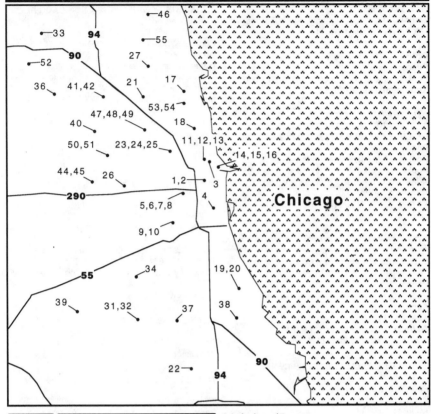

| CHICAGO | CONTINUED |

16. HOTEL INTER•CONTINENTAL CHICAGO 505
N. Michigan Ave.
Phone: 944-4100. **Reservations:** 800-327-0200.
Pool: 25y, rectangular, indoors, heated, 83°.
Admission: $10. Registered guests NC for pool
and sauna.

17. GILL PARK POOL 833 W. Sheridan Rd.
Phone: 525-7238.
Pool: 25y x 42f, 6 lanes, indoors, heated, 79°.
Admission: NC.
Masters: Hosts a Masters swim club.

18. LAKESHORE ATHLETIC CLUB 1320 W.
Fullerton
Phone: 477-9888.
Pool: 25m, 9 lanes, indoors, heated, 78°.
Admission: $10.
Affiliate: IHRSA Call.

19. WASHINGTON PARK YMCA 5000 S. Indiana
Ave.
Phone: 538-5200.
Pool: 20m, indoors, heated, 82°.
Admission: $7.
Affiliate: Y AWAY NC.

20. DYETT PARK POOL 513 E. 51st St.
Phone: 548-1816.
Pool: 25y x 42f, 6 lanes, indoors, heated, 79°.
Admission: NC.

21. INDEPENDENCE PARK POOL 3945 N.
Springfield
Phone: 478-1039.
Pool: 20y x 25f, 5 lanes, indoors, heated, 79°.
Admission: NC.

22. FOSTER PARK POOL 1440 W. Chicago
Phone: 723-7215.
Pool: 25y x 42f, 6 lanes, indoors, heated, 79°.
Admission: NC.

23. NEW CITY YMCA 1515 N. Halsted
Phone: 266-1242.
Pool: 25m x 33f, 6 lanes, indoors, heated, 83°.
Admission: $7.
Affiliate: YMCA NC.
To find: On Halsted, one block south of North Ave.
Masters: The Flying Carp. Contact Jeff Putnam at
281-6168(h).

24. CLEMENTE PARK POOL 2334 W. Division St.
Phone: 486-9052.
Pool: 25y x 42f, 6 lanes, indoors, heated, 79°.
Admission: NC.

25. ECKHART PARK POOL 1330 W. Chicago
Phone: 294-4671.
Pool: 25y x 42f, 6 lanes, indoors, heated, 79°.
Admission: NC.

26. JACKSON PARK POOL 3506 W. Fillmore
Phone: 643-6363.
Pool: 20y x 30f, 5 lanes, indoors, heated, 79°.
Admission: NC.

27. WELLES PARK POOL 2333 W. Sunnyside
Ave.
Phone: 561-1832.
Pool: 25y x 42f, 6 lanes, indoors, heated, 79°.
Admission: NC.

28. CARVER PARK POOL 939 E. 132nd St.
Phone: 821-9534.
Pool: 25y x 42f, 6 lanes, indoors, heated, 79°.
Admission: NC.

29. WEST PULLMAN POOL 12300 S. Stewart
Phone: 785-6963.
Pool: 25y x 42f, 6 lanes, indoors, heated, 79°.
Admission: NC.

30. GRIFFITH PARK POOL 346 W. 104th St.
Phone: 821-9475.
Pool: 20y x 30f, 5 lanes, indoors, heated, 79°.
Admission: NC.

31. WEST COMMUNITIES YMCA 6235 S. Homan
Ave.
Phone: 434-0300.
Pool: 20y x 30f, 4 lanes, indoors, heated, 84°.
Admission: $7.
Affiliate: Y AWAY NC.
To find: Three blocks off 63rd and Kedzie W.

32. BOGAN POOL 3939 W. 79th St.
Phone: 582-4464.
Pool: 20y x 30f, 5 lanes, indoors, heated, 79°.
Admission: NC.

33. PRESIDENT'S FITNESS CENTER 8600 W.
Bryn Mawr Ave.
Phone: 693-6500.
Pool: 20y, indoors, heated, 82°.
Admission: $8.
Affiliate: IHRSA $4.

34. MADAM CURIE POOL 4949 S. Archer Ave.
Phone: 535-2020.
Pool: 25y x 42f, 6 lanes, indoors, heated, 79°.
Admission: NC.

35. MANN POOL 130th & Carondolet
Phone: 646-9612.
Pool: 25y x 42f, 6 lanes, indoors, heated, 79°.
Admission: NC.

36. SHABBONA PARK POOL 6935 W. Addison
St.
Phone: 283-9554.
Pool: 25y x 42f, 6 lanes, indoors, heated, 79°.
Admission: NC.
Masters: Hosts a Masters swim club.

37. KELLY PARK POOL 4150 S. California Ave.
Phone: 927-1663.
Pool: 20y x 30f, 5 lanes, indoors, heated, 79°.
Admission: NC.

38. SOUTH SIDE YMCA 6330 S. Stony Island Ave.
Phone: 947-0700.
Pool: 25y, 6 lanes, indoors, heated, 82°.
Admission: $8.
Affiliate: Y AWAY NC.

39. WENTWORTH-KENNEDY PARK POOL 5625
S. Mobile
Phone: 585-1881.
Pool: 25y x 42f, 6 lanes, indoors, heated, 79°.
Admission: NC.

40. BLACK HAWK PARK POOL 2318 N. Lavergne
Phone: 237-3877.
Pool: 20y x 25f, 4 lanes, indoors, heated, 79°.
Admission: NC.

41. IRVING PARK YMCA 4251 W. Irving Park Rd.
Phone: 777-7500.
Pool: 20y x 30f, 4 lanes, indoors, heated, 82°.
Admission: $9.
Affiliate: Y AWAY NC.
To find: On Irving Park Rd. two blocks west of
Pulaski.

42. PORTAGE PARK POOL 4100 N. Long
Phone: 545-4337.
Pool: 20y x 30f, 5 lanes, indoors, heated, 79°.
Admission: NC.
Masters: Hosts a Masters swim club.

43. RIDGE PARK POOL 9625 S. Longwood Dr.
Phone: 238-1655.
Pool: 25y x 42f, 6 lanes, indoors, heated, 79°.
Admission: NC.

44. AUSTIN YMCA 501 N. Central Ave.
Phone: 287-9120 ext. 262.
Pool: 20y, 4 lanes, indoors, heated, 82°.
Admission: Before 6PM $1, after 6PM $2.
Affiliate: YMCA NC.

45. AUSTIN TOWN HALL POOL 5610 Lake St.
Phone: 378-0126.

CHICAGO   CONTINUED
Pool: 20y x 25f, 4 lanes, indoors, heated, 79°.
Admission: NC.

46. HIGH RIDGE YMCA 2424 W. Touhy Ave.
Phone: 262-8300.
Pool: 25y x 30f, 5 lanes, indoors, heated, 83°.
Admission: $8.
Affiliate: Y AWAY NC.

47. LOGAN SQUARE YMCA 3600 W. Fullerton
Ave.
Phone: 235-5150.
Pool: 25y, indoors, heated, 82°-86°.
Admission: $5.
Affiliate: YMCA Call.

48. KOSCIUSZKO PARK POOL 2732 N. Avers
Phone: 278-6756.
Pool: 25y x 42f, 6 lanes, indoor/outdoor, heated,
79°.
Admission: NC.

49. BEILFUSS NATATORIUM 1725 N. Springfield
Phone: 235-0282.
Pool: 20y x 30f, 4 lanes, indoors, heated, 79°.
Admission: NC.

50. ORR PARK POOL 730 N. Pulaski Rd.
Phone: 826-3713.
Pool: 25y x 42f, 6 lanes, indoors, heated, 79°.
Admission: NC.

51. LAFOLLETTE PARK POOL 1333 N. Laramie
Phone: 378-0124.
Pool: 20y x 30f, 5 lanes, indoors, heated, 79°.
Admission: NC.

52. BALLY'S CHICAGO HEALTH CLUB 5444 N.
Cumberland Ave.
Phone: 380-8600.
Pool: 25m, indoors, heated, 75°-80°.
Admission: Call.
Affiliate: Bally's NC.
Hotel: O'Hare Plaza NC.

53. LINCOLN-BELMONT YMCA 3333 N.
Marshfield Ave.
Phone: 248-3333.
Pool: 20y x 25f, 3 lanes, indoors, heated, 82°-84°.
Admission: $8.
Affiliate: Out-of-state Y AWAY NC.
To find: One half block north of the intersection of
School St. and Lincoln Ave.

54. BALLY'S CHICAGO HEALTH CLUB Century
Mall, 2828 Clark St.
Phone: 929-6900.
Pool: 25y, indoors, heated, 82°-85°.
Admission: Call.
Affiliate: Bally's NC.

55. MATHER PARK POOL 5835 N. Lincoln Ave.
Phone: 561-1460.
Pool: 20y x 30f, 5 lanes, indoors, heated, 79°.
Admission: NC.

COUNTRYSIDE   708
BALLY'S CHICAGO HEALTH CLUB 5917 S.
LaGrange Rd.
Phone: 482-4700.
Pool: 20y, indoors, heated, 82°.
Admission: Call.
Affiliate: Bally's NC.

CRYSTAL LAKE   815
LAKE REGION YMCA 7315 S. Route 31
Phone: 459-4455.
Pool: 25y, indoors, heated, 82°-84°.
Admission: $6.
Affiliate: YMCA Call.

DANVILLE   217
DANVILLE FAMILY YMCA 1111 N. Vermillion St.
Phone: 442-0563.
Pool: 25y, indoors, heated, 83°-85°.
Admission: $5.
Affiliate: YMCA NC.
Hotel: Days Inn (443-6600) & Ramada Inn (446-
2400): $2.50.

YWCA OF DANVILLE 201 N. Hazel St.
Phone: 446-1217.
Pool: 20y x 20f, indoors, heated, 84°.
Admission: $2.

DECATUR   217
DECATUR ATHLETIC CLUB 1010 Southside Dr.
Phone: 423-7020.
Pool: 25y, indoor/outdoor, heated, 83°.
Admission: $5.

YWCA OF DECATUR 436 N. Main St.
Phone: 423-3415.
Pool: 25y, indoors, heated, 86°.
Admission: $2.50.

DEERFIELD   708
MULTIPLEX 491 Lake Cook Rd.
Phone: 498-4030.
Pool: 20y, 4 lanes, indoors, heated, 81°.
Affiliate: IHRSA $12.
Hotel: Hyatt (945-3400), Embassy Suites (945-
4500), Courtyards by Marriott (940-8222),
Residence Inn (940-4666), Sheraton Inn (498-
6500), Red Roof Inn (205-1755), Marriott (634-
0100), & Chicago Marriott Suites (405-9666): $12
with room key.
To find: In the Lake Cook Shopping Plaza.

BALLY'S CHICAGO HEALTH CLUB 260 Waukegan Rd.
Phone: 480-0770.
Pool: 25m, indoors, heated, 78°-80°.
Admission: Call.
Affiliate: Bally's NC.

DEKALB   815

KISHWAUKEE YMCA 2500 Bethany Rd.
Phone: 756-9577.
Pool: 25y, indoors, heated, 84°.
Affiliate: Y AWAY NC.
To find: Near the hospital.

DES PLAINES   708

LATTOF INTERNATIONAL YMCA 300 E.
Northwest Hwy.
Phone: 296-3376.
Pool 1: 25y, 6 lanes, indoors, heated, 80°.
Pool 2: 25y, 4 lanes, indoors, heated, 84°.
Admission: $8.
Affiliate: Y AWAY NC.
To find: Just north of O'Hare Airport, one mile west I-294 on Dempster.

DOWNERS GROVE   708

THE ESPLANADE FITNESS CENTER 2001
Butterfield Rd.
Phone: 963-3360.
Pool: 25y, indoors, heated, 80°-82°.
Affiliate: IHRSA $7.
Hotel: Radisson Suite Hotel Downers Grove (971-2000) NC with guest pass from the hotel.
Masters: A Masters swim club is in formation. Contact Susie Pokuta at 963-3360.

DOWNERS GROVE NORTH HIGH SCHOOL POOL 4435 Prince St.
Phone: Recorded schedule: 963-0575. Rec. Dept: 963-1300.
Pool: 50y, indoors, heated, 80°-82°.
Admission: Residents $2, non-residents $3. SC(60) NC.
Notes: Park at the Saratoga parking lot.

INDIAN BOUNDARY YMCA 711 - 59th St.
Phone: 968-8400.
Pool: 25y x 60f, 6 lanes, indoors, heated, 84°.
Admission: $7.
Affiliate: Y AWAY NC.

DOWNERS GROVE SOUTH HIGH SCHOOL POOL 1436 Norfolk
Phone: Recorded schedule: 963-0575. Rec. Dept: 963-1300.
Pool: 50y, indoors, heated, 80°-82°.
Admission: Residents $2, non-residents $3. SC(60) NC.

EAST MOLINE   309

EAST MOLINE MUNICIPAL POOL 4011 Archer Dr.
Phone: 752-1624.
Pool: 25y x 45f, 6 lanes, indoors, heated, 82°.
Admission: Lap swims $1.50. Rec. swims: $2, SC(60) $1.50.
To find: At the northeast corner of United Township High School.

EDWARDSVILLE   618

EDWARDSVILLE YMCA 1200 Esic Dr.
Phone: 656-0436.
Pool: 25y, indoors, heated, 83°-84°.
Admission: $2.
Affiliate: YMCA $1.

ELGIN   708

CHANNING YMCA 111 N. Channing St.
Phone: 888-7406.
Pool: 25y x 25f, 4 lanes, indoors, heated, 83°.
Admission: $6.
Affiliate: Y AWAY 2 weeks NC.
To find: On Channing St., two blocks west of Route 25.

ELK GROVE VILLAGE   708

ELK GROVE PARK DISTRICT-DISNEY POOL 999 Liecaster Rd.
Phone: Pool: 593-6248 or 288-3521. Parks & Rec. Dept: 437-9494.
Pool: 25y x 45f, 6 lanes, indoors, heated, 82°.
Admission: Residents $2, non-residents $3.
To find: Four blocks east of Route 53 on Biesterfield Exit, turn right on Leicaster.
Masters: The Elk Grove Masters. Contact Pam Van Den Bussche at 288-3521 or James Klotz at 593-6248.

ELMHURST   708

ELMHURST YMCA 211 W. 1st St.
Phone: 834-9200.
Pool: 25y, 4 lanes, indoors, heated, 83°-86°.
Admission: $8.
Affiliate: YMCA NC.
To find: Near Elmhurst College.

HOLIDAY INN CHICAGO ELMHURST 624 N. York Rd.
Phone: 279-1100. **Reservations:** 800-HOLIDAY.
Pool: 20y, rectangular, indoors, heated, 80°-82°.
Admission: Registered guests only NC.

EVANSTON   708

MCGAW YMCA 1000 Grove St.
Phone: 475-7400.
Pool 1: 25y x 48f, indoors, heated, 81°.
Pool 2: 25y x 27f, indoors, heated, 85°.

EVANSTON   CONTINUED

Admission: $6.
Affiliate: Y AWAY NC. Chicago Metro YMCA 1
visit per week NC.
To find: Two and a half blocks east of Ridge Ave.

YWCA OF EVANSTON / NORTH SHORE 1215
Church St.
Phone: 864-8445.
Pool: 25y, indoors, heated, 84°.
Admission: 2 visits $5.
Masters: A Masters group is in formation. Contact
Peter Cragher at 864-8445.

FAIRVIEW HEIGHTS   618

BALLY'S VIC TANNY 5925 N. Illinois
Phone: 277-1450.
Pool: 25m, indoors, heated, 84°.
Admission: Call.
Affiliate: Bally's NC.
Hotel: Ramada Inn (632-4747) & Drury Inn (398-
8530): NC.

FREEPORT   815

FAMILY YMCA OF NORTHWEST ILLINOIS 2998
Pearl City Rd.
Phone: 235-9622.
Pool: 25m x 42f, 6 lanes, indoors, heated, 84°.
Admission: $6.
Affiliate: Out-of-area YMCA NC. In-area YMCA
$3.
To find: In the Highland Community College Sports
Complex.

YWCA OF FREEPORT 641 W. Stephenson St.
Phone: 235-9421.
Pool: 25y, indoors, heated, 86°.
Admission: $3.
Affiliate: YWCA Call.

GALESBURG   309

HAWTHORNE POOL Carl Sandburg Dr.
Phone: Pool: 345-3694. Parks & Rec. Dept: 345-
3683.
Pool: 100f x 42f, indoors, heated, 85°-86°.
Admission: $2.50, SC(65) $1.50.

GLEN ELLYN   708

B.R. RYALL YMCA 49 Deicke Dr.
Phone: 858-0100.
Pool: 25y, indoors, heated, 80°-85°.
Admission: 2 visits NC.
Affiliate: YMCA NC.

GLENDALE HEIGHTS   708

BALLY'S CHICAGO HEALTH CLUB 265 Army
Trail Rd.

Phone: 893-0600.
Pool: 20y, indoors, heated, 82°-85°.
Admission: Call.
Affiliate: Bally's NC.

HIGHLAND PARK   708

FORTY-ONE SPORTS CLUB 2829 Skokie Hwy.
Phone: 433-7611.
Pool: 25m, indoors, heated, water temperature not
reported.
Admission: $11.
Affiliate: IHRSA $5.

HOMEWOOD   708

**HOMEWOOD-FLOSSMOOR RACQUET &
FITNESS CLUB** 2920 W. 183rd St.
Phone: 799-1323.
Pool: 25y x 25f, 4 lanes, indoors, heated, 80°.
Admission: $6.
To find: On 183rd St., two blocks east of Kedzie
Ave.

ITASCA   708

WYNDHAM HAMILTON HOTEL 400 Park Blvd.
Phone: 773-4000. **Reservations:** 800-822-4200.
Pool: 20y, rectangular, indoors, heated, 82°-85°.
Admission: $10. Registered guests NC.

JACKSONVILLE   217

SHERWOOD EDDY MEMORIAL YMCA 1000
Sherwood Lane
Phone: 245-2141.
Pool: 25y, 6 lanes, indoors, heated, 83°.
Affiliate: Y AWAY 3 visits per year NC.
Hotel: All local hotels NC with advance notification
to the Y by the hotel.

JOLIET   815

BRIGGS STREET YMCA 1350 Briggs St.
Phone: 726-3939.
Pool: 25y x 45f, 6 lanes, indoors, heated, 84°.
Admission: $5.
Affiliate: YMCA NC.
To find: One half mile south of I-80 on Briggs St.

GALOWICH YMCA 749 Houbolt Ave.
Phone: 744-3939.
Pool: 25y x 45f, 6 lanes, indoors, heated, 84°.
Admission: $5.
Affiliate: YMCA NC.
To find: One quarter of a mile north of Joliet Junior
College.

CHARLIE FITNESS CLUB 2701 Black Rd.
Phone: 729-4503.
Pool: 20y x 25f, indoors, heated, 82°.
Affiliate: IHRSA Call.

KANKAKEE   815

KANKAKEE YMCA 1075 Kennedy Dr.
Phone: 933-1741.
Pool: 25y x 30f, 6 lanes, indoors, heated, 81°.
Admission: $6.
Affiliate: YMCA 10 visits NC.

KEWANEE   309

KEWANEE YMCA 315 W. 1st St.
Phone: 853-4431.
Pool: 20y, 4 lanes, indoors, heated, 85°-86°.
Admission: $5.
Affiliate: YMCA 3 visits NC, then $2.50.

LA GRANGE   708

RICH PORT YMCA 31 E. Ogden Ave.
Phone: 352-7600.
Pool: 25m, 6 lanes, indoors, heated, 79°-80°.
Admission: M-Th $8.
Affiliate: Y AWAY NC.
Masters: The Rich Port Masters. Contact Sandra Krol at 352-7600.

LAKE VILLA   708

HASTINGS LAKE YMCA Grass Lake Rd.
Phone: 356-4006.
Pool: 25y x 42f, indoors, heated, 83°-84°.
Admission: $7.

LIBERTYVILLE   708

CENTRE CLUB 200 W. Golf
Phone: 816-6100.
Pool: 25m, indoors, heated, 82°.
Affiliate: IHRSA outside a 75 mile radius $10.

LINCOLNWOOD   708

RADISSON HOTEL LINCOLNWOOD 4500 W. Touhy Ave.
Phone: 677-1234. **Reservations:** 800-252-1227.
Pool: 20y, rectangular, indoor/outdoor, heated, 80°.
Admission: Registered guests NC.
Memberships: $300/year.

LISLE   708

CENTRAL PARK ATHLETIC CLUB 4225 Naperville Rd.
Phone: 505-7799.
Pool: 20y x 30f, 4 lanes, indoors, heated, 81°.
Affiliate: IHRSA $7.
Hotel: TraveLodge Naperville (505-0200) $4. Hilton Inn (505-0900), Hyatt (852-1234), Radisson (505-1000), Holiday Inn (505-1000), & Hampton Inn (505-1400): $9.
To find: At the intersection of Naperville and Warrenville Rds., right off the I-88 Tollway at the Naperville Rd. Exit.

LOCKPORT   815

DENICK POOL 1911 S. Lawrence Ave.
Phone: 838-4988.
Pool: 25y, 6 lanes, indoors, heated, 85°.
Admission: $5.

LOMBARD   708

BALLY'S CHICAGO HEALTH CLUB 455 E. Butterfield Rd.
Phone: 963-3600.
Pool: 25m, indoors, heated, 78°-82°.
Admission: Call.
Affiliate: Bally's NC.

MACOMB   309

YMCA OF MCDONOUGH COUNTY 400 E. Calhoun St.
Phone: 833-2129.
Pool: 25y x 33.5f, 6 lanes, indoors, heated, 83°.
Admission: $5.
Affiliate: YMCA 3 visits NC, then $2.50.
To find: Two blocks east of the train station.

MATTESON   708

BALLY'S CHICAGO HEALTH CLUB 4701 Lincoln Mall Dr.
Phone: 481-9191.
Pool: 25y, indoors, heated, 78°-80°.
Admission: Call.
Affiliate: Bally's NC.

MELROSE PARK   708

LEO MEMORIAL POOL 800 N. 17th Ave.
Phone: 865-9184.
Pool: 25m, indoors, heated, 80°.
Admission: $4.

GOTTLIEB HEALTH & FITNESS CENTER 551 W. North Ave.
Phone: 450-5790.
Pool 1: 25y, 4 lanes, indoors, heated, 78°.
Pool 2: 20y, indoors, heated, 86°.
Affiliate: IHRSA outside a 50 mile radius 2 visits per month $10 each.

BALLY'S CHICAGO HEALTH CLUB 950 W. North Ave.
Phone: 345-8700.
Pool: 25m, indoors, heated, 80°.
Admission: Call.
Affiliate: Bally's NC.

MOLINE   309

MOLINE YMCA 2040 - 53rd St.
Phone: 797-3945.
Pool: 25y, 6 lanes, indoors, heated, 84°.

Admission: $6.
Affiliate: Y AWAY NC.

MONMOUTH   309

WARREN COUNTY YMCA 700 W. Harlem Ave.
Phone: 734-3183.
Pool: 25m, indoors, heated, 86°.
Admission: $6.
Affiliate: YMCA NC.

MORTON GROVE   708

BALLY'S NORTH SHORE HEALTH CLUB 6821
Dempster St.
Phone: 967-5800.
Pool: 25m, indoors, heated, 77°-81°.
Affiliate: Bally's NC.

MOUNT PROSPECT   708

BALLY'S CHICAGO HEALTH CLUB 225 W. Rand
Rd.
Phone: 398-4500.
Pool: 24y, indoors, heated, 71°-74°.
Affiliate: Bally's NC.

RECPLEX 420 W. Dempster
Phone: 640-1000.
Pool: 25y, 8 lanes, indoors, heated, 83°-85°.
Admission: Residents $5, non-residents $7.

CHARLIE CLUB 501 Midway Dr. (Route 83, North
of Oakton)
Phone: 364-6415.
Pool: 25y, indoors, heated, 80°-84°.
Admission: $10.

NAPERVILLE   708

EDWARD HEALTH & FITNESS CENTER 775
Brom Dr.
Phone: 717-0500.
Pool: 25y x 24f, 6 lanes, indoors, heated, 79°.
Admission: $10.
To find: On the Edward Hospital Campus.

KROEHLER CENTER YMCA 34 S. Washington St.
Phone: 420-6270.
Pool: 25y, indoors, heated, 83°.
Admission: Call.
Affiliate: YMCA NC.

NILES   708

LEANING TOWER YMCA 6300 W. Touhy Ave.
Phone: 647-8222.
Pool: 25m, indoors, heated, 78°-79°.
Admission: $12.
Affiliate: YMCA NC.

NORTHBROOK   708

NORTH SUBURBAN YMCA 2705 Techny Rd.
Phone: 272-7250.
Pool: 25y x 45f, 6 lanes, indoors, heated, 83°.
Affiliate: YMCA NC.

NORTHFIELD   708

NEW TRIER WEST CENTER POOL Winnetka
Park District, 7 Happ Rd., Bldg. F
Phone: 501-2920.
Pool: 25y x 60f, 6 lanes, indoors, heated, 82°.
Admission: Residents $3.50, non-residents $5.

OAK LAWN   708

BALLY'S CHICAGO HEALTH CLUB 6700 W. 95th
St.
Phone: 430-3500.
Pool: 25y, indoors, heated, 78°-79°.
Admission: $5.
Affiliate: Bally's NC.

OAK PARK   708

BALLY'S CHICAGO HEALTH CLUB 345 Madison
St.
Phone: 386-8020.
Pool: 25m, indoors, heated, 78°-81°.
Admission: Call.
Affiliate: Bally's NC.

OAK PARK YMCA 255 S. Marion St.
Phone: 383-5200.
Pool: 25y, 4 lanes, indoors, heated, 83°.
Affiliate: YMCA NC.
To find: One mile north of I-290 and Harlem Ave.

OAKBROOK TERRACE   708

THE EXERCISE PLAYCE 1 Tower Lane
Phone: 954-0450.
Pool: 25y, 4 lanes, indoors, heated, 84°.
Admission: $12.
Hotel: Hilton Suites-Oakbrook Terrace (941-0100)
& Drake Hotel (574-5400): NC with room key.
To find: In the basement of the tall green tower
behind Oakbrook Center Shopping Mall.

OREGON   815

OREGON PARK DISTRICT POOL 5th St.
Phone: 732-3101.
Pool: 25m, 6 lanes, indoors, heated, 82°-85°.
Admission: Residents: $2.25, SC(65) $1.50. Non-
residents: $3.25, SC $2.

ORLAND PARK   708

BALLY'S CHICAGO HEALTH CLUB 14701 La
Grange Rd.

Phone: 349-0100.
Pool: 25y, indoors, heated, 72°.
Admission: Call.
Affiliate: Bally's NC.

OTTAWA   815

OTTAWA YMCA 201 E. Jackson St.
Phone: 433-2395.
Pool: 20y, 4 lanes, indoors, heated, 85°.
Admission: $4.
Affiliate: Y AWAY NC.
To find: One block east of Washington Park.

PALATINE   708

BUEHLER YMCA 1400 W. Northwest Hwy.
Phone: 359-2400.
Pool: 25y, 6 lanes, indoors, heated, 82°.
Admission: $8.
Affiliate: YMCA NC.
To find: Seven miles west of Route 53 on
Northwest Hwy.
Masters: The Buehler Breakers. Contact Mary
Koskowski or David Zielinski at 359-2400.

RAMADA WOODFIELD HOTEL 920 E. Northwest
Hwy.
Phone: 359-6900. **Reservations:** 800-221-2222.
Pool: 50f x 24f, rectangular, indoors, heated, 84°.
Admission: $5. Registered guests NC.
Memberships: $100/year.

THE HOTEL & FITNESS CENTER 1500 E.
Dundee
Phone: 934-4900.
Pool: 20y, indoors, heated, 85°.
Admission: Registered guests NC.
Notes: In mid-1994, the hotel was in the process of
changing ownership and was expected to have a
new name after this edition of *Swimmers Guide*
goes to press. The telephone number will remain
the same and the pool will still be there, so if they
answer the phone differently when you make your
reservations, don't be surprised.

FOREST GROVE ATHLETIC CLUB 1760 N. Hicks
Rd.
Phone: 991-4646.
Pool: 20y, indoors, heated, 84°.
Affiliate: IHRSA $10 per day, $25 per week.

PALOS HILLS   708

PALOS OLYMPIC HEALTH & RACQUET CLUB
11050 S. Roberts Rd.
Phone: 974-1900.
Pool: 20y, indoors, heated, 82°-83°.
Affiliate: IHRSA $5.

PARK RIDGE   708

LUTHERAN GENERAL FITNESS CENTER 1875
Dempster St., Suite G-01

Phone: 696-8714.
Pool: 20y x 60f, 4 lanes, indoors, heated, 82°.
Admission: 3 visits per year $7 each.
To find: In the Parkside Professional Building, adja-
cent to Lutheran General Hospital.

PEKIN   309

YWCA OF PEKIN 315 Buena Vista
Phone: 347-2104.
Pool: 25y x 25f, 4 lanes, indoors, heated, 84°.
Admission: $3.25.
To find: Off Broadway St., between the library and
the Post Office.

PEORIA   309

YWCA OF PEORIA 301 N.E. Jefferson St.
Phone: 674-1167.
Pool: 20y, indoors, heated, 88°.
Admission: 1 visit NC, then $2.50.

GREATER PEORIA FAMILY YMCA 714 Hamilton
Blvd.
Phone: 671-2700.
Pool: 25y x 35f, 4 lanes, indoors, heated, 82°-83°.
Affiliate: Y AWAY 12 visits per year NC. YMCA
$5.
Hotel: Père Marquette Hotel (637-6500) & Holiday
Inn (674-2500): $5 with room key.
To find: At the intersection of Glendale and
Hamilton Blvd., right off I-74. Glendale is Exit 92.

CENTRAL PARK POOL 415 W. Richmond Ave.
Phone: 686-3370*.
Pool: 25y, 8 lanes, indoors, heated, 80°.
Admission: $1.75, SC(65) $1.25.
Notes: *During the fall, winter, and spring, it's best
to call after 5PM. The pool closes from Aug. 15 to
Sep. 15.

PROPHETSTOWN   815

PROPHETSTOWN SWIMMING POOL 410 W.
Riverside Dr.
Phone: 537-2093.
Pool: 25y, indoors, heated, 85°.
Admission: $2.

QUINCY   217

QUINCY COUNTY YMCA 3101 Maine St.
Phone: 222-1400.
Pool: 25y, indoors, heated, 84°.
Admission: $5.
Affiliate: YMCA $1.

ROCHELLE   815

HOLIDAY INN ROCHELLE Hwy. 251 & Route 38
Phone: 562-5551.
Pool: 25m, indoors, heated, 83°.
Admission: $5. Registered guests NC.

ROCK ISLAND   309

YWCA OF THE QUAD CITIES 229 - 16th St.
Phone: 788-3479.
Pool: 20y x 20f, 4 lanes, indoors, heated, 88°.
Admission: $8, SC(60) $6.50.
Affiliate: YWCA $4.50, SC $3.50.
Hotel: All Quad Cities hotels 1 visit $4.50 with room key, SC $3.50.
To find: In downtown Rock Island or 'The District', one block west of the Plaza One Hotel.

ROCKFORD   815

ROCKFORD YMCA 200 'Y' Blvd.
Phone: 987-2288.
Pool 1: 25y x 42f, 6 lanes, indoors, heated, 78°-80°.
Pool 2: 25y x 30f, 3 lanes, indoors, heated, 84°-86°.
Admission: Call.
Affiliate: YMCA outside a 75 mile radius NC.
Masters: The Rockford YMCA Masters. Contact Patrick M. Burns at 987-2288.

YWCA OF ROCKFORD 220 S. Madison St.
Phone: 968-9681.
Pool: 20y, 4 lanes, indoors, heated, 88°.
Affiliate: YWCA $2.
To find: In the downtown area, two blocks south of E. State St. Parking is in the rear.

BALLY'S ROCKFORD HEALTH CLUB 3800 E. State St.
Phone: 398-8293.
Pool: 25m, indoors, heated, 76°-78°.
Admission: 1 visit per 90 days NC.
Affiliate: Bally's NC.

ROSEMONT   708

ROSEMONT'S WILLOW CREEK CLUB 10225 W. Higgins
Phone: 698-2582.
Pool: 20m x 20f, 4 lanes, indoors, heated, 82°.
Affiliate: IHRSA $5.

ROSEMONT ELEMENTARY SCHOOL POOL 6101 Ruby St.
Phone: 823-6685.
Pool: 20y, indoors, heated, 81°.
Admission: Residents $1, non-residents $2.

SAVANA   815

SAVANA HIGH SCHOOL 500 Craigmore
Phone: 273-3887.
Pool: 24y, indoors, heated, 82°.
Admission: $2.50, SC(60) $1.50.

SCHAUMBURG   708

HYATT REGENCY WOODFIELD 1800 E. Golf Rd.
Phone: 605-1234. **Reservations:** 800-233-1234.
Pool: 22y, rectangular, indoors, heated, 80°.
Admission: Registered guests only NC.
Notes: There is also a 22y, outdoor pool operated from Jun. to Sep.

YMCA TWINBROOK 300 W. Wise Rd.
Phone: 893-9622.
Pool: 25y, 6 lanes, indoors, heated, 82°.
Affiliate: YMCA Call.

SKOKIE   708

NORTH SHORE HILTON 9599 Skokie Blvd.
Phone: 679-7000. **Reservations:** 800-TRY HILT.
Pool: 20y, rectangular, indoor/outdoor, heated, 78°.
Admission: Registered guests NC.
Memberships: $400/family/year.

HOWARD JOHNSON HOTEL 9333 Skokie Blvd.
Phone: 679-4200. **Reservations:** 800-654-2000.
Pool: 51f, rectangular, indoors, heated, 82°.
Admission: Registered guests NC.
Memberships: 6/12 months $195/$295.

SPRINGFIELD   217

YWCA OF SPRINGFIELD 421 E. Jackson St.
Phone: 522-8828.
Pool: 20y, indoors, heated, 87°.
Admission: $6.

SPRINGFIELD YMCA 701 S. 4th St.
Phone: 544-9846.
Pool: 25y x 25f, 4 lanes, indoors, heated, 82°-84°.
Admission: Out-of-town visitors with picture ID $6. All SC(50) Th 10:45-11:15AM during the school year $2.
Affiliate: YMCA NC.
To find: Near the south side of the downtown area, on the corner of 4th and Cook.
Masters: The Springfield YMCA Masters. Contact Nick Merrill at 544-9846.

CLUB WEST 2811 W. Lawrence Ave.
Phone: 787-1111.
Pool: 20y x 30f, 5 lanes, indoors, heated, 82°.
Admission: $8.
Affiliate: IHRSA $5.
Hotel: Springfield Hilton (789-1530), Holiday Inn South (529-7131), & Days Inn (529-0171): NC with a pass from the hotel.

STERLING   815

DUIS CENTER 211 E. St. Mary's Rd.
Phone: 622-6200.
Pool: 25m, indoors, heated, 82°-85°.
Admission: $2.50, SC(55) $1.

VERNON HILLS — 708

BALLY'S CHICAGO HEALTH CLUB 33 Phillips Rd.
Phone: 680-3000.
Pool: 25y, indoors, heated, 79°.
Affiliate: Bally's NC.

WAUKEGAN — 708

LAKE COUNTY FAMILY YMCA 2000 Western Ave.
Phone: 360-9622.
Pool: 25m, indoors, heated, 80°.
Affiliate: Y AWAY NC.

WEST CHICAGO — 708

WEST CHICAGO PARK DISTRICT POOL 157 W. Washington St.
Phone: 231-9474.
Pool: 25y x 25m, 6 lanes, indoors, heated, 82°.
Admission: $2.50, SC $2.
To find: The pool is in a high school. Call for directions.

WHEATON — 708

WHEATON SPORTS CENTER 1000 W. Prairie Ave.
Phone: 690-0887.

Pool: 25y, 6 lanes, indoors, heated, 81°.
Affiliate: IHRSA $8.
Hotel: Holiday Inn Carol Stream (665-3000) $8.

WHEELING — 708

NEPTUNE POOL Wheeling High School, 900 S. Elmhurst Rd.
Phone: 537-2930.
Pool: 25y, indoors, heated, 80°.
Admission: $3-$4.
Notes: This pool operates during the school year. There is an outdoor swim center available in the summer, call 537-2930 for information.

WILLOWBROOK — 708

WILLOWBROOK ATHLETIC CLUB 215 W. 63rd St.
Phone: 323-3918.
Pool: 20y, indoors, heated, 78°-82°.
Affiliate: IHRSA $10.50.

WOOD DALE — 708

WYNDHAM GARDEN HOTEL-WOOD DALE 1200 N. Mittel Blvd.
Phone: 860-2900. **Reservations:** 800-WYND-HAM.
Pool: 50f, rectangular, indoors, heated, 73°.
Admission: Registered guests only NC.

HELP MAKE THE NEXT *SWIMMERS GUIDE* EVEN BETTER

To receive a free copy of the next *Swimmers Guide* tell us about pools you know of that aren't in this edition. See page 14 for details.

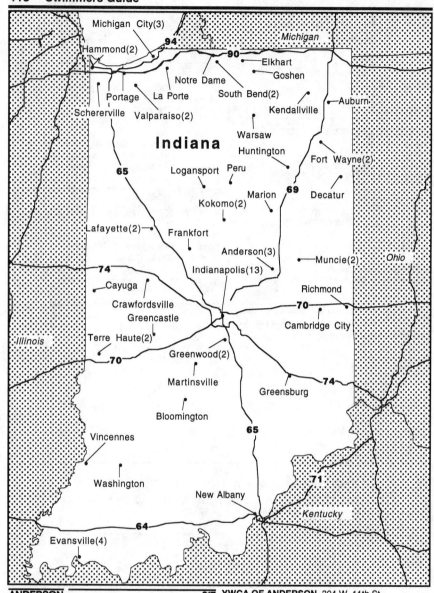

Michigan City(3)
Hammond(2)
94
Michigan
90
Elkhart
Goshen
Notre Dame
Portage La Porte South Bend(2)
Schererville Valparaiso(2) Kendallville
Auburn
65
Warsaw
Huntington
Fort Wayne(2)
Indiana
Logansport Peru
Marion
69
Decatur
Kokomo(2)
Lafayette(2)
Frankfort
74
Anderson(3)
Muncie(2)
Ohio
Cayuga
Indianapolis(13)
Crawfordsville
Richmond
Greencastle
70
Terre Haute(2)
Cambridge City
Illinois
70
Greenwood(2)
Martinsville
74
Greensburg
Bloomington
65
Vincennes
71
Washington
New Albany
Kentucky
64
Evansville(4)

ANDERSON   317

EXCEL FITNESS CENTER 2519 E. 10th St., Suite C
Phone: 649-5565.
Pool: 18m, indoors, heated, 84°.
Admission: $10.

ANDERSON YMCA 28 W. 12th St.
Phone: 644-7796.
Pool: 25y x 50f, 6 lanes, indoors, heated, 84°.
Admission: $4, SC(62) $2.
Affiliate: YMCA & U.S. Military: NC.
To find: Four blocks south of historic 8th St.

YWCA OF ANDERSON 304 W. 11th St.
Phone: 642-0211.
Pool: 20y x 25f, 5 lanes, indoors, heated, 84°.
Admission: 3 visits $2 each.

AUBURN   219

DEKALB COUNTY YMCA 310 N. Main St.
Phone: 925-4112.
Pool: 25m x 25f, 4 lanes, indoors, heated, 84°.
Admission: $5.
Affiliate: Y AWAY NC.

Hotel: Some local hotels have free pass cards. Call the Y for names of participating properties.

BLOOMINGTON   812

MONROE COUNTY YMCA 2125 S. Highland
Phone: 332-5555.
Pool: 25m x 34f, 6 lanes, indoors, heated, 82°.
Admission: $6.
Affiliate: Y AWAY NC. YMCA Call.
Hotel: Ramada Inn (332-9453) NC.

CAMBRIDGE CITY   317

GOLAY COMMUNITY CENTER 1007 E. Main St.
Phone: 478-5565.
Pool: 25m x 15m, 6 lanes, indoors, heated, 85°.
Admission: $5.
To find: At the intersection of State Route 1 and U.S. 40.

CAYUGA   317

NORTH VERMILLION HIGH SCHOOL State Rd. 63 N.
Phone: 492-3364.
Pool: 25y, 6 lanes, indoors, heated, 83°.
Admission: $1 per hour.
To find: One mile north of U.S. 234 on State Rd. 63.

CRAWFORDSVILLE   317

CRAWFORDSVILLE AQUATIC CENTER at Crawfordsville High School, 1 Athenian Dr.
Phone: 364-3247.
Pool: 50m x 25y, 8 x 14 lanes, indoors, heated, 83°.
Admission: Residents: $2.25, SC(60) $2. Nonresidents $3.25, SC $3.
Masters: The Sugar Creek Masters. Contact Aquatic Director Gus Arzner at 364-3247.

DECATUR   219

BELLMONT HIGH SCHOOL 1000 N. Adams Dr.
Phone: 724-7121.
Pool: 25y x 45f, 6 lanes, indoors, heated, 83°.
Admission: NC.
To find: Five blocks east of downtown on State Route 224 E.
Masters: The Decatur Otters Swim Club. Contact Mark Young at 724-7121 ext. 2123.

ELKHART   219

ELKHART YMCA 200 E. Jackson Blvd.
Phone: 295-6915.
Pool: 25y x 42f, 6 lanes, indoors, heated, 82°-84°.
Admission: $5.
Affiliate: YMCA NC. U.S. Military $2.
Notes: There is also a 28f x 20f, 85°-90°, shallow water, therapy pool.
To find: Two blocks east of Main St. (U.S. 33).

EVANSVILLE   812

YWCA OF EVANSVILLE 118 Vine St.
Phone: 422-1191.
Pool: 20y, indoors, heated, 86°.
Admission: $2.

YMCA OF SOUTHWESTERN INDIANA 222 N.W. 6th St.
Phone: 423-9622.
Pool: 25m x 30f, 6 lanes, indoors, heated, 85°.
Admission: Out-of-town visitors: Contact the Aquatic Director.
Affiliate: YMCA outside a 30 mile radius NC. U.S. Military NC.
To find: At the corner of 6th and Court Sts., one block east of the courthouse.
Masters: Contact Kelly Arnold at 423-9622.

UNIVERSITY OF SOUTHERN INDIANA 8600 University Blvd.
Phone: 464-1863.
Pool: 25m x 40f, 6 lanes, indoors, heated, 84°.
Admission: $2.
Memberships: $45/semester.
To find: The pool is in the PAC (Physical Activity Center) Building, which is the only building on the left side of University Blvd.

TRI-STATE ATHLETIC CLUB 555 Tennis Lane
Phone: 479-3111.
Pool: 25m x 75f, 6 lanes, indoor/outdoor, heated, 82°.
Admission: $9.
Hotel: Hampton Inn (473-5000), Holiday Inn East (473-0171), & Lee's Inn (477-6663): NC.
To find: Off Greenriver Rd. behind Darryl's Restaurant.

FORT WAYNE   219

YMCA OF GREATER FORT WAYNE - CENTRAL BRANCH 1020 Barr St.
Phone: 422-6486.
Pool: 25y x 28f, 4 lanes, indoors, heated, 84°.
Affiliate: Y AWAY NC.
Hotel: Holiday Inn Downtown Ft. Wayne (422-5511) & Ft. Wayne Hilton at the Convention Center (420-1100): Call the Y for details.
To find: Next to the Holiday Inn Downtown Ft. Wayne.

YWCA OF FORT WAYNE 2000 N. Wells St.
Phone: 424-4908.
Pool: 25y, indoors, heated, 85°.
Admission: $3.
Affiliate: YWCA $2.

FRANKFORT   317

CLINTON COUNTY YMCA 950 S. Maish Rd.
Phone: 654-9622.
Pool: 25y, indoors, heated, 82°-84°.

Admission: $5.
Affiliate: Y AWAY NC.

GOSHEN   219

GOSHEN HIGH SCHOOL 1 Redskin Rd.
Phone: 533-8651 ext. 644.
Pool: 25y x 49f, 7 lanes, indoors, heated, 82°.
Admission: $1.

GREENCASTLE   317

LILLY CENTER De Pauw University
Phone: 658-4012.
Pool: 25y x 25m, 10 lanes, indoors, heated, 80°.
Hotel: Walden Inn (653-2761) NC.

GREENSBURG   812

DECATUR COUNTY YMCA 225 N. Broadway
Phone: 663-9622.
Pool: 20y x 21f, 3 lanes, indoors, heated, 88°.
Admission: $5.
Affiliate: YMCA, YWCA, & U.S. Military on leave:
NC.
To find: Two blocks north of Courthouse Square.

GREENWOOD   317

BALLY'S SCANDINAVIAN HEALTH SPA 517
U.S. 31 S.
Phone: 885-0242.
Pool: 25m, indoors, heated, 78°-82°.
Admission: Call.
Affiliate: Bally's & IPFA: NC.
Hotel: Holiday Inn NC.

GREENWOOD HIGH SCHOOL 615 W. Smith
Valley Rd.
Phone: 889-4025.
Pool: 25y x 25m, 6 x 6 lanes, indoors, heated,
water temperature not reported.
Admission: If prior arrangements are made with
the Pool Director NC.
To find: Fifteen miles from downtown Indianapolis,
three miles from I-65.

HAMMOND   219

YWCA OF CALUMET AREA 250 Ogden St.
Phone: 931-2922.
Pool: 25y x 28f, indoors, heated, 88°-89°.
Admission: $4.

HAMMOND AREA YMCA 7322 Southeastern Ave.
Phone: 845-1507.
Pool: 25y, indoors, heated, 83°.
Admission: $4.
Affiliate: YMCA NC.

HUNTINGTON   219

HUNTINGTON YMCA 607 Warren St.

Phone: 356-4200.
Pool: 20y, indoors, heated, 87°.
Affiliate: YMCA NC.

INDIANAPOLIS   317

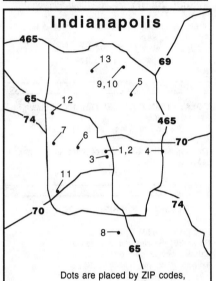

Dots are placed by ZIP codes,
not by street addresses.

**1. YMCA OF GREATER INDIANAPOLIS - FALL
CREEK PARKWAY BRANCH** 860 W. 10th St.
Phone: 634-2478.
Pool: 20y x 36f, 4 lanes, indoors, heated, 86°.
Admission: $6.
Affiliate: YMCA NC.

2. I. U. NATATORIUM / IUPUI SPORTS COMPLEX
IUPUI - 901 W. New York
Phone: 274-3518.
Pool: 50m x 25y, 8 x 16 lanes, indoors, heated,
79°.
Admission: $3.
Hotel: All local hotels $2 with room key.

3. INDIANAPOLIS ATHLETIC CLUB 350 N.
Meridian
Phone: 634-4331.
Pool: 25y, 5 lanes, indoors, heated, 82°.
Memberships: I/S $600 + $79/month base dues +
$16/month for unlimited athletic use.
Notes: This is an 'Executive Athletic Club' with din-
ing rooms, a pub, and reciprocity with 70 similarly
prestigious clubs worldwide.

4. RANSBURG YMCA 501 N. Shortridge Rd.
Phone: 357-8441.
Pool: 20y x 30f, 4 lanes, indoors, heated, 84°.
Admission: $6.
Affiliate: YMCA NC.

Hotel: Signature Inn (353-6966) $5 with room key.
Notes: There is also a 50m x 20m, 8 lane, heated, outdoor pool operated from Memorial day to Labor Day.
To find: On the east side of Indianapolis.

5. LIVRITE FITNESS CENTER 6220 N. Butler Ave.
Phone: 257-1004.
Pool: 25y, 5 lanes, indoors, heated, 84°.
Admission: $10.

6. THATCHER POOL 4649 W. Vermont
Phone: 484-3270.
Pool: 25y, indoors, heated, water temperature not reported.
Admission: $2.25.

7. SUPER SPA FITNESS CENTER 6020 Crawfordsville Rd.
Phone: 247-9100.
Pool: 80f, indoors, heated, 78°-80°.
Admission: Call.
Affiliate: IPFA NC.

8. ARTHUR BAXTER BRANCH YMCA 7900 S. Shelby St.
Phone: 881-9347.
Pool: 25y, 4 lanes, indoors, heated, 86°.
Affiliate: YMCA 3 visits NC, then $5.

9. A. JORDAN YMCA 8400 Westfield Blvd.
Phone: 253-3206.
Pool: 25y x 40f, 5 lanes, indoors, heated, 84°-85°.
Admission: $6.
Affiliate: YMCA NC.
Notes: There is also a 50m x 50f, 6 lane, outdoor, heated, 76°-78°, summer pool.
To find: On the north side of Indianapolis. Keystone Exit off I-465, west on 86th St. to Nora, left on Westfield Blvd.
Masters: The Jordan Y Masters. Contact Mel Goldstein at 253-8289.

10. BALLY'S SCANDINAVIAN HEALTH SPA 8831 Keystone Crossing
Phone: 844-1515.
Pool: 25m, indoors, heated, 78°-82°.
Affiliate: Bally's & IPFA: NC.
Hotel: Radisson Hotel (846-2700) — Call Bally's for information.

11. KRANNERT POOL 605 S. High School Rd.
Phone: Pool: 484-5200. Center: 484-3250.
Pool: 25y, indoors, heated, 80°.
Admission: $3.
Notes: There is a 25m, outdoor, summer pool. When the outdoor pool is open, the indoor pool is closed.

12. BALLY'S SCANDINAVIAN HEALTH SPA 5435 Pike Plaza Rd.
Phone: 293-9436.
Pool: 25m, indoors, heated, 78°-82°.

Admission: Call.
Affiliate: Bally's & IPFA: NC.

13. JEWISH COMMUNITY CENTER 6701 Hoover Rd.
Phone: 251-9467.
Pool: 25y, 6 lanes, indoors, heated, 84°.
Affiliate: JCC Call.
Notes: There is also an 'Olympic Size', outdoor, summer pool.

KENDALLVILLE   219

COLE CENTER FAMILY YMCA 700 S. Garden St.
Phone: 347-4200.
Pool: 25y x 45f, 6 lanes, indoors, heated, 83°.
Admission: $5.
Affiliate: YMCA NC. USMS & USS: 1 visit NC.
Hotel: Days Inn (347-5263) 1 visit NC.
To find: At the corner of Lisle and Garden Sts., across from East Noble High School. Take Lisle St. east from S. Main St.

COLE CENTER YMCA MASTERS at the Cole Center Family YMCA
Masters: Contact Coach Cindy Miller at 347-4200.
Affiliate: YMCA 1 month $5 per workout.
Notes: Coached workouts: Tu,Th: 8-9PM.

KOKOMO   317

KOKOMO YMCA 200 N. Union St.
Phone: 457-4447.
Pool: 25y, indoors, heated, 82°.
Admission: $6.
Affiliate: YMCA NC.

YWCA OF KOKOMO 406 E. Sycamore St.
Phone: 457-3293.
Pool: 25y x 25f, 4 lanes, indoors, heated, 85°.
Admission: $2.
Affiliate: YWCA $1.

LA PORTE   219

LA PORTE FAMILY YMCA 901 Michigan Ave.
Phone: 325-9622.
Pool: 25y, 6 lanes, indoors, heated, 84°.
Admission: $4.
Affiliate: YMCA & U.S. Military: NC.

LAFAYETTE   317

YWCA OF GREATER LAFAYETTE 605 N. 6th St.
Phone: 742-0075.
Pool: 25y x 42f, 6 lanes, indoors, heated, 83°.
Admission: $3.
Affiliate: YWCA $1.75.
To find: Near downtown, one block south of Union St., five minutes from Purdue University.

LAFAYETTE FAMILY YMCA 1950 S. 18th St.
Phone: 474-3448.

Pool: 25y x 45f, 6 lanes, indoors, heated, 83°.
Admission: $5.
Affiliate: Y AWAY NC.
To find: Across from Jefferson High School and next to the Tippecanoe County Fairgrounds.

LOGANSPORT   219

CASS COUNTY FAMILY YMCA 905 E. Broadway
Phone: 753-5141.
Pool: 25y, 4 lanes, indoors, heated, 82°.
Admission: $4.
Affiliate: Y AWAY NC. YMCA 3 visits NC.
Hotel: Holiday Inn Logansport (753-6351) NC.

MARION   317

GRANT COUNTY YMCA 418 W. 3rd
Phone: 664-0544.
Pool: 25y, 4 lanes, indoors, heated, 84°.
Admission: $2.
Affiliate: YMCA NC.

MARTINSVILLE   317

BARBARA B. JORDAN YMCA 2039 E. Morgan St.
Phone: 342-6688.
Pool: 25y x 25f, 4 lanes, indoors, heated, 87°.
Admission: 1 visit NC, 2nd and 3rd visits $6 each.
Affiliate: YMCA NC.

MICHIGAN CITY   219

ROGERS HIGH SCHOOL 8466 Palts Rd.
Phone: 874-2335.
Pool: 25y x 36f, 6 lanes, indoors, heated, 81°.
Admission: $1.50.

HOLIDAY INN OF MICHIGAN CITY 5820 S.
Franklin St.
Phone: 879-0311. **Reservations:** 800-HOLIDAY.
Pool: 50f, rectangular, indoors, heated, 83°.
Admission: Registered guests only NC.

MICHIGAN CITY FAMILY YMCA 1001 E.
Coolspring Ave.
Phone: 872-9622.
Pool: 25y, 6 lanes, indoors, heated, 83°.
Admission: Basic $5. Fitness Center $7.
Affiliate: Y AWAY outside a 30 mile radius NC.
To find: Off Hwy. 421 turn east onto Coolspring Ave. at the Park-N-Shop. Off Hwy. 20 turn north onto Woodland at Eagle Grocery to the light and left onto Coolspring.

MUNCIE   317

YWCA OF MUNCIE 310 E. Charles St.
Phone: 284-3345.
Pool: 20y, 4 lanes, indoors, heated, 84°.
Affiliate: YWCA $2.

MUNCIE FAMILY YMCA 500 S. Mulberry
Phone: 288-4448.
Pool: 25y x 36f, 6 lanes, indoors, heated, 83°-85°.
Admission: $8.75.
Affiliate: YMCA outside a 30 mile radius NC.
USMS & U.S. Military: NC.
Hotel: Hotel Roberts (741-7777), Signature Inn (284-4200), & Lee Inn (282-7557): $3.25 with a voucher from the hotel.
To find: Two blocks east of Hotel Roberts.
Masters: The Muncie YMCA Masters. Contact Tony Santino at 741-5541.

NEW ALBANY   812

HOLIDAY INN LOUISVILLE N.W. AT NEW ALBANY 411 W. Spring St.
Phone: 945-2771.
Pool: 50f, rectangular, indoors, heated, 92°.
Admission: Registered guests only NC.

NOTRE DAME   219

ROLFS AQUATIC CENTER University of Notre Dame, Joyce Athletic Convocation Center across from Gate 5
Phone: 631-5980.
Pool: 50m x 25y, 8 x 18 lanes, indoors, heated, 81°.
Hotel: Morris Inn on Notre Dame Campus (234-0141) $2.
To find: Across from the Notre Dame Football Stadium.

PERU   317

MIAMI COUNTY YMCA 34 E. 6th St.
Phone: 472-1979.
Pool: 20m x 25f, 4 lanes, indoors, heated, 85°.
Admission: $2.
Affiliate: YMCA outside a 50 mile radius NC.

PORTAGE   219

PORTAGE YMCA at Portage High School West, 6240 U.S. Hwy. 6
Phone: 762-2012.
Pool: 25y x 36f, 6 lanes, indoors, heated, 80°.
Admission: $2.
Affiliate: Y AWAY NC.

RICHMOND   317

RICHMOND YMCA 50 N. 8th St.
Phone: 962-7504.
Pool: 25y, indoors, heated, 84°.
Admission: $3.
Affiliate: YMCA 6 visits NC.

SCHERERVILLE   219

OMNI 41 SPORTS & FITNESS CENTER 221 U.S.
Hwy. 41

Phone: 865-6969.
Pool: 20y, indoors, heated, 83°-85°.
Admission: $15.
Affiliate: IHRSA $5.

SOUTH BEND   219

YMCA OF MICHIANA 1201 Northside Blvd.
Phone: 287-9622.
Pool: 25y x 30f, 3-4 lanes, indoors, heated, 82°.
Admission: $5.
Affiliate: Y AWAY, USMS, & U.S. Military: NC.

MICHIANA YMCA MASTERS at the YMCA of
Michiana
Masters: Contact Jim Milliken at 287-9622.
Affiliate: YMCA NC, includes pool fees.
Notes: Uncoached workouts: Tu,Th: 8:30-10PM.

HEALTH & LIFESTYLE CENTER 401 E. Colfax
Phone: 233-7877.
Pool: 25m, 2 lanes, indoors, heated, 82°.
Hotel: All local hotels $6 with room key.
To find: Across the street from the Wharf
Restaurant, on the East Race, in the Commerce
Center Building.

TERRE HAUTE   812

YWCA OF TERRE HAUTE 951 Dresser Dr.
Phone: 232-3358.
Pool: 25y x 35f, 5 lanes, indoors, heated, 84°.
Admission: $5.
Affiliate: YWCA $4.
To find: Two blocks south and one block east of
Larry Bird's Boston Connection.

TERRE HAUTE FAMILY YMCA 200 S. 6th St.
Phone: 232-2361.
Pool: 25y x 25f, 4 lanes, indoors, heated, 84°.
Admission: $6.
Affiliate: YMCA 3 visits NC.
Hotel: Larry Bird's Boston Connection (235-3333) &
Signature Inn (238-1461): NC with a pass from the
hotel.
To find: At the intersection of 6th and Walnut Sts.,
two blocks south of Wabash Ave. and three blocks
east of U.S. 41.

VALPARAISO   219

VALPARAISO YMCA 55 Chicago St.
Phone: 462-4185.
Pool 1: 20y, 4 lanes, indoors, heated, 85°.
Pool 2: 25m, indoors, heated, water temperature
not reported.
Admission: $6.
Affiliate: YMCA 4 visits per month NC.
Masters: Contact Aquatics Director Michelle Dierks
at 462-4185 ext. 25.

VALPARAISO HIGH SCHOOL 2727 Campbell St.
Phone: 531-3080.
Pool: 25y x 25m, 6 x 6 lanes, 'L' shape, indoors,
heated, 78°-80°.
Affiliate: Residents $1.

VINCENNES   812

VINCENNES YMCA 2010 College Ave.
Phone: 882-3828.
Pool: 25m, 6 lanes, indoors, heated, 86°.
Admission: $6.
Affiliate: YMCA NC.
Hotel: Executive Inn (886-5000) NC with a pass
from the hotel.
Masters: A Masters group is in formation. Contact
Sandy Bohmeier at 882-3828.

WARSAW   219

KOSCIUSKO COMMUNITY YMCA 1401 E. Smith
St.
Phone: 269-9622.
Pool: 25y x 18f, 4 lanes, indoors, heated, 84°-86°.
Admission: $8.
Affiliate: YMCA NC.
To find: Across the street from the Fairgrounds.
Masters: The Warsaw YMCA Masters. Contact
Aquatics Director Pat Burkey at 269-9622.

WASHINGTON   812

DAVIESS COUNTY FAMILY YMCA 405 N.E. 3rd
St.
Phone: 254-9622.
Pool: 25m, 6 lanes, indoors, heated, 82°.
Admission: $4.
Affiliate: Y AWAY NC.
To find: Two blocks north of the Daviess County
Courthouse.

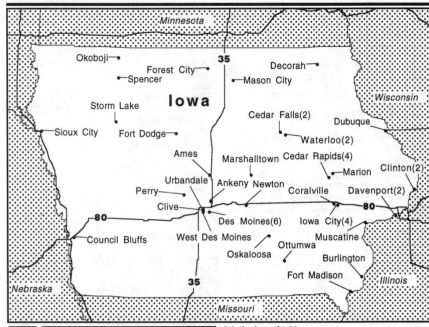

AMES   515

AMES MUNICIPAL POOL 20th & Ridgewood
Phone: 232-4561.
Pool: 25m, indoors, heated, 80°.
Admission: $2.

ANKENY   515

ANKENY FAMILY YMCA 1102 N. Ankeny Blvd.
Phone: 965-8800.
Pool: 25m, 8 lanes, indoors, heated, 88°-90°.
Admission: $10.
Affiliate: YMCA Call.

BURLINGTON   319

YM / YWCA OF BURLINGTON 2410 Mt. Pleasant
St.
Phone: 753-6734.
Pool: 25y, indoors, heated, 83°.
Admission: $5.50.
Affiliate: YMCA & YWCA: NC.

CEDAR FALLS   319

PEET JUNIOR HIGH SCHOOL 525 E. Seerley
Blvd.
Phone: 273-8636.
Pool: 25y x 45f, 6 lanes, indoors, heated, 81°-84°.
Admission: $1.50.

HOLMES JUNIOR HIGH SCHOOL 505 Holmes Dr.
Phone: 273-8636.
Pool: 25y x 45f, 6 lanes, indoors, heated, 85°.

Admission: $1.50.
Notes: There is also a 105° therapy pool.

CEDAR RAPIDS   319

CENTRAL YMCA 500 1st Ave. N.E.
Phone: 366-6421.
Pool: 25y x 36f, 6 lanes, indoors, heated, 84°.
Admission: $5.25.
Affiliate: YMCA & U.S. Military: $2.75.
Hotel: Five Seasons Hotel (363-8161) $2.75.
To find: Near downtown, two blocks east of the
Five Seasons Hotel and Civic Center.

BENDER POOL 940 - 14th Ave. S.E.
Phone: 398-5103.
Pool: 25y, indoors, heated, 86°.
Admission: Lap swimming $1.50.

NEW LIFE FITNESS WORLD 3950 Wilson Ave.
Phone: 396-1000.
Pool: 20y, indoors, heated, 82°.
Admission: $10.

COE COLLEGE NATATORIUM 1220 - 1st Ave.
N.E
Phone: 399-8659.
Pool: 25y x 60f, 8 lanes, indoors, heated, 81.5°.
Affiliate: USMS Call.
Memberships: $150/year, SC(55) $50.
Notes: The pool closes for the month of Aug.
To find: At the far north end of campus, across
from the tennis courts.

CLINTON   319

CLINTON FAMILY YMCA 300 - 5th Ave. S.
Phone: 243-1364.
Pool 1: 25y, 4 lanes, indoors, heated, 80°.
Pool 2: 20y, 4 lanes, indoors, heated, 88°.
Admission: $5.
Affiliate: Y AWAY 3 visits per month NC. Visiting U.S. Military NC.
Hotel: All local hotels $2.50.

GATEWAY YWCA 317 - 7th Ave. S.
Phone: 242-2110.
Pool: 25y, indoors, heated, 86°-88°.
Admission: $3.

CLIVE   515

SEVEN FLAGS FITNESS & RACQUET CLUB
2100 - 100th St.
Phone: 278-8888.
Pool: 25m, indoors, heated, 83°.
Admission: $10.50.
Hotel: Several local hotels. Call the club for details.
Notes: There is also a 25m, outdoor, summer pool.

CORALVILLE   319

CORALVILLE RECREATION CENTER 1506 - 8th St.
Phone: 354-3006.
Pool: 25y, 8 lanes, indoors, heated, 82°-84°.
Admission: $1.50.

COUNCIL BLUFFS   712

COUNCIL BLUFFS YMCA / CITY POOL 7 - 4th St.
Phone: 322-6606.
Pool: 25m, 6 lanes, indoors, heated, 85°.
Admission: $2.75.
Affiliate: Y AWAY NC.
To find: One half block south of Broadway.

DAVENPORT   319

SCOTT COUNTY FAMILY YMCA 606 W. 2nd St.
Phone: 322-7171.
Pool: 25y x 25f, 3 lanes, indoors, heated, 83°.
Admission: Basic $8. Fitness Center $13.
Affiliate: YMCA Call.
Hotel: Black Hawk Hotel (328-6000): Basic $5. Fitness Center $10.
To find: One block north of the baseball stadium.
Masters: The Quad Cities Masters Club. Contact Aquatic Director Bridget Cullen at 322-7171.

RAMADA INN 6263 N. Brady
Phone: 386-1940. **Reservations:** 800-2RAMADA.
Pool: 20y, oval or kidney shape, indoors, heated, 82°-84°.
Admission: Registered guests NC.
Memberships: 6 months $100.

DECORAH   319

REGENTS SWIMMING POOL Luther College, 700 College Dr.
Phone: 387-1575 or 387-1578.
Pool: 25y x 42f, 6 lanes, indoors, heated, 80°.
Admission: $2.
Memberships: $7.50/year.

DES MOINES   515

RIVERFRONT YMCA 101 Locust St.
Phone: 288-0131.
Pool: 25y x 25f, 4 lanes, indoors, heated, 82°.
Admission: $9.
Affiliate: YMCA Call.
Hotel: Embassy Suites-On the River (244-1700) $4.50.
To find: One block east of the Civic Center, four blocks east of the Convention Center.

YWCA OF GREATER DES MOINES 717 Grand Ave.
Phone: 244-8961.
Pool: 25y x 42f, 6 lanes, indoors, heated, 83°.
Admission: $7, SC(60) $3.50.
Hotel: Des Moines Marriott (245-5500) & Savery Hotel (244-2151): $3.50.
To find: At the intersection of 8th and Grand Ave., next to 801 Grand, the largest building in Des Moines.

YWCA MASTERS at the YWCA of Greater Des Moines
Masters: Contact Della Tapscott at 244-8961(w).
Non-member participation: $3.50, includes pool fees.
Notes: Uncoached workouts: M-F: 6-7AM*, 11:30AM-12:30PM. *Sometimes coached.

WALNUT CREEK FAMILY YMCA 948 - 73rd St.
Phone: 224-1888.
Pool: 25y, 6 lanes, indoors, heated, 83°.
Admission: $8.
Affiliate: Y AWAY NC.
To find: Just north of the 8th St. Exit off I-235, across the street from Wal-Mart.

BEST WESTERN BAVARIAN INN 5220 N.E. 14th St.
Phone: 265-5611. **Reservations:** 800-383-7378.
Pool: 20y, oval or kidney shape, indoors, heated, 82°.
Admission: Registered guests only NC.

RODEWAY INN 4995 Merle Hay Rd.
Phone: 278-2381. **Reservations:** 800-237-7633.
Pool: 20y, rectangular, indoors, heated, 84°.
Admission: $2. Registered guests NC.
Memberships: 3 months $35.
Notes: There is also a 20y, outdoor, unheated, summer pool.

DES MOINES　　　　　　CONTINUED

OAKMOOR RACQUETBALL - HEALTH CENTER
4731 Merle Hay Rd.
Phone: 270-2222.
Pool: 20y, indoors, heated, 84°-86°.
Admission: $10.

DUBUQUE　　　　　　　　319

YM / YWCA OF DUBUQUE 35 N. Booth St.
Phone: 556-3371.
Pool: 25y x 37f, indoors, heated, water temperature not reported.
Admission: $10.
Affiliate: YMCA & YWCA: NC.

FOREST CITY　　　　　　　515

FOREST CITY YMCA 916 W. 'I' St.
Phone: 582-5220.
Pool: 25y, indoors, heated, 83°.
Admission: $5.
Affiliate: YMCA NC.

FORT DODGE　　　　　　　515

FORT DODGE YMCA 1422 - 1st Ave. S.
Phone: 573-7107.
Pool: 25y, indoors, heated, 83°-84°.
Admission: $6.
Affiliate: Y AWAY NC.

FORT MADISON　　　　　　319

FORT MADISON FAMILY YMCA 220 - 26th St.
Phone: 372-2403.
Pool: 25y x 25f, 5 lanes, indoors, heated, 83°.
Admission: $4.
Affiliate: YMCA 3 visits per month NC, then $2.
To find: Near Aquinas High School, take Hwy. 61 to 26th St.

IOWA CITY　　　　　　　　319

NEW LIFE FITNESS WORLD 2220 Mormon Track
Phone: 351-1000.
Pool: 21m, indoors, heated, 81°.
Admission: $5.

ROBERT A. LEE COMMUNITY RECREATION CENTER 220 S. Gilbert St.
Phone: 356-5100.
Pool: 25y, indoors, heated, 83°.
Admission: $1.50.

MERCER PARK AQUATIC CENTER 2701
Bradford Dr.
Phone: 356-5109.
Pool: 25y x 20y, 4 x 8 lanes, indoors, heated, 82°.
Admission: $1.50.
To find: From Hwy. 6 E. exit 1st Ave. to Bradford Dr.

UNIVERSITY OF IOWA SWIMMING POOL Field House, University of Iowa
Phone: 335-9293.
Pool: 50m x 25y, 8 lanes, indoors, heated, water temperature not reported.
Admission: $1.

MARION　　　　　　　　　319

MARION YMCA 3100 - 10th Ave.
Phone: 377-7361.
Pool: 25y, 6 lanes, indoors, heated, 82°-84°.
Admission: $5.
Affiliate: YMCA NC.
To find: Seventh Ave. to 31st St., on the east edge of Marion.

MARSHALLTOWN　　　　　515

MARSHALLTOWN YMCA 705 S. Center St.
Phone: 752-9622.
Pool: 25m, indoors, heated, 84°.
Admission: $5.
Affiliate: YMCA NC.

MASON CITY　　　　　　　515

MASON CITY FAMILY YMCA 15 N. Pennsylvania
Phone: 423-5526.
Pool: 20y x 20f, 6 lanes, indoors, heated, 84°.
Admission: $5.
Affiliate: YMCA 4 visits per month NC. U.S. Military $3.
To find: Two blocks north of the Mason City Library. One block east of the Liberty Bank & Trust.

MUSCATINE　　　　　　　319

MUSCATINE FAMILY YMCA & YWCA 1823
Logan St.
Phone: 263-9996.
Pool: 25y x 45f, 6 lanes, indoors, heated, 81°.
Admission: $8.
Affiliate: YMCA & YWCA: 3 visits per month NC.
To find: At the intersection of Cedar and Logan Sts. Enter Cedar St. off the Hwy. 61 By-pass.

NEWTON　　　　　　　　　515

NEWTON YMCA 1701 S. 8th Ave. E.
Phone: 792-4006.
Pool: 25m, indoors, heated, 84°-85°.
Admission: $5.
Affiliate: YMCA NC.

OKOBOJI　　　　　　　　　712

THE ATHLETIC CLUB AT VILLAGE EAST at the Village Resort, Hwy. 71 N.
Phone: Club: 332-7173. Hotel: 337-3223.
Reservations: 800-727-4561.
Pool: 25y x 22f, indoors, heated, 82°.

Admission: $7. Registered guests NC.
Memberships: Call.

OSKALOOSA `515`

MAHASKA COMMUNITY CENTER YMCA 414 N. 3rd St.
Phone: 673-8411.
Pool: 25y, indoors, heated, 84°.
Admission: $6, SC(60) $4.
Affiliate: YMCA NC.

OTTUMWA `515`

YWCA OF OTTUMWA 133 W. 2nd St.
Phone: 682-5473.
Pool: 25y, indoors, heated, 86°-89°.
Admission: $3.25.

PERRY `515`

MCCREARY COMMUNITY BUILDING 1800 Patee St.
Phone: 465-5621.
Pool: 25m, indoors, heated, 82°.
Admission: Residents $3.25, non-residents $3.75.

SIOUX CITY `712`

SIOUXLAND Y 722 Nebraska St.
Phone: 252-3276.
Pool: 25y x 25f, 4 lanes, indoors, heated, 83°-84°.
Admission: $5.
Affiliate: Y AWAY & YWCA: NC.

SPENCER `712`

SPENCER FAMILY YMCA 1001 - 11th Ave. W.
Phone: 262-3782.
Pool: 25y x 25f, 4 lanes, indoors, heated, 87°.
Admission: $5.
Affiliate: YMCA NC.
To find: At the southwest corner of 11th Ave. W. and 11th St. N.

STORM LAKE `712`

FINKBINE NATATORIUM Buena Vista College
Phone: 749-2256.
Pool: 25y, 6 lanes, indoors, heated, 80°.
Admission: $1.
Memberships: $15/month. $100/academic year.
To find: Across the street from the football stadium.

URBANDALE `515`

URBANDALE POOL 7201 Aurora Ave.
Phone: 278-3959.
Pool: 31.77y, indoors, heated, 82°-84°.
Admission: $1.50, SC(65) 65¢.

WATERLOO `319`

BLACK HAWK COUNTY FAMILY YMCA 669 S. Hackett Rd.
Phone: 233-3531.
Pool: 25y x 50f, 6 lanes, indoors, heated, 85°.
Admission: $8.
Affiliate: YMCA NC.
Hotel: Holiday Inn Civic Center (233-7560) & Excel Inn (235-2165): $2.

YWCA OF BLACK HAWK COUNTY 425 Lafayette St.
Phone: 234-7589.
Pool: 20y x 20f, 4 lanes, indoors, heated, 80°.
Admission: $2.50.
Affiliate: YWCA Call.

WEST DES MOINES `515`

FITNESS WORLD WEST 3200 Westown Pkwy.
Phone: 223-5111.
Pool: 22y, indoors, heated, 90°.
Admission: 3 visits per year $10 each.
Affiliate: IHRSA $5.

ALWAYS CALL FIRST

Pools close, they change names, affiliations, admission policies, and rates. And just because a pool is listed in *Swimmers Guide* doesn't mean it's open all day, every day, for just the type of workout you want to do. Spend a quarter to save time and aggravation. . . always call first!

ARKANSAS CITY   316

ARKANSAS CITY HIGH SCHOOL POOL
Phone: 441-2018.
Pool: 25y, indoors, heated, 86°.
Admission: $1.75.

ATCHISON   913

ATCHISON YMCA 321 Commercial St.
Phone: 367-4948.
Pool: 25m, indoors, heated, 86°.
Admission: $2.50.
Affiliate: YMCA NC.

BURLINGTON   316

U.S.D. 244 RECREATION CENTER 1110 Shea
Phone: 364-8484.
Pool: 25y, indoors, heated, 84°.
Admission: Residents NC, non-residents $2.

DERBY   316

DERBY RECREATION CENTER 801 E. Market
Phone: 788-3781.
Pool 1: 25y x 45f, indoors, heated, 82°-84°.
Pool 2: 25y x 30f, indoors, heated, 82°-84°.
Admission: $5, SC(60) $4.50.
Masters: Contact Jack Belsche at 788-3781.

EMPORIA   316

RECREATION COMPLEX Emporia State
University, 1200 Commercial
Phone: 343-5668.
Pool: 25y, indoors, heated, water temperature not
reported.
Memberships: $45/semester. $85/year.

THE EMPORIA RECREATION CENTER 313 W.
4th
Phone: 342-5582.
Pool: 25y, indoors, heated, 88°.
Admission: Lap swimming 75¢. Aquacize $2.
Arthritis Exercise Class $1.25. Senior Exercise
Class 75¢.

KANSAS CITY   913

CENTRAL YMCA 900 N. 8th St.
Phone: 371-4400.
Pool: 20y x 20f, 3 lanes, indoors, heated, 85°-87°.
Affiliate: YMCA NC.

LAWRENCE   913

ROBINSON CENTER University of Kansas
Phone: 864-3385.
Pool 1: 25y, indoors, heated, 82°.
Pool 2: 25m, indoors, heated, 85°.
Memberships: $20/semester*.
Notes: *Access limited to M-F: 6-8AM.

LAWRENCE HIGH SCHOOL POOL 1901
Louisiana
Phone: 841-2091.
Pool: 25y, 6 lanes, indoors, heated, 80°-83°.
Admission: $1.50.

LEAVENWORTH   913

RIVERFRONT COMMUNITY CENTER 123 S.
Esplanade
Phone: 651-2203 ext. 27.
Pool: 25y x 45f, 6 lanes, indoors, heated, 83°.
Admission: $1.50, SC(55) $1.
To find: Where Delaware (a one-way street) ends
at Esplanade.

LIBERAL   316

SEWARD COUNTY COMMUNITY COLLEGE 1801
N. Kansas
Phone: 624-1951.
Pool: 25y, indoors, heated, 84°-86°.
Admission: $2.

MCPHERSON   316

MCPHERSON FAMILY YMCA 220 N. Walnut St.
Phone: 241-0363.
Pool: 25y x 28f, 4 lanes, indoors, heated, 85°.
Admission: $3.
Affiliate: YMCA NC.
Notes: The pool closes in August for maintenance.
To find: One block north of the Courthouse.

NEWTON   316

RECREATION CENTER POOL 415 N. Poplar
Phone: 283-7330.
Pool: 20y x 30f, indoors, heated, 86°-87°.
Admission: $1.

OVERLAND PARK   913

**HEALTHPLUS FITNESS & REHABILITATION
CENTER** 4500 W. 107th St.
Phone: 649-7433.
Pool: 25m, indoors, heated, 85°.
Admission: $10.

BALLY'S HEALTH & RACQUET 6700 W. 110th
St.
Phone: 491-0200.
Pool: 25m, indoors, heated, 79°.
Affiliate: Bally's NC.
Hotel: Drury Inn (345-1500) NC.

THE ATHLETIC CLUB OF OVERLAND PARK
10440 Marty St.
Phone: 383-9060.
Pool: 25m, 4 double lanes, indoors, heated, 80°.
Admission: $10.
Hotel: Hampton Inn (341-1551) & Holiday Inn
Express (648-7858): Purchase passes at the
hotel.
To find: One block west of Metcalf at 104th, in front
of the car wash.

OVERLAND PARK YMCA 9557 Santa Fe
Phone: 642-6800.
Pool: 25y, indoors, heated, 84°.
Admission: $10.
Affiliate: YMCA NC.

DALES ATHLETIC CLUB 11301 W. 88th St.
Phone: 888-9247.
Pool: 25y, indoors, heated, 83°-85°.
Admission: $8.
Affiliate: IHRSA $6.

PITTSBURG   316

PITTSBURG FAMILY YMCA 1100 N. Miles
Phone: 231-1100.
Pool: 25y, 6 lanes, indoors, heated, 87°.
Admission: $3.
Affiliate: YMCA NC.

PRAIRIE VILLAGE   913

JOHNSON COUNTY YMCA 4200 W. 79th St.
Phone: 642-6800.
Pool: 25y x 45f, 5 lanes, indoors, heated, 84°-86°.
Admission: $10.
Affiliate: Y AWAY NC.
To find: From I-35, take the 75th St. Exit east to
Roe Ave., turn right onto 79th St. and go one block.

SALINA   913

SALINA FAMILY YMCA 570 YMCA Dr.
Phone: 825-2151.
Pool: 25m, 6 lanes, indoors, heated, 83°.
Admission: $6.
Affiliate: YMCA NC.
To find: YMCA Dr. intersects with Westchester.

YWCA OF SALINA 651 E. Prescott
Phone: 825-4626.
Pool: 25y, indoors, heated, 88°.
Admission: 1 visit NC, then $3.

TOPEKA   913

DOWNTOWN TOPEKA YMCA 421 Van Buren
Phone: 354-8591.
Pool: 25y x 42f, 6 lanes, indoors, heated, 85°.
Admission: $10.
Affiliate: YMCA 1 visit per week NC.
Hotel: Ramada Inn Downtown (234-5400), Holiday
Inn Topeka West (272-8040), & Senate Suites
(233-5050): $5 with room key.
To find: One and a half blocks east of Topeka Blvd.
and six blocks west of the Ramada Inn Downtown.

TOPEKA YWCA 225 W. 12th St.
Phone: 233-1750.
Pool: 25y x 30f, 5 lanes, indoors, heated, 82°.
Admission: 1 visit $3.75, SC (65) $2.70.
Affiliate: YWCA $2.40, SC $1.90.
Notes: The pool closes for cleaning the last week
of Aug.
To find: At 12th and Van Buren, a couple of blocks
from the Capitol Building. Use the south entrance.
Masters: The Topeka Masters Swim Association.
Contact Fitness Director Linda Weaver at 233-
1750.

ULYSSES   316

GRANT COUNTY AQUATICS FACILITY 204 E.
Wheat
Phone: 356-4244.
Pool: 25m x 25y, 6 lanes, indoors, heated, 86°.

Admission: $1.50, SC(55) $1.25.
Notes: There is also a 25m, 8 lane, outdoor, summer pool.

WICHITA   316

CENTRAL BRANCH YMCA 402 N. Market St.
Phone: 264-9374.
Pool: 25y x 40f, 4 lanes, indoors, heated, 83°.
Admission: $7.
Affiliate: Out-of-town YMCA NC.
To find: Just off Kellogg and directly across from the courthouse.

WICHITA SWIM CLUB 8323 E. Douglas
Phone: 683-1491.
Pool: 50m x 25y, 8 x 18 lanes, indoors, heated, 81°.

Memberships: $15/half-month.
To find: Three blocks east of Town East Mall and behind the Independent School.
Masters: The Wichita Swim Club Masters. Contact Rob Snowberger at 683-1491.

WICHITA RACQUET CLUB 1551 N. Rock Rd.
Phone: 634-0094.
Pool: 25m, indoors, heated, 84°.
Admission: $10.

WEST - WICHITA YMCA 6940 Newell
Phone: 942-2271.
Pool: 25m x 42f, 6 lanes, indoors, heated, 84°-85°.
Admission: $6.
Affiliate: YMCA NC.

HELP MAKE THE NEXT *SWIMMERS GUIDE* EVEN BETTER

To receive a free copy of the next *Swimmers Guide* tell us about pools you know of that aren't in this edition. See page 14 for details.

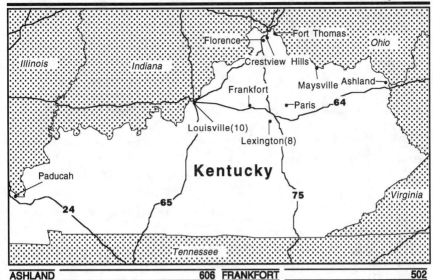

ASHLAND   606

ASHLAND AREA YMCA 3232 - 13th St.
Phone: 324-6191.
Pool: 25y, indoors, heated, 84°.
Admission: Basic $4. Health Center $6. SC(65)
50% discount.
Affiliate: YMCA $2.

CRESTVIEW HILLS   606

FOUR SEASONS SPORTS COUNTRY CLUB 345
Thomas More Pkwy.
Phone: 341-3687.
Pool: 25y, indoors, heated, 81°-83°.
Affiliate: IHRSA $10.
Hotel: Commonwealth Hilton (371-4400) — Call the
club for information.

FLORENCE   606

TRI-CITY YMCA 212 Main St.
Phone: 371-4680.
Pool: 25y, 4 lanes, indoors, heated, 82°.
Admission: $6.
Affiliate: Y AWAY NC.
To find: Next door to the Post Office.

FORT THOMAS   606

CAMPBELL COUNTY YMCA 1437 S. Fort Thomas
Ave.
Phone: 781-1814.
Pool: 25y, 4 lanes, indoors, heated, 84°.
Affiliate: YMCA outside a 50 mile radius NC, within
50 miles $2.50.
To find: On Route 27, one mile from Hwy. 471.

FRANKFORT   502

FRANKFORT YMCA on Broadway, next to the
Holiday Inn
Phone: 227-9637.
Pool: 25y, indoors, heated, 84°-85°.
Admission: 1 visit $5.
Affiliate: YMCA NC.

LEXINGTON   606

LEXINGTON ATHLETIC CLUB 3992 W. Tiverton
Court
Phone: 273-3163.
Pool: 25y x 54f, 6 lanes, indoors, heated, 82°.
Admission: 1 visit per month $10, limit 3 visits per
year.
Affiliate: IHRSA: 1 visit per month, maximum 3
visits per year, NC, then $10. 3 day pass $15. 7
day pass $25.
Hotel: Lexington Green Hotel — NC with a pass
from the hotel.
Notes: Lanes are 1.5 ft. wider than standard.
To find: Just off Nicholasville Rd., behind the
Fayette Place Shopping Center.

CROSS KEYS ROAD YWCA 1060 Cross Keys Rd.
Phone: 276-4457.
Pool: 25m x 30f, indoors, heated, 82°-85°.
Admission: $5.
Affiliate: YWCA $3.
Notes: In summer, a bulkhead is removed and the
pool width expands to the outdoors.
To find: Three miles from Lexington Airport.

CAMPBELL HOUSE INN 1375 Harrodsburg Rd.
Phone: 255-4281. **Reservations:** National: 800-
354-9235. Kentucky only: 800-432-9254.
Pool: 70f x 32f, indoors, heated, 90°.
Admission: Registered guests only NC.

Notes: There is also an 85f x 40f, outdoor, summer pool.

CONTINENTAL INN 801 New Circle Rd. N.E.
Phone: 299-5281. **Reservations:** 800-432-9388.
Pool: 83f, rectangular, 3 lanes, indoor/outdoor, heated, 88°.
Admission: Registered guests only NC.

YMCA OF CENTRAL KENTUCKY 239 E. High St.
Phone: 254-9622.
Pool: 25y x 21f, indoors, heated, 82°.
Admission: $10.
Affiliate: YMCA outside a 50 mile radius 1 month NC.
To find: In downtown Lexington.

LEXINGTON SPORTS CLUB 230 W. Main St.
Phone: 281-5110.
Pool: 20m, indoors, heated, 82°.
Affiliate: IHRSA $5.
Hotel: Radisson Plaza Hotel (231-9000) & Hyatt Regency (253-1234): $8.

HOLIDAY INN LEXINGTON-NORTH 1950
Newtown Pike
Phone: 233-0512. **Reservations:** 800-465-4329.
Pool: 50f, rectangular, indoors, heated, 84°.
Admission: Registered guests only NC.

HARLEY HOTEL OF LEXINGTON 2143 N.
Broadway
Phone: 299-1261. **Reservations:** 800-321-2323.
Pool: 20y x 25f, rectangular, indoors, heated, 82°.
Admission: Registered guests only NC.
Notes: There is also a 20y, outdoor, unheated 74°-79° pool operated from May to Sep.

LOUISVILLE   502

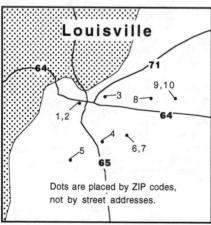

Louisville

Dots are placed by ZIP codes,
not by street addresses.

1. DOWNTOWN CENTER YMCA 555 S. 2nd St.
Phone: 587-6700.
Pool: 25y, 5 lanes, indoors, heated, 84°.
Affiliate: Out-of-state YMCA NC.
Hotel: All local hotels — Fitness center $8, basic $6. Room key and out-of-town ID required.
To find: At the intersection of Chestnut and 2nd St.

2. DOWNTOWN ATHLETIC CLUB 233 W.
Broadway
Phone: 582-2295.
Pool: 25y x 40f, 5 lanes, indoors, heated, 83°.
Hotel: All local hotels — $5 per day or $15 per week.
To find: At the intersection of Broadway and 3rd, next to McDonalds.

3. CRESCENT HILL BUBBLE POOL 201
Reservoir Ave.
Phone: 897-9949.
Pool: 50m OR 25y + 25y x 90f, 10 OR 20 lanes, indoor/outdoor, heated, 83°.
Admission: $3, SC $2.
To find: On the first fairway of the Crescent Hill Golf Course.
Masters: The Crescent Hill Bubble Sharks. Contact Tom Mester at 495-6755(h) or 426-5280(w).

4. EXECUTIVE INN 978 Phillips Lane
Phone: 367-6161. **Reservations:** 800-626-2706.
Pool: 25m, rectangular, indoors, heated, 82°.
Admission: Registered guests NC.
Memberships: $200/year.
Notes: There is also a 20y, outdoor, heated, 83° pool operated from May to Oct.

5. SOUTHWEST FAMILY YMCA 2800 Fordhaven
Rd.
Phone: 933-9622.
Pool: 25m x 36f, 6 lanes, indoor/outdoor, heated, 82°-84°.
Affiliate: YMCA outside a 50 mile radius NC.

6. SOUTHEAST FAMILY YMCA 5930 Six Mile
Lane
Phone: 491-9622.
Pool: 25m, 5 lanes, indoors, heated, 84°-86°.
Affiliate: Out-of-area Y AWAY NC.

7. AMERICAN FITNESS CENTERS 4150 Outer
Loop
Phone: 966-2814.
Pool: 22.5m, indoors, heated, 83°-84°.
Affiliate: IPFA NC. IHRSA Call.

8. BLAIRWOOD CLUB 9300 Blairwood Rd.
Phone: 426-8820.
Pool: 25y, 9 lanes, indoors, heated, 80°-85°.
Affiliate: IHRSA $10.
Hotel: All local hotels $10 with room key.

9. NORTHEAST YMCA 9400 Millbrook Rd.
Phone: 425-1271.
Pool: 25m, indoors, heated, 84°.
Affiliate: YMCA NC.

10. AMERICAN FITNESS CENTERS 9913 Shelbyville Rd.
Phone: 425-4471.
Pool: 25m, indoors, heated, 80°.
Admission: $10.
Affiliate: IPFA Call.

MAYSVILLE 606

LIMESTONE YMCA 1080 U.S. 68
Phone: 564-6772.
Pool: 25y, 5 lanes, indoors, heated, 83°-86°.
Affiliate: YMCA NC.

Hotel: Ramada Inn (564-6793) & Super 8 (759-8888): $5.

PADUCAH 502

NAUTILUS RACQUET & SWIM CLUB 950 Stonebrook Lane
Phone: 443-7529.
Pool: 25y, indoors, heated, 84°.
Admission: $10.

PARIS 606

PARIS-BOURBON COUNTY YMCA 917 Main St.
Phone: 987-1395.
Pool: 25y, indoors, heated, 85°.
Admission: $5.
Affiliate: YMCA Call.

ALWAYS CALL FIRST

Pools close, they change names, affiliations, admission policies, and rates. And just because a pool is listed in *Swimmers Guide* doesn't mean it's open all day, every day, for just the type of workout you want to do. Spend a quarter to save time and aggravation. . . always call first!

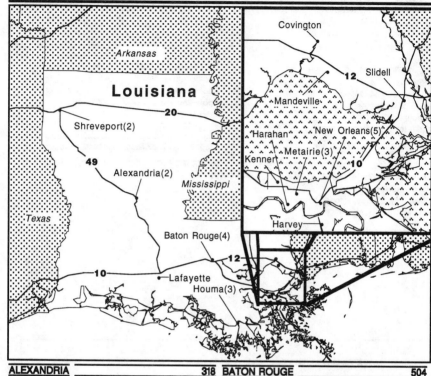

Arkansas

Louisiana

20

Shreveport(2)

49

Alexandria(2)

Mississippi

Texas

10

Baton Rouge(4)

12

Lafayette

Houma(3)

Covington

12   Slidell

Mandeville

Harahan   New Orleans(5)

Kenner   Metairie(3)

10

Harvey

ALEXANDRIA   318

YMCA OF CENTRAL LOUISIANA 1831 Turner St.
Phone: 445-8261.
Pool 1: 25y, 5 lanes, indoors, heated, 80°.
Pool 2: 25y, 3 lanes, indoors, heated, 88°.
Admission: $5.
Affiliate: YMCA NC.

ALEXANDRIA SENIOR HIGH SCHOOL 800 Ola
Lane
Phone: 443-5359.
Pool: 25y x 40f, 6 lanes, indoors, heated, 84°.
Admission: $3.
Memberships: $25 per month. Sale of member-
ships is by appointment only.
Notes: This pool does not operate in the summer.
To find: Behind the school building, beside the ten-
nis courts.

CITY OF ALEXANDRIA SWIM TEAM at Alexandria
Senior High School
Masters: Contact Coach Wally Fall at 443-5359 or
443-4426(h).
Non-member participation: Out-of-town visitors
NC.
Notes: From May through Aug., the team swims at
the 50m, outdoor, Alexandria Aquatic & Racquet
Club pool at 2001 Brentwood (442-8501).

BATON ROUGE   504

CRAWFISH MASTERS at L.S.U. Natatorium,
Nicholson Dr., Louisiana State University
Pool phone: 388-8207. **Masters:** Contact Coach
Scott Rabalais at 928-5596(h).
Pool 1: 50m x 25y, 8 x 22 lanes, indoors, heated,
80°.
Pool 2: Diving well: 25y x 60f, 6 lanes, indoors,
heated, 85°.
Affiliate: USMS 3 workouts per stay NC, then $10
per week, includes pool fees.
Notes: Coached workouts: M-F: 5:45-7AM, 6-
7:15PM. Sa: 10AM-Noon.

ARTHUR CULLEN LEWIS BRANCH YMCA 350 S.
Foster
Phone: 923-0653.
Pool: 25m, indoors, heated, 83°-86°.
Affiliate: YMCA 1 visit $2, then NC.
Hotel: Hilton Hotel (924-5000), The General
Lafayette (387-0421), Radisson Hotel (925-2244),
& Crown Sterling Suites (924-6566): Call the Y for
information.

LA SPORTS FITNESS CENTER 3103 Monterrey
Dr.
Phone: 926-7222.
Pool: 18m, indoors, heated, 80°-85°.
Admission: $10.

FOXY'S HEALTH CLUB 4343 Rhoda Dr.
Phone: 293-9301.
Pool: 25y x 30f, 5 lanes, indoors, heated, 80°-82°.
Admission: $5.
Notes: There is also a year-round, outdoor, unheated, recreation pool.
To find: Approximately one mile south of I-12 on Airline Hwy.

COVINGTON   504

WEST ST. TAMMANY YMCA 19335 N. 9th St.
Phone: 893-4800.
Pool: 20y x 30f, 5 lanes, indoor/outdoor, heated, 82°.
Admission: $8.
Affiliate: Out-of-state YMCA NC.
To find: Behind South China Restaurant on Hwy. 190.

HARAHAN   504

ELMWOOD FITNESS CENTER 1200 S. Clearview Pwy.
Phone: 733-1600.
Pool 1: 25y, indoors, heated, 80°.
Pool 2: 25y, outdoors, heated, 80°.
Admission: $10.

HARVEY   504

MANHATTAN ATHLETIC CLUB 4162 Manhattan Blvd.
Phone: 362-2200.
Pool: 25y x 31f, 6 lanes, indoors, heated, 82°.
Admission: 1 visit per month $10.
Affiliate: U.S. Military 1 visit per month $7.50.
To find: Two miles from the intersection of Manhattan Blvd. and Lapalco.

HOUMA   504

BAYOULAND YMCA 103 Valhi Blvd.
Phone: 873-9622.
Pool: 25y x 60f, 8 lanes, indoors, heated, 83°-84°.
Admission: $5.
Hotel: All local hotels 1 week pass $10.

QUALITY INN 1400 W. Tunnel Blvd.
Phone: 879-4871. **Reservations:** 800-221-2222.
Pool: 50.25f, rectangular, outdoors, unheated, the range of water temperatures was not reported.
Admission: Registered guests only NC.

RENAISSANCE II 106 S. Down West Blvd.
Phone: 872-2582.
Pool: 20y, outdoors, unheated, the range of water temperatures was not reported.
Admission: $7.

KENNER   504

KENNER BRANCH YMCA 2121 - 38th St.
Phone: 443-6363.
Pool: 25y, indoor/outdoor, heated, 88°.
Affiliate: YMCA NC.
Hotel: Days Inn-Airport (469-2531), TraveLodge (469-7341), Radisson (467-3111), Comfort Inn (457-1300), & Holiday Inn (467-5611): $5 with room key.

LAFAYETTE   318

RED LERILLE'S HEALTH & RACQUET CLUB 301 Ducet Rd.
Phone: 984-7738.
Pool: 25m, outdoors, heated, 79°-80°.
Admission: $8.

MANDEVILLE   504

FRANCO'S ATHLETIC CLUB 100 Bon Temps Roulé
Phone: 845-2639.
Pool: 22m, outdoors, heated, 84°.
Admission: $7.
Affiliate: IHRSA $5.
Masters: Contact Bill Babcock at 845-2639.

METAIRIE   504

DICK BOWER SWIM CLUB 'BOLTS' at St. Martin's School Pool, 600 Haring Rd.
Masters: Contact Dick Bower, Head Coach, at 456-9569.
Pool: 25y x 60f, 8 lanes, indoors, heated, 83°.
Affiliate: YMCA & USMS: 1 week $5 per visit, then pay monthly dues.
Notes: Workouts: M,W: 5:30-7AM, 8-9:30AM, Noon-1:30PM, 7:30-9PM. F: 5:30-7AM, 8-9:30AM, Noon-1:30PM, 6-7:30PM. Sa: Noon-1:30PM.

PREMIER ATHLETIC CLUB 1 Galleria Blvd., Suite 800
Phone: 836-5100.
Pool: 25y, indoors, heated, 82°.
Admission: $10.

METAIRIE BRANCH YMCA 3726 Houma Blvd.
Phone: 888-9622.
Pool: 25y, indoors, heated, 84°.
Admission: $8.
Affiliate: YMCA NC.
Masters: The Aqua Jet Masters. Contact Chris Prator at 888-9622.

NEW ORLEANS   504

NEW ORLEANS ATHLETIC CLUB 222 N. Rampert St.
Phone: 525-2375.
Pool: 20m, indoors, heated, 78°-82°.
Affiliate: IHRSA $20.

NEW ORLEANS   CONTINUED

Hotel: Holiday Inn Chateau LeMoyne (581-1303) & Hyatt Regency (561-1234): $20.

ISIDORE NEWMAN SCHOOL 1903 Jefferson Ave.
Phone: 896-8567.
Pool: 25y, indoors, heated, 84°.
Admission: $5*
Memberships: $42/month.
Notes: *Available M,Tu,Th,F: 5:45-7:15AM only.
Masters: The NU Wave Masters. Contact Jorge Blasini at 896-8567.

GERT TOWN POOL 7400 Stroelitz
Phone: 483-2530.
Pool: 25m, 8 lanes, indoors, heated, water temperature not reported.
Admission: $1.

TREME POOL 1600 St. Phillips
Phone: 565-7290.
Pool: 25m, 8 lanes, indoors, heated, water temperature not reported.
Admission: NC.

LEE CIRCLE YMCA 920 St. Charles Ave.
Phone: 568-9622.

Pool: 20y x 20f, 4 lanes, indoors, heated, 84°.
Admission: Out-of-town visitors $10.
Affiliate: Y AWAY $2.
Hotel: YMCA Hotel NC. All other local hotels $5 with room key and out-of-town picture ID.
To find: Next to Lee Circle on St. Charles.

SHREVEPORT   318

WILLIS KINGHTON HEALTH & FITNESS CENTER 2600 Greenwood Rd.
Phone: 632-4475.
Pool: 25m, indoors, heated, 84°-86°.
Admission: $5.

DOWNTOWN BRANCH YMCA at the corner of Travis & McNeal
Phone: 674-9622.
Pool: 20y, 4 lanes, indoors, heated, 83°.
Affiliate: YMCA NC.

SLIDELL   504

CROSS GATES ATHLETIC CLUB 200 N. Military Rd.
Phone: 643-8194.
Pool: 25y, outdoors, heated, 85°.
Admission: $7.

HELP MAKE THE NEXT *SWIMMERS GUIDE* EVEN BETTER

To receive a free copy of the next ***Swimmers Guide*** tell us about pools you know of that aren't in this edition. See page 14 for details.

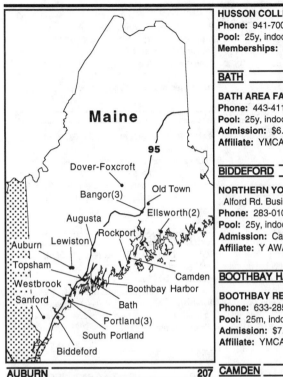

Maine

95

Dover-Foxcroft

Bangor(3)   Old Town

Augusta   Ellsworth(2)

Rockport

Auburn   Lewiston

Topsham

Westbrook   Camden

Boothbay Harbor

Sanford   Bath

Portland(3)

South Portland

Biddeford

HUSSON COLLEGE 1 College Circle
Phone: 941-7000.
Pool: 25y, indoors, heated, 81°-82°.
Memberships: $147/year, SC(55) $118.

BATH 207

BATH AREA FAMILY YMCA 26 Summer St.
Phone: 443-4112.
Pool: 25y, indoors, heated, 80°-82°.
Admission: $6.
Affiliate: YMCA $2.50.

BIDDEFORD 207

NORTHERN YORK COUNTY FAMILY YMCA
Alford Rd. Business Park
Phone: 283-0100.
Pool: 25y, indoors, heated, 80°-82°.
Admission: Call.
Affiliate: Y AWAY NC. YMCA $2.50.

BOOTHBAY HARBOR 207

BOOTHBAY REGION YMCA Townsend Ave.
Phone: 633-2855.
Pool: 25m, indoors, heated, 84°.
Admission: $7.
Affiliate: YMCA NC.

AUBURN 207

AUBURN-LEWISTON YMCA 62 Turner St.
Phone: 795-4095.
Pool: 20y x 20f, 3 lanes, indoors, heated, 82°.
Admission: Lap swims $3. Rec. swims $2.
Affiliate: Out-of-town YMCA 2 visits NC.

AUGUSTA 207

KENNEBEC VALLEY YMCA 33 Winthrop St.
Phone: 626-3488.
Pool: 25y, indoors, heated, 82°-85°.
Admission: $7.
Affiliate: YMCA 5 visits per year NC, then $3.50.

BANGOR 207

BANGOR YMCA 127 Hammond St.
Phone: 941-2815.
Pool: 25y, 4 lanes, indoors, heated, 84°-86°.
Admission: $8.
Affiliate: Y AWAY NC.

BANGOR BREWER YWCA 17 - 2nd St.
Phone: 941-2808.
Pool 1: 25y, 6 lanes, indoors, heated, 80°.
Pool 2: 25y, 4 lanes, indoors, heated, 86°.
Admission: $3.
Affiliate: YWCA $2.
Notes: Both pools are closed on Saturdays and
Sundays in the summer.

CAMDEN 207

CAMDEN AREA YMCA 50 Chestnut St.
Phone: 236-3375.
Pool: 25y, indoors, heated, 82°-84°.
Admission: $5.
Affiliate: Y AWAY 2 weeks NC.

DOVER-FOXCROFT 207

PISCATAQUIS REGIONAL YMCA 30 Park St.
Phone: 564-7111.
Pool: 25y, indoors, heated, 84°.
Admission: Call.
Affiliate: YMCA NC.

ELLSWORTH 207

DOWN EAST FAMILY YMCA Route 1 A Upper
State St.
Phone: 667-3086.
Pool: 25y x 48f, 6 lanes, indoors, heated, 83°.
Admission: $5.
Affiliate: Y AWAY Call.
Masters: The Down East Family YMCA Masters.
Contact Bill Reeve at 667-3997(h&w).

FITNESS EAST HEALTH & RACQUET CLUB
Phone: 667-3341.
Pool: 25y, indoors, heated, 83°.
Admission: $10.

LEWISTON 207

YWCA OF LEWISTON-AUBURN 130 East Ave.
Phone: 795-4050.
Pool: 25y, indoors, heated, 86°.
Admission: $5.

OLD TOWN 207

OLD TOWN COMMUNITY SWIMMING POOL 240 Stillwater Ave.
Phone: 827-3969.
Pool: 25y, 6 lanes, indoors, heated, 80°.
Admission: Non-residents $1.25.

PORTLAND 207

YWCA OF PORTLAND 87 Spring St.
Phone: 874-1130.
Pool: 25y x 28f, 4 lanes, indoors, heated, 83°.
Admission: $4, SC(60) $3.60.
Affiliate: YWCA $3, SC $2.70.
To find: Across the street from Holiday Inn by the Bay, next to the Civic Center.

GREATER PORTLAND YMCA 70 Forest Ave.
Phone: 874-1111.
Pool 1: 25y x 39f, 6 lanes, indoors, heated, 81°-83°.
Pool 2: 20y x 45f, indoors, heated, 85°.
Admission: $5.
Hotel: Sonesta Hotel Portland (775-5411) NC with room key.
To find: From I-295 take Exit 5A if north bound or 5B if south bound. Go up the hill on Forest Ave., the Y is on the right.

RIVERTON POOL 1600 Forest Ave.
Phone: 874-8456.
Pool: 25m x 45f, 6 lanes, indoors, heated, 82°-84°.
Admission: Residents $2, SC(60) $1.75. Non-residents $2.75, SC $2.

ROCKPORT 207

SAMOSET RESORT ON THE OCEAN 220 Warrenton St.

Phone: 594-2511. **Reservations:** 800-341-1650.
Pool: 50f x 30f, indoors, heated, 81°.
Admission: Before 4PM $6, after 4PM $8. Registered guests NC.
Affiliate: IHRSA 2 visits per month $6 each.
Notes: There is also a 25y x 40f, outdoor, unheated pool operated from Memorial Day to Labor Day.

SANFORD 207

SANFORD SPRINGVALE YMCA River Rd.
Phone: 324-4942.
Pool: 25y x 38f, 6 lanes, indoors, heated, 80°-83°.
Affiliate: Y AWAY $2.
To find: One mile west of Route 111 on River Rd. River Rd. is midway between Route 109 and Goodall Hospital.

SOUTH PORTLAND 207

SOUTH PORTLAND MUNICIPAL POOL 21 Nelson Rd.
Phone: 767-7655.
Pool: 25m, 6 lanes, indoors, heated, 83°.
Admission: $2.
To find: Two blocks from the intersection of Broadway and Evan St.

TOPSHAM 207

MERRYMEETING HEALTH & RACQUET CLUB 126 Main St.
Phone: 729-0129.
Pool: 25y, indoors, heated, 82°-83°.
Admission: $8.

WESTBROOK 207

JOHN P. DAVAN POOL 426 Bridge St.
Phone: 854-0834.
Pool: 25y x 42f, 6 lanes, indoors, heated, 80°.
Admission: $3.
To find: At Westbrook Junior High School.
Masters: The Westbrook Seals. Contact Dennis Connolly at 854-0834.

ALWAYS CALL FIRST

Pools close, they change names, affiliations, admission policies, and rates. And just because a pool is listed in *Swimmers Guide* doesn't mean it's open all day, every day, for just the type of workout you want to do. Spend a quarter to save time and aggravation. . . always call first!

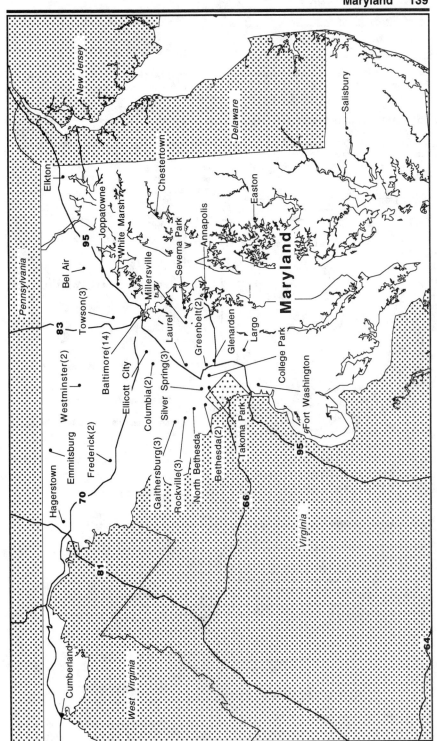

ANNAPOLIS 410

ARUNDEL OLYMPIC SWIM CENTER 2690 Riva Rd.
Phone: 222-7933.
Pool: 25y x 50m, 22 lanes, indoors, heated, 82°.
Admission: $3.50, SC(62) $2.50.
To find: On the campus of Annapolis High School.

MARYLAND MASTERS SWIM TEAM at Arundel Olympic Swim Center
Masters: Contact Carla Mazyck at 805-0222.
Affiliate: USMS Pool fees only.
Notes: Coached workouts: M, Th: 8:30-9:45PM. Sa: 8:15-9:30AM.

BALTIMORE 410

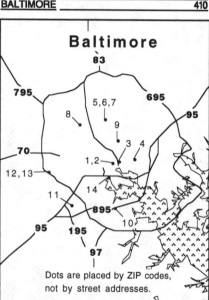

Baltimore

Dots are placed by ZIP codes, not by street addresses.

1. BALTIMORE SPORTS CLUB 218 N. Charles St.
Phone: 547-0053.
Pool: 20y, 4 lanes, indoors, heated, 79°.
Admission: $15.
Hotel: The Brookshire Hotel (625-1300), Treemont Plaza (727-2222), & Days Inn Inner Harbor (576-1000): NC to $6, depending on the hotel. Call the club for details.
To find: Directly opposite the Omni International Hotel on Fayette St., on the ground floor of the Park Charles Apartment Building.

2. HOLIDAY INN INNER HARBOR 301 W. Lombard St.
Phone: 685-3500.
Pool: 51.5f x 25.75f, rectangular, indoors, heated, 78°.
Admission: Registered guests only NC.

3. DOWNTOWN ATHLETIC CLUB 210 E. Centre St.
Phone: 332-0906.
Pool: 20y, 3 lanes, indoors, heated, 81°.
Admission: Owners of the current edition of *Swimmers Guide* $18. You must call first and show your copy of the book at check in.
Affiliate: IHRSA $12.
Hotel: Latham Hotel (727-7101) NC. All other local hotels $18 with room key.

4. CHICK WEBB RECREATION CENTER POOL 623 N. Eden St.
Phone: 396-7593.
Pool: 25y, indoors, heated, 85°.
Admission: 75¢.

5. LOYOLA COLLEGE 4501 N. Charles St.
Phone: 323-1010.
Pool: 25m, 6 lanes, indoors, heated, water temperature not reported.
Memberships: $350/year.

6. COLLEGE OF NOTRE DAME SWIM CLUB 4701 N. Charles St.
Phone: Recorded schedule: 532-3587. Information: 532-3588.
Pool: 20y, 4 lanes, indoors, heated, 79°-81°.
Memberships: $170/academic year, SC(60) $153.

7. MARYLAND MASTERS SWIM TEAM at Gilman School, 5407 Roland Ave.
Masters: Contact Shawn Fischer at 323-7395(w).
Pool: 25y, 6 lanes, indoors, heated, 85°.
Affiliate: USMS $5.
Notes: Coached workouts: Tu,Th: 8:30-10PM. Su: 8-9:30PM.

8. CALLOWHILL AQUATIC CENTER 2821 Oakley Ave.
Phone: 396-0677.
Pool: 25m, indoors, heated, 82°-83°.
Admission: $1.
Masters: The Baltimore City Masters. Contact Ernestine Toney at 396-0677.

9. MARYLAND MASTERS SWIM TEAM - ANCIENT MARINERS at Johns Hopkins University, 2715 N. Charles St.
Masters: Contact Shawn Fischer at 323-7395(w).
Pool: 25y, 6 lanes, indoors, heated, 84°.
Affiliate: USMS $5.
Notes: Coached workouts: M-F: 5:30-6:40AM. Sa: 7-8:30AM.

10. CHERRY HILL AQUATICS CENTER 2600 Giles Rd.
Phone: 396-1938.
Pool: 25y, indoors, heated, 88°-90°.
Admission: 75¢.

11. THE BALTIMORE SPORTS CLUB 6801-A Douglas Legum Dr.

Phone: 796-2582.
Pool: 68f, 3 lanes, indoors, heated, 78°.
Admission: $10.
Affiliate: IPFA NC.
Hotel: Ramada (712-4300) & Holiday Inn (799-7500): NC with a pass from the hotel.
To find: Seven miles from BWI Airport on Route 176 or two miles off I-295.

12. WESTERN FAMILY YMCA 850 S. Rolling Rd.
Phone: 747-9622.
Pool: 25y x 45f, 6 lanes, indoors, heated, 83°.
Affiliate: Y AWAY $5.

13. UNIVERSITY OF MARYLAND - BALTIMORE COUNTY POOL 5401 Wilkens Ave.
Phone: 455-2126.
Pool: 25y, 8 lanes, indoors, heated, 79°.
Admission: $3.

MARYLAND MASTERS SWIM TEAM at the University of Maryland - Baltimore County Pool
Masters: Contact Patty Devanny at 727-3777(w).
Affiliate: USMS NC.
Notes: Coached workouts: M,W,F: 5:30-7AM. Tu,Th: 6-7:30AM, 8:30-10PM. Sa,Su: 8-10AM.

14. HARBOR VIEW HEALTH CLUB 100 Harbor View Dr.
Phone: 752-3488.
Pool: 20y, indoors, heated, 82°.
Admission: $7.
Affiliate: IHRSA Call.

BEL AIR   **410**

BEL AIR ATHLETIC CLUB 658 Bolton St.
Phone: 838-2670.
Pool: 25y, 6 lanes, indoor/outdoor, heated, 82°.
Admission: $8.
Notes: There is also a 25y, 6 lane pool, and a 15y, 4 lane, instructional pool; both are outdoor, summer pools.
To find: Behind Harford Mall.

BETHESDA   **301**

BETHESDA-CHEVY CHASE YMCA 9401 Old Georgetown Rd.
Phone: 530-3725.
Pool 1: 25y x 32f, 4 lanes, indoors, heated, 83°.
Pool 2: 25y x 24f, 3 lanes, indoors, heated, 85°.
Pool 3: 25m x 48f, 6 lanes, outdoors, heated, 80°.
Affiliate: Y AWAY $2.50.
Notes: Pool 3 is operated from Apr. to early Dec.

BETHESDA SPORTS & HEALTH 4400 Montgomery Ave.
Phone: 656-9570.
Pool: 25y, indoors, heated, 80°-84°.
Affiliate: IHRSA $10.70.

CHESTERTOWN   **410**

CASEY SWIM CENTER Washington College, 300 Washington Ave.
Phone: 778-7241.
Pool: 25y x 45f, 6 lanes, indoors, heated, 83°.
Affiliate: USMS $4.
Hotel: Imperial Hotel (778-5000) NC with a pass from the hotel.
Memberships: $100/year, SC $76.50.
To find: Next to the Cain Gym and lacrosse fields.

COLLEGE PARK   **301**

TERRAPIN MASTERS at Cole Field House, Campus Dr., University of Maryland
Masters: Contact Coach Jim Wenhold at 314-7031.
Pool: 25y x 45f, 6 lanes, indoors, heated, 82°-84°.
Affiliate: USMS $3 + pool fees.
Notes: Workouts: M: 6-7:30PM. Tu,Th: 6:30-8:30AM. W: 7-8:30PM. Sa: 7AM-8:30PM.

COLUMBIA   **410**

COLUMBIA SWIM CENTER 10400 Crossfox Lane
Phone: 730-7000.
Pool: 25y, 8 lanes, indoors, heated, 85°.
Admission: $9.
Hotel: Columbia Inn (730-3900) NC.

THE SUPREME SPORTS CLUB 7080 Deepage Dr.
Phone: 381-5355.
Pool: 25y x 60f, 8 lanes, indoors, heated, 81°.
Admission: $12.
Hotel: Columbia Inn (730-3900) NC.

CUMBERLAND   **301**

CUMBERLAND YMCA 205 Baltimore Ave.
Phone: 724-5445.
Pool: 20y x 20f, 3 lanes, indoors, heated, 83°.
Admission: $3.
Affiliate: YMCA NC.

CUMBERLAND YMCA MASTERS (THE AQUANUTS) at Cumberland YMCA
Masters: Contact Executive Director Laurie Robinson at 724-5445.
Non-member participation: $3.
Affiliate: YMCA NC.
Notes: Coached workouts: M,W: Lunchtime. Tu,Th,F: Lunchtime & evening.

EASTON   **410**

TALBOT YMCA 202 Peachblossom Rd.
Phone: 822-0566.
Pool: 25y x 40f, 5 lanes, indoors, heated, 83°.
Admission: $4.50.
Affiliate: Y AWAY NC. U.S. Military $1.
To find: Route 50 East, turn right onto Route 322 (Easton By-pass), then left at the third traffic light (Peachblossom Rd.)

Masters: The Talbot County YMCA Masters. Contact Christine Lovell at 822-0566.

ELKTON   410

CECIL COUNTY YMCA 1275 W. Pulaski Hwy.
Phone: 398-2333.
Pool: 25y, 4 lanes, indoors, heated, 84°.
Admission: $5.

ELLICOTT CITY   410

HOWARD COUNTY YMCA 4331 Montgomery Rd.
Phone: 465-4334.
Pool: 25y x 42f, 6 lanes, indoors, heated, 83°.
Affiliate: YMCA outside of the Baltimore area NC.

HOWARD COUNTY YMCA MASTERS at the Howard County YMCA
Pool phone: 465-4334. **Masters:** Contact Ned Daly at 461-6054(h).
Affiliate: YMCA NC.
Notes: Coached workouts: M,W,Th: 8:45-10PM. Sa: 6-7:30PM. Su: 8-10AM.

EMMITSBURG   301

KNOTT ATHLETIC RECREATION CONVOCATION COMPLEX Mt. Saint Mary's College
Phone: 447-5290 or 447-6122.
Pool: 25m, indoors, heated, 84°-86°.
Hotel: All local hotels and motels $3 with a phone call to the Recreational Services Office (447-5290) prior to a visit.
Memberships: $150/Academic year, SC(60) $95.

FORT WASHINGTON   301

ALLENTOWN ROAD FITNESS CENTER 7210 Allentown Rd.
Phone: 449-5567.
Pool: 25y x 45f, 6 lanes, indoors, heated, 84°.
Admission: Residents: $3, SC(60) $2. Non-residents: $4, SC $3.

FREDERICK   301

FREDERICK COUNTY YMCA 1000 N. Market St.
Phone: 663-5131.
Pool: 25y, indoors, heated, 84°.
Affiliate: YMCA NC.

HOOD COLLEGE Rosemont Ave.
Phone: 663-3131.
Pool: 25y, indoors, heated, 84°-86°.
Admission: $6.75.
Memberships: $210/year.

GAITHERSBURG   301

ATHLETIC EXPRESS RACQUET & HEALTH CLUB 700 Russell Ave.

Phone: 258-0661.
Pool: 25m x 18f, 3 lanes, indoors, heated, 83°.
Admission: $12.50.
Affiliate: IHRSA $10.
Hotel: Gaithersburg Marriott (977-8900) $7.50.
To find: Across from Lakeforest Mall.

RIO SPORTS & HEALTH CLUB 9811 Washingtonian Blvd.
Phone: 258-5100.
Pool: 25m, 8 lanes, indoors, heated, 82°.
Affiliate: IHRSA $10.70.

UPPER MONTGOMERY COUNTY YMCA 10011 Stedwick Rd.
Phone: 948-9622.
Pool: 25y, 6 lanes, indoors, heated, 82°-84°.
Affiliate: Y AWAY $3.
To find: Approximately two miles off I-270 past Lakeforest Mall.

GLENARDEN   301

THERESA BANKS POOL 8615-A McLain Ave.
Phone: 772-5515.
Pool: 25y, indoors, heated, 85°.
Admission: $2.50, SC(55) $1.50.

GREENBELT   301

GREENBELT AQUATIC & FITNESS CENTER 101 Centerway
Phone: 513-0390.
Pool: 25y x 60f, 7 lanes, indoor/outdoor, heated, 82°.
Admission: Residents $3.50, SC(60) $2.25. Non-residents $4, SC $2.75.
Notes: There is a similar size outdoor pool, lap lanes go width-wise.
To find: In the center of the city, behind the historic Roosevelt Center (shopping center).

BALLY'S HOLIDAY HEALTH SPA 7415 Greenbelt Rd.
Phone: 441-8300.
Pool: 25m, indoors, heated, 83°.
Affiliate: Bally's NC.
Hotel: Holiday Inn (927-7000) NC.

HAGERSTOWN   301

HAGERSTOWN YMCA 149 N. Potomac St.
Phone: 739-3990.
Pool: 25y x 25f, 5 lanes, indoors, heated, 82°-83°.
Admission: $7.
Affiliate: YMCA outside a 50 mile radius NC, within 50 miles $2.50.

JOPPATOWNE   410

MAGNOLIA MIDDLE SCHOOL 299 Fort Hoyle Rd.
Phone: 612-1608.
Pool: 25y x 15y, 6 lanes, indoors, heated, 80°.

Memberships: Adult Swimming Program 10 weeks $18.

LARGO   301

ROBERT I. BICKFORD NATATORIUM Prince George's Community College, 301 Largo Rd.
Phone: 322-0980.
Pool: 25y x 50m, 19 lanes, indoors, heated, 84°.
Admission: $3.
To find: Two miles east of USAir Arena on Route 202.

LAUREL   301

FAIRLAND AQUATICS CENTER 13820 Old Gunpowder Rd.
Phone: 206-2359.
Pool: 25y x 25y, indoors, heated, 82°.
Admission: $3, SC(60) $2.

MILLERSVILLE   410

MARYLAND MASTERS SWIM TEAM at Severna Park Racquet & Fitness Center, 8514 Veterans Hwy.
Pool phone: 987-0980. **Masters:** Contact Nancy Brown at 255-0699.
Pool: 25m, 5 lanes, indoors, heated, 82°.
Non-member participation: Pool admission only.
Notes: Coached workouts: M,W: 6:15-7:15PM, 8-9PM, 9-10:30PM. F: 5:30-6:30AM. Su: 7-8AM, 8-9AM, 9-10:30AM.

NORTH BETHESDA   301

MONTGOMERY AQUATIC CENTER 5900 Executive Blvd.
Phone: 468-4211.
Pool: 25m + 25m x 20y, 16 lanes, indoors, heated, 83°.
Admission: $6, SC(60) $5.
To find: One block west of the White Flint Metro Station.
Masters: The Montgomery Masters. Contact Clay Britt by leaving a message with the Center at 468-4211.

ROCKVILLE   301

ROCKVILLE MUNICIPAL SWIM CENTER 355 Martins Lane
Phone: 309-3040.
Pool 1: 25y x 42f, 6 lanes, indoors, heated, 83°.
Pool 2: 25m x 45f, 6 lanes, indoors, heated, 83°.
Admission: Residents* $4, SC(60) $3.20. Non-residents $5, SC $4.
Notes: *$2 City ID required. There is also a 50m x 25m, 8 x 18 lane, outdoor, heated, 80°, summer pool.
To find: Three blocks west of the downtown Rockville Post Office (North Washington), directly across the street from Rock Terrace High School.

BALLY'S HOLIDAY HEALTH SPA 11820 Rockville Pike
Phone: 984-6262.
Pool: 25m, indoors, heated, 80°.
Affiliate: Bally's NC.
Hotel: Holiday Inn Bethesda (652-2000) NC.

JEWISH COMMUNITY CENTER 6125 Montrose Rd.
Phone: 881-0100.
Pool: 25m, indoors, heated, 82°.
Affiliate: JCC NC.

SALISBURY   301

MID-DELMARVA FAMILY YMCA 715 S. Schumaker Dr.
Phone: 749-0101.
Pool: 25y, indoors, heated, 80°-82°.
Admission: Before 3PM $5.
Affiliate: YMCA 2 visits NC.

SEVERNA PARK   410

SEVERNA PARK YMCA 623 Baltimore-Annapolis Blvd.
Phone: 647-3800.
Pool: 25y x 54f, 6 lanes, indoors, heated, 82°.
Admission: $7.
Affiliate: Y AWAY $2.

SILVER SPRING   301

SILVER SPRING YMCA 9800 Hasting Dr.
Phone: 585-2120.
Pool: 25y, 6 lanes, indoor/outdoor, heated, 84°.
Admission: $12.
Affiliate: Out-of-state YMCA $1.50.

M. L. KING SWIM CENTER 1201 Jackson Rd.
Phone: 989-1206.
Pool: 42y x 22y (25y lap lanes), indoors, heated, 84°.
Admission: Residents $3.25, SC(65) $2.75. Non-residents $4, SC $3.
Masters: The Ancient Mariners. Contact the Montgomery County Recreation Aquatics Section at 217-6840.

THE ASPEN HILL CLUB 14501 Homecrest Rd.
Phone: 598-5200.
Pool: 25m x 12m, 4 lanes, indoors, heated, 83°.
Affiliate: IHRSA & MACMA: $15.

TAKOMA PARK   301

PINEY BRANCH POOL 7510 Maple Ave.
Phone: Pool: 270-9361. Parks & Rec. Dept: 217-6840.
Pool: 25y, 3 lap lanes, indoors, heated, 84°.
Admission: Residents $2.50, non-residents $4.
Notes: Located at a school, the pool may be closed for some school holidays, but is open in summer.

TOWSON 410

TOWSON FAMILY YMCA 600 W. Chesapeake Ave.
Phone: 823-8870.
Pool: 25y x 35f, 5 lanes, indoors, heated, 83°.
Affiliate: Y AWAY $5.
To find: Two blocks from Towson State University off Bosley Ave.
Masters: The Towson YMCA Masters. Contact Dominic Garrett at 442-9312(h).

VON BORRIES SWIMMING POOL Goucher College, 1021 Dulaney Valley Rd.
Phone: 337-6388.
Pool: 25y x 60f, 6 lanes, indoors, heated, 80°.
Memberships: $185/academic year.

BU POOL Towson State University
Phone: 830-2205.
Pool: 25y x 56f, 8 lanes, indoors, heated, 82°.
Memberships: Sep.-Aug $195. Mar.-Aug $110. Ten week summer $100.
Notes: The pool is closed when classes are not in session.

WESTMINSTER 410

CARROLL COUNTY FAMILY YMCA 1719 Sykesville Rd.
Phone: 848-3660.

Pool: 25y, 6 lanes, indoors, heated, 83°.
Affiliate: YMCA $5.
To find: One quarter mile from the intersection of Routes 32 & 97. One quarter mile from Carroll County Community College.

HARLOW NATATORIUM Western Maryland College, 2 College Hill
Phone: 857-2717.
Pool: 25y x 36f, 5 lanes, indoors, heated, 81°.
Admission: $1.
To find: In Englar Hall, the first building on the right from the east entrance off Pennsylvania Ave., the pool is one floor below the cafeteria.

WHITE MARSH 410

BALLY'S HOLIDAY HEALTH SPA 8221 Towncenter Dr.
Phone: 931-8080.
Pool: 25y, indoors, heated, 80°-83°.
Admission: One week guest passes may be available. Call.
Affiliate: Bally's NC.
Masters: The Bally's Holiday Spa Masters. Contact Ed Page at 931-8080.

HELP MAKE THE NEXT *SWIMMERS GUIDE* EVEN BETTER

To receive a free copy of the next *Swimmers Guide* tell us about pools you know of that aren't in this edition. See page 14 for details.

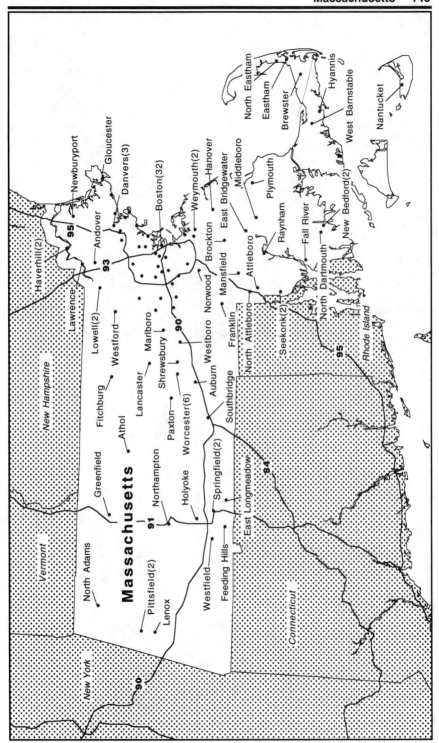

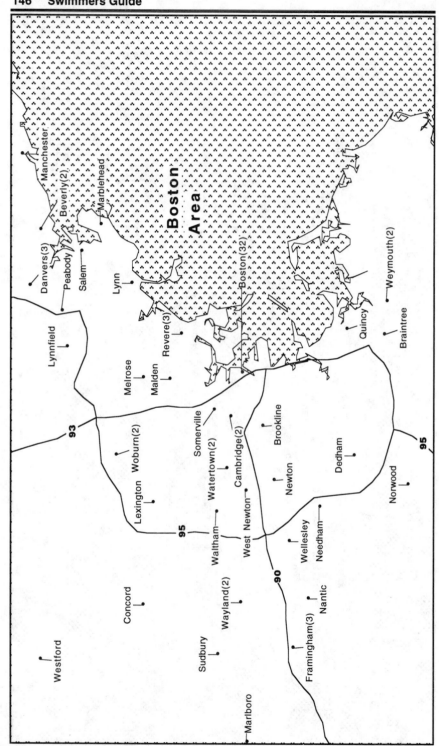

Boston Area

Manchester
Beverly(2)
Marblehead
Danvers(3)
Peabody
Salem
Lynn
Revere(3)
Boston(32)
Weymouth(2)
Quincy
Braintree
Lynnfield
Melrose
Malden
93
Somerville
Woburn(2)
Watertown(2)
Brookline
Cambridge(2)
Dedham
Newton
95
Norwood
Lexington
Waltham
West Newton
Wellesley
Needham
95
Concord
Wayland(2)
90
Framingham(3)
Nantic
Westford
Sudbury
Marlboro

ANDOVER · 508

ANDOVER-NORTH ANDOVER BRANCH YMCA
165 Haverhill St.
Phone: 685-3541.
Pool: 25y, indoors, heated, 80°-82°.
Admission: $6.
Affiliate: Y AWAY $3.

ATHOL · 508

ATHOL YMCA 545 Main St.
Phone: 249-3305.
Pool: 25y x 25f, indoors, heated, 82°-84°.
Admission: 1 visit NC, then $3.
Affiliate: YMCA outside a 50 mile radius NC, within 50 miles $1.50.

ATTLEBORO · 508

ATTLEBORO YMCA 63 N. Main St.
Phone: 222-7422.
Pool: 25y, indoors, heated, 83°-84°.
Admission: $5.
Affiliate: Y AWAY outside an unspecified radius NC.

AUBURN · 508

AUBURN RACQUET & HEALTH CLUB Route 20
Phone: 832-3236.
Pool: 25y x 35f, 3 lanes, indoors, heated, 81°.
Admission: $10.
Affiliate: IHRSA $5.
Hotel: Days Inn (832-8300) NC with room key. Ramada Inn (832-3221) $8 with room key.

BEVERLY · 508

BEVERLY REGIONAL YMCA 254 Essex St.
Phone: 922-0990.
Pool: 25y x 42f, 6 lanes, indoors, heated, 84°.
Admission: $7.
Affiliate: YMCA Call.
Masters: The Beverly Y Masters. Contact Coach Tom Lowery 927-6855 or Aquatic Director Adam Hickey at 922-0990.

NEW ENGLAND HEALTH & RACQUET CLUB 7 Reservoir Rd.
Phone: 927-0920.
Pool: 65f, indoor/outdoor, heated, 80°-84°.
Admission: $15.
Affiliate: IHRSA $10.
Hotel: Kings Grant Inn NC.

BOSTON · 617

1. ROWES WHARF HEALTH CLUB & SPA 70 Rowes Wharf
Phone: 439-3914.
Pool: 20y x 30f, indoors, heated, 82°.
Hotel: Boston Harbor Hotel (439-7000) NC.

2. SWISSOTEL BOSTON 1 Ave. de Lafayette
Phone: 451-2600. **Reservations:** 800-621-9200.
Pool: 20y, rectangular, indoors, heated, 82°.
Admission: $10. Registered guests NC.

3. QUINCY COMMUNITY CENTER 885 Washington St., Chinatown
Phone: 635-5129.
Pool: 25y, indoors, heated, 85°.
Admission: Lap swims $3, SC(65) NC. Open swims $1.50.
Memberships: $7/quarter. $25/year.

4. WELLBRIDGE CLUB 695 Atlantic Ave.
Phone: 439-9600.
Pool: 70f x 30f, indoors, heated, 80°-82°.
Admission: $10.

5. YMCA OF GREATER BOSTON - CENTRAL BRANCH 316 Huntington Ave.
Phone: 536-7800.
Pool: 25y x 25f, 3 lanes, indoors, heated, 81°.
Admission: $10.
Affiliate: Out-of-state YMCA $5.
Hotel: American Youth Hostel $4.
To find: Next to Northeastern University and Symphony Hall.

6. YWCA OF BOSTON 140 Clarendon St.
Phone: 351-7600.
Pool: 25y, indoors, heated, 80°.
Admission: $10.
Affiliate: YWCA $5, SC(62) $3. Tufts Plan $3.

7. BLACKSTONE COMMUNITY CENTER 50 W. Brookline St., South End
Phone: 635-5162.
Pool: 25y, indoors, heated, 73°.
Admission: $3.

8. MASON POOL 176 Norfolk Ave., Roxbury
Phone: 635-5218.
Pool: 25y, indoors, heated, 78°.
Memberships: Residents $4/year, non-residents $25.

9. SOUTH END FITNESS CENTER 35 Northampton St.
Phone: 534-5822.
Pool: 25y x 45f, 6 lanes, indoors, heated, 81°.
Admission: $5.
Affiliate: USMS 10 swims $35.
Notes: Affiliated with the Boston City Hospital, the Center offers membership discounts to participants in a number of HMOs.
To find: Northampton is one block south of and runs parallel to Massachusetts Ave. The Center is located between Harrison and Albany, near Boston City Hospital.
Masters: Contact Steve Sirabella at 534-5822.

10. ROXBURY FAMILY BRANCH YMCA 285 M. L. King Blvd., Roxbury

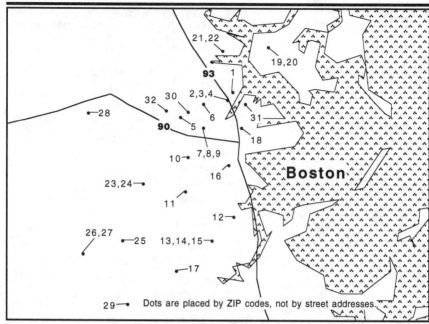

Dots are placed by ZIP codes, not by street addresses.

BOSTON ══════════ **CONTINUED**

Phone: 427-5300.
Pool: 25y, indoors, heated, 82°.
Admission: $7.
Affiliate: Y AWAY NC.

11. HOLLAND COMMUNITY CENTER 85 Olney St., Dorchester
Phone: 635-5144.
Pool: 25y, indoors, heated, 78°.
Admission: $1.

12. MURPHY COMMUNITY CENTER 1 Worrell St., Dorchester
Phone: 635-5150.
Pool: 25y, indoors, heated, 78°.
Admission: 50¢.

13. DORCHESTER FAMILY YMCA 776 Washington St., Dorchester
Phone: 436-7750.
Pool: 25y x 30f, 5 lanes, indoors, heated, 82°.
Admission: $8.
Affiliate: Y AWAY $4. Tufts Plan $3.

14. MARSHALL COMMUNITY CENTER 35 Westville Ave., Dorchester
Phone: 635-5148.
Pool: 25y, indoors, heated, 78°.
Admission: Summer $1.
Memberships: Oct.-Jun. $4.

15. ANTHONY PERKINS COMMUNITY CENTER 155 Talbot Ave., Dorchester

Phone: 635-5146.
Pool: 25y, indoors, heated, water temperature not reported.
Admission: NC.

16. CLARK ATHLETIC CENTER University of Massachusetts - Boston, Dorchester
Phone: 287-7800.
Pool: 25y x 25m, indoors, heated, 79°-81°.
Memberships: $100/year.

17. MATTAHUNT COMMUNITY CENTER 100 Hebron St., Mattapan
Phone: 635-5159.
Pool: 25y, indoors, heated, water temperature not reported.
Admission: $2.

18. CONDON COMMUNITY CENTER 200 'D' St., South Boston
Phone: 635-5100.
Pool: 25y, indoors, heated, 72°-77°.
Admission: 50¢.

19. EAST BOSTON HARBORSIDE COMMUNITY CENTER 312 Border St., East Boston
Phone: 635-5114.
Pool: 25y x 45f, 6 lanes, indoors, heated, 78°.
Admission: 25¢.
Masters: Contact Mark Sarro at 635-5114.

20. PARIS STREET COMMUNITY CENTER 113 Paris St., East Boston
Phone: 635-5125.

Pool: 25y, indoors, heated, 78°.
Memberships: Call.

21. CHARLESTOWN COMMUNITY CENTER 50
Bunker Hill St., Charlestown
Phone: 635-5169.
Pool: 25y, indoors, heated, 78°.
Admission: NC.

22. BOSTON ARMED SERVICES YMCA 150 - 2nd
Ave.
Phone: 241-8400.
Pool: 25y x 35f, indoors, heated, water temperature
not reported.
Admission: $8.
Affiliate: No reciprocity with other YMCAs.

23. HENNIGAN COMMUNITY CENTER 200 Health
St., Jamaica Plain
Phone: 635-5198.
Pool: 25y, indoors, heated, 75°-80°.
Admission: $1.

24. CURTIS HALL COMMUNITY CENTER 20
South St., Jamaica Plain
Phone: 635-5193.
Pool: 25y, indoors, heated, 80°.
Admission: $1.

25. FLAHERTY POOL 160 Florence St., Roslindale
Phone: 635-5181.
Pool: 25y, indoors, heated, 79°-81°.
Memberships: $5/year + $1.50/swim.

26. WEST ROXBURY / ROSLINDALE YMCA 15
Bellevue St., West Roxbury
Phone: 323-3200.
Pool: 20y x 36f, 4 lanes, indoors, heated, 84°.
Admission: $8, SC(60) $4.
Affiliate: Y AWAY $4. Tufts Plan $3.

27. WEST ROXBURY COMMUNITY CENTER
1205 V.F.W. Pkwy., West Roxbury
Phone: 635-5189.
Pool: 25y, indoors, heated, 75°-80°.
Admission: $2.

**28. ALLSTON / BRIGHTON FAMILY BRANCH
YMCA** 470 Washington St., Allston/Brighton
Phone: 782-3535.
Pool: 20y, indoors, heated, 82°-84°.
Affiliate: Out-of-state YMCA NC.
Masters: Contact Tim Mahoney at 782-3535.

29. HYDE PARK FAMILY BRANCH YMCA 1137
River St., Hyde Park
Phone: 364-9622.
Pool: 20y x 21f, 3 lanes, indoors, heated, 84°.
Admission: $6, SC(65) $3.
Affiliate: Y AWAY 8 visits per year NC. YMCA &
YWCA: $3.

30. SHERATON BOSTON HOTEL & TOWERS 39
Dalton St.
Phone: 236-2000.
Pool: 20y x 20f, indoor/outdoor, heated, 82°.
Admission: $10. Registered guests NC.

31. BOSTON ATHLETIC CLUB 653 Summer St.
Phone: 269-4300.
Pool: 20y x 30f, 8 lanes, indoors, heated, 82°.
Affiliate: IHRSA $10.
Hotel: All local hotels $20 with room key.
To find: One and a half miles from South Station
towards South Boston.

32. CASE CENTER POOL Boston University, 285
Babcock St.
Phone: 353-2748.
Pool: 25y x 36f, 6 lanes, indoors, heated, 80°-82°.
Affiliate: Out-of-town USMS $5.
Memberships: I/S $135 + $310/year. I/S $50 +
$85/semester.
To find: Off Commonwealth Ave., at the end of
Babcock St. across from T. Anthony's restaurant.
Masters: Boston University Masters Swimming
(BUMS). Contact Maureen Travers at 353-2748.

BRAINTREE   **617**

SHERATON TARA HOTEL, BRAINTREE 37
Forbes Rd.
Phone: 848-0600. **Reservations:** 800-325-3535.
Pool: 50f x 25f, 2 lap lanes + 1 water walking lane,
indoors, heated, 80°-82°.
Admission: $12. Registered guests NC.
Notes: The pool operates as part of a health club
within the hotel.

BREWSTER   **508**

OCEAN EDGE RESORT & GOLF CLUB 832
Villages Dr.
Phone: Pool: 896-8671. Hotel: 896-9000.
Reservations: 800-343-6074.
Pool: 25y, rectangular, indoors, heated, 82°.
Admission: Labor Day-Memorial Day $10.
Registered guests NC.
Memberships: Memorial Day-Labor Day $125/family/week.

BROCKTON   **508**

OLD COLONY YMCA 320 Main St.
Phone: 583-2155.
Pool: 20y, indoors, heated, water temperature not
reported.
Admission: $10.
Affiliate: YMCA 4 visits per month NC.

BROOKLINE   **617**

BROOKLINE SWIMMING POOL 60 Tappan St.
Phone: Pool: 730-2778. Rec. Dept: 730-2069.
Pool: 25y, 6 lanes, indoors, heated, 80°-81°.

Admission: Residents $3, SC(60) $2. Non-residents $4, SC $3.

CAMBRIDGE   617

CAMBRIDGE FAMILY YMCA 820 Massachusetts Ave.
Phone: 661-9622.
Pool: 20y, indoors, heated, 82°.
Affiliate: YMCA 2 visits per month NC, then $5. YWCA $4.
Hotel: The Inn at Harvard NC.

BALLY'S HOLIDAY HEALTH CLUB 1815 Massachusetts Ave.
Phone: 868-5100.
Pool: 20y, indoors, heated, 78°-82°.
Affiliate: Bally's NC.

CONCORD   508

THE THOREAU CLUB 1045 Old Marlboro Rd.
Phone: 369-7349.
Pool: 25y x 36f, 6 lanes, indoor/outdoor, heated, 80°-82°.
Affiliate: IHRSA $10.
Notes: The club offers 'Nifty Fifty Water Exercise/Aerobics Classes' to non-members at $5 per class.

DANVERS   508

DANVERS COMMUNITY YMCA 34 Pickering St.
Phone: 744-2055.
Pool: 25y x 36f, 5 lanes, indoors, heated, 85°.
Admission: $6.
Affiliate: Out-of-state YMCA NC, in-state $3.

THE FERNCROFT CLUB at the Sheraton Tara Hotel & Resort, 50 Ferncroft Rd.
Phone: Club: 777-2500 ext. 7929. Hotel: 777-2500. **Reservations:** 800-325-3535.
Pool: 20y x 40f, 2 lanes, indoors, heated, 82°.
Admission: $12. Registered guests NC.
Memberships: $63/month.
Notes: There is also an outdoor, summer pool.
To find: Follow signs for Ferncroft Rd., Exit 50 off I-95.

PAUL J. LYDON AQUATIC CENTER 200 Commonwealth Ave.
Phone: 774-9335.
Pool 1: 25y x 42f, 6 lanes, indoors, heated, 78°-80°.
Pool 2: 25y x 42f, indoors, heated, 84°-86°.
Hotel: All local hotels & motels $5 with room key.
Passes: 12 swims $50.
To find: At the Liberty Tree Mall on Route 128.

DEDHAM   617

DEDHAM RACQUETIME ATHLETIC CLUB 200 V.F.W. Pkwy.
Phone: 326-2900.
Pool: 82f x 32f, 4 lanes, indoors, heated, 80°.
Affiliate: IHRSA: $15. M-F 6AM to 5PM & Sa,Su 5PM to closing $10.
To find: Behind the Dedham Mall off Route 1.

EAST BRIDGEWATER   508

EAST BRIDGEWATER FAMILY YMCA 635 Plymouth St.
Phone: 378-3913.
Pool: 25y x 18y, 5 lanes, indoors, heated, 83°.
Admission: $6.
Affiliate: Y AWAY NC.
Notes: There is also a 20y, outdoor, unheated summer pool.

EAST LONGMEADOW   413

NEW ENGLAND HEALTH & RACQUET CLUB Crane Ave.
Phone: 525-3931.
Pool: 20y, indoor/outdoor, heated, 80°-82°.
Admission: $7.

EASTHAM   508

SHERATON INN EASTHAM Route 6
Phone: 255-5000. **Reservations:** 800-533-3986.
Pool: 50f, rectangular, indoors, heated, water temperature not reported.
Admission: Registered guests only NC.

FALL RIVER   508

YMCA OF GREATER FALL RIVER 199 N. Main St.
Phone: 675-7841.
Pool: 70f, indoors, heated, 82°-84°.
Admission: $7.50.
Affiliate: Y AWAY NC.

FEEDING HILLS   413

FITNESS FIRST RACQUET & FITNESS CENTER 60 N. Westfield St.
Phone: 786-1460.
Pool: 20y x 24f, indoors, heated, 82°.
Admission: $10.

FITCHBURG   508

FITCHBURG YMCA 55 Wallace Ave.
Phone: 343-4847.
Pool: 20y, indoors, heated, 82°.
Admission: $6.
Affiliate: YMCA $3.

FRAMINGHAM   508

METRO WEST YMCA - FRAMINGHAM 280 Old Connecticut Path

Phone: 879-4420.
Pool: 25y x 40f, 5 lanes, indoors, heated, 84°.
Admission: $6.
Affiliate: Y AWAY NC.
Masters: The Tsunami Masters Swim Team.
Contact Tom Wolfe at 879-4420 ext. 41.

SUBURBAN ATHLETIC CLUB 21 Blandin Ave.
Phone: 879-6544.
Pool: 25m x 10m, 5 lanes, indoors, heated, 81°.
Affiliate: IHRSA $10.
Hotel: All local hotels $15. Call the club to make arrangements.
To find: Easily accessible from Route 9 and the Massachusetts Tpk. Call the club for directions.

THE FRAMINGHAM CLUB at the Sheraton Tara Hotel, 1657 Worcester Rd.
Phone: Club and Hotel: 879-0111. Reservations: 800-325-3535.
Pool: 20y, 3 lanes, indoors, heated, 82°.
Admission: $10. Registered guests NC for pool.
Affiliate: IHRSA $5.
Notes: Sheraton Hotel guests are charged for the use of club facilities other than the pool.

FRANKLIN 508

SILVER'S HEALTH & FITNESS CENTER 750 Union St.
Phone: 528-5960.
Pool: 25m x 20f, 4 lanes, indoors, heated, 79°.
Admission: $10.
Affiliate: IHRSA $5.

GLOUCESTER 508

CAPE ANN YMCA 71 Middle St.
Phone: 283-0470.
Pool: 25y, 6 lanes, indoors, heated, 82°.
Admission: $10.
Affiliate: Y AWAY $3.

GREENFIELD 413

GREENFIELD YMCA 451 Main St.
Phone: 773-3646.
Pool: 20y, 2 lanes, indoors, heated, 83°.
Admission: $5.
Affiliate: Y AWAY 6 visits NC.

HANOVER 617

NEW ENGLAND HEALTH & RACQUET CLUB 20 East St.
Phone: 826-1300.
Pool: 25m, 4 lanes, indoors, heated, 82°.
Admission: $15.
Affiliate: IHRSA $7.50.
To find: East St. is one and three quarter miles south of the Hanover Mall on Route 53. Route 53 is Exit 13 off Route 3.

HAVERHILL 508

GREATER HAVERHILL YMCA 81 Winter St.
Phone: 374-0506.
Pool: 20y x 25f, 5 lanes, indoors, heated, 86°.
Admission: 3 visits per year $5 each.
Affiliate: YMCA outside a 50 mile radius 2 visits per month NC.
To find: One quarter of a mile west of City Hall & the library.

CEDARDALE ATHLETIC CLUB 931 Boston Rd.
Phone: 373-1596.
Pool: 20y, indoors, heated, 84°.
Affiliate: IHRSA $10.

HOLYOKE 413

GREATER HOLYOKE YMCA 171 Pine St.
Phone: 534-5631.
Pool: 20y, indoors, heated, 80°-82°.
Admission: Call.
Affiliate: YMCA NC or $2.50 depending on the location of the home Y.

HYANNIS 508

THE TARA CLUB at the Tara Hyannis Hotel & Resort, West End Circle
Phone: Club: 775-7775 ext. 171. Hotel: 775-7775. Reservations: 800-843-8272.
Pool: 22y x 33f, 2 lanes, indoors, heated, 80°.
Admission: $10. Registered guests: Pool NC. Full facility $4.
Hotel: The Cape Codder Hotel (771-3000): Pool NC. Full facility $4.
Affiliate: IHRSA $8.
Memberships: $25/week.
To find: Across from the Paddock Restaurant and the rear of the Melody Tent.

LANCASTER 508

ORCHARD HILLS ATHLETIC CLUB 90 Duval Rd.
Phone: 537-8387.
Pool: 20y x 30f, 4 lanes, indoors, heated, 83°.
Admission: $12.
Affiliate: IHRSA $6.
Notes: There is also a 100f x 100f, outdoor, summer pool.
To find: Just off Route 2, Mechanic St. / Harvard St. Exit next to the roller skating rink. Five minutes from Searstown Mall.

LAWRENCE 508

MERRIMACK VALLEY YMCA - LAWRENCE BRANCH 40 Lawrence St.
Phone: 686-6191.
Pool: 25y x 24f, 4 lanes, indoors, heated, 84°.
Admission: $6.50.
Affiliate: Y AWAY & Tufts Plan: NC.
To find: Across from the park.

LENOX   413

CANYON RANCH IN THE BERKSHIRES 91
Kimbel St.
Phone: 637-4400. **Reservations:** 800-726-9900.
Pool: 73.3f, indoors, heated, 85°.
Admission: Registered guests only NC.

LEXINGTON   617

THE LEXINGTON CLUB 475 Bedford St.
Phone: 861-8600.
Pool: 25y, 6 lanes, indoors, heated, 82°.
Admission: Owners of the current edition of
Swimmers Guide $10. You must call first and
show your copy of the book at check in.
Affiliate: IHRSA $10.
To find: One quarter of a mile off Route 128 Exit
31B.

LOWELL   508

BALLY'S HOLIDAY HEALTH CLUB 203 Plain St.
Phone: 441-0000.
Pool: 25y, indoors, heated, 80°-82°.
Admission: Call.
Affiliate: Bally's NC.

GREATER LOWELL FAMILY YMCA 35 YMCA Dr.
Phone: 454-7825.
Pool: 25y, indoors, heated, 82°-83°.
Admission: $10.
Affiliate: Y AWAY Call.

LYNN   617

GREATER LYNN YMCA 20 Neptune Blvd.
Phone: 581-3105.
Pool: 25y, 6 lanes, indoors, heated, 82°-83°.
Admission: $7.
Affiliate: YMCA $3.

LYNNFIELD   617

THE COLONIAL CLUB 425 Walnut St.
Phone: 246-7500.
Pool: 23y x 36f, 4 lanes, indoors, heated, 82°.
Admission: $12.
Affiliate: IHRSA $10.
Hotel: Colonial Hilton (245-9300) $7.
To find: Off Route 128 behind the Colonial Hilton,
between Exits 42 and 43.

MALDEN   617

MALDEN YMCA 83 Pleasant St.
Phone: 324-7680.
Pool: 20y x 20f, 4 lanes, indoors, heated, 85°.
Admission: $7.
Affiliate: Y AWAY NC. YMCA $3.
To find: On Malden Square, one block north of
Route 60.

MANCHESTER   508

MANCHESTER ATHLETIC CLUB 8 Atwater Ave.
Phone: 526-1681.
Pool: 20y x 30f, 4 lanes, indoors, heated, 83°.
Admission: $20.
Affiliate: IHRSA $10.

MANSFIELD   508

MANSFIELD FITNESS CENTER 31 Hamshire St.
Phone: 339-3991.
Pool: 20y x 25f, kidney shape, indoors, heated,
84°.
Admission: $10.
Hotel: Holiday Inn-Mansfield (339-2200) NC with
room key.

MARBLEHEAD   617

MARBLEHEAD / SWAMPSCOTT YMCA 104
Pleasant St.
Phone: 631-0870.
Pool: 20y x 20f, 3 lanes, indoors, heated, 83°.
Admission: $7.
Affiliate: Y AWAY NC.
To find: Across from the National Grand Bank, one
block from the Warwick Theatre.

MARLBORO   508

WAYSIDE RACQUET & SWIM CLUB 80
Broadmeadow Rd.
Phone: 481-1797.
Pool: 25y x 35f, 5 lanes, indoors, heated, 80°.
Affiliate: IHRSA $10.
Hotel: Quality Suites Hotel in Marlboro (485-5900)
& Holiday Inn Marlboro (481-3000): NC.
To find: Off Route 20, next to the airport.

MELROSE   617

MELROSE YMCA 497 Main St.
Phone: 665-4360.
Pool: 25y, indoors, heated, 83°-84°.
Admission: Out-of-state visitors $7.
Affiliate: Out-of-state YMCA NC.

MIDDLEBORO   508

OLD COLONY YMCA 61 E. Grove St.
Phone: 947-1390.
Pool: 25y, 6 lanes, indoors, heated, 84°.
Admission: $4, SC(60) $2.50.
Affiliate: YMCA 2 visits per month NC, then $2.
U.S. Military $2.
To find: Five miles south of the Middleboro rotary.

NANTIC   508

LONGFELLOW SPORTS CLUB 203 Oak St.
Phone: 653-4633.
Pool: 25y x 42f, indoor/outdoor, heated, 82°.

Admission: $15.
Affiliate: IHRSA $10.

NANTUCKET 508

NANTUCKET COMMUNITY POOL at the corner of Atlantic & Sparks Ave.
Phone: 228-7262.
Pool: 25y x 45f, indoors, heated, 85°.
Admission: $4.

NEEDHAM 617

CHARLES RIVER FAMILY YMCA 863 Great Plain Ave.
Phone: 444-6400.
Pool: 25y x 30f, 3 lanes, indoors, heated, 82°-84°.
Admission: $7, SC(65) $4.
Affiliate: YMCA $3 to $7.
Notes: Bathing caps are required for all swimmers. Masks, fins and snorkels are not permitted in the pool.

NEW BEDFORD 508

GREATER NEW BEDFORD YMCA 25 S. Water St.
Phone: 997-0734.
Pool: 25y, indoors, heated, 82°.
Admission: $7.
Affiliate: YMCA 3 visits NC, then $3.

YWCA OF NEW BEDFORD 66 Spring St.
Phone: 999-3255.
Pool: 20y, 3 lanes, indoors, heated, 86°-87°.
Admission: $2 or $4.

NEWBURYPORT 508

YWCA OF NEWBURYPORT 13 Market St.
Phone: Pool: 462-7622. Main office: 465-0981.
Pool: 25y x 30f, indoors, heated, 84°-86°.
Admission: $6.

NEWTON 617

WEST SUBURBAN YMCA 276 Church St.
Phone: 244-6050.
Pool: 20y, indoors, heated, 81°.
Admission: $9.
Affiliate: Out-of-state YMCA 1 week NC. In-state YMCA $4.

NORTH ADAMS 413

NORTHERN BERKSHIRE YMCA 22 Brickyard Court
Phone: 663-6529.
Pool: 25y, indoors, heated, 82°-84°.
Admission: $5.
Affiliate: Y AWAY NC.

NORTH ATTLEBORO 508

HOCKOMOCK AREA YMCA 300 Elmwood St.
Phone: 695-7001.
Pool: 25y x 35f, 6 lanes, indoors, heated, 83°.
Admission: $4.
Affiliate: YMCA outside a 50 mile radius NC.
Notes: There is also a 25y, 5 lane, outdoor summer pool.

NORTH DARTMOUTH 508

NEW ENGLAND HEALTH & RACQUET CLUB 250 Faunce Corner Rd.
Phone: 999-2171.
Pool: 25y x 30f, 4 lanes, indoors, heated, 82°.
Admission: $14.
Affiliate: IHRSA $7.

NORTH EASTHAM 508

NORSEMAN ATHLETIC CLUB Route 6
Phone: 255-6370.
Pool: 25y x 30f, 5 lanes, indoors, heated, 83°.
Admission: $12, SC(65) $5.
Affiliate: IHRSA $6.
Hotel: All local hotels $10 with room key.
Masters: The Norseman Masters. Contact Tonia Stafford at 255-6370.

NORTHAMPTON 413

HAMPSHIRE REGIONAL YMCA 286 Prospect St.
Phone: 584-7086.
Pool: 25y, 6 lanes, indoors, heated, 81°.
Admission: $5.
Affiliate: Y AWAY $2.50.
To find: At Prospect St. and Massasoit, near Smith College and the Autumn Inn.
Masters: The HRY Masters. Contact Marcia Samsel or Deborah Krasnor at 584-7086.

NORWOOD 617

MAD MAGGIE'S HEALTH & RACQUETBALL CLUB 45 Vanderbilt Ave.
Phone: 769-2340.
Pool: 25y, 5 lanes, indoor/outdoor, heated, 80°.
Admission: Pool $6. Full facility $10.
Affiliate: IHRSA full facility $8.
Hotel: Comfort Inn Norwood NC with a pass from the hotel. Courtyards by Marriott (762-4700), Super 8 Sharon Motel (784-1000), & Factory Mutual (769-7900): $5 with room key.

PAXTON 508

PAXTON SPORTS CENTER 603 Pleasant St.
Phone: 755-0089.
Pool: 20y, indoors, heated, 82°.
Memberships: I/S $60 + $30/month.
Notes: There is also a 25y, outdoor, summer pool.

PEABODY   508

BALLY'S HOLIDAY HEALTH CLUB Northshore
Mall, Routes 128 & 114
Phone: 532-6666.
Pool: 25y, 3 lanes, indoors, heated, 80°.
Affiliate: Bally's NC.

PITTSFIELD   413

PITTSFIELD YMCA 292 North St.
Phone: 499-7650.
Pool: 25m x 43f, 6 lanes, indoors, heated, 83°.
Admission: $5.
Affiliate: Y AWAY NC. YMCA $3.
To find: Three blocks north of Park Square Rotary.

BERKSHIRE WEST ATHLETIC CLUB Dan Fox Dr.
Phone: 499-4600.
Pool: 20y x 30f, 5 lanes, indoor/outdoor, heated,
80°-82°.
Admission: $15.
Affiliate: IHRSA $7.50.

PLYMOUTH   508

PLYMOUTH ATHLETIC CLUB Aldrin Rd.
Phone: 746-7448.
Pool: 25y x 25f, indoors, heated, 81°.
Admission: $10.
Affiliate: IHRSA $5.
Masters: The Plymouth Athletic Club Masters.
Contact Ron Lotto at 746-7448.

QUINCY   617

SOUTH SHORE YMCA 79 Coddinton St.
Phone: 479-8500.
Pool: 25y, indoors, heated, 82°-83°.
Admission: $7 or $8.
Affiliate: Y AWAY NC.

RAYNHAM   508

RAYNHAM ATHLETIC CLUB 1250 New State
Hwy., Route 44
Phone: 823-5440.
Pool: 20y x 30f, 5 lanes, indoors, heated, 82°.
Memberships: $55/month.
To find: Off Route 24 exit for Route 44 (east), one
mile on the left.

REVERE   617

BALLY'S HOLIDAY HEALTH CLUB 1 Wesley Rd.
at Squire Rd.
Phone: 286-5400.
Pool: 25y, indoors, heated, 80°-82°.
Admission: Call.
Affiliate: Bally's NC.
Hotel: Days Inn Sagus (233-1800) NC.

NAUTILUS PLUS HEALTH CLUB 321 Charger St.
Phone: 286-0232.
Pool: 80f, 4 lanes, indoors, heated, 78°-79°.
Admission: $8.

NORTH SHORE ATHLETIC CLUB 794 Broadway
Phone: 284-2216.
Pool: 20y, 3 lanes, indoors, heated, 80°.
Admission: $10.
Affiliate: IHRSA $5.

SALEM   508

SALEM YMCA 1 Sewall St.
Phone: 744-0351.
Pool 1: 25m, 6 lanes, indoors, heated, 83°.
Pool 2: 25y, 6 lanes, indoors, heated, 83°.
Admission: $5.
Affiliate: YMCA & Tufts Plan $3.

SEEKONK   508

NEWMAN YMCA 472 Taunton Ave.
Phone: 336-7103.
Pool: 25m x 32f, 4 lanes, indoors, heated, 83°-85°.
Affiliate: YMCA NC.
Hotel: Johnson & Wales Inn (336-8700) — Call the
Y for details.

SHERWOOD ULTRA SPORT 1314 Fall River Ave.
(Route 6)
Phone: 336-6565.
Pool: 20y, indoors, heated, 80°.
Admission: $5.

SHREWSBURY   508

MASSACHUSETTS HEALTH & FITNESS, INC. 3
Tennis Dr.
Phone: 845-1000.
Pool: 20y, indoors, heated, 83°.
Admission: $5.

SOMERVILLE   617

SOMERVILLE YMCA 101 Highland Ave.
Phone: 625-5050.
Pool: 20y, indoors, heated, 83°-84°.
Admission: $7.
Affiliate: YMCA 2 visits NC, then $5.

SOUTHBRIDGE   508

TRI-COMMUNITY YMCA 43 Everett St.
Phone: 765-5466.
Pool: 25y, indoors, heated, 84°.
Admission: $8, SC(62) $2.
Affiliate: Active duty U.S. Military 30 days NC.
YMCA Call.
Masters: The Tri-Community YMCA Tritons.
Contact Robin Lataille at 765-5466.

SPRINGFIELD 413

METROPOLITAN SPRINGFIELD YMCA 275 Chestnut St.
Phone: 739-6951.
Pool: 25y x 24f, 4 lanes, indoors, heated, 85°.
Admission: $10.
Affiliate: Y AWAY outside a 50 mile radius NC. YMCA $3.

SHERATON SPRINGFIELD MONARCH PLACE HOTEL 1 Monarch Place
Phone: 781-1010. **Reservations:** 800-426-9004.
Pool: 50f, rectangular, indoors, heated, water temperature not reported.
Admission: Registered guests only NC.

SUDBURY 508

ATKINSON POOL 40 Fair Bank Rd.
Phone: 443-5658.
Pool: 25y, 8 lanes, indoors, heated, 82°.
Admission: Residents $5, non-residents $6.
Masters: The New England Masters. Contact Cathy Lynch Harris at 371-0847(h).

WALTHAM 617

WALTHAM YMCA 725 Lexington St.
Phone: 894-5295.
Pool: 25y, indoors, heated, 82°-86°.
Affiliate: YMCA Call.

WATERTOWN 617

WATERTOWN BOYS & GIRLS CLUB 25 Whites Ave.
Phone: 926-0968.
Pool: 25y, indoors, heated, 78°-82°.
Admission: $5.

THE MOUNT AUBURN CLUB 57 Coolidge Ave.
Phone: 923-2255.
Pool: 25y, indoors, heated, 80°.
Affiliate: IHRSA $10.

WAYLAND 508

METRO WEST YMCA - WAYLAND 258 Old Connecticut Path
Phone: 358-4200.
Pool: 25y x 40f, 4 lanes, indoors, heated, 84°.
Admission: $6.
Affiliate: Y AWAY NC.

LONGFELLOW TENNIS & FITNESS CLUB 524 Boston Post Rd.
Phone: 358-7355.
Pool: 25y x 35f, indoor/outdoor, heated, 83°.
Affiliate: IHRSA $8.

WELLESLEY 617

BABSON RECREATION CENTER, INC. 150 Great Plain Ave.
Phone: 239-6000.
Pool: 25y x 36f, 6 lanes, indoors, heated, 81°-83°.
Affiliate: IHRSA outside a 50 mile radius 3 visits per month $10 each.
Notes: There is also an outdoor, summer pool.
To find: Wellesley / Needham line on Route 135.

WEST BARNSTABLE 508

YMCA OF CAPE COD 2245 Ivannough Rd. / Route 132
Phone: 362-6500.
Pool: 25y x 40f, 6 lanes, indoors, heated, 80°.
Admission: $5.
Affiliate: Y AWAY 12 visits per month NC.
Notes: There is also a shallow water, 88°, therapy pool.
To find: Exit 6 off Mid Cape Hwy., across from Cape Cod Community College.

WEST NEWTON 617

DIVERSIFIED AQUATICS MASTERS at Fessenden School, 250 Waltham St.
Masters: Contact Reid Christen at 894-2261(h&w).
Pool: 25y x 35f, 5 lanes, indoor/outdoor, heated, 80°-82°.
Non-member participation: Call.
Notes: Coached workouts: M-F: 7-8PM.

WESTBORO 508

WESTBORO TENNIS & SWIM CLUB 35 Chauncy St.
Phone: 366-1222.
Pool: 25y, 6 lanes, indoor/outdoor, heated, 80°.
Affiliate: IHRSA $5.
Hotel: Ramada Inn Westboro (366-0202) $10 with room key.
Masters: A Masters group is in formation. Contact Sharyn Thurber at 366-1222.

WESTFIELD 413

YMCA OF GREATER WESTFIELD 67 Court St.
Phone: 568-8631.
Pool 1: 25y, 6 lanes, indoors, heated, 82°.
Pool 2: 20y, 4 lanes, indoors, heated, 86°.
Affiliate: Y AWAY outside a 50 mile radius NC.

WESTFORD 508

WESTFORD RACQUET & FITNESS CLUB 4 Littleton Rd.
Phone: 692-7597.
Pool: 25y, indoors, heated, 81°.
Affiliate: IHRSA Call.

WEYMOUTH   617

WEYMOUTH CLUB 75 Finnell Dr.
Phone: 337-4600.
Pool: 25y x 42f, 6 lanes, indoor/outdoor, heated,
78°-80°.
Admission: $8.
Affiliate: IHRSA Call.
To find: A half mile west of Route 18S at the
Stetson Shoe Building.
Masters: The Weymouth Club Masters. Contact
Aquatics Director Catherine Vaughn at 337-4600.

WEYMOUTH-CONNELL MEMORIAL POOL 220
Broad St. (Rear)
Phone: 335-2090.
Pool: 25y, 6 lanes, indoors, heated, 82°-86°.
Admission: NC.

WOBURN   617

RAMADA HOTEL 15 Middlesex Canal Park Rd.
Phone: 935-8760. **Reservations:** 800-2RAMADA.
Pool: 72-80f x 40-60f, quadrilateral, indoors, heat-
ed, 78°.
Admission: Registered guests only NC.

NORTH SUBURBAN FAMILY BRANCH YMCA
137 Lexington St.
Phone: 935-3270.
Pool: 25y, indoors, heated, 82°.
Admission: $7.
Affiliate: YMCA outside a 50 mile radius NC.

WORCESTER   508

WORCESTER ATHLETIC CLUB 440 Grove St.
Phone: 852-8209.
Pool: 25m, 4 lanes, indoors, heated, 81°.

Admission: $10.
Affiliate: IHRSA outside a 25 mile radius $5.
To find: Next to Boston Billiards.

BALLY'S HOLIDAY HEALTH CLUB 535 Lincoln
St.
Phone: 854-2100.
Pool: 23m, indoors, heated, 79°-81°.
Affiliate: Bally's NC.
Hotel: Holiday Inn (852-4000), Comfort Inn, &
Hampton Inn (757-0400): NC.

GREENDALE BRANCH YMCA 100 Shore Rd.
Phone: 852-6694.
Pool 1: 25m, indoors, heated, 83°.
Pool 2: 25y, indoors, heated, 88°.
Admission: $8.
Affiliate: Y AWAY Call.

YWCA OF CENTRAL MASSACHUSETTS 1 Salem
Square
Phone: 791-3181.
Pool: 25y, indoors, heated, 84°.
Admission: $7.
Hotel: Clarion Suites Hotel (753-3512) — Call the
hotel for information.

WORCESTER JCC 633 Salisbury St.
Phone: 756-7109.
Pool: 20y, indoors, heated, 78°-80°.
Affiliate: JCC Call.
Notes: There is also an outdoor, seasonal pool.

**YMCA OF GREATER WORCESTER - CENTRAL
BRANCH** 766 Main St.
Phone: 755-6101.
Pool: 25y x 25f, 4 lanes, indoors, heated, 82°.
Admission: Weekdays $7. Weekends $10.
Affiliate: YMCA 50% of general admission.

ALWAYS CALL FIRST

Pools close, they change names, affiliations, admission policies, and rates. And
just because a pool is listed in *Swimmers Guide* doesn't mean it's open all day,
every day, for just the type of workout you want to do. Spend a quarter to save
time and aggravation. . . always call first!

Houghton

Marquette

Stambaugh

Iron Mountain

Escanaba

Menominee

Michigan

Harbor Springs

East Jordan
Bellaire

Alpena

Traverse City

Wisconsin

75

Scottville

Big Rapids

Midland

Saginaw

Bay City(2)

Caro

Flint(4) Port Huron(2)

Muskegon
Grand Haven

Grand Rapids(9)
Rockford(2)

Flushing

Davison

69

Allendale
Holland

Grandville

East Lansing(2)

Waterford(2)

Illinois

Covert

Lansing(4)

Battle Creek
Kalamazoo

Howell

Okemos

96

Jackson Ann Arbor(8)

Detroit(17)

Benton Harbor(2)

Saint Joseph

Niles(2)

94

Portage

Marshall

Saline

69

Hillsdale

Adrian

Monroe

Wyandotte(2)

90

Indiana

Ohio

96

YMCA OF LENAWEE COUNTY 638 W. Maumee
St.
Phone: 263-2151.
Pool: 25y, indoors, heated, 84°.
Admission: $4.
Affiliate: YMCA NC.

GRAND VALLEY STATE UNIVERSITY 1 Campus
Dr.
Phone: 895-3313.

Pool: 25y x 50f, 6 lanes, indoors, heated, 80°.
Admission: $4.25.
Memberships: $22.50/month.

**ALPENA COUNTY RECREATIONAL PLAZA
POOL** 3303 S. 3rd St.
Phone: 354-8287.
Pool: 25y x 45f, 4 lap lanes, indoors, heated, 84°.
Admission: $2.
To find: Connected to Alpena High School.

Detroit Area

Howell • Waterford(2) • Sterling Heights • 94 • Bloomfield Hills • 75 • Troy • Mount Clemens • West Bloomfield • Warren • Farmington Hills • Birmingham(2) • Roseville • Brighton • Royal Oak(2) • Novi • Southfield(3) • Saint Clair Shores • Livonia(2) • Redford(2) • Highland Park • 96 • Plymouth • Westland(2) • Dearborn(3) • Detroit(17) • Ann Arbor(8) • 94 • 75 • Saline • Southgate • Wyandotte(2)

ANN ARBOR   313

LIBERTY SPORTS COMPLEX 2975 W. Liberty
Phone: 665-3738.
Pool: 25y, indoors, heated, 82°-84°.
Admission: $10.

MACK POOL 715 Brooks St.
Phone: Recorded schedule: 994-2898.
 Information: 994-2899.
Pool: 25m, indoors, heated, 82°.
Admission: $2.50, SC(62) $1.50. Summer: $2,
 SC $1.25.
To find: At Mack School.
Masters: The City of Ann Arbor Masters. Contact
 Don Swalwell or the Pool Manager at 994-2899.

ANN ARBOR YMCA 350 S. 5th Ave.
Phone: 663-0536.
Pool: 20y x 15f, 4 lanes, indoors, heated, 82°.
Admission: $5.
Affiliate: YMCA 3 visits per year NC.
Notes: There is also a 10y x 15f, indoor, heated,
 92°, shallow, therapeutic pool for water walking,
 stretching, etc. Arthritis and aqua-exercise classes
 are available.
To find: In downtown Ann Arbor, across from the
 public library.

BALLY'S VIC TANNY 615 Briarwood Dr.
Phone: 769-6600.
Pool: 25y, indoors, heated, 79°-82°.
Admission: 1 visit NC, then $10.
Affiliate: Bally's & IPFA: NC.

WASHTENAW COUNTY RECREATION CENTER
 2960 Washtenaw Ave. at Platt Ave.
Phone: 971-6337.

Pool: 25y, indoors, heated, 82°.
Admission: $2.

ANN ARBOR HILTON INN 610 Hilton Blvd.
Phone: 761-7800. **Reservations:** 800-344-7829.
Pool: 20y, rectangular, indoors, heated, 82°.
Admission: Registered guests only NC.

BALLY'S VIC TANNY 4860 Washtenaw Ave.
Phone: 434-5000.
Pool: 23y, indoors, heated, 74°.
Admission: $10.
Affiliate: Bally's NC.

**UNIVERSITY OF MICHIGAN NORTH CAMPUS
 RECREATION BUILDING** 2375 Hubbard
Phone: 763-4560.
Pool: 25y x 24f, 6 lanes, indoors, heated, 81°.
Memberships: $75/semester.

BATTLE CREEK   616

Y-CENTER 182 Capital Ave. N.E.
Phone: 962-7551.
Pool: 25y, indoors, heated, 80°.
Admission: $8.
Affiliate: Y AWAY NC.

BAY CITY   517

YWCA OF BAY COUNTY 3405 E. Midland Rd.
Phone: 686-4800.
Pool: 25y x 35f, 4 lanes, indoors, heated, 84°-86°.
Admission: $3, SC(60) $2.
Affiliate: YWCA $1.50, SC $1.
To find: Three blocks west of Euclid on Midland
 Rd.

BAY AREA FAMILY YMCA 111 N. Madison Ave.
Phone: 895-8596.
Pool: 20y, indoors, heated, 84°-85°.
Admission: $7.50.
Affiliate: YMCA NC.

BELLAIRE 616

SHANTY CREEK RESORT 1 Shanty Creek Rd.
Phone: 533-8621. **Reservations:** 800-678-4111.
Pool 1: 20y, indoors, heated, 80-82°.
Pool 2: 20y, outdoors, heated, 80°-82°.
Admission: Registered guests only NC.
Notes: The resort features golf in summer and skiing in winter.

BENTON HARBOR 616

U.S.A. FITNESS 233-A Michigan Ave.
Phone: 927-3313.
Pool: 20y, indoors, heated, 82°-84°.
Admission: $10.

THE TEEN CENTER 801 - 9th St.
Phone: 927-0612.
Pool: 25m x 40f, indoors, heated, 76°.
Notes: The pool was not open to the public during the 1994-1995 school year. The status of future operations is uncertain.

BIG RAPIDS 616

HEALTH & PHYSICAL EDUCATION BLDG. Ferris State University, 401 South St.
Phone: 592-2679.
Pool: 25y x 45f, 6 lanes, indoors, heated, 82°.
Admission: $2, SC(65) $1.
Memberships: $45/semester. $100/year.
To find: The pool is located behind the football stadium on campus.
Masters: The Big Rapids Masters Swim Club. Contact Jennifer Parks at 592-2673(w).

BIRMINGHAM 810

METRO DETROIT YMCA - BIRMINGHAM BRANCH 400 E. Lincoln
Phone: 644-9036.
Pool: 25y x 30f, 5 lanes, indoors, heated, 84°.
Admission: $10.
Affiliate: YMCA & U.S. Military: NC.
To find: On the south side of Lincoln (14.5 mile), two blocks west of Woodward Ave.

BEVERLY HILLS RACQUET & HEALTH CLUB 31555 Southfield Rd.
Phone: 642-8500.
Pool: 25y x 30f, 3 double lanes, indoors, heated, 80°.
Affiliate: IHRSA $10.
Hotel: Townsend Hotel (642-7900) NC with a pass from the hotel.
To find: Just north of 13 mile on Southfield Rd.

BLOOMFIELD HILLS 810

BALLY'S VIC TANNY 6420 Telegraph Rd.
Phone: 855-2300.
Pool: 25y, indoors, heated, 83°.
Admission: Call.
Affiliate: Bally's NC.

BRIGHTON 810

BRIGHTON HIGH SCHOOL 7878 Brighton Rd.
Phone: 229-1419.
Pool: 25y, 6 lanes, indoors, heated, 82°.
Admission: $1.50.
To find: Six blocks south of Grand River St.

CARO 517

CARO COMMUNITY POOL 301 Hooper St.
Phone: 673-3166.
Pool: 25m x 11.5m, 6 lanes, indoors, heated, 82°.
Admission: $1.
To find: The pool is in the high school complex.

COVERT 616

COVERT HIGH SCHOOL COMMUNITY POOL 35323 M-140 Hwy.
Phone: 764-0241.
Pool: 25y x 45f, 6 lanes, indoors, heated, 88°.
Admission: $1. Resident SC(65) NC.

DAVISON 810

DAVISON ATHLETIC CLUB G 2140 Fairway Dr.
Phone: 653-9602.
Pool: 25m, indoors, heated, 82°-84°.
Affiliate: IHRSA $7.
Hotel: Comfort Inn Davison (658-2700) Passes are sold at the hotel.

DEARBORN 313

BALLY'S VIC TANNY 22340 Michigan Ave.
Phone: 561-3320.
Pool: 25m, indoors, heated, 82°.
Admission: $10.
Affiliate: Bally's & IPFA: NC.
Hotel: Hampton Inn (436-9600) NC.

DEARBORN RACQUET & HEALTH CLUB 2727 S. Gulley Rd.
Phone: 562-1296.
Pool: 20y, indoors, heated, 80°.
Admission: $5.

FAIRLANE CLUB 5000 Fairlane Woods
Phone: 336-4400.
Pool: 25m, 5 lanes, indoors, heated, 82°.
Affiliate: Club Corp. of America NC.
Hotel: Hyatt Regency (593-1234), Dearborn Inn (271-2700), & Ritz Carlton (441-2000): $10.

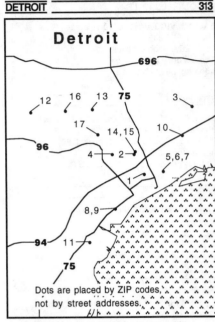

DETROIT ════════════════ 313

Detroit

696

12 16 13 **75**   3

17

14,15   10

96

4   2

5,6,7

1

8,9

94 11

75

Dots are placed by ZIP codes,
not by street addresses.

1. WHEELER RECREATION CENTER 637
Brewster St.
Phone: 833-9777.
Pool: 25y, indoors, heated, water temperature not reported.
Admission: Call.

2. DETROIT CONSIDINE CENTER 8904
Woodward Ave.
Phone: Pool: 876-0130. Center: 876-0131.
Pool: 25y, indoors, heated, 82°.
Memberships: $6/year.

3. HARRY HEILMANN RECREATION CENTER
19601 Crusade St.
Phone: 267-7153.
Pool: 25y, indoors, heated, 83°-84°.
Memberships: $6/year.

4. JOSEPH WALKER WILLIAMS CENTER 8431
Rosa Parks Blvd.
Phone: Pool: 898-2097. Center: 898-6584.
Pool: 25m, indoors, heated, water temperature not reported.
Memberships: $10/year.

5. THE RIVER PLACE: A GRAND HERITAGE
HOTEL 1000 River Place
Phone: 259-9500. **Reservations:** 800-890-9505.
Pool: 20y x 20f, 3 lanes, indoors, heated, 82°.
Admission: $5. Registered guests NC with room key.
Memberships: I/S $50 + $25/month.
To find: One mile east of downtown Detroit.

6. DETROIT YACHT CLUB Belle Isle Island
Phone: 824-1200.
Pool: 25y, indoors, heated, 76°-80°.
Memberships: I/S $1,000 + $125/month.
Notes: A private, social/yacht club, the Detroit Yacht Club has racquetball, squash, a fitness center, restaurant, and an outdoor, seasonal pool.

7. COLEMAN A. YOUNG RECREATION CENTER
1500 Chene
Phone: 224-0530.
Pool: 25y, indoors, heated, 82°-83°.
Memberships: $7/year.

8. WESTERN BRANCH YMCA 1601 Clark St.
Phone: 554-2136.
Pool: 20y, 5 lanes, indoors, heated, 72°.
Admission: $6.
Affiliate: YMCA Call.

9. PATTON RECREATION CENTER 2301
Woodmere
Phone: 297-9337.
Pool: 25y, indoors, heated, 75°-80°.
Admission: $1.

10. EASTSIDE BRANCH YMCA 10100 Harper
Ave.
Phone: 921-0770.
Pool: 20y, indoors, heated, 82°.
Admission: $1.
Affiliate: YMCA NC.

11. KEMENY RECREATION CENTER 2260 S. Fort
St.
Phone: Pool: 297-9233. Center: 297-9332.
Pool: 25y, indoors, heated, 84°.
Memberships: $6/year.

12. NORTHWESTERN YMCA 21755 W. Seven
Mile Rd.
Phone: 533-3700.
Pool: 25y x 25f, 4 lanes, indoors, heated, 85°.
Admission: 3 visits per year $7.
Affiliate: YMCA NC.
To find: At Seven Mile Rd. and Lasher, across the street from the Royal Golf Course.

13. JOHNSON RECREATION CENTER 8640
Chippewa
Phone: Pool: 935-3122. Center: 935-3121.
Pool: 25y, indoors, heated, 80°.
Memberships: $6/year.

14. DOWNTOWN DETROIT YMCA 2020 Witherell
St.
Phone: 962-6126.
Pool: 25y x 30f, 4 lanes, indoors, heated, 83°-84°.
Admission: $6.
Affiliate: YMCA NC.
To find: North of Grand Circus Park.

15. DETROIT ATHLETIC CLUB 241 Madison Ave.
Phone: 963-9200.
Pool: 25y, indoors, heated, 81°-83°.
Memberships: I/S $750 + $178/month.

16. NORTHWEST ACTIVITIES CENTER 18100
Meyers Rd.
Phone: 935-3733.
Pool: 26m, indoors, heated, 80°.
Admission: $5.

17. BUTZEL ADAMS RECREATION COMPLEX
10500 Lyndon
Phone: 935-3119.
Pool: 25y, indoors, heated, 82°.
Admission: $1.

EAST JORDAN   616

EAST JORDAN COMMUNITY POOL 240 N. Maple
St.
Phone: 536-2250.
Pool: 25y x 33f, 5 lanes, indoors, heated, 82°-84°.
Admission: Residents $2, SC(60) $1.50. Non-residents $2.50, SC $2.
To find: Attached to East Jordan High School.

EAST LANSING   517

YMCA OF LANSING - PARKWOOD BRANCH
2306 Haslett Rd.
Phone: 332-8657.
Pool: 25y x 35f, 5 lanes, indoors, heated, 83°.
Affiliate: YMCA NC.
To find: I-96 to Okemos Rd. Exit. Go north on
Okemos Rd. to Haslett Rd. and turn west. Go one
half mile.

MICHIGAN ATHLETIC CLUB / LANSING 2900
Hannah Blvd.
Phone: 337-0002.
Pool: 25m, indoors, heated, 80°.
Admission: $15.
Affiliate: IHRSA $7.

ESCANABA   906

YMCA OF DELTA COUNTY 2001 N. Lincoln Rd.
Phone: 789-0005.
Pool: 25y x 36f, 6 lanes, indoors, heated, 83°.
Admission: $7.
Affiliate: YMCA 1 visit NC.
To find: On the southeast corner of the Bay De
Noc Community College Campus on Hwy. 2/41 in
Escanaba.

FARMINGTON HILLS   810

FARMINGTON AREA YMCA 28100 Farmington
Rd.
Phone: 553-4020.
Pool: 25m x 13m, 6 lanes, indoors, heated, 84°.
Admission: $12.

Affiliate: YMCA NC.
Hotel: Comfort Inn (471-9220) NC with a pass from
the hotel.

FLINT   810

RECREATION BUILDING University of Michigan -
Flint, 303 E. Kearsley St.
Phone: 762-3441.
Pool: 25y x 32f, 4 lanes, indoors, heated, 82°.
Admission: $5, SC(62) $2.50.
Hotel: Hampton Inn (238-7744) NC with a pass
from the hotel.
Memberships: 1/12 months $60/$316, SC
$30/$158.
To find: Two blocks east of downtown Flint.
Kearsley St. at Chavez Dr.

YWCA OF GREATER FLINT 310 E. 3rd St.
Phone: 238-7621.
Pool: 25y, indoors, heated, 86°.
Admission: $3.75-$7.
Affiliate: YWCA $3.75.

FLINT YMCA 411 E. 3rd St.
Phone: 232-9622.
Pool: 25y x 40f, 5 lanes, indoors, heated, 82°.
Admission: $5.50.
Affiliate: Y AWAY NC.
Masters: The Flint YMCA Masters. Contact Patrice
Hirr at 695-1773(h).

HURLEY HEALTH & FITNESS CENTER 4500 S.
Saginaw St.
Phone: 733-2363.
Pool: 25y x 32f, 4 lanes, indoors, heated, 83°.
Admission: $7. 'Masters Swim' Wed. 7-8:30PM
$3.
Affiliate: IHRSA $3.50.
To find: At the intersection of Hemphill and
Saginaw St. just east of I-475.

FLUSHING   810

YMCA OF FLINT G-5219 W. Pierson Rd.
Phone: 732-9622.
Pool: 24y, indoors, heated, 82°.
Admission: $6.50.
Affiliate: Y AWAY NC. YMCA $3.25.

GRAND HAVEN   616

TRI-CITIES FAMILY YMCA 1 'Y' Dr.
Phone: 842-7051.
Pool: 25m x 36f, 6 lanes, indoors, heated, 82°.
Admission: $5.
Affiliate: YMCA $1.
To find: Just before the state park and across from
the U.S. Coast Guard Station.
Masters: The Westshore Waves. Contact Kristen
Schattey at 842-7051.

GRAND RAPIDS   616

FORD NATATORIUM Grand Rapids Community
College, 143 Bostwick N.E.
Phone: 771-4266.
Pool: 25y, 6 lanes, indoors, heated, 80°.
Admission: Pool 50¢. Full facility $5.
Memberships: 1/12 months $25/$125.
Notes: The pool closes for the month of Jul.
To find: Next to Butterworth Hospital.
Masters: The West Michigan Masters. Contact
Brad Henson at 771-4266.

YWCA OF GRAND RAPIDS 25 Sheldon Blvd. S.E.
Phone: 459-4681.
Pool: 22y x 18f, 4 lanes, indoors, heated, 83°-86°.
Admission: $5.
To find: One block south of Fulton St., across the
street from Veterans Memorial Park. Use the park-
ing lot entrance on Weston St.

CHARLEVOIX CLUB 975 Ottawa Ave. N.W.
Phone: 235-4580.
Pool: 25y, indoors, heated, 83°-85°.
Admission: $8.

WEST FAMILY YMCA 902 Leonard N.W.
Phone: 458-1147.
Pool: 20y, 4 lanes, indoors, heated, 86°.
Admission: $7.
Affiliate: Y AWAY $3.50.

CRESTON HIGH SCHOOL SWIMMING POOL
1720 Plainfield N.E.
Phone: 771-2430.
Pool: 25y x 52f, 6 lanes, indoors, heated, 81°.
Admission: NC.
Notes: The pool operates from Aug. to Mar.
To find: From U.S. 131 take the Ann St. Exit east
to the end. The pool is on the southeast corner of
the school.

SOUTHEAST YMCA 730 Forest Hill S.E.
Phone: 285-9077.
Pool: 25m x 15m, 6 lanes, indoors, heated, 84°.
Admission: $7.
Affiliate: Y AWAY $3.50.

EAST HILLS ATHLETIC CLUB 1640 E. Paris
Phone: 942-9521.
Pool: 25m, indoors, heated, 84°.
Affiliate: IHRSA $8.
Hotel: Some local hotels $12 with room key. Call
the Club for participating locations.

MICHIGAN ATHLETIC CLUB 2500 Burton St. S.E.
Phone: 956-0944.
Pool: 25m, indoors, heated, 82°.
Affiliate: IHRSA $7.

**FOREST HILLS COMMUNITY & AQUATIC
CENTER** 660 Forest Hill Ave. S.E.

Phone: 285-8775.
Pool: 25y x 25m, 8 x 6 lanes, indoors, heated, 80°-
81°.
Admission: Residents $1, SC(60) NC. Non-resi-
dents $2, SC $1 with Golden Age Card.

GRANDVILLE   616

PREMIER ATHLETIC CENTER 2828 - 28th St.
S.W.
Phone: 538-4270.
Pool: 20y x 40f, indoors, heated, 84°.
Affiliate: IPFA NC.

HARBOR SPRINGS   616

HARBOR SPRINGS COMMUNITY POOL 327 E.
Bluff Dr.
Phone: 526-9212.
Pool: 25y, 6 lanes, indoors, heated, 82°.
Admission: $3.
To find: Adjacent to the Harbor Springs High
School, enter off Pine St.
Masters: The Harbor Masters. Contact Marilyn
Early at 526-9824.

HIGHLAND PARK   313

HIGHLAND PARK FAMILY YMCA 13220
Woodward Ave.
Phone: 868-1946.
Pool: 20m, 4 lanes, indoors, heated, 74°.
Admission: $2.

HILLSDALE   517

GEORGE ROCHE FIELD HOUSE Hillsdale
College, 201 Oak St.
Phone: 437-2590.
Pool: 25m, 6 lanes, indoors, heated, 80°.
Admission: Call.

HOLLAND   616

HOLLAND COMMUNITY SWIMMING POOL 170
W. 22nd St.
Phone: 393-7595.
Pool: 25y x 45f, 6 lanes, indoors, heated, 83°.
Admission: 75¢.
Notes: There is also a 15y x 30f, 82°, deep water
pool.
To find: Two blocks west of River Ave. (the main
north/south road).

HOUGHTON   906

STUDENT DEVELOPMENT COMPLEX Michigan
Technological University, 1400 Townsend Dr.
Phone: 487-2578.
Pool: 25y, 8 lanes, indoors, heated, 79°-81°.
Admission: $3.
Memberships: 1 week $25. 1/3/12 months
$50/$70/$175.
To find: On McInnis Dr.

HOWELL   517

HOWELL AREA AQUATIC CENTER 1200 W. Grand River
Phone: 548-6355.
Pool: 25m x 25y, 6 lanes, indoors, heated, 83°-84°.
Admission: $3, SC(55) $2.50.
To find: The pool is attached to the high school field house.

IRON MOUNTAIN   906

CRYSTAL LAKE COMMUNITY CENTER 800 Crystal Lake Blvd.
Phone: 774-9003.
Pool: 25y x 42f, 6 lanes, indoors, heated, 81°.
Admission: $2.

JACKSON   517

Y-CENTER 127 W. Wesley St.
Phone: 782-0537.
Pool: 25y, indoors, heated, 82°.
Admission: $5.
Affiliate: YMCA NC.

KALAMAZOO   616

KALAMAZOO FAMILY YMCA 1001 W. Maple St.
Phone: 345-9622.
Pool: 25y, indoors, heated, 82°.
Admission: $11.
Affiliate: YMCA NC.

LANSING   517

LANSING YWCA 217 Townsend St.
Phone: 485-7201.
Pool: 20y x 30f, 4 lanes, indoors, heated, 85°.
Admission: $5, SC(60) $2.50.
Affiliate: YWCA $2.50, SC $1.75.
To find: At the intersection of Allegan and Townsend, across the street from the Capitol and the Post Office.

HARLEY HOTEL OF LANSING 3600 Dunckel Dr.
Phone: 351-7600. **Reservations:** 800-321-2323.
Pool: 20y x 30f, indoors, heated, 82°.
Admission: Registered guests only NC.
Notes: There is also an outdoor pool operated from May to Sep.

OAK PARK YMCA 900 Long Blvd.
Phone: 694-3901.
Pool: 30m x 60f, 3 lanes, indoors, heated, 81°.
Affiliate: YMCA 1 week NC.
To find: Long Blvd. is at the first traffic light south of the I-96 overpass that crosses S. Cedar St.
Masters: Contact Wally Dobler by leaving a message at 694-3901.

DOWNTOWN YMCA 301 W. Lenawee St.
Phone: 484-4000.

Pool: 20y x 20f, 3 lanes, indoors, heated, 81°.
Affiliate: YMCA NC.
Hotel: Radisson Hotel (482-0188) $6.
To find: Four blocks south of the State Capitol.

LIVONIA   313

PARK PLACE ATHLETIC CLUB 37684 W. Six Mile
Phone: 462-3880.
Pool: 20m, 4 double lanes, indoors, heated, 80°-83°.
Affiliate: IHRSA $6.
Hotel: Marriott (462-3100), Courtyard by Marriott (462-2000), & Holiday Inn (464-1300): $4.

LIVONIA YMCA 14255 Stark Rd.
Phone: 261-2161.
Pool: 25y, indoors, heated, 84°.
Affiliate: YMCA NC.
Masters: Contact Shirley Ritter at 261-2161.

MARQUETTE   906

PHYSICAL EDUCATION INSTRUCTION FACILITY (PEIF) Northern Michigan University, Fair Ave. at Presque Isle Ave.
Phone: 227-2414.
Pool: 25y x 60f, 8 lanes, indoors, heated, 80°.
Admission: $5.
Memberships: $215/year (Aug. 1 - Jul. 31).
To find: Behind Hardee's Restaurant on Presque Isle Ave.

MARSHALL   616

MARSHALL HIGH SCHOOL 701 N. Marshall Ave.
Phone: 781-1331.
Pool: 25y x 45f, 6 lanes, indoors, heated, 80°.
Admission: $1.50. Resident SC(62) NC.
To find: Two blocks south of I-94.

MENOMINEE   906

MARINETTE-MENOMINEE YMCA 1600 West Dr.
Phone: 863-9983.
Pool: 25y x 25f, 4 lanes, indoors, heated, 85°.
Admission: $6.
Affiliate: YMCA NC.
To find: At the intersection of West Dr. and 14th Ave. West Dr. is parallel to and one block west of 25th St.

MIDLAND   517

MIDLAND COMMUNITY CENTER 2001 George St.
Phone: 832-7936.
Pool: 25y, 4 lanes, indoors, heated, 84°.
Admission: $3.

MONROE   313

MONROE FAMILY YMCA 1111 W. Elm
Phone: 241-2606.
Pool: 25y, 6 lanes, indoors, heated, 84°.
Admission: $6.
Affiliate: YM/WCA & YM/WHA, both outside a 25
mile radius: 3 visits per year NC. U.S. Military NC.
To find: From I-75 take the Elm Ave. Exit, turn west
after the fourth light. The YMCA is on the left after
the railroad tracks.

MOUNT CLEMENS   810

MACOMB YMCA 10 N. River Rd.
Phone: 468-1411.
Pool: 25y, indoors, heated, 80°.
Affiliate: YMCA $1.

MUSKEGON   616

MUSKEGON YFCA 900 W. Western Ave.
Phone: 722-9322.
Pool: 25m x 42f, 6 lanes, indoors, heated, 84°.
Admission: $10.
Affiliate: Y AWAY NC.
Hotel: Holiday Inn Harbor (722-0100) $6 with a
pass from the hotel.

NILES   616

NILES-BUCHANAN YMCA FAMILY CENTER 315
W. Main St.
Phone: 683-1552.
Pool: 20y x 20f, 4 lanes, indoors, heated, 85°.
Admission: $6.
Affiliate: Y AWAY NC. YMCA 2 weeks NC.
To find: Two blocks west of downtown Niles.

HONG'S TAE KWAN DO 1118 Ontario Rd.
Phone: 684-5951.
Pool: 25y, indoors, heated, 78°-80°.
Memberships: $35/month (3 year minimum mem-
bership).

NOVI   810

BALLY'S VIC TANNY 43055 Crescent Blvd.
Phone: 349-7410.
Pool: 25y, indoors, heated, 78°-82°.
Admission: $10.
Affiliate: Bally's & IPFA: NC.
Hotel: Wyndham Garden Hotel (344-8800) NC.

OKEMOS   517

COURT ONE ATHLETIC CLUBS 2291 Research
Circle
Phone: 349-1199.
Pool: 25y, 5 lanes, indoors, heated, 83°.
Affiliate: IHRSA $5.

PLYMOUTH   313

BALLY'S VIC TANNY 40700 Ann Arbor Rd.
Phone: 459-8890.
Pool: 25m, indoors, heated, 82°-84°.
Affiliate: Bally's & IPFA: NC.

PORT HURON   810

BIRCHWOOD ATHLETIC CLUB 2900 Krafft Rd.
Phone: 385-4475.
Pool: 20y x 40f, 3 lanes, indoors, heated, 82°.
Admission: $10.
Affiliate: IHRSA outside a 60 mile radius $7.
To find: At the corner of Pine Grove & Krafft, direct-
ly behind the Denny's restaurant.

BLUE WATER YMCA 700 Fort St.
Phone: 987-6400.
Pool: 20y, 4 lanes, indoors, heated, 82°.
Admission: Out-of-town visitors — Call.
Affiliate: YMCA NC.
To find: Two blocks east of downtown next to the
National Bank of Detroit (NBD) Building on the St.
Clair River.

PORTAGE   616

PORTAGE FAMILY YMCA PROGRAM CENTER
2900 W. Centre Ave.
Phone: 329-9622.
Pool: 25y, indoors, heated, 82°.
Admission: $11.
Affiliate: YMCA NC.

REDFORD   313

NORTHWEST YWCA 25940 Grand River Ave.
Phone: 537-8500.
Pool: 25y x 15m, indoors, heated, 84°.
Memberships: I/S $35 + $35/month + $2/swim,
SC(55) + $25 + $2.

BALLY'S VIC TANNY 9359 Telegraph Rd.
Phone: 535-5010.
Pool: 25y, indoors, heated, 84°.
Admission: Call.
Affiliate: Bally's & IPFA: NC.

ROCKFORD   616

ROCKFORD HIGH SCHOOL POOL 4100 Kroes
Phone: 866-9855.
Pool: 25y x 20y, 8 lanes, indoors, heated, 80°.
Admission: Residents $1, SC(60) 50¢. Non-resi-
dents $2, SC $1.
Masters: The West Michigan Masters. Contact
Richard Ten Hoor at 866-6328.

ROCKFORD MIDDLE SCHOOL POOL 397 E.
Division

Phone: 866-7144.
Pool: 25y x 40f, 6 lanes, indoors, heated, 84°.
Admission: Residents $1, SC(60) 50¢. Non-residents $2, SC $1.
To find: At the northwest corner of Wolverine Blvd. and Ten Mile Rd.

ROSEVILLE 810

ROSE SHORES FITNESS & RACQUET CLUB at the Days Inn of Roseville, 31950 Little Mack
Phone: Club: 296-2200. Hotel: 296-6700.
Reservations: 800-437-2747.
Pool: 25y x 33f, 5 lanes, indoors, heated, 84°.
Admission: $10. M-Th before 4PM $6.
Registered guests NC with room key.
Affiliate: IHRSA Call.
Memberships: 3/6/12 months $90/$150/$288, SC(55) $81/$135/$259.20.
To find: At the corner of Masonic and Little Mack.

ROYAL OAK 810

SOUTH OAKLAND FAMILY YMCA 1016 W. 11 Mile Rd.
Phone: 547-0030.
Pool: 25y x 30f, 5 lanes, indoors, heated, 82°-86°.
Admission: $7.
Affiliate: YMCA NC.
To find: Two blocks east of Woodward Ave.
Masters: S.O.A.K. Contact Mike Conley by leaving a message at 547-0030.

GEORGE A. DONDERO HIGH SCHOOL 709 N. Washington
Phone: 435-8400 ext. 208.
Pool: 25y x 25m, 8 lanes, indoors, heated, 78°.
Admission: $1, SC(65) NC.
To find: Between 11 Mile Rd. and Catalpa.

SAGINAW 517

SAGINAW YMCA 1915 Fordney St.
Phone: 753-7721.
Pool: 20y, 4 lanes, indoors, heated, 80°-82°.
Admission: $6.
Affiliate: YMCA NC.
Notes: A new, 25y, 6 lane pool will open in 1995.

SAINT CLAIR SHORES 810

BALLY'S VIC TANNY 20701 E. 8 Mile Rd.
Phone: 772-0005.
Pool: 25m, indoors, heated, 82°.
Affiliate: Bally's & IPFA: NC.

SAINT JOSEPH 616

BENTON HARBOR-ST. JOSEPH YMCA 3665 Hollywood Rd.
Phone: 429-9727.
Pool: 25m x 37f, 6 lanes, indoors, heated, 83°.
Admission: $8.
Affiliate: YMCA 12 visits per year NC.

SALINE 313

SALINE RECREATION COMPLEX 1866 Woodland Dr.
Phone: 429-3502.
Pool: 25y x 60f, 6 lanes, indoors, heated, 82°.
Admission: $5, SC(60) $3.
To find: South off Textile between Ann Arbor Saline Rd. and State St.

SCOTTVILLE 616

WEST SHORE COMMUNITY COLLEGE RECREATION CENTER 3000 N. Stiles Rd.
Phone: 845-6211.
Pool: 25m, 6 lanes, indoors, heated, 82°.
Admission: $2, SC(60) $1.
Memberships: 1/3/6/9/12 months $20/$40/$55/$65/$85.
To find: Three miles north on Stiles Rd. and three miles east of Ludington.

SOUTHFIELD 810

FRANKLIN FITNESS & RACQUET CLUB 29350 Northwestern Hwy.
Phone: 352-8000.
Pool: 20y x 30f, 4 lanes, indoors, heated, 82°.
Affiliate: IHRSA $12.
Hotel: All local hotels $12. Call the club for details.
Notes: There is also a 25y x 60f, 6 lane, outdoor, summer pool.
To find: On Northwestern Hwy. between 12 Mile and 13 Mile Rds.

BALLY'S VIC TANNY 16000 Northland Dr.
Phone: 557-4700.
Pool: 24y, indoors, heated, 84°.
Admission: Call.
Affiliate: Bally's & IPFA: NC.

CMI-HEALTH & TENNIS CLUB INC. 30333 Southfield Rd.
Phone: 646-8990.
Pool: 20y, indoors, heated, 78°-82°.
Affiliate: IHRSA $10.
Notes: There is also a 25y, outdoor, heated 78°, summer pool.

SOUTHGATE 313

RAMADA HERITAGE CENTER 17201 Northline Rd.
Phone: 283-4400. **Reservations:** 800-2-RAMA-DA.
Pool: 21y x 28f, rectangular, indoors, heated, 79°-82°.
Admission: Registered guests only NC.

STAMBAUGH 906

GEORGE YOUNG RECREATIONAL COMPLEX Youngs Lane off C.R. 424

Phone: 265-3401.
Pool: 20y, indoors, heated, 82°.
Admission: $5.

STERLING HEIGHTS   810

BALLY'S VIC TANNY 44987 Schoenherr Rd.
Phone: 254-4411.
Pool: 25y, indoors, heated, 82°.
Admission: $10.
Affiliate: Bally's & IPFA: NC.

TRAVERSE CITY   616

GRAND TRAVERSE COUNTY CIVIC CENTER
POOL 1125 W. Civic Center Dr.
Phone: 922-4814.
Pool: 25y x 42f, 6 lanes, indoors, heated, 82°.
Admission: $2, SC(62) $1.50.

TROY   810

BALLY'S VIC TANNY 2501 W. Big Beaver Rd.
Phone: 649-0555.
Pool: 25y, indoors, heated, 80°.
Admission: $10.
Affiliate: Bally's & IPFA: NC.
Hotel: Somerset Inn NC.

WARREN   810

WARREN CITY POOL 27400 Campbell
Phone: 754-1570.
Pool: 25y, indoor/outdoor, heated, 86°-87°.
Admission: Residents: $1.50, SC(55) $1. Non-
residents $2.50, SC $2.
Hotel: All local hotels — Resident rate with current
hotel receipt.

WATERFORD   810

BALLY'S VIC TANNY 1490 N. Oakland Blvd.
Phone: 666-3611.
Pool: 25y, indoors, heated, 78°.
Admission: Call.
Affiliate: Bally's & IPFA: NC.

PRESCRIPTION FITNESS INC. 5210 Highland Rd.
Phone: 674-8855.
Pool: 68f, indoors, heated, 82°.
Admission: $6.

WEST BLOOMFIELD   810

JEWISH COMMUNITY CENTER 6600 W. Maple
Rd.
Phone: 661-1000.
Pool: 25y, indoors, heated, 85°.
Admission: $8.
Affiliate: JCC NC.

WESTLAND   313

FORUM HEALTH SPA 34250 Ford Rd.
Phone: 729-0600.
Pool: 20y x 30f, indoors, heated, 80°.
Admission: $5.

WAYNE-WESTLAND YMCA 827 S. Wayne Rd.
Phone: 721-7044.
Pool: 25m x 40f, 6 lanes, indoors, heated, 85°.
Admission: $5, SC(62) $2.
Affiliate: YMCA 3 visits per year NC.
To find: East of I-275 on Wayne Rd., between Ford
Rd. and Michigan Ave.

WYANDOTTE   313

WYANDOTTE MEMORIAL SWIM POOL 1931
Ludington St.
Phone: 246-4437.
Pool: 25m, indoors, heated, 85°.
Admission: $1.50.

DOWNRIVER FAMILY YMCA 3211 Fort St.
Phone: 281-2600.
Pool: 25y, 5 lanes, indoors, heated, 80°.
Admission: $5.
Affiliate: Y AWAY NC.
To find: At the northeast corner of Eureka and Fort
St.

Minnesota

North Dakota

Grand Rapids

Virginia

Duluth(2)

Breezy Point

Brainerd

Fergus Falls

29

Alexandria

35

Wisconsin

94

Lindstrom

Ramsey

Stillwater

Brooklyn Park

Saint Paul(7)

Minneapolis(8)

Eden Prairie(3)

Cottage Grove

South Dakota

Chaska

Eagan

Red Wing

94

Lakeville(2)

Northfield

Winona(2)

Mankato

Faribault

Worthington

Albert Lea(2)

Austin

Rochester(3)

90

LeRoy

Iowa

35

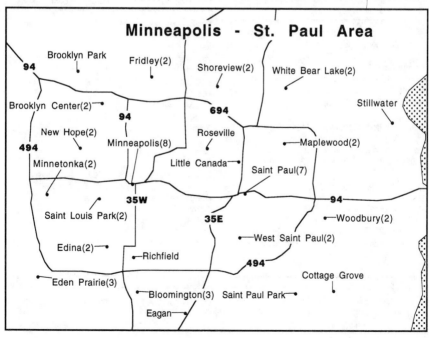

Minneapolis - St. Paul Area

Brooklyn Park

Fridley(2)

Shoreview(2)

White Bear Lake(2)

94

Stillwater

Brooklyn Center(2)

694

New Hope(2)

Roseville

Maplewood(2)

494

Minneapolis(8)

Minnetonka(2)

Little Canada

Saint Paul(7)

Saint Louis Park(2)

35W

94

Woodbury(2)

35E

Edina(2)

West Saint Paul(2)

Richfield

494

Eden Prairie(3)

Cottage Grove

Bloomington(3)

Saint Paul Park

Eagan

ALBERT LEA   507

DAYS INN OF ALBERT LEA 2306 E. Main St.
Phone: 373-6471. **Reservations:** 800-325-2525.
Pool: 50f x 25f, rectangular, indoors, heated, 83°.
Admission: $3. Registered guests NC.
Notes: Non-guest swimmers must bring their own towels.

ALBERT LEA YMCA 2021 W. Main St.
Phone: 373-8228.
Pool: 25y, indoors, heated, 78°.
Admission: $8.55.
Affiliate: YMCA NC.

ALEXANDRIA   612

DOUGLAS COUNTY SERVICES CENTER 715 Elm St.
Phone: 762-2868.
Pool: 25y x 36f, 5 lanes, indoors, heated, 84°.
Admission: Lap swimming $2. Water exercise $3.
To find: At 9th Ave. and Fillmore, one block west of Broadway.

AUSTIN   507

AUSTIN YMCA 704 - 1st Dr. N.W.
Phone: 433-1804.
Pool: 25y x 42f, 6 lanes, indoors, heated, 86°.
Admission: Out-of-county visitors $5.
Affiliate: YMCA & U.S. Military: NC.
To find: Take 4th St. N.W. off I-90 to 1st Dr. and turn left. The YMCA is three blocks down on the left.

BLOOMINGTON   612

DECATHLON ATHLETIC CLUB 7800 Cedar Ave. S.
Phone: 854-7777.
Pool: 25y, 4 lanes, indoors, heated, 78°-80°.
Hotel: Registered guests NC.
Memberships: Call.

HOLIDAY INN AIRPORT 2 5401 Green Valley Dr.
Phone: 831-8000. **Reservations:** 800-HOLIDAY.
Pool: 20y, rectangular, indoors, heated, 82°.
Admission: Registered guests only NC.

BALLY'S U.S. SWIM & FITNESS 4951 W. 80th St.
Phone: 896-1000.
Pool: 25m, 5 lanes, indoors, heated, 75°.
Admission: $10.
Affiliate: Bally's & IPFA: NC.
Hotel: Holiday Inn (831-9595), Embassy Suites (884-4811), & Hotel Seville: NC.

BRAINERD   218

BRAINERD FAMILY YMCA 602 Oak St.
Phone: 829-4767.
Pool: 25y, 4 lanes, indoors, heated, 84°.

Admission: $4.25, SC(62) $3.20.
Affiliate: YMCA & YWCA: NC.

BREEZY POINT   218

BREEZY POINT RESORT
Phone: 562-7811. **Reservations:** 800-432-3777.
Pool: 58f, rectangular, indoors, heated, 88°.
Admission: Registered guests only NC.

BROOKLYN CENTER   612

HIGHWAY 100 NORTH FRANCE RACQUET,
SWIM & HEALTH CLUB 4001 Lake Breeze Ave.
Phone: 435-3157.
Pool: 82.25f x 39.5f, 6 lanes, indoors, heated, 83°.
Admission: $15.
Affiliate: IHRSA $10, 1 week $20.
Hotel: Omni Northstar (338-2288), Minneapolis Marriott Southwest (935-5500), Marquette (332-2351), Whitney (339-9300), Sheraton Park Place (542-8600), & Crown Sterling Downtown (333-3111): Purchase passes at the hotels.

BROOKLYN CENTER COMMUNITY CENTER
6301 Shingle Creek Pkwy.
Phone: 569-3400.
Pool: 50m x 50f, 2 x 2 lanes for lap swimming, indoors, heated, 85°, in summer 82°.
Admission: $2.75, SC(62) $2.
To find: One block north of the Target Store.

BROOKLYN PARK   612

LIFETIME FITNESS 7970 Brooklyn Blvd.
Phone: 493-9393.
Pool: 25m, indoors, heated, 80°-82°.
Admission: $5.

CHASKA   612

CHASKA COMMUNITY CENTER 1661 Park Ridge Dr.
Phone: 448-5633.
Pool: 25y, indoors, heated, 82°.
Admission: Residents $2.25, non-residents $3.75.

COTTAGE GROVE   612

PARK SENIOR HIGH SCHOOL 8040 - 80th St.
Phone: Community Education Dept: 458-6600.
Pool: 25y, 5 lanes, indoors, heated, 82°.
Admission: $2.
Notes: The school district will be adding a second pool in Cottage Grove in the fall of 1995. For particulars, call the Community Education Department at 458-6600.

DULUTH   218

DULUTH AREA FAMILY YMCA 302 W. 1st St.
Phone: 722-4745.
Pool: 25y x 30f, 4 lanes, indoors, heated, 81°.

Admission: $6.
Affiliate: YMCA NC.
To find: One block from Superior St., in the block next to the Holiday Inn/Holiday Center.

CENTER FOR PERSONAL FITNESS 402 E. 2nd St.
Phone: 725-5400.
Pool: 25m, indoors, heated, 83°.
Admission: $6.
Masters: The CPF Masters. Contact Gregg Batinich at 725-5400.

EAGAN _____ **612**

BALLY'S U.S SWIM & FITNESS 3970 Sibley Memorial Hwy.
Phone: 452-0044.
Pool: 20y, 4 lanes, indoors, heated, 80°-81°.
Admission: $10.
Affiliate: Bally's NC.

EDEN PRAIRIE _____ **612**

FLAGSHIP ATHLETIC CLUB 755 Prairie Center Dr.
Phone: 941-2000.
Pool: 25m, indoors, heated, 84°.
Affiliate: IHRSA $10.

EDEN PRAIRIE COMMUNITY CENTER 16700 Valley View Rd.
Phone: 949-8470.
Pool: 25y, indoors, heated, 82°-83°.
Admission: $2.

CROSSTOWN RACQUET, SWIM & HEALTH CLUB 6233 Baker Rd.
Phone: 435-3157.
Pool: 25y x 40f, 6 lanes, indoors, heated, 83°.
Admission: $15.
Affiliate: IHRSA $10, 1 week $20.
Hotel: Omni Northstar (338-2288), Minneapolis Marriott Southwest (935-5500), Marquette (332-2351), Whitney (339-9300), Sheraton Park Place (542-8600), & Crown Sterling Downtown (333-3111): Purchase passes at the hotels.

EDINA _____ **612**

EDINBOROUGH PARK POOL 7700 York Ave. S.
Phone: 893-9890.
Pool: 25y x 46f, 6 lanes, indoors, heated, 84°.
Admission: $3.
Hotel: Hawthorn Suites Hotel (893-9300) NC with a pass from the hotel.

SOUTHDALE YMCA 7355 York Ave.
Phone: 835-2567.
Pool: 25y x 36f, 6 lanes, indoors, heated, 83°.
Affiliate: YMCA NC.

FARIBAULT _____ **507**

FARIBAULT COMMUNITY CENTER 15 W. Division
Phone: 334-2064.
Pool: 25y, 6 lanes, indoors, heated, 86°.
Admission: $2.55.

FERGUS FALLS _____ **218**

FERGUS FALLS YMCA 1164 N. Friberg
Phone: 739-4489.
Pool: 25m x 28f, 4 lanes, indoors, heated, 84°.
Admission: $4.50.
Affiliate: YMCA NC.
To find: On the northeast side of town, north of the high school and the middle school.

FRIDLEY _____ **612**

MOORE LAKE NORTHWEST RACQUET, SWIM & HEALTH CLUB 1200 Moore Lake Dr.
Phone: 435-3157.
Pool: 25y x 40f, 6 lanes, indoors, heated, 83°.
Admission: $15.
Affiliate: IHRSA $10, 1 week $20.
Hotel: Omni Northstar (338-2288), Minneapolis Marriott Southwest (935-5500), Marquette (332-2351), Whitney (339-9300), Sheraton Park Place (542-8600), & Crown Sterling Downtown (333-3111): Purchase passes at the hotels.
Notes: There is also a 25y x 40f, 6 lane, outdoor, summer pool.

BALLY'S U.S. SWIM & FITNESS 7200 University Ave. N.E.
Phone: 574-8888.
Pool: 25y, 5 lanes, indoors, heated, 80°-82°.
Admission: $10.
Affiliate: Bally's NC.
Hotel: Country Suites Hotel NC.

GRAND RAPIDS _____ **218**

ITASCA COUNTY FAMILY YMCA 400 River Rd.
Phone: 327-1161.
Pool: 25y, indoors, heated, 79°-84°.
Admission: $6.
Affiliate: YMCA NC.

LAKEVILLE _____ **612**

KENWOOD TRAIL JUNIOR HIGH SCHOOL 19455 Kenwood Trail
Phone: 469-7178.
Pool: 25y x 60f, 8 x 8 lanes, indoors, heated, 82°.
Admission: $1.50.
Affiliate: USMS $1.
Masters: The Lakeville Swim Club. Contact Heide Gross at 724-6252(h).

MCGUIRE JUNIOR HIGH SCHOOL 21220 Holy Oak Ave.

Phone: 469-7218.
Pool: 25y x 45f, 6 lanes, indoors, heated, 80°.
Admission: $1.50.
Affiliate: USMS $1.
Masters: The Lakeville Swim Club. Contact Heide Gross at 724-6252(h).

LEROY   507

LEROY OSTRANDER COMMUNITY POOL at Hwy. 14 & Hwy. 56
Phone: 324-5742.
Pool: 25y, indoors, heated, 85°.
Admission: $3.
Masters: Contact Pool Manager Kathy Roe at 324-5742.

LINDSTROM   612

CHISAGO SWIM POOL 29400 Olinda Trail
Phone: 257-5788.
Pool: 25y x 25m, 8 lanes, indoors, heated, 82°-84°.
Admission: $2.25.
To find: At the south end of Chisago High School.

LITTLE CANADA   612

BALLY'S U.S. SWIM & FITNESS 71 Minnesota Ave.
Phone: 484-4444.
Pool: 25y, 5 lanes, indoors, heated, 81°.
Admission: $10.
Affiliate: Bally's NC.

MANKATO   507

MANKATO FAMILY YMCA 1401 S. Riverfront Dr.
Phone: 387-8255.
Pool: 25y, indoors, heated, 84°.
Admission: $5.
Affiliate: YMCA 2 visits per month NC.

MAPLEWOOD   612

JOHN GLENN MIDDLE SCHOOL 1560 E. County Rd. 'B'
Phone: 770-4745.
Pool: 25y x 45f, 6 lanes, indoors, heated, 82°.
Admission: $1.50.
To find: Two blocks west of the Group Health Building on White Bear Ave.

MAPLEWOOD MIDDLE SCHOOL 2410 Holloway Ave.
Phone: 770-4745.
Pool: 25y x 45f, 6 lanes, indoors, heated, 84°-85°.
Admission: $1.50.
Notes: Water exercise classes are offered. Call for rates.

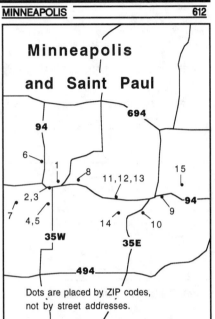

MINNEAPOLIS   612

Minneapolis
and Saint Paul

Dots are placed by ZIP codes, not by street addresses.

1. DOWNTOWN MINNEAPOLIS YMCA 30 S. 9th St.
Phone: 371-8750.
Pool: 25y x 56f, 8 lanes, indoors, heated, 82°-84°.
Admission: $10.70.
Affiliate: YMCA Call.

2. ARENA CLUB 600 1st Ave. N.
Phone: 435-3157.
Pool: 25y x 40f, 6 lanes, indoors, heated, 83°.
Admission: $15.
Affiliate: IHRSA $10, 1 week $20.
Hotel: Omni Northstar (338-2288), Minneapolis Marriott Southwest (935-5500), Marquette (332-2351), Whitney (339-9300), Sheraton Park Place (542-8600), & Crown Sterling Downtown (333-3111): Purchase passes at the hotels.

3. YWCA OF MINNEAPOLIS 1130 Nicollet Mall
Phone: 332-0501.
Pool: 25m, 5 lanes, indoors, heated, 82°-84°.
Admission: $10, SC(55) $5.
Affiliate: YWCA $5, SC $3.
Hotel: All local hotels $6.
Masters: Contact Brian Gutzmann or Susie George at the Uptown YWCA, 874-7131.

4. BLAISDELL BRANCH YMCA 3335 Blaisdell Ave. S.
Phone: 827-5401.
Pool: 25y, 6 lanes, indoors, heated, 84°.
Admission: $5.30.
To find: Four blocks south of Lake St., behind Burger King.

5. UPTOWN YWCA 2808 Hennepin Ave. S.
Phone: 874-7131.
Pool: 25y, 7 lanes, indoors, heated, 82°.
Admission: $10.
Affiliate: YWCA $5.
Masters: Contact Brian Gutzmann or Susie George at 874-7131.

6. NORTH COMMUNITY YMCA 1711 W. Broadway
Phone: 588-9484.
Pool: 25y x 38f, 6 lanes, indoors, heated, 80°-82°.
Admission: $5.
Affiliate: YMCA NC.
To find: Approximately two miles west of I-94, take the W. Broadway Exit.

7. CALHOUN BEACH CLUB 2925 Dean Pkwy.
Phone: 927-9951.
Pool: 20y, indoors, heated, 82°-83°.
Admission: Call.
Affiliate: IHRSA NC.

8. UNIVERSITY OF MINNESOTA AQUATIC CENTER 1900 University Ave. S.E.
Phone: 626-1352.
Pool: 50m x 25y, 8 x 18 lanes, indoors, heated, 80°.
Admission: $2 for two hours.
Hotel: Radisson Hotel Metrodome (379-8888) $5 for a full day's access to all recreational facilities.
To find: Behind the Radisson Metrodome/University of Minnesota Hotel.
Masters: The Gopher Swim Club. Contact Jim Anderson at 626-1352.

MINNETONKA   612

RIDGEDALE YMCA 12301 Ridgedale Dr.
Phone: 544-7708.
Pool: 25y, 6 lanes, indoors, heated, 82°-83°.
Admission: $10.65, SC(62) $4.
Affiliate: YMCA 2 weeks NC.
Hotel: Ramada Inn (592-0000) NC with a pass from the hotel.
To find: Located on the south side of Ridgedale Mall, next to the Ramada Plaza.

RUTH STRICKER'S THE MARSH - A CENTER FOR BALANCE & FITNESS 15000 Minnetonka Blvd.
Phone: 935-2202.
Pool: 73f, indoors, heated, 84°-85°.
Affiliate: IHRSA $15.

NEW HOPE   612

NORTHWEST YMCA 7601 - 42nd Ave. N.
Phone: 535-4800.
Pool: 25y, 6 lanes, indoors, heated, 83°.
Admission: $10.
Affiliate: Y AWAY NC.

BALLY'S U.S. SWIM & FITNESS 4239 Winnetka Ave. N.
Phone: 533-0101.
Pool: 25m, 5 lanes, indoors, heated, 82°-84°.
Admission: $10.
Affiliate: Bally's NC.

NORTHFIELD   507

THORPE POOL, WEST GYM Carleton College, 1 N. College St.
Phone: 663-4052.
Pool: 25y, 6 lanes, indoors, heated, 80°.
Admission: Call.
Memberships: Call.
Notes: There is also a 25y, 5 lane, 84° pool on the opposite side of the campus (Cowling Pool).
To find: On Hwy. 19, next to the large Physical Plant steam stack with a 'C' on it.

RAMSEY   612

HEALTHQUEST ATHLETIC CLUB 14100 Sunfish Lake Blvd.
Phone: 421-8103.
Pool: 25y x 24f, 5 lanes, indoors, heated, 82°.
Admission: $6.
Affiliate: IHRSA $4.
Hotel: Call the club for information about hotel guest rates.
To find: Sunfish Lake Blvd. is off Hwy. 10.

RED WING   612

RED WING YMCA Main & Broad St.
Phone: 388-4724.
Pool: 25y x 36f, 6 lanes, indoors, heated, 85°.
Admission: Out-of-town visitors $5.33.
Affiliate: YMCA & U.S. Military: NC.
Masters: Contact Paul Windrath by leaving a message at 388-4724.

RICHFIELD   612

BALLY'S U.S. SWIM & FITNESS 100 W. 66th St.
Phone: 861-5505.
Pool: 20y, 5 lanes, indoors, heated, 82°.
Admission: $10.
Affiliate: Bally's NC.

ROCHESTER   507

ROCHESTER / OLMSTED RECREATION CENTER 21 Elton Hills Dr.
Phone: 281-6167.
Pool: 50m OR 25y + 27m, 8 OR 16 lanes, indoors, heated, 82°-83°.
Admission: $2.75.
Notes: The pool is configured for long course swimming in the summer.
Masters: The Rochester Swim Club. Contact John Sfire at 252-8569(w).

ROCHESTER   CONTINUED

ROCHESTER ATHLETIC CLUB 3100 - 19th St.
S.W.
Phone: 282-6000.
Pool: 25m, 5 lanes, indoors, heated, 77°-79°.
Affiliate: IHRSA $10.

ROCHESTER AREA FAMILY YMCA 709 - 1st
Ave. S.W.
Phone: 287-2260.
Pool: 25y x 35f, 5 lanes, indoors, heated, 83°.
Admission: $7.50.
Affiliate: Y AWAY & U.S. Military: NC.

ROSEVILLE   612

FAIRVIEW COMMUNITY CENTER POOL 1910 W.
County Rd. 'B'
Phone: 631-1013.
Pool: 25y, 6 lane, indoors, heated, 85°-86°.
Admission: $1.75, SC(60) $1.50.

SAINT LOUIS PARK   612

THE ST. LOUIS PARK MASTERS SWIM
Masters: Contact Marilyn Franzen at 893-1319(w).
Affiliate: USMS Call.
Notes: Workouts: Tu: 6:30-7:30PM. F: 6-7PM.
The Club swims at the 25y, 5 lane St. Louis Park
Senior High School Pool; the 25m, 6 lane, 84° Park
Junior High School Pool; and the Central
Community Center (listed below) on a rotating
basis. Call to find the current workout location and
times.

CENTRAL COMMUNITY CENTER 6300 Walker St.
Phone: Pool: 928-6791. Coordinator: 928-6780.
Pool: 25m, 6 lanes, indoors, heated, 84°.
Admission: $1.

NORTHWEST RACQUET, SWIM & HEALTH
CLUB 5525 Cedar Lake Rd.
Phone: 435-3157.
Pool: 66.5f x 35f, 5 lanes, indoors, heated, 83°.
Admission: $15.
Affiliate: IHRSA $10, 1 week $20.
Hotel: Omni Northstar (338-2288), Minneapolis
Marriott Southwest (935-5500), Marquette (332-
2351), Whitney (339-9300), Sheraton Park Place
(542-8600), & Crown Sterling Downtown (333-
3111): Purchase passes at the hotels.

SAINT PAUL   612

9. SKYWAY YMCA 194 E. 6th St.
Phone: 292-4130.
Pool: 25m x 25f, 6 lanes, indoors, heated, 82°-84°.
Admission: $8.
Affiliate: YMCA NC.
Hotel: St. Paul Hotel & Radisson Hotel St. Paul
(224-8999): NC with room key.

10. YWCA OF ST. PAUL 198 Western Ave. N.
Phone: 222-3741.
Pool: 25y, 6 lanes, indoors, heated, 83°-86°.
Admission: $5.

11. OXFORD POOL 1079 Iglehart Ave.
Phone: 647-9925.
Pool: 25y x 60f, 8 lanes, indoors, heated, 82°.
Admission: $2.50, SC(62) $2.
Notes: The pool closes on holidays and the last two
weeks in Aug.

12. MIDWAY YMCA 1761 University Ave.
Phone: 646-4557.
Pool: 20y, 4 lanes, indoors, heated, 81°-85°.
Affiliate: YMCA NC.
To find: I-94 to Snelling, Snelling north to
University Ave., University Ave. west about five
blocks, across the street from Wendy's.

13. BALLY'S U.S. SWIM & FITNESS 1166
University Ave.
Phone: 644-2444.
Pool: 25m, 5 lanes, indoors, heated, 82°.
Admission: $10.
Affiliate: Bally's NC.
Hotel: Crown Sterling Hotel (224-5400) $5.

14. BUTLER CENTER POOL College of St.
Catherine, 2004 Randolph Ave.
Phone: 690-6732.
Pool: 25y x 60f, 8 lanes, indoors, heated, 81°.
Admission: $3.
To find: Butler Center is directly west into campus
from the Fairview Ave. entrance (Gate 6).

15. EAST YMCA 1075 Arcade St.
Phone: 771-8881.
Pool: 20y x 15f, 4 lanes, indoors, heated, 84°-86°.
Admission: $8.
Affiliate: YMCA NC.
Hotel: St. Paul Hotel & Radisson Hotel St. Paul
(224-8999): NC with room key.

SAINT PAUL PARK   612

OLTMAN JUNIOR HIGH SCHOOL 1020 - 3rd St.
Phone: Community Education Dept: 458-6600.
Pool: 25y, 6 lanes, indoors, heated, 82°.
Admission: $2.

SHOREVIEW   612

NORTHWEST FAMILY BRANCH YMCA 3760 N.
Lexington Ave.
Phone: 483-2671.
Pool: 25y x 35f, 5 lanes, indoors, heated, 83°.
Admission: Out-of-town visitors $8.52.
Affiliate: YMCA NC.
Notes: There is also a 50m, 6 lane, outdoor, heat-
ed, 83°, summer pool.
To find: Two blocks south of I-694, next door to the
Target Store.

SHOREVIEW COMMUNITY CENTER 4600 N.
Victoria St.
Phone: 490-4700.
Pool: 25y, 6 lanes, indoors, heated, 84°.
Admission: Residents $3.50, SC(65) $2.50. Non-residents $4.75, SC $3.75.
To find: At the corner of N. Victoria St. and Hwy. 96.
Masters: The Northern Shores Masters. Call 490-4700.

STILLWATER   612

RIVER VALLEY ATHLETIC CLUB 1826
Northwestern Ave.
Phone: 439-7611.
Pool: 25y, indoors, heated, 83°.
Admission: $10.

VIRGINIA   218

MESABI FAMILY YMCA 8367 S. 8th St.
Phone: 749-8020.
Pool: 25y x 22f, 4 lanes, indoors, heated, 82°.
Admission: $5.
Affiliate: Y AWAY NC.
To find: At the intersection of Hwys. 53 and 169.

WEST SAINT PAUL   612

SOUTH FAMILY BRANCH YMCA 150 E.
Thompson Ave.
Phone: 457-0048.
Pool: 25y x 75f, 6 lanes, indoors, heated, 85°.
Affiliate: YMCA NC.

SOUTHVIEW ATHLETIC CLUB 260 Marie Ave. E.
Phone: 450-1660.
Pool: 20y x 27f, indoors, heated, 80°.
Admission: $10.
Hotel: All local hotels NC with room key.

WHITE BEAR LAKE   612

NORTHEAST YMCA 2100 Orchard Lane
Phone: 777-8103.
Pool: 25y x 60f, 5 lanes, indoors, heated, 79°.
Affiliate: YMCA NC.
Hotel: Best Western (770-2811) NC with a pass from the hotel.
To find: Four blocks north of Maplewood Mall on White Bear Ave.

WHITE BEAR RACQUET & SWIM 4800 White
Bear Pkwy.
Phone: 426-1308.
Pool: 25y, indoors, heated, 83°-84°.
Affiliate: IHRSA $8.
Masters: The White Bear Masters. Contact Kristina Roan at 426-2750 ext. 136.

WINONA   507

WINONA FAMILY YMCA 207 Winona St.
Phone: 454-1520.
Pool: 25y, indoors, heated, 80°.
Admission: $4.
Affiliate: YMCA NC.

YWCA OF WINONA 223 Center St.
Phone: 454-4345.
Pool: 20y, indoors, heated, 84°.
Admission: $3.50.
Affiliate: YWCA Call.

WOODBURY   612

WOODBURY JUNIOR HIGH SCHOOL POOL
1425 School Dr.
Phone: Community Education Dept: 458-6600.
Pool: 25y x 45f, 6 lanes, indoors, heated, 82°.
Admission: $2.
To find: Two miles from I-494.
Masters: Contact Sharon Simpson at 459-8076(h). USMS registration required.

WOODBURY SENIOR HIGH SCHOOL POOL
2665 Woodlane Dr.
Phone: Community Education Dept: 458-6600.
Pool: 25y x 45f, 6 lanes, indoors, heated, 82°.
Admission: $2.
Notes: The school district will be adding a third pool in Woodbury in the fall of 1995. For particulars, contact the Community Education Department at 458-6600.
Masters: Contact Sharon Simpson at 459-8076(h). USMS registration required.

WORTHINGTON   507

WORTHINGTON YMCA 211 - 11th St.
Phone: 376-6197.
Pool: 25y, 4 lanes, indoors, heated, 82°.
Admission: $5.
Affiliate: YMCA NC.

ALWAYS CALL FIRST

Pools close, they change names, affiliations, admission policies, and rates. And just because a pool is listed in *Swimmers Guide* doesn't mean it's open all day, every day, for just the type of workout you want to do. Spend a quarter to save time and aggravation. . . always call first!

Tennessee

Arkansas

Tupelo

Mississippi

Alabama

55

Vicksburg Brandon

20

Clinton Jackson(4)

59

Hattiesburg

Louisiana

Ocean Springs

Biloxi

pool is through the blue door at the back of Alumni Hall.

HATTIESBURG 601

INSTITUTE FOR WELLNESS & SPORTS MEDICINE Methodist Hospital Campus, 210 W. Hospital Blvd. - Hwy. 98 W.
Phone: 268-5010.
Pool: 25y x 35f, 5 lanes, indoors, heated, 82°.
Admission: Out-of-town visitors 3 visits per quarter $7 each.
Hotel: Hampton Inn (264-8080) NC.
Masters: IWSM Masters. Contact Jeanne Franks at 268-5010.

JACKSON 601

MISSISSIPPI BAPTIST SPORTS / LIFE FITNESS CENTER 717 Manship St.
Phone: 968-1766.
Pool: 20m x 30f, 5 lanes, indoors, heated, 86°.
Affiliate: USMS pool only, lap swimming hours only $5.
Hotel: Cabot Lodge Millsaps (948-8650) $5 with voucher card. Millsaps Buie House Bed & Breakfast Inn (352-0221) $10 with voucher card.
To find: Across the street and one block south of the Mississippi Baptist Medical Center, in the Medical Arts East Building on State St.

MISSISSIPPI BAPTIST FITNESS CENTER MASTERS at the Mississippi Baptist Sports/Life Fitness Center
Masters: Contact Aquatics Coordinator Mary Lou Brantley at 968-1766.
Affiliate: USMS 3 workouts per week $5 each.
Notes: Uncoached Masters workouts: Tu: 7-8:45PM. Th: 7-8PM. Sa: 7-9AM. Lap swimming: M-Sa: Noon-1PM.

DOWNTOWN YMCA 800 E. River Place
Phone: 948-3090.
Pool: 25y x 60f, 8 lanes, indoor/outdoor, heated, 82°.
Affiliate: Y AWAY NC. YMCA $3.50. USMS $7.
Hotel: Residence Inn (355-3599) & Quality Inn North (982-1044): NC with room key. All other local hotels $5 with room key.
Masters: The Jackson Y Masters Swim Team. Contact Candace Loper at 977-0444.

THE COURTHOUSE RACQUET CLUB 2631 Courthouse Rd.
Phone: 932-4800.
Pool: 50m x 25y, indoor/outdoor, heated, 80°.
Affiliate: IHRSA $10, before 4:30PM $5.

COURTHOUSE RACQUET CLUB NORTHEAST 46 Northtown Dr.
Phone: 956-1300.
Pool: 25y, indoors, heated, 83°.
Affiliate: IHRSA $10.

BILOXI 601

BILOXI NATATORIUM 1384 Father Ryan Ave.
Phone: 435-6108 or 435-6205.
Pool: 25y x 50m, indoor/outdoor, heated, 82°-84°.
Admission: $1.
To find: Across the street from Keesler Air Force Base, next to Biloxi High School.
Masters: Are invited to join 'South Mississippi Surf' age group workouts. Contact Coach Kevin Stanton at 435-6108 or 435-6205.

BRANDON 601

FITNESS PLUS 336 Crossgates Blvd.
Phone: 825-9181.
Pool: 25y, indoor/outdoor, heated, 85°-86°.
Admission: $5.

CLINTON 601

MISSISSIPPI COLLEGE POOL Hwy. 80 W.
Phone: 925-3857.
Pool: 25y x 25f, indoors, heated, 85°.
Admission: $3.
To find: On the Mississippi College Campus, across from the tennis courts. The entrance to the

OCEAN SPRINGS   601

MISSISSIPPI GULF COAST YMCA 1810
Government St.
Phone: 875-5050.
Pool: 25y, 8 lanes, indoors, heated, 84°.
Admission: Out-of-town visitors — Call.
Affiliate: Y AWAY 2 weeks NC.

TUPELO   601

N.M.M.C. WELLNESS CENTER 1030 S. Madison
St.
Phone: 841-4141.
Pool: 25y x 24f, 4 lanes, indoors, heated, 82°.
Admission: $5.
To find: One block east of the North Mississippi
Medical Center, at the intersection of S. Madison
and Garfield Sts.

TUPELO AQUATIC CLUB at N.M.M.C. Wellness
Center
Masters: Contact Head Coach Barbara Aguirre at
842-1996(w) or 842-2358(h).
Affiliate: USS & USMS: Pool fees only, limit 5
workouts and one week.
Notes: Workouts: M-F: 5:45-7AM, 7:30-9PM. Sa:
10:30AM-12:30PM. The N.M.M.C. pool is used
Nov.-Mar. In April and May, the club swims at the
25m, 4 lane, outdoor, heated, 83°, Lee Acres Pool
on Fillmore St. In summer, the club swims at the
50m x 25y, 8 lane, outdoor, unheated, 78°-82°,
City Park Pool on Joyner St.

VICKSBURG   601

VICKSBURG YMCA 821 Clay St.
Phone: 638-1071.
Pool: 20y, indoors, heated, 86°.
Admission: $6.
Affiliate: YMCA $3.

HELP MAKE THE NEXT *SWIMMERS GUIDE* EVEN BETTER

To receive a free copy of the next *Swimmers Guide* tell us about pools you
know of that aren't in this edition. See page 14 for details.

BLUE SPRINGS   816

CENTENNIAL POOL-PLEX 2401 Ashton Dr.
Phone: 228-0188.
Pool: 25y x 44f, 6 lanes, indoors, heated, 81°.
Admission: $2.
Notes: There is also a 50m, outdoor, summer pool.
To find: Across Ashton Dr. from Blue Springs High School.
Masters: The Blue Springs Masters. Contact Aquatics Coordinator David Stevens at 228-0137.

BRENTWOOD   314

MID COUNTY YMCA 1900 Urban Dr.
Phone: 962-9450.
Pool: 27m x 25m, indoors, heated, 83°-84°.
Affiliate: Y AWAY 2 weeks NC.

BRIDGETON   314

BRIDGETON COMMUNITY CENTER 4201 Feefee Rd.
Phone: 739-5599.
Pool: 25y, indoors, heated, 83°-84°.
Admission: Residents $1.25, non-residents $2.

CAPE GIRARDEAU   314

CENTRAL POOL 205 Caruthers St.
Phone: 335-4040.
Pool: 25y x 50m, indoor/outdoor, heated, 82°.
Admission: $2.

CHESTERFIELD   314

WEST COUNTY YMCA 16464 Burkhardt Place
Phone: 532-3100.
Pool: 25m, 8 lanes, indoors, heated, 83°.
Admission: $10.
Affiliate: Y AWAY Call.
Hotel: Marriott Residence Inn (537-1444) NC.
To find: Behind Chesterfield Shopping Mall off Chesterfield Pkwy. Rd.
Masters: The West County YMCA Masters. Contact Jan McGah at 532-3100.

ST. LOUIS MASTERS at Marquette High School, 2351 Clarkson
Masters: Contact Susan Richmond at 225-0618.
Pool: 25y, 8 lanes, indoors, heated, 81°.
Affiliate: USMS NC, includes pool fees.
Notes: Fall, winter, & spring: Coached workouts: M-Sa: 5:30-7AM. Su: 8:30-10AM*. Uncoached workouts: M,W,Th,F: 11:30AM-1PM. *At John Burroughs High School 755 S. Price Rd. From Memorial Day to Labor Day, the club works out at the 50m x 25y, 8 lane, outdoor, unheated, 75°-85° Maplewood Community Center pool at 7550 Lohmeyer in Maplewood (781-1625).

CLAYTON   314

BALLY'S VIC TANNY 7393 Forsyth
Phone: 725-1777.
Pool: 25m, indoors, heated, 80°-81°.
Affiliate: Bally's NC.
Hotel: Ritz-Carlton (863-6300), Seven Gables, & Residence Inn (862-1900): NC.

COLUMBIA   314

HICKMAN POOL 1104 N. Providence Rd.
Phone: 874-7476.
Pool: 25y, indoors, heated, 84°.
Admission: $2.50.

CRESTWOOD   314

BALLY'S VIC TANNY 9744 Watson Rd.
Phone: 822-8100.
Pool: 20y, indoors, heated, 82°-84°.
Admission: Call.
Affiliate: Bally's NC.

FESTUS   314

JEFFERSON COUNTY YMCA 1303 YMCA Dr.
Phone: 937-1562.
Pool: 25m, 6 lanes, indoors, heated, 82°-86°.
Affiliate: YMCA NC.

FULTON   314

CALLAWAY COUNTY YMCA 103 W. 5th St.
Phone: 642-1065.
Pool: 25y, 6 lanes, indoors, heated, 82°.
Admission: $5.
Affiliate: YMCA NC.

INDEPENDENCE   816

INDEPENDENCE YMCA 14001 E. 32nd St.
Phone: 254-9622.
Pool: 25y, 6 lanes, indoors, heated, 86°.
Affiliate: Y AWAY NC.
To find: Off Noland Rd.

BALLY'S HEALTH & RACQUET 13801 E. 42nd
  Terrace
Phone: 373-1600.
Pool: 20m, indoors, heated, 81°.
Affiliate: Bally's NC.
Hotel: Drury Inn (923-3000) & Red Roof Inn (373-2800): NC.

JEFFERSON CITY   314

JEFFERSON CITY FAMILY YMCA 424 Stadium
Phone: 635-9136.
Pool: 25y x 40f, 6 lanes, indoors, heated, 85°.
Admission: $6.
Affiliate: YMCA $3.
Notes: There is also a 25m, outdoor, summer pool.

KANSAS CITY   816

GOLD'S GYM 106 W. 11th St.
Phone: 471-2677.
Pool: 25y, indoors, heated, 80°.
Admission: $11.
Affiliate: IPFA NC.

DERAMUS YWCA 1000 Charlotte St.
Phone: 842-7535.
Pool: 25y x 30f, 4 lanes, indoors, heated, 83°.
Admission: $4.50.
Affiliate: YWCA $2.25.

THE WESTIN CROWN CENTER 1 Pershing Rd.
Phone: 474-4400. **Reservations:** 800-228-3000.
Pool: 25y, half circle shape, outdoors, heated, 83°.
Admission: Registered guests NC.
Memberships: I/S $50 + $42/month.

CLAY-PLATTE YMCA 1101 N.E. 47th St.
Phone: 453-6600.
Pool: 25y x 45f, 6 lanes, indoors, heated, 84°.
Affiliate: Y AWAY & USMS: $10.
Hotel: All local hotels $10.
Notes: There is also a 50m x 20y, 8 lane, outdoor, summer pool.
To find: Off I-29 and Northoak, call for directions.

RED BRIDGE UNIT YMCA 11300 Holmes Rd.
Phone: 942-2020.
Pool: 25y x 20y, 6 lanes, indoors, heated, 84°.
Admission: 3 visits per year $5 each.
Affiliate: YMCA NC.
Notes: There is also a 25y x 75f, 6 lane, outdoor pool operated from Memorial Day to Labor Day.

PARK HILL AQUATIC CENTER 8152 N. Congress
Phone: 741-7963.
Pool: 25m x 40f, 3-6 lanes, indoors, heated, 79°-83°.
Admission: $1.75.
To find: Exit I-29 to Barry Rd., go west three traffic lights to Congress St. Turn left (south) onto Congress St. The Aquatic Center is near the football field.

KIRKSVILLE   816

NORTHEAST MISSOURI STATE UNIVERSITY NATATORIUM Pershing Building
Phone: 785-4470.
Pool: 25y x 42f, 6 lanes, indoors, heated, 82°.
Passes: 10 swims $15.
Memberships: $30/semester.
Notes: The facility closes for semester and holiday breaks.
Masters: The Kirksville Masters (NEMO Masters). Contact David Fraseur at 785-4470.

LEES SUMMIT   816

SUMMIT FITNESS 178 N.W. Oldham Pkwy.
Phone: 525-5040.
Pool: 20m, indoors, heated, 82°.
Admission: $5.
Affiliate: IPFA NC.

MANCHESTER 314

BALLY'S VIC TANNY 14015 Manchester Rd.
Phone: 391-1600.
Pool: 25y, indoors, heated, 81°.
Admission: Call.
Affiliate: Bally's NC.

MARYLAND HEIGHTS 314

BALLY'S VIC TANNY 12703 Dorsett Rd.
Phone: 576-5300.
Pool: 25y, indoors, heated, 82°.
Affiliate: Bally's NC.
Hotel: Holiday Inn (291-5100), Marriott (423-9700),
& Sheraton West Port Plaza (878-1500): NC.

MEXICO 314

MEXICO AREA FAMILY YMCA 1127 Adams St.
Phone: 581-1540.
Pool: 20y x 30f, 4 lanes, indoors, heated, 82°.
Admission: $3.
Affiliate: YMCA NC.

RAYTOWN 816

SUBURBAN YWCA 9110 E. 63rd St.
Phone: 353-9246.
Pool: 25y x 30f, 4 lanes, indoors, heated, 83°.
Admission: $4.50.
Affiliate: YWCA $2.25.
To find: Three blocks east of Appleby's Restaurant.

RAYTOWN YMCA 11811 E. 75th St.
Phone: 356-9622.
Pool: 25y x 36f, 6 lanes, indoors, heated, 85°.
Admission: $5.
Affiliate: YMCA NC.

SAINT ANN 314

BALLY'S VIC TANNY 10417 St. Charles Rock Rd.
Phone: 423-3004.
Pool: 25y, indoors, heated, 80°-82°.
Affiliate: Bally's NC.

SAINT CHARLES 314

BALLY'S VIC TANNY 1540 - 1st Capitol S.
Phone: 946-8090.
Pool: 25y, indoors, heated, 84°.
Affiliate: Bally's NC.
Hotel: Comfort Inn (949-8700) NC.

SAINT JOSEPH 816

ST. JOSEPH YMCA 315 S. 6th St.
Phone: 232-3344.
Pool: 25m, indoors, heated, 82°.
Admission: $5.
Affiliate: YMCA NC.

SAINT LOUIS 314

Saint Louis

Dots are placed by ZIP codes, not by street addresses.

1. DOWNTOWN YMCA 1528 Locust St.
Phone: 436-4100.
Pool: 25y x 25f, 3 lanes, indoors, heated, 85°.
Admission: $10.
Affiliate: Y AWAY $4.
Hotel: Hyatt Regency St. Louis (231-1234), Hotel
Majestic (436-2355), & Holiday Inn Downtown
Riverfront (621-8200): NC with a pass from the
hotel.
To find: Four blocks north of Union Station,
between 15th and 16th Sts.

2. SOUTH SIDE YMCA 2232 S. Grand Blvd.
Phone: 865-3500.
Pool: 20y x 20f, 4 lanes, indoors, heated, 88°.
Admission: $5.
Affiliate: Y AWAY Call.

3. MISSOURI ATHLETIC CLUB 405 Washington
Ave.
Phone: 231-7220.
Pool: 25y, 6 lanes, indoors, heated, 82°-83°.
Memberships: I/S $1,000 + $137/month dues +
$50/quarter food and beverage minimum.
Notes: This is an 'Executive Athletic Club', with
restaurants, a hotel, and numerous other amenities.

4. CARONDOLET BRANCH YWCA 4510 S. Kings
Hwy.
Phone: 832-2000.
Pool: 25y x 33f, 6 lanes, indoors, heated, 89°.
Admission: Out-of-town visitors $1.75 for less than
one hour, $2 more than one hour.
To find: Next to the White Castle restaurant.

5. CARONDELET BRANCH YMCA 600
Loughborough Ave.
Phone: 353-4960.

Pool: 20y x 20f, 4 lanes, indoors, heated, 88°.
Admission: $5.
Affiliate: Y AWAY NC.

6. MONSANTO YMCA 5555 Page Ave.
Phone: 367-4646.
Pool: 25y x 36f, 6 lanes, indoors, heated, 83°.
Admission: $5.
Affiliate: Out-of-town YMCA NC.

7. NORTHWEST COUNTY YMCA 9116 Lackland Rd.
Phone: 428-0840.
Pool: 20y, 4 lanes, indoors, heated, 86°.
Admission: $5.
Affiliate: YMCA outside a 60 mile radius NC.
To find: Across from Overland City Hall, one block west of the Post Office.

8. CHEROKEE CENTER 3200 S. Jefferson
Phone: 664-0582.
Pool: 25y, indoors, heated, 82°-84°.
Admission: NC.

9. WEBSTER YMCA 226 E. Lockwood Ave.
Phone: 962-9622.
Pool: 25y x 25f, 4 lanes, indoors, heated, 85°.
Admission: $10.
Affiliate: Y AWAY NC. YMCA $5.
To find: One block west of Webster University.
Masters: The Kirkwood-Webster YMCA Masters. Contact Liz Stroh at 962-9622.

10. KIRKWOOD YMCA 325 N. Taylor
Phone: 965-9622.
Pool: 25y x 25f, 4 lanes, indoors, heated, 85°.
Admission: $10.
Affiliate: Y AWAY NC. YMCA $5.
Hotel: Kirkwood Inn NC with card from the hotel.
To find: One block east of Kirkwood Rd. off Adams.

11. SOUTH COUNTY YMCA 12736 Southfork Rd.
Phone: 843-6703.
Pool: 25m, indoors, heated, 84°.
Affiliate: YMCA NC.

12. EMERSON FAMILY YMCA 3390 Pershall Rd.
Phone: 522-1822.
Pool: 25y x 28f, 4 lanes, indoors, heated, 84°.
Admission: $8.
Affiliate: Y Away NC.
To find: Next to Florissant Valley Community College.

13. JEWISH COMMUNITY CENTERS ASSOCIATION 2 Millstone Campus Dr.
Phone: 432-5700.
Pool 1: 25y, 6 lanes, indoors, heated, 82°.
Pool 2: 25y, 6 lanes, indoors, heated, 88°.
Admission: $5.50, Specialty Club $7.
Affiliate: JCC 1 week NC.
Notes: There is also a 50y, 6 lane, unheated, outdoor, summer pool.

14. WESTPORT ATHLETIC CLUB 2388 Chaffee
Phone: 569-0648.
Pool: 25y, indoors, heated, 82°-88°.
Admission: $5.

SAINT PETERS   314

ST. CHARLES COUNTY YMCA 3900 Ehlmann Rd.
Phone: 928-1928.
Pool: 25y, 6 lanes, indoors, heated, 85°.
Admission: $10.
Affiliate: Out-of-area Y AWAY 2 or 3 visits NC.

ST. PETERS RECPLEX 5200 Mexico Rd.
Phone: 939-2386.
Pool: 50m x 25y, indoors, heated, 80°.
Admission: Residents $3, non-residents $6.
Notes: This pool was the site of the 1994 U.S. Olympic Festival's swimming events. Admission includes use of a weight room, track, hot tub, sauna, and ice rink.

SPRINGFIELD   417

NORTHPARK FITNESS CENTER 2610 N. Glenstone
Phone: 866-0099.
Pool: 25y, indoors, heated, 84°.
Affiliate: IPFA NC.
Hotel: Comfort Inn (866-5255) NC.

HAMMONS POOL Southwest Missouri State University, 901 S. National
Phone: 836-5466.
Pool: 25y x 60f, 8 lanes, indoors, heated, 80°.
Affiliate: USMS Call.
To find: In Hammons Center.

SPRINGFIELD FAMILY YMCA - JONES BRANCH 1901 E. Republic Rd.
Phone: 881-1599.
Pool: 25m x 30f, 6 lanes, indoors, heated, 84°-86°.
Admission: $7.50.
Affiliate: Y AWAY 30 days NC. YMCA 30 days $2.50 per day.
To find: One block south of the James River Frwy., between Glenstone and Fremont.

SPRINGFIELD FAMILY YMCA - WARD BRANCH 417 S. Jefferson
Phone: 862-7456.
Pool: 25y x 20f, 4 lanes, indoors, heated, 86°-87°.
Admission: $5.
Affiliate: Y AWAY 30 days NC. YMCA 30 days $2.50 per day.
To find: Four blocks south of Square.

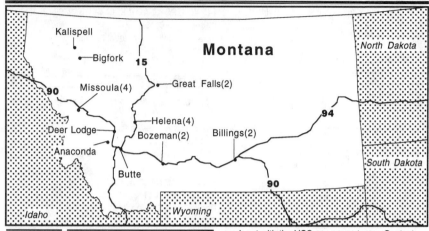

ANACONDA 406

FAIRMONT HOT SPRINGS RESORT 1500
Fairmont
Phone: 797-3241. **Reservations:** 800-443-2381.
Pool: 105f 1in, rectangular, partly indoors, partly
outdoors, heated, 88°-92°.
Admission: $6.50. Registered guests NC.

BIGFORK 406

BIG FORK ATHLETIC CLUB 850 Holt Dr.
Phone: 837-2582.
Pool: 25y, indoors, heated, 80°.
Admission: $5.

BILLINGS 406

BILLINGS YMCA 402 N. 32nd St.
Phone: 248-1685.
Pool 1: 25y, indoors, heated, 80°-84°.
Pool 2: 25y, indoors, heated, 80°-84°.
Affiliate: YMCA NC.
Hotel: Billings TraveLodge $5 with a pass from the
hotel. Radisson Northern Hotel (245-5121) —
Purchase passes at the hotel.
Masters: Contact Donna Hirt at 248-1685 ext. 208.

BILLINGS ATHLETIC CLUB 777 - 15th St. W.
Phone: 259-2626.
Pool: 20y, indoors, heated, 83°.
Affiliate: IHRSA $3.50.

BOZEMAN 406

BOZEMAN SWIM CENTER 1211 W. Main
Phone: 587-4724.
Pool: 50m x 58f, 8 lanes, indoors, heated, 83°-84°.
Admission: $2, SC(55) $1.
Notes: Offers lap swimming, day and evening
recreation swimming, lessons and technique clin-
ics. Call for hours and details.
To find: Adjacent to a high school.
Masters: Visiting USMS registered Masters may

work out with the USS age group team. Contact
Janice Lopez at 763-4136(h).

PHYSICAL EDUCATION COMPLEX Montana
State University
Phone: 994-5000.
Pool: 25y x 75f, 8 lanes, indoors, heated, 84°.
Admission: 5 visits $5 each.
Memberships: $250/year.

BUTTE 406

BUTTE FAMILY YMCA 405 W. Park St.
Phone: 782-1266.
Pool: 20y x 20f, 5 lanes, indoors, heated, 86°.
Admission: Pool $3. Full facility $5.
Affiliate: YMCA NC.

DEER LODGE 406

CENTRAL PARK CENTER 444 Montana Ave.
Phone: 846-1553.
Pool: 82f x 45f, 6 lanes, indoors, heated, 86°.
Admission: NC.
Notes: Our respondent indicated that lap swimming
is not a major activity at this school district operat-
ed pool.
To find: One city block east of Main St. on Montana
Ave.

GREAT FALLS 406

MORONY NATATORIUM 12th St. & 2nd Ave.
Phone: 771-1265.
Pool: 25m, indoors, heated, 84°.
Admission: Lap swimming $1.50.

COLLEGE OF GREAT FALLS 1301 - 20th St. S.
Phone: 761-8210.
Pool: 25y, indoors, heated, 83°-84°.
Admission: $1.50.

HELENA   406

CROSSROADS SPORTS & FITNESS CENTER
1013 Dearborn Ave.
Phone: 442-6733.
Pool: 25y, indoors, heated, 84°.
Admission: $6.
Affiliate: IHRSA $5.

HELENA YMCA 1200 N. Last Chance Gulch
Phone: 442-9622.
Pool: 25y, indoors, heated, 82°.
Admission: Call.
Affiliate: YMCA NC.

BROADWATER ATHLETIC CLUB & HOT SPRINGS 4920 Hwy. 12W
Phone: 443-5777.
Pool 1: 20y, outdoors, naturally heated, 87°-91°.
Pool 2: 25y, outdoors, naturally heated, 92°.
Admission: $9, SC(60) $5.
Affiliate: IHRSA $3.50.

CARROLL COLLEGE P.E. CENTER 1601 N.
Benton Ave.
Phone: 447-4484.
Pool: 25y x 46f, indoors, heated, 84°.
Admission: $2.50, SC(55) $1.
To find: The campus is at the corner of Benton & Euclid Aves., next to Lundy Shopping Center. The P.E. Center is at the north end of the campus.

KALISPELL   406

SECOND WIND SPORT & FITNESS CENTER 205
Sunnyview Lane
Phone: 752-4100.
Pool: 25y x 42f, 6 lanes, indoors, heated, 82°.
Admission: $4.
Affiliate: IHRSA $2.

MISSOULA   406

MISSOULA FAMILY YMCA 3000 Russell St.
Phone: 721-9622.
Pool: 25y x 36f, 6 lanes, indoors, heated, 84°.
Admission: $5, SC(62) $3.
Affiliate: Y AWAY NC.
Masters: The Montana Masters. Contact Coach Steven Holloway or Director Mike Boyle at 721-9622.

MISSOULA ATHLETIC CLUB 1311 E. Broadway
Phone: 728-0714.
Pool: 25y, 3 lanes, indoors, heated, 78°-80°.
Admission: $7, SC(62) $3.
Hotel: Holiday Inn (721-8550) & Village Red Lion: $6 with room key, SC $2.

WESTERN MONTANA SPORTS MEDICINE & FITNESS CENTER 5000 Blue Mountain Rd.
Phone: 251-3344.
Pool: 25y, indoors, heated, 83°.
Affiliate: IHRSA $8.

GRIZZLY POOL University of Montana
Phone: 243-2763.
Pool: 25y x 50f, 7 lanes, indoors, heated, 84°.
Admission: $1.75.
To find: On the University of Montana Campus, directly south of the Harry Adams Field House.

ALWAYS CALL FIRST

Pools close, they change names, affiliations, admission policies, and rates. And just because a pool is listed in *Swimmers Guide* doesn't mean it's open all day, every day, for just the type of workout you want to do. Spend a quarter to save time and aggravation. . . always call first!

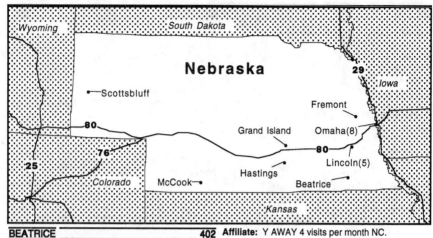

BEATRICE   402

MARY YMCA 1801 Scott St.
Phone: 223-5266.
Pool: 25m, indoors, heated, 82°-84°.
Admission: $7.50.
Affiliate: YMCA NC.

FREMONT   402

FREMONT FAMILY YMCA 810 N. Lincoln
Phone: 721-6952.
Pool 1: 25y, 6 lanes, indoors, heated, 85°.
Pool 2: 25y, 6 lanes, indoors, heated, 85°.
Admission: $4.
Affiliate: YMCA NC.

GRAND ISLAND   308

GRAND ISLAND YMCA 222 E. 3rd St.
Phone: 384-8181.
Pool: 25m, 6 lanes, indoors, heated, 84°-86°.
Admission: Open swim $2. Day pass $5.
Affiliate: Y AWAY NC.
Hotel: Holiday Inn-Midtown (384-1330) NC with
room key.

HASTINGS   402

HASTINGS FAMILY YMCA 1430 W. 16th St.
Phone: 463-3139.
Pool: 25y x 60f, 8 lanes, indoors, heated, 83°.
Admission: $5.
Affiliate: YMCA NC.
To find: Two blocks west of the senior high school.

LINCOLN   402

NORTHEAST YMCA 2601 N. 70th St.
Phone: 434-9252.
Pool: 25y x 36f, 6 lanes, indoors, heated, 83°.
Admission: $8.52.
Affiliate: Y AWAY 4 visits per month NC.
Masters: The Y-nauts. Contact Anne Lenz at
434–9252.

DOWNTOWN LINCOLN YMCA 1039 'P' St.
Phone: 434-9230.
Pool: 25y x 37.5f, 6 lanes, indoors, heated, 82°.
Admission: $8.52.
Affiliate: YMCA 4 visits per month NC.
Hotel: Ramada Hotel (475-4011) & Corn Husker
Hotel (474-7474): NC with a card from the hotel.

YWCA OF LINCOLN 1432 'N' St.
Phone: 476-2802.
Pool: 20y x 20f, indoors, heated, 85°.
Admission: $2.25.

LINCOLN RACQUET CLUB 5300 Old Cheney Rd.
Phone: 423-2511.
Pool: 20y, indoors, heated, 82°-84°.
Admission: $8.
Affiliate: IHRSA $5.
Hotel: Harvester Motel (423-3131) $5 with a vouch-
er from the motel.
Masters: Contact Linda L. Stansbury at 423-2511.

COTTONWOOD CLUB 330 W. 'P' St.
Phone: 475-3386.
Pool: 20m x 15m, 4 lanes, indoors, heated, 79°.
Admission: $8.50.
Affiliate: IHRSA $3.25.
Hotel: Comfort Inn (475-2200) & Hampton Inn
(474-2080): NC with a pass from the hotel.

MCCOOK   308

MCCOOK YMCA 901 W. 'E' St.
Phone: 345-6228.
Pool: 25y, indoors, heated, 85°.
Admission: $6.50.
Affiliate: YMCA NC.

OMAHA 402

THE PINNACLE CLUB 2027 Dodge St.
Phone: 342-2582.
Pool: 25y, indoors, heated, 80°-82°.
Admission: $7.50.

DOWNTOWN YMCA 430 S. 20th St.
Phone: 341-1600.
Pool: 25y, 6 lanes, indoors, heated, 72°-76°.
Admission: $5.33.
Affiliate: YMCA NC.

PARK AVENUE HEALTH CLUB 501 Park Ave.
Phone: 345-8175.
Pool: 20y, 5 lanes, indoors, heated, water temperature not reported.
Admission: $10.65.

THE WESTROADS CLUB 1212 N. 102nd St.
Phone: 393-7710.
Pool: 25y, indoors, heated, 79°-82°.
Affiliate: IHRSA $5.

MOCKINGBIRD HILLS POOL 10242 Mockingbird Dr.
Phone: 444-6103.
Pool: 25y, indoors, heated, 84°.
Admission: $1.50.

WEST YMCA 7502 Maple St.
Phone: 393-3700.

Pool: 25y x 25f, 4 lanes, indoors, heated, 86°-89°.
Admission: $5.35.
Affiliate: YMCA NC.

MONTCLAIR POOL 2304 S. 135th Ave.
Phone: 444-4957.
Pool: 25m, indoors, heated, 83°-84°.
Admission: $1.50.

MAVERICK ADULT SWIM PROGRAM at the University of Nebraska at Omaha, 60th & Dodge Sts.
Masters: Contact Coach Todd Samland at 554-2539 or 496-7390(h).
Pool: 25y x 45f, 6 lanes, indoors, heated, 81°.
Non-member participation: 4 workouts per month $4 each, includes pool fees.
Notes: Coached workouts: M-Th: 6:30-7:30AM, 8-9AM, 11:15AM-Noon, 5:30-6:30PM, 6:30-7:30PM. F: 6:30-7:30AM, 8-9AM, 11:15AM-Noon. Sa: 8:45-9:45AM, 9:45-10:45AM. Su: 6:30-7:30PM.

SCOTTSBLUFF 308

SCOTTSBLUFF FAMILY YMCA 22 S. Beltline Hwy.
Phone: 635-2318.
Pool: 25y x 42f, 6 lanes, indoors, heated, 84°.
Admission: $6.
Affiliate: YMCA subject to unspecified frequency restrictions NC.

HELP MAKE THE NEXT *SWIMMERS GUIDE* EVEN BETTER
To receive a free copy of the next *Swimmers Guide* tell us about pools you know of that aren't in this edition. See page 14 for details.

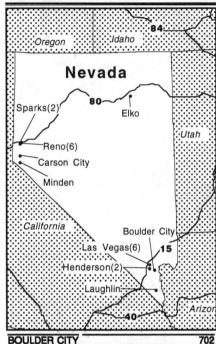

Phone: 454-6000 ext. 249.
Pool: 25m, 4 lanes, indoors, heated, 81°-83°.
Affiliate: IHRSA $15.
Notes: There is also a 25m, outdoor, heated, 81°-83° pool open Mar. 1 to Nov. 1.
To find: Off Sunset Rd. east of Las Vegas Blvd.

LORN WILLIAMS POOL 500 Palo Verde Dr.
Phone: 565-2123.
Pool: 25y, 8 lanes, indoors, heated, 82°.
Admission: $1.

LAS VEGAS   702

LAS VEGAS MUNICIPAL POOL 430 E. Bonanza
Phone: 229-6309.
Pool: 25y x 80f, 16 lanes, indoor/outdoor, heated, 80°.
Admission: $1.50.

BENNETT FAMILY YMCA 4141 Meadows Lane
Phone: 877-9622.
Pool: 25m, 4 lanes, indoors, heated, 78°.
Admission: $10, SC(55) $5.
Affiliate: Y AWAY 14 days NC.
To find: On Meadows Lane, just off Valley View, across the street from Meadows Mall.

BOULDER CITY   702

BOULDER CITY POOL 861 Ave. 'B'
Phone: 293-9286.
Pool: 25m x 25y, 8 x 8 lanes, indoor/outdoor, heated, 84°.
Admission: $1.25, SC(60) $1.
Notes: There is also a diving well with 1m and 3m boards which is open from May to Sep.

CARSON CITY   702

CARSON CITY AQUATIC FACILITY 851 E. William
Phone: 887-2242.
Pool: 25y x 60f, 6 lanes, indoors, heated, 80°-82°.
Admission: $2.25, SC(55) $1.50.
Notes: There is also a 50m x 25y, outdoor, heated, 80°-82°, summer pool.

ELKO   702

ELKO MUNICIPAL POOL 1501 College
Phone: 738-5670.
Pool: 25y x 45f, 6 lanes, indoors, heated, 82°.
Admission: $2, SC(60) 75¢.
Notes: The pool closes for the month of Jan.
To find: On College Ave. one block west of the Convention Center in the northwest corner of City Park.

HENDERSON   702

GREEN VALLEY ATHLETIC CLUB 2100 Olympic Ave.

SPORTING HOUSE OF LAS VEGAS 3025 Industrial Rd.
Phone: 733-8999.
Pool: 20m x 31f, 5 lanes, indoors, heated, 80°-82°.
Admission: $20.
Affiliate: IHRSA $10.
Hotel: Stardust Hotel (732-6111) & Circus Circus: $12. All other local hotels $15.
To find: One block west of 'The Strip' (Las Vegas Blvd.) directly behind the Stardust Hotel.

LAS VEGAS HILTON 3000 Paradise Rd.
Phone: 732-5111. **Reservations:** 800-732-7117.
Pool: 25m, triangular shape, outdoors, heated, 75°, but the temperature varies by season.
Admission: Registered guests only NC.

SHERATON DESERT INN 3145 Las Vegas Blvd.
Phone: 733-4444. **Reservations:** 800-634-6906.
Pool: 88f, 'L' shape, outdoors, heated, water temperature not reported.
Admission: Registered guests only NC.

CAESERS PALACE 3570 Las Vegas Blvd. S.
Phone: 731-7110. **Reservations:** 800-634-6661.
Pool: 25m, roman shield shape, outdoors, heated, 80°.
Admission: Registered guests only NC.

LAUGHLIN   702

FLAMINGO HILTON LAUGHLIN 1900 S. Casino Dr.
Phone: 298-5111. **Reservations:** 800-FLAMINGO.

Pool: 20y, rectangular, outdoors, heated, 78°.
Admission: Registered guests only NC.

MINDEN   702

CARSON VALLEY SWIM CENTER 1600 Hwy. 88
Phone: 782-8840.
Pool: 25y x 25m, 6 x 6 lanes, 'L' shape, indoors,
heated, 81°.
Admission: $2.50, SC(55) $1.
Notes: There are also indoor and outdoor therapy
pools, an indoor tot pool, and an outdoor 25y, 8
lane pool. The Swim Center won the National
Recreation & Park Award for Excellence in
Aquatics.
To find: On State Hwy. 88 just south of Hwy. 395,
next to Douglas High School.
Masters: The Carson Valley Masters. Contact Kirk
Chapella at 782-8840.

RENO   702

SPORTS WEST ATHLETIC CLUB 1575 S. Virginia
Phone: 348-6666.
Pool: 25y, indoors, heated, 80°.
Admission: $10.
Affiliate: IHRSA $5.
Hotel: John Ascaguas Nugget Hotel (356-3300)
[See that listing under Sparks, NV] & the Eldorado
Hotel: $8.

NORTHWEST POOL 2925 Apollo Way
Phone: 334-2203.
Pool: 25y, indoors, heated, 82°-84°.
Admission: $2.50.

SIERRA NEVADA MASTERS at Northwest Pool
Masters: Contact Coach Steve Lintz at 334-
2203(w) or Sally Dillon at (916) 583-7439(h).
Non-member participation: Pool fees only.
Notes: From Sep. to May: Coached workouts:
M,W,F: 6-7:15AM. Tu,Th: Noon-1PM. Sa: 7-
8AM. Lap swimming: M-F: 6-7PM. Su: Noon-
1PM, 5-6PM. From May to Sep., the club swims at
the 50m x 65f, 8 lane, outdoor, heated, 83°,
Idlewild Pool at 1805 Idlewild Dr. (334-2267).
Workouts are: M,W,F: 6-7:15AM. Tu,Th: 5-6PM.
Sa: 7-8AM.

**YMCA OF THE SIERRA - RENO FAMILY
BRANCH** 1300 Foster Dr.
Phone: 329-1311.

Pool: 25y x 25f, 4 lanes, indoors, heated, 80°.
Admission: $8. After 7PM $4.
Affiliate: YMCA NC.
To find: From I-80 take the Keystone Exit to Booth
St., across from the Reno High School football
field.
Masters: The Prairie Otters. Contact Mike Bowe at
329-1311.

LAKERIDGE TENNIS CLUB 6000 Plumas
Phone: 827-3300.
Pool: 25m, indoors, heated, 82°.
Affiliate: IHRSA $8.

MOANA POOL 240 W. Moana Lane
Phone: 334-2268.
Pool: 40m, indoors, heated, 85°.
Admission: $2.50.

RENO YWCA 1301 Valley Rd.
Phone: 322-4531.
Pool: 25y x 51f, 4 lanes, indoors, heated, 86°.
Admission: $4.
Affiliate: YWCA $2.50.
To find: Two blocks east of the University of
Nevada at Reno.

SPARKS   702

ALF SORENSEN COMMUNITY POOL 1400
Baring Blvd.
Phone: 353-2385.
Pool: 25y x 60f, 8 lanes, indoors, heated, 84°.
Admission: Lap swimming: Residents $3, non-
residents $3.50. Rec. swimming: Residents
$2.25, non-residents $2.75. All SC(55) $1.50 for
both.
To find: Off McCarran Blvd. by Reed High School.

JOHN ASCUAGA'S NUGGET HOTEL 1100
Nugget Ave.
Phone: 356-3300. **Reservations:** 800-648-1177.
Pool: 24y x 32f, rectangular, indoors, heated, water
temperature not reported.
Admission: Non-guests receive a pool pass for
every $10 purchase at Chonne's Salon.
Registered guests NC.
Notes: Guests also have discounted access to the
facilities at Sports West Athletic Club. [See that
listing under Reno, NV.]

To find: Behind Butterfield Gymnasium and across from Fosters Daily Democrat. From Central Ave. take Henry Law Ave.
Masters: The Seacoast Masters. Contact Hilary J. Grabe at 743-6056.

EXETER   603

RESULTS SWIM & FITNESS 64 Epping Rd.
Phone: 778-1818.
Pool: 20y, indoors, heated, 82°.
Admission: $12.
Affiliate: IHRSA $7.50.
Masters: Call 778-1818.

GORHAM   603

ROYALTY ATHLETIC CLUB 138 Main St.
Phone: 466-5422.
Pool: 25y, indoors, heated, 75°.
Admission: $9.

HANOVER   603

KARL B. MICHAEL POOL Alumni Gym, Dartmouth College
Phone: 346-3654.
Pool: 25y x 60f, 8 lanes, indoors, heated, 80°.
Admission: $10.
Memberships: $260/year.

LACONIA   603

LACONIA ATHLETIC & SWIM CLUB 827 N. Main St.
Phone: 524-9252.
Pool: 25y, indoors, heated, 83°-84°.
Admission: $8.
Affiliate: IHRSA $4.

LINCOLN   603

LOON MOUNTAIN RECREATION Kancamagus Hwy.
Phone: 745-8111.
Pool: 20y, indoors, heated, 79°-82°.
Admission: $12.
Hotel: Marriott Hotel (745-8111) NC.

MANCHESTER   603

GREATER MANCHESTER FAMILY YMCA 30 Mechanic St.
Phone: 623-3558.
Pool: 25y x 25f, 4 lanes, indoors, heated, 81°-83°.
Affiliate: YMCA 10 visits NC.
Hotel: Holiday Inn-Center of New Hampshire Complex (625-1000): Basic $5. Fitness Plus $8.

EXECUTIVE HEALTH & SPORTS CENTER - AIRPORT 1 Highlander Way
Phone: 668-4753.
Pool: 25y, indoors, heated, 78°-80°.

CONCORD   603

THE RACQUET CLUB OF CONCORD 10 Garvins Falls Rd.
Phone: 224-7787.
Pool: 25y x 35f, 5 lanes, indoors, heated, 82°.
Admission: $6.

CONCORD YMCA 15 N. State St.
Phone: 228-9622.
Pool: 80f, indoors, heated, 83°.
Admission: Basic $5.50, SC(65) $4.20. Fitness Center $8.80, SC $7.25.
Affiliate: YMCA 4 visits per year NC, then 50% off the applicable admission rates.
Masters: Contact Liz McBride at 228-9622.

DOVER   603

DOVER INDOOR POOL 6 Washington St., Henry Law Park
Phone: 743-6056.
Pool: 25y x 40f, 6 lanes, indoors, heated, 82°.
Admission: Residents: $2.25, SC(60) $1.75. Non-residents: $3.25, SC $2.75.

Admission: $12.
Affiliate: IHRSA Call.

MERRIMACK   603

MERRIMACK YMCA 6 Henry Clay Dr.
Phone: 881-7778.
Pool: 25y, 5 lanes, indoors, heated, 81°-82°.
Affiliate: YMCA $5.

MILFORD   603

HAMPSHIRE HILLS SPORTS & FITNESS
Emerson & Federal Hill Rds.
Phone: 673-7123.
Pool: 25y, 6 lanes, indoors, heated, 79°-80°.
Admission: $7.
Affiliate: IHRSA NC.
Masters: Contact Pool Coordinator Scott McQuade
at 673-7123 ext. 278.

NASHUA   603

NASHUA YMCA & YWCA OF NASHUA 17
Prospect St.
Phone: YMCA: 882-2011. YWCA: 883-3081.
Pool: 25y x 25f, 4 lanes, indoors, heated, 82°.
Admission: YMCA side $7. YWCA side $3.75.
Affiliate: YMCA $3.50.
Notes: The YMCA and YWCA share the building
and the pool, but operate separately.

NASHUA BOYS CLUB 47 Grand Ave.
Phone: 883-0523.
Pool: 25y, indoors, heated, 78°.
Admission: $5.

THE ROYAL RIDGE CLUB at the Sheraton Hotel,
11 Tara Blvd.
Phone: Club: 891-1119. Hotel: 888-9970.
Reservations: 800-325-3535.

Pool: 50f, indoors, heated, 82°-83°.
Admission: $10. Registered guests NC for pool.
Affiliate: IHRSA $5.
Notes: There is also an outdoor, summer pool.

PORTSMOUTH   603

GOLD'S GYM & ATHLETIC CLUB 8 Greenleaf
Woods Dr.
Phone: 436-6664.
Pool: 20y x 30f, 6 lanes, indoors, heated, 80°.
Admission: $10.
Affiliate: Gold's Gym Travel Card — Call.
Hotel: Howard Johnsons Hotel (436-7600) NC.
To find: Off Route 1, behind the Bournival Auto
Dealership.

COMFORT INN AT YOKEN'S 1390 Lafayette Rd.
Phone: 443-3338. Reservations: 800-552-8484.
Pool: 50f, rectangular, indoors, heated, 82°.
Admission: Registered guests only NC.

SALEM   603

SALEM ATHLETIC CLUB 16 Manor Pkwy.
Phone: 893-8612.
Pool: 25y x 35f, 5 lanes, indoors, heated, 85°.
Admission: $12, SC(55) $6.
Affiliate: IHRSA $6.
To find: Take Exit 2 off Route 93. Turn left at the
end of the exit. The first right is Manor Pkwy.

SOMERSWORTH   603

THE WORKS ATHLETIC CLUB 246 Route 108
Phone: 742-2163.
Pool: 25y, indoors, heated, 82°.
Admission: $10.
Affiliate: IHRSA Call.

HELP MAKE THE NEXT *SWIMMERS GUIDE* EVEN BETTER

To receive a free copy of the next *Swimmers Guide* tell us about pools you
know of that aren't in this edition. See page 14 for details.

Paramus

Mount Arlington

Mountain Lakes

Paterson

Hackensack

Tenafly

Randolph

80

Passaic

Englewood Cliffs

Clifton

Garfield

Cedar Knolls

Montclair

Morristown

Livingston

West Orange

Newark

95A

Madison

Short Hills

Orange

Basking Ridge Summit(2)

78

Hoboken

Berkeley Heights

Springfield

Elizabeth

Union

Jersey City(3)

Cranford

Scotch Plains Westfield Rahway

Bayonne

New York

Bridgewater South Plainfield(2)

Somerville

Metuchen

Piscataway

95

Northeast New Jersey

New Brunswick

ALLENWOOD   908

THE ATLANTIC CLUB 1904 Atlantic Ave.
Phone: 223-2100.
Pool: 25m, indoors, heated, 82°.
Affiliate: IHRSA $15.

ATLANTIC CITY   609

THE SPA AT BALLY'S PARK PLACE HOTEL
  Park Place & The Boardwalk
Phone: 340-4600.
Pool: 20y x 30f, indoors, heated, 85°.
Admission: $30.
Affiliate: IHRSA $20.
Hotel: Bally's Park Place Hotel (340-4600) $10.

BASKING RIDGE   908

SOMERSET HILLS YMCA 140 Mt. Airy Rd.
Phone: 766-7898.
Pool: 25y x 36f, 6 lanes, indoors, heated, 83°.
Admission: 'Try the Y' pass 2 visits NC.
Affiliate: YMCA from out-of-state or outside a 50
  mile radius NC, within 50 miles $4.
Hotel: Somerset Hills Hotel & Bernardsville Inn:
  NC with a pass from the hotel.

Masters: The Somerset Hills YMCA Masters Team.
  Contact John Barnes at 766-7898 ext. 531.

BAYONNE   201

BAYONNE YMCA 259 Ave. 'E'
Phone: 339-2330.
Pool: 20y x 30f, indoors, heated, 84°.
Admission: 5 visit pass NC.

BERKELEY HEIGHTS   908

BERKELEY AQUATIC CLUB MASTERS at the
  Berkeley Aquatic Club, 649 Springfield Ave.
Masters: Contact Coach Cathy Copeland at 464-
  0574.
Pool: 25y x 36f, 6 lanes, indoors, heated, 80°.
Affiliate: USMS $3 per workout.
Notes: Coached workouts: M: 8:30-9:30PM. W:
  8-9:15PM. F: 8-9PM. Su: 8:30-10:30AM.

BRICK   201

BALLY'S JACK LALANNE 193 Chambers Bridge
Rd.
Phone: 920-3377.
Pool: 20y, indoors, heated, 83°.

Admission: Call.
Affiliate: Bally's NC.

Memberships: Resident and non-resident memberships are available. Call for rates.

BRIDGEWATER   908

SOMERSET VALLEY YMCA 601 Garretson Rd.
Phone: 526-0688.
Pool: 25y x 75f, 10 lanes, indoors, heated, 82°.
Admission: $7, SC(62) $3.
Affiliate: Y AWAY $3.50, SC $1.50.
Masters: Contact Coach Paul H. Casazza at 526-0688.

CAMDEN   609

CAMDEN CITY YMCA 3rd & Federal St.
Phone: 963-0151.
Pool: 25y x 42f, 6 lanes, indoors, heated, 86°.
Admission: $10.
Affiliate: YMCA outside a 100 mile radius NC, within 100 miles $2.50.
To find: Behind the New Jersey State Aquarium.

CEDAR KNOLLS   201

MORRIS CENTER YMCA 79 Horsehill Rd.
Phone: 267-0704.
Pool: 25m x 42f, 6 lanes, indoors, heated, 82°-84°.
Admission: $10.
Affiliate: YMCA NC.

CHERRY HILL   609

JEWISH COMMUNITY CENTER OF SOUTHERN NEW JERSEY 2395 W. Marlton Pike
Phone: 662-8800.
Pool: 20y, indoors, heated, 80°-85°.
Affiliate: JCC NC.

FITQUEST 14 Olney Ave.
Phone: 751-5177.
Pool: 20m x 40f, 4 lanes, indoors, heated, 80°.
Admission: $10.
Affiliate: IHRSA $8.
Hotel: Mt. Laurel Hilton (234-7300) & Hampton Inn (346-4500): NC with a pass from the hotel.
To find: At the intersection of Olney Ave. and Esterbrook Lane. Esterbrook Lane is off Springdale Rd. between Route 70 and Church Rd.

CLIFTON   201

RAMADA HOTEL 265 Route 3 E.
Phone: 778-6500. **Reservations:** 800-772-2816.
Pool: 50f x 30f, rectangular, indoors, heated, 68°.
Admission: Registered guests only NC.

CRANFORD   908

CRANFORD CENTENNIAL POOL 401 Centennial Ave.
Phone: 709-7260.
Pool: 25y, 8 lanes, indoors, heated, 81°-82°.

DEPTFORD   609

HADDONWOOD TENNIS / SWIM & HEALTH CLUB Route 41, 200 N. Hurffville Rd.
Phone: 227-4141.
Pool: 25y x 36f, 6 lanes, indoors, heated, 86°.
Admission: Owners of the current edition of *Swimmers Guide* $6. You must call first and show your copy of the book at check in.
Affiliate: IHRSA $6.
Hotel: Several local hotels — Call the club for details.
Notes: There is also a 25y x 36f, 6 lane, outdoor, summer pool.
To find: Six minutes from Center City Philadelphia over the Walt Whitman Bridge and just south of the Deptford Mall.

EAST BRUNSWICK   908

BALLY'S JACK LALANNE 8 Edgeboro Rd.
Phone: 254-7373.
Pool: 25m, indoors, heated, 79°-80°.
Admission: 1 visit per 6 months NC.
Affiliate: Bally's NC.
Hotel: Motel 6 NC.

EGG HARBOR TOWNSHIP   609

TILTON ATHLETIC CLUB Tilton Rd. & Hingston Ave.
Phone: 646-2590.
Pool: 20y x 20f, 3 lanes, indoors, heated, 80°.
Admission: Pool $7. Full facility $15.
Affiliate: IHRSA full facility $7.50.
To find: On Tilton Rd., one mile east of the Shore Mall, behind Atlantic Chrysler-Plymouth.

ELIZABETH   908

NEWARK AIRPORT HILTON HOTEL 1170 Spring St.
Phone: 351-3900. **Reservations:** 800-HILTONS.
Pool: 18y, rectangular, indoors, heated, 86°.
Admission: Registered guests NC.
Memberships: $300/year.

ENGLEWOOD CLIFFS   201

BALLY'S JACK LALANNE 150 Sylvan Ave.
Phone: 871-9600.
Pool: 20y x 20f, indoors, heated, 78°-82°.
Admission: Call.
Affiliate: Bally's NC.

FLEMINGTON   908

DEER PATH FAMILY YMCA 144 W. Woodschurch Rd.
Phone: 782-1030.
Pool: 25m, 6 lanes, indoors, heated, 84°.

Admission: $5.
Affiliate: Y AWAY $2.50.
To find: From Route 31 S., turn right onto
Woodschurch Rd.

FREEHOLD 908

FREEHOLD AREA YMCA 470 E. Freehold Rd.
Phone: 462-0464.
Pool: 25y, indoors, heated, water temperature not
reported.
Admission: Call.
Affiliate: YMCA $6 for pool.

GARFIELD 201

GARFIELD YMCA 33 Outwater Lane
Phone: 772-7450.
Pool: 20y, 4 lanes, indoors, heated, 83°.
Admission: $7.50.
Affiliate: Y AWAY NC. YMCA $2.
To find: Two blocks from the Passaic River.

HACKENSACK 201

GREATER BERGEN COUNTY YMCA 360 Main
St.
Phone: 487-6600.
Pool: 25y, indoors, heated, 80°-82°.
Admission: $7.
Affiliate: YMCA $3.50.

HOBOKEN 201

HOBOKEN YMCA 1301 Washington St.
Phone: 963-4100.
Pool: 20y, indoors, heated, 81°-82°.
Admission: $10.
Affiliate: YMCA outside a 60 mile radius NC.

JERSEY CITY 201

YMCA OF JERSEY CITY 654 Bergen Ave.
Phone: 434-3211.
Pool: 25y x 25f, 4 lanes, indoors, heated, 75°.
Admission: $5, SC(65, 62 if retired) $3.
Affiliate: Y AWAY $3.

YWCA OF HUDSON COUNTY 270 Fairmont Ave.
Phone: 333-5700.
Pool: 25y, indoors, heated, 88°.
Memberships: $35/year.

PERSHING FIELD POOL & ICE RINK 1 Pershing
Plaza
Phone 547-6886.
Pool: 25m x 58f, indoors, heated, water tempera-
ture not reported.
Admission: $3, SC(62) $1.

LIVINGSTON 201

WEST ESSEX BRANCH YMCA 321 S. Livingston
Ave.
Phone: 992-7500.
Pool: 25y x 35f, indoors, heated, 82°.
Admission: $10.
Affiliate: Out-of-state YMCA NC.

MADISON 201

MADISON AREA YMCA 1 Ralph Stoddard Dr.
Phone: 377-6200.
Pool: 25y x 25f, 4 lanes, indoors, heated, 84°.
Admission: Residents $3, non-residents $8.
Affiliate: Y AWAY NC.
Masters: The Madison Masters. Contact Chris
Collier at 377-6200.

MANAHAWKIN 609

STAFFORD POOL & FITNESS CENTER 700 S.
Mains St.
Phone: 597-6084.
Pool: 25y, indoors, heated, 83°.
Admission: $10.
Affiliate: IPFA NC.

MARGATE 609

JEWISH COMMUNITY CENTER 501 N. Jerome
Ave.
Phone: 822-1167.
Pool: 25m, indoors, heated, 80°.
Affiliate: JCC $5.

MEDFORD 609

EASTERN ATHLETIC CLUB 3 Nelson Dr.
Phone: 654-1440.
Pool: 25m x 30f, 4 lanes, indoors, heated, 82°.
Affiliate: IHRSA Call.

METUCHEN 908

METUCHEN-EDISON YMCA 65 High St.
Phone: 548-2044.
Pool: 25y x 25f, indoors, heated, 82°.
Admission: $8.
Affiliate: Out-of-state YMCA $1.

MONTCLAIR 201

MONTCLAIR YMCA 25 Park St.
Phone: 744-3400.
Pool 1: 25y, 6 lanes, indoors, heated, 80°.
Pool 2: 25y, 4 lanes, indoors, heated, 85°.
Admission: Call.
Affiliate: YMCA outside a 50 mile radius NC.
Masters: The Montclair YMCA Masters. Contact
Margaret Mulford at 744-3400.

MORRISTOWN   201

**HEADQUARTERS HEALTH & RACQUETBALL
CLUB** 118 Headquarters Plaza
Phone: 644-9600.
Pool: 22y, indoors, heated, 84°-88°.
Admission: $20.
Affiliate: IHRSA $12.
Hotel: Headquarters Hotel (898-9100) NC.

MOUNT ARLINGTON   201

SHERATON INN 15 Howard Blvd.
Phone: 770-2000. **Reservations:** 800-325-3535.
Pool: 50f x 25f, rectangular, indoors, heated, 70°-
80°.
Admission: Registered guests only NC.

MOUNT LAUREL   609

FAMILY Y OF BURLINGTON COUNTY 5001
Centerton Rd.
Phone: 234-6200.
Pool: 25y x 45f, 6 lanes, indoors, heated, 83°.
Admission: $6.
Affiliate: Y AWAY outside a 50 mile radius NC,
within 50 miles $3.
To find: In Laurel Corporate Center, off Marter
Ave., near Route 38 and I-295.

OMNIFIT 130 Gaither Dr., Suite 136
Phone: 722-1001.
Pool: 20y, indoors, heated, 88°.
Admission: $5.

JERSEY WAHOOS SWIM CLUB 4101 Church Rd.
Phone: 234-5898.
Pool: 25y, 7 lanes, indoors, heated, 80°.
Admission: $5.
To find: Exit 4 off the New Jersey Tpk. The club is
behind Bennigan's Restaurant on Route 73.
Masters: The Jersey Wahoos Swim Club Masters.
Contact Chris Gally at 234-5898.

MOUNTAIN LAKES   201

LAKELAND HILLS FAMILY YMCA 100 Fanny Rd.
Phone: 334-2820.
Pool: 25y x 24f, 6 lanes, indoors, heated, 84°.
Affiliate: YMCA $5.
Hotel: Embassy Suites in Parsippany (334-1440)
NC with room key.
To find: One quarter mile off The Boulevard and
three miles off Route 46.

NEW BRUNSWICK   908

YWCA OF CENTRAL JERSEY 51 Livingston Ave.
Phone: 545-6622.
Pool: 25y x 30f, 4 lanes, indoors, heated, 82°.
Admission: $3, SC(60) $2.
To find: One block from Fountain on George St.

NEWARK   201

NEWARK YM/WCA 600 Broad St.
Phone: 624-8900.
Pool: 25y, 4 lanes, indoors, heated, 84°.
Admission: $10.
Affiliate: Y AWAY outside a 50 mile radius NC.
YMCA outside a 50 mile radius $5.

ORANGE   201

YWCA OF ESSEX & WEST HUDSON 395 Main St.
Phone: 672-9500.
Pool: 25y x 30f, 5 lanes, indoors, heated, 82°.
Affiliate: YWCA $3, SC(62) $2.50.
To find: Across the street from the Orange Post
Office and two blocks north of the Orange Library.

PARAMUS   201

THE HEALTH SPA 2 Bergen Mall, Route 4 and
Forest Ave.
Phone: 843-3131.
Pool: 20y x 35f, 5 lanes, indoors, heated, 81°-83°.
Admission: $15.
Affiliate: IHRSA $8.

PASSAIC   201

YMCA OF PASSAIC-CLIFTON 45 River Dr.
Phone: 777-0123.
Pool: 20y x 20f, 2 lanes, indoors, heated, 82°.
Admission: 1 visit $15, then $5 per day.
Affiliate: YMCA $5.

PATERSON   201

PATERSON YMCA 128 Ward St.
Phone: 684-2320.
Pool: 20y x 36f, 5 lanes, indoors, heated, 83°.
Admission: $5.
Affiliate: Y AWAY outside a 50 mile radius NC.

PEMBERTON   609

BURLINGTON COUNTY COLLEGE County Route
530
Phone: Recorded schedules: 894-9311 ext. 436.
Information: 894-9311 ext. 496.
Pool: 25y x 45f, 6 x 3 lanes, indoors, heated, 86°.
Admission: $2*, SC $1*.
Notes: *All pool users must have a Facility Use
Card photo ID, available for $2 at the Physical
Education Building.

PISCATAWAY   908

SONNY WERBLIN RECREATION CENTER
Rutgers University - Busch Campus
Phone: 932-0462.
Pool: 50m OR 25y + 25y x 25y, 8 OR 16 lanes,
indoors, heated, 79°.
Affiliate: USMS Call.
To find: One block from Rutgers Stadium.

Masters: The Rutgers Masters Club. Contact Alex Antoniou at 932-0462.

84°.
Admission: $5.

POMPTON PLAINS 201

SPA 23 & RACQUET CLUB 381 Route 23
Phone: 839-8823.
Pool: 25y x 24f, 4 lanes, indoors, heated, 83°.
Admission: $12.
Affiliate: IHRSA $6.

PRINCETON 609

YWCA OF PRINCETON Paul Robeson Place
Phone: 497-2100. **Pool:** 497-2148.
Pool: 25y, indoors, heated, 85°.
Affiliate: YWCA $4.

RAHWAY 908

RAHWAY YMCA 1564 Irving St.
Phone: 388-0057.
Pool: 25y x 42f, 6 lanes, indoors, heated, water temperature not reported.
Admission: $6.
Affiliate: Y AWAY outside a 50 mile radius NC.
To find: Across the street from the Union County Arts Center.

RANDOLPH 201

WEST MORRIS AREA YMCA 140 Dover Chester Rd.
Phone: 366-1120.
Pool: 25m, indoors, heated, 82°.
Affiliate: YMCA $3.

RED BANK 908

RED BANK YMCA 166 Maple Ave.
Phone: 741-2504.
Pool: 25y x 43f, indoors, heated, 82°.
Affiliate: Y AWAY $4.50.
Notes: There is also a 40f x 18f, indoor, heated, 88° pool.
Masters: The Red Bank YMCA Masters. Contact Doug Rice or Marc T. Riker at 741-2504.

RIDGEWOOD 201

YM / YWCA OF BERGEN COUNTY 112 Oak St.
Phone: 444-5600.
Pool 1: 25y, indoors, heated, 82°.
Pool 2: 25y, indoors, heated, 85°.
Admission: $5.

SALEM 609

LIFESTYLES FAMILY FITNESS & AQUATIC CENTER 73 Maskill's Rd.
Phone: 935-0837.
Pool: 25m x 15m, 6 lanes, indoor/outdoor, heated,

SCOTCH PLAINS 908

FANWOOD-SCOTCH PLAINS YMCA 1340 Martine Ave.
Phone: 889-8880.
Pool: 25y, indoors, heated, 83°.
Affiliate: Y AWAY NC.

SHORT HILLS 201

THE HILTON AT SHORT HILLS 41 John F. Kennedy Pkwy.
Phone: 379-0100. **Reservations:** 800-HILTONS.
Pool: 50f, indoors, heated, 83°-84°.
Admission: Registered guests NC.
Affiliate: IHRSA $20.

SOMERS POINT 609

EASTERN ATHLETIC CLUB 7th St. & New Hampshire Ave.
Phone: 926-1515.
Pool: 25m x 30f, 4 lanes, indoors, heated, 82°.
Affiliate: IHRSA Call.

SOMERVILLE 908

SOMERSET VALLEY YMCA N. Bridge & Green Sts.
Phone: 722-4567.
Pool: 25y x 35f, 6 lanes, indoors, heated, 85°.
Admission: $7.
Affiliate: Y AWAY $3.50.

SOUTH PLAINFIELD 908

HOLIDAY INN OF SOUTH PLAINFIELD 4701 Stelton Rd. at Route 287
Phone: 753-5500.
Pool: 20y, irregularly shaped, indoor/outdoor, heated, 80°.
Admission: Registered guests only NC.

RICOCHET HEALTH & RACQUET CLUB 219 St. Nicholas Ave.
Phone: 753-2300.
Pool: 25y, indoors, heated, 85°-86°.
Memberships: 3 months $169, daytime hours only. I/S $99 + $39 to $59/month.

SPRINGFIELD 201

BALLY'S JACK LALANNE 99 U.S. Hwy. 22
Phone: 376-6886.
Pool: 25y, indoors, heated, 81°-83°.
Admission: 1 visit NC.
Affiliate: Bally's NC.
Hotel: Holiday Inn (376-9400) NC.

SUMMIT   908

SUMMIT AREA YMCA 67 Maple St.
Phone: 273-3330.
Pool: 25y, indoors, heated, 80°-82°.
Affiliate: YMCA outside a 75 mile radius NC.

YWCA OF SUMMIT 79 Maple St.
Phone: 273-4242.
Pool: 25y x 35f, indoors, heated, 82°.
Admission: $4.

TENAFLY   201

JEWISH COMMUNITY CENTER 411 E. Clinton
Ave.
Phone: 569-7900.
Pool: 25m, indoors, heated, 80°.
Affiliate: JCC NC.

TOMS RIVER   908

OCEAN COUNTY YMCA 1088 Whitty Rd.
Phone: 341-9622.
Pool: 25y x 45f, 6 lanes, indoors, heated, 85°.
Affiliate: YMCA $3.
Notes: There is also a 25m, outdoor, summer pool.

OCEAN COUNTY YMCA MASTERS at the Ocean
County YMCA
Masters: Contact Maureen Rohrs or Coach Herb
Roeschke at 341-9622.
Affiliate: YMCA Call.
Notes: Coached workouts: Tu,Th: 6-7PM. Su: 8-
10AM.

TRENTON   609

YWCA OF TRENTON 140 E. Hanover St.
Phone: 396-8291.
Pool: 20y, indoors, heated, 84°-85°.
Affiliate: YWCA $5.

AQUATICS CENTER Trenton State College
Phone: 771-2383.
Pool: 25y or 25m, 8 lanes, indoors, heated, 80°-
83°.
Admission: Out-of-town adult visitors $2.
Memberships: $150/year.
Masters: TSC Masters Swimming. Contact Chris
Denn at 771-3249(w).

UNION   908

BOYS & GIRLS CLUB OF UNION 1050 Jeanett
Ave.
Phone: 687-2697.
Pool: 25y, indoors, heated, water temperature not
reported.
Admission: $2.

VINELAND   609

VINELAND YMCA 1159 E. Landis Ave.
Phone: 691-0030.
Pool: 25y, indoors, heated, 84°.
Affiliate: YMCA NC.

VOORHEES   609

ECHELON YMCA 120 Britton Place
Phone: 772-9622.
Pool: 25y x 36f, 6 lanes, indoors, heated, 84°.
Admission: $3.
Affiliate: Y AWAY NC.
To find: Across from Echelon Mall.
Masters: The Echelon YMCA Electric Eels.
Contact Aquatic Director Ken MacKenzie at 772-
9622.

BALLY'S HOLIDAY FITNESS CENTER 1160
White Horse Rd.
Phone: 346-4700.
Pool: 25m, indoors, heated, 82°.
Affiliate: Bally's NC.
Hotel: Hampton Inn (346-4500) NC.

COLISEUM SPORTS CENTER 333 Preston Ave.
Phone: 429-6908.
Pool: 25y, indoors, heated, water temperature not
reported.
Admission: 1 visit NC, 2 additional visits $10 each.

WEST ORANGE   201

JEWISH COMMUNITY CENTER METRO WEST
760 Northfield Ave.
Phone: 736-3200 ext. 303.
Pool: 25y x 35f, 5 lanes, indoors, heated, 82°.
Affiliate: Out-of-state YM-YWHA & JCC: NC.
Masters: The Metro Express. Contact Edward
Nessel at (908) 561-5339.

WESTFIELD   908

WESTFIELD YMCA 220 Clark St.
Phone: 233-2700.
Pool: 25y, 6 lanes, indoors, heated, 82°.
Affiliate: Y AWAY NC. YMCA $5.
Hotel: Westfield Motor Inn $10.
To find: One block from Lord & Taylor Department
Store.

WOODBURY   609

YMCA OF GLOUCESTER COUNTY 235 E. Red
Bank Ave.
Phone: 845-0720.
Pool: 25y x 35f, 6 lanes, indoors, heated, 84°-86°.
Admission: $7.
Affiliate: Y AWAY outside a 50 mile radius 4 visits
per month NC. YMCA outside a 50 mile radius
$3.50.
To find: One block east of Underwood Hospital.

Admission: Out-of-town visitors — Call.
Affiliate: Y AWAY 2 visits NC. YMCA $3.

LOS ALTOS POOL 10100 Lomas Blvd. N.E.
Phone: 291-6290/1.
Pool: 25m x 56f, 9 lanes, indoors, heated, 83°.
Admission: $1.84, SC(65) $26¢.
To find: In Los Altos Park, at Eubank & Lomas N.E.

SANDIA POOL 7801 Candelaria N.E.
Phone: 291-6278.
Pool: 25y x 56f, 8 lanes, indoors, heated, 82°.
Admission: $1.84, SC(65) $26¢.
To find: One block north of Pennsylvania and
    Candelaria, at Sandia High School.
Masters: Duke City Aquatics. Contact Reed
    Barnitz at 256-7727(w&h).

HIGHPOINT RACQUET & SWIM CLUB 4300
    Landau N.E.
Phone: 293-5820.
Pool: 20y, indoors, heated, 84°-86°.
Admission: $7. M-F before 4PM & Sa,Su after
    3PM $3.

RIVER POINT SWIM & RACQUET CLUB, INC.
    9190 Coors Blvd. N. W.
Phone: 897-3716.
Pool: 25m, 4 lanes, indoors, heated, 82°.
Admission: $8.
Affiliate: IHRSA $5.
Notes: There is also a 25y, 6 lane, outdoor, sum-
    mer pool.
To find: At the southeast corner of Paseo del Norte
    and Coors Blvd. in northwest Albuquerque.

HOLIDAY INN EXPRESS 10330 Hotel Ave. N.E.
Phone: 275-8900. **Reservations:** 800-HOLIDAY.
Pool: 25y x 24f, rectangular, indoors, heated, 78°.
Admission: Registered guests only NC.

FARMINGTON   505

ROYAL SPA & COURT CLUB 2101 Bloomfield
    Hwy.
Phone: 326-2211.
Pool: 20m, indoors, heated, 84°.
Admission: $10.
Affiliate: IHRSA Call.
Hotel: All local hotels $6 with room key.

FARMINGTON AQUATIC CENTER 1151 Sullivan
Phone: 599-1167.
Pool: 25y x 50m, 8 x 8 lanes, indoors, heated, 82°.
Admission: $2.50.
Notes: There's also a 150 ft. water slide, for an
    additional charge.
To find: Between Main and 20th St. on Sullivan.
Masters: The Four Corners Aquatic Team
    (F.C.A.T.) Contact Greg Maxwell at 599-1167.

ALBUQUERQUE   505

VALLEY HIGH POOL 1505 Candelaria N.W.
Phone: 761-4806.
Pool: 25y x 56f, 9 lanes, indoors, heated, 82°.
Admission: $1.84, SC(65) $26¢.
To find: Behind Valley High School. Enter through
    the main entrance off Candelaria N.W.
Masters: Duke City Aquatics. Contact Reed
    Barnitz at 256-7727(w&h).

HIGHLAND SWIMMING POOL 400 Jackson St.
    S.E.
Phone: 256-2096/7.
Pool: 25y x 25m, 11 lanes, indoors, heated, 82°.
Admission: $1.84, SC(65) $26¢.
Masters: Duke City Aquatics. Contact Reed
    Barnitz at 256-7727(w&h).

MIDTOWN SPORTS & WELLNESS 4100 Prospect
    Ave. N.E.
Phone: 888-4811.
Pool: 25y x 42f, 6 lanes, indoor/outdoor, heated,
    82°.
Affiliate: IHRSA $5 or $7, depending on the hour.
Hotel: Radisson Inn Albuquerque Airport (247-
    0512) NC. Quality Hotel Four Seasons (888-3311)
    $2.50 or $5.
To find: Adjacent to the Quality Inn Four Seasons
    off I-40.

HEIGHTS FAMILY YMCA 4901 Indian School Rd.
    N.E.
Phone: 265-6971.
Pool: 25y x 25f, 2 lanes, indoors, heated, 85°.

GALLUP   505

HOWARD RUNNELS POOL COMPLEX 720 E. Wilson
Phone: 722-7107.
Pool: 25m, indoors, heated, 84°.
Admission: $1.60, SC(60) $1.05.

HOBBS   505

HOBBS HIGH SCHOOL POOL at Jefferson & Sanger
Phone: Pool: 397-9326. Rec. Dept: 397-9293.
Pool: 25m, 6 lanes, indoors, heated, 82°.
Admission: $1.50.

LAS VEGAS   505

NEW MEXICO HIGHLANDS UNIVERSITY National Ave. & 11th St.
Phone: Pool: 454-3073. University: 425-7511.
Pool: 25y, indoors, heated, water temperature not reported.
Admission: $1.

LOS ALAMOS   505

LARRY R. WALKUP AQUATICS CENTER 2760 Canyon Rd.
Phone: 662-8037.
Pool: 25y x 50m, 22 x 8 lanes, indoors, heated, 82°.
Admission: $2.75, SC(65) $2.25.
Notes: There is also a 20f x 40f, 94° therapy pool. The center is at an altitude of 7,500 feet.
To find: At the junction of Central & Canyon at the western end of Central.
Masters: The Los Alamos Swim Team. Contact Phil Coe at 662-8037.

SANTA FE   505

FORT MARCY COMPLEX 490 Washington
Phone: 984-6725.
Pool: 25y x 45f, 6 lanes, indoors, heated, 82°.
Admission: $1.25, SC(60) NC.
Hotel: La Posada Inn (986-0000) NC.
Masters: The Master Swim Club of Santa Fe. Contact Andrea Ortiz at 984-6725.

TINO GRIEGO SWIMMING POOL 1730 Llano
Phone: 473-7270.
Pool: 25y x 45f, 6 lanes, indoors, heated, 84°.
Admission: $1.25, SC(60) NC.

SALVADOR PEREZ SWIMMING POOL 601 Alta Vista
Phone: 984-6755.
Pool: 25y x 45f, 7 lanes, indoors, heated, 84°.
Admission: $1.25, SC(60) NC.

THE CLUB EL GANCHO Las Vegas Hwy.
Phone: 988-5000.
Pool: 20y, indoors, heated, 83°.
Affiliate: IHRSA $7.50.
To find: Call for directions.

QUAIL RUN CLUB 3101 Old Pecos Trail
Phone: 986-2222.
Pool: 20y, indoors, heated, 85°.
Affiliate: IHRSA $20.

TAOS   505

DON FERNANDO POOL 124 Civic Plaza Dr.
Phone: 758-9171.
Pool: 70f x 35f, 6 lanes, indoors, heated, 85°.
Admission: $2, SC(60) NC.

ALWAYS CALL FIRST

Pools close, they change names, affiliations, admission policies, and rates. And just because a pool is listed in *Swimmers Guide* doesn't mean it's open all day, every day, for just the type of workout you want to do. Spend a quarter to save time and aggravation. . . always call first!

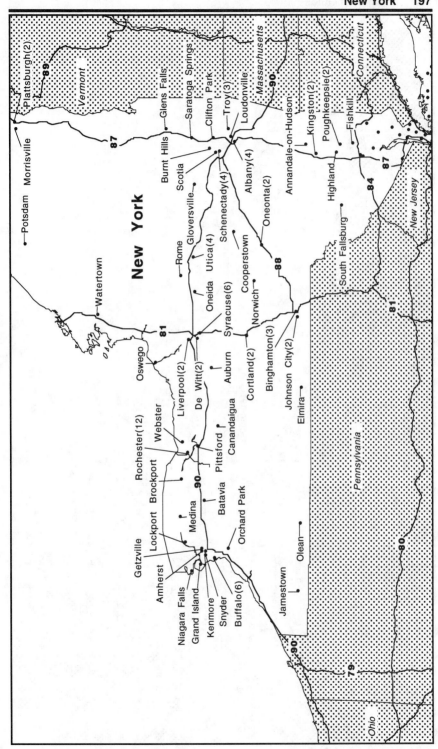

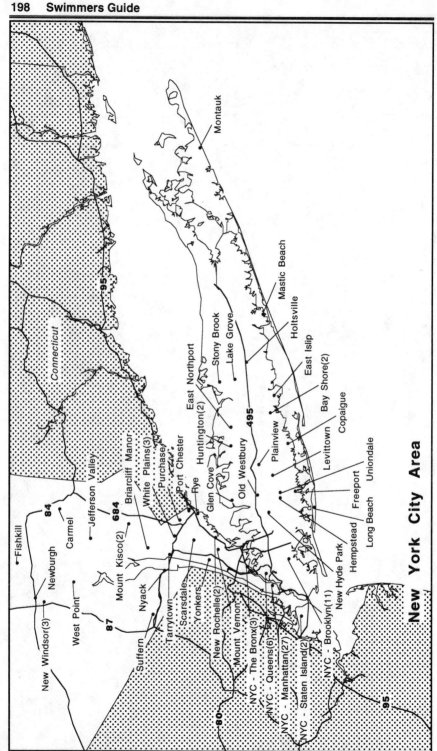

Montauk

Mastic Beach

Holtsville

Stony Brook

Lake Grove

East Islip

East Northport

Huntington(2)

Bay Shore(2)

Copaigue

Plainview

Old Westbury

Glen Cove

Levittown

Port Chester

Rye

Freeport

Uniondale

Purchase

White Plains(3)

Hempstead

Long Beach

Briarcliff Manor

New Hyde Park

Jefferson Valley

NYC - Brooklyn(11)

Mount Kisco(2)

NYC - Staten Island(2)

Carmel

NYC - Manhattan(27)

Nyack

NYC - Queens(6)

NYC - The Bronx(3)

Newburgh

Mount Vernon

New Rochelle(2)

West Point

Yonkers

Scarsdale

New Windsor(3)

Tarrytown

Fishkill

Suffern

Connecticut

New York City Area

ALBANY 518

ALBANY YMCA 274 Washington Ave.
Phone: 449-7196.
Pool 1: 25y x 48f, 6 lanes, indoors, heated, 82°.
Pool 2: 20y x 40f, 4 lanes, indoors, heated, 86°.
Affiliate: Y AWAY NC. YMCA $3.50.

ALBANY JEWISH COMMUNITY CENTER 340
Whitehall Rd.
Phone: 438-6651.
Pool: 20y x 30f, 5 lanes, indoors, heated, 83°.
Admission: 3 visits per year $5 each.
Affiliate: JCC outside a 50 mile radius NC.
Notes: There is also a 25y x 45f, 6 lane, outdoor,
78°-80° pool operated from Memorial Day to Labor
Day.
To find: Between Main St. & Manning Blvd., two
blocks south of St. Peters Hospital.
Masters: The AJCC Masters. Contact Coach Boris
Gybatskaya or Jeanette Gottlieb at 438-6651.

THE ALBANY ACADEMY Academy Rd.
Phone: 465-1461 ask for Dan Hanifin.
Pool: 25y x 45f, 6 lanes, indoors, heated, 79°.
Admission: $5 per hour.
Memberships: $20/week. $50/month.
Notes: The pool offers early morning lap swimming
and Masters workouts.
Masters: Albany Masters Swimming. Contact Dan
Hanifin at 465-1461.

THE UNIVERSITY AT ALBANY 1400 Washington
Ave.
Phone: Alumni Assn: 442-3080. Recreation facili-
ties: 442-3310.
Pool: 25y, 6 lanes, indoors, heated, 77°-78°.
Memberships: $129/year (annual Alumni Assn.
contribution of $30 + $99 facility dues).

AMHERST 716

BALLY MATRIX FITNESS CENTER 3880 E.
Robinson Rd.
Phone: 691-4292.
Pool: 25y, indoors, heated, 78°-82°.
Admission: $15.
Affiliate: Bally's NC.
Hotel: Holiday Inn (691-8181) & Residence Inn
(632-6622): NC.

ANNANDALE-ON-HUDSON 914

BARD TIDAL WAVES at Stevenson Gymnasium,
Bard College
Pool phone: 758-7527. **Masters:** Contact Kay
Moore at 758-6473(h).
Pool: 25y x 42f, 6 lanes, indoors, heated, 79°-81°.
Non-member participation: $5*, includes pool
fees.
Notes: Sep.-May: Coached workouts: M,W,F: 4-
5PM. *Visitors are admitted only as guests of
members.

AUBURN 315

AUBURN YMCA-WEIU 27 William St.
Phone: 253-5304.
Pool: 25y x 31f, 6 lanes, indoors, heated, 85°.
Affiliate: YMCA Call.

BATAVIA 716

GENESEE AREA YMCA 209 E. Main St.
Phone: 344-1664.
Pool: 25y, 6 lanes, indoors, heated, 84°.
Admission: Swim $2.50. Day Pass $9.
Affiliate: YMCA NC.

BAY SHORE 516

GREAT SOUTH BAY YMCA 200 W. Main St.
Phone: 665-4255.
Pool: 25y x 42f, 6 lanes, indoors, heated, 84°.
Admission: $7.
Affiliate: Out-of-state YMCA NC.

BALLY'S JACK LALANNE 1175 Sunrise Hwy.
Phone: 666-5533.
Pool: 20y, indoors, heated, 82°.
Admission: Call.
Affiliate: Bally's NC.

BINGHAMTON 607

BINGHAMTON YMCA 61 Susquehanna St.
Phone: 772-0560.
Pool: 25y, 3 double lanes, indoors, heated, 85°.
Admission: $10.
Affiliate: Y AWAY NC. YMCA 1 visit NC, then $3.
Hotel: Holiday Inn Downtown-Arena Area (722-
1212), Hotel DeVille, Ramada Inn (724-2412), &
Residence Inn (770-8500): NC.
To find: Behind the New York State Office Building.

EAST GYM POOL SUNY - Binghamton, Vestal
Pkwy. E.
Phone: 777-4257.
Pool: 25y, indoors, heated, 80°.
Admission: $3.

SNEAKERS FITNESS CENTER 67 Robinson St.
Phone: 723-1000.
Pool: 25y, indoors, heated, 86°.
Admission: $10.
Affiliate: IPFA NC.

BRIARCLIFF MANOR 914

CLUB FIT N. State Rd.
Phone: 762-3444.
Pool: 20y x 33f, indoors, heated, 78°-80°.
Affiliate: IHRSA $15.

BROCKPORT   716

TUTTLE NORTH ATHLETIC COMPLEX SUNY - Brockport
Phone: 395-5344.
Pool: 50m x 25y, indoors, heated, 78°-82°.
Admission: $1.

BUFFALO   716

YWCA OF WESTERN NEW YORK 190 Franklin St.
Phone: 852-6120.
Pool: 20y x 24f, 4-6 lanes, indoors, heated, 82°.
Admission: $5, SC(60) $4.
To find: Across from the Convention Center.

THE OLYMPIA CLUB 300 Pearl St.
Phone: 847-6000.
Pool: 20y, indoors, heated, 83°.
Admission: $15.

WILLIAM EMSLIE BRANCH YMCA 585 William St.
Phone: 845-5440.
Pool: 25y, indoors, heated, 82°-84°.
Admission: $6.
Affiliate: YMCA Call.

JEWISH CENTER 787 Delaware Ave.
Phone: 886-3145.
Pool: 25y, 4 lanes, indoors, heated, 83°.
Admission: $5.
Affiliate: JCC NC.

DELAWARE FAMILY YMCA 2564 Delaware Ave.
Phone: 875-1283.
Pool: 20y x 20f, 4 lanes, indoors, heated, 84°.
Admission: $8.
Affiliate: Out-of-area Y AWAY 7 visits per year NC.
To find: In north Buffalo between Hertel and Kenmore Aves.

AQUATIC & FITNESS CENTER 1 Pool Plaza
Phone: 876-7424.
Pool: 50m OR 25y + 25y, indoors, heated, 82°.
Admission: Non-residents $6.25.

BURNT HILLS   518

BURNT HILLS HIGH SCHOOL Lakehill Rd.
Phone: 399-9141.
Pool: 25y x 45f, 6 lanes, indoors, heated, 82°.
Admission: $2.
Notes: The pool closes for the months of Jul. and Aug.

CANANDAIGUA   716

CANANDAIGUA MASTER SWIM CLUB ('THE SAWBELLIES') at Canandaigua Academy Pool, 435 East St.

Pool phone: 396-3827. **Masters:** Contact Vern Heckler at 394-4075(h) evenings.
Pool: 25y x 56f, 8 lanes, indoors, heated, 79°-81°.
Affiliate: USMS $2, includes pool fees.
Notes: Coached workouts: M,Tu,Th,F: 8:30-10PM.

CARMEL   914

CARMEL FITNESS & RACQUET CLUB Old Route 6
Phone: 225-0888.
Pool: 20y x 24f, 4 lanes, indoors, heated, 83°.
Admission: $5.

CLIFTON PARK   518

SOUTHERN SARATOGA YMCA 1 Wall St.
Phone: 371-2139.
Pool: 25y x 56f, 8 lanes, indoors, heated, 83°.
Affiliate: Y AWAY outside a 50 mile radius NC.
To find: Wall St. is between the Shop 'n Save Plaza and the Clifton Park Library. It dead ends at the YMCA entrance.
Masters: The Southern Saratoga Y Masters. Contact Alex Walker at 371-2139 ext. 33.

COOPERSTOWN   607

CLARK SPORTS CENTER Susquehanna Ave.
Phone: 547-2800.
Pool: 25y x 45f, 6 lanes, indoors, heated, 82°.
Admission: $7.
Notes: There is a 15y x 35f, indoor, heated, 82° diving pool with a 1m board which is also used for aqua jogging.

COPAIGUE   516

BALLY'S JACK LALANNE 1147 Sunrise Hwy.
Phone: 842-7000.
Pool: 25m, indoors, heated, 79°.
Admission: Call.
Affiliate: Bally's NC.

CORTLAND   607

CORTLAND COUNTY FAMILY YMCA 22 Tompkins St.
Phone: 756-2893.
Pool: 25y x 30f, 4 lanes, indoors, heated, 82°.
Admission: 3 visits per year $8 each.
Affiliate: YMCA $1. U.S. Military NC.

YWCA OF CORTLAND 14 Clayton Ave.
Phone: 753-9651.
Pool: 24y, indoors, heated, 87°-90°.
Admission: $3.

DE WITT   315

BALLY MATRIX FITNESS CENTER 5801 Bridge St.

Phone: 445-9370.
Pool: 25m, indoors, heated, 78°-81°.
Admission: $10.
Affiliate: Bally's NC.
Hotel: Genesee Inn & Marriott's Fairfield Inn (432-9333): NC.

GOLD'S GYM AT SUNDOWN 5791 Widewaters Pkwy.
Phone: 446-0376.
Pool: 25m, 3 lanes, indoors, heated, 80°.
Admission: $10.
Affiliate: Gold's Gym Travel Card — NC to $10.
To find: Off Erie Blvd., behind Hills Plaza and Shoppingtown.

EAST ISLIP   516

BELFRAN HEALTH & FITNESS CENTER 265 E. Main St.
Phone: 277-7610.
Pool: 22y, indoors, heated, 80°.
Admission: $12.
Affiliate: IPFA & IHRSA: Call.
Masters: The Belfran Barracudas. Contact John Connor at 277-7610.

EAST NORTHPORT   516

THE FITNESS CLUB 1960 Jericho Tpk.
Phone: 462-6400.
Pool: 20y x 25f, 4 lanes, indoors, heated, 82°.
Affiliate: IHRSA $5, peak hours $10.
To find: On Jericho Tpk., a quarter of a mile east of Deer Park Ave.

ELMIRA   607

YWCA OF CHEMUNG COUNTY 211 Lake St.
Phone: 733-5575.
Pool: 20y x 20f, indoors, heated, 86°-88°.
Admission: $3.

FISHKILL   914

ALL SPORT FITNESS & RACQUET CLUB 17 Old Main St.
Phone: 896-5678.
Pool: 25m, indoors, heated, 83°.
Affiliate: IHRSA $10.
Hotel: Holiday Inn (896-6281), Courtyards by Marriott (897-2400), & Wellesley Inn: NC.

FREEPORT   516

FREEPORT RECREATION CENTER 130 E. Merrick Rd.
Phone: 223-8000.
Pool: 25y, 6 lanes, indoors, heated, 80°.
Affiliate: Residents $3.
Memberships: Residents $125/year, non-residents $190.

FREEPORT WRECKS at the Freeport Recreation Center
Masters: Contact Kitty Kessler at 367-4092(h).
Non-member participation: $6, SC $4. Both rates include pool fees.
Notes: Uncoached workouts: Tu-Sa: 11AM-12:30PM. Su: Noon-1:30PM.

GETZVILLE   716

JEWISH CENTER OF GREATER BUFFALO, INC. 2640 N. Forest
Phone: 688-4033.
Pool: 25y, indoors, heated, 82°.
Admission: $5.
Affiliate: JCC NC.
Hotel: University Inn & Conference Center (636-7500) NC with a pass from the hotel.
Notes: There is also a seasonal outdoor pool complex. Admission is $5 for all.

GLEN COVE   516

YMCA AT GLEN COVE Dosoris Lane
Phone: 671-8270.
Pool: 25y x 36f, 6 lanes, indoors, heated, 84°.
Admission: $7.
Affiliate: YMCA $3.50.
To find: Call for directions.

GLENS FALLS   518

GLENS FALLS YMCA 600 Upper Glen St.
Phone: 793-3878.
Pool: 25y x 40f, 6 lanes, indoors, heated, 82°.
Admission: $7.
Affiliate: Y AWAY outside a 60 mile radius NC. YMCA $3.50.

GLENS FALLS YMCA MASTERS at the Glens Falls YMCA
Pool phone: 793-3878. **Masters:** Contact Masters Coach John Ogden at 792-3603(h).
Affiliate: USMS & YMCA: $5, includes pool fees.
Notes: Workouts: M,W,F: 5:30-7AM. Tu,Th: 8-9PM. Su: 10AM-Noon.

GLOVERSVILLE   518

GLOVERSVILLE YMCA 19 E. Fulton St.
Phone: 725-0627.
Pool: 20y, indoors, heated, 86°.
Admission: $10.
Affiliate: YMCA $5.

GRAND ISLAND   716

HOLIDAY INN GRAND ISLAND 100 Whitehaven Rd.
Phone: 773-1111. **Reservations:** 800-HOLIDAY.
Pool: 20y, rectangular, indoors, heated, 84°.
Admission: $5. Registered guests NC.
Memberships: $220/year.

HEMPSTEAD 516

HOFSTRA UNIVERSITY SWIM CENTER 240
Hofstra University
Phone: 463-5081.
Pool: 50m, 8 lanes, indoors, heated, 81°.
Memberships: 1/3/12 months $60/$115/$345. SC
10% discount.

JACKSON EXPRESS MASTERS at Hofstra
University Swim Center
Masters: Contact Christine Zimmet at 368-8353(h).
Non-member participation: $3, includes pool fees.
Notes: Fall, winter, and spring: Uncoached work-
outs: Sa: 11AM-12:30PM. Su: Noon-1:30PM.

HIGHLAND 914

ROCKING HORSE RANCH 600 Route 44-55
Phone: 691-2927. **Reservations:** 800-647-2624.
Pool: 50f, rectangular, indoors, heated, 82°.
Admission: Registered guests only NC.

HOLTSVILLE 516

BROOKHAVEN-ROE YMCA 155 Buckley Rd.
Phone: 289-4440.
Pool: 25m, 6 lanes, indoors, heated, 83°-84°.
Admission: $7.
Affiliate: YMCA 2 visits NC, then $3.50.
To find: Off Patchogue-Holbrook Rd., south of
Woodside Ave. (Route 99), across from the IRS.
Masters: The Brookhaven Clammers. Contact
Linda Relethford or Joan Zullo by leaving a mes-
sage with the Y at 289-4440.

HUNTINGTON 516

HUNTINGTON YMCA 60 Main St.
Phone: 421-4242.
Pool 1: 25y x 42f, 6 lanes, indoors, heated, 83°-
85°.
Pool 2: 25y x 25f, 4 lanes, indoors, heated, 83°-
85°.
Admission: $10.
Affiliate: YMCA $3. U.S. Military & Clergy: $5.

HUNTINGTON YMCA MASTERS SWIM CLUB at
the Huntington YMCA
Masters: Contact Aquatics Director Jane Maresco
at 421-4242.
Non-member participation: $10, includes pool
fees.
Affiliate: YMCA $5, includes pool fees.
Notes: Workouts: M,W: 7-9AM, 11:30AM-1PM, 5-
6PM, 8-9PM. Tu,Th: 7-9AM, 11:30AM-1PM. 6-
7PM, 7:45-9PM. F: 7-9AM, 11:30AM-1PM, 7-
8:30PM. Sa: 8-9:30AM, 5-7PM. Su: 7:30AM-
Noon.

NORTH SHORE SWIM CLUB 214 Wall St.
Phone: 271-7946.

Pool: 33y, 4 lanes, indoors, heated, 81°-84°.
Admission: $10.

JAMESTOWN 716

JAMESTOWN YMCA 101 E. 4th St.
Phone: 664-2802.
Pool 1: 25y, indoors, heated, 82°-85°.
Pool 2: 20y, indoors, heated, 85°-87°.
Admission: $4.
Affiliate: YMCA NC.
Hotel: Holiday Inn (664-3400) $2 with room key.
Masters: The Muskies Swim Team. Contact Deb
Peters or Missy Denault at 664-2802.

JEFFERSON VALLEY 914

CLUB FIT Bank Rd.
Phone: 245-4040.
Pool: 20y x 26f, 4 lanes, indoors, heated, 83°.
Affiliate: IHRSA 2 visits per month $15 each.
To find: Off Route 6, across from the Jefferson
Valley Mall.

JOHNSON CITY 607

COURT JESTER ATHLETIC CLUB 216 Reynolds
Rd.
Phone: 729-3332.
Pool: 25y, 3 lanes, indoors, heated, 84°-86°.
Admission: $12.
Affiliate: IPFA NC.

WEST BRANCH YMCA 740 Main St.
Phone: 729-4976.
Pool: 25y, indoors, heated, 84°-86°.
Admission: $10.
Affiliate: YMCA NC.
Masters: Contact Bob Benninger at 770-9622 or
748-0808(h).

KENMORE 716

KENTON FAMILY YMCA 535 Belmont Ave.
Phone: 874-5051.
Pool: 25y, 4 lane, indoors, heated, 81°-83°.
Admission: $7.
Affiliate: Y AWAY NC.
Masters: Contact Coach Keith Bollion or Dawn
Hambleton at 874-5051.

KINGSTON 914

KINGSTON MASTERS SWIM CLUB at Kingston
High School, Broadway
Masters: Contact Ron Keillor at 626-0044(h).
Pool: 25y x 50f, 6 lanes, indoors, heated, 80°.
Affiliate: USMS NC, includes pool fees.
Notes: Uncoached lap swimming: M-F: 6-7AM.
Sa: 8-9AM.

KINGSTON & ULSTER COUNTY YMCA 507
Broadway

Phone: 338-3810.
Pool: 25y, indoors, heated, 78°-80°.
Admission: $11.
Affiliate: YMCA NC.

LAKE GROVE   516

BALLY'S JACK LALANNE FITNESS CENTER 22
Middle Country Rd.
Phone: 471-6000.
Pool: 25m, indoors, heated, 80°.
Admission: Call.
Affiliate: Bally's NC.

LEVITTOWN   516

BALLY'S JACK LALANNE FITNESS CENTER
2935 Hempstead Tpk.
Phone: 579-3900.
Pool: 22m, indoors, heated, 81°.
Admission: Call.
Affiliate: Bally's NC.

LIVERPOOL   315

**YMCA OF GREATER SYRACUSE - NORTH AREA
BRANCH** 4775 Wetzel Rd.
Phone: 451-2562.
Pool: 25y x 42f, 6 lanes, indoors, heated, 84°.
Admission: $8.
Affiliate: Y AWAY outside a 50 mile radius $1.

GOLD'S GYM AT SUNDOWN 7455 Morgan Rd.
Phone: 451-5050.
Pool: 25m, indoors, heated, 75°-82°.
Admission: $10.

LOCKPORT   716

LOCKPORT YMCA 19 East Ave.
Phone: 434-8887.
Pool: 20y x 20f, 4 lanes, indoors, heated, 86°.
Admission: $2, SC(55) $1.
To find: In downtown Lockport, between the Old
Post Office and the public library.

LONG BEACH   516

LONG BEACH MUNICIPAL POOL Magnolia Blvd.
& W. Bay Dr.
Phone: 431-5533 or 431-3890.
Pool: 25y x 42f, 6 lanes, indoors, heated, 72°.
Admission: $4, SC(60) & Disabled $2.

LOUDONVILLE   518

COLONIE ATHLETIC CLUB, INC.* 636 Albany-
Shaker Rd.
Phone: 458-7400.
Pool: 20y x 50f, indoors, heated, 86°-88°.
Admission: $8.
Affiliate: IHRSA $5.
Hotel: Hampton Inn-Wolf Road (438-2822) &

Howard Johnson (785-5891): NC with a pass from
the hotel.
Notes: *The pool is expected to open in March,
1995.

MASTIC BEACH   516

YMCA - EAST BROOKHAVEN TOWN POOL 300
Mastic Beach Rd.
Phone: 281-1710.
Pool: 25m, 6 lanes, indoors, heated, 84°.
Admission: $3.75, SC(55) $2.50.
Affiliate: YMCA 1 visit NC, then $1.75 per visit,
combined limit 2 weeks.
To find: Across the street from the William Floyd
High School athletic fields.

MEDINA   716

LAKE PLAINS YMCA at Wise Middle School Pool,
Gwinn St.
Phone: 798-2040.
Pool: 25y, 6 lanes, indoors, heated, 78°-80°.
Admission: $5*, SC(60) $4*.
Affiliate: YMCA NC.
Notes: *This is an 'Extension Site' facility. Pool
passes are sold at the Y's main facility at 306 Pearl
St, they are not available at the pool.

MONTAUK   516

GURNEY'S INT'L HEALTH & BEAUTY SPA Old
Montauk Hwy.
Phone: 668-2345. **Reservations:** 800-8-GUR-
NEYS.
Pool: 20y x 35f, salt water, rectangular, indoors,
heated, 82°.
Admission: $16.50. Registered guests NC.

MORRISVILLE   315

SUNY AGRI-TECH MORRISVILLE Route 20
Phone: 684-6072.
Pool: 25y, indoors, heated, 80°-82°.
Admission: NC.
Notes: Operates during the academic year only.

MOUNT KISCO   914

MT. KISCO BOYS & GIRLS CLUB 351 Main St.
Phone: 666-8069.
Pool: 25y x 28f, indoors, heated, 84°-85°.
Admission: $5.

SAW MILL RIVER CLUB 77 Kensico Dr.
Phone: 241-0797.
Pool: 25y, 3 lanes, indoors, heated, 80°-82°.
Affiliate: IHRSA $16.

SAW MILL ACE MASTERS at the Saw Mill River
Club
Masters: Contact Head Coach Gretchen Normann
at 241-0797.

Notes: Coached workouts: M,W,F: 9:30-10:30AM.
Th: 7-8:30PM.

MOUNT VERNON   914

MOUNT VERNON YMCA FAMILY CENTER 20 S.
2nd Ave.
Phone: 668-4041.
Pool: 25y, 3 lanes, indoors, heated, 83°.
Admission: $8.
Affiliate: YMCA $4.

NEW HYDE PARK   516

THE PHYSICAL ACTIVITIES CENTER 1801
Evergreen Ave.
Phone: 327-3100.
Pool: 25y, indoors, heated, 80°.
Affiliate: Town of North Hempstead residents $4.

NEW ROCHELLE   914

MULCAHY CAMPUS CENTER Iona College, 715
North Ave.
Phone: 633-2323.
Pool: 25y x 44f, 6 lanes, indoors, heated, 81°.
Admission: $5.
Memberships: $275/year.

NEW ROCHELLE YMCA 50 Weyman Ave.
Phone: 632-1818.
Pool: 25y, indoors, heated, 82°-85°.
Admission: $10.
Affiliate: Y AWAY $1.

NEW WINDSOR   914

HUDSON VALLEY CLUB 72 Route 9W
Phone: 565-7600.
Pool: 25y x 25f, 3 lanes, indoors, heated, 82°.
Affiliate: IHRSA $10.
To find: On Route 9W approximately three miles
south off Route 84.

YWCA OF ORANGE COUNTY 565 Union Ave.
Phone: 561-8050.
Pool: 25m x 15m, 6 lanes, indoors, heated, 82°.
Admission: $7.50.
Affiliate: YWCA & USMS: $5.

NEW WINDSOR ≈ NEW WAVE MASTERS at the
YWCA of Orange County
Masters: Contact the YWCA at 561-8050.
Pool: 25m, 6 lanes, indoors, heated, 83°.
Non-member participation: $5.
Notes: Coached workouts: Tu,Th: 7:30-8:30PM.

NEW YORK CITY - THE BRONX   718

1. ST. MARY'S RECREATION CENTER 450 St.
Ann's Ave.
Phone: 402-5155.
Pool: 25y x 25f, 5 lanes, indoors, heated, water

temperature not reported.
Memberships: $15/year, SC $5.
To find: In the South Bronx area, off 149th St.

2. BALLY'S JACK LALANNE 298 W. 231st St.
Phone: 796-9000.
Pool: 22y, indoors, heated, 75°.
Affiliate: Bally's & IPFA: NC.

3. RIVERDALE YM-YWHA 5625 Arlington Ave.
Phone: 548-8200.
Pool: 25y x 32f, 4 lanes, indoors, heated, 82°.
Admission: $10.
Affiliate: YM/WHA & JCC both outside a 60 mile
radius NC.
To find: At 256th & Riverdale Ave.

NEW YORK CITY - BROOKLYN   718

4. TWELVE TOWNS YMCA 570 Jamaica Ave.
Phone: 277-1600.
Pool: 20y x 20f, 4 lanes, indoors, heated, 86°.
Admission: $10.
Affiliate: YMCA $3.
To find: Take the Cypress Hills St. Exit off the
Interborough Pkwy., south to Jamaica Ave.

5. BAY RIDGE MASTERS at Ft. Hamilton High
School Natatorium, 8301 Shore Rd.
Pool phone: 630-5842. **Masters:** Contact Siem
John Berkhout at 836-1264(h).
Pool: 25y, 6 lanes, indoors, heated, 79°.
Affiliate: USMS with photocopy of current USMS
card NC.
Notes: Uncoached Masters workouts: M,W: 8:30-
10PM. Sa: 8:30-10AM.

6. METROPOLITAN COMMUNITY CENTER 261
Bedford Ave.
Phone: 965-6541.
Pool: 25y, indoors, heated, 80°.
Admission: NC.
To find: At Bedford & Metropolitan Aves.

7. BROWNSVILLE RECREATION CENTER 1555
Linden Blvd.
Phone: 485-4633.
Pool: 25y, indoors, heated, 80°.
Admission: NC.
To find: At Linden and Mother Gaston Blvds.

8. ST. JOHNS RECREATION CENTER POOL
1251 Prospect Place
Phone: 771-2787.
Pool: 25y x 45f, indoors, heated, 86°.
Memberships: $10/year*.
Notes: *Memberships are sold only on Mondays
10AM-Noon and 8-10PM. Payment must be made
by money order. No cash, checks, or credit cards
accepted.

9. PROSPECT PARK YMCA 357 - 9th St.
Phone: 768-7100.

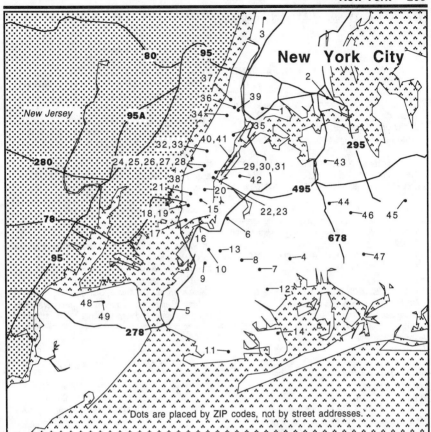

New Jersey

New York City

Dots are placed by ZIP codes, not by street addresses.

Pool: 20y x 20f, 3 lanes, indoors, heated, 84°.
Admission: $15.
Affiliate: YMCA 3 visits NC, then $5.
To find: Midway between the 4th Ave. and the 7th Ave. 'F' train stations on 9th St. Next to McCrory's 5¢ & 10¢.

10. YWCA OF BROOKLYN 30 - 3rd Ave.
Phone: 875-1190.
Pool: 20y x 25f, 3 double lanes, indoors, heated, 84°.
Affiliate: YWCA $5.
To find: At the corner of 3rd & Atlantic Aves.

11. BALLY'S JACK LALANNE 1720 Sheepshead Bay Rd.
Phone: 332-8282.
Pool: 20y, indoors, heated, 82°.
Admission: Call.
Affiliate: Bally's NC.

12. PAERDEGAT ATHLETIC CLUB 1500 Paerdegat Ave.
Phone: 209-1010.
Pool: 20y, indoors, heated, 80°.
Affiliate: IHRSA $10.

13. EASTERN ATHLETIC CLUB 17 Eastern Pkwy.
Phone: 789-4600.
Pool: 25y x 25f, 4 lanes, indoors, heated, 79°.
Admission: $14.
To find: On Grand Army Plaza, directly across Eastern Pkwy. from the public library.

14. STARRETT AT SPRING CREEK POOL, FITNESS & TENNIS 1540 Van Siclen Ave.
Phone: 642-2720.
Pool: 100f, 6 lanes, indoors, heated, 81°.
Affiliate: IHRSA 50% discount on current guest pass rates.

NEW YORK CITY - MANHATTAN   212

15. EDUCATIONAL ALLIANCE EMANU-EL MIDTOWN Y 344 E. 14th St.
Phone: 674-7200.
Pool: 20y x 25f, 4 lanes, indoors, heated, 82°.
Admission: 3 visits per year $7 each.
To find: On 14th St. between 1st and 2nd Aves.

16. DOWNTOWN ATHLETIC CLUB 19 West St.
Phone: 425-7000.
Pool: 25y x 35f, 4 lanes, indoors, heated, 80°.

Affiliate: 10K $20, Sa,Su $5.
Memberships: $1,800/year.

17. NEW YORK MARRIOTT FINANCIAL CENTER
85 West St.
Phone: 385-4900. **Reservations:** 800-228-9290.
Pool: 50f, indoors, heated, water temperature not reported.
Admission: Registered guests NC.
Memberships: $545/year.

18. BOROUGH OF MANHATTAN COMMUNITY COLLEGE 199 Chambers St.
Phone: Registration information: 346-2450 or 346-8390.
Pool: 25y, indoors, heated, 78°-80°.
Memberships: $424/year. Sep.-Dec. & Jan.-May: $175. Jun.-Aug. $125. SC(60) NC, registration required.
Notes: Two hours of early morning lap/open swimming available per day.

19. BALLY'S JACK LALANNE HEALTH SPA
Woolworth Building, 233 Broadway
Phone: 227-5977.
Pool: 65f x 25f, indoors, heated, 80°-82°.
Admission: Call.
Affiliate: Bally's NC.

20. ASSER LEVY RECREATION CENTER E. 23rd St. & F.D.R. Dr.
Phone: 447-2020.
Pool: 64f x 21f, 3 lanes, indoors, heated, 79°.
Memberships: $25*/year, SC(55) $10*.
Notes: *Call for information about membership registration times and requirements. Memberships honored at all Manhattan Municipal Recreation Centers.

21. CARMINE ST. RECREATION CENTER
Clarkson St. & 7th Ave. S.
Phone: 242-5228.
Pool: 24y x 23f, 3 lanes, indoors, heated, water temperature not reported.
Memberships: $25*/year, SC(55) $10*.
Notes: *Call for information about membership registration times and requirements. Memberships honored at all Municipal Recreation Centers.

22. VANDERBILT YMCA 224 E. 47th St.
Phone: 756-9600.
Pool 1: 25y x 40f, 6 lanes, indoors, heated, 80°-82°.
Pool 2: 20y x 20f, 3 lanes, indoors, heated, 83°-86°.
Admission: $15.
Affiliate: YMCA out of the N.Y. area 6 visits NC.
To find: Near the United Nations and Grand Central Station, in Midtown, on the east side of Manhattan.

23. BALLY'S THE VERTICAL CLUB 335 Madison Ave.
Phone: 983-5320.
Pool: 25y, indoors, heated, 78°-81°.
Affiliate: Bally's NC.
Hotel: Grand Hyatt Hotel (883-1234), Royalton Hotel, & Roosevelt Hotel: Passes may be available. Contact the hotels for details.

24. NEW YORK SPORTS CLUB at the Crowne Plaza - Manhattan, 1605 Broadway, 15th Floor
Phone: Club: 977-8800. Hotel: 977-4000.
Reservations: 800-243-NYNY.
Pool: 50f, rectangular, indoors, heated, 82°.
Admission: Registered guests: Pool NC. Full facility $10. Concierge Level guests: Full facility NC.
Affiliate: Town Sports International — NC.
Memberships: Call.

25. WEST 59TH STREET RECREATION CENTER
533 W. 59th St.
Phone: 397-3159.
Pool: 20y, 4 lanes, indoors, heated, 79°.
Memberships: $25*/year, SC(55) $10*.
Notes: *Call for information about membership registration times and requirements. Memberships honored at all Manhattan Municipal Recreation Centers.

26. RED TIDE OF NYC at John Jay College, 899 - 10th Ave.
Masters: Contact Dana Evans at 989-0417(h).
Pool: 25y, 5 lanes, indoors, heated, 84°.
Affiliate: USMS $5, includes pool fees.
Notes: Coached workouts: M-F: 7-8:30AM.

27. BALLY'S THE VERTICAL CLUB 350 W. 50th St.
Phone: 265-9400.
Pool: 25m, indoors, heated, 80°.
Affiliate: Bally's NC.
Hotel: Passes may be available from the Hotel Edison. Contact the hotel for details.

28. SHERATON MANHATTAN HEALTH CLUB at the Sheraton Manhattan Hotel, 790 - 7th Ave. at 52nd St.
Phone: Club: 621-8591. Hotel: 581-3300.
Reservations: 800-325-3535.
Pool: 50f x 25f, 2-3 lanes, indoors, heated, 83°.
Admission: $20. Registered guests NC.
Hotel: Sheraton New York (581-1000): NC with room key. Sheraton Park Avenue (685-7676) & The St. Regis Hotel (756-4500): $10 with room key.
Affiliate: IHRSA $10.
Memberships: $599/year.
To find: On the 5th floor of the Sheraton Manhattan Hotel.

29. NEW YORK CITY YWCA 610 Lexington Ave.
Phone: 735-9755.

Pool: 25y x 36f, 6 lanes, indoors, heated, 81°-83°.
Admission: $15.
Affiliate: YWCA & USMS: $6.

30. ST. BART'S COMMUNITY CLUB 109 E. 50th St.
Phone: 751-1616 ext. 242.
Pool: 65f x 64f, 6 lanes, indoors, heated, 80°.
Memberships: I/S $50 + $450/year.

31. BALLY'S THE VERTICAL CLUB 139 W. 32nd St.
Phone: 465-1750.
Pool: 80f, indoors, heated, 77°-78°.
Affiliate: Bally's NC.
Hotel: Best Western New York Hotel Pennsylvania (736-5000). Contact the hotel for details.

32. EAST 54TH ST. RECREATION CENTER 348 E. 54th St.
Phone: 397-3154.
Pool: 18y x 48f, 6 lanes, indoors, heated, 79°.
Memberships: $25*/year, SC(55) $10*.
Notes: *Call for information about membership registration times and requirements. Memberships honored at all Manhattan Municipal Recreation Centers.

33. WEST SIDE YMCA 5 W. 63rd St.
Phone: 787-1301.
Pool: 25y, 6 lanes, indoors, heated, 80°.
Affiliate: YMCA 6 visits per year NC, then $10.

34. RED TIDE OF NYC at City College, Convent Ave. at 137th St.
Masters: Contact Dana Evans at 989-0417(h).
Pool: 25y, 6 lanes, indoors, heated, 85°.
Affiliate: USMS $5, includes pool fees.
Notes: Coached workouts: Sep.-Jun: M,W: 7-8:30PM. Sa: 7-9AM. No summer workouts.

35. 1199 PLAZA RECREATION CENTER 2116 - 1st Ave.
Phone: 289-8100.
Pool: 25m, indoors, heated, 81°-83°.
Admission: $7, SC(50) $3.50.
Affiliate: U.S. Military — Call.

36. HARLEM YMCA 180 W. 135th St.
Phone: 281-4100 ext. 222 or 223.
Pool: 20y x 20f, 5 lanes, indoors, heated, 83°.
Admission: $10.
Affiliate: Out-of-town YMCA NC.

37. RIVERBANK STATE PARK POOL 679 Riverside Dr. at W. 145th St.
Phone: 694-3665.
Pool: 50m x 60f, 8 lanes, indoors, heated, 82°-84°.
Admission: Lap swims $2. Recreation swims $1. SC(60): Weekdays NC. Weekends 50¢.
Notes: There is also a 25y x 46f, 6 lane, outdoor, summer pool.
To find: One block west of Broadway at 145th St.

38. MANHATTAN PLAZA HEALTH CLUB 482 W. 43rd St.
Phone: 563-7001.
Pool: 25y x 35f, 4 lanes, indoors, heated, 79°-81°.
Affiliate: IHRSA outside a 75 mile radius 4 visits per month $15 each.
To find: On 43rd St. between 9th & 10th Aves.

MPHC MASTERS at Manhattan Plaza Health Club
Masters: Contact Aquatic Director Miguel Ortiz at 563-7001 ext. 312.
Non-member participation: Masters workouts $15.
Notes: Coached workouts: M-F: 6-7AM, Sa: 7-8:30AM. Uncoached workouts: M-F: 7:30-8:30AM. Local Masters swimmers may want to inquire about MHPC Masters membership which can be obtained without joining the host facility.

39. HANSBOROUGH RECREATION CENTER 35 W. 134th St.
Phone: 234-9603.
Pool: 25y, indoors, heated, 80°-82°.
Memberships: $25*/year, SC(55) $10*.
Notes: *Call for information about membership registration times and requirements. Memberships honored at all Manhattan Municipal Recreation Centers.

40. CENTER FOR HEALTH, FITNESS & SPORT
The 92nd St. YM/YWHA, 1395 Lexington Ave.
Phone: 415-5729.
Pool: 25y x 30f, 3-4 lanes, indoors, heated, 80°.
Affiliate: YM/YWHA & JCC: 1 week NC.
To find: Lexington Ave. at 92nd St.

41. ASPHALT GREEN AQUACENTER 1750 York Ave.
Phone: 369-8890.
Pool: 50m OR 25y + 25m x 20y, 8 or 16 lanes, indoors, heated, 79°-80°.
Admission: Pool: $14, SC(62) $10. Pool & Fitness Center: $25, SC $15.
Notes: There is also a 26f x 18f, warm water, exercise pool.
Masters: The Asphalt Green Masters. Contact Lorraine Martinelli at 369-8890 ext. 213.

NEW YORK CITY - QUEENS   718

42. LAGUARDIA COMMUNITY COLLEGE POOL
3110 Thomson Ave., Long Island City
Phone: 482-5044.
Pool: 25y, indoors, heated, 81°-82°.
Admission: $5.
Memberships: 3/12 months $65/$240.

43. FLUSHING YMCA 138-46 Northern Blvd., Flushing
Phone: 961-6880.
Pool: 25y x 45f, 6 lanes, indoors, heated, 80°-82°.
Admission: $15.
Affiliate: YMCA $3.

NEW YORK CITY - QUEENS   CONTINUED

44. QUEENS COLLEGE 65-30 Kissena Blvd.,
Flushing
Phone: 520-7775.
Pool: 25y x 42f, indoors, heated, 80°.
Memberships: Sep.- Jun. $125. Jul.- Aug. $125.
SC(65) 25% discount.

45. CROSS ISLAND YMCA 238-10 Hillside Ave.,
Bellrose
Phone: 479-0505.
Pool 1: 25y, 4 lanes, indoors, heated, 80°-83°.
Pool 2: 25y, 6 lanes, indoors, heated, 84°-88°.
Admission: 3 visits $10 each.
Affiliate: YMCA outside a 50 mile radius 5 visits
per year NC, then $5; within 50 miles 5 visits per
month $2 each, then $5.

CROSS ISLAND MASTERS at the Cross Island
YMCA
Masters: Contact Coach Kathy Madigan at 479-
0505.
Non-member participation: $10.
Notes: Coached workouts: M,W,F: 7:30-8:45PM.

46. CENTRAL QUEENS YMCA 89-25 Parsons
Blvd., Jamaica
Phone: 739-6600.
Pool: 20y x 20f, 4 lanes, indoors, heated, 84°-87°.
Affiliate: Y AWAY & Out-of-state YMCA: NC.

47. ROY WILKINS RECREATION CENTER 177
Baisley Blvd., Jamaica
Phone: 276-8696 or 276-8690.
Pool: 25y x 30f, indoors, heated, 82°-84°.
Admission: NC.

NEW YORK CITY - STATEN ISLAND   718

48. STATEN ISLAND YMCA 651 Broadway
Phone: 981-4933.
Pool: 20y x 40f, 4 lanes, indoors, heated, 84°-86°.
Affiliate: YMCA $5.
To find: Across the street from the main entrance
to the Staten Island Zoo.

STATEN ISLAND YMCA PSYQUATICS at the
Staten Island YMCA
Masters: Contact Janet Panza at 273-7969(h).
Affiliate: USMS & YMCA: Pool fees only.
Notes: Workouts: Su: 9-11AM.

49. STATEN ISLAND AQUATICS MASTERS 734
Post Ave.
Masters: Contact the pool staff at 273-7151.
Pool: 25m x 74f, 6 lanes, indoors, heated, 80°.
Affiliate: USMS $10.
Notes: Workouts: M-F: 6AM-Noon, 9-10PM. Call
for weekend workout times.

NEWBURGH   914

GOLDS GYM & ATHLETIC CLUB 260 Route 17K
Phone: 564-7500.
Pool: 20y x 25f, indoors, heated, 82°.
Admission: $10.
Affiliate: IHRSA $5. Golds Gyms NC to $5.
Hotel: Howard Johnson (564-4000) & Holiday Inn
(564-9020): NC with a pass from the hotel.

NIAGARA FALLS   716

NIAGARA FALLS FAMILY YMCA 1317 Portage
Rd.
Phone: 285-8491.
Pool: 20y, indoors, heated, 83°.
Admission: $10.
Affiliate: YMCA outside a 75 mile radius NC.

NORWICH   607

NORWICH YMCA 68-70 N. Broad St.
Phone: 336-9622.
Pool: 20y x 21f, 3 lanes, indoors, heated, 81°.
Admission: $5.
Affiliate: Y AWAY NC.
To find: Across the street from Howard Johnson's
Motel on N. Broad St. (Route 12).

NYACK   914

NYACK BRANCH YMCA 35 S. Broadway
Phone: 358-0245.
Pool: 20y x 20f, 4 lanes, indoors, heated, 83.5°.
Admission: $8, SC(60) $4.
Affiliate: YMCA outside a 50 mile radius 3 visits
per month NC.
To find: Two blocks south of Main St.

OLD WESTBURY   516

SUNY - OLD WESTBURY
Phone: 876-3353.
Pool: 25y, indoors, heated, 80°.
Admission: $5.

OLEAN   716

OLEAN YMCA 130 S. Union
Phone: 373-2400.
Pool 1: 20y x 30f, 4 lanes, indoors, heated, 79°.
Pool 2: 20y, 4 lanes, indoors, heated, 88°.
Affiliate: Y AWAY NC.
Hotel: Old Library Bed & Breakfast at 120 S. Union
St. — Call the Y for information.
To find: Two blocks south of the 'four corners'.

ONEIDA   315

TRI-VALLEY YMCA 701 Seneca St.
Phone: 363-7788.
Pool: 25y x 42f, 6 lanes, indoors, heated, 84°.
Admission: $5.

Affiliate: YMCA 10 visits per year NC.
To find: Up the hill from Oneida City Hospital.

TRI-VALLEY Y MASTERS at Tri-Valley YMCA
Masters: Contact the Y at 363-7788.
Non-member participation: $5.
Notes: Coached workouts: W: 7:30-9PM. Lap
swimming M-F: 6-7AM.

ONEONTA 607

ONEONTA FAMILY YMCA 20-26 Ford Ave.
Phone: 432-0010.
Pool: 25y x 36f, 4 lanes, indoors, heated, 82°.
Admission: $5.
Affiliate: YMCA NC.

BINDER GYMNASIUM POOL Hartwick College,
West St.
Phone: 431-4719 or 431-4714.
Pool: 25y x 66f, 8 lanes, indoors, heated, 78°-82°.
Affiliate: YMCA & USMS: 5 visits per 6 months
NC.
Memberships: $250/year, SC $225.

ORCHARD PARK 716

SOUTHTOWNS YMCA at Erie Community College,
4140 Southwestern Blvd.
Phone: 662-9369.
Pool: 25y, 6 lanes, indoors, heated, 79°.
Admission: $2.
To find: This is a YMCA 'Extension Site' pool at
Building 6, ECC South Campus, next to the Buffalo
Bills Football Stadium on Abbot Rd. in Orchard
Park.

OSWEGO 315

OSWEGO YMCA 249 W. 1st St.
Phone: 343-1981.
Pool: 25y x 60f, 4 lanes, indoors, heated, 84°.
Admission: $5.
Affiliate: YMCA outside a 50 mile radius NC.
To find: Two blocks south of downtown at 1st &
Bridge Sts.

PITTSFORD 716

SOUTHEAST FAMILY YMCA 111 E. Jefferson Rd.
Phone: 385-4665.
Pool: 25y, 6 lanes, indoors, heated, 84°.
Admission: $8.
Affiliate: Y AWAY NC. YMCA $4.
To find: E. Jefferson Rd. is also Route 96.

PLAINVIEW 516

MID ISLAND Y JCC 45 Manetto Hill Rd.
Phone: 822-3535.
Pool: 25m, 6 lanes, indoors, heated, 81°.
Admission: Non-residents $10.

Affiliate: JCC NC.
To find: One block west of Old Country Rd.

PLATTSBURGH 518

COMFORT INN 411 Route 3
Phone: 562-2730. **Reservations:** 800-950-0403.
Pool: 50f x 22f, 'L' shape, indoors, heated, 83°.
Admission: $7. Registered guests NC.
Memberships: 9/12 months $324/$384.

PLATTSBURGH YMCA 17 Oak St.
Phone: 561-4290.
Pool: 20y, indoors, heated, 82°-84°.
Admission: $6.
Affiliate: YMCA $3.

PORT CHESTER 914

PORT CHESTER YMCA 400 Westchester Ave.
Phone: 939-7800.
Pool: 25y, indoors, heated, 86°.
Admission: $10.
Affiliate: YMCA NC.

POTSDAM 315

MAXCY HALL Potsdam College, Pierpont Ave.
Phone: 267-2305.
Pool: 25y, indoors, heated, 80°.
Memberships: 6 months $65.

POUGHKEEPSIE 914

DUTCHESS COUNTY YMCA Eastman Park
Phone: 471-9622.
Pool: 25y x 35f, 6 lanes, indoors, heated, 84°.
Admission: $7.
Affiliate: YMCA $3.
Hotel: Radisson Hotel (475-1910) NC with room
key.
Masters: The Dutchess County Masters Swim
Team. Contact Don Gringras or Margaret T. Craig
at 471-9622.

YWCA OF DUTCHESS COUNTY 18 Bancroft Rd.
Phone: 462-3162.
Pool: 20y x 20f, 3 lanes, indoors, heated, 85°.
Affiliate: YWCA $2.
To find: About a mile and a half from Route 9 and
the Holiday Inn Express in Poughkeepsie.

PURCHASE 914

PURCHASE COLLEGE FITNESS SUNY
Purchase, 735 Anderson Hill Rd.
Phone: 251-6530.
Pool: 25y, 6 lanes, indoors, heated, 80°.
Admission: $7 by arrangement with the Aquatic
Director only.
Memberships: $105-$145/semester.
Notes: The pool is closed in late Aug. and late May.
To find: Across the street from Pepsi-Cola.

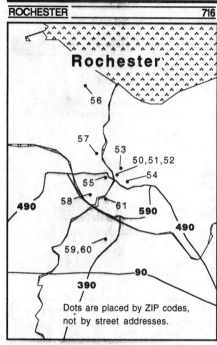

Dots are placed by ZIP codes,
not by street addresses.

50. CARLSON METROCENTER YMCA 444 E.
Main St.
Phone: 325-2880.
Pool: 25y x 36f, 6 lanes, indoors, heated, 84°.
Admission: 3 visits per year $10 each.
Affiliate: YMCA $3.50.
Hotel: All Rochester hotels $10.

51. HARRO EAST ATHLETIC CLUB 400 Andrews
St.
Phone: 546-1000.
Pool: 25y, indoors, heated, 82°.
Admission: $7.
Hotel: Strathallen (461-5010), Hyatt (546-1234),
and all downtown hotels: $6.

52. PLAZA ATHLETIC CLUB 50 Chestnut Plaza
Phone: 546-7350.
Pool: 25y, indoors, heated, 82°.
Admission: $10.

53. CLINTON BADEN COMMUNITY CENTER 485
N. Clinton Ave.
Phone: 428-6589.
Pool: 25y, 6 lanes, indoors, heated, 82°.
Admission: NC.

54. MONROE BRANCH YMCA 797 Monroe Ave.
Phone: 271-5320.
Pool: 20y, indoors, heated, 80°.
Affiliate: Y AWAY NC.

55. ADAMS STREET RECREATION CENTER 85
Adams St.
Phone: 428-7456.
Pool: 25y, 6 lanes, indoors, heated, 82°.
Admission: $2. Resident SC(65) $1*.
Notes: *With city issued 'Good Time' pass.

56. NORTHWEST FAMILY YMCA 730 Long Pond
Rd.
Phone: 227-3900.
Pool: 25y x 38f, 6 lanes, indoors, heated, 83°-84°.
Affiliate: YMCA $4.
To find: Located 3.7 miles north of Route 104 W.

57. MAPLEWOOD FAMILY YMCA 25 Driving Park
Ave.
Phone: 647-3600.
Pool: 25y x 37f, 6 lanes, indoors, heated, 84°.
Affiliate: YMCA NC.

58. ARNETT FAMILY YMCA 240 Arnett Blvd.
Phone: 328-9330.
Pool: 20y, 4 lanes, indoors, heated, 84°.
Admission: $5.
Affiliate: YMCA $2.50.
To find: Near the Rochester Airport.

**59. BALLY'S HOLIDAY HEALTH & FITNESS
CENTER** 3195 Brighton Henrietta Town Line Rd.
Phone: 427-7890.
Pool: 20y, indoors, heated, 79°-84°.
Admission: $10.
Affiliate: Bally's & IPFA: NC.
Hotel: Radisson Inn (475-1910), Wellsley Inn, &
Residence Inn (272-8850): NC.

60. MCC MASTERS at Monroe Community College,
1000 E. Henrietta Rd.
Masters: Contact George McVey at 271-2323.
Pool: 25y, 6 lanes, indoors, heated, 78°-80°.
Affiliate: USMS NC, includes pool fees.
Notes: Coached workouts: M-Th: 8:15-9:45PM.
Sa: 10:30AM-12:30PM. Su: 9:30-11:30AM.
There is also a diving well.

61. RIVER CAMPUS SPORTS COMPLEX
University of Rochester
Phone: Membership information: 275-5135. Pool:
275-4883.
Pool: 25y x 25m, indoors, heated, 78°-80°.
Memberships: $243/year, 3 University affiliated ref-
erences required.

ROME _____ 315

ROME FAMILY YMCA 301 W. Bloomfield St.
Phone: 336-3500.
Pool: 25y x 45f, 6 lanes, indoors, heated, 81°.
Admission: $8.
Affiliate: YMCA 12 visits per year NC.
Notes: There is also an 89°, therapeutic pool and a
special locker room accessible by the disabled.

To find: Three blocks northwest of downtown City Hall; three blocks west of Black River Blvd.

RYE   914

RYE YMCA 21 Locust Ave.
Phone: 967-6363.
Pool: 25y, indoors, heated, 84°.
Affiliate: YMCA NC.

SARATOGA SPRINGS   518

SARATOGA YMCA 262 Broadway
Phone: 584-6840.
Pool: 25y, 5 lanes, indoors, heated, 82°-83°.
Admission: $7.
Affiliate: YMCA $3.50.
Hotel: Several local hotels NC with room key. Call the Y for details.

SCARSDALE   914

YM / YWHA OF MID-WESTCHESTER 999 Wilmont Rd.
Phone: 472-3300.
Pool: 25y, indoors, heated, water temperature not reported.
Affiliate: JCC $7.50.
Notes: Call between 9AM and 5PM only.

SCHENECTADY   518

SCHENECTADY YWCA 44 Washington Ave.
Phone: 374-3394.
Pool: 20y x 28f, 5 lanes, indoors, heated, 85°.
Admission: $5.
Affiliate: YWCA $2.50.
To find: In the historic Stockade District at the foot of Union St. One block north of Schenectady County Community College, Route 5.

DOWNTOWN BRANCH YMCA 13 State St.
Phone: 374-9136.
Pool: 20y, 5 lanes, indoors, heated, 83°.
Affiliate: YMCA Call.

UNION COLLEGE MASTERS at Alumni Gym Swimming Pool, Union College, Union Ave.
Masters: Contact T.J. Davis at 388-6190.
Pool: 25y, 8 lanes, indoors, heated, 79°.
Affiliate: USMS NC, includes pool fees.
Notes: Coached workouts: M-F: 6-7PM.

JEWISH COMMUNITY CENTER OF SCHENECTADY 2565 Balltown Rd.
Phone: 377-8803.
Pool: 20y, indoors, heated, 82°-83°.
Affiliate: JCC 3 visits NC.

SCOTIA   518

PARKSIDE YMCA 127 Droms Rd.

Phone: 399-8118.
Pool: 25y, indoors, heated, 84°.
Admission: $7.
Affiliate: YMCA NC.

SNYDER   716

NORTHEAST YMCA 4433 Main St.
Phone: 839-2543.
Pool: 25y, indoors, heated, 84°.
Admission: $7.
Affiliate: YMCA 7 visits NC, then $3.50.

SOUTH FALLSBURG   914

THE PINES RESORT HOTEL Laurel Ave.
Phone: 434-6000. **Reservations:** 800-367-4637.
Pool: 25y, square, indoors, heated, 78°.
Admission: Registered guests only NC.
Notes: There is also a large seasonal outdoor pool.

STONY BROOK   516

INDOOR SPORTS COMPLEX SUNY - Stony Brook
Phone: 632-7200.
Pool: 25y, 6 lanes, indoors, heated, 85°.
Memberships: $150/year.

SUFFERN   914

ROCKLAND COMMUNITY COLLEGE 145 College Rd.
Phone: 574-4455.
Pool: 25y x 42f, 6 lanes, indoors, heated, 82°.
Admission: $4.
Memberships: $95 for 5 months.
Notes: The pool closes Jun. through Aug.
To find: In the college's field house.

SYRACUSE   315

DOWNTOWN BRANCH OF THE YMCA OF GREATER SYRACUSE 340 Montgomery St.
Phone: 474-0784.
Pool: 25y x 38f, 5 lanes, indoors, heated, 84°.
Admission: $8.
Affiliate: Y AWAY outside a 50 mile radius $1.

SOUTHWEST POOL 200 Block of Lincoln Ave. at Clover St.
Phone: 473-4336.
Pool: 25y x 42f, 6 lanes, indoor/outdoor, heated, 80°-84°.
Admission: NC.
To find: In the downtown area, seven blocks west of the Hotel Syracuse.

VALLEY POOL Amidon Dr. off the 4900 block of S. Salina St.
Phone: 473-4336.
Pool: 25y x 42f, 6 lanes, indoors, heated, 82°-84°.
Admission: NC.

SYRACUSE   CONTINUED

To find: One block south of Seneca Tpk. and S. Salina St., behind Clary Middle School.

HUNTINGTON SCHOOL 400 Sunnycrest Rd.
Phone: 473-4336.
Pool: 25y, 6 lanes, indoors, heated, 73°-78°.
Admission: NC.
Notes: Evening access during the school year, afternoon access in the summer. The pool is closed in Sep. and the last two weeks in June.

GRANT MIDDLE SCHOOL 2400 Grant Blvd.
Phone: 473-4336.
Pool: 25y, 6 lanes, indoors, heated, 73°-78°.
Admission: NC.
Notes: Evening access during the school year, afternoon access in the summer. The pool is closed in Sep. and the last two weeks in June.

NOTTINGHAM HIGH SCHOOL 3100 E. Genesee St.
Phone: 435-5874.
Pool: 25y + 25y x 60f, 8 + 8 lanes, indoor/outdoor, heated, 80°.
Admission: Adults $1.

SYRACUSE MASTERS SWIM CLUB at Nottingham High School
Masters: Contact Amy S. Wisner at 435-5874.
Affiliate: USMS NC, includes pool fees.
Notes: Workouts: M-F: 5:30-7PM. All workouts have 3 written programs provided for members of different ability levels.

TARRYTOWN   914

TARRYTOWN YMCA 62 Main St.
Phone: 631-4807.
Pool: 25y, 4 lanes, indoors, heated, 85°.
Affiliate: YMCA outside a 50 mile radius NC, within 50 miles $5.

TROY   518

TROY-COHOES YWCA 21 - 1st St.
Phone: 274-7100.
Pool: 20y x 20f, 3-4 lanes, indoors, heated, 86°.
Admission: 1 visit $3.25.
Affiliate: YWCA $3.25.
To find: At the intersection of 1st St. and State, one block north of Russell Sage College.

TROY FAMILY YMCA 2500 - 21st St.
Phone: 272-5900.
Pool: 20y x 30f, 4 lanes, indoors, heated, 83°.
Admission: $8.
Affiliate: Y AWAY NC.

RPI MASTERS at Robison Pool, 15th St.
Masters: Contact Jane H. Moir at 271-8623(h).
Pool: 25m x 25y, 8 lanes, indoors, heated, 80°.

Non-member participation: $5.
Notes: Coached workouts: M-F: 6:30-7:30AM.

UNIONDALE   516

OMNI ATHLETIC CLUB 333 Earl Ovington Blvd., Lower Level
Phone: 222-7900.
Pool: 25y, indoors, heated, 78°-80°.
Admission: $10.

UTICA   315

MOHAWK VALLEY COMMUNITY COLLEGE POOL 1101 Sherman Dr.
Phone: 792-5570.
Pool: 25y, indoors, heated, 78°.
Admission: $1.

YWCA OF UTICA 1000 Cornelia St.
Phone: 732-2159.
Pool: 20y, indoors, heated, 86°-87°.
Admission: 1 visit NC, then $1.

UTICA YMCA 726 Washington St.
Phone: 735-8581.
Pool: 20y, indoors, heated, 80°-85°.
Admission: $8.
Affiliate: YMCA NC.

UTICA COLLEGE 1600 Burrstone Rd.
Phone: Athletic Dept: 792-3051. Registration Information: 792-3344.
Pool: 25y x 25m, 10 lanes, indoors, heated, 78°-82°.
Memberships: $150/semester. $300/year.

WATERTOWN   315

WATERTOWN FAMILY YMCA 6 Public Square
Phone: 782-3100.
Pool: 20y, 3 lanes, indoors, heated, 86°.
Admission: $6.
Affiliate: YMCA $1.

WEBSTER   716

BAY VIEW FAMILY BRANCH YMCA 1209 Bay Rd.
Phone: 671-8414.
Pool: 25y x 35f, 6 lanes, indoors, heated, 83°-84°.
Affiliate: YMCA $3.75.

WEST POINT   914

WEST POINT MASTERS SWIM CLUB at Arvin Gym, U.S. Military Academy
Masters: Contact Norman Sheldon at 800-431-1404 ext. 120(w) or 446-6745(h).
Pool: 25y x 50m, 14 x 6 lanes, indoors, heated, 80°.
Affiliate: USMS 2 weeks NC.
Notes: Workouts: M,W,F: Noon-1PM. Tu: Noon-

1PM, 6-8PM. Th: 6-8PM. Sa: 8-11AM. Su: Noon-4PM.

WHITE PLAINS   914

CLUB FIT 1 N. Broadway
Phone: 946-0404.
Pool: 20y, indoors, heated, 83°.
Affiliate: IHRSA $15.

WHITE PLAINS YMCA 250 Mamaroneck Ave.
Phone: 949-8030.
Pool: 25y, 6 lanes, indoors, heated, 78°-80°.
Admission: $10.
Affiliate: Y AWAY outside a 75 mile radius NC, within 75 miles $5.
Hotel: Holiday Inn Crown Plaza (682-0050) NC with a pass from the hotel.
To find: At the intersection of Mamaroneck and Maple Aves.

WHITE PLAINS YWCA 515 North St.
Phone: 949-6227.
Pool: 25y x 45f, 6 lanes, indoors, heated, 83°.
Admission: $6, SC(62) $3.
Affiliate: YWCA & USMS: NC.
To find: Across from a high school, one half mile from Exit 25 of the Hutchinson River Pkwy.
Masters: The YWCA Masters Swim Club. Contact Coach Don Sandford or Aquatic Director Sally Petrone at 949-6227.

YONKERS   914

YONKERS YMCA 17 Riverdale Ave.
Phone: 963-0183/4.
Pool: 20y, indoors, heated, 82°-84°.
Admission: $10.
Affiliate: YMCA $5.

HELP MAKE THE NEXT *SWIMMERS GUIDE* EVEN BETTER

To receive a free copy of the next ***Swimmers Guide*** tell us about pools you know of that aren't in this edition. See page 14 for details.

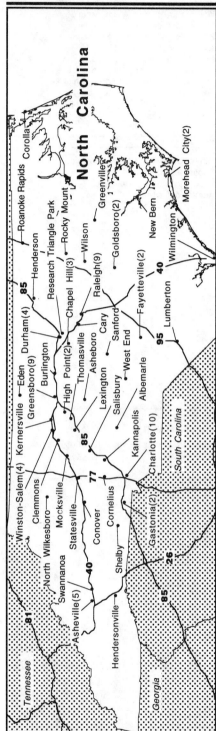

ALBEMARLE   704

STANLEY COUNTY FAMILY YMCA 427 N. 1st St.
Phone: 982-1916.
Pool: 25y x 30f, 6 lanes, indoors, heated, 85°.
Admission: $10.
Affiliate: YMCA 2 visits per month NC.

ASHEBORO   910

RANDOLPH-ASHEBORO YMCA 430 Hwy. 42N.
Phone: 625-1976.
Pool: 25m, indoors, heated, 81°-86°.
Admission: $5.
Affiliate: YMCA NC.
Masters: Contact Angela Queen at 625-1976.

ASHEVILLE   704

YMCA OF ASHEVILLE & BUNCOMBE COUNTY
30 Woodfin St.
Phone: 252-4726.
Pool 1: 25y, 4 lanes, indoors, heated, 80°.
Pool 2: 25y, 4 lanes, indoors, heated, 86°.
Affiliate: YMCA $6.
Hotel: Radisson Hotel Asheville (252-8211) & Best
   Western Asheville Central (253-1851): $6 passes
   are sold at the hotels.

YWCA OF ASHEVILLE 185 S. French Broad Ave.
Phone: 254-7206.
Pool: 25y x 20f, 4 lanes, indoors, heated, 88°.
Admission: $4.50.
Affiliate: YWCA $2.
To find: Three blocks south of the Chamber of
   Commerce.

GOLD'S GYM & ATHLETIC CLUB 711 Biltmore
Ave.
Phone: 253-5555.
Pool: 25m, indoors, heated, 84°.
Admission: $10. Mention *Swimmers Guide* for a
   discount on daily admission rates.
Affiliate: IPFA & Gold's Gym: NC.
Hotel: Quality Inn Biltmore (274-1800) NC with
   room key.

JUSTICE CENTER University of North Carolina at
   Asheville, 1 University Heights
Phone: 251-6459.
Pool: 25y, 6 lanes, indoors, heated, 80°.
Admission: $3.
Memberships: 3 months $55.

BLUE RIDGE MASTERS at Justice Center,
   University of North Carolina
Masters: Contact Michael Witaszek at 684-5491(h).
Affiliate: USMS $4, includes pool fees.
Notes: Workouts: Sa: 7-8:30AM.

SPA HEALTH CLUB 30 Westgate Pkwy.
Phone: 254-4946.
Pool: 20y, indoors, heated, 83°-84°.

Admission: $5.
Affiliate: IPFA & AHA: NC.

BURLINGTON 910

ALAMANCE COUNTY YMCA 1346 S. Main St.
Phone: 227-2061.
Pool: 25y x 35f, 5 lanes, indoors, heated, 84°-86°.
Affiliate: YMCA $2.

CARY 919

CARY FAMILY YMCA 101 YMCA Dr.
Phone: 469-9622.
Pool: 25y, indoor/outdoor, heated, 82°-84°.
Admission: Call.
Affiliate: YMCA Call.

CHAPEL HILL 919

CHAPEL HILL / CARRBORO YMCA 980 Airport Rd.
Phone: 942-5156.
Pool: 25y x 37f, 6 lanes, indoors, heated, 83°.
Admission: $10.
Affiliate: YMCA NC.

CHAPEL HILL COMMUNITY CENTER POOL 120 S. Estes Dr.
Phone: 968-2790.
Pool: 25m x 42f, 6 lanes, indoors, heated, 82°.
Admission: Residents $2, non-residents $2.50.
To find: Across from the main Post Office.
Masters: The Chapel Hill Masters. Contact Center Supervisor Dallas Myatt at 968-2790.

NORTH CAROLINA AQUATIC MASTERS at Koury Natatorium, University of North Carolina, Skipper Bowles Drive.
Masters: Contact Coach Barrett Hahn at 966-1900(w).
Pool: 50m x 25y, 8 x 18 lanes, indoors, heated, 81°.
Affiliate: USMS $5, includes pool fees.
Notes: Coached workouts: M,Th: 12:15-1:15PM, 7-8:30PM. Tu: 12:15-1:15PM. W,F: 6-7AM, 12:15-1:15PM, 7-8:30PM. Su: 8-9:30AM.

CHARLOTTE 704

1. UPTOWN YMCA 200 One First Union Center, Level A, 301 S. College St.
Phone: 333-9622.
Pool: 25y x 39f, 5 lanes, indoors, heated, 82°.
Admission: $10.
Affiliate: YMCA 3 visits per month NC.
Hotel: Omni Charlotte Hotel (377-6664) — Reduced admission.
To find: At the intersection of 2nd and College Sts.

2. CENTRAL BRANCH YMCA 400 E. Morehead St.
Phone: 333-7771.

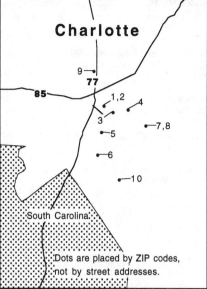

Charlotte

Dots are placed by ZIP codes, not by street addresses.

Pool 1: 25m, 4 lanes, indoors, heated, 81°.
Pool 2: 25m, 4 lanes, indoors, heated, 88°.
Admission: $10.
Affiliate: Out-of-town YMCA 3 visits per month NC, then $10.

3. MECKLENBURG COUNTY AQUATIC CENTER 800 E. 2nd St.
Phone: 336-3483.
Pool 1: 50m x 25y, 8 x 20 lanes, indoors, heated, 81°.
Pool 2: 25y x 24f, 4 lanes, indoors, heated, 86°.
Admission: Residents: $3, SC(60) & Disabled $2.50. Non-residents: $4, SC & Disabled $3.50.
Hotel: Government House Hotel (372-7550) NC.
To find: At the intersection of McDowell and 2nd St. in Uptown Charlotte, across from the Adam's Mark Hotel.
Masters: The Atom Masters. Contact Mollie Snyder at 336-3483.

4. JOHNSTON MEMORIAL BRANCH YMCA 3025 N. Davidson St.
Phone: 333-6206.
Pool: 25y x 30f, 6 lanes, indoors, heated, 85°.
Admission: $4.
Affiliate: YMCA NC.
To find: At the corner of 33rd & N. Davidson Sts.

5. YWCA OF THE CENTRAL CAROLINAS 3420 Park Rd.
Phone: 525-5770.
Pool: 25y, 5 lanes, indoors, heated, 84°-86°.
Admission: $4, SC(60) $3.50.
Affiliate: YWCA $2.50, SC $2.25.
To find: One mile from the Woodlawn/Park Rd. intersection, between Hillside Dr. & Marsh Rd.

CHARLOTTE   CONTINUED

There is a yellow blinking traffic signal in front of the building.

6. JAMES J. HARRIS FAMILY BRANCH YMCA 5900 Quail Hollow Rd.
Phone: 552-9622.
Pool: 25y, indoors, heated, 86°.
Admission: $10.
Affiliate: Y AWAY NC.

7. GEORGE E. SIMMONS BRANCH YMCA 6824 Democracy Dr.
Phone: 536-1714.
Pool: 25y, 6 lanes, indoors, heated, 86°.
Affiliate: YMCA Call.
To find: One block south of Harris Blvd. and Albemarle Rd.

8. BALLY'S HOLIDAY HEALTH CLUB 5404 Central Ave.
Phone: 537-2600.
Pool: 25m, indoors, heated, 89°.
Admission: Call.
Affiliate: Bally's NC.

9. MCCROREY YMCA 3801 Beatties Ford Rd.
Phone: 394-2356.
Pool: 25y x 25f, 4 lanes, indoors, heated, 85°-88°.
Admission: $3.
Affiliate: YMCA NC.
To find: From I-85 North going out of town, take Beatties Ford Rd.

10. MECKLENBURG AQUATIC CLUB 9850 Providence Rd.
Phone: 846-5335.
Pool: 50m x 25y, 10 x 22 lanes, indoors, heated, 80°-82°.
Admission: $3.
To find: One and a half miles southeast of the intersection of 51 and Providence Rd., which is the location of Arboretum Shopping Center.
Masters: MAC Masters. Contact Rick Fenton at 846-5335.

CLEMMONS   910

WEST FORSYTH YMCA 1150 S. Peacehaven Rd.
Phone: 712-2000.
Pool: 25y, indoors, heated, 84°-85°.
Admission: $6.

CONOVER   704

CATAWBA COUNTY YMCA 1104 Conover Blvd. E.
Phone: 464-6130.
Pool: 25m, 6 lanes, indoors, heated, 84°.
Admission: Call.
Affiliate: YMCA NC.

CORNELIUS   704

LAKE NORMAN YMCA 21300 Davidson St.
Phone: 892-9622.
Pool: 25y x 36f, 5 lanes, indoors, heated, 84°-85°.
Admission: $8.
Affiliate: YMCA out of the Charlotte Metro Area 3 visits per month NC, then $8.

COROLLA   919

B & B ON THE BEACH 1023 Ocean Trail
Phone: 453-3033. **Reservations:** 800-962-0201.
Pool: 25m, rectangular, indoors, heated, 80°.
Admission: Registered guests only NC.

DURHAM   919

ROCK QUARRY INDOOR POOL 600 W. Murray Ave.
Phone: 560-4265.
Pool: 25y x 60f, 8 lanes, indoors, heated, 83.5°.
Admission: Residents $1. Non-residents $1.25, SC(60) $1.
To find: Located behind the North Carolina Museum of Life & Science.

METROSPORT ATHLETIC CLUB 501 Douglas St.
Phone: 286-7529.
Pool: 25y x 45f, 6 lanes, indoor/outdoor, heated, 81°.
Admission: $10.
To find: Behind the Brownstone Inn on Erwin.

DURHAM FAMILY YMCA 2119 Chapel Hill Rd.
Phone: 493-4502.
Pool: 25y x 30f, 4 lanes, indoors, heated, 83°.
Admission: $8.
Affiliate: Y AWAY NC. YMCA $4.

IRWIN R. HOLMES INDOOR POOL 2000 S. Alston Ave.
Phone: 560-4444.
Pool: 25y x 60f, 8 lanes, indoors, heated, 83°.
Admission: Residents $1. Non-residents $1.25, SC(60) $1.
Masters: The Durham Aquatic Masters. Contact Janelle E. Morrow at 560-4444.

EDEN   910

EDEN YMCA 301 Kennedy Ave.
Phone: 623-8496.
Pool: 25y, indoors, heated, water temperature not reported.
Admission: $8.
Affiliate: YMCA NC.

FAYETTEVILLE   910

FAYETTEVILLE YMCA 2717 Ft. Bragg Rd.
Phone: 323-0800.
Pool: 25y, indoors, heated, 86°-87°.

Admission: Call.
Affiliate: YMCA NC.

THE SPORTS CENTER 5951 Cliffdale Rd.
Phone: 864-3303.
Pool: 21m, indoor/outdoor, heated, 82° in fall and winter, unheated in the summer, 78°-86°.
Admission: $10.
Affiliate: IHRSA $5.
Hotel: Inn Keeper Hotel, Comfort Inn (867-1777), Fairfield Inn by Marriott (487-1400), & Prince Charles Radisson Hotel Fayetteville (433-4444): $5.
To find: The club is about an eighth of a mile off the road. Look for the Sports Center sign.

GASTONIA   704

GASTON COUNTY FAMILY YMCA - CENTRAL BRANCH 615 W. Franklin Blvd.
Phone: 865-8551.
Pool: 20y x 40f, indoors, heated, 85°-87°.
Admission: 1 visit NC, then $5.
Affiliate: YMCA & U.S. Military on leave: NC.

GAC FITNESS TODAY 3240 Union Rd.
Phone: 865-2193.
Pool: 25y, indoors, heated, 82°-86°.
Admission: $7.
Affiliate: IPFA NC.

GOLDSBORO   919

WAYNE COUNTY MEMORIAL COMMUNITY BUILDING 239 N. Walnut St.
Phone: 734-2105.
Pool: 25y x 42f, 5 lanes, indoors, heated, 86°.
Admission: $1.
To find: Downtown, directly across from the Wayne County Courthouse.

GOLDSBORO FAMILY YMCA 1105 Pkwy. Dr.
Phone: 778-8557.
Pool: 50m x 25y, 8 lanes, indoors, heated, 82°-84°.
Admission: $15.
Affiliate: YMCA $3.
Hotel: Holiday Inn (735-7901) NC. All other local hotels — $5 with room key.

GREENSBORO   910

GREENSBORO CENTRAL YMCA 1015 W. Market St.
Phone: 272-4146.
Pool: 25y, 6 lanes, indoors, heated, 84°.
Admission: 3 visits per year $5 each.
Affiliate: YMCA $1.50.
To find: At the intersection of W. Market and Tate Sts., between Greensboro College and the University of North Carolina at Greensboro.

HANES GYMNASIUM POOL Greensboro College,

815 W. Market St.
Phone: Sep.-May*: 272-7102 ext. 250.
Pool: 25y, 5 lanes, indoors, heated, 80°-82°.
Memberships: $50 minimum annual dues to the college's athletic booster club.
Notes: *In the summer, the pool is operated by the Westover Swim Club. For information call 230-0430.

YWCA OF GREENSBORO 1 YWCA Place
Phone: 273-3461.
Pool: 25y x 35f, 5 lanes, indoors, heated, 87°-88°.
Admission: $2.25.
To find: Off Church St., between the Greensboro Historical Museum and the Cultural Arts Center; behind Duke Power.

HAYES-TAYLOR MEMORIAL BRANCH YMCA 1101 E. Market St.
Phone: 272-2131.
Pool: 25y, indoors, heated, 80°.
Admission: $5.
Affiliate: YMCA $2.

BEN L. SMITH HIGH SCHOOL POOL 2407 S. Holden Rd.
Phone: Pool: 852-6645. School: 294-7300.
Pool: 25y, indoors, heated, 87°-88°.
Admission: $1.25.

GRIMSLEY HIGH SCHOOL POOL 801 Westover Terrace
Phone: 274-4247.
Pool: 25y, 8 lanes, indoors, heated, 86°.
Admission: $1.25.

TRIAD MASTERS SWIMMING at Grimsley High School
Masters: Contact Mike Wynns at 869-4788(h).
Affiliate: USMS $2, includes pool fees.
Notes: Coached workouts: M,W: 8:30-9:45PM. Th: 8:30-9:30PM. From Jun. to Aug., the club swims at the 50m x 25y, outdoor, unheated, Lindley Park Pool at 2914 Springwood Dr. (373-2574). Summer workouts: M,W: 8:15-9:30PM and F: 7:45-9PM.

SPORTIME RACQUET & ATHLETIC CLUB 1909 Lendew St.
Phone: 275-1391.
Pool: 25m, 4 lanes, indoors, heated, 83°.
Admission: $10.
Affiliate: IHRSA $6.

GUILFORD COLLEGE YMCA 5800 W. Friendly Ave.
Phone: 316-2311.
Pool: 25m x 30f, 6 lanes, indoors, heated, 85°.
Admission: $4.
Affiliate: YMCA $2.

GREENVILLE   919

GREENVILLE ATHLETIC CLUB 140 Oakmont Dr.
Phone: 756-9175.
Pool: 25y, 4 lanes, indoor/outdoor, heated, 84°.
Admission: $12.
Affiliate: IHRSA $8.
Hotel: Hilton Inn (355-5000) NC with guest card from the hotel. Hampton Inn (355-2521) $6 with guest card from the hotel.
Masters: The Dolphins. Contact Matt Maloney or Breon Klopp at 756-9175.

HENDERSON   919

HENDERSON FAMILY YMCA 1925 Ruin Creek Rd.
Phone: 438-2144.
Pool: 25y, indoors, heated, 82°-84°.
Admission: Call.
Affiliate: YMCA 5 visits NC.

HENDERSONVILLE   704

HENDERSON COUNTY FAMILY YMCA 810 - 6th Ave. W.
Phone: 692-5774.
Pool: 25m, 5 lanes, indoors, heated, 83°-84°.
Admission: $5, SC(55) $4.
Affiliate: Y AWAY 1 visit NC, then $1.

HIGH POINT   910

ADAMS MEMORIAL YWCA 112 Gatewood Ave.
Phone: 882-4126.
Pool: 25y, indoors, heated, 85°-86°.
Admission: $3.
Affiliate: YWCA $2.

HIGH POINT CENTRAL FAMILY YMCA 150 W. Hartley Drive
Phone: 869-0151.
Pool: 25m x 65f, 6 lanes, indoors, heated, 84°.
Admission: $9.
Affiliate: Y AWAY Call.

KANNAPOLIS   704

CANNON MEMORIAL YMCA & COMMUNITY CENTER YMCA Dr. off W. 'C' St.
Phone: 933-5121.
Pool: 28y x 45f, indoors, heated, 86°-87°.
Affiliate: YMCA outside a 50 mile radius NC.
Masters: The YMCA Whalers. Contact David K. White at 933-5121.

KERNERSVILLE   910

KERNERSVILLE BRANCH YMCA 1113 W. Mountain St.
Phone: 996-2231.
Pool: 25y, indoors, heated, 85°.
Admission: $6.
Affiliate: YMCA $3.

LEXINGTON   704

LEXINGTON AREA YMCA 119 W. 3rd Ave.
Phone: 249-2177.
Pool: 25y x 45f, 6 lanes, indoors, heated, 84°.
Admission: $7.
Affiliate: Y AWAY NC.
To find: At the corner of Hargrave & W. 3rd Ave.

LUMBERTON   910

LIFESTYLE FITNESS CENTER of the Southeast General Hospital, 4895 Fayetteville Rd.
Phone: 738-5433.
Pool: 25y x 28f, 7 lanes, indoors, heated, 85°.
Affiliate: Out-of-town USMS & USS: Call for workout information.
Hotel: Holiday Inn (671-1166), Comfort Suites (739-8800), & Ramada Inn (738-8261): NC with room key.
Masters: The Lumberton Lightning Bolts. Contact John Caliri at 738-5433.

MOCKSVILLE   704

DAVIE FAMILY YMCA 215 Cemetery St.
Phone: 634-9622.
Pool: 25y x 60f, 6 lanes, indoors, heated, 84°.
Affiliate: Y AWAY $2. YMCA $5.
Notes: There is also an outdoor pool operated Jun. through Aug. Daily admission is $2.

MOREHEAD CITY   919

SPORTS CENTER 701 Camp Glenn Dr.
Phone: 726-7070.
Pool: 25y x 30f, 5 lanes, indoors, heated, 84°.
Admission: $5.
Affiliate: IHRSA $4.

SPORTS CENTER 'UNDERTOADS' at the Sports Center
Masters: Contact Aquatic Director Deanna McElmon at 726-7070.
Non-member participation: 1 visit per week $5, includes pool fees.
Affiliate: IHRSA $4, includes pool fees.
Notes: Coached workouts: M,W,F: 7:30-8:30PM.

NEW BERN   919

TWIN RIVERS YMCA 100 YMCA Lane
Phone: 638-8799.
Pool: 25y x 45f, 6 lanes, indoors, heated, 84°.
Affiliate: YMCA $2.
Hotel: All New Bern hotels $3.
To find: Take the Trentwoods and Pembroke Exit off the Hwy. 70 By-pass, turn onto Rhem St. next to Exxon, turn left onto Park Ave., turn left onto YMCA Lane.

NORTH WILKESBORO   910

YMCA OF WILKESBORO 418 Wilkesboro Blvd.

Phone: 838-3991.
Pool: 25y, indoors, heated, 85°.
Admission: $5.
Affiliate: YMCA outside a 50 mile radius NC.
Hotel: The Addison of North Wilkesboro — Call the
Y for details.

RALEIGH   919

RADISSON PLAZA HOTEL 421 S. Salisbury St.
Phone: 834-9900. Reservations: 800-333-3333.
Pool: 25y, rectangular, indoors, heated, 82°.
Admission: Registered guests only NC.

YWCA OF WAKE COUNTY 1012 Oberlin Rd.
Phone: 828-3205.
Pool: 25y x 36f, 6 lanes, indoors, heated, 83°.
Admission: Out-of-town visitors $2.
Affiliate: YWCA Call.
To find: Just off Wade Ave., near Cameron Village
and North Carolina State University.

RALEIGH YMCA 1601 Hillsborough St.
Phone: 832-6601.
Pool: 25y, indoors, heated, 83°-85°.
Affiliate: YMCA $3.

PULLEN AQUATIC CENTER 410 Ashe Ave.
Phone: 831-6197.
Pool: 50m x 25y, 8 x 19 lanes, indoor/outdoor,
heated, 82°.
Admission: $2, SC(62) $1.
Masters: The Raleigh Area Masters. Contact Ceil
Blackwell at 787-8325(h).

REX WELLNESS CENTER Rex Hospital, 4400
Lake Boone Trail
Phone: 781-1371.
Pool: 25y, indoors, heated, 83°.
Admission: $8.

OPTIMIST PARK POOL 5902 Whittier Dr.
Phone: 870-2882.
Pool: 50m x 25y, 8 x 19 lanes, indoor/outdoor,
heated, 82°.
Admission: $2, SC(62) $1.
Notes: The pool closes for the last week of May
and the first two weeks of Sep.
To find: Three miles north of North Hills Mall.
Whittier Dr. is off N. Cliff.
Masters: The Raleigh Area Masters. Contact Ceil
Blackwell at 787-8325(h).

GARNER ROAD YMCA 2235 Garner Rd.
Phone: 833-4430.
Pool: 25y, indoors, heated, 83°-85°.
Admission: $1.75.

HOLIDAY INN-CRABTREE 4100 Glenwood Ave.
Phone: 782-8600. Reservations: 800-465-4329.
Pool: 50f, oval or kidney shape, indoors, heated,
80°.
Admission: Registered guests only NC.

RALEIGH ATHLETIC CLUB 7339 Six Forks Rd.
Phone: 847-8189.
Pool: 25y, indoors, heated, 84°.
Affiliate: IHRSA $8.

RESEARCH TRIANGLE PARK   919

IMPERIAL ATHLETIC CLUB 4700 Emperor Blvd.
Phone: 941-9010.
Pool: 25y x 24f, 4 lanes, indoors, heated, 82°.
Admission: $15.
Affiliate: IHRSA $8.
Hotel: Sheraton Imperial Hotel & Convention
Center (941-5050) $8.
To find: Just off I-40, Page Rd. Exit beside the
Sheraton Imperial Hotel.

ROANOKE RAPIDS   919

ROANOKE ATHLETIC CLUB 539 Becker Dr.
Phone: 537-7946.
Pool: 25y, 4 lanes, indoors, heated, 83°.
Admission: Residents 4 visits per year $7.50 each.
Non-residents $5. All SC(60) M,W,F $2.
Affiliate: IHRSA outside a 30 mile radius $5.
Hotel: Hampton Inn (537-7555) & Holiday Inn (537-
1031): NC with a pass from the hotel.

ROCKY MOUNT   919

ROCKY MOUNT FAMILY YMCA 427 S. Church St.
Phone: 972-9622.
Pool: 25y, indoors, heated, 85°.
Admission: $6.
Affiliate: YMCA $3.

SALISBURY   704

ROWAN COUNTY YMCA 220 N. Fulton St.
Phone: 636-0111.
Pool: 25m, indoors, heated, 85°.
Admission: $10.
Affiliate: YMCA NC.
Masters: The Rowan County Aquatic Club.
Contact Nikki Rosenbluth at 636-0111.

SANFORD   919

SANFORD NAUTILUS & RACQUET CLUB 1907
K. M. Wicker Dr.
Phone: 774-4532.
Pool: 25y x 30f, 6 lanes, indoors, heated, 81°.
Admission: $10.
Affiliate: IHRSA $5.
Hotel: Hampton Inn (775-2000) $5.
To find: Across from the AMI C.C.H. Hospital.

SHELBY   704

SHELBY HIGH SCHOOL POOL Hwy. 74 & Dekalb
St.
Phone: 484-6821.
Pool: 25m, indoors, heated, 85°.
Admission: $1.25.

STATESVILLE   919

IREDELL COUNTY YMCA 828 Wesley Dr.
Phone: 972-9622.
Pool: 25m, 6 lanes, indoors, heated, 84°-86°.
Admission: $6.
Affiliate: YMCA NC.

SWANNANOA   704

DEVRIES RECREATION CENTER Warren Wilson
College, 701 Warren Wilson Rd.
Phone: 298-3325 ext. 271.
Pool: 25y x 45f, 6 lanes, indoors, heated, 84°-86°.
Admission: $3.
Memberships: $160/year.

THOMASVILLE   910

TOM A. FINCH COMMUNITY YMCA 1010
Mendenhall Rd.
Phone: 475-6125.
Pool: 25m, indoors, heated, 86°.
Affiliate: YMCA NC.

WEST END   910

FOREVER FIT NAUTILUS Edgewater Dr.
Phone: 673-1180.
Pool: 25y x 40f, 4 lanes, indoors, heated, 82°-83°.
Admission: $10.
Affiliate: IPFA NC.
To find: Two miles from Hwy. 211, just outside of
West End, in the Seven Lakes North Development.

WILMINGTON   910

WILMINGTON YMCA 2710 Market St.
Phone: 251-9622.
Pool 1: 25y, indoors, heated, 84°.
Pool 2: 25y, indoors, heated, 86°.
Admission: Call.
Affiliate: YMCA NC.

WILSON   919

WILSON RECREATION POOL 500 Sunset Rd.
Phone: 399-2269.
Pool: 25y, 8 lanes, indoor/outdoor, heated, water
temperature not reported.
Admission: $1.50.

WINSTON-SALEM   910

YWCA OF WINSTON-SALEM 1201 Glade St.
Phone: 722-5138.
Pool: 25y, indoors, heated, 86°.
Admission: $5.
CENTRAL YMCA OF WINSTON-SALEM 775 West
End Blvd.
Phone: 721-2100.
Pool: 25m x 75f, 6 lanes, indoors, heated, 85°.
Affiliate: YMCA outside a 50 mile radius NC, within
50 miles $3.
To find: Near Baptist Hospital off I-40's Cloverdale
Exit.
Masters: Contact Robby Goodwin at 721-2100 ext.
2156.

WINSTON LAKE FAMILY BRANCH YMCA 901
Waterworks Rd.
Phone: 724-9205.
Pool: 25y, indoors, heated, 85°.
Admission: $4.

WINSTON-SALEM Y MASTERS at the Winston
Lake Family Branch YMCA
Masters: Contact The Central YMCA Swim Office
at 721-2100 or Sandra Cathey at (704) 872-
0364(h).
Notes: This is a new Masters group in formation;
visitor policies and workout schedules had not
been established when we contacted them.

ALWAYS CALL FIRST

Pools close, they change names, affiliations, admission policies, and rates. And
just because a pool is listed in *Swimmers Guide* doesn't mean it's open all day,
every day, for just the type of workout you want to do. Spend a quarter to save
time and aggravation. . . always call first!

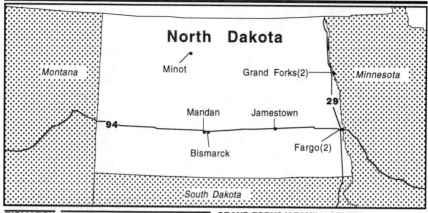

North Dakota

Montana

Minot

Grand Forks(2)

Minnesota

29

Mandan   Jamestown

94

Bismarck

Fargo(2)

South Dakota

BISMARCK   701

MISSOURI VALLEY FAMILY YMCA 1608 N. Washington St.
Phone: 255-1525.
Pool 1: 25y, 8 lanes, indoors, heated, 80°-83°.
Pool 2: 25y, 6 lanes, indoors, heated, 86°.
Admission: $5.
Affiliate: YMCA NC.
To find: At the corner of Washington St. & Divide Ave.

FARGO   701

HOLIDAY INN 3803 - 13th Ave. S.
Phone: 282-2700. **Reservations:** 800-465-4329.
Pool: 20y, kidney shape, indoors, heated, 86°.
Admission: Registered guests only NC.

FARGO-MOORHEAD YMCA 400 - 1st Ave. S.
Phone: 293-9622.
Pool: 25y x 20f, 4 lanes, indoors, heated, 82°.
Admission: $4.
Affiliate: YMCA Call.
To find: In downtown Fargo.

GRAND FORKS   701

HYSLOP SPORTS CENTER University of N. Dakota
Phone: 777-4330 or 777-2766.
Pool: 50m OR 25y + 25y x 60f, 8 OR 16 lanes, indoors, heated, 80°.
Admission: Lap swimming: Winter NC. Summer $1.
Masters: The Dakota Masters. Contact Will Gosnold at 777-2631(w).

GRAND FORKS Y FAMILY CENTER 215 N. 7th St.
Phone: 775-2586.
Pool: 25y x 38f, 5 lanes, indoors, heated, 83°-84°.
Admission: $4.50.
Affiliate: YMCA NC.
Hotel: Best Western Town House (746-5411) NC with a pass from the hotel.
To find: One block west and one block south of the Civic Center.

JAMESTOWN   701

JAMES RIVER FAMILY YMCA 918 - 7th St. N.E.
Phone: 253-4101.
Pool: 25m, indoors, heated, 82°-83°.
Admission: $5.
Affiliate: YMCA NC.

MANDAN   701

MANDAN COMMUNITY CENTER 901 Division St. N.W.
Phone: 667-3260.
Pool: 50m x 60f, 8 lanes, indoors, heated, 82°.
Admission: $2, SC(62) $1.50.
Notes: There is also a 24f x 24f, indoor, heated, 82° diving well.
To find: Three quarters of a mile south of the Sunset Dr. interchange on I-94.

MINOT   701

MINOT FAMILY YMCA 1st Ave. & 1st St. S.E.
Phone: 852-0141.
Pool: 20y x 20f, 4 lanes, indoors, heated, 85°.
Admission: $5.
Affiliate: Y AWAY NC.
To find: Three blocks north of Burdick Expressway.

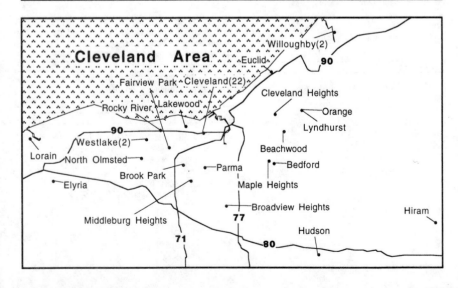

AKRON   216

CITICENTER ATHLETIC CLUB 146 S. High St.
Phone: 762-2582.
Pool: 20y, 5 lanes (3 for lap swimming), indoors, heated, 85°.
Admission: Call.
Affiliate: IHRSA $10.
Hotel: Akron Hilton Inn at Quaker Square (253-5970) $7.50 with room key.

CANAL SQUARE YMCA 80 W. Center St.
Phone: 434-9622 or 376-1335.
Pool: 25y, indoors, heated, 84°.
Admission: $7.
Affiliate: Y AWAY $3.50.

SPRINGFIELD NATATORIUM at Springfield High School, 2966 Sanitarium Rd.
Phone: 794-0207.
Pool: 25y, indoors, heated, 84°.
Admission: $3.50.

BALLY'S SCANDINAVIAN HEALTH SPA 1653 Merriman Rd.
Phone: 867-5262.
Pool: 25y, indoors, heated, 74°.
Affiliate: Bally's & IPFA: NC.

ALLIANCE   216

ALLIANCE FAMILY YMCA 205 S. Union Ave.
Phone: 823-1930.
Pool: 20y x 20f, 4 lanes, indoors, heated, 83°.
Admission: $6.
Affiliate: Y AWAY NC.

ASHLAND   419

ASHLAND YMCA 207 Miller St.
Phone: 289-0626.
Pool 1: 25m, indoors, heated, 80°.
Pool 2: 20y, indoors, heated, 87°.
Admission: $5.
Affiliate: YMCA & U.S. Military: NC.
Masters: The Ashland Masters. Contact Melody Nealis at 289-0626.

ASHTABULA   216

ASHTABULA COUNTY YMCA 263 Prospect Rd.
Phone: 997-5321.
Pool: 25y, indoors, heated, 86°.
Admission: $6.
Affiliate: YMCA 3 visits per month NC.

ATHENS   614

OHIO UNIVERSITY AQUATIC CENTER Oxbow Trail
Phone: 593-4670.
Pool: 25y x 50m, 10 lanes, indoors, heated, 81°.
Admission: $2.25.

Memberships: $40/quarter*. $120/year.
Notes: *Annual membership includes access during between-quarter breaks, quarterly membership does not.

BATAVIA   513

CLERMONT COUNTY YMCA 2075 Front Wheel Dr.
Phone: 724-9622.
Pool: 25m, 6 lanes, indoors, heated, 83°.
Affiliate: YMCA $3.
Notes: There is also a 25y x 50m, outdoor, unheated pool operated from Memorial Day to Labor Day.
To find: Exit Front Wheel Dr. off State Route 32, go east one mile.

BEACHWOOD   216

BALLY'S SCANDINAVIAN HEALTH SPA 3600 Park E.
Phone: 765-8085.
Pool: 25m, indoors, heated, 78°-84°.
Admission: Call.
Affiliate: Bally's & IPFA: NC.

BEAVERCREEK   513

BEAVERCREEK YMCA 560 Grange Hall Rd.
Phone: 426-9622.
Pool: 25y x 25m, 8 x 6 lanes, 'L' shape, indoors, heated, 84°.
Admission: 3 visits per calendar year $4 each.
Affiliate: YMCA 6 visits per year NC.
To find: A 15 minute drive east from downtown Dayton, via Route 35. Exit at Dayton-Xenia Rd., turn left at the end of the ramp, then right onto Grange Hall Rd.
Masters: Call 462-9622.

BEDFORD   216

SOUTHEAST BRANCH YMCA 460 Northfield Rd.
Phone: 663-7522.
Pool: 20y, 4 lanes, indoors, heated, 84°.
Admission: $6.
Affiliate: YMCA NC.

BERLIN   216

HOLMES HEALTH & FITNESS CENTER 5336 County Rd. 201
Phone: 893-3101.
Pool: 20y x 30f, indoors, heated, 80°-85°.
Admission: $5.

BROADVIEW HEIGHTS   216

EAGLE VALLEY HEALTH & ATHLETIC CLUB 1 Eagle Valley Court
Phone: 838-5600.
Pool: 25m, indoors, heated, 80°.
Admission: $12.

BROOK PARK   216

BALLY'S SCANDINAVIAN HEALTH SPA 14571 Snow Rd.
Phone: 267-3500.
Pool: 25y, indoors, heated, 82°.
Affiliate: Bally's & IPFA: NC.
Hotel: Holiday Inn Airport (252-7700), Holiday Inn Middleburg Heights (243-4040), & Fairfield Inn (676-5200): NC.

BRYAN   419

YWCA OF WILLIAMS COUNTY 1 Faber Dr.
Phone: 636-6185.
Pool: 25y, indoors, heated, 86°.
Admission: $5.

CAMBRIDGE   614

CAMBRIDGE AREA YMCA 703 N. 7th St.
Phone: 432-6318.
Pool: 20y x 30f, 4 lanes, indoors, heated, 84°.
Admission: $3.50.
Affiliate: YMCA & U.S. Military: NC.
Hotel: Holiday Inn (432-2337) & TraveLodge (432-7375): NC with room key.

CANTON   216

CANTON DOWNTOWN YMCA 405 2nd St. N.W.
Phone: 456-7141.
Pool 1: 25m, indoors, heated, 82°-83°.
Pool 2: 20y, indoors, heated, 86°-89°.
Admission: $5.
Affiliate: YMCA 2 weeks NC. U.S.Military NC.

C.T. BRANIN NATATORIUM 1715 Harrison Ave. N.W.
Phone: 438-2738.
Pool: 50m x 25y, 8 lanes, indoors, heated, 78°-80°.
Admission: $1.50.

BALLY'S SCANDINAVIAN HEALTH SPA 4733 Hills & Dales Rd. N.W.
Phone: 478-8363.
Pool: 25y, indoors, heated, 84°-86°.
Admission: Call.
Affiliate: Bally's & IPFA: NC.
Hotel: Park Hotel (499-9410) NC.

HALL OF FAME FITNESS CENTER, INC. 2700 Roberts Ave. N.W.
Phone: 455-4348.
Pool: 25y x 52f, 4 lanes, indoors, heated, 82°.
Admission: $8.
Hotel: Holiday Inn (494-2770) NC.
Notes: There is also a 50y x 25y, 4 lane, outdoor, summer pool.

CELINA   419

LAKE FRONT RACQUET & HEALTH CLUB 6301 U.S. 127 S.
Phone: 586-6688.
Pool: 25m, 6 lanes, indoors, heated, 84°.
Admission: $8.
Affiliate: IHRSA $5.
Hotel: S & W Motel — NC with room key.
To find: On U.S. 127 S. about a half mile from the center of Celina.

CENTERVILLE   513

BALLY'S VIC TANNY 1530 Miamisburg-Centerville Rd.
Phone: 435-3042.
Pool: 25m, indoors, heated, 78°-82°.
Admission: Call.
Affiliate: Bally's NC.
Hotel: Days Inn (847-8422), Courtyards (433-3131), & Marriott (223-1000): NC.

WASHINGTON TOWNSHIP RECREATION CENTER 895 Miamisburg-Centerville Rd.
Phone: 433-0130.
Pool: 25y x 65f, 8 lanes, indoors, heated, 82°.
Admission: Residents $2, SC(60) $1. Non-residents $4, SC $2.
Notes: There is also a 20y, 0-3.5f deep, indoor, 86°-88° pool.
To find: Off I-75 and I-675, on State Route 725, two miles east of the Dayton Mall.
Masters: The Washington Township Masters. Contact Anne Phillips at 433-0130.

CINCINNATI   513

1. YWCA 898 Walnut St.
Phone: 241-7090 ext. 116.
Pool: 25y x 24f, indoors, heated, 85°.
Admission: $5, SC(60) $3.
To find: On the corner of 9th & Walnut, across from the Main Library.

2. W.J. WILLIAMS BRANCH YMCA 1228 E. McMillan St.
Phone: 961-7552.
Pool: 20y x 45f, 3 lanes, indoors, heated, 80°.
Admission: $8.
Affiliate: YMCA outside a 50 mile radius 3 visits per month NC, within 50 miles $3.
To find: Near Eden Park.

3. MELROSE BRANCH YMCA 2840 Melrose Ave.
Phone: 961-3510.
Pool: 25y x 30f, 4 lanes, indoors, heated, 82°.
Admission: $6.
Affiliate: YMCA 3 visits NC, then $3.
To find: Two blocks south of the intersection of Gilbert Ave. and Martin Luther King Dr.

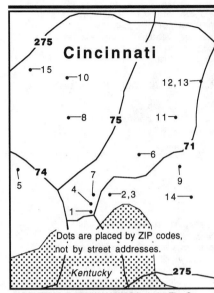

Cincinnati

275

←15 ←10

12,13

←8 **75** 11→

←6 **71**

74 7 9

5 4 ←2,3 14→

1

Dots are placed by ZIP codes, not by street addresses.

Kentucky 275

4. CENTRAL PARKWAY YMCA 1105 Elm St.
Phone: 241-5348.
Pool: 25y, 3 lanes, indoors, heated, 79°-81°.
Admission: $10.
Affiliate: YMCA outside a 50 mile radius 3 visits NC, then $5.

5. GAMBLE-NIPPERT BRANCH YMCA 3159 Montana Ave.
Phone: 661-1105.
Pool: 25y, indoors, heated, 80°.
Affiliate: YMCA Call.

6. RICHARD E. LINDNER FAMILY YMCA Sherman & Walter Aves.
Phone: 731-0115.
Pool: 20y, indoors, heated, 82°.
Affiliate: Y AWAY 3 visits NC.
Notes: There is also an outdoor, summer pool.

7. THE FRIARS CLUB 65 W. McMillan
Phone: 381-5432.
Pool: 25.2y, indoors, heated, 80°.
Admission: $7.

8. KEATING NATATORIUM St. Xavier High School, 616 W. North Bend Rd.
Phone: 761-3320.
Pool: 50m OR 25y + 25y x 20y, 8 OR 16 lanes, indoors, heated, 79°.
Admission: $5.
To find: At the top of North Bend Hill, about a half mile from Winton Rd.
Masters: The Cincinnati Marlins Masters. Call 761-3320.

9. CINCINNATI SPORTS CLUB 3950 Redbank Rd.
Phone: 527-4550.

Pool: 25y x 27f, 3 lanes, indoors, heated, 81°.
Affiliate: IHRSA: Weekdays $6. Weekends $10.
Masters: The Cincinnati Sports Club Masters. Contact the Program Director at 527-4550.

10. POWEL CROSLEY JUNIOR YMCA 9601 Winton Rd.
Phone: 521-7112.
Pool: 25y x 38f, 6 lanes, indoors, heated, 82°.
Affiliate: YMCA outside a 50 mile radius 3 visits NC, within 50 miles $3.

11. HARLEY HOTEL OF CINCINNATI 8020 Montgomery Rd.
Phone: 793-4300. **Reservations:** 800-321-2323.
Pool: 20y x 30f, indoors, heated, 82°.
Admission: Registered guests only NC.
Notes: There is also an outdoor, unheated, 78°-84° pool operated May through Sep.

12. BLUE ASH YMCA 5000 YMCA Dr.
Phone: 791-5000.
Pool 1: 25y x 42f, 6 lanes, indoors, heated, 82°.
Pool 2: 25y x 42f, 6 lanes, indoors, heated, 86°.
Affiliate: Y AWAY 3 visits per month NC.
To find: Three miles north of Kenwood Towne Center on Kenwood Rd.

13. BALLY'S SCANDINAVIAN 9675 Montgomery Rd.
Phone: 984-4811.
Pool: 23y, 4 lanes, indoors, heated, 80°-82°.
Admission: Call.
Affiliate: Bally's & IPFA: NC.

14. M.E. LYONS FAMILY BRANCH YMCA 8108 Clough Pike
Phone: 474-1400.
Pool: 25y x 45f, 6 lanes, indoors, heated, 82°-84°.
Affiliate: Y AWAY NC. YMCA $3.

15. CLIPPARD YMCA 8920 Cheviot Rd.
Phone: 923-4466.
Pool: 25m, indoors, heated, 80°.
Affiliate: Y AWAY 3 visits per month NC, then $6.

CIRCLEVILLE _____ **614**

PICKAWAY COUNTY YMCA 440 Nicholas Dr.
Phone: 477-1661.
Pool: 25y x 48f, 6 lanes, indoors, heated, 84°.
Admission: $5.
Affiliate: YMCA NC.

CLEVELAND _____ **216**

16. CLARK RECREATION CENTER 5706 Clark Ave.
Phone: 664-4657.
Pool: 20y x 25f, indoors, heated, 82°.
Admission: NC.

CLEVELAND **CONTINUED**

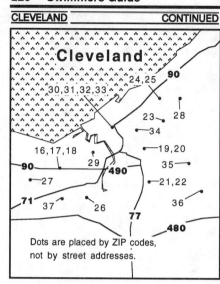

Cleveland

Dots are placed by ZIP codes, not by street addresses.

17. CUDELL RECREATION CENTER 1910 West Blvd.
Phone: 664-4137.
Pool: 25y x 42f, indoors, heated, 82°.
Admission: NC.

18. ZONE RECREATION CENTER 6301 Lorain Ave.
Phone: 664-3373.
Pool: 25y x 45f, indoors, heated, 82°.
Admission: NC.

19. FAIRFAX RECREATION CENTER 2335 E. 82nd St.
Phone: 664-4132.
Pool: 25y x 42f, indoors, heated, 82°.
Admission: NC.

20. LONNIE BURTEN RECREATION CENTER 2511 E. 46th St.
Phone: 664-4139.
Pool: 25y x 25f, indoors, heated, 82°.
Admission: NC.

21. STELLA WALSH RECREATION CENTER 7345 Broadway Ave.
Phone: 664-4658.
Pool: 25y x 45f, indoors, heated, 82°.
Admission: NC.

22. BROADWAY BRANCH YMCA 11300 Miles Ave.
Phone: 341-1860.
Pool: 20y, indoors, heated, 86°.
Admission: $4.
Affiliate: YMCA NC.

23. THURGOOD MARSHALL RECREATION CENTER 8611 Hough Ave.
Phone: 664-4045.
Pool: 25y x 45f, indoors, heated, 82°.
Admission: NC.

24. CORY RECREATION CENTER 10510 Drexel Ave.
Phone: 664-3389.
Pool: 24y x 30f, indoors, heated, 82°.
Admission: NC.

25. GLENVILLE RECREATION CENTER 680 E. 113th St.
Phone: 664-2516.
Pool: 25y x 42f, indoors, heated, 82°.
Admission: NC.

26. BROOKLYN YMCA 3881 Pearl Rd.
Phone: 749-2355.
Pool: 20y x 20f, 4 lanes, indoors, heated, 83°.
Admission: $6.
Affiliate: Y AWAY NC. YMCA $2.
To find: One mile from I-71 heading south on Pearl Rd., just past Denison Ave.

27. WEST PARK-FAIRVIEW BRANCH YMCA 15501 Lorain Ave.
Phone: 941-5410.
Pool: 20y x 20f, 4 lanes, indoors, heated, 84°-86°.
Admission: $6.
Affiliate: YMCA NC to $3, depending on the type of membership.

28. YWCA NORTH CENTRAL 1831 Lee Blvd.
Phone: 451-3425.
Pool: 20y, indoors, heated, 83°-86°.
Affiliate: YWCA $2.

29. WEST SIDE YMCA 3200 Franklin Blvd.
Phone: 961-3277.
Pool: 20y x 20f, 4 lanes, indoors, heated, 86°.
Admission: $6.
Affiliate: YMCA Call.
To find: West of Fulton Rd. and W. 25th, two blocks south of Detroit Ave.

30. STERLING RECREATION CENTER 1380 E. 32nd St.
Phone: 664-2573.
Pool: 25y x 45f, indoors, heated, 82°.
Admission: NC.

31. ATHLETIC CLUB AT ONE CLEVELAND CENTER 1375 E. 9th St.
Phone: 621-0770.
Pool: 20y x 60f, 4 lanes, indoors, heated, 81°.
Admission: $15.
Affiliate: CSI NC. IHRSA $8.
Hotel: Sheraton Cleveland City Centre Hotel (771-7600) & Holiday Inn: $8.
To find: At the intersection of E. 9th and St. Clair, across from the Galleria. The club is on the 7th

floor of the parking complex at One Cleveland Center.
Masters: Contact Paul James at 621-0770.

32. HOLIDAY INN LAKESIDE 1111 Lakeside Ave.
Phone: 241-5100. **Reservations:** 800-HOLIDAY.
Pool: 50f, rectangular, indoors, heated, 82°.
Admission: Registered guests only NC.

33. RADISSON PLAZA HOTEL CLEVELAND 1701 E. 12th St.
Phone: 523-8000. **Reservations:** 800-333-3333.
Pool: 50f x 25f, rectangular, indoors, heated, 82°.
Admission: Registered guests NC.
Memberships: $35/month.

34. CLEVELAND ATHLETIC CLUB 1118 Euclid Ave.
Phone: 621-8900.
Pool: 20y, indoors, heated, 84°-86°.
Admission: $7.

35. ALEXANDER HAMILTON RECREATION CENTER 13200 Kinsman Rd.
Phone: 664-4121.
Pool: 25y x 42f, indoors, heated, 82°.
Admission: NC.

36. JOHN F. KENNEDY RECREATION CENTER 17300 Harvard Ave.
Phone: 664-2572.
Pool: 25y x 45f, indoors, heated, 82°.
Admission: NC.

37. ESTABROOK RECREATION CENTER 4125 Fulton Rd.
Phone: 664-4149.
Pool: 25y x 42f, indoors, heated, 82°.
Admission: NC.

CLEVELAND HEIGHTS   **216**

HEIGHTS YMCA 2340 Lee Rd.
Phone: 371-2323.
Pool: 20y x 25f, 4 lanes, indoors, heated, 82°-84°.
Admission: $4.
Affiliate: YMCA NC.

COLUMBUS   **614**

SWIM CENTER 1160 Hunter Ave.
Phone: 645-6122.
Pool: 25m, indoors, heated, water temperature not reported.
Admission: 25¢.

ELDON W. WARD BRANCH YMCA 130 Woodland Ave.
Phone: 252-3166.
Pool: 25y x 10y, 4 lanes, indoors, heated, 83°.
Admission: $5.
Affiliate: Y AWAY 5 visits per month NC.

To find: Three and a half miles east of downtown, one and a half blocks south of Franklin Park.

CENTRAL BRANCH YMCA 40 W. Long St.
Phone: 224-1131.
Pool: 20y, indoors, heated, 84°.
Admission: $5.
Affiliate: YMCA $3.
Hotel: Holiday Inn Crowne Plaza (461-4100) NC with a voucher from the hotel.

YWCA OF COLUMBUS 60 S. 4th St.
Phone: 224-9121.
Pool: 20y, indoors, heated, 80°.
Admission: $5.

YMCA NORTH 1640 Sandalwood Place
Phone: 885-4252.
Pool: 25y x 40f, 6 lanes, indoors, heated, 82°.
Admission: $8. Before 2PM $6.
Affiliate: YMCA $1.
To find: Four blocks north of Morse Rd. off Karl Rd.

COLUMBUS NORTH SPORTS CLUB at the Best Western Columbus North, 888 E. Dublin Granville Rd.
Phone: Club: 888-1565. Hotel: 888-8230.
Reservations: 800-528-1234.
Pool: 25y, indoors, heated, 81°.
Admission: $8. Registered guests NC.

BALLY'S SCANDINAVIAN HOLIDAY SPA 2439 Fuji Rd.
Phone: 899-1133.
Pool: 23y, indoors, heated, 80°.
Affiliate: Bally's & IPFA: NC.
Hotel: Embassy Suits (890-8600), Days Inn (885-9696), & AmeriSuites: NC.

CONTINENTAL ATHLETIC CLUB 6124 Busch
Phone: 846-8400.
Pool: 20y, indoors, heated, 82°.
Admission: $14.
Affiliate: IHRSA $8.

SAWMILL ATHLETIC CLUB 3111 Hayden Rd.
Phone: 889-7698.
Pool: 25m, 6 lanes, indoors, heated, 82°-84°.
Admission: $12.
Affiliate: IHRSA $8.
Hotel: Cross Country Inn $5. Hyatt Regency Columbus (463-1234), Buckeye Inn (261-7141), Studio Plus (764-0159), Worthington (885-2600), Howard Johnsons (486-4554), Stouffer Dublin Hotel (764-2200), & Dublin Inn: $8.
Notes: There is also a 20y, 4 lane, outdoor, heated, 82°-84° pool operated from early May through late Oct.
To find: One half mile west of the intersection of Sawmill and Bethel.

CUYAHOGA FALLS 216

CUYAHOGA FALLS BRANCH FAMILY YMCA
544 Broad Blvd.
Phone: 923-5223.
Pool: 20y x 25f, 4 lanes, indoors, heated, 89°.
Affiliate: Y AWAY NC.

SHERATON SUITES AKRON / CUYAHOGA FALLS 1989 Front St.
Phone: 929-3000. **Reservations:** 800-325-5788.
Pool: 50f, rectangular, indoors, heated, 82°.
Admission: Registered guests only NC.

THE NATATORIUM IN CUYAHOGA FALLS 2351 - 4th St.
Phone: 971-8080.
Pool 1: 25y, indoors, heated, 83°.
Pool 2: 25y, indoors, heated, 85°.
Admission: Residents $4, non-residents $5.
Hotel: Sheraton Suites Cuyahoga Falls (929-3000) NC.
Masters: The Cuyahoga Falls Masters. Contact the pool staff at 971-8080.

DAYTON 513

DOWNTOWN YMCA 316 N. Wilkenson
Phone: 228-9622.
Pool: 25y, 4 lanes, indoors, heated, 81°-83°.
Admission: $10.
Affiliate: YMCA Call.
Hotel: Radisson Hotel (278-5711) & Stouffers Hotel (224-0800): $4 with room key.

DABNEY POOL 1600 Princeton Dr.
Phone: 277-4122.
Pool: 25m, 6 lanes, indoor/outdoor, heated, 86°.
Admission: $1, SC(55) 50¢.
To find: Two minutes from downtown Dayton, eight blocks west of I-75 in northwest Daytonview, between Salem Ave. & Philadelphia Dr.

ROOSEVELT CENTER 2013 W. 3rd St.
Phone: 263-3576.
Pool: 23y, indoors, heated, water temperature not reported.
Admission: NC.

WEST AREA YMCA 4415 Dayton-Liberty Rd.
Phone: 268-6741.
Pool: 25m, 6 lanes, indoors, heated, 88°.
Admission: $3.
Affiliate: YMCA NC.

LOHREY CENTER 2366 Glenarm Ave.
Phone: 253-0526.
Pool: 25y, indoors, heated, 83°-84°.
Admission: $1.
Masters: The Dayton Synchronettes. Contact Lieneke Keihl at 253-9676(w).

KETTERING BRANCH YMCA 4545 Marshall Rd.
Phone: 434-1964.
Pool: 25y, indoors, heated, 85°-86°.
Admission: $5.
Affiliate: YMCA NC.

DEFIANCE 419

DEFIANCE AREA YMCA 1599 Palmer Dr.
Phone: 784-4747.
Pool: 25y x 45f, 6 lanes, indoors, heated, 82°.
Admission: $5.
Affiliate: YMCA NC.

DOVER 216

TUSCARAWAS COUNTY YMCA 600 Monroe St.
Phone: 364-5511.
Pool: 25y, 6 lanes, indoors, heated, 83°.
Admission: $4.
Affiliate: YMCA NC.

DUBLIN 614

ATHLETIC CLUB AT METRO V 655 Metro Place S.
Phone: 889-4717.
Pool: 25m, indoors, heated, 81°.
Admission: $15.
Hotel: Stouffer Dublin Hotel (764-2200) NC.

EAST LIVERPOOL 216

SKYLIGHT HEALTH SPA at the East Liverpool Motor Lodge, 2340 Dresden Ave.
Phone: Spa 386-5858 ext. 41. Hotel: 386-5858 ext. 0.
Pool: 20y x 20f, indoors, heated, 84°.
Admission: Registered guests: Pool NC. Full facility $5.
Affiliate: IHRSA $5.
Memberships: Call.

EAST LIVERPOOL YMCA 134 E. 4th St.
Phone: 385-0663.
Pool: 20y, indoors, heated, 86°.
Admission: $4.
Affiliate: YMCA $1.50.

ELYRIA 216

ELYRIA FAMILY YMCA 265 Washington Ave.
Phone: 323-5500.
Pool: 25y, indoors, heated, 86°.
Affiliate: YMCA NC.

ENGLEWOOD 513

HOLIDAY INN DAYTON N.W. AIRPORT 10 Rockridge Rd.
Phone: 832-1234. **Reservations:** 800 HOLIDAY.
Pool: 50f x 26f, rectangular, indoors, heated, 82°.
Admission: Registered guests only NC.

EUCLID   216

EUCLID YMCA 631 Babbitt Rd.
Phone: 731-7454.
Pool: 20y, 4 lanes, indoors, heated, 84°.
Admission: $5.
Affiliate: YMCA NC.

FAIRBORN   513

FAIRBORN YMCA 300 S. Central Ave.
Phone: 878-8122.
Pool: 25y, 4 lanes, indoors, heated, 84°.
Admission: $5.
Affiliate: YMCA 6 visits NC, then $5.
Hotel: Ramada Inn (879-3920) $3.50 with room
key.

FAIRFIELD   513

FAIRFIELD YMCA 5220 Bibury Rd.
Phone: 829-3091.
Pool: 25y x 45f, 6 lanes, indoors, heated, 82°.
Admission: $10.
Affiliate: Y AWAY NC. YMCA within a 50 mile
radius 1 visit per month NC.
To find: One block from Krogers Savon East.

FAIRVIEW PARK   216

O*H*I*O* MASTERS SWIM CLUB at Fairview High
School, 4507 W. 213th St.
Masters: Contact Judith Norton at 228-3686(h).
Pool: 25y, 6 lanes, indoors, heated, 78°.
Affiliate: USMS 4 workouts per week NC.
Notes: Coached workouts: M,W,Th: 9-10PM. Sa:
7:30-9AM. See the club's listing under Orange,
Ohio, for Tu,Th,Su workout times. The pool is
closed from mid-Jun. through Aug.

FINDLAY   419

FINDLAY YMCA 300 E. Lincoln St.
Phone: 422-4424.
Pool: 25y x 30f, 6 lanes, indoors, heated, 80°.
Admission: Call.
Affiliate: Y AWAY NC.
Hotel: Country Hearth Inn (423-4303) & the Findlay
Inn & Conference Center: NC.
To find: Go east off S. Main at the southern end of
the business district. The intersection of Main and
Lincoln has a Marathon gas station and a church.
Masters: The Findlay Y Masters. Contact Sandra
Yuenger at 422-4424.

FOSTORIA   419

GEARY FAMILY YMCA 154 W. Center St.
Phone: 435-6608.
Pool: 25y x 25f, 4 lanes, indoors, heated, 86.5°.
Admission: $5.
Affiliate: YMCA NC.
To find: Easy to find, small town, BIG Y.

FREMONT   419

SANDUSKY COUNTY YMCA 1000 North St.
Phone: 332-1531.
Pool: 25y x 30f, 4 lanes, indoors, heated, 85°.
Affiliate: YMCA NC.

GAHANNA   614

GAHANNA FITNESS CLUB 501 Morrison Rd.
Phone: 476-1165.
Pool: 20y, indoors, heated, 84°.
Admission: $5.

GALION   419

GALION COMMUNITY YMCA 500 Gill Ave.
Phone: 468-7754.
Pool: 25y, 4 lanes, indoors, heated, 82°.
Admission: $4.
Affiliate: YMCA NC.

HAMILTON   513

HAMILTON CENTRAL BRANCH YMCA 105 N.
2nd St.
Phone: 887-0001.
Pool: 20y, indoors, heated, 83°.
Admission: $10.
Affiliate: YMCA NC.

HAMILTON WEST YMCA 1307 N.W. Washington
Blvd.
Phone: 869-8550.
Pool: 25y x 42f, 6 lanes, indoors, heated, 84°.
Admission: $10.
Affiliate: Y AWAY NC.
Masters: Hamilton West YMCA Masters. Contact
Claudia Multer at 869-8550.

HIRAM   216

HIRAM COLLEGE
Phone: 569-5340.
Pool: 25m, 5 lanes, indoors, heated, 84°.
Memberships: Pool: $130/calendar year. Full
facility: $200/year.

HUDSON   216

LIFECENTER PLUS FITNESS CENTER 5133
Darrow Rd.
Phone: 655-2377.
Pool: 25m, indoors, heated, 84°.
Admission: $8.50.

KETTERING   513

KETTERING RECREATION COMPLEX 2900
Glengarry Dr.
Phone: 296-2587.
Pool: 25y x 60f, 8 lanes, indoor/outdoor, heated,
84°.

Admission: Residents $2, SC(55) $1.75. Non-residents $4, SC $3.50.

SOUTH COMMUNITY FAMILY YMCA 4545 Marshall Rd.
Phone: 434-1964.
Pool: 25y, 4 lanes, indoors, heated, 83°.
Admission: $5.
Affiliate: YMCA NC.
Masters: The South Community Family YMCA - KEY. Contact Gary Galbreath or Denise Houk at 434-1964.

BALLY'S VIC TANNY 4084 Wilmington Pike
Phone: 299-0101.
Pool: 25y, indoors, heated, 82°.
Affiliate: Bally's & IPFA: NC.

LAKEWOOD   216

LAKEWOOD Y 16915 Detroit Ave.
Phone: 521-8400.
Pool: 20y x 40f, 4 lanes, indoors, heated, 84°-86°.
Admission: $5.
Affiliate: YMCA & YWCA: NC.

LANCASTER   614

LANCASTER FAMILY YMCA 465 W. 6th Ave.
Phone: 654-0616.
Pool: 20y x 21f, 4 lanes, indoors, heated, 84°.
Affiliate: YMCA & U.S. Military personnel on leave: NC.
Hotel: Holiday Inn Lancaster (653-3040) & Shaw's Inn (653-5522): NC.

LEBANON   513

COUNTRYSIDE YMCA 1699 Deerfield Rd.
Phone: 932-1424.
Pool: 25m x 56f, 8 lanes, indoors, heated, 81°-82°.
Affiliate: YMCA 1 visit per month NC. Y AWAY outside a 50 mile radius $1.75 (after NC visit). U.S. Military on leave NC.
To find: There is also a 50f x 30f, indoor, heated, 84°-86°, instructional pool and an outdoor, seasonal pool.

LIMA   419

LIMA FAMILY YMCA 136 S. West St.
Phone: 223-6045.
Pool: 25y x 32f, 4 lanes, indoors, heated, 80°-82°.
Admission: Basic $6. Health Center $10.
Affiliate: YMCA 12 visits per year NC.
Hotel: Ho Jo by Howard Johnson (228-2525) 50% of general admission rates.
To find: Two blocks southwest of the Civic Center in downtown, at the intersection of West and Spring Sts.

YWCA OF LIMA 649 W. Market St.
Phone: 228-8664.
Pool: 25y x 30f, 4 lanes, indoors, heated, 86°.
Admission: $5.
Affiliate: YWCA $2.50, SC(62) $1.50.
To find: Across from the public library.

LORAIN   216

LORAIN FAMILY YMCA 1121 Tower Blvd.
Phone: 282-4414.
Pool: 25y x 35f, 6 lanes, indoors, heated, 84°.
Admission: $6.
Affiliate: YMCA & U.S. Military on leave: NC.
Hotel: Spitzer Plaza (246-5767) NC with membership card from the hotel.
Notes: This Y also operates three city owned outdoor pools in the summer. Call the Y for information.
To find: Located behind Bank One.

LOUISVILLE   216

LOUISVILE YMCA 1421 Nickleplate Ave. S.
Phone: 875-1611.
Pool: 25m, indoors, heated, 82°-83°.
Admission: $5.
Affiliate: Y AWAY 1 week NC. YMCA $2.50.
Masters: The Canton Area Masters. Contact Cindy Virdo at 875-1611.

LYNDHURST   216

HILLCREST FAMILY YMCA 5000 Mayfield Rd.
Phone: 382-4300.
Pool: 20y x 20f, 4 lanes, indoors, heated, 83°.
Admission: Lap swimming 1 visit $4. Open swims $4.
Affiliate: YMCA NC.
To find: Near the intersection of Richmond and Mayfield Rd.

MADISON   216

EAST END BRANCH YMCA 730 N. Lake St.
Phone: 428-5125.
Pool: 25y x 45f, 6 lanes, indoors, heated, 85°.
Admission: 3 visits per year $5 each.
Affiliate: YMCA NC on an irregular basis.
To find: From I-90 proceed north on Route 528 into Madison Village. Turn right at the stop sign and left at the traffic light. Proceed north on Route 528 (Lake St.) crossing the R.R. tracks. The Y is one quarter mile on right.

MANSFIELD   419

MANSFIELD YMCA 455 Park Ave. W.
Phone: 522-3511.
Pool: 20y x 24f, 4 lanes, indoors, heated, 84°.
Affiliate: YMCA outside a 30 mile radius NC.
Hotel: Holiday Inn (525-6000) $5.

MAPLE HEIGHTS — 216

BALLY'S SCANDINAVIAN HEALTH SPA 5510 Warrensville Center Rd.
Phone: 662-1500.
Pool: 25m, indoors, heated, 82°.
Affiliate: Bally's NC.

MARIETTA — 614

MARIETTA FAMILY YMCA 300 - 7th St.
Phone: 373-2250.
Pool: 25y x 30f, 6 lanes, indoors, heated, 82°-84°.
Admission: $6.
Affiliate: Y AWAY $3.
Hotel: Lafayette Hotel (373-5522), Holiday Inn (374-9660), & Best Western (374-7211): NC with a pass from the hotel.

MASSILLON — 216

PERRY HIGH SCHOOL 3737 Harsh Ave. S.W.
Phone: 478-6157 ext. 137.
Pool: 25m x 45f, 6 lanes, indoors, heated, 81°.
Admission: $1.25, SC(60) NC.
Affiliate: USMS NC.
Notes: The pool closes for the month of Aug.
To find: One block south of the intersection of Genoa and Route 172.

THE YMCA-YWCA OF WESTERN STARK COUNTY 131 Tremont Ave. S.E.
Phone: 837-5116.
Pool: 25m x 45f, 6 lanes, indoors, heated, 86°.
Affiliate: Y AWAY & YWCA: NC.
To find: Across the street from the police station.

MAUMEE — 419

SOUTHWEST FAMILY YMCA 2100 S. Holland-Sylvania Rd.
Phone: 866-9622.
Pool: 25m, 6 lanes, indoors, heated, 85°-86°.
Affiliate: YMCA NC.
To find: One half mile south of Airport Hwy. (Route 2) near the I-475 interchange.

MIDDLEBURG HEIGHTS — 216

YWCA 13169 Smith Rd.
Phone: 842-4242.
Pool: 25y, indoors, heated, 84°.
Admission: $2.

MILFORD — 513

ROYAL HEALTH & FITNESS Milford Shopping Center, 930 Lila Ave.
Phone: 831-0006.
Pool: 20y, 4 lanes, indoors, heated, 82°-84°.
Affiliate: IPFA NC.
Notes: A new pool, completed in late 1994.

MORAINE — 513

MORAINE NATATORIUM 4000 Trail On Rd.
Phone: 859-3250.
Pool: 25y, 5 lanes, indoor/outdoor, heated, 82°.
Admission: $2, SC(55) $1.
To find: The pool may be difficult to locate, visitors should call for directions.

MOUNT VERNON — 614

MOUNT VERNON YMCA 103 N. Main St.
Phone: 392-9622.
Pool: 25y, indoors, heated, 82°-85°.
Admission: $5.
Affiliate: YMCA NC.

NEWARK — 614

NORTHTOWNE ATHLETIC CLUB 140 Derby Downs Rd.
Phone: 366-7331.
Pool: 20y, indoor/outdoor, heated, 83°.
Admission: $7.

YWCA OF LICKING COUNTY 140 W. Church & 6th Sts.
Phone: 345-4084.
Pool: 25y, indoors, heated, 89°.
Admission: $2.75.

NILES — 216

TRUMBULL COUNTY YMCA - EASTWOOD BRANCH 995 Youngstown-Warren Rd.
Phone: 544-2383.
Pool: 25y x 36f, 6 lanes, indoors, heated, 84°-86°.
Affiliate: YMCA NC.
To find: On Route 422 less than a block east of Route 46.

NORTH CANTON — 216

NORTH CANTON YMCA 200 S. Main St.
Phone: 499-2587.
Pool: 25y, indoors, heated, 84°.
Affiliate: YMCA $3.

NORTH OLMSTED — 216

NORTH OLMSTED RECREATION CENTER 26000 Lorian Rd.
Phone: 734-8200.
Pool: 25y, indoors, heated, 83°.
Admission: Non-residents $3.50.

ORANGE — 216

O*H*I*O* MASTERS SWIM CLUB at Orange High School, 32000 Chagrin Blvd.
Masters: Contact Jennifer A. Savage at 349-4186(h) or 535-5711(w).
Pool: 25y, 6 lanes, indoors, heated, 78°.

Affiliate: USMS 4 workouts per week NC.
Notes: Workouts: Tu,Th: 8-9:30PM. Sa: 7:30-9AM. Su: 10-11:30AM. See the club's listing under Fairview Park, Ohio, for M,W workout times. The pool is closed from May through mid-Sep.

OREGON   419

EASTERN COMMUNITY BRANCH YMCA 2960 Pickle Rd.
Phone: 691-3523.
Pool: 25y, indoors, heated, 84°.
Admission: $5.
Affiliate: YMCA NC.
Hotel: Local hotels $3 with room key.

PARMA   216

RIDGEWOOD YMCA 6840 Ridge Rd.
Phone: 842-5200.
Pool: 25y x 36f, 6 lanes, indoors, heated, 86°.
Admission: $6.
Affiliate: YMCA NC.
Masters: Contact Cindy Strebig at 842-5200.

PIQUA   513

MIAMI COUNTY YMCA 223 W. High St.
Phone: 773-4305.
Pool: 25m, indoors, heated, 82°.
Affiliate: YMCA NC.

ROCKY RIVER   216

RIVER OAKS RACQUET & FITNESS CENTER 21220 Center Ridge Rd.
Phone: 331-4980.
Pool: 21y, indoors, heated, 84°.
Admission: $6.

SANDUSKY   419

SANDUSKY AREA YMCA 2101 W. Perkins Ave.
Phone: 621-9622.
Pool 1: 25m, 6 lanes, indoors, heated, 82°.
Pool 2: 25y, 4 lanes, indoors, heated, 86°.
Admission: NC with 24 hours notice.
Affiliate: YMCA & U.S. Military: NC.
Masters: The Sandusky Area YMCA Masters. Contact Jim Caldwell at 621-9622 ext. 419.

SIDNEY   513

SIDNEY-SHELBY COUNTY YMCA 300 Parkwood St.
Phone: 492-9622.
Pool: 25y x 42f, 6 lanes, indoors, heated, 82°.
Affiliate: YMCA: Basic $3. Fitness Center $5.
Hotel: Holiday Inn (492-1131): Basic $3. Fitness Center $5.

SPRINGFIELD   513

SPRINGFIELD YMCA 300 S. Limestone
Phone: 323-3781.
Pool: 25y, indoors, heated, 83°.
Admission: Out-of-state visitors $5.
Affiliate: Out-of-state YMCA NC.

SYLVANIA   419

BALLY'S VIC TANNY 5215 Monroe St.
Phone: 885-4627.
Pool: 80f x 20f, indoors, heated, 84°.
Admission: $5.
Affiliate: Bally's & IPFA: NC.

TALLMADGE   216

YWCA 111 West Ave.
Phone: 633-4983.
Pool: 25y, indoors, heated, 84°-88°.
Admission: $4.

TOLEDO   419

AQUARIUS ATHLETIC CLUB 5730 Opportunity Dr.
Phone: 476-4884.
Pool: 25y x 25f, 5 lanes, indoors, heated, 83°.
Admission: $5.
Affiliate: IPFA NC. IHRSA $3.
To find: On Opportunity Dr., one block west of the intersection of Lewis Ave. and Alexis Rd.

SOUTH YMCA - TOLEDO 1226 Woodsdale Park Dr.
Phone: 385-9622.
Pool: 25y x 28f, 4 lanes, indoors, heated, 85°.
Admission: $5.
Affiliate: YMCA NC.
To find: Off the Anthony Wayne Trail across from the Toledo Zoo parking lot.

ST. JAMES CLUB 7337 W. Bancroft St.
Phone: 841-5597.
Pool: 25y x 25f, 5 lanes, indoors, heated, 84°.
Admission: $5.
Affiliate: IPFA outside a 25 mile radius 30 days NC. IHRSA outside a 25 mile radius $3.
Notes: There is also a 25 meter, outdoor, summer pool.
To find: One half mile west of McCord Rd.

BALLY'S VIC TANNY 5424 Airport Hwy.
Phone: 866-8276.
Pool: 25m, indoors, heated, 80°.
Admission: Out-of-state visitors NC.
Affiliate: Bally's & IPFA: NC.

AQUARIUS ATHLETIC CLUB SOUTH 630 S. Reynolds Rd.
Phone: 536-4064.
Pool: 25y, indoors, heated, 83°.

Admission: $5.
Affiliate: IHRSA & IPFA: $3.

TOLEDO YWCA 1018 Jefferson Ave.
Phone: 241-3235.
Pool: 25y x 35f, 5 lanes, indoors, heated, 86°.
Admission: $2.
Affiliate: YWCA NC.
Masters: Contact Aquatics Coordinator Julie Miller at 241-3235.

VAN WERT   419

VAN WERT YMCA 241 W. Main St.
Phone: 238-0443.
Pool: 25m, 7 lanes, indoors, heated, 84°.
Admission: $3.
Affiliate: YWCA NC.

WARREN   216

TRUMBULL COUNTY YMCA - WARREN FAMILY BRANCH 210 High St.
Phone: 394-1565.
Pool 1: 25y x 24f, 4 lanes, indoors, heated, 82°.
Pool 2: 20y x 24f, 4 lanes, indoors, heated, 86°.
Admission: $6.
Affiliate: YMCA NC.
To find: Directly across from the Trumbull County Courthouse.

YWCA OF WARREN 375 N. Park Ave.
Phone: 373-1010.
Pool 1: 25y x 35f, 5 lanes, indoors, heated, 83°-84°.
Pool 2: 20y, indoors, heated, 88°.
Admission: $5.
Affiliate: YWCA NC.
To find: Two blocks northeast of the Trumbull County Courthouse.

AVALON INN & RESORT 9519 E. Market St.
Phone: 856-1900. **Reservations:** Out-of-state: 800-221-1549. In Ohio: 800-828-2566.
Pool: 25y x 42f, 7 Lanes, indoors, heated, 87°-88°.
Admission: Registered guests NC.
Memberships: $250/year.

WESTERVILLE   614

WESTERVILLE ATHLETIC CLUB 939 S. State St.
Phone: 882-7331.
Pool: 25m, indoors, heated, 84°.
Admission: $12.
Affiliate: IHRSA $8.

WESTLAKE   216

BALLY'S SCANDINAVIAN HEALTH SPA 1255 Columbia Rd.
Phone: 835-8230.
Pool: 25y, indoors, heated, 78°-82°.
Admission: Call.

Affiliate: Bally's & IPFA: NC.
Hotel: Hampton Inn (892-0333), Holiday Inn (871-6000), & Red Roof Inn (892-7920): NC.
Masters: Contact General Manager Pam Braithwaite at 835-8230.

WEST SHORE FAMILY YMCA 1575 Columbia Rd.
Phone: 871-6885.
Pool: 20y, indoors, heated, 83°.
Admission: $6.
Affiliate: YMCA NC.

WILLOUGHBY   216

WEST END YMCA 37100 Euclid Ave.
Phone: 946-1160.
Pool: 25y, indoors, heated, 84°.
Affiliate: Y AWAY NC.

BALLY'S SCANDINAVIAN HEALTH SPA 5880 S.O.M. Center Rd.
Phone: 944-6888.
Pool: 25y, indoors, heated, 78°-82°.
Affiliate: Bally's & IPFA: NC.
Hotel: Fairfield Inn (975-9922), Harley Hotel (944-4300), & Holiday Inn in Euclid (585-2750): NC.

WILMINGTON   513

CLINTON COUNTY YMCA 700 Elm St.
Phone: 382-9622.
Pool: 25m, indoors, heated, 84°.
Affiliate: YMCA 6 visits NC.

WOOSTER   216

WOOSTER YMCA POOL at 515 Oldman Rd.
Phone: Pool: 345-4000. YMCA: 264-3131.
Pool: 50m x 25y, indoors, heated, 82°.
Admission: $3, SC(60) $2.
Affiliate: YMCA NC.
Notes: The address above is for the pool, the other YMCA facilities are at 680 Woodland Ave.
Masters: The Wooster YMCA Masters Swim Team. Contact Aquatics Director Carolyn Bare at 345-4000.

YOUNGSTOWN   216

CENTRAL BRANCH YMCA 17 N. Champion St.
Phone: 744-8411.
Pool 1: 25y, indoors, heated, 80°.
Pool 2: 25y, indoors, heated, 86°.
Admission: $8.
Affiliate: YMCA NC.
Masters: Contact Janine Meily at 744-8411.

YWCA OF YOUNGSTOWN 25 W. Rayen Ave.
Phone: 746-6361.
Pool: 20y x 30f, 5 lanes, indoors, heated, 85°.

YOUNGSTOWN   CONTINUED

Affiliate: YWCA $1.50, SC(65) $1.25.
To find: Across the street from Youngstown State University.

YOUNGSTOWN AREA JEWISH FEDERATION (JCC) 505 Gypsy Lane
Phone: 746-3251.
Pool: 25y, indoors, heated, 86°.

Admission: $5.
Affiliate: YM-YWHA, JCC, & U.S. Military: Call.

ZANESVILLE   614

HOLIDAY INN 4645 E. Pike
Phone: 453-0771. **Reservations:** 800 HOLIDAY.
Pool: 50f, rectangular, indoors, heated, 85°.
Admission: Registered guests only NC.

HELP MAKE THE NEXT *SWIMMERS GUIDE* EVEN BETTER

To receive a free copy of the next ***Swimmers Guide*** tell us about pools you know of that aren't in this edition. See page 14 for details.

ALTUS 405

ALTUS CITY / SCHOOL SWIMMING FACILITY
121 N. Park Lane
Phone: 481-2137.
Pool: 25m x 45f, 6 lanes, indoors, heated, 85°.
Admission: $2, SC(55) NC.
Notes: There is also a 25m x 25y, outdoor, unheated, seasonal pool.
To find: At the corner of Park Lane and Broadway.

ARDMORE 405

ARDMORE FAMILY YMCA 920 - 15th N.W.
Phone: 223-3990.
Pool: 25y, indoors, heated, 82°.
Admission: $5.
Affiliate: YMCA NC.

BARTLESVILLE 918

BARTLESVILLE YMCA 101 N. Osage
Phone: 336-0713.
Pool: 25m, indoors, heated, 83.5°.
Admission: $5.
Affiliate: YMCA $2.50.

BETHANY 405

WESTSIDE YMCA 3400 N. Mueller
Phone: 789-0231.
Pool: 25y x 60f, 3 - 4 lanes, indoors, heated, 85°.
Admission: $4.
Affiliate: Y AWAY 2 weeks NC. YMCA $4.
To find: Between Rockwell and MacArthur at the corner of 32nd and Mueller.

BIXBY 918

BIXBY PUBLIC SCHOOLS Riverview & Stadium Rd.
Phone: 366-4427.
Pool: 25m x 48f, 6 lanes, indoors, heated, 82°.
Admission: $2.
To find: On the Bixby High School Campus.

DAILY FAMILY YMCA 7910 E. 134th St. S.
Phone: 369-9622.
Pool: 25y, indoors, heated, 87°.
Admission: $5.
Affiliate: YMCA outside a 50 mile radius 3 visits per year NC.

EDMOND 405

EDMOND YMCA 1220 S. Rankin
Phone: 348-9622.
Pool: 25y, 4 lanes, indoors, heated, 84°.
Admission: $7.
Affiliate: Y AWAY NC. YMCA outside a 50 mile radius 3 visits per month NC.

ENID 405

ENID & GARFIELD COUNTY YMCA 415 W. Cherokee
Phone: 237-4645.
Pool: 20y, indoors, heated, 86°-87°.
Admission: $5.
Affiliate: YMCA NC.

LAWTON 405

LAWTON YMCA 5 S.W. 5th St.
Phone: 355-9622.
Pool 1: 25y x 37f, 6 lanes, indoors, heated, 82°.
Pool 2: 20m x 42f, 6 lanes, indoors, heated, 84°.
Admission: $5.
Affiliate: Y AWAY NC.
Hotel: Ramada Inn (355-7155) NC with a pass from the hotel.

To find: At the intersection of 5th St. and Gore Blvd.

MIDWEST CITY   405

TINKER AREA YMCA 2817 N. Woodcrest Dr.
Phone: 733-9622.
Pool: 25y, 4 lanes, indoors, heated, 85°.
Admission: $7.
Affiliate: YMCA NC.
To find: One block west of Heritage Park Shopping Mall.

NORMAN   405

MURRAY CASE SELLS MEMORIAL SWIM COMPLEX University of Oklahoma, 1401 Asp Ave.
Phone: 325-4837.
Pool: 25y x 60f, 8 lanes, indoors, heated, 82°.
Admission: Lap swims $1. Other swims $2, SC(65) $1.
Notes: There is also a 50m x 25y, 10 lane, outdoor, summer pool.
To find: Three blocks south of Oklahoma University's Owen Stadium.

CLEVELAND COUNTY FAMILY YMCA 1801 Halley Ave.
Phone: 364-9200.
Pool: 25y x 25m, 3 lanes, indoors, heated, 85°-86°.
Admission: $10.
Affiliate: Y AWAY NC. Out-of-town YMCA $2.
Hotel: Residence Inn (366-0900) NC with room key.
To find: On the University of Oklahoma North Campus / Research Park.

OKLAHOMA CITY   405

CENTRAL BRANCH YMCA 125 N.W. 5th St.
Phone: 297-7700.
Pool: 25y x 25f, 4 lanes, indoors, heated, 83°.
Admission: $10.
Affiliate: YMCA NC.
Hotel: Century Plaza Inn (232-5624) $5 with room key.

FOSTER INDOOR POOL 6140 N.W. 4th St. (off Lincoln)
Phone: 239-6898.
Pool: 20y, 4 lanes, indoors, heated, 86°.
Admission: $1.

SOUTH OKLAHOMA CITY YMCA 5325 S. Pennsylvania
Phone: 681-6636.
Pool: 25y x 25f, 4 lanes, indoors, heated, 86°.
Admission: $7.
Affiliate: Y AWAY 5 visits NC. YMCA 3 visits NC.

NORTH SIDE YMCA 10000 N. Pennsylvania
Phone: 751-6363.

Pool: 25y, 4 lanes, indoors, heated, 83°-84°.
Admission: $7.
Affiliate: YMCA 5 visits NC.

IONE BRANCH YWCA 6103 N.W. 58th
Phone: 721-2485.
Pool: 25y x 25f, 4 lanes, indoors, heated, 84°.
Admission: $5.
Affiliate: YWCA $2.
To find: Located four blocks west of MacArthur on 58th.

ALL AMERICAN FITNESS CENTER 6920 N.W. Expressway
Phone: 728-3600.
Pool: 23m, indoors, heated, 85°.
Affiliate: IPFA NC.

OKLAHOMA CITY COMMUNITY COLLEGE AQUATIC CENTER 7777 S. May Ave.
Phone: 682-7560.
Pool: 50m x 25y, 8 x 14 lanes, indoors, heated, 82°-84°.
Admission: $1.25, SC(60) 75¢.
Memberships: $50/semester (16 weeks), $125/year. SC 50% discount on both rates.
To find: In southwest Oklahoma City, near the airport, at the intersection of May Ave. and 74th.

PERRY   405

NOBLE COUNTY FAMILY YMCA 107 - 7th St.
Phone: 336-4411.
Pool: 25y, indoors, heated, 86°-87°.
Admission: Out-of-town visitors NC.

SAND SPRINGS   918

THE SALVATION ARMY BOY'S & GIRL'S CLUB / COMMUNITY CENTER 4403 S. 129th W. Ave.
Phone: 245-2237.
Pool: 20y, 4 lanes, indoors, heated, 82°.
Admission: $3.
To find: Take Hwy. 97 to 41st, go about two miles on 41st to 129th W. Ave., turn left and go one block.

TULSA   918

DOWNTOWN TULSA YMCA 515 S. Denver
Phone: 583-6201.
Pool: 25y x 25f, 5 lanes, indoors, heated, 78°-82°.
Admission: $8, photo ID required.
Affiliate: YMCA NC.
Hotel: Downtown Tulsa Hotel & Doubletree Hotel Downtown Tulsa (587-8000): NC with a pass from the hotel.
To find: At the intersection of S. Denver and 6th, across from the Tulsa County Courthouse.

PATTI JOHNSON WILSON YWCA 1910 S. Lewis
Phone: 749-2519.

Pool: 25m x 20f, 4 lanes, indoor/outdoor, heated, 85°.
Affiliate: YWCA $3.
To find: One block north of 21st on Lewis.

UNIVERSITY OF TULSA 600 S. College Ave.
Phone: 631-2000.
Pool: 25y, indoors, heated, 78°-82°.
Memberships: $75/semester.

W. L. HUTCHERSON BRANCH YMCA 1120 E. Pine St.
Phone: 585-1171.
Pool: 20y, indoors, heated, 84°-85°.
Admission: $3.

EAST YWCA 8145 E. 17th St.
Phone: 628-1030.
Pool: 25y, indoors, heated, 87°-88°.
Affiliate: YWCA $2.50.

SALVATION ARMY BOYS & GIRLS CLUB 1231 N. Harvard
Phone: 834-2464.
Pool: 25y, indoors, heated, 82°.
Memberships: $50/year.

BALLY'S HEALTH CLUB 8306 E. 61st St.
Phone: 250-7010.
Pool: 25m, indoors, heated, 83°.
Affiliate: Bally's NC.

THORNTON YMCA 5002 S. Fulton
Phone: 622-4500.
Pool: 25y, indoor/outdoor, heated, 82°-86°.
Admission: $8.
Affiliate: YMCA NC.
Hotel: Ramada Inn (622-7000) $4 with room key.

DOUBLETREE HOTEL AT WARREN PLACE 6110 S. Yale Ave.
Phone: 495-1000. **Reservations:** 800-528-0444.
Pool: 50f x 30f, rectangular, indoors, heated, 85°.
Admission: Registered guests only NC.

ALWAYS CALL FIRST

Pools close, they change names, affiliations, admission policies, and rates. And just because a pool is listed in *Swimmers Guide* doesn't mean it's open all day, every day, for just the type of workout you want to do. Spend a quarter to save time and aggravation. . . always call first!

ALBANY COMMUNITY POOL 2150 - 36th Ave. S.E.
Phone: 967-4521.
Pool: 50m OR 25y + 30y, indoors, heated, 83°-84°.
Admission: $2, SC(55) $1.75.
Notes: The pool is operated long course (50m lanes) in summer.

MID-WILLAMETTE FAMILY YMCA 3311 Pacific Blvd. S.W.
Phone: 926-4488.
Pool: 25y, 4 lanes, indoors, heated, 84°.
Admission: $5, SC(62) $2.50.
Affiliate: YMCA NC.
To find: On Pacific Blvd. S.W., near the intersection with 34th St.

ALOHA   503

ALOHA SWIM CENTER 18650 S.W. Kinnaman Rd.
Phone: 642-1586.
Pool: 25y x 42f, indoors, heated, 84°-86°.
Admission: $1.75, SC(62) $1.
To find: Next to Aloha High School. Tri-Met Bus #52 & #88.

ASHLAND   503

MCNEAL HALL Southern Oregon State College, 1250 Siskiyou Blvd.
Phone: 552-6236.
Pool: 25y, 6 lanes, indoors, heated, 68°-72°.
Admission: $2.
Memberships: $25/term (10-11 weeks).

BEAVERTON   503

HARMAN SWIM CENTER 7300 S.W. Scholls Ferry Rd.
Phone: 643-6681.
Pool: 25y x 42f, indoors, heated, 88°-90°.
Admission: $1.75, SC(62) $1.
To find: A few blocks from McKinley Grade School. Tri-Met Bus #56.

BEAVERTON SWIM CENTER 12850 S.W. 3rd St.
Phone: 644-1111.
Pool: 25y x 42f, indoors, heated, 84°-86°.
Admission: $1.75, SC(62) $1.
To find: Next to Beaverton High School. Tri-Met Bus #52 & #78.

GRIFFITH PARK ATHLETIC CLUB 4925 S.W. Griffith Dr.
Phone: 644-3900.
Pool: 25y, 4 lanes, indoors, heated, water temperature not reported.
Affiliate: IHRSA $6.
Hotel: Greenwood Inn (643-7444) & Residence Inn (288-1400): NC.

RECREATION SWIM CENTER 15707 S.W. Walker Rd.
Phone: 645-7454.
Pool: 50m x 25y, indoors, heated, 83°-84°.
Admission: $1.75, SC(62) $1.
To find: One mile south of the Cornell Rd. Exit off Sunset Hwy., across the street from the Fred Meyer Store. Tri-Met Bus #60.
Masters: The Tualatin Hills Barracudas Masters Swim Club. Contact Ben Davis at 629-5568(w) between 9AM and noon, or leave a message.

BEND   503

JUNIPER AQUATIC CENTER 800 N.E. 6th St.
Phone: 389-7665.
Pool: 25m, indoors, heated, 83°.
Admission: $2.75.
Masters: Contact Matt Mercer at 389-7665.

ATHLETIC CLUB OF BEND 61615 Mount Bachelor Dr.
Phone: 385-3062.
Pool: 25y, indoors, heated, 79°.
Affiliate: NACA $5. IHRSA $8.

CLACKAMAS   503

EAST SIDE ATHLETIC CLUB 9100 S. E. Sunnyside Rd.
Phone: 659-3846.
Pool: 25y, indoors, heated, 83°.
Affiliate: NACA NC.
Hotel: Monarch Hotel, Sunnyside Hotel, & Days Inn (654-1699): $6.

COOS BAY   503

BAY AREA ATHLETIC CLUB 985 Newmark
Phone: 888-5507.
Pool: 25y x 20f, 4 lanes, indoors, heated, 87°.
Admission: $7.
Affiliate: NACA NC.
Hotel: Pony Village Motor Lodge (756-3191) NC with room key. Red Lion Motel (267-4141) NC with a pass from the hotel.

CORVALLIS   503

OSBORN AQUATIC CENTER 1940 N.W. Highland Dr.
Phone: 757-5854.
Pool: 25y x 56f, 8 lanes, indoors, heated, 82°.
Admission: $2.25.
To find: At the corner of Higland Dr. and Circle. The Center shares a parking lot with the Highland View Middle School.
Masters: The Corvallis Aquatic Master Team. Contact Judy Storie at 757-5854.

THE DALLES   503

THE DALLES FITNESS & COURT CLUB 731 Pomona W.
Phone: 298-8508.
Pool: 20y x 30f, 4 lanes, indoors, heated, 85°.
Admission: $10.
Affiliate: NACA NC.
Hotel: Quality Inn The Dalles (298-5161) NC.

EUGENE   503

DOWNTOWN ATHLETIC CLUB 999 Willamette St.
Phone: 484-4011.
Pool: 25y x 45f, 4 lanes, indoors, heated, 82°.
Affiliate: NACA NC. IHRSA $7.
Hotel: Eugene Hilton (342-2000) & Valley River Inn (687-0123): $6 with a pass from the hotel.
Notes: There is also an 20f x 20f, indoor, heated, 86° pool.

EUGENE   CONTINUED

SHELDON POOL 2445 Willakenzie Rd.
Phone: 687-5314.
Pool: 25y x 42f, 6 lanes, indoors, heated, 85°.
Admission: $2.50, SC(62) $2.
To find: Off Coburg Rd., next to Sheldon High School.
Masters: Contact the pool staff at 687-5314.

COURTSPORTS ATHLETIC CLUB 4242 Commerce
Phone: 687-2255.
Pool: 25y, indoors, heated, 79°.
Affiliate: IHRSA Call.

RIVER ROAD PARK AND RECREATION DISTRICT POOL 1400 Lake Dr.
Phone: 461-7777.
Pool: 25y x 45f, indoors, heated, 84°.
Admission: Residents $1.75, SC(55) NC. Non-residents $2.25, SC $1.75.

EUGENE FAMILY YMCA 2055 Patterson St.
Phone: 686-9622.
Pool: 25y x 24f, 4 lanes, indoors, heated, 82°.
Admission: $5.
Affiliate: Y AWAY NC.
Masters: Contact Dick Moody or Aquatic Director Diane Plante at 686-9622.

FOREST GROVE   503

FOREST GROVE AQUATIC CENTER 2300 Sunset Dr.
Phone: 359-3238.
Pool: 25y x 42f, 6 lanes, indoors, heated, 86°.
Admission: Residents $2, SC(65) $1.25. Non-residents $2.80, SC $1.70.
Notes: There is also a 33m, outdoor, summer pool.
To find: Two blocks north of Pacific University.

GLENEDEN BEACH   503

SALISHAN LODGE Hwy. 101
Phone: 764-3600. **Reservations:** 800-452-2300.
Pool: 20y x 20f, rectangular, indoors, heated, 82°-84°.
Admission: $10. Registered guests NC.

GRANTS PASS   503

GRANTS PASS FAMILY YMCA 1000 Redwood Ave.
Phone: 474-0001.
Pool: 25m x 75f, 6 lanes, indoors, heated, 83°.
Admission: $3.50.
Affiliate: YMCA NC.
To find: Just south of the Fairgrounds on the Redwood Hwy.
Masters: The Grants Pass YMCA Masters. Contact Lisa Glen or leave a message for Coach Kjell Moline at 474-0001.

GRESHAM   503

CASCADE ATHLETIC CLUB 19201 S.E. Division
Phone: 665-4142.
Pool: 25y, indoors, heated, 81°.
Affiliate: IHRSA $8.

HILLSBORO   503

HILLSBORO AQUATIC CENTER 953 S.E. Maple St.
Phone: 681-6127.
Pool: 25m x 60f, 6 lanes, indoors, heated, 85°.
Admission: Residents $2.25, SC(62) $1.50. Non-residents $3.25, SC $2.50.

HOOD RIVER   503

HOOD RIVER SPORTS CLUB 3230 Brookside Dr.
Phone: 386-3230.
Pool: 25y x 27f, 4 lanes, indoors, heated, 84°.
Admission: $10.
Affiliate: NACA NC.
Hotel: The Inn at Hood River (386-2200) 1 visit per day NC with a pass from the hotel.
To find: On 13th St. (Tucker Rd.), turn right after NAPA Auto Parts. The club is the first building on the right.

KEIZER   503

COURTHOUSE ATHLETIC CLUB 6425 Wheatland Rd.
Phone: 391-5220.
Pool: 25y x 30f, 4 lanes, indoors, heated, 83°.
Affiliate: NACA NC. IHRSA $7.

KLAMATH FALLS   503

KLAMATH COUNTY FAMILY YMCA 1221 S. Alameda
Phone: 884-4149.
Pool: 25y x 27f, 4 lanes, indoors, heated, 86°.
Admission: $4.50.
Affiliate: YMCA NC.

LAKE OSWEGO   503

LAKE OSWEGO DISTRICT SWIM POOL 2400 Country Club Rd.
Phone: 635-0330.
Pool: 25y x 54f, 8 lanes, indoors, heated, 84°.
Admission: Residents $2, SC(55) $1. Non-residents $2.50, SC $1.50.
To find: On the campus of the Lake Oswego High School.

RIVER'S EDGE ATHLETIC CLUB 5450 S.W. Childs Rd.
Phone: 620-7322.
Pool: 20y x 40f, 5 lanes, indoors, heated, 84°.
Affiliate: NACA NC.
To find: One and a half miles from I-5. Take the Lake Oswego Exit (Exit 290).

LINCOLN CITY — 503

LINCOLN CITY COMMUNITY CENTER POOL
2850 N.E. Oar Place
Phone: 994-5208.
Pool: 25m x 42f, 6 lanes, indoors, heated, 85°.
Admission: Residents $1.50, SC(62) $1. Non-residents $1.75, SC $1.25. Disabled 50% of the applicable rate.
To find: Turn east from Hwy. 101 onto N.E. 21st, then take the first right.
Masters: The Lincoln City Masters. Contact Gail Kimberling at 994-7595(h).

MCMINNVILLE — 503

MCMINNVILLE AQUATIC CENTER 138 Park Dr.
Phone: 434-7309.
Pool 1: 25y, indoors, heated, 82°.
Pool 2: 20y, indoors, heated, 86°.
Admission: $2.

MEDFORD — 503

ROGUE VALLEY FAMILY YMCA 522 W. 6th St.
Phone: 772-6295.
Pool: 25y, 8 lanes, indoors, heated, 84°.
Admission: $5, SC $3. Non-member use restricted to off peak hours. Call.
Affiliate: YMCA NC.
To find: At the convergence of Main and 6th Sts.

SUPERIOR ATHLETIC CLUB 727 Cardley Ave.
Phone: 779-7529.
Pool: 25y, 6 lanes, indoors, heated, 82°-83°.
Admission: $7.

MILWAUKIE — 503

NORTH CLACKAMAS AQUATIC PARK 7300 S.E. Harmony Rd.
Phone: 557-7873.
Pool: 25y x 45f, 6 lanes, indoors, heated, 84°.
Admission: Lap swimming: Residents $2, non-residents $3. Higher prices for open swims.
To find: Behind the Toys 'R' Us on 82nd & Harmony Rd. One mile west of the Clackamas Town Center, off I-205.

EAST SIDE ATHLETIC CLUB 4606 S.E. Boardman
Phone: 659-3845.
Pool: 20y, indoors, heated, 84°.
Affiliate: NACA NC. IHRSA Call.

NEHALEM — 503

NEHALEM BAY CENTER Tillamook Bay Community College
Phone: 368-7121.
Pool: 25y x 35f, 4 lanes, indoors, heated, 85°.
Admission: $2.
Memberships: 1/3 months $22.50/$45. SC $22.50/quarter.
To find: Off Hwy. 101 north on 9th St. one block.

NEWBERG — 503

CHEHALEM POOL 1802 Haworth Ave.
Phone: 538-4813.
Pool: 25y, indoors, heated, 86°.
Admission: $2, SC(60) $1.50.
Masters: The Chehalem Masters Swim Team. Contact Coach Steve Roth at 538-7454(w).

NEWPORT — 503

NEWPORT YMCA SWIMMING POOL 1212 N.E. Fogarty
Phone: 265-7770.
Pool: 25y x 42f, 6 lanes, indoors, heated, 83°.
Admission: $2, SC(62) $1.50.
Affiliate: YMCA NC.

NORTH BEND — 503

NORTH BEND MUNICIPAL SWIMMING POOL
2401 Pacific St. (15th & Pacific)
Phone: 756-4915.
Pool: 25m x 25y, 6 x 6 lanes, indoors, heated, 84°.
Admission: Residents $1.50, SC(60) $1.25. Non-residents $2.25, SC $2.
To find: Next to North Bend High School, directly behind (south of) Pony Village Shopping Mall.
Masters: The North Bend Masters. Contact Alice Parsons at 756-4915.

ONTARIO — 503

ONTARIO AQUATIC & FITNESS CENTER 790 S.W. 3rd Ave.
Phone: 889-7946.
Pool: 25m x 45f, 6 lanes, indoors, heated, 84°.
Admission: $2.25, SC(55) $1.25.
To find: Below the hospital on S.W. 4th Ave. in Lions Park.

OREGON CITY — 503

OREGON CITY MUNICIPAL SWIMMING POOL
1211 Jackson
Phone: 657-8273.
Pool: 25m x 42f, 6 lanes, indoors, heated, 84°.
Admission: $1.50, SC(55) $1.
To find: Across the street from Oregon City High School.

PENDLETON — 503

ROUNDUP ATHLETIC CLUB 1415 Southgate
Phone: 276-0880.
Pool: 25m x 28f, 4 lanes, indoors, heated, 83°.
Admission: $7.
Affiliate: NACA & IHRSA: NC.
Hotel: Red Lion Motor Inn (276-6111) NC with room key. Tapadera Inn (276-3231) NC with a pass from the hotel.

PORTLAND 503

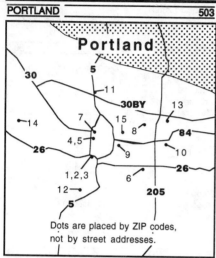

Portland

30
5
11
30BY 13
14
7 15
8
84
4,5
26
9 10
1,2,3 26
6
12 205
5

Dots are placed by ZIP codes, not by street addresses.

6. SOUTHEAST FAMILY YMCA 6036 S.E. Foster Rd.
Phone: 294-3311.
Pool: 20y x 30f, 5 lanes, indoors, heated, 86°.
Admission: $4, SC(55) $1.50.
Affiliate: Y AWAY NC.
To find: Foster Rd. is in front of the building, Holgate is in back.

7. METROPOLITAN LEARNING CENTER POOL 2033 N.W. Glisan St.
Phone: 823-3671.
Pool: 20y x 21f, indoors, heated, 86°.
Admission: $1.75.
To find: On the lower level of the Metropolitan Learning Center School.

8. DISHMAN POOL 77 N.E. Knott
Phone: 823-3673.
Pool: 25y, indoors, heated, 82°-84°.
Admission: $1.75.
Masters: The Portland Parks Masters Swim Team. Contact John Zell at 282-9347(h).

9. BUCKMAN POOL 320 S.E. 16th Ave.
Phone: 823-3668.
Pool: 20y x 24f, indoors, heated, 84°-86°.
Admission: $1.75.
To find: On the lower level of Buckman Elementary School.

10. CASCADE ATHLETIC CLUB 9260 S.E. Stark
Phone: 257-4142.
Pool: 25y, indoors, heated, 81°-82°.
Affiliate: IHRSA $6.

11. COLUMBIA POOL 7701 N. Chautauqua Blvd.
Phone: 823-3669.
Pool 1: 25y x 36f, indoors, heated, 84°-86°.
Pool 2: 25y x 36f, indoors, heated, 84°-86°.
Admission: $1.75.
To find: One block north of Lombard, in Columbia Park.

12. PORTLAND COMMUNITY COLLEGE 12000 S.W. 49th Ave.
Phone: 244-6111 ext. 4210.
Pool: 25y, 6 lanes, indoors, heated, 84°.
Memberships: $37*/college term, SC(62) $22*.
Notes: *Plus $18 parking permit.

13. USA OREGON ATHLETIC CLUB 8333 N.E. Russell St.
Phone: 254-5546.
Pool: 25m, indoors, heated, 80°-82°.
Affiliate: IPFA NC.

14. SUNSET SWIM CENTER 13707 N.W. Science Park Dr.
Phone: 644-9770.
Pool: 25y x 42f, indoors, heated, 84°-86°.
Admission: $1.75, SC(62) $1.

1. WILLAMETTE ATHLETIC CLUB 4949 S.W. Landing Dr.
Phone: 225-1068.
Pool: 25y, 4 lanes, indoors, heated, 82°.
Affiliate: NACA & IHRSA: $10.
To find: South of downtown, in John's Landing District, off Macadan Ave.

2. METRO FAMILY YMCA 2831 S.W. Barbur Blvd.
Phone: 294-3366.
Pool: 25m, 6 lanes, indoors, heated, 83°.
Admission: $10.
Affiliate: YMCA 7 visits per year NC, then $5.
Masters: The Metro Masters. Contact Dirk Marshall or Charles Von Rosen at 294-3366.

3. RIVER PLACE ATHLETIC CLUB 0150 S.W. Montgomery
Phone: 221-1212.
Pool: 25y, indoors, heated, 82°-85°.
Hotel: River Place Hotel $8. Other Portland hotels $15.

4. YWCA FITNESS & SWIM CENTER 1111 S.W. 10th Ave.
Phone: 223-6281 ext. 3033.
Pool: 25y x 30f, 4 lanes, indoors, heated, 84.5°.
Admission: $5.50, SC(62) $3.75.
Affiliate: YWCA $3.75.
To find: Four blocks west of the downtown Hilton.

5. PRINCETON ATHLETIC CLUB 614 S.W. 11th Ave.
Phone: 222-2639.
Pool: 20y x 40f, 3 lanes, indoors, heated, 80°.
Admission: $15.
Affiliate: USMS & U.S. Military: $10.
Hotel: Heathman Hotel (241-4100) & Vintage Hotel: $8 with a voucher from the hotel. Governor Hotel (224-3400) $10 with a voucher from the hotel.
To find: In the Govenor Hotel, 11th Ave. at Alder.

To find: Next to Sunset High School. Tri-Met Bus #89 & #67.

15. NORTHEAST FAMILY YMCA 1630 N.E. 38th Ave.
Phone: 294-3377.
Pool: 20y, 4 lanes, indoors, heated, 86°.
Admission: $9.
Affiliate: YMCA outside a 50 mile radius NC.

ROSEBURG   503

DOUGLAS COUNTY FAMILY YMCA 1151 Stewart Pkwy.
Phone: 440-9622.
Pool 1: 25y x 42f, 6 lanes, indoors, heated, 82°.
Pool 2: 25y x 25f, 4 lanes, indoors, heated, 87°.
Admission: $5.
Affiliate: YMCA NC.
Masters: The Umpqua Valley Masters. Contact Terry McCurdy at 440-9622.

SALEM   503

OLINGER POOL 1310 'A' St. N.E.
Phone: 588-6332.
Pool: 25y, indoors, heated, 84°.
Admission: $2.50, SC(55) $1.75.

SALEM FAMILY YMCA 685 Court St. N.E.
Phone: 581-9622.
Pool: 20y, 4 lanes, indoors, heated, 83°-84°.
Admission: $6.
Affiliate: Y AWAY NC.

YWCA OF SALEM 768 State St.
Phone: 581-9922.
Pool: 20y x 28f, 5 lanes, indoors, heated, 88°.
Admission: $3.
To find: Behind the Capitol and across from Willamette University.

COURTHOUSE ATHLETIC CLUB 2975 River Rd. S.
Phone: 364-8463.
Pool: 25y x 30f, 4 lanes, indoors, heated, 83°.
Affiliate: NACA NC. IHRSA $7.

COURTHOUSE ATHLETIC CLUB 4132 Devonshire Court N.E.
Phone: 585-2582.
Pool: 25y x 30f, 4 lanes, indoors, heated, 83°.
Affiliate: NACA NC. IHRSA $7.

SEASIDE   503

SUNSET POOL 1140 E. Broadway
Phone: 738-3311.

Pool: 25y x 38f, 6 lanes, indoors, heated, 86°.
Admission: Residents $2, SC(65) $1.25. Non-residents $2.25, SC $1.50.
To find: One half block east of Hwy. 101.

SPRINGFIELD   503

WILLAMALANE PARK SWIM CENTER 1276 'G' St.
Phone: 726-4366.
Pool: 25y, 6 lanes, indoors, heated, 84°.
Admission: Residents $1.50, SC(55) $1. Non-residents $2.25, SC $1.50.

LIVELY PARK SWIM CENTER 6100 Thurston Rd.
Phone: 747-9283 or 726-2752.
Pool: 25y, 6 lanes, indoors, heated, 84°-86°.
Admission: Residents $1.50, SC(55) $1. Non-residents $2.25, SC $1.50.

SWEET HOME   503

SWEET HOME POOL 1641 Long St.
Phone: 367-7169.
Pool: 25y, indoors, heated, water temperature not reported.
Admission: $2.

TIGARD   503

TIGARD SWIM CENTER 8680 S.W. Durham Rd.
Phone: 684-2100.
Pool: 25y x 45f, 6 lanes, indoors, heated, 84°.
Admission: $2.
To find: At the corner of Hall Blvd. and Durham Rd.

TILLAMOOK   503

TILLAMOOK COUNTY FAMILY YMCA 610 Stillwell Ave.
Phone: 842-9622.
Pool: 25y x 40f, 6 lanes, indoors, heated, 84°-85°.
Admission: $6, SC(60) $5.50.
Affiliate: Y AWAY NC.
To find: One block west of Hwy. 101 between 6th and 7th Sts.

TOLEDO   503

TOLEDO CITY POOL 174 N.W. 7th St.
Phone: 336-3181.
Pool: 25y x 45f, 5 lanes, indoors, heated, 86°.
Admission: $2, SC(60) $1.
To find: At the 'A' St. Park next to the library and tennis courts.

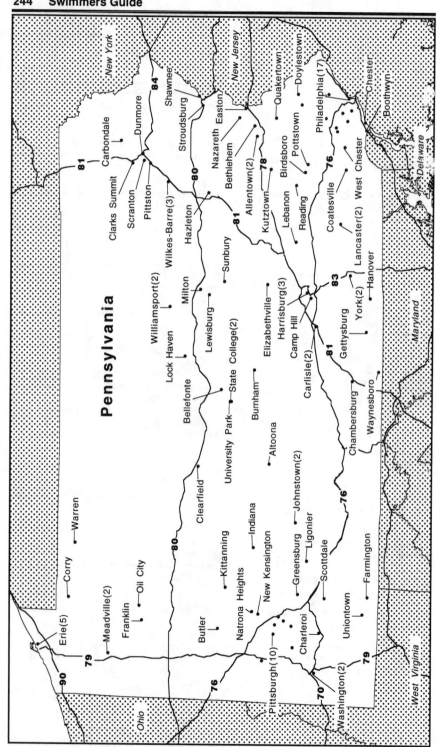

Philadelphia Area

Doylestown
Chalfont
Hatboro
Willow Grove
Lansdale Ambler
Feasterville
Fairless Hills
Phoenixville
Abington
276
Jenkintown
Berwyn
76
King of Prussia
Ardmore
West Chester
Philadelphia(17)
New Jersey
Broomall
476 Lansdowne
Chester 95
Boothwyn
295
Delaware
295

Pittsburgh Area

Sewickley
Natrona Heights
New Kensington
279
Penn Hills
Pittsburgh(10)
376
Monroeville 76
79
Wilmerding
Bethel Park McKeesport
Washington(2)
Charleroi 70

ABINGTON   215

ABINGTON YMCA 1073 Old York Rd.
Phone: 884-9622.
Pool: 20y, 3 lanes, indoors, heated, 86°.
Admission: $5.
Affiliate: YMCA $2.50.

ALLENTOWN   610

ALLENTOWN YM / YWCA 425 S. 15th St.
Phone: 432-6821.
Pool: 25y, 5 lanes, indoors, heated, 85°.
Admission: $8.
Affiliate: Y AWAY & YWCA both outside a 35 mile radius NC, within 35 miles $4.

WESTEND RACQUET CLUB 4636 Crackersport Rd.
Phone: 395-3337.
Pool: 25m x 54f, 6 lanes, indoor/outdoor, heated, 82°.
Admission: $12. M-F 4PM-8PM $15.
Hotel: Days Inn Conference Center (395-3731) 1 visit NC.

ALTOONA 814

THE SUMMIT ATHLETIC CLUB Regency Square, Plank Rd. & Route 220
Phone: 946-1668.
Pool: 25y, 4 lanes, indoors, heated, 83°-84°.
Admission: $10.
Affiliate: IHRSA $5.
Hotel: Days Inn Altoona (944-9661) & Ho Jo Inn Altoona (946-7601): Passes available at the hotels for $5. Holiday Inn Altoona (944-4581) $5 with room key.

AMBLER 215

AMBLER AREA YMCA 400 Bethlehem Pike
Phone: 628-9950.
Pool: 25y, 6 lanes, indoors, heated, 85°.
Admission: $8.
Affiliate: Y AWAY NC.

ARDMORE 610

MAIN LINE YMCA 100 St. George's Rd.
Phone: 649-0700.
Pool: 25y, 4 lanes, indoors, heated, 85°.
Admission: $5.
Affiliate: Y AWAY outside a 50 mile radius NC, within 50 miles $2.50.
To find: Across the street from the Suburban Square Shopping Center.

BELLEFONTE 814

BELLEFONTE FAMILY YMCA 125 W. High St.
Phone: 355-5551.
Pool: 23.5y, 4 lanes, indoors, heated, 82°.
Admission: $5.
Affiliate: Y AWAY 3 visits per month NC, then $2.50.
To find: Down the street from the Centre County Courthouse.
Masters: The Bellefonte Masters Swim Team. Contact John R. Shipp at 237-9515(h).

BERWYN 610

UPPER MAIN LINE YMCA 1416 Berwyn-Paoli Rd.
Phone: 647-9622.
Pool 1: 25y x 45f, 6 lanes, indoors, heated, 80°.
Pool 2: 25y x 45f, 6 lanes, indoors, heated, 86°.
Affiliate: Y AWAY outside a 50 mile radius NC.
Notes: There is also a 50m, 6 lane, outdoor, heated, 80°-82° pool operated from Apr. through Oct.
Masters: The Upper Main Line Y Masters. Contact Ruth Small at 649-9622 ext. 267.

BETHEL PARK 412

BALLY'S SCANDINAVIAN HEALTH SPA 3000 Oxford Dr.
Phone: 833-7200.
Pool: 25y, indoors, heated, 84°.

Affiliate: Bally's & IPFA: NC.
Hotel: Holiday Inn South Hills NC.

BETHLEHEM 610

BETHLEHEM YMCA 430 E. Broad St.
Phone: 867-7588.
Pool: 25y, indoors, heated, 80°-85°.
Affiliate: YMCA 3 visits NC, then $3.

BIRDSBORO 610

AQUABILITIES SWIM SCHOOL & AQUATIC FITNESS CENTER 320 W. Main St.
Phone: 582-2348.
Pool: 25y x 24f, 3 lanes, indoors, heated, 86°.
Admission: $6.
To find: Next door to a pharmacy.

BOOTHWYN 610

CHICHESTER HIGH SCHOOL Chichester Community Aquatic Program, 3333 Chichester Ave.
Phone: 485-6888.
Pool: 25y x 42f, 6 lanes, indoors, heated, 82°.
Admission: $1.
Notes: The pool is closed in Jul. and Aug.

BROOMALL 610

SUSSEX FITNESS CENTER 1101 Sussex Blvd.
Phone: 328-2610.
Pool: 25y x 20f, 4 lanes, indoors, heated, 83°.
Admission: $5.
Affiliate: IHRSA outside a 50 mile radius $2.50.
Notes: Baby sitting is available M-F 9AM-Noon.
To find: In the Lawrence Park Industrial Center.

BURNHAM 717

JUNIATA VALLEY YMCA 105 - 1st Ave.
Phone: 248-5019.
Pool: 25y x 35f, 4 lanes, indoors, heated, 78°-80°.
Admission: Out-of-town visitors — Call.
Affiliate: YMCA & YWCA: NC.

BUTLER 412

BUTLER COUNTY FAMILY YMCA 339 N. Washington Blvd.
Phone: 287-4733.
Pool: 25m, indoors, heated, 82°-84°.
Admission: $5.
Affiliate: Y AWAY $2.50.

CAMP HILL 717

WEST SHORE YMCA 410 Fallowfield Rd.
Phone: 737-0511.
Pool 1: 25y x 45f, 6 lanes, indoors, heated, 84°-85°.

Pool 2: 25y x 45f, 6 lanes, indoors, heated, 84°-85°.
Admission: Basic $15. Health & Fitness Center $20.
Affiliate: Y AWAY NC. YMCA: Basic $3, Health & Fitness Center $5.
To find: One half mile west of the Camp Hill Mall off Trindale Rd.
Masters: The West Shore YMCA Masters. Contact Mike Gobrecht at 737-0511.

CARBONDALE   717

CARBONDALE YMCA 82 N. Main St.
Phone: 282-2210.
Pool: 64f x 25f, 3 lanes, indoors, heated, 86°.
Admission: Basic $2. Full facility $5.
Affiliate: Y AWAY NC. YMCA full facility $2.50.
To find: On Main St., two blocks north of City Hall. Main St. is U.S. Route 6.

CARLISLE   717

CLARKE AQUATIC CENTER Kline Center, Dickinson College
Phone: 245-1523.
Pool: 25y x 52f, 8 lanes, indoors, heated, 81°.
Admission: Out-of-town visitors — Call.
Memberships: 4 months $52.
To find: In Kline Center, the large gymnasium on campus.

CARLISLE YMCA 311 S. West St.
Phone: 243-2525.
Pool: 25y, indoors, heated, 84°-85°.
Affiliate: YMCA outside an unspecified radius NC. U.S. Military $3.
Masters: The Carlisle Masters. Contact Bill Pappalardo at 243-2525.

CHALFONT   215

HIGHPOINT ATHLETIC CLUB 1 Highpoint Dr.
Phone: 822-2303.
Pool: 25y, 6 lanes, indoor/outdoor, heated, 80°.
Admission: 3 visits per year $10 each.
Affiliate: IHRSA $5.

CHAMBERSBURG   717

CHAMBERSBURG YMCA 570 E. McKinley
Phone: 263-8508.
Pool 1: 25y, indoors, heated, 80°-85°.
Pool 2: 25y, indoors, heated, 80°-85°.
Admission: $3.50.
Affiliate: YMCA NC.

CHARLEROI   412

MON VALLEY YMCA Route 88, Taylor Run Rd.
Phone: 483-8077.
Pool: 25y, indoors, heated, 85°.
Admission: $8.

Affiliate: YMCA outside a 30 mile radius NC, within 30 miles 2 visits per month NC.

CHESTER   610

YWCA OF CHESTER 7th & Sproul Sts.
Phone: 876-8226.
Pool: 25y, 3 lanes, indoors, heated, water temperature not reported.
Admission: $1.50.

CLARKS SUMMIT   717

ABINGTON HEIGHTS HIGH SCHOOL, NORTH CAMPUS Noble Rd.
Phone: 586-2511.
Pool: 25y, 6 lanes, indoors, heated, 82°.
Admission: $2, SC with Gold Card NC.

CLEARFIELD   814

CLEARFIELD YMCA 21 N. 2nd St.
Phone: 765-5521.
Pool: 20y x 45f, 3 lanes, indoors, heated, 84°.
Admission: $3.50.
Affiliate: Y AWAY NC.
Masters: The Allegheny Mt. YMCA Masters Swim League. Contact Christal Jensen at 765-5521.

COATESVILLE   610

BRANDYWINE YMCA 650 Hurley Rd.
Phone: 384-5084.
Pool: 25m, 6 lanes, indoors, heated, water temperature not reported.
Admission: Out-of-town visitors — Call.
Affiliate: YMCA outside a 50 mile radius 5 visits per year NC.
Notes: There is also an outdoor, summer pool.
To find: One quarter mile from the Route 30 Bypass. Take the Brandywine Hospital Exit.

CORRY   814

CORRY YMCA 906 N. Center St.
Phone: 664-7757.
Pool: 20y x 32f, 4 lanes, indoors, heated, 84°.
Admission: $3.
Affiliate: Y AWAY & U.S. Military: NC. YMCA Call.
To find: Next to a church and Quality Market Food Store.

DOYLESTOWN   215

CENTRAL BUCKS FAMILY YMCA 2500 Lower State Rd.
Phone: 348-8131.
Pool: 25m, 6 lanes, indoors, heated, 86°.
Affiliate: Y AWAY outside a 60 mile radius NC.

DUNMORE 717

GREATER SCRANTON YMCA 706 N. Blakely St.
Phone: 342-8115.
Pool: 25y x 48f, 6 lanes, indoors, heated, 85°.
Admission: $12.
Affiliate: YMCA NC.
To find: Behind Friendly's Restaurant.
Masters: The Stingrays. Contact Diana Dempsey at 342-8115.

EASTON 610

THIRD STREET ALLIANCE FOR WOMEN & CHILDREN 41 N. 3rd St.
Phone: 258-6271.
Pool: 20y, indoors, heated, 88°-90°.
Admission: $2.50, SC(62) $2.

ELIZABETHVILLE 717

NORTHERN DAUPHIN COUNTY YMCA W. Church St.
Phone: 362-9494.
Pool: 25y, 6 lanes, indoors, heated, 84°.
Admission: $6.
Affiliate: Y AWAY $3.
Notes: A new facility, the pool and Y opened in mid-1994.

ERIE 814

DOWNTOWN BRANCH YMCA 31 W. 10th St.
Phone: 452-3261.
Pool: 20y, indoors, heated, 83°.
Admission: $7.
Affiliate: Y AWAY NC.

NAUTILUS FITNESS & RACQUET CLUB 2312 W. 15th St.
Phone: 459-3033.
Pool: 25y, indoors, heated, 82°.
Admission: $10.

YWCA OF ERIE 4247 W. Ridge Rd.
Phone: 838-9671.
Pool: 25y, indoors, heated, 88°.
Admission: $3.

GLENWOOD PARK FAMILY BRANCH YMCA 3727 Cherry St.
Phone: 868-0867.
Pool: 25y, 4 lanes, indoors, heated, 82°.
Admission: $7.
Affiliate: Y AWAY NC.

THE PENNBRIAR ATHLETIC CLUB 100 Pennbriar Dr.
Phone: 825-8111.
Pool: 25y x 30f, 2 lanes, indoors, heated, 84°.
Admission: $12.
Affiliate: IHRSA $7.
Hotel: Holiday Inn-South (864-4911) & Holiday Inn-

Downtown (456-2961): NC.
To find: Turn right one light north of I-90 on Route 97 N.

FAIRLESS HILLS 215

LOWER BUCKS COUNTY YMCA Oxford Valley Rd.
Phone: 949-3400.
Pool: 25y, indoors, heated, 86°.
Affiliate: YMCA $3.

FARMINGTON 412

NEMACOLIN WOODLANDS RESORT Route 40
Phone: 329-8555. **Reservations:** 800-422-2736.
Pool: 63.5f x 22.5f, rectangular, indoors, heated, 84°.
Admission: Registered guests only NC.

FEASTERVILLE 215

B & R FULL HEALTH & FITNESS CLUB 1040 Mill Creek Dr.
Phone: 355-2700.
Pool: 25m, 6 lanes, indoors, heated, 85°.
Affiliate: IHRSA $10.

FRANKLIN 814

FRANKLIN YMCA Otter & W. Park St.
Phone: 432-2138.
Pool: 25y, indoors, heated, 82°-84°.
Admission: $5.
Hotel: The Inn at Franklin (437-3031) NC.

GETTYSBURG 717

GETTYSBURG YWCA 909 Fairfield Rd.
Phone: 334-9171.
Pool: 25m x 46f, 6 lanes, indoors, heated, 84°.
Admission: $3.
To find: Behind the Lutheran Theological Seminary on Route 116 W.

GREENSBURG 412

GREENSBURG YMCA 101 S. Maple Ave.
Phone: 834-0150.
Pool: 25y, indoors, heated, 85°.
Admission: 1 visit $5.
Affiliate: YMCA 3 visits NC, then $5.
Hotel: Knights Inn (836-7100) & Sheraton Inn (836-6060): Call the Y for information.
Masters: The Greensburg YMCA Masters. Contact the Aquatic Office at 834-0150.

HANOVER 717

HANOVER AREA YMCA 500 N. George St.
Phone: 632-8211.
Pool: 25m, 6 lanes, indoors, heated, 82°-84°.
Affiliate: Y AWAY NC.

HARRISBURG   717

EAST SHORE YMCA Front & North St.
Phone: 232-9622.
Pool: 70f x 35f, 4 lanes, indoors, heated, 86°.
Affiliate: Y AWAY outside a 50 mile radius 4 visits
per month NC, then $2.50.
To find: Two blocks from the Capitol Complex.

CENTRAL PENN FITNESS CENTER 450 Powers
Ave. #103
Phone: 564-4171.
Pool: 25y, indoors, heated, 85°.
Admission: $10.

SHERATON INN-HARRISBURG 800 E. Park Dr.
Phone: 561-2800. **Reservations:** 800-325-3535.
Pool: 50f, rectangular, indoors, heated, 78°.
Admission: $5. Registered guests NC.

HATBORO   215

HATBORO AREA YMCA 440 S. York Rd.
Phone: 674-4545.
Pool: 25y, 6 lanes, indoors, heated, 85°.
Admission: $5.
Affiliate: YMCA $3.
Masters: Contact C.R. Levy at 674-4545.

HAZLETON   717

HAZLETON YMCA & YWCA 75 S. Church St.
Phone: 455-2046.
Pool: 25y x 25f, 4 lanes, indoors, heated, 86°.
Admission: 3 visits per year $6 each.
Affiliate: Y AWAY & YWCA: 3 visits NC, then
$1.50. YMCA $1.50.

INDIANA   412

INDIANA COUNTY YMCA Ben Franklin Rd. & 422
W.
Phone: 463-9622 or 465-2655.
Pool: 25y, 6 lanes, indoors, heated, 85°.
Admission: 1 visit NC.
Affiliate: Y AWAY NC.
Hotel: Holiday Inn (463-3561) NC with room key.
Masters: The Indiana County YMCA Masters.
Contact Eric Neel at 463-9622 or 465-2655.

JENKINTOWN   215

THE ABINGTON FITNESS & COUNTRY CLUB
300 Meeting House Rd.
Phone: 885-0734.
Pool: 25y x 35f, 7 lanes, indoors, heated, 82°.
Admission: $8.
To find: Off State Route 611 directly behind the
Benjamin Fox Pavillion.

JOHNSTOWN   814

JOHNSTOWN YMCA 100 Haynes St.

Phone: 535-8381.
Pool: 25m, 6 lanes, indoors, heated, 86°.
Admission: $10.
Affiliate: YMCA NC.

YWCA OF JOHNSTOWN 526 Somerset St.
Phone: 536-3519.
Pool: 25y, indoors, heated, 87°.
Admission: $3.50.

KING OF PRUSSIA   610

BALLY'S HOLIDAY SPA 256 Goddard Blvd.
Phone: 768-0710.
Pool: 25y, indoors, heated, 80°.
Admission: Call.
Affiliate: Bally's NC.
Hotel: Holiday Inn (265-7500) NC.

KITTANNING   412

ARMSTRONG COUNTY YMCA 138 N. Water St.
Phone: 543-1045.
Pool: 20y x 25f, 4 lanes, indoors, heated, 85°.
Admission: $3.
Affiliate: Y AWAY & U.S. Military: NC. YMCA out-
side a 50 mile radius 3 visits NC, then 3 visits $3
each.

KUTZTOWN   610

KEYSTONE POOL Keystone Hall, Kutztown
University
Phone: 683-4359.
Pool: 25y, 6 lanes, indoors, heated, 80°.
Admission: $1*.
Memberships: $40/semester.
Notes: *Passes are sold at the Athletic Office, M-F
8:30AM-4:30PM.

LANCASTER   717

YWCA OF LANCASTER 110 N. Lime St.
Phone: 393-1735.
Pool: 20y, indoors, heated, 86°.
Admission: Call.

LANCASTER FAMILY YMCA 572 N. Queen St.
Phone: 397-7474.
Pool: 25y, 6 lanes, indoors, heated, 83°.
Admission: $8-$11. Call the Aquatic Director.
Affiliate: Y AWAY outside a 50 mile radius NC,
within 50 miles 50% of applicable 'admission' rate.
YMCA Call.
To find: Across from Lane General Hospital.
Masters: Contact Cece O'Day at 393-4178(h).

LANSDALE   215

NORTH PENN YMCA 608 E. Main St.
Phone: 368-1601.
Pool 1: 25y, 6 lanes, indoors, heated, 82°-88°.
Pool 2: 25y, 4 lanes, indoors, heated, 82°-88°.

Affiliate: Y AWAY NC.
Masters: The Colonials. Contact Christal Jensen at 368-1601 ext. 211.

LANSDOWNE   610

COMMUNITY YMCA OF EASTERN DELAWARE COUNTY 2110 Garrett Rd.
Phone: 259-1661.
Pool: 25y x 42f, 6 lanes, indoors, heated, 85°.
Admission: $5.
Affiliate: YMCA outside a 50 mile radius $2.50.
To find: At the intersection of Garrett Rd. and Lansdowne Ave., across from Trolley tracks.
Masters: The CY Masters. Contact Tom Newsham at 259-1661.

LEBANON   717

LEBANON VALLEY FAMILY YMCA 201 N. 7th St.
Phone: 273-2691.
Pool: 25m, indoors, heated, 85°-86°.
Admission: $10.
Affiliate: Y AWAY NC.
Masters: The Leby Masters. Contact Karen Mailen or Jim Gichener at 273-2691.

LEWISBURG   717

FREAS-ROOKE POOL Bucknell University
Phone: 524-1211 or 524-1232.
Pool: 25y x 42f, 6 lanes, indoors, heated, 80°-82°.
Memberships: 6/12 months $150/$250. SC(62) $50 one-time fee.

LIGONIER   412

LIGONIER YMCA 110 W. Church St.
Phone: 238-7580.
Pool: 25y, indoors, heated, 86°.
Admission: $5.
Affiliate: YMCA NC.

LOCK HAVEN   717

LOCK HAVEN AREA YMCA Grove & Water Sts.
Phone: 748-6727.
Pool: 25y, indoors, heated, 83°-84°.
Admission: $3.
Affiliate: YMCA Call.
Hotel: Lindsay Place (748-3297) NC with room key.

MCKEESPORT   412

MCKEESPORT YMCA 523 Sinclair St.
Phone: 664-9168.
Pool: 25m, indoors, heated, 84°-89°.
Affiliate: YMCA NC.

MEADVILLE   814

MEADVILLE YMCA 356 Chestnut St.
Phone: 336-2196.

Pool: 20y, 4 lanes, indoors, heated, 88° in winter, 84° in summer.
Admission: $4.
Affiliate: YMCA NC.

YWCA OF MEADVILLE 378 Chestnut St.
Phone: 337-4279.
Pool: 25y x 50f, 6 lanes, indoors, heated, 84°.
Admission: $3.
Affiliate: YWCA $2.
Notes: One side of the pool is reserved for laps. Arthritis, Senior Swim, and Aqua Dance are also offered.
To find: The 6th building on the right from Diamond Park, when heading west on Chestnut St.
Masters: The YWCA Masters. Contact Dick Fryling at 337-4279.

MILTON   717

MILTON YMCA 12 Bound Ave.
Phone: 742-7321.
Pool: 20y, indoors, heated, 85°.
Admission: $6.
Affiliate: Y AWAY NC.

MONROEVILLE   412

THE RACQUET CLUB OF PITTSBURGH 1 Racquet Lane
Phone: 856-3930.
Pool: 25m, indoors, heated, 82°-84°.
Affiliate: IHRSA $10.
Hotel: Radisson Hotel (373-7300) NC with a voucher from the hotel.

NATRONA HEIGHTS   412

ALLEGHENY VALLEY YMCA 5021 Freeport Rd.
Phone: 295-9400.
Pool: 25m, indoors, heated, 84°-86°.
Affiliate: YMCA NC.

NAZARETH   610

NAZARETH YMCA 33 S. Main St.
Phone: 759-3440.
Pool: 25y x 75f, 6 lanes, indoors, heated, 85°.
Admission: $7.
Affiliate: Y AWAY $2.50.

NEW KENSINGTON   412

YMCA OF NEW KENSINGTON 800 Constitution Blvd.
Phone: 335-9191.
Pool: 20y x 37.5f, 4 lanes, indoors, heated, 84°.
Admission: $5.
Affiliate: YMCA outside a 50 mile radius & U.S. Military: NC.
Hotel: Days Inn New Kensington (335-9171) $5 per day or $15 per week, with a receipt from the hotel.

OIL CITY — 814

OIL CITY YMCA 7 Petroleum St.
Phone: 677-3000.
Pool: 25y, indoors, heated, 86°.
Admission: $5.
Affiliate: YMCA outside a 50 mile radius NC, within 50 miles $2.50.
Hotel: Oil City Holiday Inn (677-1221) NC with room key.

PENN HILLS — 412

BALLY'S SCANDINAVIAN HEALTH SPA 310 Rodi Rd.
Phone: 241-4282.
Pool: 25y, indoors, heated, 72°.
Affiliate: Bally's NC.
Hotel: Harley Hotel (244-1600) NC.

PHILADELPHIA — 215

Philadelphia

Dots are placed by ZIP codes, not by street addresses.

1. CENTRAL YMCA 1425 Arch St.
Phone: 557-0082.
Pool: 25y, 4 lanes, indoors, heated, 83°.
Admission: $12.
Affiliate: Y AWAY outside a 50 mile radius NC. YMCA 3 visits NC, then $6.

2. THE SPORTING CLUB AT THE BELLEVUE HOTEL 224 S. Broad St.
Phone: Club: 985-9876. Hotel: 893-1776.
Reservations: 800-221-0833.
Pool: 25m, 4 lanes, indoors, heated, 75°.
Admission: Registered guests NC.
Affiliate: IHRSA $12.

3. PENNYPACK AQUATIC & FITNESS CENTER 3600 Grant Ave.
Phone: 677-0400.
Pool: 50m x 60f, 8 lanes, indoors, heated, 83°.

Admission: $10.
Affiliate: IPFA outside a 25 mile radius 4 visits per month NC.
To find: One mile from the I-95 Academy Rd. Exit, one half mile east of Northeast Philadelphia Airport.
Masters: Team Pennypack. Contact Dick Jackson at 677-0400.

4. NIRVANA 4401 'G' St.
Phone: 289-4200.
Pool: 25y, indoors, heated, 82°-84°.
Admission: Call.
Affiliate: IPFA NC.

5. COLUMBIA NORTH YMCA 1400-26 N. Broad St.
Phone: 235-6440.
Pool: 25m, 6 lanes, indoors, heated, 82°.
Admission: $6.
Affiliate: Y AWAY NC. YMCA $3.

6. ROXBORO YMCA Ridge Ave. & Domino Lane
Phone: 482-3900.
Pool: 25y x 25f, 4 lanes, indoors, heated, 85°.
Affiliate: Y AWAY outside a 50 mile radius NC, within 50 miles $4.

7. ST. JOSEPH'S UNIVERSITY MASTERS/TRIATHLON CLUB at St. Joseph's University Pool, 5600 City Ave.
Masters: Contact Bob Krotee, Aquatics Director, at (610) 660-1717.
Pool: 25m x 60f, 8 lanes, indoors, heated, 81°.
Affiliate: USMS $5, includes pool fees.
Notes: Coached workouts: M-Th: 6-7:30PM. Lap swimming: F: 6-7:30PM. Sa,Su: Noon-2PM.
To find: At 54th and City Ave. in west Philadelphia.

8. LINCOLN RECREATION CENTER Rowland & Shelmire
Phone: After 5 PM: 335-8751. Parks & Recreation Dept: 686-3649.
Pool: 25m, indoors, heated, 85°.
Admission: NC.

9. WEST PHILADELPHIA YMCA 5120 Chestnut St.
Phone: 476-2700.
Pool: 25y x 32m, 6 lanes, indoors, heated, 84°-86°.
Admission: $5.
Affiliate: YMCA $2.50.

10. SAYRE / MORRIS POOL 59th & Spruce Sts.
Phone: After 5 PM: 472-5801. Parks & Recreation Dept: 686-3649.
Pool: 25y, indoors, heated, 82°.
Admission: NC.

11. LASALLE UNIVERSITY 1900 W. Olney Ave.
Phone: 951-1520.
Pool: 25y 1in x 50f, 6 lanes, indoors, heated, 80°.
Admission: $3.

PHILADELPHIA   CONTINUED

12. YMCA OF GERMANTOWN 5722 Greene St.
Phone: 844-3281.
Pool: 25y, indoors, heated, 85°.
Admission: $5.

13. PICKETT POOL Wayne & Chelten Aves.
Phone: After 5 PM: 685-2196. Parks & Recreation
Dept: 686-3649.
Pool: 25y, indoors, heated, 82°.
Admission: NC.

14. CHRISTIAN STREET BRANCH YMCA 1724
Christian St.
Phone: 735-5800.
Pool: 25y x 25f, 6 lanes, indoors, heated, 84°.
Admission: $5.
Affiliate: YMCA $2.50.
To find: Four blocks south of South St.

15. GERSHMAN YM / YWHA 401 S. Broad St.
Phone: 545-4400.
Pool: 25y x 35f, 6 lanes, indoors, heated, 83°.
Admission: Residents $8, non-residents $5.
To find: On Broad St., four blocks south of City
Hall.

**16. YWCA OF PHILADELPHIA - NORTHEAST
BRANCH** 2840 Holme Ave.
Phone: 335-1222.
Pool: 25y x 42f, indoors, heated, water temperature
not reported.
Admission: $6, SC(65) $4.
Affiliate: YWCA $4, SC $3.

17. BALLY'S HOLIDAY FITNESS CENTER 851
Franklin Mills Circle
Phone: 637-1580.
Pool: 25m, indoors, heated, 80°-82°.
Affiliate: Bally's & IPFA: NC.
Hotel: Holiday Inn on Street Rd. (364-2000) NC.

PHOENIXVILLE   610

PHOENIXVILLE AREA YMCA 400 E. Pothouse
Rd.
Phone: 933-5861.
Pool: 25m, indoors, heated, water temperature not
reported.
Admission: Call.
Affiliate: YMCA outside a 50 mile radius NC.
Masters: Contact Joe Cushing at 933-5861.

PITTSBURGH   412

18. CLUB ONE 6325 Penn Ave.
Phone: 362-4806.
Pool: 25y, 6 lanes, indoors, heated, 83°.
Affiliate: IHRSA NC.

19. OLIVER BATH HOUSE S. 10th St.
Phone: 431-9650.

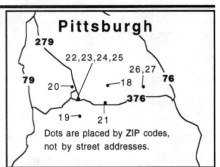

Pittsburgh

Dots are placed by ZIP codes,
not by street addresses.

Pool: 20y, indoors, heated, 80°.
Memberships: Residents $10/year, non-residents
$25.
Notes: Memberships are sold at the pool except in
the summer months. In summer, purchase memberships in the City & County Building, at Grant St.
and Forbes Ave., 4th floor.

**20. YMCA OF PITTSBURGH - ALLEGHENY
BRANCH** 600 W. North Ave.
Phone: 321-8594.
Pool: 20y, 4 lanes, indoors, heated, 82°.
Affiliate: Y AWAY outside a 50 mile radius NC.
To find: At the intersection of W. North Ave. and
Monterey St.

21. JEWISH COMMUNITY CENTER 5738 Forbes
Ave.
Phone: 521-8010.
Pool: 25y, indoors, heated, water temperature not
reported.
Admission: 2 visits per year $5 each.
Affiliate: JCC NC.

22. EXECUTIVE FITNESS CENTER at the Vista
Hotel, 1000 Penn Ave.
Phone: Fitness Center: 227-4482. Hotel: 281-
3700. **Reservations:** 800-367-8478.
Pool: 20y x 20f, 3 lanes, indoors, heated, 78°-80°.
Admission: $9. Registered guests NC.
Affiliate: IHRSA $6.
To find: Across the street from the Convention
Center on the 4th floor of the Vista Hotel.

23. DOWNTOWN PITTSBURGH YMCA 330 Blvd.
of the Allies
Phone: 227-6420.
Pool: 25m x 38f, 6 lanes, indoors, heated, 82°.
Admission: 3 visits per year $7 each.
Affiliate: YMCA outside a 50 mile radius 2 visits
per month $3 each.
Masters: The YMCA Masters. Contact Craig White
at 227-6432(w).

24. CURZONS CITY CLUB 119 - 6th St.
Phone: 391-3300.
Pool: 65f x 18f, 3 lanes, indoors, heated, 80°.
Admission: $10.
To find: One and a half blocks from Heinz Hall.

25. YWCA OF GREATER PITTSBURGH 305 Wood St.
Phone: 391-5100.
Pool: 25y x 35f, 6 lanes, indoors, heated, 85°.
Admission: 1 week $4 per visit.
Affiliate: YWCA $3, SC(62) $2.50.
Notes: This YWCA offers a wide range of aquatic exercise classes. Hydro-Fit, Wet Vests, and Aqua Jogger equipment is available.
To find: Two blocks south of 5th Ave., across from Point Park College, in the same block as the PPG Place Complex.

26. HARLEY HOTEL OF PITTSBURGH 699 Rodi Rd.
Phone: 244-1600. **Reservations:** 800-321-2323.
Pool: 20y, rectangular, indoors, heated, 90°.
Admission: Registered guests only NC.
Notes: There is also a 20y, rectangular, outdoor, summer pool. Guests also have access to the Bally's Scandinavian Health Spa. See that listing under Penn Hills, Pennsylvania.

27. OLYMPIC SWIM & HEALTH CLUB 517 Twin Oaks Dr.
Phone: 793-8503.
Pool: 25y, 6 lanes, indoors, heated, 85° in winter, 80° in summer.
Memberships: $10/week.

PITTSTON 717

GREATER PITTSTON YMCA 10 N. Main St.
Phone: 655-2255.
Pool: 20y x 30f, indoors, heated, 85°.
Admission: $5.

POTTSTOWN 610

POTTSTOWN YMCA Adams & Jackson Sts.
Phone: 323-7300.
Pool: 25y, 6 lanes, indoors, heated, 82°.
Admission: Call.
Affiliate: YMCA NC.

QUAKERTOWN 215

UPPER BUCKS COUNTY YMCA POOL at 151 S. 14th St.
Phone: Pool: 536-8409. YMCA: 536-8841.
Pool: 25y x 42f, indoors, heated, 85°.
Admission: $5.
Affiliate: YMCA 3 visits NC.
Notes: The pool is at the address shown, about a mile away from the main YMCA facility.

READING 610

CENTRAL YMCA Reed & Washington Sts.
Phone: 378-4700.
Pool: 25m, indoors, heated, 82°.
Affiliate: YMCA 4 visits NC, then $1.75.

SCOTTDALE 412

SCOTTDALE YMCA 106 Spring St.
Phone: 887-8730.
Pool: 25m, indoors, heated, 84°.
Admission: $5.
Affiliate: YMCA $4.

SCRANTON 717

WESTON FIELD HOUSE 982 Providence Rd.
Phone: 348-4186.
Pool: 25y, indoors, heated, 78°-80°.
Admission: Residents $1, non-residents $2.

SEWICKLEY 412

SEWICKLEY VALLEY YMCA 625 Blackburn Rd.
Phone: 741-9622.
Pool: 25y, 6 lanes, indoors, heated, 82°-83°.
Affiliate: Y AWAY NC.
Hotel: Local hotels (not members of national chains) NC. Call the Y for specifics.
To find: Across the street from Sewickley Valley Hospital.
Masters: The Sewickley Valley YMCA Masters. Contact Colleen Fedor at 741-9622.

SHAWNEE 717

SHAWNEE INN & GOLF RESORT River Rd., Shawnee-on-Delaware
Phone: 421-1500. **Reservations:** 800-742-9633.
Pool: 25y, rectangular, indoors, heated, 80°.
Admission: Registered guests only NC.
Notes: There is also an outdoor, summer pool.

STATE COLLEGE 814

CENTRE REGION PARKS & RECREATION DEPT. at the State College High School Natatorium, 653 Westerly Pkwy.
Phone: Information: 231-3071. Pool office: 231-4161.
Pool: 25y, indoors, heated, 78°-90°.
Memberships: Early AM Lap swimming: Mid-Sep. to mid-Dec. $40. Mid-Jan. to mid-May $40.
Notes: Enrollment is limited to prevent crowding.

THE ATHLETIC CLUB 1445 W. College Ave.
Phone: 237-5108.
Pool: 25y, indoors, heated, 82°.
Admission: $8.
Hotel: Atherton Hilton (231-2100) NC. Holiday Inn (238-3001) & Hampton Inn (231-1590): $5.

STROUDSBURG 717

POCONO FAMILY YMCA 809 Main St.
Phone: 421-2525.
Pool: 20y x 25f, 3 lanes, indoors, heated, 86°.
Admission: $6, SC(62) $5.
Affiliate: YMCA NC.

SUNBURY   717

SUNBURY AREA YMCA 1150 N. 4th St.
Phone: 286-5636.
Pool: 25y x 36f, 4 lanes, indoors, heated, 84°.
Admission: $6.
Affiliate: Y AWAY outside a 50 mile radius NC.

UNIONTOWN   412

UNIONTOWN AREA YMCA 1 YMCA Dr.
Phone: 438-2584.
Pool: 25y x 42f, 6 lanes, indoors, heated, 86°.
Admission: $6.
Affiliate: Y AWAY NC.
Hotel: Holiday Inn (437-2816) $3 with room key.
To find: Behind the South Union Township Fire
Department.

UNIVERSITY PARK   814

MCCOY NATATORIUM Penn State University,
Bigler & Curtin Rds.
Phone: Recorded schedules: 863-1311.
Information: 865-1432.
Pool 1: 25y, 6 lanes, indoors, heated, 80°.
Pool 2: 25m, 6 lanes, indoors, heated, 84°.
Admission: $2.
Memberships: $50/semester.
Notes: There is also a 25y, 4 lane, indoor, heated,
84° pool in the White Building near the HUB; and a
50m x 25y, 7 lane, outdoor, heated, 84°, seasonal
pool, reserved for lap swimming. Admission to the
outdoor pool is $1.50.

WARREN   814

WARREN YMCA 212 Lexington Ave.
Phone: 726-0110.
Pool: 25m, indoors, heated, 84°.
Admission: Call.
Affiliate: YMCA NC.

WASHINGTON   412

WASHINGTON YMCA 99 W. Beau St.
Phone: 225-0811.
Pool: 25y x 30f, 5 lanes, indoors, heated, 86°-89°.
Admission: $8.
Affiliate: Y AWAY NC. YMCA outside a 60 mile
radius NC.

YWCA OF WASHINGTON COUNTY 42 W. Maiden
St.
Phone: 222-3200.
Pool: 20y x 20f, indoors, heated, 89°.
Admission: 1 visit NC, then $3.25.
Affiliate: YWCA $1.75.
Notes: This YWCA does not encourage lap swim-
ming.
To find: One half block west of Main St. on Route
40 West.

WAYNESBORO   717

WAYNESBORO YMCA 810 E. Main St.
Phone: 762-6012.
Pool: 25m x 45f, 6 lanes, indoors, heated, 85°.
Admission: $5.
Affiliate: Y AWAY outside a 50 mile radius NC.

WEST CHESTER   610

CENTRAL CHESTER COUNTY YMCA 1 E.
Chestnut St.
Phone: 692-8440.
Pool: 25m, indoors, heated, 82°.
Admission: $8.
Affiliate: YMCA outside a 50 mile radius 5 visits
per year NC.

WILKES-BARRE   717

CATHOLIC YOUTH CENTER 36 S. Washington St.
Phone: 823-6121.
Pool: 25y, indoors, heated, 82°-85°.
Admission: $3.

ODYSSEY TOTAL FITNESS CENTER 401 Coal
St.
Phone: 829-2661.
Pool: 20y x 30f, 5 lanes, indoors, heated, 82°.
Admission: $10.
Affiliate: IHRSA $7.
Hotel: All local hotels $7 with room key.

WILKES-BARRE YMCA 40 W. Northampton St.
Phone: 823-2191.
Pool: 25y, 4 lanes, indoors, heated, 84°.
Admission: $6.
Affiliate: Y AWAY 6 visits NC.
To find: One block from the square.
Masters: The Wilkes-Barre Family YMCA
Stingrays. Contact Elaine Moore at 823-2191.

WILLIAMSPORT   717

WILLIAMSPORT YMCA 320 Elmira St.
Phone: 323-7134.
Pool: 25m x 45f, 6 lanes, indoors, heated, 86°.
Admission: $8. SC(65) $3, M-F 2-3PM $1.75.
Affiliate: Y AWAY NC.
Hotel: Reighard House Hotel NC. Sheraton Inn
Williamsport (327-8231), Genetti Hotel &
Convention Center (326-6600), & Snyder House:
$1.25.
To find: Between 3rd and 4th Sts., one block west
of City Hall.

YWCA OF WILLIAMSPORT 815 W. 4th St.
Phone: 322-4637.
Pool: 20y, indoors, heated, 87°-90°.
Admission: Lap swimming $3.50.

WILLOW GROVE   215

BALLY'S HOLIDAY SPA 151 N. York Rd.
Phone: 657-8500.
Pool: 25m, indoors, heated, 78°-82°.
Admission: Call.
Affiliate: Bally's NC.
Hotel: Hampton Inn (659-3535) NC.

WILMERDING   412

SOUTHEAST AREA YMCA Memorial Field
Phone: 823-9000.
Pool: 20y, 4 lanes, indoors, heated, 83°-85°.
Admission: $6. M-F before 6PM $4. SC(62) $1
  per swim with $9 'Senior ID', valid for limited days
  and times.
Affiliate: Y AWAY 30 days NC.
To find: On Ice Plant Hill, two quick turns from
  Route 30 East.

YORK   717

YMCA OF YORK COUNTY 90 N. Newberry St.
Phone: 843-7884.
Pool: 25y, indoors, heated, water temperature not
  reported.
Affiliate: YMCA outside a 50 mile radius NC.

YWCA OF YORK 320 E. Market St.
Phone: 845-2631.
Pool: 21y, indoors, heated, 85°-88°.
Admission: $1.50.
To find: Three blocks east of the York Towne
  Hotel.

HELP MAKE THE NEXT *SWIMMERS GUIDE* EVEN BETTER

To receive a free copy of the next ***Swimmers Guide*** tell us about pools you
know of that aren't in this edition. See page 14 for details.

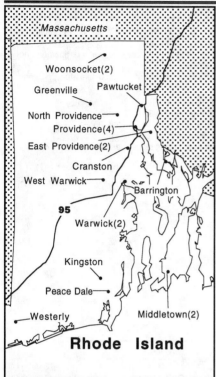

Massachusetts

Woonsocket(2)

Greenville   Pawtucket

North Providence

Providence(4)

East Providence(2)

Cranston

West Warwick

Barrington

95

Warwick(2)

Kingston

Peace Dale

Westerly   Middletown(2)

Rhode Island

BARRINGTON   401

BARRINGTON YMCA 70 West St.
Phone: 245-2444.
Pool: 25y x 28f, 4 lanes, indoors, heated, 82.5°.
Affiliate: YMCA $2.50.
Notes: There is also a 25y x 42f, 6 lane, outdoor,
unheated, 78°-81°, summer pool.

BARRINGTON YMCA MASTERS SWIMMING at
the Barrington YMCA
Masters: Contact Head Coach Eric Hecker at 245-
2444.
Non-member participation: Call for information.
Notes: Fall, winter, spring: Coached workouts:
M,W: 7:45-9:15PM. Structured workouts, not
always coached: Tu,Th: 8-8:45PM. Summer:
Coached workouts: M-Th: 7:15-9PM. Summer
workouts are in the outdoor pool.

CRANSTON   401

CRANSTON BRANCH YMCA 1225 Park Ave.
Phone: 943-0444.
Pool: 25y, indoors, heated, 82°-84°.
Admission: $10.
Affiliate: YMCA 1 visit NC, then $2.50.
Masters: Contact Scott Stevens or Carolyn
Stevens at 943-0444.

EAST PROVIDENCE   401

NEW ENGLAND HEALTH & RACQUET CLUB 15
Catamore Blvd.
Phone: 434-3600.
Pool: 20y x 30f, 4 lanes, indoor/outdoor, heated,
82°.
Admission: $14. M-F before 4PM $7.
Affiliate: IHRSA $7.
Hotel: Ramada Inn Seekonk (336-7300) $7 with
room key.
To find: Just off Route 6 in East Providence, Exit 7
on I-95.

BALLY'S HOLIDAY HEALTH CENTER 50
Narragansett Dr.
Phone: 722-6900.
Pool: 25m, indoors, heated, 80°.
Affiliate: Bally's NC.

GREENVILLE   401

SMITHFIELD YMCA Deerfield Dr.
Phone: 949-2480.
Pool: 25y, indoors, heated, 82°-85°.
Admission: Call.
Affiliate: YMCA Call.

KINGSTON   401

TOOTELL AQUATIC CENTER Mackal Field
House, University of Rhode Island
Phone: 792-2029.
Pool: 25y x 60f, 8 lanes, indoors, heated, 78°-80°.
Admission: $2.
Memberships: Sep. to May $90. Jun. to Aug. $60.
To find: The Mackal-Keaney-Tootell Complex is
located off Route 138.

MIDDLETOWN   401

NEWPORT ATHLETIC CLUB 66 Valley Rd.
Phone: 846-7723.
Pool: 25y, indoor/outdoor, heated, 80°-81°.
Admission: $10.
Hotel: Newport Bay Club (849-8600) NC with a
pass from the hotel.

NEWPORT COUNTY YMCA 792 Valley Rd.
Phone: 847-9200.
Pool: 25y x 35f, 6 lanes, indoors, heated, 83°.
Admission: $7.50. M-F before 4PM $5.
Affiliate: Out-of-state YMCA NC.
Hotel: Seaview Inn (847-0110) NC with a voucher
from the Inn.
To find: One mile from the 'Cliff-Walk' and Easton's
Beach.

NORTH PROVIDENCE   401

NORTH PROVIDENCE NATATORIUM 1810 Mill
Spring Ave.
Phone: 353-7007.

Pool: 25m, indoors, heated, 83.5°.
Memberships: North Providence residents $20/year.

PAWTUCKET ━━━━━━━━━━ **401**

PAWTUCKET YMCA 20 Summer St.
Phone: 727-7900.
Pool: 25y, 4 lanes, indoors, heated, 82°.
Admission: $8.
Affiliate: YMCA $4.

PEACE DALE ━━━━━━━━━━ **401**

SOUTH COUNTY BRANCH YMCA 165 Broad Rock Rd.
Phone: 783-3900.
Pool: 25m, indoors, heated, 83°-84°.
Admission: 1 visit NC.
Affiliate: YMCA Call.
Masters: A Masters group is in formation. Contact the Aquatic Director at 783-3900.

PROVIDENCE ━━━━━━━━━━ **401**

IN-TOWN PROVIDENCE YMCA 164 Broad St.
Phone: 456-0100.
Pool: 20y x 20f, 3 lanes, indoors, heated, 80°-84°.
Admission: $5.
Affiliate: YMCA NC.
To find: In downtown Providence, overlooking I-95 / I-195.

EAST SIDE MT. HOPE YMCA 438 Hope St.
Phone: 521-0155.
Pool: 25y x 32f, 5 lanes, indoors, heated, 84°-86°.
Admission: 3 visits per year $10 each.
Affiliate: Out-of-state Y AWAY NC.
To find: Near Hope High School, at the intersection of Hope St. and Doyle.

SMITH SWIM CENTER Brown University
Phone: Pool: 863-2204. Membership information: 863-2773.
Pool: 50m x 25y, indoors, heated, 82°.
Memberships: $150/academic year. $150/summer.

TAYLOR NATATORIUM Providence College, River & Eaton St.
Phone: 865-2268.

Pool: 25m, 6 lanes, indoors, heated, 79°.
Passes: 20 swims $100.

WARWICK ━━━━━━━━━━ **401**

NEW ENGLAND HEALTH & RACQUET CLUB 2191 Post Rd.
Phone: 732-2413.
Pool: 21y, indoor/outdoor, heated, 82°.
Admission: $3.50 to $14.
Affiliate: IHRSA 50% off the applicable 'admission' rate.
Hotel: Johnson & Wales Hotel NC with a pass from the hotel.

KENT COUNTY BRANCH YMCA 900 Centerville Rd.
Phone: 828-0130.
Pool: 25y, indoors, heated, 82°-84°.
Admission: $5.
Affiliate: YMCA NC.

WEST WARWICK ━━━━━━━━━━ **401**

AMERICAN HEALTH FITNESS CENTER 555 Quaker Lane
Phone: 828-3458.
Pool: 20y, indoors, heated, 80°.
Admission: $5.
Affiliate: IPFA NC.

WESTERLY ━━━━━━━━━━ **401**

WESTERLY-PAWCATUCK YMCA 95 High St.
Phone: 596-2894.
Pool: 20y, indoors, heated, 86°.
Admission: $8.
Affiliate: YMCA NC.

WOONSOCKET ━━━━━━━━━━ **401**

WOONSOCKET YMCA 18 Federal St.
Phone: 769-0791.
Pool: 25y, indoors, heated, 82°.
Admission: $7.
Affiliate: Y AWAY NC.

NEW ENGLAND HEALTH & RACQUET CLUB 600 Social St.
Phone: 766-6766.
Pool: 20y x 20f, indoors, heated, 83°-84°.
Admission: $10.

ALWAYS CALL FIRST

Pools close, they change names, affiliations, admission policies, and rates. And just because a pool is listed in *Swimmers Guide* doesn't mean it's open all day, every day, for just the type of workout you want to do. Spend a quarter to save time and aggravation. . . always call first!

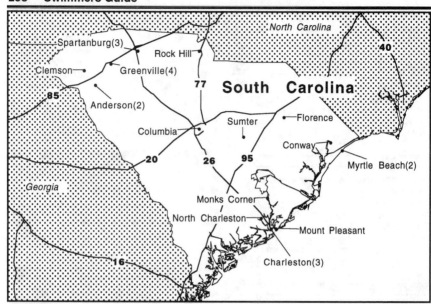

ANDERSON   803

SHEPPARD SWIM CENTER 1115 Cornelia Rd.
Phone: 260-5170.
Pool: 25m x 50f, 7 lanes, indoors, heated, 83°-84°.
Admission: $2, SC(62) $1.50.

HUDGENS SWIM CENTER 710 Burdine Rd.
Phone: 260-5176.
Pool: 25m x 50f, 7 lanes, indoors, heated, 83°-84°.
Admission: $2, SC(62) $1.50.

ANDERSON MASTERS at Sheppard Swim Center
and at Hudgens Swim Center
Masters: Contact Centers Director Steve Wycoff at
260-5170.
Non-member participation: $2, SC(62) $1.50.
Notes: Sheppard Swim Center: Uncoached work-
outs: M,W: 5:15-6:15PM. Hudgens Swim Center:
Coached workouts: Tu,W,F,Su: 7-8:30PM.

CHARLESTON   803

CHRISTIAN FAMILY Y OF CHARLESTON 21
George St.
Phone: 723-6473.
Pool: 25y x 21f 7in, 4 lanes, indoors, heated, 83°.
Affiliate: No reciprocity with other YMCAs.
Memberships: $275/year.
Notes: There is also an indoor, heated, 86°-90°,
therapy pool.

W.L. STEPHENS, JR. AQUATIC CENTER 780 W.
Oak Forest Dr.
Phone: 724-7342.
Pool: 25y x 40f, 6 lanes, indoor/outdoor, tempera-
ture controlled, 82.5°.

Admission: Residents $2, SC(55) $1. Non-residents $4, SC $2.
Affiliate: NRPA outside a 60 mile radius 4 visits per
month $2 each, SC $1. USMS outside a 75 mile
radius 4 visits per month $2 each, SC $1.
To find: Leaving downtown Charleston on Hwy. 17
south (Savannah Hwy.), two stop lights after St.
Andrews Shopping Center, turn right onto W. Oak
Forest Dr. Proceed one to one and a half miles to
the pool which is on the right.

PALMETTO MASTERS SWIMMING at the W.L.
Stephens Aquatic Center
Pool phone: 724-7342. **Masters:** Contact Hugh
Wilder at 853-1308(h) or 953-5491(w).
Affiliate: USMS 10 workouts per year NC.
Notes: Workouts: M-F: 6:30-8AM. Sa: 9-
10:30AM. From Memorial Day to Labor Day, the
club works out at the 50m, outdoor Martin Luther
King Pool (724-7327).

ST. ANDREWS PARK & PLAYGROUND 1642
Sam Rittenberg Blvd.
Phone: 763-3850.
Pool: 25m x 25y, indoors, heated, 82°.
Admission: $6.

CLEMSON   803

RAMADA INN & CONFERENCE CENTER Hwys.
123 & 76
Phone: 654-7501. **Reservations:** 800-272-6232.
Pool: 25y, 'L' shape, indoors, heated, 86°.
Admission: Registered guests only NC.

COLUMBIA 803

COLUMBIA YMCA 1420 Sumter St.
Phone: 799-9187.
Pool: 20y x 20f, indoors, heated, 82°-85°.
Affiliate: YMCA $3.
Masters: The Columbia YMCA Masters. Contact Cheryl Stevenson at 799-9187.

CONWAY 803

COASTAL CAROLINA UNIVERSITY
Phone: 448-1481.
Pool: 25y, indoors, heated, 80°-81°.
Admission: $4.

FLORENCE 803

FLORENCE FAMILY YMCA 1700 S. Rutherford Rd.
Phone: 665-1234.
Pool: 25y, indoors, heated, 85°-86°.
Admission: $5.
Affiliate: YMCA NC.

GREENVILLE 803

YWCA OF GREENVILLE 700 Augusta St.
Phone: 467-3700.
Pool: 25y x 35f, 4 lanes, indoors, heated, 86°.
Admission: Out-of-town visitors — Call.
Affiliate: YWCA $3, SC(62) $2.50.
To find: Turn right at the intersection of Church St. & Augusta Rd. The YWCA is one half mile on the left.

LIFE CENTER HEALTH & CONDITIONING CLUB 875 W. Faris Rd.
Phone: 455-8446.
Pool: 25m, indoors, heated, 84°.
Memberships: Call.

WESTSIDE AQUATIC CENTER 2700 Blue Ridge Dr. (Hwy. 253)
Phone: 295-0032.
Pool: 50m x 25y, indoors, heated, 81°.
Admission: $3, SC(65) $1.50.
To find: On Hwy. 253 between Cedar Lane Rd. & Hwy. 25, one mile north of Berea Wal-Mart.
Masters: Team Greenville. Contact Jim Keogh at 295-0032.

CLEVELAND STREET YMCA 721 Cleveland St.
Phone: 242-4651.
Pool: 25y, 6 lanes, indoors, heated, 83°.
Admission: Visitors from outside a 50 mile radius $10.
Affiliate: YMCA & YWCA, both outside a 50 mile radius: NC.
Hotel: Holiday Inn Greenville I-85 (277-8921) NC.

MONKS CORNER 803

BERKELEY COUNTY YMCA 210 Rembert Dennis Blvd.
Phone: 761-9622.
Pool: 25y, indoors, heated, 82°-83°.
Admission: $5.
Affiliate: YMCA NC.

MOUNT PLEASANT 803

R.L. JONES RECREATION CENTER 391 Egypt Rd.
Phone: 884-2528.
Pool: 25y, 6 lanes, indoors, heated, 81°-84°.
Admission: $2.
Masters: The Palmetto Masters of Mt. Pleasant. Contact Marty Hamburger at 884-2528.

MYRTLE BEACH 803

SPORT & HEALTH CLUB AT KINGSTON PLANTATION 9760 Kings Rd.
Phone: 497-2444.
Pool: 25y, indoors, heated, 84°.
Admission: $12.50.

PEPPER GEDDINGS RECREATION CENTER 3205 Oak St.
Phone: 448-8578.
Pool: 25y x 45f, 6 lanes, indoors, heated, 83°.
Admission: $2.50, SC(55) $2.
Hotel: Yachtsman Resort Hotel (448-1441) — Call the Recreation Center for information.
To find: Twelve blocks north of the Myrtle Beach Convention Center and Myrtle Square Mall, between the elementary and middle schools.

NORTH CHARLESTON 803

THE ATHLETIC & FITNESS CLUB 8545 Dorchester Rd.
Phone: 767-3706.
Pool: 25m, indoors, heated, 85°.
Admission: $10.

ROCK HILL 803

ROCK HILL YMCA 402 Charlotte Ave.
Phone: 327-2063.
Pool: 25y, indoors, heated, 86°.
Admission: $5.
Affiliate: YMCA NC.

SPARTANBURG 803

SPARTANBURG SWIM CENTER 447 S. Church St.
Phone: 596-3900.
Pool: 25y x 60f, 8 lanes, indoors, heated, 86°.
Admission: $1.
To find: At the first traffic signal south of the Main Post Office, on the east side of S. Church St.

SPARTANBURG   CONTINUED

SPARTANBURG YMCA FAMILY CENTER 266 S. Pine St.
Phone: 585-0306.
Pool 1: 25y, 12 lanes, indoors, heated, 82°.
Pool 2: 25y, 5 lanes, indoors, heated, 88°.
Admission: Out-of-town visitors — Call.
Affiliate: Y AWAY NC.
Hotel: Several local hotels NC. Call the Y for participating locations.
To find: Three blocks from the Chamber of Commerce, next to Wendy's Restaurant and across the street from the public library.

SPARTANBURG ATHLETIC CLUB 2420 Andrews Rd.
Phone: 582-5050.
Pool: 25m, indoors, heated, 80°-85°.
Admission: $10.
Affiliate: IHRSA Call.

SUMTER   803

SUMTER YMCA 50 Willow Dr.
Phone: 773-1404.
Pool: 25y, 5 lanes, indoors, heated, 86°.
Admission: Call.
Affiliate: YMCA Call.

HELP MAKE THE NEXT *SWIMMERS GUIDE* EVEN BETTER

To receive a free copy of the next *Swimmers Guide* tell us about pools you know of that aren't in this edition. See page 14 for details.

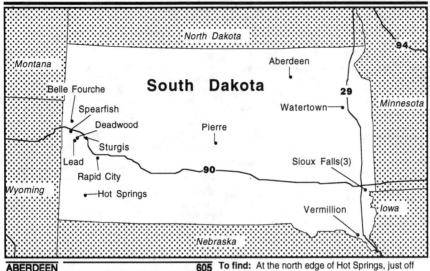

ABERDEEN   605

ABERDEEN YMCA 420 S. Lincoln St.
Phone: 225-4910.
Pool: 20y, indoors, heated, 84°.
Admission: $5.
Affiliate: YMCA NC.

BELLE FOURCHE   605

BELLE FOURCHE AREA COMMUNITY CENTER
1111 National Ave.
Phone: 892-2467.
Pool: 25m x 45f, 6 lanes, indoors, heated, 82°.
Admission: $3.25.
To find: Hwy. 85 North, turn right onto National
Ave. and go up the hill. The complex is located in
Highland Park.

DEADWOOD   605

DEADWOOD RECREATION CENTER 105
Sherman St.
Phone: 578-3729.
Pool: 64f x 44f, 6 lanes, indoors, heated, 82°.
Admission: $2, SC(60) $1.
Hotel: Bullock Hotel (578-1745) NC with a pass
from the hotel.
To find: One block south of the Deadwood Post
Office, across the street from Deckers Food Center
and the Baptist Church.

HOT SPRINGS   605

EVANS PLUNGE 1145 N. River
Phone: 745-5165.
Pool: 200f x 50f, indoor/outdoor, spring fed, natu-
rally temperature controlled, 87°.
Admission: $7.
Hotel: Battle Mountain Motel (745-3182) $6.50,
purchase tickets at the Motel.

To find: At the north edge of Hot Springs, just off
Hwy. 385.

LEAD   605

NORTHERN HILLS YMCA 845 Miners Ave.
Phone: 584-1113.
Pool: 25y, indoors, heated, 83°.
Admission: $3.
Affiliate: YMCA NC.
Hotel: Golden Hills Resort (584-1800) $2 with room
key.

PIERRE   605

OAHE YMCA 900 E. Church St.
Phone: 224-1683.
Pool: 25y x 20f, 3 lanes, indoors, heated, 86°.
Admission: $4.
Affiliate: YMCA Call.
To find: Across the street from Riggs High School
and next door to Rawlins Library.

RAPID CITY   605

RAPID CITY YMCA 815 Kansas City St.
Phone: 342-8538.
Pool: 25y x 25f, 4 lanes, indoors, heated, 83°.
Admission: $5.
Affiliate: YMCA NC.

SIOUX FALLS   605

SIOUX FALLS YWCA 300 W. 11th St.
Phone: 336-3660.
Pool: 25y x 36f, 6 lanes, indoors, heated, 82°-85°.
Admission: $5.
Affiliate: YWCA $2.50.
To find: One block north and one block east of the
Best Western Townhouse Motel.

SIOUX FALLS   CONTINUED

Masters: The Snowfox. Contact Tom Herder at 330-9553(h&w).

SIOUX FALLS YMCA 230 S. Minnesota Ave.
Phone: 336-3190.
Pool 1: 25y x 40f, indoors, heated, 83°.
Pool 2: 20y x 20f, indoors, heated, 83°.
Admission: $6.
Affiliate: Y AWAY NC.
Notes: There is also a 15y x 25f, indoor, 88°-90°, training pool.
Masters: The Prairie Masters. Contact Coach Tom Herder at 330-9553(h&w).

SIOUX VALLEY HOSPITAL WELLNESS CENTER 4201 S. Oxbow Ave.
Phone: 333-1633.
Pool: 25y x 50f, 5 lanes, indoors, heated, 84°.
Admission: $5.
Masters: The Sioux Valley Masters. Contact Kathy Grady at 333-1633.

SPEARFISH   605

DONALD E. YOUNG SPORTS & FITNESS CENTER Black Hills State University, 1200 University St.
Phone: 642-6196.
Pool: 25m x 45f, 6 lanes, indoors, heated, 81°.
Admission: Pool $1. Full facility $6.

STURGIS   605

STURGIS COMMUNITY CENTER POOL 1400 Lazelle
Phone: 347-6513.
Pool: 25y, 6 lanes, indoors, heated, 81°.
Admission: $3, SC(62) $1.75.
Affiliate: USS & USMS: NC for USS workouts.
To find: Across the street from Rockingtree Landscape.
Masters: USMS registered swimmers are invited to join the Sturgis USS Swim Team's workouts. Contact Andrew Hollanderx347-0004.

VERMILLION   605

DAKOTA DOME POOL University of South Dakota, 414 E. Clark St.
Phone: Pool: 677-5931. Information: 677-5324.
Pool: 25m x 40f, 6 lanes, indoors, heated, 81°.
Admission: $2.
Memberships: $50/year (Sep.-Aug.).
To find: Look for the dome.

WATERTOWN   605

WATERTOWN COMMUNITY RECREATION CENTER 200 - 9th St. N.E.
Phone: 886-7715.
Pool: 25m x 20m, 8 lanes, indoors, heated, 84°.
Admission: $3.
To find: West of the Lake Area Technical Institute, north of the high school and Civic Arena.

ALWAYS CALL FIRST

Pools close, they change names, affiliations, admission policies, and rates. And just because a pool is listed in *Swimmers Guide* doesn't mean it's open all day, every day, for just the type of workout you want to do. Spend a quarter to save time and aggravation. . . always call first!

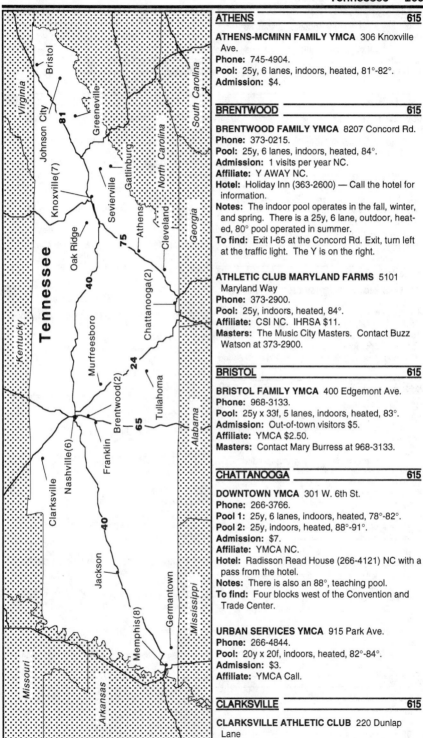

ATHENS 615

ATHENS-MCMINN FAMILY YMCA 306 Knoxville Ave.
Phone: 745-4904.
Pool: 25y, 6 lanes, indoors, heated, 81°-82°.
Admission: $4.

BRENTWOOD 615

BRENTWOOD FAMILY YMCA 8207 Concord Rd.
Phone: 373-0215.
Pool: 25y, 6 lanes, indoors, heated, 84°.
Admission: 1 visits per year NC.
Affiliate: Y AWAY NC.
Hotel: Holiday Inn (363-2600) — Call the hotel for information.
Notes: The indoor pool operates in the fall, winter, and spring. There is a 25y, 6 lane, outdoor, heated, 80° pool operated in summer.
To find: Exit I-65 at the Concord Rd. Exit, turn left at the traffic light. The Y is on the right.

ATHLETIC CLUB MARYLAND FARMS 5101 Maryland Way
Phone: 373-2900.
Pool: 25y, indoors, heated, 84°.
Affiliate: CSI NC. IHRSA $11.
Masters: The Music City Masters. Contact Buzz Watson at 373-2900.

BRISTOL 615

BRISTOL FAMILY YMCA 400 Edgemont Ave.
Phone: 968-3133.
Pool: 25y x 33f, 5 lanes, indoors, heated, 83°.
Admission: Out-of-town visitors $5.
Affiliate: YMCA $2.50.
Masters: Contact Mary Burress at 968-3133.

CHATTANOOGA 615

DOWNTOWN YMCA 301 W. 6th St.
Phone: 266-3766.
Pool 1: 25y, 6 lanes, indoors, heated, 78°-82°.
Pool 2: 25y, indoors, heated, 88°-91°.
Admission: $7.
Affiliate: YMCA NC.
Hotel: Radisson Read House (266-4121) NC with a pass from the hotel.
Notes: There is also an 88°, teaching pool.
To find: Four blocks west of the Convention and Trade Center.

URBAN SERVICES YMCA 915 Park Ave.
Phone: 266-4844.
Pool: 20y x 20f, indoors, heated, 82°-84°.
Admission: $3.
Affiliate: YMCA Call.

CLARKSVILLE 615

CLARKSVILLE ATHLETIC CLUB 220 Dunlap Lane

Phone: 645-4313.
Pool: 25y x 42f, 6 lanes, indoors, heated, 80°.
Admission: $7.
Hotel: TraveLodge (645-1400) NC with a pass from the hotel.
To find: Next to Governors Square Mall.

CLEVELAND   615

CLEVELAND FAMILY YMCA 350 Central Ave.
Phone: 476-5573.
Pool: 25y x 25f, indoors, heated, 86°.
Affiliate: YMCA NC.

FRANKLIN   615

FRANKLIN-WILLIAMSON COUNTY PARKS & RECREATION POOL 1120 Hillsboro Rd.
Phone: 790-5719.
Pool: 25y, indoors, heated, 83°.
Admission: $2.

GATLINBURG   615

GATLINBURG COMMUNITY CENTER Mills Park Rd.
Phone: 436-4990.
Pool: 25y x 42f, 6 lanes, indoors, heated, 85°.
Admission: $1.50, SC(65) 75¢.
To find: About four miles from downtown Gatlinburg, behind Gatlinburg-Pittman High School.

GERMANTOWN   901

GERMANTOWN CENTRE 1801 Exeter Rd.
Phone: 757-7370.
Pool: 25y OR 25m x 22.5y, 8 lanes, indoors, heated, 84°.
Admission: Residents $5, non-residents $7.50.
Notes: The length of the pool is variable and changed according to the time of year.
To find: One block east of Germantown Pkwy.
Masters: Contact Aquatics Director René Drain at 757-7366.

GREENEVILLE   615

GREENE COUNTY YMCA 404 'Y' St.
Phone: 639-6107.
Pool: 25y x 45f, 6 lanes, indoors, heated, 86°.
Admission: W,Su $3.
Affiliate: YMCA 2 weeks NC.
Notes: Members of other YMCAs and non-member children are admitted every day; non-member adults are admitted only on Wednesdays and Sundays.
To find: Six blocks from Main St.

JACKSON   901

JACKSON FAMILY YMCA 1515 Campbell St.
Phone: 424-0912.
Pool: 25y, indoors, heated, 85°-87°.
Affiliate: YMCA NC.

JOHNSON CITY   615

FREEDOM HALL POOL 1320 Pactolas Rd.
Phone: 461-4872.
Pool: 25m, indoors, heated, 78°.
Admission: $1.

KNOXVILLE   615

NEW DOWNTOWN YMCA 605 W. Clinch Ave.
Phone: 522-9622.
Pool: 20y, 4 lanes, indoors, heated, 81°.
Admission: $12.
Affiliate: YMCA 14 visits NC, then $2.
Hotel: Knoxville Hilton (523-2300) & Holiday Inn-World's Fair (522-2800): NC with a pass from the hotel.
To find: Across the street from the Holiday Inn-World's Fair.

YWCA OF KNOXVILLE 420 W. Clinch Ave.
Phone: 523-6126.
Pool: 20y x 30f, indoors, heated, 85°.
Admission: 1 visit $2.
Affiliate: YWCA Call.

WEST SIDE FAMILY CENTER YMCA 400 Winston Rd.
Phone: 690-9622.
Pool: 95f x 57f, indoors, heated, 87°-91°.
Admission: $5.
Affiliate: YMCA NC.

BALLY'S HOLIDAY FITNESS CENTER 1501 Kirby Rd.
Phone: 588-6461.
Pool: 25y, indoors, heated, 76°.
Affiliate: Bally's NC.
Hotel: Holiday Inn Knoxville West (584-3911) & Quality Inn (546-0954): NC.

SOUTH KNOXVILLE COMMUNITY CENTER 522 Old Maryville Pike
Phone: 577-7591.
Pool: 25y, indoors, heated, 88°-90°.
Admission: NC.

FORT SANDERS HEALTH & FITNESS CENTER 270 Fort Sanders W. Blvd.
Phone: 531-5000.
Pool: 25y, indoors, heated, 84°.
Admission: $8.

NEW NORTH SIDE YMCA 7609 Maynardville Hwy.
Phone: 922-9622.
Pool: 25y x 42f, 6 lanes, indoor/outdoor, heated, 86°-88°.
Admission: $7.
Affiliate: Y AWAY NC.
To find: In the community of Halls Crossroads in northern Knoxville, one half mile past Halls High School.

MEMPHIS   901

LOUIS T. FOGELMAN DOWNTOWN YMCA 245
Madison Ave.
Phone: 527-9622.
Pool: 25y x 36f, 6 lanes, indoors, heated, 83°.
Admission: $8.
Affiliate: Y AWAY NC.

THE PEABODY 149 Union Ave.
Phone: 529-4000. **Reservations:** 800-PEABODY.
Pool: 50f x 30f, rectangular, indoors, heated, 82°.
Admission: $5. Registered guests NC.

MASON YMCA 3458 Walker Ave.
Phone: 323-4505.
Pool: 25y x 45f, 4 lanes, indoors, heated, 89°.
Admission: $7.
Affiliate: YMCA 3 visits NC, then $3.
To find: Between Highland and the University of
Memphis, just north of Southern Ave.
Masters: The Mason YMCA Masters. Contact
Obel James at 323-4505.

DAVIS YMCA 4727 Elvis Presley Blvd.
Phone: 398-2366.
Pool: 25y, 5 lanes, indoor/outdoor, heated, 87°.
Affiliate: YMCA outside the Metro Memphis Area
NC.
Hotel: Holiday Inn Graceland Area (398-9211) $1
with room key.
To find: Across the street from Southland Mall.

'Q' THE SPORTS CLUB 1285 Ridgeway Rd.
Phone: 763-3265.
Pool: 25m, indoors, heated, 85°.
Affiliate: IHRSA NC.
Hotel: Embassy Suites (684-1777), Courtyards by
Marriott (761-0330), & Adam's Mark Hotel (684-
6664): NC with a pass from the hotel.

EAST MEMPHIS BRANCH YMCA 5885 Quince
Rd.
Phone: 682-8025.
Pool: 25y x 24y, indoor/outdoor, heated, 86°.
Affiliate: YMCA NC.

JEWISH COMMUNITY CENTER 6560 Poplar Ave.
Phone: 761-0810.
Pool: 25y, 6 lanes, indoors, heated, 80°.
Affiliate: JCC NC.
Notes: There is also a 50m, outdoor, unheated pool
with a 25y lap swimming lane operated from
Memorial Day to Labor Day. When the outdoor
pool is open, the indoor pool is only open a few
hours a day.

WIMBLETON SPORTSPLEX 6161 Shelby Oaks
Dr.
Phone: 388-6580.
Pool: 25y, 4 lanes, indoors, heated, 82°-84°.
Admission: $20.
Affiliate: IHRSA $10.

Hotel: Holiday Inn (388-7050) & Hampton Inn (388-
4881): $10*.
Notes: There is also a 25y, 6 lane, outdoor, unheated, 76°-82° summer pool. *N/C for Holiday Inn
Priority Club members.

MURFREESBORO   615

SPORTSCOM POOL 2310 Memorial Blvd.
Phone: 895-5040.
Pool: 25y x 60f, indoors, heated, 82°.
Admission: $3, SC(60) $2.

NASHVILLE   615

CENTENNIAL SPORTSPLEX 222 - 25th Ave. N.
Phone: 862-8480.
Pool 1: 50m x 25y, 8 lanes, indoors, heated, 80°.
Pool 2: 25y, 6 lane 'recreation pool', indoors, heat-
ed, 85°.
Admission: $4.
To find: Next to Centennial Park in downtown
Nashville.

DOWNTOWN YMCA 1000 Church St.
Phone: 254-0631.
Pool: 25m, indoors, heated, 81°.
Admission: $10.
Affiliate: Y AWAY NC.
Masters: The Downtown YMCA Masters. Contact
Ray Mullican at 329-2573(w).

WESTSIDE ATHLETIC CLUB 11 Vaughns Gap
Rd.
Phone: 352-8500.
Pool: 25m x 42f, 6 lanes, outdoors, heated, 82°.
Affiliate: IHRSA $6.
Hotel: Stouffer Nashville Hotel (255-8400) &
Holiday Inn Crown Plaza (259-2000): $6 with prior
arrangement by the hotel.

DONELSON-HERMITAGE YMCA 3001 Lebanon
Rd.
Phone: 889-2632.
Pool: 25y x 36f, 6 lanes, indoors, heated, 84°-85°.
Admission: 1 visit per year, with tour, NC.
Affiliate: Y AWAY NC.
To find: Close to the Nashville Airport.

GREEN HILLS YMCA 4041 Hillsboro Circle
Phone: 297-6529.
Pool: 25y, 7 lanes, indoor/outdoor, heated, 84°.
Admission: 1 visit per calendar year NC.
Affiliate: Y AWAY NC.

EAST YMCA 2624 Gallatin Rd.
Phone: 228-5525.
Pool: 25y x 20f, 4 lanes, indoors, heated, 84°-86°.
Affiliate: YMCA NC.
To find: Five minutes from downtown Nashville.

OAK RIDGE   615

OAK RIDGE CIVIC CENTER POOL 1403 Oak Ridge Tpk.
Phone: 482-8450.
Pool: 25y x 48f, 7 lanes, indoors, heated, 82°.
Admission: $1.50.

OAK RIDGE MASTERS SWIM CLUB at Oak Ridge Civic Center Pool
Pool phone: 482-8450. **Masters:** Contact Elwood Gift at 482-1806(h).
Affiliate: USMS $3, includes pool fees.
Notes: Coached workouts: M,W,Th: 8:30-9:30PM.

SEVIERVILLE   615

COMMUNITY CENTER POOL 200 Gary Wade Blvd.
Phone: 453-5441.
Pool: 25m, indoors, heated, 83°-84°.
Admission: $2, SC(55) $1.35.
Masters: The Greater Knoxville Swim Team. Contact Susan Curtis at 584-2999(w).

TULLAHOMA   615

WILSON COMMUNITY POOL 501 N. Collins
Phone: Parks Department: 455-1121.
Pool: 25m, indoors, heated, 82°-86°.
Admission: $2.
Notes: This pool closes in the summer when the city's outdoor pool is in operation. For the location of the outdoor pool, call the Parks Dept.

HELP MAKE THE NEXT *SWIMMERS GUIDE* EVEN BETTER

To receive a free copy of the next *Swimmers Guide* tell us about pools you know of that aren't in this edition. See page 14 for details.

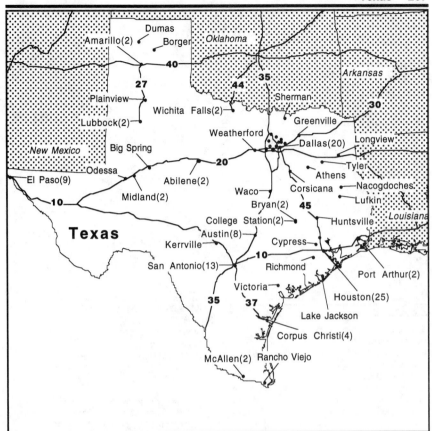

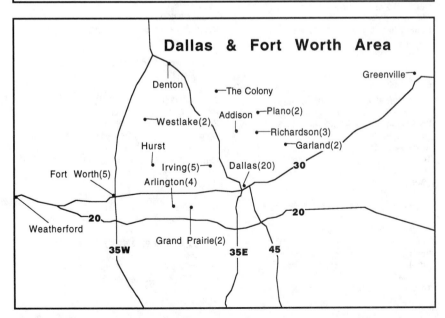

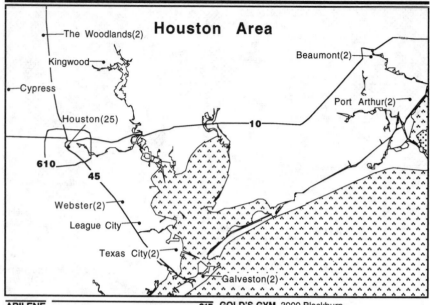

Houston Area

The Woodlands(2)
Kingwood
Cypress
Houston(25)
610
45
Webster(2)
League City
Texas City(2)
Galveston(2)
Beaumont(2)
Port Arthur(2)
10

ABILENE   915

STATE STREET YMCA 3250 State St.
Phone: 677-8144.
Pool: 25y x 40f, 5 lanes, indoors, heated, 84°.
Admission: $5, SC $3.
Affiliate: YMCA NC.
To find: Two blocks west of Abilene High School
on State St. which runs along the north side of the
high school campus.

REDBUD PARK BRANCH YMCA 3125 S. 32nd St.
Phone: 695-3400.
Pool: 25y, indoors, heated, 84°-85°.
Admission: $5.
Affiliate: YMCA NC.

ADDISON   214

LOOS SWIMMING CENTER 3815 Spring Valley
Phone: 888-3191. Call between 9AM and 2PM.
Pool: 50m OR 25y + 25y x 20m, 8 OR 16 lanes,
indoors, heated, 83°.
Admission: $2.
To find: On Spring Valley, between Marsh and
Midway, on the west side of Loos Athletic
Complex.

AMARILLO   806

DOWNTOWN YMCA 816 S. Van Buren
Phone: 374-4651.
Pool: 20y x 21f, 5 lanes, indoors, heated, 86°.
Admission: 2 visits per year $5 each.
Affiliate: YMCA NC.
To find: West of downtown between 8th and 9th.

GOLD'S GYM 3000 Blackburn
Phone: 359-5438.
Pool: 25y, indoors, heated, 84°.
Admission: $8.
Affiliate: Gold's Gym NC. IHRSA $6.
Hotel: TraveLodge West (353-3541) — Call the
club for information.

ARLINGTON   817

1. HUGH SMITH RECREATION CENTER 1815
New York Ave.
Phone: 275-0513.
Pool: 25y x 36f, 5 lanes, indoors, heated, 87°.
Admission: $3.
To find: One quarter to one half mile west of Hwy.
360, between Park Row on the north and Pioneer
Pkwy. on the south.

2. CHARLIE'S CLUB & HOTEL 117 S. Watson Rd.
Phone: 633-4000.
Pool: 20y, indoors, heated, 80°-81°.
Admission: $10. Registered guests NC.

3. UNIVERSITY OF TEXAS AT ARLINGTON
Behind 500 W. Nedderman
Phone: 273-3277.
Pool: 25m, indoors, heated, 80°-84°.
Admission: $1.
Notes: There is also an outdoor, summer pool.

4. BALLY'S PRESIDENT'S HEALTH CLUB 2306
S. Collins
Phone: 274-7177.
Pool: 25y, indoors, heated, 85°.
Admission: Call.
Affiliate: Bally's NC.

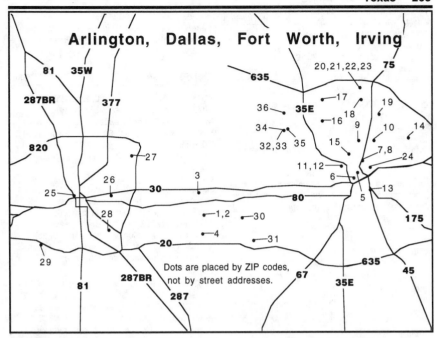

Arlington, Dallas, Fort Worth, Irving

Dots are placed by ZIP codes, not by street addresses.

ATHENS   903

CAIN CENTER, INC. Civic & Fitness Center, 915 S. Palestine
Phone: 677-2000.
Pool: 25m, 7 lanes, indoors, heated, 83°-86°.
Admission: $2.

AUSTIN   512

TOWN LAKE YMCA 1100 W. 1st St.
Phone: 476-6705.
Pool: 25y x 48f, 6 lanes, indoors, heated, 82°.
Admission: $10.
Affiliate: YMCA 5 visits per year NC.
To find: On the west side of downtown, at 1st St. and Lamar.

STACY POOL 800 E. Live Oak, off Congress
Phone: Parks & Rec. Dept: 476-4521.
Pool: 100f, 6 lanes, outdoors, spring fed, naturally temperature controlled, 75°.
Admission: NC.
Notes: The city operates several seasonal pools in addition to the year-round Stacy Pool. Although none of the other pools operates long enough to qualify for listing, the season in Austin begins before Memorial Day and ends after Labor Day. When you call, ask if a more convenient pool is open.

BARTON SPRINGS POOL 2201 Barton Springs Rd.
Phone: 476-9044.
Pool: 1/8 mile lap swim area, outdoors, spring fed,
naturally temperature controlled, 68°.
Admission: Weekdays $2*. Weekends $2.25.*.
Notes: *From 5-9AM, the pool is unguarded and swimming is free. At 9AM, the pool is cleared and admission is charged. In summer, lap swimming may be difficult after 10AM.

ST. EDWARDS UNIVERSITY POOL 3001 S. Congress Ave.
Phone: 448-8519.
Pool: 25m, 6 lanes, indoors, heated, 79°-82°.
Admission: NC.

SOUTHWEST FAMILY BRANCH YMCA 6219 Oakclaire
Phone: 891-9622.
Pool: 20y, 3 lanes, indoors, heated, 84°.
Admission: 1 visit NC, then $10.
Affiliate: YMCA NC.
To find: On Hwy. 290 W, one and a half miles west of Mopac, across from Diamond Shamrock.

THE HILLS FITNESS CENTER 4615 Bee Caves Rd.
Phone: 327-4881.
Pool 1: 25y x 20f, 4 lanes, indoors, heated, 82°.
Pool 2: 25y x 20f, 4 lanes, outdoors, heated, 82°.
Admission: $12.50.
Affiliate: IHRSA Call.
To find: On Bee Caves Rd. between Hwy. 360 and Mopac 1.
Masters: Austin Swims. Contact Jimmy Bynum at 327-4881.

AUSTIN   CONTINUED

HQ FITNESS 2215 E. Riverside
Phone: 440-7711.
Pool: 25y, indoors, heated, 78°-82°.
Admission: $10.
Affiliate: IPFA NC.

'Q' THE SPORTS CLUB 10616 Research Blvd.
Phone: 794-9151.
Pool: 25m, indoors, heated, 80°-83°.
Affiliate: IHRSA NC.
Hotel: Hawthorne Suites (477-1234) NC with room key.

BEAUMONT   409

YWCA OF BEAUMONT 660 Calder St.
Phone: 832-7765.
Pool: 25y x 20f, indoors, heated, 90° in winter, 80° in summer.
Affiliate: YWCA $2.

DOWNTOWN BRANCH YMCA 934 Calder Ave.
Phone: 833-3341.
Pool: 20y, indoors, heated, water temperature not reported.
Admission: 1 visit NC, then $5.
Affiliate: YMCA NC.

BIG SPRING   915

YMCA OF BIG SPRING 801 Owens
Phone: 267-8234.
Pool: 25y, 6 lanes, indoors, heated, 76°-80°.
Admission: $7.
Affiliate: Y AWAY NC.

BORGER   806

BORGER COMMUNITY ACTIVITY CENTER 1300 Roosevelt
Phone: 274-5318.
Pool: 25m, indoors, heated, 80°-82°.
Admission: $5.

BRYAN   409

BRYAN AQUATIC CENTER 3100 Oak Ridge
Phone: 361-3650.
Pool: 50m x 65f, 8 lanes, outdoors, temperature controlled, 82°.
Admission: $2, SC(55) $1.50.
To find: Located one block behind the Wal-Mart Supercenter on Briarcrest Dr.

AEROFIT HEALTH & FITNESS CENTER 1900 W. Villa Maria Rd.
Phone: 823-0971.
Pool: 25y x 72f, 8 lanes, indoors, heated, 84°.
Admission: $6.
Hotel: College Station Hilton (693-7500), Comfort Inn (846-7333), Hampton Inn (846-0184) & Manor House: $5.

To find: One block west of Hwy. 2818.
Masters: The Masters of Brazos. Contact Judy Wagner at 690-1123(h) or Cindy Hallaran at 764-3442(w).

COLLEGE STATION   409

WOFFORD CAIN POOL & P.L. DOWN'S NATATORIUM Texas A&M University
Phone: 845-4918 or 845-3021.
Pool 1: Cain: 50m x 60f, 8 lanes, outdoors, heated, 80°-83°.
Pool 2: Down's: 25y x 60f, 8 lanes, indoors, heated, 80°-83°.
Admission: $2.
Memberships: $20/semester.
Notes: A new Recreation Center with swimming facilities is expected to open in mid-1995, at which time these pools will be closed. We have no descriptive information on the replacement(s).
To find: On the west side of the football stadium. Parking is on the east side of the stadium.

SOUTHWOOD POOL 1000 Rock Prairie Rd.
Phone: 764-3787.
Pool: 25y x 60f, 6 lanes, outdoors, heated, 83°.
Admission: $1.25.
Notes: The pool is open from mid-Mar. through Nov.
To find: Down the street from Brazos Valley Medical Center.

MASTERS OF BRAZOS at Southwood Pool
Pool phone: 764-3787. **Masters:** Contact Cindy Hallaran at 764-3442(w).
Non-member participation: $3.25, includes pool fees.
Notes: Workouts: M,W: 7-7:45PM. Tu,Th: 5:30-7:30PM and/or 7-7:45PM. In Summer, the club works out at Thomas Pool, 1000 James Pkwy. (764-3735).

THE COLONY   214

THE COLONY AQUATIC PARK 5580 N. Colony Blvd.
Phone: 370-SWIM.
Pool: 25y, indoors, heated, 84°.
Admission: $1.50.
Masters: The Colony Aqua CATS. Contact Tip Spence at 335-0324(h).

CORPUS CHRISTI   512

YMCA OF CORPUS CHRISTI 417 S. Broadway
Phone: 882-1741.
Pool: 20y x 20f, 3 lanes, indoors, heated, 82°.
Admission: $5.
Affiliate: YMCA NC.
Hotel: Radisson Marina Hotel Corpus Christi (883-5111) NC. Quality Inn (882-8100), Sheraton (882-1700), & Marriott (887-1600): $3.

COLLIER POOL 3801 Harris Dr.
Phone: 852-0243.
Pool: 25m, outdoors, heated from mid-Oct. to mid-May, 83°.
Admission: $1.50, SC(65) $1.

YWCA OF CORPUS CHRISTI 4601 Corona Dr.
Phone: 857-5661.
Pool: 25y, indoors, heated, 86°.
Admission: $4.

CORPUS CHRISTI ATHLETIC CLUB 2101 Airline Rd.
Phone: 992-7100.
Pool: 25y x 50f, 6 lanes, indoors, heated, 82°-84°.
Admission: $15.
Affiliate: IHRSA $10.
Hotel: Holiday Inn Emerald Beach (883-5731) NC with a pass from the hotel.
To find: At the intersection of Airline and Holly Rds.

CORSICANA   903

THE YMCA OF CORSICANA 400 Oaklawn
Phone: 872-2412.
Pool: 25y, indoors, heated, 83°.
Admission: $4.
Affiliate: Y AWAY NC.

CYPRESS   713

THE MET FAMILY LIFE CENTER 11403 Regency Green Dr.
Phone: 890-7788.
Pool: 25m x 15m, 6 lanes, indoors, heated, 88°.
Admission: $5.
Notes: There is also a seasonally operated, unheated, outdoor 'volleyball' pool.

DALLAS   214

5. DOWNTOWN DALLAS YMCA 601 N. Akard St.
Phone: 954-0500.
Pool: 25m, 8 lanes, indoors, heated, 82°.
Admission: $10.
Affiliate: Y AWAY NC.
To find: On Akard St. between Ross and San Jacinto.

6. TEXAS CLUB 800 Main St.
Phone: 761-6300.
Pool: 20y, indoors, heated, 76°-80°.
Affiliate: IHRSA $10.
Hotel: Hyatt Regency Dallas (651-1234) & The Adolphus (742-8200): $15.

7. BALLY'S PRESIDENT'S HEALTH CLUB 3232 McKinney Ave., Suite 400
Phone: 871-7700.
Pool: 25y, outdoors, heated, 80°.
Admission: Call.
Affiliate: Bally's NC.

8. YWCA OF METROPOLITAN DALLAS 4621 Ross Ave.
Phone: 827-5600.
Pool: 25m, 3 double lanes, indoors, heated, 82°-85°.
Admission: $4.
Affiliate: YWCA $2.
Masters: Team Dallas Aquatics. Call 827-5600.

9. PARK-NORTH DALLAS BRANCH YMCA 6000 Preston Rd.
Phone: 526-7293.
Pool: 25y, 6 lanes, indoors, heated, 82°-84°.
Admission: $10.
Affiliate: YMCA NC.

10. THE PREMIER ATHLETIC CLUB 5910 N. Central
Phone: 891-6600.
Pool: 20m, indoors, heated, 80°-84°.
Affiliate: IHRSA $8.

11. STOUFFER DALLAS HOTEL 2222 Stemmons Frwy.
Phone: 631-2222. **Reservations:** 800 HOTELS-1.
Pool: 56.25f, rectangular, outdoors, heated, 72°-76°.
Admission: Registered guests NC.
Memberships: 6 months $125.

12. THE VERANDAH CLUB 2201 Stemmons Frwy.
Phone: 761-7878.
Pool 1: 25m x 30f, 7 lanes, indoors, heated, 82°.
Pool 2: 25y, 4 lanes, outdoors, heated, 75°-80° in winter, summer temperatures may reach 88°.
Hotel: Loews Anatole Hotel Dallas (720-2020) $10 with room key.
To find: Adjacent to Loews Anatole Hotel at Stemmons Frwy. (I-35) & Wycliff St.
Masters: The Verandah Aquatic Club. Contact Lisa Hawk at 761-7895.

13. PARK SOUTH BRANCH YMCA 2500 Romine
Phone: 421-5301.
Pool: 25m, indoors, heated, 82°.
Admission: $5.
Affiliate: YMCA Call.

14. WHITE ROCK ATHLETIC CLUB, INC. 718 N. Buckner
Phone: 320-0446.
Pool: 79f, indoor/outdoor, heated, 82°.
Admission: $5.

15. CENTRUM SPORTS CLUB 3102 Oak Lawn Ave., Suite 400
Phone: 522-4100.
Pool: 20y x 23f, 4 lanes, indoors, heated, 81°-84°.
Admission: $12.99.
Affiliate: IHRSA $8.66.

DALLAS   CONTINUED

Hotel: Hotel St. Germaine (871-2516), Dallas Marriott Suites Market Center (747-3000), Mansion Hotel (559-2100), Omni Melrose Hotel (521-5151), & Stoneleigh Hotel (871-7111): NC with a pass from the hotel.
To find: At the intersection of Oak Lawn and Cedar Springs, on the 4th floor of the Centrum Building.

16. BALLY'S PRESIDENT'S HEALTH CLUB 9655 Webb Chapel
Phone: 353-2999.
Pool: 25m, indoors, heated, 78°-83°.
Affiliate: Bally's NC.

17. TOWN NORTH YMCA 4332 Northaven Rd.
Phone: 357-8431.
Pool: 25y x 30f, 6 lanes, indoors, heated, 84°.
Admission: $10.
Affiliate: YMCA $5.
To find: One and a half miles south of I-635 on Midway Rd.

18. THE COOPER FITNESS CENTER 12100 Preston Rd.
Phone: 233-4832.
Pool: 25y, outdoors, heated, 83°-85°.
Admission: $10.
Masters: The Cooper Fitness Center - S.W.A.M. Contact Jerry Heidrich at 233-4832.

19. BALLY'S PRESIDENT'S HEALTH CLUB 6508 Skillman, Suite100
Phone: 349-6186.
Pool: 20y, indoors, heated, 80°-82°.
Admission: Call.
Affiliate: Bally's NC.

20. THE WESTIN HOTEL, GALLERIA DALLAS 13340 Dallas Pkwy.
Phone: 934-9494. **Reservations:** 800-228-3000.
Pool: 20y, rectangular, outdoors, heated, 72°.
Admission: Registered guests only NC.

21. NORTH DALLAS ATHLETIC CLUB 13701 N. Dallas Pkwy.
Phone: 458-2582.
Pool: 25m, outdoors, heated, 75°-80°.
Affiliate: IHRSA $10.

22. SIGNATURE ATHLETIC CLUB 14725 Preston Rd.
Phone: 490-7777.
Pool: 25m x 15m, 4 lanes, outdoors, heated, 82°.
Affiliate: CSI outside a 50 mile radius NC. IHRSA outside a 50 mile radius 2 visits per month $12 each.
To find: One block south of Belt Line Rd., at the corner of Alexis and Preston Rd.

23. LINCOLN CITY CLUB 5440 L.B.J. Frwy.
Phone: 239-8900.
Pool: 20m, indoors, heated, 84°.
Affiliate: IHRSA $10.
Hotel: Doubletree at Lincoln Center (934-8400) $11.

24. TOM LANDRY SPORTS MEDICINE & RESEARCH CENTER 411 N. Washington
Phone: 820-7800.
Pool 1: 25m x 25y, 9 x 10 lanes, indoors, heated, 81°.
Pool 2: 20y x 30f, indoors, heated, 87°.
Admission: $7.
Affiliate: IHRSA NC.
To find: Four minutes east of downtown Dallas, on the Campus of Baylor University Medical Center.

BAYLOR / LONE STAR MASTERS at Tom Landry Sports Medicine & Research Center
Pool phone: 820-7800. **Masters:** Contact Head Coach Bobby Patten at 820-7860.
Affiliate: USMS 5 workouts per week $7 each + pool fees.
Notes: Workouts: M,W: 5-8AM, Noon-1PM, 6-8PM. Tu,Th: 6-8AM, Noon-1PM, 6-8PM. F: 5-8AM. Sa: 7-10AM.

DENTON   817

GOLD'S GYM 723 I-35 South
Phone: 382-0234.
Pool: 25m, indoors, heated, 84°.
Admission: $10.

DUMAS   806

DUMAS & VICINITY YMCA 1400 S. Maddox
Phone: 935-4136.
Pool: 25m, indoors, heated, 85°.
Admission: $6.
Affiliate: YMCA NC.

EL PASO   915

JOYCE WHITFIELD JAYNES BRANCH YWCA 1600 Brown St.
Phone: 533-7475.
Pool: 25y x 45f, 6 lanes, indoors, heated, 86°-88°.
Admission: $3.
Affiliate: YWCA $1.

CENTRAL YMCA OF EL PASO 701 Montana Ave.
Phone: 533-3941.
Pool: 25y x 36f, 5 lanes, indoors, heated, 84°.
Admission: $7.
Affiliate: Y AWAY 5 visits per year NC.

SHAWBER POOL 8100 Independence
Phone: 860-2349.
Pool: 25y, indoors, heated, 82°.
Admission: $1.

WESTSIDE POOL 650 Wallenberg
Phone: 584-9848.
Pool: 25y, indoors, heated, 84°.
Admission: $1.

WASHINGTON POOL 4210 Paisano
Phone: 542-0087.
Pool: 25y, indoors, heated, 84°-85°.
Admission: $1.

NORTHEAST FAMILY YMCA 5509 Will Ruth Ave.
Phone: 755-9622.
Pool: 25m x 42f, 5 lanes, indoors, heated, 84°.
Admission: $5, SC(65) $3.
Affiliate: Y AWAY NC.
Masters: Contact Aquatic Director Karen Fuller at
755-9622.

VETERANS POOL 6301 Salem
Phone: 821-0142.
Pool: 25y, indoors, heated, water temperature not
reported.
Admission: $1.

EL PASO AIRPORT HILTON 2027 Airway Blvd.
Phone: 778-4241. **Reservations:** 800-742-7248.
Pool: 25y, free form, outdoors, heated, 82°.
Admission: Registered guests only NC.

HAWKINS POOL 1500 Hawkins Blvd.
Phone: 594-8031.
Pool: 25y, indoors, heated, 85°.
Admission: $1.

FORT WORTH   817

25. AMON CARTER JR. DOWNTOWN YMCA 512
Lamar St.
Phone: 332-3281.
Pool: 25m x 36f, 6 lanes, indoors, heated, 85°.
Admission: $10.
Affiliate: Y AWAY NC.
Hotel: All downtown hotels $5 with room key.
To find: At the intersection of 4th and Lamar St.

26. BALLY'S PRESIDENT'S HEALTH CLUB 1201
Oakland Blvd.
Phone: 457-2393.
Pool: 20y, indoors, heated, 84°.
Admission: Call.
Affiliate: Bally's NC.

27. RIVERBEND ATHLETIC CLUB 2201 E. Loop
820 N.
Phone: 284-3353.
Pool: 25m, outdoors, heated, 81°.
Admission: $4.

28. THE FT. WORTH-ARLINGTON SWIM TEAM at
Wilkerson-Greines Aquatic Center, 5101 Folwell
Masters: Contact Aquatics Coordinator Rob Ingle
at 531-6348.

Pool: 25y x 50m, 17 lanes, indoors, heated, 81°-
82°.
Affiliate: USMS Call.

29. THE HEALTH & FITNESS CONNECTION 6242
Hulen Bend Blvd.
Phone: 346-6161.
Pool: 25y, indoors, heated, 82°-84°.
Admission: $5.
Notes: The pool was completely renovated in 1994.

GALVESTON   409

GALVESTON YMCA 2222 Ave. 'L'
Phone: 763-4607.
Pool: 25y x 27f, 2 lap lanes, indoors, heated, 85°.
Admission: $4.
Affiliate: YMCA NC.
To find: Two blocks south of Broadway on 23rd
(Tremont St.) and Ave. 'L'.

GALVESTON HEALTH & RACQUET CLUB 83rd
& Airport
Phone: 744-3651.
Pool: 25y, outdoors, heated, 80°.
Admission: $10.

GARLAND   214

NORTHSTAR ATHLETIC CLUB 1332 Beltline Rd.
Phone: 495-7501.
Pool: 20y, indoors, heated, 84°-86°.
Admission: $5.
Affiliate: IHRSA NC.

BALLY'S PRESIDENT'S HEALTH CLUB 1121
Northwest Hwy.
Phone: 271-4614.
Pool: 20y, indoors, heated, 78°-80°.
Admission: Call.
Affiliate: Bally's NC.

GRAND PRAIRIE   214

30. FITNESS UNIQUE 545 W. Hwy. 303
Phone: 642-0785.
Pool: 70f x 20f, 4 lanes, indoor/outdoor, heated,
84°.
Admission: $10.

31. KIRBY CREEK NATATORIUM 3201 Corn
Valley Rd.
Phone: 263-8174.
Pool: 25m x 46f, indoors, heated, 86°.
Admission: $2.

GREENVILLE   903

GREENVILLE / HUNT COUNTY YMCA 1915
Stanford
Phone: 455-5405.
Pool: 25y x 30f, indoors, heated, 84°.
Admission: $5.

Affiliate: YMCA Call.
Hotel: Holiday Inn (454-7000) $4 with room key.

HOUSTON _____ 713

Houston

290
610
90
90PR
10
10

Dots are placed by ZIP codes, not by street addresses.

37. THE TEXAS CLUB 601 Travis
Phone: 227-7000.
Pool: 25y x 36f, 4 lanes, indoors, heated, 82°.
Admission: Weekdays $10. Weekends $5. Limit 3 visits per month.
Hotel: Lancaster Hotel (228-9500) & Hyatt Regency Houston (654-1234): NC.
To find: At the intersection of Capital and Travis, atop the Texas Commerce Center.
Masters: The Texas Club Masters. Contact Jody Johnston at 227-7000.

38. DOWNTOWN BRANCH YMCA 1600 Louisiana St.
Phone: 659-8501.
Pool: 25y, 4 lanes, indoors, heated, 72°.
Affiliate: YMCA 3 visits per month NC.

39. H₂OUSTON SWIMS at the University of Houston Natatorium, 3855 Holmann
Pool phone: 743-9500. **Masters:** Contact Head Coach Emmett Hines at 748-7946.
Pool: 25y x 42f, 6 lanes, indoors, heated, 80°.
Affiliate: USMS 2 workouts per month NC, then $5 per workout, includes pool fees.
Notes: Coached workouts: M-F: 6-7:30PM. Su: 9-10:30AM. In summer, add M,W,F: 6-7:30AM and Sa: 8-9:30AM.
To find: The campus is at I-45 and Cullen, the facility is attached to the Hofheinz Pavilion.

40. BALLY'S PRESIDENT & FIRST LADY HEALTH CLUB 2500 Dunstan

Phone: 521-3113.
Pool: 25m, indoors, heated, 80°.
Affiliate: Bally's NC.

41. RICE UNIVERSITY POOL 6100 S. Main St.
Phone: 527-4710.
Pool: 25y, 6 lanes, indoors, heated, 80°.
Memberships: $175/year.
Masters: Contact Coach Kris Wingenroth at 527-4710.

42. YWCA OF HOUSTON 3621 Willia
Phone: 868-6075.
Pool: 25y, indoors, heated, 86°.
Admission: 1 visit NC, then $7.50.

43. BAYOU PARK CLUB 4400 Memorial Dr.
Phone: 880-9330.
Pool: 25y, outdoors, heated, 82°-83°.
Admission: $10.

44. COSSABOOM FAMILY YMCA 7903 S. Loop E.
Phone: 643-4396.
Pool 1: 20y x 25f, 4 lanes, indoors, heated, 82°-84°.
Pool 2: 25y x 30f, 4 lanes, outdoors, unheated, the range of water temperatures was not reported.
Admission: $6.
Affiliate: YMCA $3.
To find: At Gulfgate area, near I-45 and 610 Loop.

45. THE HOUSTONIAN HOTEL & CLUB 111 N. Post Oak Blvd.
Phone: 680-2626. **Reservations:** 800-231-2759.
Pool: 25y, rectangular, outdoors, heated, 82°.
Admission: Registered guests NC.
Affiliate: IHRSA $15.
To find: At Woodway and I-610, just west of the Galleria area.

H₂OUSTON SWIMS at The Houstonian Hotel & Club
Masters: Contact Head Coach Emmett Hines at 748-7946.
Hotel: The Houstonian Hotel & Club NC.
Notes: Coached workouts: M,W,F: Noon-1PM. Tu,Th: 6-7AM, Noon-1PM, 6-7PM. Sa: 9-10:30AM. Access to workouts is restricted to members of the Houstonian Club and guests at the Houstonian Hotel.

46. BALLY'S PRESIDENT & FIRST LADY HEALTH CLUB 9825 Katy Rd.
Phone: 467-8181.
Pool: 25m, indoors, heated, 80°.
Affiliate: Bally's NC.

47. HOUSTON SWIM CLUB 8307 Augustine
Phone: 774-7946.
Pool 1: 25y x 180f, 7 lanes, outdoors, heated, 80°.
Pool 2: 20y x 120f, 4 lanes, indoors, heated, 92°.
Admission: $3.

To find: Four blocks west and south of the intersection of Beechnut and Gessner.

48. BALLY'S PRESIDENT & FIRST LADY
HEALTH CLUB 13350 Northwest Frwy.
Phone: 690-1006.
Pool: 25m, indoors, heated, 78°-82°.
Admission: Call.
Affiliate: Bally's NC.

49. H₂OUSTON SWIMS at the University of Texas
Health Sciences Center, 7779 Knight Rd.
Pool phone: 792-4920. **Masters:** Contact Head Coach Emmett Hines at 748-7946.
Pool: 25y x 50m, 17 x 9 lanes, outdoors, heated, 80°-85°.
Affiliate: USMS $5 per workout.
Notes: Coached workouts: M,W,F: 6-7:30AM. Sa: 8-9:30AM. Workouts are held here in the fall, winter, and spring. In summer, workouts continue at the University of Houston. (See #39, above.)

50. WESTSIDE FAMILY YMCA 1006 Voss Rd.
Phone: 467-9622.
Pool 1: 50m x 25y, 10 x 22 lanes, outdoors, heated, 80°.
Pool 2: 25y x 45f, 7 lanes, indoors, heated, 81°.
Admission: $5.
Affiliate: Y AWAY NC.
To find: On the north side of I-10, between Bingle and Campbell.
Masters: The Westside Masters. Contact Larry Glass at 467-9622.

51. BALLY'S PRESIDENT & FIRST LADY
HEALTH CLUB 1980A S. Post Oak Rd.
Phone: 960-1037.
Pool: 25m, indoors, heated, 80°-82°.
Affiliate: Bally's NC.

52. POST OAK FAMILY YMCA 1331 Augusta Dr.
Phone: 781-1061.
Pool: 25y x 48f, 8 lanes, outdoors, heated, 82°-84°.
Admission: $10.
Affiliate: Out-of-town YMCA 30 days NC.
To find: In the Galleria area.

53. BALLY'S PRESIDENT & FIRST LADY
HEALTH CLUB 430 W. Greens Rd.
Phone: 872-1130.
Pool: 25m, indoors, heated, 78°-80°.
Affiliate: Bally's NC.

54. BALLY'S PRESIDENT & FIRST LADY
HEALTH CLUB 5215 FM 1960 W.
Phone: 440-9835.
Pool: 22m, indoors, heated, 78°-80°.
Affiliate: Bally's NC.

55. BALLY'S PRESIDENT & FIRST LADY
HEALTH CLUB 7737 W. Bellfort

Phone: 729-7049.
Pool: 25m, indoors, heated, 78°-82°.
Admission: Call.
Affiliate: Bally's NC.

56. OLYMPIA FITNESS & RACQUETBALL CLUB
8313 Southwest Frwy.
Phone: 988-8787.
Pool: 65f x 15f, 2 lanes, indoors, heated, 80°.
Admission: $5.
Affiliate: IPFA & AHA: NC.
Hotel: La Quinta (772-3626) NC with room key.
To find: On the in-bound side of Southwest Frwy., between Gessner and Beechnut, next to Channel 2 TV, in the middle building of 'THE CENTER' office complex.

57. MEMORIAL ATHLETIC CLUB 14690 Memorial Dr.
Phone: 497-7570.
Pool: 25y, 5 lanes, outdoors, heated, 72°-75° in winter, 80°-82° in summer.
Admission: $8.

58. BALLY'S PRESIDENT & FIRST LADY
HEALTH CLUB 15415 Katy Frwy.
Phone: 578-9191.
Pool: 25m, indoors, heated, 78°-82°.
Affiliate: Bally's NC.

59. FIT INN / CHARLIE CLUB HOTEL 9009 Boone Rd.
Phone: 530-0000.
Pool 1: 70f x 30f, 3 lanes, indoors, heated, 73°-74°.
Pool 2: 25y, 2 lanes, outdoors, unheated, the range of water temperatures was not reported.
Admission: $10. Registered guests NC.
Affiliate: IHRSA $5.
Memberships: $50/month.
To find: Exit Hwy. 59 at Bissonett, one mile west to Boone, two blocks north.

60. BALLY'S PRESIDENT & FIRST LADY
HEALTH CLUB 19304 Hwy. 59
Phone: 446-5114.
Pool: 25m, indoors, heated, 80°-84°.
Affiliate: Bally's NC.

61. BALLY'S PRESIDENT & FIRST LADY
HEALTH CLUB 1418 Spencer Hwy.
Phone: 941-3584.
Pool: 20m, indoors, heated, 82°.
Admission: Call.
Affiliate: Bally's NC.

HUNTSVILLE   409

WATERWOOD NATIONAL RESORT 1 Waterwood
Phone: 891-5211. **Reservations:** 800-441-5211.
Pool: 25m, rectangular, outdoors, unheated, 75°-90°.
Admission: Registered guests only NC.
Notes: The pool is closed Dec. through Mar.

HURST   817

BALLY'S PRESIDENT'S HEALTH CLUB 650
Grapevine Hwy.
Phone: 281-6043.
Pool: 20y, indoors, heated, 80°-85°.
Admission: Call.
Affiliate: Bally's NC.

IRVING   214

32. FOUR SEASONS RESORT & CLUB 4150 N.
MacArthur Blvd.
Phone: 717-0700. **Reservations:** 800-332-3442.
Pool: 25m, indoors, heated, 80°.
Admission: Registered guests only NC.
Notes: Also see Las Colinas Sports Club listed
below.

33. LAS COLINAS SPORTS CLUB 4200 N.
MacArthur
Phone: 717-2500.
Pool 1: 25y, 4 lanes, indoors, heated, 82.5°.
Pool 2: 25m, 4 lanes, outdoors, unheated, the
range of water temperatures was not reported.
Admission: $12.
Hotel: Four Seasons Resort & Club (717-0700)
[see previous listing] NC with room key or guest
pass from the hotel.

34. NORTHLAKE AQUATIC CENTER Northlake
Community College Pool, 5001 N. MacArthur Blvd.
Phone: 659-5360.
Pool: 50m OR 25y + 27m, indoor/outdoor, heated,
82°-84°.
Admission: $1.50.

35. WYNDHAM GARDEN HOTEL-LAS COLINAS
110 W. Carpenter Frwy.
Phone: 650-1600. **Reservations:** 800-WYND-
HAM.
Pool: 65f, rectangular, indoors, heated, 72°.
Admission: Registered guests only NC.

36. DALLAS / FT. WORTH AIRPORT MARRIOTT
8440 Freeport Pkwy.
Phone: 929-8800. **Reservations:** 800-228-9290.
Pool: 27y, oval or kidney shape, indoor/outdoor,
heated, 80°.
Admission: $5. Registered guests NC.
Notes: The indoor section of the pool is 19 yards
long.

KERRVILLE   210

FAMILY SPORTS CENTER 1107 Junction Hwy.
Phone: 895-5555.
Pool: 20y x 30f, indoors, heated, 88°.
Admission: $10.

KINGWOOD   713

KINGWOOD ATHLETIC CLUB 806 Russell Palmer
Dr.
Phone: 358-7765.
Pool 1: 25y, indoors, heated, 82°.
Pool 2: 25m, outdoors, unheated, the range of
water temperatures was not reported.
Admission: $8.
Affiliate: IHRSA & CSI: Call.
Masters: The Kingwood Athletic Club Masters.
Contact Mary Tipton at 358-7765.

LAKE JACKSON   409

LAKE JACKSON RECREATION CENTER 335 E.
Hwy. 332
Phone: 297-4533.
Pool: 25m, indoors, heated, 81°-82°.
Admission: $2, SC(60) $1.

LEAGUE CITY   713

**THE FITNESS CENTER AT SOUTH SHORE
HARBOUR** 3000 Invincible Dr.
Phone: 334-2560.
Pool: 25y x 21f, 3 lanes, indoors, heated, 83°.
Affiliate: IHRSA $10 per day, $12.50 per week.
Hotel: South Shore Harbour Resort & Conference
Center (334-1000) $5 per day, $12.50 per week.

LONGVIEW   903

LONGVIEW AQUATIC CENTER 201 E. Hawkins
Pkwy.
Phone: 663-2744 or 663-2636.
Pool: 25m, indoors, heated, 82°.
Admission: $2.

LUBBOCK   806

TEXAS TECH AQUATIC CENTER at the corner of
Hartford & Main
Phone: 742-3351.
Pool: 50m x 25y, indoor/outdoor, heated, 81°-82°.
Memberships: Annual Alumni Century Club contri-
bution of $100 + $85/semester facility dues.

YWCA OF LUBBOCK 3101 - 35th St.
Phone: 792-2723.
Pool: 25y x 45f, 6 lanes, indoors, heated, 85°.
Admission: $3.50.
Affiliate: YWCA $2.
To find: At the corner of Flint and 35th St., east of
Indian Ave.

LUFKIN   409

LIVE WELL ATHLETIC CLUB 1616 Tulane
Phone: 639-5483.
Pool: 25y, outdoors, heated, 80°.
Admission: $8.50.
Hotel: Ramada Inn (639-1122) $7.50 with Livewell
Discount Card from the hotel.

To find: Behind Lufkin Mall (Loop 287 at 59).
Masters: The Lufkin Sharks. Contact Julie
Johnston at 639-5483.

MCALLEN   210

CITY OF MCALLEN SWIMMING POOL 1921 N.
Bicentennial Blvd.
Phone: 682-2392.
Pool: 50m, outdoors, heated, 80°-84°.
Admission: $1.
Notes: In winter, the pool is open only for lap swim-
ming and water aerobics.

SUMMIT SPORTS CLUB 1500 W. Hall Acres
Phone: 630-2722.
Pool: 25y, 6 lanes, indoors, heated, 84°.
Affiliate: IHRSA $5.
To find: From Expressway 83 go 2.5 miles south
on Jackson Rd. to Hall Acres, turn west and the
club is about one quarter mile.

MIDLAND   915

MIDLAND METRO YMCA 800 N. Big Springs
Phone: 682-2551.
Pool: 25y x 30f, 4 lanes, indoors, heated, 83°-84°.
Admission: $5.
Affiliate: YMCA outside a 50 mile radius NC.
To find: On the main north/south downtown street,
next to Dinero Plaza.

ALAMO YMCA 901 N. Midland Dr.
Phone: 694-2528.
Pool: 25y x 44f, 6 lanes, indoors, heated, 88°.
Admission: $5.
Affiliate: Y AWAY NC.
Notes: There is also an outdoor, summer pool.

NACOGDOCHES   409

THE COURT CLUB 4822 N. University Dr.
Phone: 569-0068.
Pool: 25y, indoor/outdoor, heated, 80°.
Admission: $5.

ODESSA   915

YMCA OF ODESSA 3001 E. University Blvd.
Phone: 362-4301.
Pool: 25y, indoors, heated, 87°.
Admission: $5.
Affiliate: YMCA NC.

PLAINVIEW   806

PLAINVIEW YMCA 313 Enis
Phone: 293-8319.
Pool: 25m, indoors, heated, 87°.
Admission: $3.
Affiliate: YMCA NC.
Hotel: Best Western Conestoga (293-9454) NC
with room key.

PLANO   214

PLANO AQUATIC CENTER 2301 Westside Dr.
Phone: 964-4232.
Pool: 25y x 60f, 6 lanes, indoors, heated, 84°.
Admission: $1.
To find: On the east side of Plano Senior High
School, at the intersection of Park and
Independence.
Masters: The Plano Wetcats. Contact the Aquatics
Superintendent at 578-7250.

BALLY'S PRESIDENT'S HEALTH CLUB 910 W.
Parker Rd.
Phone: 578-7676.
Pool: 25m, indoors, heated, 79°-82°.
Admission: Call.
Affiliate: Bally's NC.

PORT ARTHUR   409

NAUTILUS TRAINING CENTER 3335 Twin City
Hwy.
Phone: 963-3344.
Pool: 20y x 40f, outdoors, heated, 82°.
Admission: $5.

YMCA OF PORT ARTHUR 6760 - 9th Ave.
Phone: 962-6644.
Pool: 25y, 6 lanes, indoors, heated, 85°.
Admission: $6.
Affiliate: YMCA NC.
Hotel: Holiday Inn-Park Central (724-5000) &
Ramada Inn of Port Arthur (962-9858): NC with
room key.

RANCHO VIEJO   210

RANCHO VIEJO RESORT & COUNTRY CLUB 1
Rancho Viejo Dr.
Phone: 350-4000. **Reservations:** 800-531-7400.
Pool: 35y, 'clover leaf' shape, outdoors, unheated,
60°-75°.
Admission: Registered guests only NC.
Notes: The pool has a waterfall and swim-up bar.

RICHARDSON   214

J. J. PEARCE HIGH SCHOOL POOL 1600 N. Coit
Phone: 238-4100.
Pool: 25m, indoors, heated, 76°-78°.
Memberships: $15 - $22/month.
Notes: Community access is managed by the
Richardson Parks & Recreation Dept.

RICHARDSON YWCA NATATORIUM 1416 E.
Collins Blvd.
Phone: 231-7201.
Pool: 25y, indoors, heated, 84°.
Admission: $3.
Affiliate: YWCA $1.50.
Masters: There is a Masters group in formation.
Contact Mike Orren at 272-4947(w).

RICHARDSON CONTINUED

BERKNER HIGH SCHOOL POOL 1600 E. Spring Valley
Phone: 238-4100.
Pool: 25m, indoors, heated, 76°-78°.
Memberships: $15 - $22/month.
Notes: Community access is managed by the Richardson Parks & Recreation Dept.

RICHMOND 713

T. W. DAVIS YMCA 911 Thompson Hwy.
Phone: 341-0791.
Pool: 25y, 6 lanes, indoors, heated, 86°.
Admission: $5.
Affiliate: Y AWAY NC.

SAN ANTONIO 210

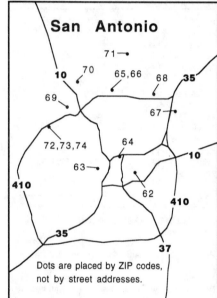

San Antonio

71 →

10   70   65,66   68   35

69

67

72,73,74   64   10

63

410

62

410

35

37

Dots are placed by ZIP codes, not by street addresses.

62. ALAMO BRANCH YMCA 1213 Iowa
Phone: 532-0932.
Pool: 25y, indoors, heated, 83°.
Admission: $3.
Affiliate: YMCA Call.

63. SAN ANTONIO NATATORIUM 1430 W. Durango
Phone: 226-8541.
Pool: 25y x 50m, indoors, heated, 82°.
Admission: $1.50.

64. DOWNTOWN YMCA OF SAN ANTONIO 903 N. St. Mary's St.

Phone: 246-9600.
Pool: 25y x 25f, 4 lanes, indoors, heated, 83°-85°.
Admission: $7.
Affiliate: YMCA NC.
To find: At the intersection of St. Mary's St. and Lexington Ave. There is a 50¢ charge in the parking lot.

65. CONCORD ATHLETIC CLUB 7700 Jones Maltsberger
Phone: 828-8880.
Pool: 25m x 15m, 5 lanes, indoors, heated, 82°.
Affiliate: IHRSA $8.50.
Hotel: Holiday Inn Riverwalk (224-2500), La Mansion Del Rio (225-2581), Embassy Suites Int'l Airport (525-9999), Hyatt Regency San Antonio (222-1234), Marriott, Hilton, & Sheraton hotels: $15.
To find: One mile south of the airport, off Hwy. 281.

66. BLOSSOM AQUATIC CENTER 12002 Jones Maltsberger Rd.
Phone: 491-6136.
Pool: 50m x 25y, 8 x 16 lanes, indoors, heated, 82°.
Admission: $2. Resident SC(65) NC.
To find: Next to the airport, at the corner of Bitters Rd. and Jones Maltsberger.
Masters: The Nemo Masters. Contact Lisa Hokett or Bill Walker at 491-6136.

67. WORLD GYM 4555 Walzem Rd.
Phone: 650-5444.
Pool: 20y, 3 lanes, indoors, heated, 78°-80°.
Admission: Out-of-town visitors $10.
Affiliate: IHRSA & IPFA: NC.
Hotel: Drury Inn East (654-1144): NC with room key.

68. WORLD GYM 13032 Nacogdoches Rd.
Phone: 655-8063.
Pool: 20y, 3 lanes, indoors, heated, 78°-80°.
Admission: Out-of-town visitors $10.
Affiliate: IHRSA & IPFA: NC.

69. WORLD GYM 7460 Callaghan Rd.
Phone: 377-3234.
Pool: 20y, 3 lanes, indoors, heated, 78°-80°.
Admission: Out-of-town visitors $10.
Affiliate: IHRSA & IPFA: NC.
Hotel: Drury Inn East (654-1144): NC with room key.

70. COLONNADE ATHLETIC CLUB 9834 Colonnade Blvd.
Phone: 694-4100.
Pool: 20y, 3 lanes, indoors, heated, 82°-86°.
Admission: $5.50.

71. RACQUETBALL & FITNESS CLUB 15759 San Pedro
Phone: 490-9161.

Pool: 20y, indoors, heated, 82°.
Admission: $6

72. NORTHSIDE AQUATIC CENTER 7001
Culebra Rd.
Phone: 706-7500.
Pool: 50m OR 25m + 25y x 60f, 8 OR 9 + 9 lanes,
indoor/outdoor, heated, 82°.
Admission: $2.
To find: At the intersection of Culebra Rd. and
Loop 410, adjacent to La Quinta-Ingram.

73. WORLD GYM 6418 Bandera Rd.
Phone: 647-0131.
Pool: 20y, 3 lanes, indoors, heated, 78°-80°.
Admission: Out-of-town visitors $10.
Affiliate: IHRSA & IPFA: NC.

74. BALLY'S PRESIDENT'S HEALTH CLUB 5819
N.W. Loop 410, Suite 150
Phone: 647-9600.
Pool: 25y, indoors, heated, 80°-82°.
Admission: Call.
Affiliate: Bally's NC.

SHERMAN   903

HANNAH NATATORIUM Austin College, 900 N.
Grand Ave.
Phone: 813-2474.
Pool: 25y x 45f, 6 lanes, indoors, heated, 80°-84°.
Memberships: $40/semester.

TEXAS CITY   409

LOWRY FITNESS CENTER 1900 - 5th Ave. N.
Phone: 643-5984.
Pool: 25y x 25f, 3 lanes, indoors, heated, 86°.
Admission: $3.75.
Notes: There is also an 'Olympic size', outdoor pool
operated in summer.
To find: Right behind City Hall on Palmer Hwy.

COLLEGE OF THE MAINLAND 1200 Amburn Rd.
Phone: 938-1211.
Pool: 25y, 6 lanes, indoors, heated, 84°.
Admission: $3.
Memberships: $15/month. $50/year (9/1-8/31),
SC $10.
Notes: The pool has a diving well.
To find: Approximately one mile east of Gulf
Greyhound Park in Texas City.

TYLER   903

TYLER METROPOLITAN YMCA 215 W. Bow
Phone: 593-7327.
Pool: 25y, indoors, heated, 85°.
Admission: $5.
Affiliate: YMCA NC.

VICTORIA   512

VICTORIA YMCA 1806 N. Nimitz
Phone: 575-0511.
Pool: 22.8m, indoors, heated, 85°.
Admission: $5.
Affiliate: YMCA NC.

WACO   817

WACO FAMILY Y 6800 Harvey
Phone: 776-6612.
Pool 1: 25y x 25m, 10 x 9 lanes, indoors, heated,
82°.
Pool 2: 20y, 5 lanes, indoors, heated, 88°.
Admission: Residents 3 visits per month $10 each.
Non-residents 4 visits per month $10 each.
Affiliate: YMCA & YWCA: 4 visits per month NC.
Notes: This is a new pool, opened in August, 1994.

WEATHERFORD   817

HEALTH FORUM 301 I-20 W. at Tintop
Phone: 594-4703.
Pool: 25y, indoors, heated, 78°.
Admission: $5.
Affiliate: IPFA NC.

WEBSTER   713

**WILLIAMS INDOOR POOL & RECREATION
CENTER** 15000 McConn
Phone: 486-2626.
Pool: 25y x 105f, 10 lanes, indoors, heated, 82°.
Admission: $3.
Affiliate: USMS outside a 50 mile radius 8 visits
per month $2.00 each.
Hotel: Holiday Inn NASA (333-2500) & Residence
Inn (486-2424): $2.00 with voucher or room key.
To find: I-45 south to Clear Lake City Blvd.
Masters: The Space City Aquatic Team (SCAT).
Contact Robert Henrick at 486-2626.

**BALLY'S PRESIDENT & FIRST LADY HEALTH
CLUB** 20761 Gulf Frwy.
Phone: 332-8746.
Pool: 25m, indoors, heated, 78°-82°.
Admission: Call.
Affiliate: Bally's NC.

WESTLAKE   817

MARRIOTT SOLANA 5 Village Circle
Phone: 430-3848. Reservations: 800-228-9290.
Pool: 26y, 'L' shape, outdoors, unheated, 60°-70°.
Admission: Registered guests only NC.
Notes: Registered guests also have access to the
Solana Club's facilities. See the listing which fol-
lows.

THE SOLANA CLUB 2902 Sams School Rd.
Phone: 491-4559.
Pool: 25y, 3 lanes, indoors, heated, 80°-83°.
Affiliate: IHRSA outside a 50 mile radius $7.51.

Hotel: Marriott Solana (430-3848) [see preceding listing] NC with hotel pass.
Notes: There is also a 30y, 3 lane, outdoor, summer pool.

WICHITA FALLS   817

WICHITA FALLS YMCA 1010 - 9th St.
Phone: 322-7816.
Pool: 20y x 25f, 5 lanes, indoors, heated, 85°.
Admission: $5.
Affiliate: YMCA NC.
Hotel: Ramada Hotel Wichita Falls (466-6000) & Sheraton Inn Wichita Falls (761-6000): NC.

YWCA OF WICHITA FALLS 801-03 Burnett St.
Phone: 723-2124.
Pool: 20y, indoors, heated, 90°.
Admission: $4.

THE WOODLANDS   713

WOODLANDS ATHLETIC CENTER 11111
Winterberry Place
Phone: 363-9500.
Pool 1: 50y x 25y, outdoors, heated, 81°-83°.
Pool 2: 25y, 6 lanes, indoors, heated, 78°-83°.
Admission: Visitors from outside a 50 mile radius $6.
Affiliate: IHRSA NC.
Masters: The Woodlands Masters. Contact Leslie Smith at 363-9500.

SOUTH MONTGOMERY COUNTY YMCA 6145
Shadowbend Place
Phone: 367-9622.
Pool: 25y, 6 lanes, outdoors, heated, 78°-80°.
Admission: $10.
Affiliate: Out-of-town YMCA NC.
To find: Exit I-45 at Research Forest Dr. heading west. Turn left at Shadowbend, the YMCA is on the right.

ALWAYS CALL FIRST

Pools close, they change names, affiliations, admission policies, and rates. And just because a pool is listed in *Swimmers Guide* doesn't mean it's open all day, every day, for just the type of workout you want to do. Spend a quarter to save time and aggravation. . . always call first!

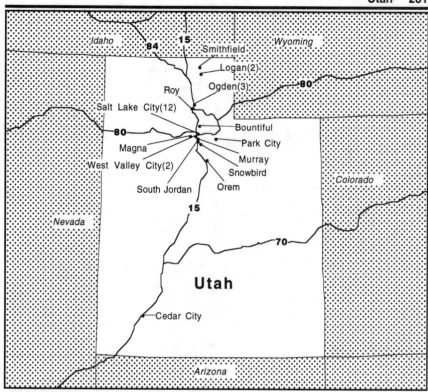

BOUNTIFUL 801

BOUNTIFUL INDOOR POOL 785 S. 1st E.
Phone: 298-6224.
Pool: 25y, indoors, heated, 86°.
Admission: $2.50.

CEDAR CITY 801

SOUTHERN UTAH UNIVERSITY 351 W. Center
Phone: 586-7829.
Pool: 25m x 12m, 7 lanes, indoors, heated, 80°.
Admission: $1.
To find: In the Physical Education Building.

LOGAN 801

LOGAN MUNICIPOOL 125 E. 1000 N.
Phone: 750-9890.
Pool: 25y x 39f, 6 lanes, indoors, heated, 88°.
Admission: Lap swims $1.25. Rec. swims $2, SC
$1.75.

HPER BUILDING - CAMPUS RECREATION Utah
State University, 700 N. 800 E.
Phone: 797-1502.
Pool: 25y, 6 lanes, indoors, heated, 84°.
Affiliate: USMS $2, 1 week $5.
Hotel: University Inn (797-1153) $2.

Masters: The USU Masters Swim. Contact the
Campus Recreation Office at 797-1502.

MAGNA 801

CYPRUS HIGH SCHOOL 8623 W. 3000 S.
Phone: 481-7194 days. 250-8613 evenings.
Pool: 25y x 36f, 5 lanes, indoors, heated, 85°.
Admission: $2. Resident SC(65) $1.
Notes: There are no lap swimming sessions at this
facility, all swims are 'rec. swims'.

MURRAY 801

MURRAY HIGH SCHOOL 5440 S. State
Phone: 264-7412.
Pool: 25y x 48f, 6 lanes, indoors, heated, 83°.
Admission: $2, SC(60) $1.

OGDEN 801

**MARSHALL WHITE COMMUNITY CENTER -
WEBER COUNTY** 222 - 28th St.
Phone: 629-8347.
Pool: 25y, indoors, heated, 84°.
Admission: 50¢.

TOTAL FITNESS CENTER 550 - 25th St.
Phone: 399-5861.
Pool: 20y x 24f, indoors, heated, 87°.

OGDEN   CONTINUED

Admission: $7.50.
Hotel: Radisson Suite Hotel Ogden (627-1900) &
Ogden Park Hotel: $5.50 with room key.

OGDEN ATHLETIC CLUB 1221 E. 5800 S.
Phone: 479-6500.
Pool: 25m, indoors, heated, 82°.
Admission: $7.

OREM   801

OREM FITNESS CENTER 165 S. 580 W.
Phone: 229-7154.
Pool: 50m x 25y, 2-3 lap swimming lanes, indoors,
heated, 85°.
Admission: $2, SC(55) $1.50.
To find: Next to Mountain View High School, six
blocks west of State St. and two blocks south of
Center St.

PARK CITY   801

PROSPECTOR ATHLETIC CLUB at the Inn at
Prospector Square, 2080 Gold Dust Lane
Phone: 649-6670.
Pool: 25y x 25f, 3 lanes, indoors, heated, 80°.
Admission: $15.
Affiliate: IHRSA $7.50.
Hotel: The Inn at Prospector Square (649-7100)
$7.50.
To find: At Gold Dust Lane and Sidewinder Dr.

ROY   801

AMERICAN FITNESS 5385 S. 1950 W.
Phone: 773-6220.
Pool: 20m, indoors, heated, 83°.
Admission: $5.

SALT LAKE CITY   801

1. RED LION HOTEL / SALT LAKE CITY 255 S.W.
Temple
Phone: 328-2000. **Reservations:** 800-547-8010.
Pool: 52f, rectangular, indoors, heated, water tem-
perature not reported.
Admission: Registered guests only NC.

2. LITTLE AMERICA HOTEL & TOWERS 500 S.
Main St.
Phone: 363-6781. **Reservations:** 800-453-9450.
Pool: 70f+, 'twisted 8' shape, indoors, heated, 86°.
Admission: Registered guests only NC.
Notes: There is also a 25y, outdoor, seasonal pool.

3. DESERET GYMNASIUM 161 N. Main
Phone: 359-3911.
Pool 1: 25y x 54f, 6 lanes, indoors, heated, 83°.
Pool 2: 20y x 60f, indoors, heated, 88°.
Admission: $5,SC(62) $3.50.
To find: One block north of Temple Square.

Salt Lake City

Dots are placed by ZIP codes,
not by street addresses.

4. GRANITE HIGH SCHOOL 3305 S. 500 E.
Phone: 481-7194 days. 481-7159 evenings.
Pool: 25y x 42f, 6 lanes, indoors, heated, 86°.
Admission: $2. Resident SC(65) $1.

5. STEINER AQUATIC CENTER 645 Guardsman
Way
Phone: 583-9713.
Pool: 25y, indoors, heated, 84°.
Admission: $3.

6. SKYLINE HIGH SCHOOL 3251 E. 3760 S.
Phone: 481-7194 days. 273-2091 evenings.
Pool: 25y x 42f, 6 lanes, indoors, heated, 85°.
Admission: $2. Resident SC(65) $1.

7. SALT LAKE CITY YWCA 322 E. 300 S.
Phone: 355-2804.
Pool: 20y x 20f, 4 lanes, indoors, heated, 92°.
Affiliate: YWCA $1-$5 depending on program.

8. NORTHWEST MULTI PURPOSE CENTER 1300
W. 300 N.
Phone: 596-0072.
Pool: 25y x 18f, 4 lanes, indoors, heated, 87.5°.
Admission: Lap swimming: $1.59, SC(65) $1.06.
Open plunge $2.65, SC $1.06.

9. SPORTS MALL 5445 S. 900 E.
Phone: 261-3426.
Pool: 25y x 45f, 6 lanes, indoor/outdoor, heated,
84°.
Admission: $10.
Affiliate: IHRSA $5.

10. COTTONWOOD HIGH SCHOOL 5717 S. 1300
E.
Phone: 481-7194 days. 273-2111 evenings.
Pool: 25y x 42f, 6 lanes, indoors, heated, 85°.
Admission: $2. Resident SC(65) $1.

11. COTTONWOOD HEIGHTS RECREATION CENTER 7500 S. 2700 E.
Phone: 943-3160.
Pool: 25m, indoors, heated, 83°.
Admission: Residents $2.10, non-residents $3.15.

12. TAYLORSVILLE HIGH SCHOOL 5225 S. Redwood Rd.
Phone: 481-7194 days. 263-6152 evenings.
Pool: 25y x 42f, 6 lanes, indoors, heated, 86°.
Admission: $2. Resident SC(65) $1.

SMITHFIELD _____ 801

SKYVIEW POOL 600 S. 250 E.
Phone: 563-5625.
Pool: 25y, indoors, heated, 88°.
Admission: $1.50.

SNOWBIRD _____ 801

SNOWBIRD SKI & SUMMER RESORT
Phone: 742-2222. **Reservations:** 800-742-3100.
Pool: 25m, rectangular, outdoors, heated, 94° in winter, 80° in summer.
Admission: $10. Registered guests NC.

SOUTH JORDAN _____ 801

QUEST SPORT & FITNESS 103rd S. Redwood Rd.
Phone: 254-6999.
Pool: 25m, indoors, heated, 84°.
Admission: $6.50.

WEST VALLEY CITY _____ 801

GRANGER HIGH SCHOOL 3690 S. 3600 W.
Phone: 481-7194 days. 964-7613 evenings.
Pool: 25y x 42f, 6 lanes, indoors, heated, 85°.
Admission: $2. Resident SC(65) $1.

HUNTER HIGH SCHOOL 4200 S. 5600 W.
Phone: 481-7194 days. 964-7962 evenings.
Pool: 25y x 46f, 6 lanes, indoors, heated, 84°.
Admission: $2. Resident SC(65) $1.
To find: In the northwest corner of the school, by the football field.

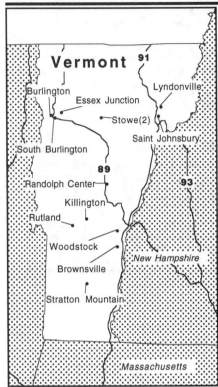

Vermont 91

Burlington
Lyndonville
Essex Junction
Stowe(2)
Saint Johnsbury
South Burlington
89
Randolph Center
93
Killington
Rutland
Woodstock
New Hampshire
Brownsville
Stratton Mountain
Massachusetts

BROWNSVILLE 802

THE ASCUTNEY MOUNTAIN RESORT
Phone: 484-7711. **Reservations:** 800-243-0011.
Pool: 25y, indoors, heated, 82°-84°.
Admission: $8. Registered guests NC.
Memberships: 1/3/6/12 months
$35/$99/$185/$290. SC(60) 10% discount.

BURLINGTON 802

GREATER BURLINGTON YMCA 266 College St.
Phone: 862-9622.
Pool 1: 25y x 36f, 6 lanes, indoors, heated, 79°-80°.
Pool 2: 20y x 20f, indoors, heated, 84°-86°.
Admission: $10.
Affiliate: YMCA 3 visits per month NC, then $2.
Hotel: Radisson Hotel (658-6500) $8.
To find: Two blocks east of the Church St.
Marketplace, three blocks west of the University of Vermont Green.

ESSEX JUNCTION 802

RACQUET'S EDGE HEALTH & FITNESS CENTER
4 Morse Dr.
Phone: 879-7734.
Pool: 25y, indoors, heated, 84°.
Admission: $12.

Affiliate: IHRSA $6.
Masters: Masters Swim Program. Contact Melissa Steininger at 879-7734.

KILLINGTON 802

INN OF THE SIX MOUNTAINS Killington Rd.
Phone: 422-4302. **Reservations:** 800-228-4676.
Pool: 21y, 'T' shape, indoors, heated, 80°.
Admission: Registered guests only NC.
Notes: There is also a 55f, rectangular, outdoor, heated, 85° pool operated from May to Oct.

LYNDONVILLE 802

LYNDON STATE COLLEGE POOL Lyndon State
College, Vail Hill
Phone: 626-9371 ext. POOL.
Pool: 25y, indoors, heated, 80°.
Admission: $1.

RANDOLPH CENTER 802

SHAPE POOL Vermont Technical College
Phone: 728-3391 ext. 385.
Pool: 25y x 42f, 6 lanes, indoors, heated, 82°.
Hotel: Three Stallion Inn NC with 'Shape' card from the Inn.
Memberships: 3/6/12 months $50/$100/$175.

RUTLAND 802

PICO SPORTS CENTER at the Pico Ski & Summer
Resort, Sherburne Pass
Phone: 773-1786. **Reservations:** 800-848-7325.
Pool: 25y x 45f, 5 lanes (3 lap lanes at all times), indoors, heated, 82°.
Admission: $10.
Hotel: Pico Resort Hotel (747-3000) & Pico Resort Condo renters (773-1786): NC.
Notes: The brochure for the Resort also shows a pretty nice looking outdoor pool.
To find: Located at the Pico Ski & Resort Area, two miles west of the Killington Ski Area.
Masters: The Green Mountain Masters. Contact Maureen Anderson at 773-1786.

SAINT JOHNSBURY 802

SAINT JOHNSBURY ACADEMY POOL Saint
Johnsbury Academy Field House, Park St.
Phone: 748-8683.
Pool: 25y x 45f, 3 lanes, indoors, heated, 82°.
Admission: $3.
Hotel: Fairbanks Inn (748-5666), Yankee Traveler Motel (748-8192), & Maple Center Motel (748-2393): NC with room key.
To find: Going south on Main St., go straight through the yellow light, then take the second left, the parking lot is on the right. Enter the building with six peaks.

SOUTH BURLINGTON 802

TWIN OAKS SPORTS & FITNESS 75 Farrell St.
Phone: 658-0002.
Pool: 25y x 56f, 8 lanes, indoors, heated, 81°.
Admission: Pool $10.50.
To find: One street behind Route 7 and the factory outlet mall.
Masters: The Twin Oaks Masters. Contact Coach Katherine Hoehl or Water Fitness Director Laurie Robinson at 658-0002.

STOWE 802

GOLDEN EAGLE RESORT The Mountain Rd., Route 108
Phone: 253-4811. **Reservations:** 800-626-1010.
Pool: 50f x 20f, rectangular, indoors, heated, 84°.
Admission: $10. Registered guests NC.
Memberships: 1/12 months $65/$350.
Notes: The pool is open 9AM-8:45PM.

TOPNOTCH AT STOWE RESORT & SPA
Mountain Rd.

Phone: 253-8585. **Reservations:** 800-451-8686.
Pool: 20y, indoors, heated, 82°.
Admission: $25. Registered guests NC.
Notes: There is also an outdoor, heated, summer pool.

STRATTON MOUNTAIN 802

STRATTON SPORTS CENTER
Phone: 297-4230.
Pool: 25y, indoors, heated, 80°-84°.
Hotel: Stratton Village Lodge & Stratton Mountain Inn (297-2500 for both): $8-$15.

WOODSTOCK 802

WOODSTOCK INN & RESORT 14 The Green
Phone: 457-1100. **Reservations:** 800-448-7900.
Pool: 20y x 30f, rectangular, indoors, heated, 83°.
Admission: Weekdays $13.75. Weekends & holidays $16.25. Registered guests NC.
Memberships: Limited hours membership $59/month.

ALWAYS CALL FIRST

Pools close, they change names, affiliations, admission policies, and rates. And just because a pool is listed in *Swimmers Guide* doesn't mean it's open all day, every day, for just the type of workout you want to do. Spend a quarter to save time and aggravation. . . always call first!

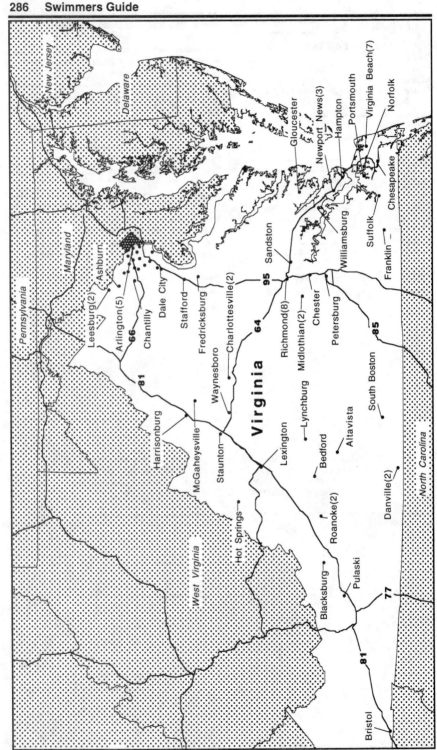

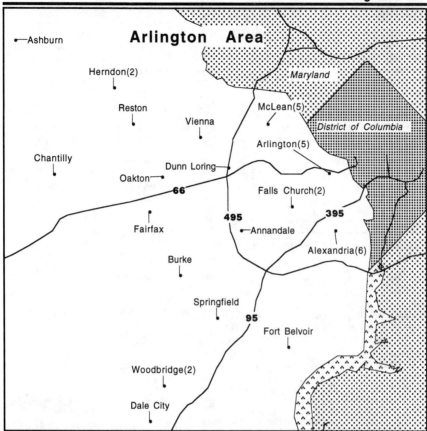

Arlington Area

←Ashburn

Herndon(2)

Reston

Vienna

Chantilly

Oakton→

Dunn Loring—

66

Fairfax

Burke

Springfield

Maryland

McLean(5)

District of Columbia

Arlington(5)

Falls Church(2)

495   395

←Annandale

Alexandria(6)

95

Fort Belvoir

Woodbridge(2)

Dale City

ALEXANDRIA 703

CHINQUAPIN PARK RECREATION CENTER
3210 King St.
Phone: 931-1127.
Pool: 25m x 25y, 8 lanes, indoors, heated, 83°.
Admission: Residents $4, SC(60) $3. Non-residents $5.50.
To find: From I-395 take the King St. Exit east one mile. From Old Town Alexandria follow King St. one mile.

THE CENTER CLUB 4300 King St.
Phone: 820-8900.
Pool: 25y, indoors, heated, 82°.
Affiliate: IHRSA $10.

MOUNT VERNON RECREATION CENTER 2017
Belle View Blvd.
Phone: 768-3224.
Pool: 25y x 25m, 10 lanes, indoors, heated, 82°-84°.
Admission: Residents $4.95, SC(60) $3.25. Non-residents $6.95.
To find: One and a half miles from Richmond Hwy. and I-495.

GEORGE WASHINGTON RECREATION CENTER
8426 Old Mt. Vernon Rd.
Phone: 780-8894.
Pool: 25y x 75f, 3 lap swimming lanes, indoors, heated, 83°.
Admission: Residents $4.95, SC(60) $3.25. Non-residents $6.95.

ROBERT E. LEE RECREATION CENTER 6601
Telegraph Rd.
Phone: 922-9841.
Pool: 25y x 50m, 13 lanes, indoors, heated, 82°-84°.
Admission: Residents $4.95, SC(60) $3.25. Non-residents $6.95.
To find: Take Telegraph Rd. (Exit 2A) off the Capitol Beltway, go approximately 2.5 miles to the traffic light, turn left into the park entrance and follow the drive up to the center.

BALLY'S HOLIDAY 6200 Little River Tpk.
Phone: 658-5000.
Pool: 25m, indoors, heated, 80°-84°.
Admission: Call.
Affiliate: Bally's & IPFA: NC.

ALTAVISTA   804

ALTAVISTA AREA YMCA 1000 Franklin Ave.
Phone: 369-9622.
Pool: 25y, 6 lanes, indoors, heated, 83°-84°.
Admission: $5.
Affiliate: YMCA Call.
Hotel: Comfort Suites (369-4000) NC.

ANNANDALE   703

WAKEFIELD RECREATION CENTER 8100
Braddock Rd.
Phone: 321-7081.
Pool: 25y x 50m, 3 lanes, indoors, heated, 83°-84°.
Admission: Residents $4.95, SC(60) $3.25. Non-
residents $6.95.

ARLINGTON   703

WASHINGTON-LEE SWIMMING POOL 1300 N.
Quincy St.
Phone: 358-6262.
Pool: 25y x 45f, 6 lanes, indoors, heated, 82°.
Admission: Residents $3, SC(60) $2. Non-resi-
dents $4, SC $2.65.
Masters: The Arlington Masters Swim Club.
Contact David Smith at 527-5980(h) or Ward Foley
at 358-4754(w).

**FITNESS CENTER AT THE DOUBLETREE
HOTEL** 300 Army/Navy Dr.
Phone: Club: 416-4100 ext. 1934. Hotel: 416-
4100. **Reservations:** 800-528-0444.
Pool: 18m, 3 lanes, indoors, heated, 83°-84°.
Admission: $15. Registered guests NC.
Affiliate: IHRSA $10. The Fitness Company Clubs
outside a 50 mile radius NC; inside 50 miles 4 vis-
its per month NC, then $7.50.
To find: Across from the Pentagon. On the mezza-
nine level of the hotel.

SKYLINE CLUB AT CRYSTAL PARK 2231 Crystal
Dr.
Phone: 486-3380.
Pool: 25y, indoors, heated, 82°.
Affiliate: IHRSA $10.
Hotel: Marriott Hotel (413-5500) $10.

WAKEFIELD SWIMMING POOL 4901 S.
Chesterfield Rd.
Phone: 578-3063.
Pool: 25y x 45f, 6 lanes, indoors, heated, 82°.
Admission: Residents $3, SC(60) $2. Non-resi-
dents $4, SC $2.65.
Masters: The Arlington Masters Swim Club.
Contact David Smith at 527-5980(h) or Ward Foley
at 358-4754(w).

YORKTOWN SWIMMING POOL 5201 N. 28th St.
Phone: 536-9739.
Pool: 25y x 45f, 6 lanes, indoors, heated, 82°.

Admission: Residents $3, SC(60) $2. Non-residents $4, SC $2.65.

ASHBURN   703

ASHBURN VILLAGE SPORTS PAVILION 20585
Ashburn Village Blvd.
Phone: 729-0581.
Pool: 25m, 6 lanes, indoors, heated, 82°.
Affiliate: IHRSA $7.
Masters: The Ashburn Sports Pavilion Masters.
Contact Doug Slitor or Jack Read at 729-0581.

BEDFORD   703

BEDFORD AREA YMCA Turnpike Dr. off 460
Phone: 586-3483.
Pool: 25y, indoors, heated, 85°.
Admission: $4.
Affiliate: YMCA NC.

BLACKSBURG   703

BLACKSBURG AQUATIC CENTER 625 Patrick
Henry Dr.
Phone: 961-1852.
Pool: 25y 1in x 45f, 6 lanes, indoors, heated, 82°-
85°.
Admission: $2, SC(65) $1.50.
To find: Three blocks west of the Virginia Tech
Campus. From N. Main St. turn onto Patrick Henry
Dr., the Aquatic Center is two blocks down on the
left.

BRISTOL   703

MARGARET H. ST. JOHN POOL at Virginia High
School, Spring Garden
Phone: 645-9662.
Pool: 25y x 25m, 6 x 6 lanes, 'L' shape, indoors,
heated, 82°.
Admission: $1.
Hotel: Comfort Inn (466-3881), Super 8 (466-8800),
& Thrifty Inn (669-6701): NC.
To find: Exit 381 off I-81.

BURKE   703

BURKE RACQUET & SWIM CLUB 6001 Burke
Commons Rd.
Phone: 250-1299.
Pool: 25y x 25m, 12 lanes, indoors, heated, 82°-
83°.
Affiliate: IHRSA outside a 50 mile radius 4 visits
per month $5 each.
Masters: The Burke Masters. Contact Pete
Morgan at 250-1299.

CHANTILLY   703

THE CLUB AT WESTFIELDS 14800 Conference
Center Dr., Suite 102
Phone: 631-9378.
Pool: 20m, 3 lanes, indoors, heated, 80°.

Affiliate: IHRSA $10.
Hotel: Westfields International Conference Center (818-0300) $14.
To find: Next to Westfields International Conference Center.

CHARLOTTESVILLE   804

CROW POOL Walker Upper Elementary School, Rose Hill Dr.
Phone: 977-1362.
Pool: 25y x 43f, 6 lanes, indoors, heated, 82°-85°.
Admission: Residents $2, SC(55) $1.50. Non-residents $3, SC $1.75.
To find: Off U.S. 250 By-pass.

SMITH POOL Buford Middle School, 10th & Cherry
Phone: 977-1960.
Pool: 25y x 43f, 6 lanes, indoors, heated, 82°-85°.
Admission: Residents $2, SC(55) $1.50. Non-residents $3, SC $1.75.

CHESAPEAKE   804

BALLY'S HOLIDAY HEALTH CLUB 1501 Ring Rd.
Phone: 420-0310.
Pool: 25y, indoors, heated, 80°.
Admission: Call.
Affiliate: Bally's & IPFA: NC.

CHESTER   804

CHESTER YMCA 3011 W. Hundred Rd.
Phone: 748-9622.
Pool: 25m, 6 lanes, indoors, heated, 86°.
Admission: $3.
Affiliate: YMCA NC.
Hotel: Holiday Inn Chester (523-1500) NC.
To find: One mile off I-95 on Route 10 (West).
Masters: Contact Michelle Reedy at 748-9622.

DALE CITY   703

DALE CITY RECREATION CENTER POOL 14300 Minnieville Rd.
Phone: Recorded schedule: 670-7111.
Information: 670-7112.
Pool: 25y, indoors, heated, 84°.
Admission: Residents $3, non-residents $4.

DANVILLE   804

YWCA OF DANVILLE / PITTSYLVANIA COUNTY 750 Main St.
Phone: 792-1522.
Pool: 25m x 37f, 6 lanes, indoors, heated, 84°.
Admission: $2.50.
Affiliate: YWCA $1.50.
To find: Near the downtown shopping area, two buildings from the Main Post Office. Once on Main St., it's easy to see the YWCA sign in the front yard.

DANVILLE YMCA 810 Main St.
Phone: 792-0621.
Pool: 25y, indoors, heated, 87°.
Affiliate: YMCA NC.

DUNN LORING   703

YWCA FITNESS CENTER AT TYSONS CORNER 8101 Wolftrap and Gallows Rd.
Phone: 560-1111.
Pool: 25y x 57f, 6 lanes, indoors, heated, 83°.
Admission: $10.
Affiliate: YWCA $6.

FAIRFAX   703

THE FITNESS CLUB OF FAIRFAX 11230 Waples Mill Rd.
Phone: 352-2280.
Pool: 25y x 45f, indoors, heated, 82°.
Admission: $10.
Affiliate: IHRSA $5.
Hotel: Holiday Inn-Fair Oaks Mall (352-2525) & Courtyards by Marriott (273-6161): $5.

FALLS CHURCH   703

THE SKYLINE CLUB 5115 Leesburg Pike
Phone: 820-4100.
Pool: 25m, 3 lanes, indoors, heated, 84°.
Admission: $22.
Hotel: Hampton Inn at Bailey's Crossroads (671-4800) $10 with voucher.
To find: In the Skyline Mall. Park in front of the Discovery Zone and take the elevator to Level 'C'.
Masters: The Skyline Masters. Contact Karen Hannam at 820-4100.

PROVIDENCE RECREATION CENTER 7525 Marc Dr.
Phone: 698-1351.
Pool: 25m x 75f, 10 lanes, indoors, heated, 82°-84°.
Admission: Residents $4.95, SC(60) $3.25. Non-residents $6.95.

FORT BELVOIR   703

BENYAURD INDOOR POOL Ft. Belvoir - Building 182, 182 Gunston Rd.
Phone: 805-2620.
Pool: 25y x 45f, 6 lanes, indoors, heated, 83°.
Affiliate: U.S. Military & Dept. of Defense: $2.

FRANKLIN   804

JAMES L. CAMP YMCA 300 Crescent Dr.
Phone: 562-3491.
Pool: 25y, indoors, heated, 85°-86°.
Affiliate: Y AWAY NC.

FREDRICKSBURG   703

RAPPAHANNOCK AREA YMCA 212 Butler Rd.
Phone: 371-9622.
Pool: 25m, indoors, heated, 84°-85°.
Admission: $6.
Affiliate: YMCA NC.

GLOUCESTER   804

**RIVERSIDE WELLNESS & FITNESS CENTER -
MIDDLE PENINSULA** Route 17
Phone: 693-8888.
Pool: 25y x 60f, indoors, heated, 84°.
Admission: $12.
Affiliate: IHRSA $9.
To find: Adjacent to Riverside Walter Reed
Hospital.

HAMPTON   804

**SENTARA HAMPTON HEALTH & FITNESS
CENTER** 300 Butler Farm Rd.
Phone: 766-2658.
Pool: 25m, indoors, heated, 84°-86°.
Admission: $12.
Affiliate: IHRSA NC.

HARRISONBURG   703

VALLEY WELLNESS CENTER 411 Stone Spring
Rd.
Phone: 434-6224.
Pool: 25m, indoors, heated, 85°.
Admission: $8. Contact the Membership
Coordinator.
Masters: Contact Deb Rigby at 434-6224.

HERNDON   703

WORLDGATE ATHLETIC CLUB 13037 Worldgate
Dr.
Phone: 709-9100.
Pool: 25y, 6 lanes, indoors, heated, 82°.
Admission: $20.
Affiliate: IHRSA $10.
Hotel: Washington Dulles Marriott Suites (709-
0400) NC.
To find: Exit 2 off the Dulles Toll Rd., at the first
traffic light turn right onto Worldgate Dr.

HERNDON COMMUNITY CENTER 814 Ferndale
Ave.
Phone: 787-7300.
Pool: 25y, 8 lanes, indoors, heated, 84°.
Admission: $3.75, SC(60) $2.75.
To find: North on Centerville Ave. and one mile
from the Dulles Toll Rd.

HOT SPRINGS   703

THE HOMESTEAD Route 220
Phone: 839-5500. **Reservations:** 800-336-5771.
Pool: 25y, rectangular, indoors, heated, 87°.

Admission: Registered guests only NC.
Notes: There are also two unheated, outdoor pools
operated from Apr. to Oct.

LEESBURG   703

LANSDOWNE RESORT 44050 Woodridge Pkwy.
Phone: 729-8400. **Reservations:** 800-541-4801.
Pool: 20y, rectangular, indoors, heated, 82°-84°.
Admission: Registered guests only NC.
Notes: There is also an outdoor pool.

IDA LEE PARK RECREATION CENTER 50 Ida
Lee Dr. N.W.
Phone: 777-1368.
Pool: 25y x 25m, 10 lanes, indoors, heated, 82°-
84°.
Admission: $4, SC(60) $2.
To find: Ida Lee Dr. is off Route 15, a quarter of a
mile north of the intersection of Routes 7 and 15
(County Courthouse).
Masters: Contact Karen Broyles at 777-1368.

LEXINGTON   703

WARNER CENTER Washington & Lee University,
Washington St.
Phone: 463-8481.
Pool: 25y, 6 lanes, indoors, heated, 79°-81°.
Admission: $2.
Memberships: 4 months $50.
Notes: The pool closes Jun. through Aug.
To find: Located at the intersection of Route 60
and Washington St., across from the Performing
Arts Center.
Masters: The Lexington Masters. Contact Coach
Kiki Jacobs at 463-8481.

LYNCHBURG   804

CENTRAL VIRGINIA YMCA 1315 Church St.
Phone: 847-5597.
Pool 1: 25m, indoors, heated, 81°.
Pool 2: 20y, indoors, heated, 88°.
Admission: $10.
Affiliate: Y AWAY NC. YMCA $2.

MCGAHEYSVILLE   703

LA CLUB AT MASSANUTTEN RESORT Hwy. 644
Phone: 289-9441.
Pool: 25y, indoors, heated, 79°.
Admission: Registered guests NC.
Memberships: $430/year.

MCLEAN   703

MCLEAN RACQUET & HEALTH CLUB 1472
Chain Bridge Rd.
Phone: 356-3300.
Pool: 20y, indoors, heated, 82°.
Affiliate: IHRSA $12.

SPRING HILL RECREATION CENTER 1239 Spring Hill Rd.
Phone: 827-0989.
Pool: 25m x 25y, indoors, heated, 82°-84°.
Admission: Residents $4.95, SC(60) $3.25. Non-residents $6.95.

MCLEAN HILTON AT TYSONS CORNER 7920 Jones Branch Dr.
Phone: 847-5000. **Reservations:** 800-HILTONS.
Pool: 50f, indoors, heated, 82°-83°.
Admission: Registered guests NC.
Affiliate: IHRSA $2.

REGENCY SPORT & HEALTH CLUB 1800 Old Meadows Rd.
Phone: 556-6550.
Pool: 25y, 8 lanes, indoors, heated, 81°-83°.
Affiliate: IHRSA $10.

SPORTING CLUB AT TYSONS CORNER 8250 Greensboro Dr.
Phone: 442-9150.
Pool: 25m, indoors, heated, 78°-80°.
Affiliate: IHRSA $12.

MIDLOTHIAN 804

WOODLAKE SWIM & RACQUET CLUB 5000 Woodlake Village Pkwy.
Phone: 739-4120.
Pool: 25y, indoors, heated, 84°.
Affiliate: IHRSA: Weekdays $2. Weekends $3.

RIVERSIDE WELLNESS & FITNESS CENTER - BRIARWOOD 11621 Robious Rd.
Phone: 378-1600.
Pool: 50m OR 25y + 25m, 8 OR 16 lanes, indoors, heated, 82°-83°.
Admission: $12.
Affiliate: IHRSA $9.

VIRGINIA MASTERS SWIM TEAM at Riverside Wellness & Fitness Center - Briarwood
Pool phone: 378-1600. **Masters:** Contact Beth Waters at 744-8225(h).
Affiliate: USMS & IHRSA: Call.
Notes: Workouts: M,Tu,Th: 6-7AM, 7-8:15PM. W: 6-7AM, 12:15-1:15PM, 7-8:15PM. F: 6-7AM, 12:15-1:15PM. Sa: 8-9AM. Su: 4-5PM.

NEWPORT NEWS 804

RIVERSIDE WELLNESS & FITNESS CENTER 12650 Jefferson Ave.
Phone: 875-7525.
Pool: 25m, 7 lanes, indoors, heated, 85°.
Admission: $12.
Affiliate: IHRSA $9.
Masters: The Wellness Aquatics Club. Contact Craig West or Steve Hennessy at 875-7525.

BALLY'S HEALTH & FITNESS 12255 Hornsby Lane
Phone: 249-1315.
Pool: 25m, indoors, heated, 82°.
Admission: Call.
Affiliate: Bally's & IPFA: NC.

PENINSULA METROPOLITAN YMCA - NEWPORT NEWS BRANCH 7827 Warwick Blvd.
Phone: 245-0047.
Pool: 25m x 36f, 6 lanes, indoors, heated, 84°-86°.
Admission: $8.
Affiliate: YMCA NC.
To find: Just before the James River Bridge next to Huntington Park.

NORFOLK 804

NORFOLK YMCA 312 W. Bute St.
Phone: 622-9622.
Pool: 25m, 6 lanes, indoors, heated, 84°.
Admission: $6.
Affiliate: YMCA NC.
Hotel: Norfolk YMCA (622-9622) $2.
To find: Two blocks west of the Scope, off Brambleton.
Masters: Contact Joe Ryan at 622-9622.

OAKTON 703

OAK MARR RECREATION CENTER 3200 Jermantown Rd.
Phone: 281-6501.
Pool: 50m x 25y, indoors, heated, 82°-84°.
Admission: Residents $4.95, SC(60) $3.25. Non-residents $6.95.

PETERSBURG 804

YMCA OF SOUTHSIDE VIRGINIA 120 N. Madison St.
Phone: 733-9333.
Pool: 25m, 6 lanes, indoors, heated, 86°.
Admission: Out-of-town visitors — Call.
Affiliate: YMCA outside a 20 mile radius NC. U.S. Military $3.50.
Hotel: Best Western Petersburg (733-1776) & Howard Johnson Hotel (732-5950): NC with room key.

PORTSMOUTH 804

MANCHESTER YMCA 4900 High St. W.
Phone: 276-9622.
Pool: 25y, indoors, heated, 84°.
Affiliate: YMCA NC.

PULASKI 703

PULASKI YMCA 615 Oakhurst Ave.
Phone: 980-3671.
Pool: 25y x 27f, 4 lanes, indoors, heated, 84°.
Admission: $5.

Affiliate: YMCA NC.
To find: Oakhurst Ave. is the third left off Route 11 after the hospital.

RESTON   703

RESTON COMMUNITY CENTER 2310 Colts Neck Rd.
Phone: 476-4500.
Pool: 25m, 6 lanes, indoors, heated, 83°-84°.
Admission: Residents $2, SC(60) $1. Non-residents $3, SC $1.50.
Hotel: Hyatt Regency Reston (709-1234) & Sheraton Reston Hotel (620-9000): $2 with a voucher from the hotel, SC $1.
Notes: The pool closes for annual cleaning from late Aug. to early Sep.
To find: To the rear of Hunterswoods Shopping Center.
Masters: The Reston Masters. Contact Tom Yorty at 476-6853(h).

RICHMOND   804

DOWNTOWN YMCA 2 W. Franklin St.
Phone: 644-9622.
Pool: 25y, 7 lanes, indoors, heated, 83°.
Affiliate: YMCA NC.
Hotel: Linden Row Inn, Jefferson Hotel (788-8000), & Holiday Inn-Downtown (644-9871): NC with room key.
To find: One half mile west of Virginia Commonwealth University and across from the Jefferson Hotel.

CALHOUN POOL 436 Calhoun St.
Phone: Pool: 780-4751. Rec. Center: 780-4403.
Pool: 25y, indoors, heated, 86°.
Admission: NC.

SWANSBORO POOL 3160 Midlothian Tpk.
Phone: 780-5088.
Pool: 25y, indoors, heated, 86°.
Admission: NC.

NORTH RICHMOND BRANCH YMCA 4207 Old Brook Rd.
Phone: 329-9622.
Pool: 25y, indoors, heated, 83°.
Admission: $6.
Affiliate: YMCA NC.

AMERICAN FAMILY FITNESS CENTER 5750 Brook Rd.
Phone: 261-1000.
Pool: 20y x 40f, indoors, heated, 82°.
Admission: $10.

TUCKAHOE FAMILY YMCA 9211 Patterson Ave.
Phone: 740-9622.
Pool: 25m x 50f, 6 lanes, indoors, heated, 81°.
Admission: 3 visits per year $5 each.
Affiliate: Y AWAY NC.

To find: In the west end of Richmond, three miles south of I-64 off the Parham Rd. Exit.
Masters: The Tuckahoe Family YMCA Masters Program. Contact Aquatic Director Mark Woodard at 740-9622.

ROBIOUS SPORTS & FITNESS CENTER 10800 Center View Dr.
Phone: 330-2222.
Pool: 25y x 42f, 6 lanes, indoors, heated, 83°.
Admission: $7-$10.
Affiliate: IHRSA Call.
Hotel: Holiday Inn-Koger Center (379-3800), Sheraton Inn Park South (323-1144), & Days Inn (794-4999): $7.
To find: Next to the Holiday Inn Koger Center and Johnston-Willis Hospital.

MANCHESTER FAMILY YMCA 7540 Hull St. Rd.
Phone: 276-9622.
Pool: 25y x 35f, 5 lanes, indoors, heated, 83°-84°.
Affiliate: YMCA NC.
To find: One mile west of Chippenham Pkwy. on U.S. Route 360.

ROANOKE   703

YWCA OF ROANOKE VALLEY 605 - 1st St. S.W.
Phone: 345-9922.
Pool: 20y x 20m, indoors, heated, 88°.
Admission: 1 visit $3.

CENTRAL BRANCH YMCA 425 Church St.
Phone: 342-9622.
Pool: 20y, indoors, heated, 82°-84°.
Admission: $10.
Affiliate: YMCA NC.

SANDSTON   804

CHICKAHOMINY BRANCH YMCA 5401 Whiteside Rd.
Phone: 737-9622.
Pool: 25m x 15m, 6 lanes, indoors, heated, 84°.
Admission: 3 visits per year $4 each.
Affiliate: Out-of-area Y AWAY NC.
Hotel: Holiday Inn-Richmond Airport (222-6450), Hampton Inn Airport (222-8200), Sheraton Inn Richmond Airport (226-4300), & Richmond Airport Hilton (226-6400): NC with a pass from the hotel.
To find: Close to Richmond Airport.

SOUTH BOSTON   804

SOUTH BOSTON / HALIFAX COUNTY YMCA 650 Hamilton Blvd.
Phone: 572-8909.
Pool: 25m, 6 lanes, indoors, heated, 84°.
Affiliate: YMCA $2 per visit or $21 per month.

SPRINGFIELD   703

SOUTH RUN RECREATION CENTER 9501 Pohick Rd.
Phone: 866-0566.
Pool: 25y x 75f, 3 lanes, indoors, heated, 83°.
Admission: Residents $4.95, SC(60) $3.25. Non-residents $6.95.

STAFFORD   703

FITNESS UNIVERSITY OF STAFFORD Aquia Town Center, 2852 Jefferson Davis Hwy. #501
Phone: 659-3488.
Pool: 25y, indoor/outdoor, heated, 84°-88°.
Admission: $5.

STAUNTON   703

STAUNTON RACQUET CLUB 708 N. Coalter St.
Phone: 885-8089.
Pool: 25y, indoors, heated, 83°.
Admission: $5.
Hotel: Staunton Holiday Inn (248-5111) NC.
Masters: Contact Joan Letizio or Bob Couch at 885-8089.

SUFFOLK   804

SUFFOLK YMCA 2769 Godwin Blvd.
Phone: 934-9622.
Pool: 25y, indoors, heated, 85°.
Admission: 1 visit $6.
Affiliate: YMCA NC.

VIENNA   703

TYSONS CORNER MARRIOTT 8028 Leesburg Pike
Phone: 318-8220.
Pool: 17y, rectangular, indoors, heated, 85°.
Admission: $5. Registered guests NC.

VIRGINIA BEACH   804

BOW CREEK CENTER 3427 Clubhouse Rd.
Phone: 431-3765.
Pool: 20y x 35f, indoors, heated, 82°.
Admission: $4.

BALLY'S HEALTH CLUB 3960 Virginia Beach Blvd.
Phone: 340-4800.
Pool: 25m, indoors, heated, 82°.
Affiliate: Bally's & IPFA: NC.

VIRGINIA BEACH BRANCH YMCA 4441 South Blvd.
Phone: 456-9622.
Pool: 25m, 6 lanes, indoors, heated, 84°.
Affiliate: YMCA $6.

GREAT NECK CENTER 2521 Shorehaven Dr.
Phone: 496-6766.
Pool: 25m x 25y, 8 lanes, indoors, heated, 82°.
Admission: $4.

BAYSIDE COMMUNITY CENTER 4420 - 1st Court Rd.
Phone: 460-7450.
Pool: 25m x 25y, 8 lanes, indoors, heated, 82°.
Admission: $4.

PRINCESS ANNE RECREATION CENTER 1400 Ferrell Pkwy.
Phone: 426-0022.
Pool: 25m x 25y, 8 lanes, indoors, heated, 82°.
Admission: $4.

KEMPSVILLE CENTER 800 Monmouth Lane
Phone: 474-8492.
Pool: 25m x 45f, 6 lanes, indoors, heated, 82°.
Admission: $4.

WAYNESBORO   703

WAYNESBORO FAMILY YMCA 648 S. Wayne Ave.
Phone: 942-5107.
Pool: 25y, indoors, heated, 85°.
Admission: $4.
Affiliate: Y AWAY NC.

WILLIAMSBURG   804

JAMES CITY-WILLIAMSBURG RECREATION CENTER 5301 Longhill Rd.
Phone: 220-4700.
Pool: 25m, indoors, heated, 80°-81°.
Admission: Residents $2, non-residents $3.

WOODBRIDGE   703

DEVIL'S REACH SPORT & HEALTH CLUB 1401 Devil's Reach Rd.
Phone: 690-1629.
Pool: 25m, indoors, heated, 80°-82°.
Affiliate: IHRSA $10.

CHINN AQUATICS & FITNESS CENTER 13025 Chinn Park Dr.
Phone: 730-1054.
Pool: 40y with bulkhead for 25y lap swimming, 8 lanes, indoors, heated, 80°.
Admission: Residents $5, SC(60) $3. Non-residents $7, SC $5.25.
Masters: The Northern Virginia Masters. Contact Harry DeLong at 368-0309(h) before 10PM, please.

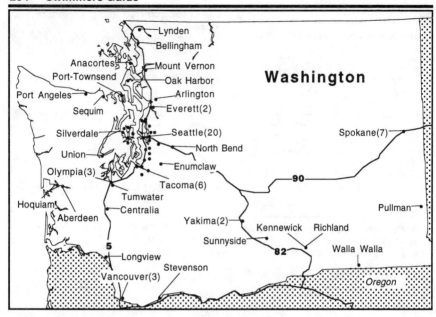

Washington

Lynden
Bellingham
Anacortes
Mount Vernon
Port-Townsend
Oak Harbor
Port Angeles
Arlington
Sequim
Everett(2)
Silverdale
Seattle(20)
Spokane(7)
North Bend
Union
Enumclaw
Olympia(3)
Tacoma(6)
90
Hoquiam
Tumwater
Pullman
Aberdeen
Centralia
Yakima(2)
Sunnyside
Kennewick
Richland
5
Longview
Walla Walla
82
Vancouver(3)
Stevenson
Oregon

Seattle Area

Port-Townsend
Arlington
Port Angeles
Marysville
Sequim
Everett(2)
Lynnwood(2)
5
Edmonds
Mountlake Terrace
Poulsbo
Bothell(3)
NSB Bangor
Kirkland(2)
Silverdale
Bainbridge Island
Redmond
Bremerton
Bellevue(7)
Seattle(20)
Mercer Island(2)
Port Orchard
Issaquah
90
Des Moines
Renton(2)
North Bend
Kent(3)
Union
Auburn(2)
Enumclaw
Federal Way(4)
Tacoma(6)
Fife
Sumner
5
Puyallup
Olympia(3)
Tumwater

ABERDEEN   360

MILLER NATATORIUM POOL Aberdeen YMCA, Willard & 'B' St.
Phone: Schedule information: 533-3881. Pool: 538-2169.
Pool: 25y x 30f, 4 lanes, indoors, heated, 89°.
Admission: Lap swim $3.
Affiliate: YMCA 6 visits per month NC.

ANACORTES   360

FIDALGO POOL & FITNESS CENTER 1603 - 22nd St.
Phone: 293-0673.
Pool: 25m x 75f, 6 lanes, indoors, heated, 85°.
Admission: $2, SC(62) $1.50.
To find: At the intersection of 'J' and 22nd Sts., two blocks south of the high school.
Masters: The Thunderbird Aquatic Club Masters. Contact Pinky Walker at 293-0673.

ARLINGTON   360

STILLAGUAMISH ATHLETIC CLUB 4417 - 172 St. N.E.
Phone: 435-9404.
Pool: 20y, indoors, heated, 84°.
Admission: Visitors from outside a 20 mile radius $5.
Affiliate: NACA NC.

AUBURN   206

AUBURN VALLEY YMCA 1005 - 12th St. S.E.
Phone: 833-2770.
Pool: 25y x 20f, 4 lanes, indoors, heated, 86°.
Admission: $4.
Affiliate: Out-of-area YMCA NC.

AUBURN POOL 516 - 4th N.E.
Phone: 939-8825.
Pool: 25y x 43f, 6 lanes, indoors, heated, 84°.
Admission: $2.25, SC(60) & Disabled $1.50.

BAINBRIDGE ISLAND   206

RAY WILLIAMSON POOL Madison & High School Rd.
Phone: 842-2302.
Pool: 25y, indoors, heated, 85°.
Admission: $2.25.

BELLEVUE   206

THE SEATTLE CLUB BELLEVUE 800 Bellevue Way N.E., Suite 200
Phone: 646-1111.
Pool: 25y, 4 lanes, indoors, heated, 83°.
Affiliate: NACA outside a 50 mile radius NC. IHRSA $10.
Hotel: Hyatt Regency Bellevue (462-1234) 7 days $12 per visit with voucher & room key.
To find: At the corner of Bellevue Way and N.E. 8th St., cater corner from Bellevue Square.
Masters: The Seattle Club Masters. Contact Donna Gedney or Kiki Benson at 646-1111.

EASTSIDE ATHLETIC CLUB 1505 - 140th Ave. N.E.
Phone: 641-1111.
Pool: 23y, indoors, heated, 78°.
Admission: $10.

NEWPORT HILLS SWIM & TENNIS CLUB MASTERS 5464 - 119th Ave. S.E.
Pool phone: 746-9510. **Masters:** Contact Club Manager Pat McCarthy at 746-9510.
Pool: 25m x 44f, 6 lanes, indoor/outdoor, heated, 83°.
Affiliate: USMS Call.
Notes: Workouts: M,W,F: 6-7PM. Tu,Th: 6:30-7:30AM.

BELLEVUE POOL 601 - 143rd Ave. N.E.
Phone: 296-4262.
Pool: 25y x 43f, 6 lanes, indoors, heated, 84°.
Admission: $2.25, SC(60) & Disabled $1.50.
Masters: Contact the pool staff at 296-4262.

BALLY'S PACIFIC WEST 3235 - 148th Ave.
Phone: 643-0060.
Pool: 25m, indoors, heated, 82°.
Affiliate: Bally's NC.
Hotel: Bellevue Hilton (455-3330) NC with a pass from the hotel.

PRO SPORTS CLUB 4455 - 148th Ave. N.E.
Phone: 885-5566.
Pool 1: 25y, indoors, heated, 78°.
Pool 2: 25y, indoors, heated, 82°.
Affiliate: IHRSA $15.
Hotel: Residence Inn (882-1222) NC with a pass from the hotel.

EASTSIDE FAMILY YMCA 14230 Bel-Red Rd.
Phone: 746-9900.
Pool: 25y, indoors, heated, 83°.
Admission: $15.
Affiliate: YMCA NC.
Masters: Contact Paul Craig at 746-9900 or 296-4262.

BELLINGHAM   360

WHATCOM FAMILY YMCA 1256 N. State St.
Phone: 733-8630.
Pool: 20y x 30f, 4 lanes, indoors, heated, 82°.
Admission: $4.
Affiliate: Y AWAY NC, a frequency restriction may apply.
Masters: The Whatcom Family YMCA Masters. Contact Karen Ackelson at 733-8630.

BOTHELL 206

ST. EDWARD POOL 14445 Juanita Dr. N.E.
Phone: 296-2970.
Pool: 25y x 42f, 6 lanes, indoors, heated, 84°.
Admission: $2.25, SC(60) & Disabled $1.50.

NORTHSHORE POOL 9815 N.E. 188th St.
Phone: 296-4333.
Pool: 25y x 43f, 6 lanes, indoors, heated, 84°.
Admission: $2.25, SC(60) & Disabled $1.50.

NORTHSHORE YMCA 11811 N.E. 195th
Phone: 485-9797.
Pool: 25y x 36f, 6 lanes, indoors, heated, 83°-86°.
Admission: $8, SC(60) $5.
Affiliate: Y AWAY 10 visits per year NC.
Hotel: Marriott's Residence Inn (485-3030) —
Passes may be purchased at the hotel.

BREMERTON 360

BREMERTON MUNICIPAL POOL 50 Magnuson
Way
Phone: 478-5376.
Pool: 25y x 43f, 6 lanes, indoors, heated, 84°.
Admission: $1.50.
Affiliate: YMCA Call.
To find: Next to the Kitsap Family YMCA. There is
a large park surrounding the pool.

CENTRALIA 360

CENTRALIA INDOOR POOL 910 Johnson Rd.
Phone: 736-0143.
Pool: 25m x 44f, 6 lanes, indoors, heated, 83°-85°.
Admission: $2, SC(60) $1.40.

DES MOINES 206

MT. RAINIER POOL 22722 - 19th Ave. S.
Phone: 296-4278.
Pool: 25y x 43f, 6 lanes, indoors, heated, 84°.
Admission: $2.25, SC(60) & Disabled $1.50.
Masters: Contact the pool staff at 296-4278.

EDMONDS 206

HARBOR SQUARE ATHLETIC CLUB 160 W.
Dayton
Phone: 778-3546.
Pool: 20y x 24f, 4 lanes, indoors, heated, 83°.
Affiliate: NACA NC. IHRSA $5.
Hotel: Harbor Inn (771-5021) $5.
To find: One block east of the Kingston Ferry dock
in Edmonds.

ENUMCLAW 206

ENUMCLAW POOL 420 Semanski St. S.
Phone: 825-1188.
Pool: 25y x 43f, 6 lanes, indoors, heated, 84°.

Admission: $2.25, SC(60) & Disabled $1.50.
Masters: Contact the pool staff at 825-1188.

EVERETT 206

EVERETT COUNTY YMCA 2720 Rockefeller Ave.
Phone: 258-9211.
Pool: 25m, indoors, heated, 81°.
Affiliate: YMCA 3 visits NC.

FOREST PARK SWIM CENTER 801 Mukilteo Blvd.
Phone: 259-0309.
Pool: 25y, indoors, heated, 83°-85°.
Admission: $1.25.

FEDERAL WAY 206

CASCADE ATHLETIC CLUB 31701 - 20th Ave. S.
Phone: 941-5990.
Pool: 20m, 5 lanes, indoors, heated, 83°.
Admission: $10.
Hotel: Best Western Federal Way Executel (941-
6000) NC with a pass from the hotel.
To find: Next to the Best Western Federal Way
Executel.

FEDERAL WAY POOL 30421 - 16th Ave. S.
Phone: 839-1000.
Pool: 25y x 43f, 6 lanes, indoors, heated, 84°.
Admission: $2.25, SC(60) & Disabled $1.50.

BALLY'S PACIFIC WEST 32818 - 1st Ave. S.
Phone: 838-3424.
Pool: 25m, indoors, heated, 85°.
Admission: $5.
Affiliate: Bally's NC.

KING COUNTY AQUATIC CENTER 650 S.W.
Campus Dr.
Phone: From Seattle 296-4444. From Tacoma
927-5173.
Pool 1: 50m x 25y, 8 x 16 lanes, indoors, heated,
82°.
Pool 2: 25y x 22f, 3 lanes, indoors, heated, 86°.
Admission: $2.25, SC(60) & Disabled $1.50.
Masters: Contact the pool staff at 296-4444 from
Seattle or 927-5173 from Tacoma.

FIFE 206

FIFE COMMUNITY POOL 5410 - 20th St. E.
Phone: 922-7665.
Pool: 25y x 42f, 6 lanes, indoors, heated, 84°-86°.
Admission: $1.75, SC(60) $1.40.
To find: From I-5, take Exit 137, east on 20th St.
one half block from the 54th Ave. intersection. The
pool is directly west of Fife High School.

HOQUIAM 360

HOQUIAM POOL 717 'K' St.
Phone: 533-3447.
Pool: 25y, 6 lanes, indoors, heated, 86°.

Admission: $2.
To find: At the Hoquiam Library.

ISSAQUAH   206

ISSAQUAH POOL 50 S.E. Clark St.
Phone: 557-3298.
Pool: 25y x 43f, 6 lanes, indoors, heated, 84°.
Admission: $3, SC(55) $2.
Affiliate: USMS NC.
Masters: This Issaquah Swim Team Masters.
Contact Coach Dave Kienlen at 557-3298 or
557-8206(h).

KENNEWICK   509

TRI-CITY COURT CLUB 1350 N. Grant St.
Phone: 783-5465.
Pool 1: 25y, 5 lanes, indoors, heated, 81°.
Pool 2: 25y, 4 lanes, indoors, heated, 83°.
Admission: $7.
Affiliate: NACA NC. IHRSA $5.
To find: Next to the Juvenile Justice Center, two
blocks west of the Oasis Water Slides off Canal Dr.
Masters: The Tri-City Court Club Masters. Contact
Todd Stafek at 783-5465.

KENT   206

KENT POOL 25316 - 101st Ave. S.E.
Phone: 296-4275.
Pool: 25y x 43f, 6 lanes, indoors, heated, 84°.
Admission: $2.25, SC(60) & Disabled $1.50.

BALLY'S PACIFIC WEST 1340 W. Smith St.
Phone: 852-9500.
Pool: 20y, indoors, heated, 83°.
Admission: $5.
Affiliate: Bally's NC.

TAHOMA POOL 18230 S.E. 240th
Phone: 296-4276.
Pool: 25y x 43f, 6 lanes, indoors, heated, 84°.
Admission: $2.25, SC(60) & Disabled $1.50.

KIRKLAND   206

BALLY'S PACIFIC WEST 6601 - 132nd Ave. N.E.
Phone: 885-2600.
Pool: 20y, indoors, heated, 85°-90°.
Admission: $5.
Affiliate: Bally's NC.

JUANITA POOL 10601 N.E. 132nd St.
Phone: 823-7627.
Pool: 25y x 45f, 6 lanes, indoors, heated, 85°.
Admission: $1, SC(65) 75¢.
Notes: There is also a 15y x 40f, indoor, heated,
85° pool.
To find: On the Juanita High School Campus.

LONGVIEW   360

YMCA OF SOUTHWEST WASHINGTON 766 -
15th Ave.
Phone: 423-4770.
Pool: 25y x 42f, 6 lanes, indoors, heated, 84°.
Admission: $5, SC(62) $3.50.
Notes: There is also a 3f deep, 94°, indoor pool.
To find: At 15th Ave. and Douglas, across from St.
Johns Hospital and Lake Sacajawea.

LYNDEN   360

LYNDEN YMCA 100 Drayton St.
Phone: 354-5000.
Pool: 25y x 37.5f, 5 lanes, indoors, heated, 84°.
Admission: $5.
Affiliate: Y AWAY NC.

LYNNWOOD   206

LYNNWOOD POOL 18900 - 44th Ave. W.
Phone: 771-4030.
Pool: 25y x 44f, 6 lanes, indoor/outdoor, heated,
85°.
Admission: $1.75, SC(62) $1.25.
Notes: Admission includes use of hot tub, sauna, &
newly remodeled weight/exercise room.
To find: Just north of Fred Meyer.

BALLY'S PACIFIC WEST 19820 Scriber Lake Rd.
Phone: 774-5338.
Pool: 20m, indoors, heated, 82°-84°.
Admission: $5.
Affiliate: Bally's NC.

MARYSVILLE   360

MARYSVILLE-PILCHUCK SWIMMING POOL
5611 - 108th St. N.E.
Phone: 653-0609.
Pool: 25y x 37.5f, 6 lanes, indoors, heated, 86°.
Admission: $1.50, SC(55) $1.
To find: The pool is on the high school campus.

MERCER ISLAND   206

MERCER ISLAND POOL 8815 S.E. 40th
Phone: 296-4370.
Pool: 25y x 43f, 6 lanes, indoors, heated, 84°.
Admission: $2.25, SC(60) & Disabled $1.50.
Masters: Contact the pool staff at 296-4370.

STROUM JEWISH COMMUNITY CENTER 3801 E.
Mercer Way
Phone: 232-7115.
Pool: 25y x 30f, 4 lanes, indoors, heated, 85°.
Affiliate: JCC NC.
To find: Take I-90 East Mercer Way Exit. The JCC
is across from the Synagogue, one block from City
Hall.
Masters: The JCC Masters Team. Contact Julie
Kari at 232-7115.

MOUNT VERNON   360

SKAGIT VALLEY FAMILY YMCA 215 E. Fulton St.
Phone: 336-9622.
Pool: 25y x 42f, 6 lanes, indoors, heated, 85°.
Admission: $4.
Affiliate: YMCA 3 visits per month NC.

MOUNTLAKE TERRACE   206

CITY OF MOUNTLAKE TERRACE 5303 - 228th
St. S.W.
Phone: 653-3116.
Pool: 25y x 75f, indoors, heated, 87°.
Admission: Residents $1.75, SC(60) $1. Non-residents $2.50, SC $1.75.
Notes: The facility has an extensive schedule of water walking, water aerobics and deep water exercise programs at a small additional charge.

NORTH BEND   206

SI VIEW POOL 400 S.E. Orchard Dr.
Phone: 888-1447.
Pool: 20y x 30f, 4 lanes, indoors, heated, 86°.
Admission: $2.25, SC(60) & Disabled $1.50.

NSB BANGOR   360

BANGOR POOL Bldg. 2700
Phone: 779-4817.
Pool: 25m, indoors, heated, 84°-86°.
Affiliate: U.S. Military & Dept. of Defense: Call.

OAK HARBOR   360

VANDERZAICHT POOL 2299 - 20th N.W.
Phone: 675-7665.
Pool: 25m, indoors, heated, 83°.
Admission: $2, SC(60) $1.75.
Masters: The Afterburners. Contact Rachel Pasteris at 675-7665.

OLYMPIA   360

OLYMPIA AREA YMCA 510 Franklin St. S.E.
Phone: 357-6609.
Pool: 20y x 20f, 2-3 lanes, indoors, heated, 85°-86°.
Admission: 1 visit NC, then $6. SC(65) M,W,F: 1-1:30PM lap swims $1.
Affiliate: Y AWAY 2 visits NC, then $1.

EVERGREEN COLLEGE RECREATION CENTER
Recreation & Athletics #210
Phone: 866-6000 ext. 6534.
Pool: 25y x 25m, 11 lanes, indoors, heated, 82°.
Admission: $5, SC(65) $2.

BALLY'S PACIFIC WEST 200 N.E. Sleater-Kinney
Rd.
Phone: 438-2800.
Pool: 24y, indoors, heated, 83°-85°.

Admission: $5.
Affiliate: Bally's NC.

PORT ANGELES   360

WILLIAMS SHORE MEMORIAL POOL 225 E. 5th
Phone: 457-0241.
Pool: 25y, indoors, heated, 84°.
Admission: $1.75, SC(60)$1.25. Early AM laps $1.25.

PORT ORCHARD   360

**SOUTH KITSAP COMMUNITY HIGH SCHOOL
SWIMMING POOL** 425 Mitchell Ave.
Phone: 876-7385.
Pool: 25m x 50m, indoors, heated, 82°.
Admission: $1.50.

PORT TOWNSEND   360

**MOUNTAIN VIEW ELEMENTARY SCHOOL
SWIMMING POOL** at the corner of Blaine & 19th
Sts.
Phone: 385-POOL.
Pool: 20y, 4 lanes, indoors, heated, 83°.
Admission: $2.85, SC(60) $1.75.
Masters: Contact Dr. Larry Little at 385-7597(h).

POULSBO   360

**NORTH KITSAP SCHOOL DISTRICT
COMMUNITY POOL** 1881 Hostmark
Phone: 779-3790.
Pool: 25y x 25y, 4 x 6 lanes, 'L' shape, indoors, heated, 82°.
Admission: $2.25, SC(60) $1.50.
To find: Four blocks east of Market Place Foods on Hwy. 305.
Masters: The Old Olympic Peninsula Swimmers. Contact Kurt Schmid at 779-3790.

PULLMAN   509

WASHINGTON STATE UNIVERSITY SWIM CLUB
at Washington State University
Masters: Contact Doug Garcia at 335-3518.
Pool: Gibb Pool: 25y x 25y, 8 lanes, indoors, heated, 80°.
Affiliate: USMS Call.
Notes: Coached workouts: M,W,F: 6-7:30AM. There are 3 pools at the University. The club uses different pools at different times, so be sure to find out where they're swimming when you call.

PUYALLUP   206

BALLY'S PACIFIC WEST 3600 - 9th St. S.W.
Phone: 845-1713.
Pool: 25m, indoors, heated, 84°.
Affiliate: Bally's NC. IHRSA $5.

REDMOND   206

REDMOND POOL 17535 N.E. 104th
Phone: 296-2961.
Pool: 25y x 43f, 6 lanes, indoors, heated, 84°.
Admission: $2.25, SC(60) & Disabled $1.50.

RENTON   206

RENTON POOL 16740 - 128th S.E.
Phone: 296-4335.
Pool: 25y x 43f, 6 lanes, indoors, heated, 84°.
Admission: $2.25, SC(60) & Disabled $1.50.
Masters: Contact the pool staff at 296-4335.

CASCADE ATHLETIC CLUB 17110 - 116th Ave.
S.E.
Phone: 271-3857.
Pool: 25y, indoors, heated, 80°-84°.
Admission: Call.

RICHLAND   509

COLUMBIA BASIN RACQUET CLUB 1776
Terminal Dr.
Phone: 943-8416.
Pool 1: 25m x 28f, 4 lanes, indoors, heated, 83°.
Pool 2: 25m x 35f, 5 lanes, indoor/outdoor, heated,
water temperature not reported.
Admission: $7.
Affiliate: NACA NC. IHRSA $6.
Hotel: Red Lion Hanford House (946-7611) NC
with a pass from the hotel. Shiloh Inn (946-4661)
$5.
To find: By-pass Hwy. and Van Giesen St.

SEATTLE   206

**1. YMCA OF GREATER SEATTLE - DOWNTOWN
BRANCH** 909 - 4th Ave.
Phone: 382-5010.
Pool: 20y x 60f, 3 lanes, indoors, heated, 83°.
Admission: $8, SC(60) $4.
Affiliate: YMCA 12 visits per year NC.
To find: On 4th Ave. between Madison and Marlon,
across the street from the Bank of California.

2. GATEWAY ATHLETIC CLUB 700 - 5th Ave.,
14th Floor
Phone: 343-4692.
Pool: 25y, indoors, heated, 82°-83°.
Affiliate: IHRSA $10.
Hotel: Vintage Hotel $10.

**3. SALVATION ARMY CORPS COMMUNITY
CENTER** 9050 - 16th Ave. S.W.
Phone: 767-3150.
Pool: 25y x 35f, 5 lanes, indoors, heated, 86°.
Admission: Lap and open swims $1.75, SC $1.25.
Water walking $1.50. Water aerobics $2.50, SC
$2.

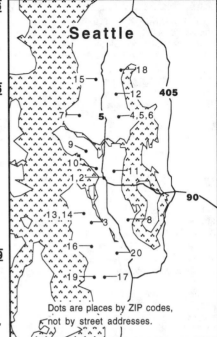

Seattle

Dots are places by ZIP codes,
not by street addresses.

4. EVANS POOL 7201 E. Green Lake Dr. N.
Phone: 684-4961.
Pool: 25y x 45f, 6 lanes, indoors, heated, 85°-86°.
Admission: $2, SC(65) $1.25.
To find: In Greenlake Park.
Masters: Contact the pool staff at 684-4961.

5. SEATTLE ATHLETIC CLUB 333 N.E. 97th St.
Phone: 522-9400.
Pool: 20y, 4 lanes, indoors, heated, 83°.
Affiliate: IHRSA: $6. M-F 4:30-7:30PM $8.

6. SANDPOINT NAVAL STATION POOL Bldg. 47,
NAVSTA Puget Sound
Phone: 526-3336 ext. 8.
Pool: 25y, 5 lanes, indoors, heated, water tempera-
ture not reported.
Affiliate: U.S. Military & Dept. of Defense: NC to
$1.25 depending on status.

7. BALLARD POOL 1471 N.W. 67th
Phone: 684-4094.
Pool: 25y x 45f, 6 lanes, indoors, heated, 85°.
Admission: $2, SC(65) & Disabled $1.25.
To find: At the corner of 15th Ave. and N.W. 67th,
next to Ballard High School.

8. RAINIER BEACH POOL 8825 Rainier Ave. S.
Phone: 386-1944.
Pool: 25y x 37f, 6 lanes, indoors, heated, 85°.
Admission: $2, SC(65) $1.25.
To find: Nine miles south of downtown Seattle on
Rainier Ave. Served by numerous bus routes.

SEATTLE   CONTINUED

9. QUEEN ANNE POOL 1920 - 1st W.
Phone: 386-4282.
Pool: 25y x 45f, 6 lanes, indoors, heated, 86°.
Admission: $2, SC(65) & Disabled $1.25.

10. THE SEATTLE CLUB 2020 Western Ave.
Phone: 443-1111.
Pool: 20y, 5 lanes, indoors, heated, 84°.
Admission: $10.
Affiliate: IHRSA NC.
To find: Located in the Pike Place Market near downtown.

11. EAST MADISON YMCA 1700 - 23rd Ave.
Phone: 322-6969.
Pool: 25y x 24f, 4 lanes, indoors, heated, 83°.
Admission: $5.
Affiliate: Y AWAY NC.
To find: At the intersection of 23rd Ave. and Olive, two blocks south of Madison St.

12. AQUA DIVE SWIM & HEALTH CLUB 12706 - 33rd Ave. N.E.
Phone: 364-2535.
Pool: 25m x 75f, 3 lanes, 'L' shape, indoors, heated, 84°.
Memberships: $625/year.
Notes: Swim and stroke analysis classes are available with membership at no additional charge, as are a number of aquatic and land-based fitness classes.

13. SOUTHWEST POOL 2801 S.W. Thistle
Phone: 684-7440.
Pool: 25y x 45f, 6 lanes, indoors, heated, 85°.
Admission: $2. SC(65) & Special populations: $1.25.

14. WEST SEATTLE FAMILY YMCA 4515 - 36th Ave. S.W.
Phone: 935-6000.
Pool: 25y x 36f, 6 lanes, indoors, heated, 86°.
Admission: $8.50, SC(60) $5.50.
Affiliate: YMCA NC.
To find: Two blocks south and one block west of the end of the W. Seattle Frwy.

15. HELENE MADISON POOL 13401 Meridian Ave. N.
Phone: 684-4979.
Pool: 110f x 45f, 6 lanes, indoors, heated, 85°.
Admission: $2, SC (65) $1.25. Coached training sessions $2.50, advance registration not required.
Masters: Contact the pool staff at 684-4979.

16. EVERGREEN POOL 606 S.W. 116th
Phone: 296-4410.
Pool: 25y x 43f, 7 lanes, indoors, heated, 84°.
Admission: $2.25, SC(60) & Disabled $1.50.

17. HIGHLINE ATHLETIC CLUB 125 S. 156th St.
Phone: 246-9000.
Pool: 20y, indoors, heated, 86°.
Admission: $10.
Affiliate: IHRSA $7.
Hotel: Local hotels $7 with room key or registration forms.
Notes: The pool uses bromine rather than chlorine for purification.

18. SHORELINE POOL 19030 - 1st Ave. N.E.
Phone: 296-4345.
Pool: 25y x 43f, 6 lanes, indoors, heated, 84°.
Admission: $2.25, SC(60) & Disabled $1.50.
Masters: Contact the pool staff at 296-4345.

19. HIGHLINE FITNESS & SWIM CLUB 626 S.W. 154th
Phone: 433-1036.
Pool: 25y, indoor/outdoor, heated, 86°.
Admission: $4.50.

20. SOUTH CENTRAL POOL 4414 S. 144th
Phone: 296-4487.
Pool: 25y x 43f, 6 lanes, indoors, heated, 84°.
Admission: $2.25, SC(60) & Disabled $1.50.

SEQUIM   360

SEQUIM AQUATIC RECREATION CENTER 610 N. 5th
Phone: 683-3344.
Pool: 25y x 45f, 6 lanes, indoors, heated, 84°.
Admission: $3.50, SC(62) $3.25.
Masters: The Sequim Masters. Contact Dr. Larry Little at 385-7597(h).

SILVERDALE   360

OLYMPIC AQUATIC CENTER 7070 Stampede Blvd.
Phone: Recorded schedule: 692-3192.
Information: 692-3217.
Pool: 25y, indoors, heated, 78°-82°.
Admission: $2.

SPOKANE   509

INLAND EMPIRE YMCA N. 507 Howard St.
Phone: 838-3577.
Pool: 25y x 24f, 4 lanes, indoors, heated, 82°.
Admission: $7.75.
Affiliate: YMCA NC.
Hotel: All downtown hotels $3.50 with room key.
To find: In the northwest corner of Riverfront Park, downtown. Cross streets are Spokane Falls Blvd. and Post St.

SHADLE PARK SWIMMING POOL 4300 N. Oak St.
Phone: 625-6200.
Pool: 25y x 48f, 6 lanes, indoors, heated, 82°.
Admission: $1.50.

To find: At the west end of Shadle Park High School.
Masters: The Spokane Masters Swim & Tri. Contact Jim McBride at 747-9043(h).

STA-FIT EAST E. 14210 Sprague
Phone: 926-1241.
Pool: 22y, indoors, heated, 85°.
Affiliate: IHRSA $7.

NORTH PARK RACQUET / ATHLETIC CLUB N. 8121 Division
Phone: 467-5124.
Pool: 25m, indoors, heated, 80°-82°.
Affiliate: NACA NC.

STA-FIT NORTH N. 8707 Division
Phone: 467-1500.
Pool: 25y, indoors, heated, 82°-84°.
Affiliate: IHRSA $7.

STA-FIT SOUTH 5501 Regal
Phone: 448-8442.
Pool: 20y, indoors, heated, 84°-85°.
Admission: $7.

WHITWORTH COLLEGE AQUATIC CENTER W. 300 Hawthorne Rd.
Phone: 466-3297.
Pool: 25y x 42f, 6 lanes, indoors, heated, 82°.
Admission: $2.
Passes: 10 swims $15.

STEVENSON — 509

SKAMANIA LODGE 1131 Skamania Lodge Way
Phone: Fitness Center 427-2529. Hotel 427-7700.
Reservations: 800-221-7117.
Pool: 20y x 20f, 3 lanes, indoors, heated, 82°.
Admission: $6.42. Registered guests NC.
Notes: The Skamania Lodge is a rustic mountain retreat in the Columbia River Gorge.

SUMNER — 206

SUMNER POOL 1707 Main St.
Phone: 863-8110.
Pool: 25y x 42f, 6 lanes, indoors, heated, 84°.
Admission: $1.75.
To find: Behind Sumner High School at the end of Mason. One block north of Main St. on Mason. Approach via Wood Ave.
Masters: The Maranha Swim Team. Contact Bill Haugen at 863-8110.

SUNNYSIDE — 509

VALLEY RACQUET & FITNESS CLUB, INC. 701 Scoon Rd.
Phone: 837-7733.
Pool: 25y, indoors, heated, 85°-87°.
Admission: $7.

TACOMA — 206

TACOMA CENTER YMCA 1144 S. Market St.
Phone: 597-6444.
Pool: 20m x 10m, 5 lanes, indoors, heated, 82°.
Affiliate: YMCA 6 visits per year NC.
Hotel: Sheraton Hotel (572-3200) NC with a pass from the hotel.

EASTSIDE COMMUNITY POOL 3524 E. 'L' St.
Phone: 591-2042.
Pool: 25m x 45f, 6 lanes, indoors, heated, 86°.
Admission: $1.25, SC(62) $1.
To find: Next to Gault Middle School, 10 blocks south of the Tacoma Dome.

PEOPLE'S CENTER POOL 1602 S. Martin Luther King Jr. Way ('K' St.)
Phone: 591-5323.
Pool: 25m x 45f, 6 lanes, indoors, heated, 86°.
Admission: $1.25, SC(63) $1.

PACIFIC LUTHERAN UNIVERSITY 124th & Yakima
Phone: 535-7370.
Pool: 25y x 42f, 6 lanes, indoors, heated, 84°.
Admission: $2.
Passes: 15 swims $25.
To find: From I-5 take Exit 127 E., go south on Pacific Ave. to 125th St., turn right and go six blocks.

TACOMA FAMILY YMCA 1002 S. Pearl St.
Phone: 564-9622.
Pool: 25m x 45f, 6 lanes, indoors, heated, 82°-84°.
Affiliate: Y AWAY 6 visits NC.
Notes: There is also a 40f x 20f, indoor, heated, 84°-86° training pool, and a 96°-98° therapy pool.

BALLY'S PACIFIC WEST 1680 S. Mildred St.
Phone: 565-4600.
Pool: 25m, indoors, heated, 84°.
Affiliate: Bally's NC.

TUMWATER — 360

VALLEY ATHLETIC CLUB POOL 4833 Tumwater Valley Dr.
Phone: 352-3400 ext. 124.
Pool: 25y x 40f, 6 lanes, indoors, heated, 83°.
Affiliate: IHRSA & IPFA: Call.
Hotel: Tyee Hotel & Westwater Hotel: $6.47 with room key.
Notes: There is also an 85°-86° diving/therapy pool and an outdoor seasonal pool.
To find: Next to the Olympia Brewery.
Masters: The Valley Masters. Contact Erik Strom at 352-3400 ext. 124.

UNION   360

**ALDERBROOK RESORT GOLF & CONFERENCE
CENTER** E. 7101 Hwy. 106
Phone: 898-3111. **Reservations:** 800-622-9370.
Pool: 54.5f, rectangular, indoors, heated, 85°.
Admission: $2.50. Registered guests NC.

VANCOUVER   360

CLARK COUNTY YMCA at Washington State
School for the Blind, McLouglin & 'W' St.
Phone: 696-6181.
Pool: 25y, 5 lanes, indoors, heated, 90°.
Admission: $2.
Affiliate: YMCA NC.
Notes: The pool closes Jun. through Aug.
To find: On the north side of Washington State
School for the Blind.

MARSHALL POOL 1009 E. McLoughlin Blvd.
Phone: 696-8239.
Pool: 25y x 37.5f, 6 lanes, indoors, heated, 85°-
86°.
Admission: Residents $1.75, SC(60)1.25. Non-
residents $2.50, SC $2.
Notes: Admission rates are subject to change.
To find: One block west of Clark College.

OXFORD ATHLETIC CLUB 7588 Delaware Lane
Phone: 694-8361.

Pool: 20y, indoors, heated, 87°-88°.
Admission: Call.

WALLA WALLA   509

WALLA WALLA YMCA 340 S. Park
Phone: 525-8863.
Pool: 25y, indoors, heated, 83°.
Admission: $5.
Affiliate: YMCA NC.

YAKIMA   509

YAKIMA YMCA 5 N. Naches Ave.
Phone: 248-1202.
Pool: 25y x 25f, 4 lanes, indoors, heated, 86°.
Admission: $6, limited hours.
Affiliate: YMCA 3 visits per month NC.
Hotel: Red Lion Motor Inn, Holiday Inn (452-6511),
& Cavanaugh's: Contact the Y for information.

YAKIMA ATHLETIC CLUB 2501 Racquet Lane
Phone: 453-6521.
Pool: 25y x 33f, 5 lanes, indoor/outdoor, heated,
82°-84°.
Admission: $10.
Affiliate: NACA NC with reciprocal card. IHRSA
$6.
To find: On S. 24th Ave., two blocks from the
Yakima Airport.

HELP MAKE THE NEXT *SWIMMERS GUIDE* EVEN BETTER

To receive a free copy of the next *Swimmers Guide* tell us about pools you
know of that aren't in this edition. See page 14 for details.

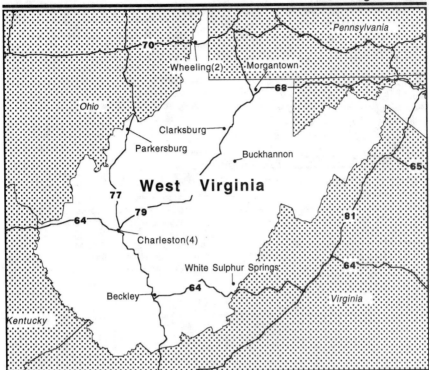

BECKLEY-RALEIGH COUNTY YMCA 121 E. Main
St.
Phone: 255-6600 or 252-0715.
Pool: 25m, 6 lanes, indoors, heated, 85.4°.
Admission: $5.
To find: Two blocks from the courthouse on Main
St.

WEST VIRGINIA WESLEYAN COLLEGE 59
College Ave.
Phone: 473-8507.
Pool: 25y, 6 lanes, indoors, heated, 80°.
Admission: $3.

CHARLESTON YWCA 1114 Quarrier St.
Phone: 340-3550.
Pool: 20y x 20f, 4 lanes, indoors, heated, 86°.
Admission: $3.

UNIVERSITY OF CHARLESTON 2300 MacCorkle
Ave. S.E.
Phone: Pool: 357-4822. Swimming Office: 357-
4825.
Pool: 25y x 45f, 6 lanes, indoors, heated, 82°-83°.
Admission: Sa,Su: $2. Out-of-town visitors may

be able to obtain guest passes for one or two
weekday visits through the UC Swimming Office.
Memberships: $30/month, SC(55) $22.50.
To find: On the south side of the Kanawha River,
across from the West Virginia State Capitol com-
plex.
Masters: The UC Aquatic Team (USS). Contact
Greg Olson at 357-4825.

**SOUTH CHARLESTON COMMUNITY CENTER
POOL** 601 Jefferson Rd.
Phone: 744-4731.
Pool: 25m, 2 lap swimming lanes, indoors, heated,
84°.
Admission: $2, SC(62) $1.
Hotel: South Charleston Red Roof Inn (744-1500)
NC with room key.

CHARLESTON FAMILY YMCA 300 Hillcrest Dr. E.
Phone: 340-3527.
Pool: 25y x 45f, 6 lanes, indoors, heated, 82°-86°.
Admission: $8.
Affiliate: Y AWAY NC.

HARRISON COUNTY YMCA Lowndes Hill Park
Phone: 623-3303.
Pool: 25y, indoors, heated, 80°-82°.
Admission: $5.
Affiliate: YMCA NC.

Masters: The Harrison County YMCA Masters. Contact Rich Ferro at 623-3303.

MORGANTOWN 304

LAKEVIEW RESORT Route 6
Phone: 594-1111. **Reservations:** 800-624-8300.
Pool 1: 50f x 16f, indoors, heated, 83°.
Pool 2: 50f x 35f, indoors, heated, 82°.
Admission: $7.50. Registered guests NC.
Memberships: $43.46/month.

PARKERSBURG 304

PARKERSBURG YMCA 1800 - 30th St.
Phone: 485-5585.
Pool: 25y x 42f, 6 lanes, indoors, heated, 84°.
Admission: $6.
Affiliate: YMCA NC.
Hotel: Blennerhasset Hotel (422-3131) NC with room key.

WHEELING 304

HOWARD LONG WELLNESS CENTER 800 Medical Park Rd.
Phone: 242-9355.
Pool: 25y x 36f, indoors, heated, 82°.
Admission: $10.

CHAMBERS YMCA Lounez Ave.
Phone: 242-8086.
Pool: 25y, 6 lanes, indoors, heated, 80°-82°.
Admission: $5.
Affiliate: Y AWAY NC.

WHITE SULPHUR SPRINGS 304

THE GREENBRIER
Phone: 536-1110. **Reservations:** 800-624-6070.
Pool: 100.4f x 42f, rectangular, indoors, heated, 78°.
Admission: Registered guests only NC.
Notes: This is a Mobil 'Five Star' and AAA 'Five Diamond' resort property.

ALWAYS CALL FIRST

Pools close, they change names, affiliations, admission policies, and rates. And just because a pool is listed in *Swimmers Guide* doesn't mean it's open all day, every day, for just the type of workout you want to do. Spend a quarter to save time and aggravation. . . always call first!

Wisconsin

Superior

Michigan

Marinette

Chippewa Falls   Wausau

Eau Claire(2)

Sturgeon Bay

Stevens Point(2)   Green Bay(5)

94

Port Edwards

Appleton(2)

43

Neenah

Tomah   Oshkosh   Maintowoc

90   Fond du Lac   Sheboygan

Minnesota   Green Lake

La Crosse(2)   Kohler

Beaver Dam   West Bend

Iowa   Menomonee Falls

Brookfield(3)

Madison(5)   Hartland   Brown Deer

94

Platteville   Waukesha   Milwaukee(5)

Janesville   Wauwatosa   West Allis

Monroe

43   Cudahy(2)

Greenfield(2)   Racine

Illinois

90   94

APPLETON FAMILY YMCA 218 E. Lawrence St.
Phone: 739-6135.
Pool 1: 25m, indoors, heated, 82°.
Pool 2: 25y, indoors, heated, 84°.
Admission: $6.
Affiliate: Y AWAY NC.
Hotel: Paper Valley Hotel (733-8000) $3 with room key.
Masters: The Appleton YMCA Marlins Masters. Contact Matt Luebbers at 954-7627(w).

BUCHANAN-KIEWIT RECREATION CENTER Lawrence University, 525 College Ave.
Phone: 832-6638.
Pool: 25y x 60f, 8 lanes, indoors, heated, 82°.
Admission: $2*.
Notes: *Visitors must call the Recreation Program Coordinator at least 3 days prior to arrival to arrange a visit.

BEAVER DAM YMCA 117 Park Ave.
Phone: 887-8811.
Pool: 25y, indoors, heated, 84°-86°.
Admission: $5.
Affiliate: YMCA NC.

HIGHLANDER ELITE FITNESS & RACQUET CLUB 13825 W. Burleigh St.
Phone: 786-0880.
Pool: 25y x 20f, 4 lanes, indoors, heated, 82°.
Affiliate: IHRSA $10.
Notes: The pool is chlorine free.
To find: About a mile off I-43 west on Burleigh St.

BALLY'S VIC TANNY 16985 W. Bluemound Rd.
Phone: 785-9475.
Pool: 25y, indoors, heated, 82°.
Admission: Call.
Affiliate: Bally's NC.

BROOKFIELD CONTINUED

BROOKFIELD CENTRAL HIGH SCHOOL 16900 W. Gebhardt Rd.
Phone: 796-6675.
Pool: 25y, 2-3 lanes, indoors, heated, 80°.
Affiliate: Residents $1.50.
Notes: *The Brookfield Park & Recreation Dept. operates a 50m, outdoor, summer pool in Wirth Park at Pilgrim & North Ave. Non-residents may swim there at the general admission rate.

BROWN DEER 414

SCHROEDER YMCA & AQUATIC CENTER 9250 N. Green Bay Rd.
Phone: 354-9622 ext. 220.
Pool: 50m OR 25m + 25m x 22m, 8 OR 16 lanes, indoors, heated, 80°.
Affiliate: Y AWAY outside a 50 mile radius NC, within 50 miles 3 visits per month NC.
Hotel: Sheraton Inn (355-8585) $4 with a pass from the hotel.

CHIPPEWA FALLS 715

CHIPPEWA VALLEY FAMILY YMCA 611 Jefferson Ave.
Phone: 723-2201.
Pool: 25m x 37f, 6 lanes, indoors, heated, 84°.
Admission: $6, SC(52) $4.
Affiliate: YMCA NC.
To find: On Jefferson Ave. between the Northern Wisconsin State Fair and Lowater Auto Parts.

CUDAHY 414

SOUTH SHORE YMCA 3244 E. College Ave.
Phone: 764-6400.
Pool: 25y, 6 lanes, indoors, heated, 82°.
Admission: $8.
Affiliate: YMCA NC.

BALLY'S VIC TANNY 2525 E. Layton Ave.
Phone: 481-2255.
Pool: 25m, indoors, heated, 82°-83°.
Admission: Call.
Affiliate: Bally's NC.

EAU CLAIRE 715

EAU CLAIRE ATHLETIC CLUB 3656 Mall Dr.
Phone: 833-2201.
Pool: 20y x 30f, 4 lanes, indoors, heated, 83°.
Admission: $8.
Affiliate: IHRSA $5.
Hotel: Holiday Inn-Gateway (834-3181), Heartland Inn (839-7100), & Howard Johnsons (834-6611): $4.
To find: On Hwy. 93, one mile north of I-94.

EAU CLAIRE YMCA 700 Graham Ave.
Phone: 836-8460.
Pool: 25y x 36f, indoors, heated, 84°.
Admission: $5.
Affiliate: YMCA NC.

FOND DU LAC 414

FOND DU LAC YMCA 90 W. 2nd St.
Phone: 921-3330.
Pool: 25y x 25f, indoors, heated, 85°.
Admission: $7.
Affiliate: YMCA NC.

GREEN BAY 414

DOWNTOWN CENTER YMCA 235 N. Jefferson St.
Phone: 435-5361.
Pool: 25y, indoors, heated, 83°.
Admission: $6.
Affiliate: YMCA NC.

BROADVIEW CENTER YMCA 380 Broadview Dr.
Phone: 336-1600.
Pool: 25y, indoors, heated, 83°-84°.
Admission: $8.
Affiliate: YMCA NC.

YWCA OF GREEN BAY-DE PERE 230 S. Madison St.
Phone: 432-5581.
Pool: 25y, indoors, heated, 88°-90°.
Admission: $4.50.
Affiliate: YWCA $3.

WEST SIDE CENTER YMCA 2630 W. Point Rd.
Phone: 494-5555.
Pool: 20y x 20f, indoors, heated, 83°.
Admission: $6.
Affiliate: YMCA NC.

PHOENIX SPORTS CENTER University of Wisconsin - Green Bay, 2420 Nicolet Dr.
Phone: 465-2449.
Pool: 25y x 60f, 8 lanes, indoors, heated, 81°.
Admission: $5.
Memberships: Fall and spring semesters: $105, SC(62) $55. Summer semester: $50, SC $45.

GREEN LAKE 414

GREEN LAKE CONFERENCE CENTER American Baptist Assembly, W. 2511 State Hwy. 23
Phone: 294-3323. **Reservations:** 800-558-8898.
Pool: 25y, rectangular, indoors, heated, 85°.
Admission: $2.50, SC(65) $2. Registered guests NC.

GREENFIELD 414

SOUTHWEST SUBURBAN BRANCH YMCA 11311 W. Howard Ave.
Phone: 546-9622.
Pool: 80f x 48f, indoors, heated, 86°.
Affiliate: YMCA NC.

CLUB UNIVERSE 5020 S. 110th St.
Phone: 529-2223.
Pool: 25y, indoors, heated, 81°.
Affiliate: IHRSA $5.

HARTLAND _____ **414**

LAKE COUNTRY RACQUET CLUB 560 Industrial Dr.
Phone: 367-4999.
Pool: 25y, indoors, heated, 83°.
Admission: $10.

JANESVILLE _____ **608**

JANESVILLE FAMILY YMCA 54 S. Franklin St.
Phone: 754-6654.
Pool: 25y x 40f, 6 lanes, indoors, heated, 81°.
Admission: $6.
Affiliate: Out-of-area Y AWAY NC.

KOHLER _____ **414**

SPORTS CORE Willow Creek Dr.
Phone: 457-4444.
Pool 1: 25y x 30f, indoors, heated, 80°.
Pool 2: 20y x 30f, indoors, heated, 84°.
Affiliate: IHRSA $10.

LA CROSSE _____ **608**

LA CROSSE FAMILY YMCA 1140 Main St.
Phone: 782-9622.
Pool: 25y x 42f, 6 lanes, indoors, heated, 83°.
Admission: $7. Masters workouts $3.25.
Affiliate: Y AWAY Call.
To find: At the corner of Main St. and West.
Masters: The La Crosse-Onalasica Swim Team (LOST). Contact Todd Ondell at 788-9260(w).

VALLEY VIEW FITNESS & RACQUET CLUB 3939 County Hwy. B
Phone: 781-4614.
Pool: 25y, indoors, heated, 81°-83°.
Admission: $10.

MADISON _____ **608**

PRINCETON CLUB 4030 E. Towne Blvd.
Phone: 241-2639.
Pool: 20y, indoors, heated, 81°-82°.
Admission: $10.
Affiliate: IPFA NC.
Hotel: Holiday Inn (244-4703), Excel Inn, & Hampton Inn (222-9400): Discount passes are available at the hotels.

BALLY'S VIC TANNY 26 Schroeder Court
Phone: 273-2110.
Pool: 20y, indoors, heated, 81°.
Admission: Call.
Affiliate: Bally's NC.

MADISON EAST YMCA 711 Cottage Grove Rd.
Phone: 221-1571.
Pool: 25y, 8 lanes, indoors, heated, 82°.
Admission: $8.
Affiliate: Y AWAY NC.
Masters: Contact Jim Burskowitz at 221-1571.

SUPREME HEALTH & FITNESS 5555 Odana Rd.
Phone: 274-5080.
Pool: 65f x 18f, 3 lanes, indoors, heated, 82°.
Admission: $6.
To find: At the intersection of Odana Rd. and Whitney Way.

WEST YMCA 5515 Medical Circle
Phone: 276-6606.
Pool: 25m, 6 lanes, indoors, heated, 82°-83°.
Admission: $8.
Affiliate: Y AWAY NC.

MAINTOWOC _____ **414**

MANITOWOC-TWO RIVERS YMCA 205 Maritime Dr.
Phone: 682-0341.
Pool: 25y x 42f, 6 lanes, indoors, heated, 85°.
Admission: $5.
Affiliate: YMCA NC.
Hotel: Inn on Maritime Bay (682-7000) NC with a pass from the hotel.

MARINETTE _____ **715**

UNIVERSITY YMCA at the intersection of University Dr. and Shore Dr.
Phone: 735-9417.
Pool: 25y x 42f, 6 lanes, indoors, heated, 84°.
Admission: $6.
Affiliate: YMCA NC.

MENOMONEE FALLS _____ **414**

TRI-COUNTY YMCA N84 W17501 Menomonee Ave.
Phone: 255-9622.
Pool: 25m, 6 lanes, indoors, heated, 84°.
Admission: $8.
Affiliate: Y AWAY outside a 40 mile radius NC.

MILWAUKEE _____ **414**

NORTH CENTRAL YMCA 2200 N. 12th St.
Phone: 374-6060.
Pool: 25y, indoors, heated, 78°-80°.
Affiliate: YMCA NC.

MOODY INDOOR POOL 2200 W. Burleigh
Phone: 445-1245.
Pool: 25m, 8 lanes, indoors, heated, 82°.
Admission: 10¢.
To find: Inner City Milwaukee.

MILWAUKEE CONTINUED

PULASKI INDOOR POOL 2701 S. 16th St.
Phone: 645-2328.
Pool: 25m, 8 lanes, indoors, heated, 82°.
Admission: $1.50. Lap swim sessions $2.
To find: On the south side of Milwaukee, four blocks north of Oklahoma Ave., on 16th and Cleveland.

BALLY'S DOWNTOWN CLUB 1237 N. Van Buren
Phone: 291-0444.
Pool: 25m, indoors, heated, 80°.
Admission: 1 visit NC.
Affiliate: Bally's NC.

NOYES INDOOR POOL 8235 W. Good Hope Rd.
Phone: 353-1252.
Pool: 25m, 8 lanes, indoors, heated, 82°.
Admission: $1.50. Lap swim sessions $2.
To find: On the northwest side of Milwaukee, three blocks west of 76th St.

MONROE 608

GREEN COUNTY FAMILY YMCA 1307 - 2nd St.
Phone: 325-2003.
Pool: 25m, 6 lanes, indoors, heated, 85°.
Admission: $7.50.
Affiliate: Y AWAY 12 visits per year NC, then $3.75.

NEENAH 414

NEENAH-MENASHA YMCA 110 W. N. Waters St.
Phone: 729-9622.
Pool 1: 25m, 6 lanes, indoors, heated, 81°.
Pool 2: 25y, 5 lanes, indoors, heated, 88°.
Admission: $6.
Affiliate: Y AWAY NC.
Hotel: Valley Inn (725-8441) NC.

OSHKOSH 414

OSHKOSH YMCA 324 Washington Ave.
Phone: 236-3380.
Pool: 25y, 4 lanes, indoors, heated, 83°.
Admission: $7.
Affiliate: YMCA NC.

PLATTEVILLE 608

PIONEER ACTIVITY CENTER-WILLIAMS FIELD HOUSE University of Wisconsin - Platteville, 1 University Plaza
Phone: 342-1577.
Pool: 25m, indoors, heated, 80°.
Admission: $5.
Memberships: $75/year.

PORT EDWARDS 715

SOUTH WOOD COUNTY YMCA 211 Wisconsin River Dr.
Phone: 887-3240.
Pool: 25y, indoors, heated, 82°-86°.
Admission: $5.
Affiliate: YMCA NC.

RACINE 414

YWCA OF RACINE 740 College Ave.
Phone: 633-3503.
Pool: 20y, indoors, heated, 87°.
Admission: $4.
Affiliate: YWCA $2.

SHEBOYGAN 414

SHEBOYGAN YMCA 812 Broughton Dr.
Phone: 451-8000.
Pool: 25m, 6 lanes, indoors, heated, 79°-80°.
Admission: Basic $5, SC(62) $1.75. Fitness Center $6, SC $2.75.
Affiliate: YMCA NC.
Masters: The Sheboygan Masters. Contact Marty Mader at 458-2861(h).

STEVENS POINT 715

STEVENS POINT AREA YMCA 1000 Division St.
Phone: 342-2980.
Pool: 25y x 42f, 6 lanes, indoors, heated, 83°.
Admission: $5, SC(60) $2.50.
Affiliate: YMCA NC. U.S. Military $2.
To find: One mile south of the Holiday Inn.
Masters: Contact Wendy Weber or Kelly Geiger at 342-2980.

UNIVERSITY OF WISCONSIN - STEVENS POINT 4th Ave.
Phone: 346-2200.
Pool: 25y x 60f, 8 lanes, indoors, heated, 80°.
Admission: $2.
Memberships: $158.25/year.

STURGEON BAY 414

DOOR COUNTY YMCA 17 S. 5th Ave.
Phone: 743-4949.
Pool: 25y, 6 lanes, indoors, heated, 83°.
Admission: $3.50, SC(62) $2.75.
Affiliate: Y AWAY NC.

SUPERIOR 715

SUPERIOR / DOUGLAS COUNTY YMCA 9 N. 21st St.
Phone: 392-5611.
Pool: 25y, 4 lanes, indoors, heated, 84°.
Admission: $5.
Affiliate: Y AWAY NC.

TOMAH 608

HOLIDAY INN Jct. I-94 & Hwy. 21
Phone: 372-3211. **Reservations:** 800 HOLIDAY.
Pool: 50f x 25f, rectangular, indoors, heated, 78°.
Admission: $3. Registered guests NC.

WAUKESHA 414

CHRISTOPH MEMORIAL YWCA 306 N. West Ave.
Phone: 547-1872.
Pool: 20y x 25f, 3 lanes, indoors, heated, 85°.
Admission: $5, SC(65) $4.75.
Affiliate: YWCA $4, SC $3.75.
Notes: There is also a 40f x 25f, 4-5.5ft deep, 90°
pool extensively used for aqua aerobics, water
walking, and arthritis classes.
To find: A half mile north of the driver license
examination building on West Ave.

WAUSAU 715

WAUSAU - WOODSON YMCA 707 - 3rd St.
Phone: 845-2177.
Pool: 25y, indoors, heated, 78°-82°.
Admission: $5.
Affiliate: Y AWAY NC.

WAUWATOSA 414

WEST SUBURBAN YMCA 2420 N. 124th St.
Phone: 778-4949.
Pool: 25y, indoors, heated, 80°.
Affiliate: YMCA NC.

WEST ALLIS 414

BALLY'S VIC TANNY 901 S. 60th St.
Phone: 475-7066.
Pool: 25m, indoors, heated, 82°.
Admission: Call.
Affiliate: Bally's NC.

WEST BEND 414

KETTLE MORAINE YMCA 1111 W. Washington
St.
Phone: 334-3405.
Pool: 82f x 42f, indoors, heated, 80°-82°.
Admission: $5.
Affiliate: YMCA 3 visits NC, then $2.50.

HELP MAKE THE NEXT *SWIMMERS GUIDE* EVEN BETTER

To receive a free copy of the next *Swimmers Guide* tell us about pools you
know of that aren't in this edition. See page 14 for details.

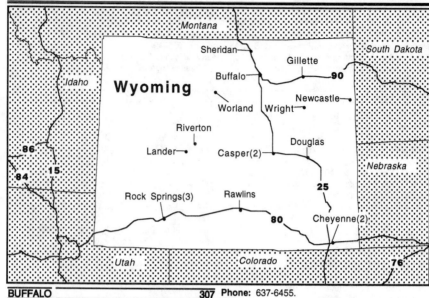

BUFFALO   307

JOHNSON COUNTY FAMILY YMCA 101 Klondike
Phone: 684-9558.
Pool: 25y, 6 lanes, indoors, heated, 82°.
Admission: $4, SC(65) $2.
Affiliate: YMCA NC.

CASPER   307

CASPER FAMILY YMCA 315 E. 15th St.
Phone: 234-9187.
Pool: 25y x 45f, 5 lanes, indoors, heated, 86°.
Admission: $2.
Affiliate: YMCA NC.
To find: Two blocks north of Casper College on
Durbin St.

WYOMING ATHLETIC CLUB 455 Thelma Dr.
Phone: 265-6928.
Pool: 25y, 4 lanes, indoors, heated, 83°.
Admission: $8.
Affiliate: IHRSA & Western Association of Clubs:
$5.
To find: Off 2nd St., behind Norwest Bank East
Branch.

CHEYENNE   307

CHEYENNE FAMILY YMCA 1426 E. Lincolnway
Phone: 634-9622.
Pool: 25m x 36f, 6 lanes, indoors, heated, 86°.
Admission: $5.
Affiliate: Y AWAY NC.
To find: Adjacent to Holiday Park and accessible
via Dunn Ave.

CITY OF CHEYENNE MUNICIPAL POOL Lions
Park, 931 Pool Dr.

Phone: 637-6455.
Pool: 25m x 75f, 6 lanes, indoor/outdoor, heated,
84°.
Admission: $1.75, SC(60) $1.50.
Affiliate: USMS $1 during lap swims.
To find: At the north end of Lions Park across from
the golf course.
Masters: The Warren Masters Swim Team.
Contact Stacy Ross at 637-6457.

DOUGLAS   307

RECREATIONAL CENTER POOL 1701 Hamilton
St.
Phone: 358-4231.
Pool: 25m, indoors, heated, 85°.
Admission: NC.

GILLETTE   307

**CAMPBELL COUNTY PARKS & RECREATION
DEPT.** 1000 Douglas Hwy.
Phone: 682-5470.
Pool: 25y, 6 lanes, indoor/outdoor, heated, 84°.
Admission: $2.50, SC(62) NC.
To find: Four blocks north of the Holiday Inn.

LANDER   307

LANDER SWIM POOL 450 S. 9th
Phone: 332-2272.
Pool: 25y, 6 lanes, indoors, heated, 83°.
Admission: $1.75, SC(60) NC.

NEWCASTLE   307

NEWCASTLE HIGH SCHOOL 116 Casper Ave.
Phone: 746-2714.

Pool: 25y, indoors, heated, 86°.
Admission: $2.

RAWLINS 307

RAWLINS HIGH SCHOOL 1401 Colorado
Phone: 328-9272.
Pool: 25y x 48f, 6 lanes, indoors, heated, 84°.
Admission: $1.
To find: At the west end of the Rawlins High School Complex.

RIVERTON 307

RIVERTON AQUATIC CENTER 2001 W. Sunset Dr.
Phone: 856-4230.
Pool: 25y, 8 lanes, indoors, heated, 86°.
Admission: $2, SC(55) $1.

ROCK SPRINGS 307

ROCK SPRINGS FAMILY RECREATION CENTER 3900 Sweetwater Rd.
Phone: 382-3265.
Pool: 25m x 10m, 4 lanes, indoors, heated, 84°.
Admission: $3.75, SC(62) $1.25.

ROCK SPRINGS CIVIC CENTER 401 'N' St.
Phone: 362-6181.
Pool: 25m x 10m, 6 lanes, indoors, heated, 84°.
Admission: $3.75, SC(62) $1.25.

WWCC AQUATIC CENTER Western Wyoming College, 2500 College Dr.
Phone: 382-1694.
Pool: 25m x 20y, 8 lanes, indoors, heated, 84°.
Admission: $1.

SHERIDAN 307

SHERIDAN COUNTY FAMILY YMCA 417 N. Jefferson
Phone: 674-7488.
Pool 1: 25y x 25f, 4 lanes, indoors, heated, 84°.
Pool 2: 25m x 25f, 4 lanes, indoors, heated, 88°.
Admission: $5.
Affiliate: YMCA NC.
To find: Two blocks west of Hardee's Restaurant.

WORLAND 307

WORLAND COMMUNITY POOL 801 S. 17th St.
Phone: 347-4113.
Pool: 25y x 42f, 6 lanes, indoors, heated, 85°.
Admission: $1.75.
To find: In the geodesic domed building next to the high school.

WRIGHT 307

WRIGHT RECREATION CENTER 225 Wright Blvd.
Phone: 464-0198.
Pool: 25y x 28f, 4 lanes, indoors, heated, 84°.
Admission: $2.50.
To find: Across from Wright Senior High School.

ALWAYS CALL FIRST

Pools close, they change names, affiliations, admission policies, and rates. And just because a pool is listed in *Swimmers Guide* doesn't mean it's open all day, every day, for just the type of workout you want to do. Spend a quarter to save time and aggravation. . . always call first!

POOL LENGTH EQUIVALENTS - LENGTHS PER MILE - PER 1000 YARDS - PER 1000 METERS

Length	No. of Pools	Equivalents Yards	Meters	Lengths per mile Precise	Whole	Lengths/1000y Precise	Whole	Lengths/1000m Precise	Whole
50 feet	50	16.67	15.24	105.60	106	60.00	60	65.62	66
50.25 feet	1	16.75	15.32	105.07	106	59.70	60	65.29	66
51 feet	1	17.00	15.54	103.53	104	58.82	59	64.33	65
51.5 feet	1	17.17	15.70	102.52	103	58.25	59	63.71	64
52 feet	3	17.33	15.85	101.54	102	57.69	58	63.09	64
54 feet	2	18.00	16.46	97.78	98	55.56	56	60.76	61
54.5 feet	2	18.17	16.61	96.88	97	55.05	56	60.20	61
55 feet	2	18.33	16.76	96.00	96	54.55	55	59.65	60
56.25 feet	1	18.75	17.15	93.87	94	53.33	54	58.33	59
58 feet	4	19.33	17.68	91.03	92	51.72	52	56.57	57
61 feet	1	20.33	18.59	86.56	87	49.18	50	53.78	54
62 feet	2	20.67	18.90	85.16	86	48.39	49	52.92	53
63.5 feet	1	21.17	19.35	83.15	84	47.24	48	51.67	52
64 feet	4	21.33	19.51	82.50	83	46.88	47	51.26	52
65 feet	8	21.67	19.81	81.23	82	46.15	47	50.47	51
66.5 feet	1	22.17	20.27	79.40	80	45.11	46	49.34	50
68 feet	2	22.67	20.73	77.65	78	44.12	45	48.25	49
70 feet	15	23.33	21.34	75.43	76	42.86	43	46.87	47
72 feet	1	24.00	21.95	73.33	74	41.67	42	45.57	46
73 feet	4	24.33	22.25	72.33	73	41.10	42	44.94	45
73.3 feet	1	24.43	22.34	72.03	73	40.93	41	44.76	45
74 feet	2	24.67	22.56	71.35	72	40.54	41	44.34	45
76 feet	5	25.33	23.16	69.47	70	39.47	40	43.17	44
79 feet	2	26.33	24.08	66.84	67	37.97	38	41.53	42
80 feet	9	26.67	24.38	66.00	66	37.50	38	41.01	42
82 feet	3	27.33	24.99	64.39	65	36.59	37	40.01	41
82.25 feet	1	27.42	25.07	64.19	65	36.47	37	39.89	40
83 feet	1	27.67	25.30	63.61	64	36.14	37	39.53	40
85 feet	1	28.33	25.91	62.12	63	35.29	36	38.60	39
88 feet	1	29.33	26.82	60.00	60	34.09	35	37.28	38
92 feet	1	30.67	28.04	57.39	58	32.61	33	35.66	36
95 feet	1	31.67	28.96	55.58	56	31.58	32	34.54	35
100 feet	25	33.33	30.48	52.80	53	30.00	30	32.81	33
100.4 feet	1	33.47	30.60	52.59	53	29.88	30	32.68	33
103 feet	1	34.33	31.39	51.26	52	29.13	30	31.85	32
105.083 feet	1	35.03	32.03	50.25	51	28.55	29	31.22	32
110 feet	1	36.67	33.53	48.00	48	27.27	28	29.83	30
137 feet	1	45.67	41.76	38.54	39	21.90	22	23.95	24
149 feet	1	49.67	45.42	35.44	36	20.13	21	22.02	23
200 feet	1	66.67	60.96	26.40	27	15.00	15	16.40	17

POOL LENGTH EQUIVALENTS - LENGTHS PER MILE - PER 1000 YARDS - PER 1000 METERS

Length	No. of Pools	Equivalents Feet	Meters	Lengths per mile Precise	Whole	Lengths/1000y Precise	Whole	Lengths/1000m Precise	Whole
17 yards	3	51.00	15.54	103.53	104	58.82	59	64.33	65
18 yards	4	54.00	16.46	97.78	98	55.56	56	60.76	61
20 yards	480	60.00	18.29	88.00	88	50.00	50	54.68	55
21 yards	7	63.00	19.20	83.81	84	47.62	48	52.08	53
21.75 yards	1	65.25	19.89	80.92	81	45.98	46	50.28	51
22 yards	16	66.00	20.12	80.00	80	45.45	46	49.71	50
23 yards	7	69.00	21.03	76.52	77	43.48	44	47.55	48
23.5 yards	1	70.50	21.49	74.89	75	42.55	43	46.54	47
24 yards	12	72.00	21.95	73.33	74	41.67	42	45.57	46
25 yards	1913	75.00	22.86	70.40	71	40.00	40	43.74	44
25.2 yards	1	75.60	23.04	69.84	70	39.68	40	43.40	44
26 yards	1	78.00	23.77	67.69	68	38.46	39	42.06	43
27 yards	3	81.00	24.69	65.19	66	37.04	38	40.50	41
28 yards	1	84.00	25.60	62.86	63	35.71	36	39.06	40
30 yards	6	90.00	27.43	58.67	59	33.33	34	36.45	37
31.77 yards	1	95.31	29.05	55.40	56	31.48	32	34.42	35
33 yards	1	99.00	30.18	53.33	54	30.30	31	33.14	34
35 yards	2	105.00	32.00	50.29	51	28.57	29	31.25	32
40 yards	4	120.00	36.58	44.00	44	25.00	25	27.34	28
42 yards	1	126.00	38.40	41.90	42	23.81	24	26.04	27
48 yards	1	144.00	43.89	36.67	37	20.83	21	22.78	23
50 yards	5	150.00	45.72	35.20	36	20.00	20	21.87	22
55 yards	1	165.00	50.29	32.00	32	18.18	19	19.88	20
100 yards	1	300.00	91.44	17.60	18	10.00	10	10.94	11

Length	No. of Pools	Equivalents Feet	Yards	Lengths per mile Precise	Whole	Lengths/1000y Precise	Whole	Lengths/1000m Precise	Whole
18 meters	4	59.06	19.69	89.41	90	50.80	51	55.56	56
18.5 meters	1	60.70	20.23	86.99	87	49.43	50	54.05	55
20 meters	49	65.62	21.87	80.47	81	45.72	46	50.00	50
21 meters	2	68.90	22.97	76.64	77	43.54	44	47.62	48
22 meters	3	72.18	24.06	73.15	74	41.56	42	45.45	46
22.5 meters	1	73.82	24.61	71.53	72	40.64	41	44.44	45
22.8 meters	1	74.80	24.93	70.59	71	40.11	41	43.86	44
23 meters	3	75.46	25.15	69.97	70	39.76	40	43.48	44
24 meters	1	78.74	26.25	67.06	68	38.10	39	41.67	42
25 meters	557	82.02	27.34	64.37	65	36.58	37	40.00	40
26 meters	1	85.30	28.43	61.90	62	35.17	36	38.46	39
27 meters	2	88.58	29.53	59.61	60	33.87	34	37.04	38
30 meters	4	98.43	32.81	53.64	54	30.48	31	33.33	34
34 meters	1	111.55	37.18	47.33	48	26.89	27	29.41	30
40 meters	2	131.23	43.74	40.23	41	22.86	23	25.00	25
50 meters	120	164.04	54.68	32.19	33	18.29	19	20.00	20
60 meters	1	196.85	65.62	26.82	27	15.24	16	16.67	17

Length	No. of Pools	Equivalents Feet	Yards	Meters	Lengths Per Mile	Lengths/1000y Precise	Whole	Lengths/1000m Precise	Whole
1/8 mile	1	660.00	220.00	201.17	8.00	4.55	5	4.97	5
1/4 mile	1	1,320.00	440.00	402.34	4.00	2.27	3	2.49	3

HOTELS WITH POOLS ON-SITE

The following are all of the listings in the main directory which are located in hotels or which have on-premises hotel accommodations, and whose guests are admitted to the pool at no additional charge. An asterisk (*) preceding the name indicates that the pool is less than 20 yards long:

ALABAMA
Mobile
    Ramada Inn Conference Center

ALASKA
Anchorage
    *Hotel Captain Cook (#1)

ARIZONA
Carefree
    The Boulders Resort
Litchfield Park
    The Wigwam Resort
Mesa
    Arizona Golf Resort
Phoenix
    Pointe Hilton Resort at Squaw
        Peak (#8)
    Arizona Sports Ranch (#12)
    *Wyndham Garden Hotel-North
        Phoenix (#13)
Scottsdale
    The Phoenician (#18)
    Marriott's Mountain Shadows
        Resort & Golf Club (#21)
    *Regal McCormick Ranch
        Resort & Villas (#23)
    Red Lion La Posada Resort
        (#20)
    Radisson Resort (#22)
    Scottsdale Princess (#24)
    Scottsdale Pima Motel (#25)
Sedona
    Sedona Health Spa at Los
        Abrigados Resort
    *Poco Diablo Resort
Sierra Vista
    *Thunder Mountain Inn
Tucson
    Ramada Downtown Tucson
        (#27)
    Canyon Ranch (#36)
    *Loews Ventana Canyon Resort
        (#35)
    Tucson National Golf &
        Conference Resort (#42)

CALIFORNIA-NORTHERN
Big Sur
    Ventana Inn
Coalinga
    The Inn at Harris Ranch
Death Valley
    Furnace Creek Ranch Resort
Fresno
    *Holiday Inn - Airport
Milpitas
    Sheraton San Jose Hotel

Oakland
    Claremont Resort, Spa &
        Tennis Club (#10)
Pebble Beach
    The Lodge at Pebble Beach
    The Inn at Spanish Bay
Sacramento
    Hyatt Regency Sacramento
        (#11)
Saint Helena
    Meadowood Resort
San Francisco
    Swimming & Fitness at the
        Sheehan Hotel (#21)
    Sheraton Palace Hotel (#27)
    *Hyatt at Fisherman's Wharf
        (#44)
San Francisco Int'l Airport
    San Francisco Airport Hilton
Santa Rosa
    Doubletree Hotel
    Montecito Heights Health &
        Racquet Club at the
        Flamingo Resort Hotel &
        Fitness Center
Sunnyvale
    Sheraton Inn Sunnyvale

CALIFORNIA-SOUTHERN
Beverly Hills
    The Beverly Hilton
    The Peninsula Beverly Hills
Borrego Springs
    La Casa del Zorro
Coronado
    Hotel del Coronado
    Le Meridien San Diego
    Loews Coronado Bay Resort
Costa Mesa
    *The Westin South Coast Plaza
Covina
    Embassy Suites
Desert Hot Springs
    Desert Hot Springs Spa Hotel
El Segundo
    Doubletree Club Hotel LAX
Irvine
    Radisson Plaza Hotel Orange
        County Airport
La Jolla
    *Radisson Hotel La Jolla
Long Beach
    Long Beach Airport Marriott
Los Angeles
    Los Angeles Athletic Club (#2)
    *Four Seasons Hotel at Beverly
        Hills (#14)
    Century Plaza Hotel & Tower
        (#17)

Manhattan Beach
    Radison Plaza Hotel/LAX South
Marina del Rey
    The Ritz-Carlton, Marina del
        Rey
Ojai
    Ojai Valley Inn
Pasadena
    The Ritz-Carlton, Huntington
        Hotel
Rancho Mirage
    Marriott's Rancho Las Palmas
        Resort
    The Ritz-Carlton, Rancho
        Mirage
Rancho Santa Fe
    *The Inn at Rancho Santa Fe
San Diego
    Hyatt Regency San Diego (#19)
    Humphrey's Half Moon Inn &
        Suites (#21)
    Doubletree Hotel at Horton
        Plaza (#27)
    San Diego Princess Resort
        (#26)
    Ramada Inn San Diego North
        (#29)
    *Doubletree Club Hotel Rancho
        Bernardo (#37)
Santa Barbara
    Fess Parker's Red Lion Resort
Santa Maria
    *Santa Maria Airport Hilton
Santa Monica
    Loews Santa Monica Beach
        Hotel

COLORADO
Breckenridge
    Breckenridge Beach Club at the
        Village of Breckenridge
        Resort
Denver
    Executive Tower Inn (#1)
    *Sheraton Inn Denver Airport
        (#8)
Durango
    Fitness Works at the Days Inn-
        Durango
Englewood
    The Scanticon Hotel & Resort
Vail
    Vail Athletic Club

DISTRICT OF COLUMBIA
Washington
    Loews L'enfant Plaza Hotel
        (#10)
    *ANA Hotel (#13)

HOTELS WITH POOLS ON-SITE   **CONTINUED**

FLORIDA
Altamonte Springs
  Holiday Inn Orlando North-
    Altamonte Springs
  Days Inn Days Lodge
Bradenton
  *Holiday Inn Riverfront
Cape Haze
  Palm Island Resort
Coral Gables
  The Biltmore Hotel, Westin
    Hotels & Resorts
Fort Lauderdale
  Sheraton Yankee Trader
    Beach Resort
Fort Myers
  Radisson Inn Sanibel Gateway
Fort Walton Beach
  *Ramada Beach Resort
Hialeah
  *Ramada Inn Miami/Hialeah
Islamorada
  Cheeca Lodge
Jacksonville
  *Doubletree Club Hotel
Key Biscayne
  Sonesta Beach Resort
Key Largo
  Sheraton Key Largo Resort
Key West
  Holiday Inn Beachside
Kissimmee
  Orange Lake Resort & Country
    Club
  Holiday Inn Main Gate East
Lake Buena Vista
  Walt Disney World Dolphin
Lakeland
  *Holiday Inn Lakeside
Longboat Key
  The Resort at Longboat Key
Miami
  The Grand Prix Hotel
Miami Beach
  The Raleigh Hotel
  The Spa at the Fontainebleau
    Hilton Resort
Naples
  The Ritz-Carlton, Naples
North Miami Beach - Aventura
  Turnberry Isle Resort & Club
Ocoee
  *Holiday Inn-Orlando West
Orlando
  The Peabody (#10)
  Best Western Plaza
    International (#11)
  *Days Inn Lakeside (#12)
Palm Beach
  The Breakers
  *Palm Beach Hilton Oceanfront
    Resort

Pensacola
  Ramada Inn North
Plantation
  Sheraton Suites Plantation
Port St. Lucie
  Club Med Village Hotel
Sanibel Island
  Sundial Beach & Tennis
    Resort
Sarasota
  *Ramada Inn Airport
Singer Island
  Holiday Inn Palm Beach
    Oceanfront Resort
Tampa
  Tampa Marriott Westshore (#16)
  Crowne Plaza at Sabal Park
    (#17)
Titusville
  Royal Oak Resort & Golf Club

GEORGIA
Atlanta
  Atlanta Marriott Marquis (#2)
  *Wyndham Garden Hotel-
    Midtown (#5)
  The Ritz-Carlton, Buckhead
    (#13)
  *Cumberland Center II Health
    Club at the Courtyard by
    Marriott (#22)
Jekyll Island
  Jekyll Island Club Hotel

HAWAII
Kailua-Kona
  Kona Surf Resort & Country
    Club
Waianae
  Sheraton Makaha Resort &
    Country Club

ILLINOIS
Alsip
  *Holiday Inn Chicago/Alsip
Chicago
  Chicago Hilton & Towers (#4)
  Courtyard By Marriott/Chicago
    Downtown (#14)
  Hotel Inter•Continental
    Chicago (#16)
Elmhurst
  Holiday Inn Chicago Elmhurst
Itasca
  Wyndham Hamilton Hotel
Lincolnwood
  Radisson Hotel Lincolnwood
Palatine
  The Hotel & Fitness Center
  *Ramada Woodfield Hotel
Rochelle
  Holiday Inn Rochelle
Schaumburg
  Hyatt Regency Woodfield

Skokie
  North Shore Hilton
  *Howard Johnson Hotel
Wood Dale
  *Wyndham Garden Hotel-
    Wood Dale

INDIANA
Michigan City
  *Holiday Inn of Michigan City
New Albany
  *Holiday Inn Louisville N.W. at
    New Albany

IOWA
Davenport
  Ramada Inn
Des Moines
  Best Western Bavarian Inn
  Rodeway Inn
Okoboji
  The Athletic Club at Village
    East at the Village Resort

KENTUCKY
Lexington
  Campbell House Inn
  Continental Inn
  *Holiday Inn Lexington-North
  Harley Hotel of Lexington
Louisville
  Executive Inn (#4)

LOUISIANA
Houma
  *Quality Inn

MAINE
Rockport
  *Samoset Resort on the Ocean

MARYLAND
Baltimore
  *Holiday Inn Inner Harbor (#2)

MASSACHUSETTS
Boston
  Swissotel Boston (#2)
  Sheraton Boston Hotel &
    Towers (#30)
Braintree
  *Sheraton Tara Hotel,
    Braintree
Brewster
  Ocean Edge Resort & Golf
    Club
Danvers
  The Ferncroft Club at the
    Sheraton Tara Hotel &
    Resort
Eastham
  *Sheraton Inn Eastham
Framingham
  The Framingham Club at the
    Sheraton Tara Hotel

Hyannis
　The Tara Club at the Tara
　　Hyannis Hotel & Resort
Lenox
　Canyon Ranch in the
　　Berkshires
Springfield
　*Sheraton Springfield Monarch
　　Place Hotel
Woburn
　Ramada Hotel

MICHIGAN
Ann Arbor
　Ann Arbor Hilton Inn
Bellaire
　Shanty Creek Resort
Detroit
　The River Place: A Grand
　　Heritage Hotel (#5)
Lansing
　Harley Hotel of Lansing
Roseville
　Rose Shores Fitness & Racquet
　　Club at the Days Inn of
　　Roseville
Southgate
　Ramada Heritage Center

MINNESOTA
Albert Lea
　*Days Inn of Albert Lea
Bloomington
　Holiday Inn Airport 2
Breezy Point
　*Breezy Point Resort

MISSOURI
Kansas City
　The Westin Crown Center

MONTANA
Anaconda
　Fairmont Hot Springs Resort

NEVADA
Las Vegas
　Las Vegas Hilton
　Caesers Palace
　Sheraton Desert Inn
Laughlin
　Flamingo Hilton Laughlin
Sparks
　John Ascuaga's Nugget Hotel

NEW HAMPSHIRE
Nashua
　*The Royal Ridge Club at the
　　Sheraton Hotel
Portsmouth
　*Comfort Inn at Yoken's

NEW JERSEY
Clifton
　*Ramada Hotel

Elizabeth
　*Newark Airport Hilton Hotel
Mount Arlington
　*Sheraton Inn
Short Hills
　*The Hilton at Short Hills
South Plainfield
　Holiday Inn of South Plainfield

NEW MEXICO
Albuquerque
　Holiday Inn Express

NEW YORK
Grand Island
　Holiday Inn Grand Island
Highland
　*Rocking Horse Ranch
Montauk
　Gurney's Int'l Health & Beauty
　　Spa
N.Y.C. - Manhattan
　*New York Marriott Financial
　　Center (#17)
　*New York Sports Club at the
　　Crowne Plaza - Manhattan
　　(#24)
　*Sheraton Manhattan Health
　　Club at the Sheraton
　　Manhattan Hotel (#28)
Plattsburgh
　*Comfort Inn
South Fallsburg
　The Pines Resort Hotel

NORTH CAROLINA
Corolla
　B & B On The Beach
Raleigh
　Radisson Plaza Hotel
　*Holiday Inn-Crabtree

NORTH DAKOTA
Fargo
　Holiday Inn

OHIO
Cincinnati
　Harley Hotel of Cincinnati (#11)
Cleveland
　*Holiday Inn Lakeside (#32)
　*Radisson Plaza Hotel
　　Cleveland (#33)
Columbus
　Columbus North Sports Club at
　　the Best Western Columbus
　　North
Cuyahoga Falls
　*Sheraton Suites
　　Akron/Cuyahoga Falls
East Liverpool
　Skylight Health Spa at the East
　　Liverpool Motor Lodge
Englewood
　*Holiday Inn Dayton N.W. Airport

Warren
　Avalon Inn & Resort
Zanesville
　*Holiday Inn

OKLAHOMA
Tulsa
　*Doubletree Hotel at Warren
　　Place

OREGON
Gleneden Beach
　Salishan Lodge

PENNSYLVANIA
Farmington
　Nemacolin Woodlands Resort
Harrisburg
　*Sheraton Inn-Harrisburg
Philadelphia
　The Sporting Club at the
　　Bellevue Hotel (#2)
Pittsburgh
　Executive Fitness Center at the
　　Vista Hotel (#22)
　Harley Hotel of Pittsburgh (#26)
Shawnee
　Shawnee Inn & Golf Resort

SOUTH CAROLINA
Clemson
　Ramada Inn & Conference
　　Center

TENNESSEE
Memphis
　*The Peabody

TEXAS
Arlington
　Charlie's Club & Hotel (#2)
Dallas
　*Stouffer Dallas Hotel (#11)
　The Westin Hotel, Galleria
　　Dallas (#20)
El Paso
　El Paso Airport Hilton
Houston
　The Houstonian Hotel & Club
　　(#45)
　Fit Inn/Charlie Club Hotel (#59)
Huntsville
　Waterwood National Resort
Irving
　Four Seasons Resort & Club
　　(#32)
　Wyndham Garden Hotel-Las
　　Colinas (#35)
　Dallas/Ft. Worth Airport Marriott
　　(#36)
Rancho Viejo
　Rancho Viejo Resort & Country
　　Club
Westlake
　Marriott Solana

HOTELS WITH POOLS ON-SITE

UTAH
Salt Lake City
  *Red Lion Hotel/Salt Lake City
    (#1)
  Little America Hotel & Towers
    (#2)
Snowbird
  Snowbird Ski & Summer Resort

VERMONT
Brownsville
  The Ascutney Mountain Resort
Killington
  Inn of the Six Mountains
Stowe
  Topnotch at Stowe Resort & Spa
  *Golden Eagle Resort
Woodstock
  Woodstock Inn & Resort

VIRGINIA
Arlington
  *Fitness Center at the
    Doubletree Hotel
Hot Springs
  The Homestead
Leesburg
  Lansdowne Resort
McGaheysville
  La Club at Massanutten Resort
McLean
  *McLean Hilton at Tysons
    Corner
Vienna
  *Tysons Corner Marriott

WASHINGTON
Stevenson
  Skamania Lodge
Union
  *Alderbrook Resort Golf &
    Conference Center

WEST VIRGINIA
Morgantown
  *Lakeview Resort
White Sulphur Springs
  The Greenbrier

WISCONSIN
Green Lake
  Green Lake Conference Center
Tomah
  *Holiday Inn

FACILITIES WHICH ADMIT HOTEL GUESTS AT DISCOUNTED RATES

The facilities named below are all of the listings in the main directory which admit guests registered at nearby hotels on a preferred basis. Please refer to the individual listings in the main directory for details. Because arrangements between hotels and the facilities are likely to change from time to time, we strongly recommend contacting both the facility and the hotel to confirm the listing information before making a reservation:

ALABAMA
Anniston
 Calhoun County YMCA
Birmingham
 Downtown Center YMCA
 Five Points South YMCA

ALASKA
Fairbanks
 Fairbanks Athletic Club
Wrangell
 Wrangell Pool

ARIZONA
Chandler
 L.A. Fitness & Sports Club
Flagstaff
 Flagstaff Athletic Club West
Phoenix
 City Square Athletic Club (#3)
 The Sports Club (#16)
Tempe
 Western Reserve Club Family
  Sports Center
Tucson
 Results Sports & Fitness
  Center (#30)
 El Conquistador Racquet Club
  (#41)

ARKANSAS
Little Rock
 Downtown YMCA
Springdale
 Northwest Athletic Club

CALIFORNIA-NORTHERN
Burlingame
 Royal Athletic Club
Chico
 Chico Sports Club
 Kangaroo Kourts
Davis
 Davis Athletic Club
Fremont
 Schoeber's Athletic Club
Gilroy
 Parkside Athletic Club
Gold River
 Gold River Racquet Club
Los Gatos
 Los Gatos Athletic Club
Madera
 Madera Athletic Club
Milpitas
 South Bay Athletic Club
Monterey
 Monterey Sports Center

Oakland
 Sports Club at City Center
  Oakland (#7)
Pebble Beach
 The Lodge at Pebble Beach
 The Inn at Spanish Bay
Pleasanton
 Schoeber's Athletic Club
Sacramento
 Capital Athletic Club (#12)
San Francisco
 Swimming & Fitness at the
  Sheehan Hotel (#21)
 Embarcadero YMCA (#26)
 San Francisco JCC (#41)
Santa Clara
 Decathlon Club
Santa Rosa
 The Parkpoint Club
Walnut Creek
 Walnut Creek Sports & Fitness
  Club
 Clarke Memorial Pool

CALIFORNIA-SOUTHERN
Atascadero
 Kennedy Nautilus Center
City of Industry
 Industry Hills Swim Stadium
Claremont
 The Claremont Club
Encinitas
 Magdalena Ecke Family YMCA
La Jolla
 Lawrence Family Jewish
  Community Center
 La Jolla YMCA
 Shiley Sports & Health Center
  of Scripps Clinic
Laguna Niguel
 Laguna Niguel Racquet Club
Los Angeles
 Ketchum-Downtown YMCA (#9)
San Clemente
 Ole Hanson Beach Club
San Diego
 Downtown YMCA (#18)
 Mission Valley Health Club (#24)
 Sporting Club at Aventine (#34)
San Luis Obispo
 Avila Hot Springs Spa & RV
  Resort
Santa Barbara
 Santa Barbara Athletic Club
 Santa Barbara Family YMCA
Santa Maria
 Santa Maria Valley YMCA

Santa Monica
 Santa Monica Family YMCA
Ventura
 Pierpont Racquet Club
Woodland Hills
 Warner Center Club

COLORADO
Boulder
 YMCA of Boulder Valley
Copper Mountain
 Copper Mountain Racquet &
  Athletic Club
Denver
 Athletic Club at Monaco (#15)
Englewood
 Athletic Club at Inverness
 American Fitness, Inc.
Fort Collins
 Fort Collins Club
 Fort Collins Pulse Aerobic &
  Fitness Center
Glendale
 Cherry Creek Sporting Club
Lakewood
 Lakewood Athletic Club
Pueblo
 Sam Jones Swimming Pool
 Pueblo YMCA

CONNECTICUT
Cromwell
 Tri-Town Sports
Enfield
 New England Health &
  Racquet Club
Mystic
 Mystic Community Center
New Britain
 New Britain-Berlin YMCA
Plainfield
 Wheeler Regional Family YMCA
Shelton
 Shelton Community Center
Stamford
 Stamford YMCA
Stratford
 Stratford Club
Wallingford
 Healthworks

DELAWARE
New Castle
 Delaware Swim & Fitness
  Center
Wilmington
 Central YMCA

FACILITIES WHICH ADMIT HOTEL GUESTS AT DISCOUNTED RATES   CONTINUED

DISTRICT OF COLUMBIA
Washington
   National Capital YMCA (#12)
   ANA Hotel, Washington, D.C.
     (#13)

FLORIDA
Altamonte Springs
   Bally's Health & Racquet Club
Boca Raton
   Bally's Scandianvian Health &
     Fitness Center
Cape Coral
   Cape Coral Yacht Club Pool
Clearwater
   Ross Norton Pool
   Bally's Total Fitness
   Long Center
Coral Gables
   Venetian Pool
Longwood
   Lake Brantley Aquatic Center
Miami
   Bally's Scandinavian Health &
     Fitness Center
Orange Park
   'Q' the Sports Club
Orlando
   Bally's Bay Hill (#7)
   International Drive YMCA &
     Aquatic Center (#9)
   Bally's South Orlando (#13)
Saint Petersburg
   The Fitness Connection
Sarasota
   Lido Pool
Sunrise
   Markham Park Swimming Pool
Tampa
   Central City YMCA (#14)
   Harbour Island Athletic Club
     (#15)
   Bally's Total Fitness (#23)
West Palm Beach
   Bally's Scandinavian Health &
     Fitness Center

GEORGIA
Atlanta
   City Athletic Club (#1)
   Peachtree Center Athletic Club
     (#3)
   Concourse Atheltic Club (#18)
   The Vinings Club (#20)
Brunswick
   YWCA of Brunswick
Marietta
   Main Event Fitness
Roswell
   Sportslife

HAWAII
Kohala Coast
   Mauna Lani Racquet Club

ILLINOIS
Alton
   Nautilus Fitness/Racquet Center
Bannockburn
   Bannockburn Bath & Tennis
     Club, Inc.
Belleville
   Belleville YMCA
   Bi-County YMCA
Bloomington
   YWCA of McLean County
Calumet City
   Bally's Chicago Health Club
Chicago
   Athletic Club at Illinois Center
     (#2)
   University of Illinois at Chicago
     Pool (#7)
   Bally's Health Club (#8)
   Downtown Sports Club (#15)
   Bally's Chicago Health Club
     (#52)
Danville
   Danville Family YMCA
Deerfield
   Multiplex
Downers Grove
   The Esplanade Fitness Center
Fairview Heights
   Bally's Vic Tanny
Jacksonville
   Sherwood Eddy Mem. YMCA
Lisle
   Central Park Athletic Club
Oakbrook Terrace
   The Exercise Playce
Peoria
   Greater Peoria Family YMCA
Rock Island
   YWCA of the Quad Cities
Springfield
   Club West
Wheaton
   Wheaton Sports Center

INDIANA
Auburn
   Dekalb County YMCA
Bloomington
   Monroe County YMCA
Evansville
   Tri-State Athletic Club
Fort Wayne
   YMCA of Greater Fort Wayne
Greencastle
   Lilly Center
Greenwood
   Bally's Scandinavian Health Spa
Indianapolis
   I. U. Natatorium / IUPUI Sports
     Complex (#2)
   Ransburg YMCA (#4)
   Bally's Scandinavian Health
     Spa (#10)

Kendallville
   Cole Center Family YMCA
Logansport
   Cass County Family YMCA
Muncie
   Muncie Family YMCA
Notre Dame
   Rolfs Aquatic Center
South Bend
   Health & Lifestyle Center
Terre Haute
   Terre Haute Family YMCA
Vincennes
   Vincennes YMCA

IOWA
Cedar Rapids
   Central YMCA
Clinton
   Clinton Family YMCA
Clive
   Seven Flags Fitness &
     Racquet Club
Davenport
   Scott County Family YMCA
Des Moines
   Riverfront YMCA
   YWCA of Greater Des Moines
Waterloo
   Black Hawk County Family
     YMCA

KANSAS
Overland Park
   Bally's Health & Racquet
   The Athletic Club of Overland
     Park
Topeka
   Downtown Topeka YMCA

KENTUCKY
Crestview Hills
   Four Seasons Sports Country
     Club
Lexington
   Lexington Athletic Club
   Lexington Sports Club
Louisville
   Downtown Center YMCA (#1)
   Downtown Athletic Club (#2)
   Blairwood Club (#8)
Maysville
   Limestone YMCA

LOUISIANA
Baton Rouge
   Arthur Cullen Lewis Branch
     YMCA
Houma
   Bayouland YMCA
Kenner
   Kenner Branch YMCA
New Orleans
   New Orleans Athletic Club
   Lee Circle YMCA

MAINE
Portland
  Greater Portland YMCA

MARYLAND
Baltimore
  Baltimore Sports Club (#1)
  Downtown Athletic Club (#3)
  The Baltimore Sports Club (#11)
Chestertown
  Casey Swim Center
Columbia
  Columbia Swim Center
  The Supreme Sports Club
Emmitsburg
  Knott Athletic Recreation
    Convocation Complex
Gaithersburg
  Athletic Express Racquet &
    Health Club
Greenbelt
  Bally's Holiday Health Spa
Rockville
  Bally's Holiday Health Spa

MASSACHUSETTS
Auburn
  Auburn Racquet & Health Club
Beverly
  New England Health &
    Racquet Club
Boston
  Rowes Wharf Health Club &
    Spa (#1)
  YMCA of Greater Boston -
    Central Branch (#5)
  Boston Athletic Club (#31)
Cambridge
  Cambridge Family YMCA
Danvers
  Paul J. Lydon Aquatic Center
Framingham
  Suburban Athletic Club
Lynnfield
  The Colonial Club
Mansfield
  Mansfield Fitness Center
Marlboro
  Wayside Racquet & Swim Club
North Eastham
  Norseman Athletic Club
Norwood
  Mad Maggie's Health &
    Racquetball Club
Revere
  Bally's Holiday Health Club
Seekonk
  Newman YMCA
Westboro
  Westboro Tennis & Swim Club
Worcester
  Bally's Holiday Health Club
  YWCA of Central
    Massachusetts

MICHIGAN
Birmingham
  Beverly Hills Racquet & Health
    Club
Davison
  Davison Athletic Club
Dearborn
  Bally's Vic Tanny
  Fairlane Club
Farmington Hills
  Farmington Area YMCA
Flint
  Recreation Building
Grand Rapids
  East Hills Athletic Club
Lansing
  Downtown YMCA
Livonia
  Park Place Athletic Club
Muskegon
  Muskegon YFCA
Novi
  Bally's Vic Tanny
Southfield
  Franklin Fitness & Racquet Club
Troy
  Bally's Vic Tanny
Warren
  Warren City Pool

MINNESOTA
Bloomington
  Decathlon Athletic Club
  Bally's U.S. Swim & Fitness
Brooklyn Center
  Highway 100 North France
    Racquet, Swim & Health
    Club
Eden Prairie
  Crosstown Racquet, Swim &
    Health Club
Edina
  Edinborough Park Pool
Fridley
  Moore Lake Northwest Racquet,
    Swim & Health Club
  Bally's U.S. Swim & Fitness
Minneapolis
  Arena Club (#2)
  YWCA of Minneapolis (#3)
  University of Minnesota (#8)
Minnetonka
  Ridgedale YMCA
Ramsey
  HealthQuest Athletic Club
Saint Louis Park
  Northwest Racquet, Swim &
    Health Club
Saint Paul
  Skyway YMCA (#9)
  Bally's U.S. Swim & Fitness
    (#13)
  East YMCA (#15)

West Saint Paul
  Southview Athletic Club
White Bear Lake
  Northeast YMCA

MISSISSIPPI
Hattiesburg
  Institute For Wellness & Sports
    Medicine
Jackson
  Mississippi Baptist Sports / Life
    Fitness Center
  Downtown YMCA

MISSOURI
Chesterfield
  West County YMCA
Clayton
  Bally's Vic Tanny
Independence
  Bally's Health & Racquet
Kansas City
  Clay-Platte YMCA
Maryland Heights
  Bally's Vic Tanny
Saint Charles
  Bally's Vic Tanny
Saint Louis
  Downtown YMCA (#1)
  Kirkwood YMCA (#10)
Springfield
  Northpark Fitness Center

MONTANA
Billings
  Billings YMCA
Missoula
  Missoula Athletic Club

NEBRASKA
Grand Island
  Grand Island YMCA
Lincoln
  Downtown Lincoln YMCA
  Lincoln Racquet Club
  Cottonwood Club

NEVADA
Las Vegas
  Sporting House of Las Vegas
Reno
  Sports West Athletic Club

NEW HAMPSHIRE
Lincoln
  Loon Mountain Recreation
Manchester
  Greater Manchester Family
    YMCA
Portsmouth
  Gold's Gym & Athletic Club

NEW JERSEY
Atlantic City
  The Spa at Bally's Park Place
    Hotel

FACILITIES WHICH ADMIT HOTEL GUESTS AT DISCOUNTED RATES   CONTINUED

Basking Ridge
  Somerset Hills YMCA
Cherry Hill
  Fitquest
Deptford
  Haddonwood Tennis/Swim &
    Health Club
East Brunswick
  Bally's Jack LaLanne
Morristown
  Headquarters Health &
    Racquetball Club
Mountain Lakes
  Lakeland Hills Family YMCA
Springfield
  Bally's Jack LaLanne
Voorhees
  Bally's Holiday Fitness Center
Westfield
  Westfield YMCA

NEW MEXICO
Albuquerque
  Midtown Sports & Wellness
Farmington
  Royal Spa & Court Club
Santa Fe
  Fort Marcy Complex

NEW YORK
Amherst
  Bally Matrix Fitness Center
Binghamton
  Binghamton YMCA
De Witt
  Bally Matrix Fitness Center
Fishkill
  All Sport Fitness & Racquet Club
Getzville
  Jewish Center of Greater
    Buffalo, Inc.
Jamestown
  Jamestown YMCA
Loudonville
  Colonie Athletic Club, Inc.
N.Y.C. - Manhattan
  Bally's The Vertical Club (#23,
    27 & 31)
  Sheraton Manhattan Health
    Club (#28)
Newburgh
  Golds Gym & Athletic Club
Olean
  Olean YMCA
Poughkeepsie
  Dutchess County YMCA
Rochester
  Carlson Metrocenter YMCA
    (#50)
  Harro East Athletic Club (#51)
  Bally's Holiday Health &
    Fitness Center (#59)
Saratoga Springs
  Saratoga YMCA

White Plains
  White Plains YMCA

NORTH CAROLINA
Asheville
  YMCA of Asheville &
    Buncombe County
  Gold's Gym & Athletic Club
Charlotte
  Uptown YMCA (#1)
  Mecklenburg County Aquatic
    Center (#3)
Fayetteville
  The Sports Center
Goldsboro
  Goldsboro Family YMCA
Greenville
  Greenville Athletic Club
Lumberton
  Lifestyle Fitness Center
New Bern
  Twin Rivers YMCA
North Wilkesboro
  YMCA of Wilkesboro
Research Triangle Park
  Imperial Athletic Club
Roanoke Rapids
  Roanoke Athletic Club
Sanford
  Sanford Nautilus & Racquet
    Club

NORTH DAKOTA
Grand Forks
  Grand Forks Y Family Center

OHIO
Akron
  CitiCenter Athletic Club
Brook Park
  Bally's Scandinavian Health Spa
Cambridge
  Cambridge Area YMCA
Canton
  Bally's Scandinavian Health Spa
  Hall of Fame Fitness Center
Celina
  Lake Front Racquet & Health
    Club
Centerville
  Bally's Vic Tanny
Cleveland
  Athletic Club at One Cleveland
    Center (#31)
Columbus
  Central Branch YMCA
  Bally's Scandinavian Holiday
    Spa
  Sawmill Athletic Club
Cuyahoga Falls
  The Natatorium in Cuyahoga
    Falls
Dayton
  Downtown YMCA

Dublin
  Athletic Club at Metro V
Fairborn
  Fairborn YMCA
Findlay
  Findlay YMCA
Lancaster
  Lancaster Family YMCA
Lima
  Lima Family YMCA
Lorain
  Lorain Family YMCA
Mansfield
  Mansfield YMCA
Marietta
  Marietta Family YMCA
Oregon
  Eastern Community Branch
    YMCA
Sidney
  Sidney-Shelby County YMCA
Westlake
  Bally's Scandinavian Health Spa
Willoughby
  Bally's Scandinavian Health Spa

OKLAHOMA
Lawton
  Lawton YMCA
Norman
  Cleveland County Family YMCA
Oklahoma City
  Central Branch YMCA
Tulsa
  Downtown Tulsa YMCA
  Thornton YMCA

OREGON
Beaverton
  Griffith Park Athletic Club
Clackamas
  East Side Athletic Club
Coos Bay
  Bay Area Athletic Club
The Dalles
  The Dalles Fitness & Court Club
Eugene
  Downtown Athletic Club
Hood River
  Hood River Sports Club
Pendleton
  Roundup Athletic Club
Portland
  River Place Athletic Club (#3)
  Princeton Athletic Club (#5)

PENNSYLVANIA
Allentown
  Westend Racquet Club
Altoona
  The Summit Athletic Club
Bethel Park
  Bally's Scandinavian Health
    Spa

FACILITIES WHICH ADMIT HOTEL GUESTS AT DISCOUNTED RATES   CONTINUED

Erie
  The Pennbriar Athletic Club
Franklin
  Franklin YMCA
Greensburg
  Greensburg YMCA
Indiana
  Indiana County YMCA
King of Prussia
  Bally's Holiday Spa
Lock Haven
  Lock Haven Area YMCA
Monroeville
  The Racquet Club of Pittsburgh
New Kensington
  YMCA of New Kensington
Oil City
  Oil City YMCA
Penn Hills
  Bally's Scandinavian Health Spa
Philadelphia
  Bally's Holiday Fitness Center
    (#17)
Sewickley
  Sewickley Valley YMCA
State College
  The Athletic Club
Uniontown
  Uniontown Area YMCA
Wilkes-Barre
  Odyssey Total Fitness Center
Williamsport
  Williamsport YMCA
Willow Grove
  Bally's Holiday Spa

RHODE ISLAND
East Providence
  New England Health &
    Racquet Club
Middletown
  Newport Athletic Club
  Newport County YMCA
Warwick
  New England Health &
    Racquet Club

SOUTH CAROLINA
Greenville
  Cleveland Street YMCA
Myrtle Beach
  Pepper Geddings Recreation
    Center
Spartanburg
  Spartanburg YMCA Family
    Center

SOUTH DAKOTA
Deadwood
  Deadwood Recreation Center
Hot Springs
  Evans Plunge
Lead
  Northern Hills YMCA

TENNESSEE
Brentwood
  Brentwood Family YMCA
Chattanooga
  Downtown YMCA
Clarksville
  Clarksville Athletic Club
Knoxville
  New Downtown YMCA
  Bally's Holiday Fitness Center
Memphis
  Davis YMCA
  'Q' The Sports Club
  Wimbleton Sportsplex
Nashville
  Westside Athletic Club

TEXAS
Amarillo
  Gold's Gym
Austin
  'Q' The Sports Club
Bryan
  Aerofit Health & Fitness Center
Corpus Christi
  YMCA of Corpus Christi
  Corpus Christi Athletic Club
Dallas
  Texas Club (#6)
  The Verandah Club (#12)
  Centrum Sports Club (#15)
  Lincoln City Club (#23)
Fort Worth
  Amon Carter Jr. Downtown
    YMCA (#25)
Greenville
  Greenville/Hunt County YMCA
Houston
  The Texas Club (#37)
  Olympia Fitness & Racquetball
    Club (#56)
Irving
  Las Colinas Sports Club (#33)
League City
  The Fitness Center at South
    Shore Harbour
Lufkin
  Live Well Athletic Club
Plainview
  Plainview YMCA
Port Arthur
  YMCA of Port Arthur
San Antonio
  Concord Athletic Club (#65)
  World Gym (#67 & 69)
Webster
  Williams Indoor Pool
Westlake
  The Solana Club
Wichita Falls
  Wichita Falls YMCA

UTAH
Logan
  HPER Building - Campus Rec.
Ogden
  Total Fitness Center
Park City
  Prospector Athletic Club

VERMONT
Burlington
  Greater Burlington YMCA
Randolph Center
  SHAPE Pool
Rutland
  Pico Sports Center
Saint Johnsbury
  Saint Johnsbury Academy
    Pool
Stratton Mountain
  Stratton Sports Center

VIRGINIA
Altavista
  Altavista Area YMCA
Arlington
  Skyline Club at Crystal Park
Bristol
  Margaret H. St. John Pool
Chantilly
  The Club at Westfields
Chester
  Chester YMCA
Fairfax
  The Fitness Club of Fairfax
Falls Church
  The Skyline Club
Herndon
  Worldgate Athletic Club
Norfolk
  Norfolk YMCA
Petersburg
  Southside Virginia YMCA
Reston
  Reston Community Center
Richmond
  Downtown YMCA
  Robious Sports & Fitness Ctr.
Sandston
  Chickahominy Branch YMCA
Staunton
  Staunton Racquet Club

WASHINGTON
Bellevue
  The Seattle Club Bellevue
  Bally's Pacific West
  PRO Sports Club
Bothell
  Northshore YMCA
Edmonds
  Harbor Square Athletic Club
Federal Way
  Cascade Athletic Club

FACILITIES WHICH ADMIT HOTEL GUESTS AT DISCOUNTED RATES   CONTINUED

Richland
  Columbia Basin Racquet Club
Seattle
  Gateway Athletic Club (#2)
  Highline Athletic Club (#17)
Spokane
  Inland Empire YMCA
Tacoma
  Tacoma Center YMCA
Tumwater
  Valley Athletic Club Pool
Yakima
  Yakima YMCA

WEST VIRGINIA
Charleston
  South Charleston Community
    Center Pool
Parkersburg
  Parkersburg YMCA

WISCONSIN
Appleton
  Appleton Family YMCA
Brown Deer
  Schroeder YMCA & Aquatic
    Center

Eau Claire
  Eau Claire Athletic Club
Madison
  Princeton Club
Maintowoc
  Manitowoc-Two Rivers YMCA
Neenah
  Neenah-Menasha YMCA

CITIES WITH RECIPROCAL YMCAS   CONTINUED

The following cities have listings of YMCA swimming facilities which admit members of other YMCAs or members of YMCAs which participate in the Y's AWAY (**A**lways **W**elcome **A**t **Y**MCAs) Program, on a more favorable basis than the general public. A number in parenthesis following the city name indicate the number of YMCAs in that city which offer preferential admission. Due to the number of listed YMCAs it is not practical to name each one individually, however, non-YMCA facilities which offer preferred access to YMCA members are individually named within the parenthesis following the city name.

If you belong to a YMCA which participates in the AWAY Program, be sure to have your home Y affix an AWAY sticker on your membership card. Many Ys will welcome you anyway, but some will charge higher fees if you don't have the sticker, and a few will not recognize your Y membership at all with out it.

ALABAMA
Anniston, Bessemer, Birmingham (3), Gadsden, Mobile, Montgomery, Tuscaloosa

ALASKA
Anchorage

ARIZONA
Mesa, Phoenix (3), Tempe, Tucson

ARKANSAS
Hot Springs, Jonesboro, Little Rock (2), North Little Rock

CALIFORNIA-NORTHERN
Berkeley, Fresno, Mountain View, Oakland, Pleasant Hill, Redwood City, Sacramento (2), Salinas, San Francisco (4 + Swimming & Fitness at the Sheehan Hotel), San Jose (2), San Rafael, Santa Rosa, Saratoga, Watsonville

CALIFORNIA-SOUTHERN
Alhambra, Anaheim, Burbank, Culver City, Downey, Encinitas, Escondido, Glendale, Hollywood, Huntington Park, La Canada, La Jolla, La Mesa, Lakewood, Long Beach (3), Los Angeles (3), Newport Beach, North Hollywood, Pacific Palisades, Pomona, Reseda, Riverside, San Bernardino (2), San Diego (4), San Pedro, Santa Barbara (2), Santa Maria, Santa Monica, South Pasadena, Torrance, Tujunga, Van Nuys, Ventura, Whittier

COLORADO
Boulder, Colorado Springs (2), Denver (3), Lakewood, Littleton, Pueblo

CONNECTICUT
Ansonia, Bridgeport, Brookfield, Danbury, Darien, Fairfield, Greenwich, Hamden, Hartford, Middletown, Milford, Naugatuck, New Britain, New Canaan, Norwalk, Norwich, Plainfield, Southington, Stamford, Stratford, Torrington, Wallingford, Waterbury, Westbrook, Westport, Wilton, Winsted

DELAWARE
Dover, Newark, Rehoboth Beach, Wilmington (3)

DISTRICT OF COLUMBIA
Washington

FLORIDA
Boca Raton, Bradenton, Clearwater, Daytona Beach, Fort Lauderdale, Fort Pierce, Fort Walton Beach, Gainesville, Hollywood, Jacksonville, Lake Mary, Lakeland, Miami, Naples, Orlando (2), Ormond Beach, Pensacola, Port Orange, Saint Petersburg, Sarasota, Seffner, Spring Hill, Stuart, Tampa (2), Venice, West Palm Beach, Winter Park

GEORGIA
Albany, Atlanta (3), Columbus (2), Decatur (2), Lawrenceville, Marietta, Moultrie, Rome, Thomasville

HAWAII
Honolulu (2)

IDAHO
Boise, Twin Falls

ILLINOIS
Aurora, Belleville (2), Belvidere, Berwyn, Bloomington, Canton, Champaign, Chicago (9), Crystal Lake, Danville, Dekalb, Des Plaines, Downers Grove, Edwardsville, Elgin, Elmhurst, Evanston, Freeport, Glen Ellyn, Jacksonville, Joliet (2), Kankakee, Kewanee, La Grange, Macomb, Moline, Monmouth, Naperville, Niles, Northbrook, Oak Park, Ottawa, Palatine, Peoria, Quincy, Rockford, Schaumburg, Springfield, Waukegan

INDIANA
Anderson, Auburn, Bloomington, Elkhart, Evansville, Fort Wayne, Frankfort, Greensburg, Hammond, Huntington, Indianapolis (4), Kendallville, Kokomo, La Porte, Lafayette, Logansport, Marion, Martinsville, Michigan City, Muncie, Peru, Portage, Richmond, South Bend, Terre Haute, Valparaiso, Vincennes, Warsaw, Washington

IOWA
Ankeny, Burlington, Cedar Rapids, Clinton, Council Bluffs, Davenport, Des Moines (2), Dubuque, Forest City, Fort Dodge, Fort Madison, Marion, Marshalltown, Mason City, Muscatine, Newton, Oskaloosa, Sioux City, Spencer, Waterloo

KANSAS
Atchison, Kansas City, McPherson, Overland Park, Pittsburg, Prarie Village, Salina, Topeka, Wichita (2)

KENTUCKY
Ashland, Florence, Fort Thomas, Frankfort, Lexington, Louisville (4), Maysville, Paris

LOUISIANA
Alexandria, Baton Rouge, Covington, Kenner, Metairie (1 YMCA + Dick Bower Swim Club 'Bolts'), New Orleans, Shreveport

MAINE
Auburn, Augusta, Bangor, Bath, Biddeford, Boothbay Harbor, Camden, Dover-Foxcroft, Ellsworth, Sanford

MARYLAND
Baltimore, Bethesda, Cumberland, Easton, Ellicott City, Frederick, Gaithersburg, Hagerstown, Salisbury, Severna Park, Silver Spring, Towson, Westminster

CITIES WITH RECIPROCAL YMCAS   CONTINUED

MASSACHUSETTS
Andover, Athol, Attleboro, Beverly, Boston (6), Brockton, Cambridge, Danvers, East Bridgewater, Fall River, Fitchburg, Framingham, Gloucester, Greenfield, Haverhill, Holyoke, Lawrence, Lowell, Lynn, Malden, Marblehead, Melrose, Middleboro, Needham, New Bedford, Newton, North Adams, North Attleboro, Northampton, Pittsfield, Quincy, Salem, Seekonk, Somerville, Southbridge, Springfield, Waltham, Wayland, West Barnstable, Westfield, Woburn, Worcester (2)

MICHIGAN
Adrian, Ann Arbor, Battle Creek, Bay City, Birmingham, Detroit (4), East Lansing, Escanaba, Farmington Hills, Flint, Flushing, Grand Haven, Grand Rapids (2), Jackson, Kalamazoo, Lansing (2), Livonia, Menominee, Monroe, Mount Clemens, Muskegon, Niles, Port Huron, Portage, Royal Oak, Saginaw, Saint Joseph, Westland, Wyandotte

MINNESOTA
Albert Lea, Austin, Brainerd, Duluth, Edina, Fergus Falls, Grand Rapids, Mankato, Minneapolis (2), Minnetonka, New Hope, Red Wing, Rochester, Saint Paul (3), Shoreview, Virginia, West Saint Paul, White Bear Lake, Winona, Worthington

MISSISSIPPI
Jackson, Ocean Springs, Vicksburg

MISSOURI
Brentwood, Chesterfield, Festus, Fulton, Independence, Jefferson City, Kansas City (2), Mexico, Raytown, Saint Joseph, Saint Louis (9), Saint Peters, Springfield (2)

MONTANA
Billings, Butte, Helena, Missoula

NEBRASKA
Beatrice, Fremont, Grand Island, Hastings, Lincoln (2), McCook, Omaha (2), Scottsbluff

NEVADA
Las Vegas, Reno

NEW HAMPSHIRE
Concord, Manchester, Merrimack, Nashua

NEW JERSEY
Basking Ridge, Bridgewater, Camden, Cedar Knolls, Flemington, Freehold, Garfield, Hackensack, Hoboken, Jersey City, Livingston, Madison, Metuchen, Montclair, Mount Laurel, Mountain Lakes, Newark, Passaic, Paterson, Rahway, Randolph, Red Bank, Scotch Plains, Somerville, Summit, Toms River, Vineland, Voorhees, Westfield, Woodbury

NEW MEXICO
Albuquerque

NEW YORK
Albany, Auburn, Batavia, Bay Shore, Binghamton, Buffalo (2), Clifton Park, Cortland, Glen Cove, Glens Falls, Gloversville, Holtsville, Huntington, Jamestown, Johnson City, Kenmore, Kingston, Liverpool, Mastic Beach, Medina, Mount Vernon, New Rochelle, N.Y.C. - Brooklyn (2), N.Y.C. - Manhattan (3), N.Y.C. - Queens(3), N.Y.C. - Staten Island, Niagara Falls, Norwich, Nyack, Olean, Oneida, Oneonta (1 YMCA + Binder Gymnasium), Oswego, Pittsford, Plattsburgh, Port Chester, Poughkeepsie, Rochester (5), Rome, Rye, Saratoga Springs, Schenectady, Scotia, Snyder, Syracuse, Tarrytown, Troy, Utica, Watertown, Webster, White Plains, Yonkers

NORTH CAROLINA
Albemarle, Asheboro, Asheville, Burlington, Cary, Chapel Hill, Charlotte (6), Conover, Cornelius, Durham, Eden, Fayetteville, Gastonia, Goldsboro, Greensboro (3), Henderson, Hendersonville, High Point, Kannapolis, Kernersville, Lexington, Mocksville, New Bern, North Wilkesboro, Raleigh, Rocky Mount, Salisbury, Statesville, Thomasville, Wilmington, Winston-Salem

NORTH DAKOTA
Bismarck, Fargo, Grand Forks, Jamestown, Minot

OHIO
Akron, Alliance, Ashland, Ashtabula, Batavia, Beavercreek, Bedford, Cambridge, Canton, Cincinnati (9), Circleville, Cleveland (4), Cleveland Heights, Columbus (3), Cuyahoga Falls, Dayton (3), Defiance, Dover, East Liverpool, Elyria, Euclid, Fairborn, Fairfield, Findlay, Fostoria, Fremont, Galion, Hamilton (2), Kettering, Lakewood, Lancaster, Lebanon, Lima, Lorain, Louisville, Lyndhurst, Madison, Mansfield, Marietta, Massillon, Maumee, Mount Vernon, Niles, North Canton, Oregon, Parma, Piqua, Sandusky, Sidney, Springfield, Toledo, Van Wert, Warren, Westlake, Willoughby, Wilmington, Wooster, Youngstown

OKLAHOMA
Ardmore, Bartlesville, Bethany, Bixby, Edmond, Enid, Lawton, Midwest City, Norman, Oklahoma City (3), Tulsa (2)

OREGON
Albany, Eugene, Grants Pass, Klamath Falls, Medford, Newport, Portland (3), Roseburg, Salem, Tillamook

PENNSYLVANIA
Abington, Allentown, Ambler, Ardmore, Bellefonte, Berwyn, Bethlehem, Burnham, Butler, Camp Hill, Carbondale, Carlisle, Chambersburg, Charleroi, Clearfield, Coatesville, Corry, Doylestown, Dunmore, Elizabethville, Erie (2), Fairless Hills, Greensburg, Hanover, Harrisburg, Hatboro, Hazleton, Indiana, Johnstown, Kittanning, Lancaster, Lansdale, Lansdowne, Lebanon, Ligonier, Lock Haven, McKeesport, Meadville, Milton, Natrona Heights, Nazareth, New Kensington, Oil City, Philadelphia (5), Phoenixville, Pittsburgh (2), Pottstown, Quakertown, Reading, Scottdale, Sewickley, Stroudsburg, Sunbury, Uniontown, Warren,

CITIES WITH RECIPROCAL YMCAS

CONTINUED

Washington, Waynesboro, West Chester, Wilkes-Barre, Williamsport, Wilmerding, York

RHODE ISLAND
Barrington, Cranston, Greenville, Middletown, Pawtucket, Peace Dale, Providence (2), Warwick, Westerly, Woonsocket

SOUTH CAROLINA
Columbia, Florence, Greenville, Monks Corner, Rock Hill, Spartanburg, Sumter

SOUTH DAKOTA
Aberdeen, Lead, Pierre, Rapid City, Sioux Falls

TENNESSEE
Brentwood, Bristol, Chattanooga (2), Cleveland, Greeneville, Jackson, Knoxville (3), Memphis (4), Nashville (4)

TEXAS
Abilene (2), Amarillo, Austin (2), Beaumont, Big Spring, Corpus Christi, Corsicana, Dallas (4), Dumas, El Paso (2), Fort Worth, Galveston, Greenville, Houston (4), Midland (2), Odessa, Plainview, Port Arthur, Richmond, San Antonio (2), Tyler, Victoria, Waco, Wichita Falls, The Woodlands

VERMONT
Burlington

VIRGINIA
Altavista, Bedford, Chester, Danville, Franklin, Fredricksburg, Lynchburg, Newport News, Norfolk, Petersburg, Portsmouth, Pulaski, Richmond (4), Roanoke, Sandston, South Boston, Suffolk, Virginia Beach, Waynesboro

WASHINGTON
Aberdeen, Auburn, Bellevue, Bellingham, Bothell, Bremerton, Everett, Lynden, Mount Vernon, Olympia, Seattle (3), Spokane, Tacoma (2), Vancouver, Walla Walla, Yakima

WEST VIRGINIA
Charleston, Clarksburg, Parkersburg, Wheeling

WISCONSIN
Appleton, Beaver Dam, Brown Deer, Chippewa Falls, Cudahy, Eau Claire, Fond du Lac, Green Bay (3), Greenfield, Janesville, La Crosse, Madison (2), Maintowoc, Marinette, Menomonee Falls, Milwaukee, Monroe, Neenah, Oshkosh, Port Edwards, Sheboygan, Stevens Point, Sturgeon Bay, Superior, Wausau, Wauwatosa, West Bend

WYOMING
Buffalo, Casper, Cheyenne, Sheridan

MASTERS LISTINGS

The following are all of the listings in the main directory which we believe will be of special interest to Masters swimmers. Most of the listings include at least the name and telephone number of a contact for a Masters group which swims at the facility. Some have special Masters admission charges but do not include contact information. For a few, those which have an asterisk (*) in front of the listing name, we noted mention of a Masters group in the literature we received, but were not given contact information, or we were given a contact name and phone number but could not obtain permission to publish the information in *Swimmers Guide*. In one case, we just happened to see a Masters workout posted on the pool bulletin board when we were visiting the club.

An 'Affiliate' rate for USMS members shown in a listing may applicable only during Masters workout times.

Masters contacts at some facilities which require local membership or affiliation with groups other than USMS have indicated they will be happy to 'sponsor' a Masters swimmer from out of town for one or two visits, as long as the visitor pays the necessary guest fees. Others require visiting Masters to meet the host pool's affiliation or membership requirements for admission or to participate in workout sessions.

If you hope to be able to use a facility on the basis of your USMS membership, be sure to have your card with you when you go there.

ALABAMA
Auburn University
    James E. Martin Aquatics
        Center
Gadsden
    Gadsden-Etowah County YMCA
Huntsville
    * Brahan Spring Natatorium
Mobile
    Masters of Mobile
Montgomery
    Montgomery YMCA Barracuda
        Masters
Tuscaloosa
    Bama Masters Swim Club

ALASKA
Anchorage
    The Alaska Club (#3)
    Anchorage Community YMCA
        (#4)
    Bartlett 50 Meter Swimming
        Pool (#11)
Juneau
    Augustus Brown Pool
Ketchikan
    Kayhi Pool
Palmer
    Wasilla Pool
Soldotna
    Skyview High School
        Swimming Pool

ARIZONA
Statewide Masters Contact
Flagstaff
    Flagstaff Athletic Club West
    Northern Arizona University
        Natatorium
Litchfield Park
    Litchfield Park Recreation
        Center Pool
Mesa
    Kino Junior High School

Phoenix
    Chris-Town YMCA (#5)
    Phoenix Swim Club (#6)
Tempe
    Western Reserve Club Family
        Sports Center
    Arizona Masters
    Tempe Rio Salado Masters
Tucson
    Hillenbrand Aquatic Masters
        (After #39)
Yuma
    Marcus Pool

ARKANSAS
Fayetteville
    Intramural/Recreational Sports
Jonesboro
    Jonesboro YMCA Aquatic
        Center
Little Rock
    War Memorial Fitness Center

CALIFORNIA-NORTHERN
Alameda
    Mariner Square Athletic Club
Arcata
    Arcata Community Pool
Berkeley
    Strawberry Canyon Recreation
        Area Pool
Burlingame
    Prime Time Athletic Club
Carmichael
    Sports Courts
Chico
    Chico Sports Club
    Kangaroo Kourts
Davis
    Davis Aquatic Masters
    * Davis Athletic Club
El Cerrito
    El Cerrito Swim Center
Elk Grove
    Laguna Creek Racquet Club

Fair Oaks
    Rollingwood Racquet Club
Fort Bragg
    Mendocino Coast Recreation &
        Park District
Gilroy
    Parkside Athletic Club
Los Gatos
    Courtside Tennis Club
    Los Gatos Swim & Racquet Club
    Addison Penzac Jewish
        Community Center
Menlo Park
    Burgess Memorial Pool
Monterey
    Monterey Sports Center
Mountain View
    El Camino YMCA
Oakland
    Temescal Pool (#3)
    Live Oak Memorial Pool (#4)
    Montclair Swim Club (#6)
Pacifica
    Oceana Pool
Palo Alto
    Rinconada Pool
Portola Valley
    Solo Masters Swim Club
Redwood City
    Sequoia YMCA
    Peninsula Covenant
        Community Center
Rocklin
    Rocklin Aquatics Masters
Sacramento
    Capital Athletic Club (#12)
    Natomas Racquet Club (#20)
San Francisco
    Embarcadero YMCA (#26)
    San Francisco Athletic Club
        (#35)
    *Hamilton Pool (#36)
    *Sava Pool (#37)
    Koret Health & Recreation
        Center (#40)

San Jose
  San Jose Aquatics
San Mateo
  San Mateo Master Marlins
San Ramon
  San Ramon Olympic Pool
Santa Clara
  Decathlon Club
  International Swim Center
Santa Cruz
  Harvey West Pool
  Santa Cruz Masters Aquatics
Santa Rosa
  Santa Rosa Swim Center
Saratoga
  Southwest YMCA
Shingle Springs
  Sports Club of El Dorado
South San Francisco
  Orange Pool
Truckee
  Truckee-Donner Community
    Pool
Ukiah
  Redwood Health Club
Walnut Creek
  Walnut Creek Masters
Yuba City
  Yuba City Racquet & Health
    Club

CALIFORNIA-SOUTHERN
Alhambra
  Alhambra Park Pool
Bakersfield
  * Hillman Aquatic Center
Barstow
  Al Vigil Community Swim Center
Carlsbad
  Carlsbad Masters
City of Industry
  Industry Hills Swim Stadium
Claremont
  The Claremont Club
Coronado
  Coronado Masters Association
Culver City
  Culver-Palms Family YMCA
El Cajon
  Grossmont High School Pool
  El Cajon Valley High School
    Pool
Fullerton
  Independence Park Pool
Irvine
  Heritage Park Aquatics Complex
La Jolla
  Lawrence Family Jewish
    Community Center
  Shiley Sports & Health Center
    of Scripps Clinic
  Canyonview Pool

La Mesa
  La Mesa Municipal Pool
Lancaster
  Eastside Pool - City of Lancaster
Los Angeles
  Los Angeles Athletic Club (#2)
  Southern California Aquatic
    Masters (After #s 5, 11 &
    #15)
  Ketchum-Downtown YMCA (#9)
Northridge
  University Student Union Pool
Pacific Palisades
  Palisades-Malibu YMCA Pool
Palm Springs
  Palm Springs Swim Center
Reseda
  Cleveland Pool
Rialto
  Rialto Racquet & Fitness Center
San Bernardino
  YWCA of San Bernadino
San Clemente
  Ole Hanson Beach Club
San Diego
  Peninsula Family YMCA (#22)
  Mission Beach Plunge (#25)
  Mission Valley YMCA (#28)
  Center for Sports Medicine (#35)
San Luis Obispo
  San Luis Aquatic Masters
Santa Barbara
  Santa Barbara Swim Club
  Santa Barbara Family YMCA
Santa Monica
  Southern California Aquatic
    Masters (2 listings)
Solana Beach
  San Dieguito Boys & Girls Club
Thousand Oaks
  Daland United Masters
Torrance
  South End Racquet & Health
    Club, Inc.
Ventura
  Ventura Aquatic Club
West Hollywood
  City of West Hollywood Pool
Woodland Hills
  Southwest Aquatic Masters

COLORADO
Arvada
  George Meyers Pool
Aspen
  James E. Moore Pool
Aurora
  * Utah Park Pool
Boulder
  YMCA of Boulder Valley
  Boulder Aquatic Masters (3
    listings)

Denver
  Central Branch YMCA (#2)
  Athletic Club at Denver Place
    (#3)
  Denver Athletic Club (#5)
Durango
  Fitness Works at the Days Inn-
    Durango
Englewood
  * Athletic Club at Inverness
Fort Collins
  Edora Pool & Ice Center (EPIC)
Glendale
  * Cherry Creek Sporting Club
Greeley
  Greeley Recreation Center
Lakewood
  Jeffco Family YMCA
  Green Mountain Rec. Center
Littleton
  Goodson Rec. Center & Pool
Longmont
  Centennial Pool

CONNECTICUT
Greenwich
  Greenwich Masters
Hartford
  Hartford Region YWCA Masters
Milford
  Milford-Orange YMCA
Orange
  Orange Town Pool
Ridgefield
  Ridgefield Parks & Recreation
    Dept. Pool
Storrs
  University of Connecticut
    Masters Swim Club
Westbrook
  Valley Shore YMCA
Wilton
  * Wilton Family Y

DELAWARE
New Castle
  Delaware Swim & Fitness
    Center
Newark
  Delaware Aquatic Masters
Wilmington
  Central YMCA
  Pike Creek Fitness Club

DISTRICT OF COLUMBIA
Washington
  YWCA Fitness Center at
    Gallery Place (#1)
  District of Columbia Aquatics
    Club (After #4)
  DCRP Masters Swim Team
    (After #5)
  St. Alban's Lawrence Pool (#6)

FLORIDA
Boca Raton
  Meadows Park Pool
Bonita Springs
  * Bonita Springs Community
    Pool
Clearwater
  Ross Norton Pool
  Clearwater Aquatic Masters
Coral Gables
  Stingray Aquatic Clubl
Coral Springs
  Coral Springs Masters Swim
    Program
Delray Beach
  Aqua Crest Pool
Fort Lauderdale
  Fort Lauderdale Swim Team
    Masters
Fort Pierce
  Indian River Community College
    Master Swim Team
Gainesville
  Florida Aquatic Mastersr
  F.A.S.T. Masters
Hialeah
  Hialeah Storm
Indian Harbour Beach
  Indian Harbour Beach
    Swimming Pool
Jacksonville
  University of North Florida
    Aquatic Center
Jupiter
  * North County Aquatic Complex
Lake Mary
  Seminole Family YMCA
Lauderhill
  Veterans Park Pool
Leesburg
  Venetian Gardens Pool
Lehigh Acres
  * Lehigh Acres Community Pool
Longwood
  Team Orlando Masters
  Longwood Aquatic Club
Miami
  Miami Olympian Swim Team
  Stingray Aquatic Club
Naples
  Swim Florida Masters
North Miami Beach
  Victory Pool
North Palm Beach
  North Palm Beach Swim Club
Ocala
  Ocala Masters Swim Club
Orlando
  Team Orlando Masters (After
    #9)
Pensacola
  Greater Pensacola Aquatic
    Club (2 listings)

Plantation
  Plantation Central Park Pool
Saint Petersburg
  St. Pete Masters
Sarasota
  Suncoast Masters
Stuart
  Martin County Community Pool
Tallahassee
  Wade Wehunt Pool
Tampa
  Central City YMCA (#14)
  The Forest Hill Aquatic Club
    (#22)
Vero Beach
  St. Edward's School
Wellington
  Palm Beach Polo & Country
    Club
West Palm Beach
  Gaines Park Pool
  * Lake Lytal Pool
  Jewish Community Center of
    the Palm Beaches
Winter Park
  Team Orlando Masters

GEORGIA
Atlanta
  Peachtree Center Athletic Club
    (#3)
  Georgia Masters Killer Whales
    (#16)
  Concourse Atheltic Club (#18)
  *The Sporting Club at Windy
    Hill (#19)
  The Vinings Club (#20)
Brunswick
  YWCA of Brunswick
Chamblee
  Dynamo Swim Center
Columbus
  * D.A. Turner YMCA
Decatur
  * Decatur / Dekalb YMCA of
    Metro Atlanta

HAWAII
Honolulu
  Rainbow Aquatics - Masters
    Swimming Division (#10)
Lahaina
  Masters at Lahaina
Wailuku
  Maui Ocean Swim Club

IDAHO
Boise
  Boise Family YMCA
  * The Court House
Idaho Falls
  Idaho Falls Aquatic Center
Nampa
  Nampa Recreation Center

ILLINOIS
Barrington
  Barrington High School
Chicago
  University of Illinois at Chicago
    Pool (#7)
  *Gill Park Pool (#17)
  New City YMCA (#23)
  *Shabbona Park Pool (#36)
  *Portage Park Pool (#42)
  * Lincoln-Belmont YMCA (#53)
Downers Grove
  The Esplanade Fitness Center
Elk Grove Village
  Elk Grove Park District-Disney
    Pool
Evanston
  YWCA of Evanston/North Shore
La Grange
  Rich Port YMCA
Palatine
  Buehler YMCA
Rockford
  Rockford YMCA
Springfield
  Springfield YMCA

INDIANA
Crawfordsville
  Crawfordsville Aquatic Center
Decatur
  Bellmont High School
Evansville
  YMCA of Southwestern Indiana
Indianapolis
  A. Jordan YMCA (#9)
Kendallville
  Cole Center YMCA Masters
Muncie
  Muncie Family YMCA
South Bend
  Michiana YMCA Masters
Valparaiso
  Valparaiso YMCA
Vincennes
  Vincennes YMCA
Warsaw
  Kosciusko Community YMCA

IOWA
Cedar Rapids
  * Coe College Natatorium
Davenport
  Scott County Family YMCA
Des Moines
  YWCA Masters

KANSAS
Derby
  Derby Recreation Center
Topeka
  Topeka YWCA
Wichita
  Wichita Swim Club

KENTUCKY
Louisville
Crescent Hill Bubble Pool (#3)

LOUISIANA
Alexandria
City of Alexandria Swim Team
Baton Rouge
Crawfish Masters
Mandeville
Franco's Athletic Club
Metairie
Dick Bower Swim Club 'Bolts'
Metairie Branch YMCA
New Orleans
Isidore Newman School

MAINE
Ellsworth
Down East Family YMCA
Westbrook
John P. Davan Pool

MARYLAND
Annapolis
Maryland Masters Swim Team
Baltimore
Maryland Masters Swim Team
(#7, 9, & After #13)
Callowhill Aquatic Center (#8)
Chestertown
* Casey Swim Center
College Park
Terrapin Masters
Cumberland
Cumberland YMCA Masters
Easton
Talbot YMCA
Ellicott City
Howard County YMCA Masters
Millersville
Maryland Masters Swim Team
North Bethesda
Montgomery Aquatic Center
Silver Spring
M. L. King Swim Center
Towson
Towson Family YMCA
White Marsh
Bally's Holiday Health Spa

MASSACHUSETTS
Beverly
Beverly Regional YMCA
Boston
South End Fitness Center (#9)
East Boston Harborside
Community Center (#19)
Allston / Brighton Family
Branch YMCA (#28)
Case Center Pool (#32)
Framingham
Metro West YMCA-Framingham
North Eastham
Norseman Athletic Club

Northampton
Hampshire Regional YMCA
Pittsfield
* Pittsfield YMCA
Plymouth
Plymouth Athletic Club
Southbridge
Tri-Community YMCA
Sudbury
Atkinson Pool
West Newton
Diversified Aquatics Masters
Westboro
Westboro Tennis & Swim Club
Weymouth
Weymouth Club

MICHIGAN
Ann Arbor
Mack Pool
Big Rapids
Health & Physical Education
Bldg.
Flint
Flint YMCA
* Hurley Health & Fitness Center
Grand Haven
Tri-Cities Family YMCA
Grand Rapids
Ford Natatorium
Harbor Springs
Harbor Springs Community Pool
Lansing
Oak Park YMCA
Livonia
Livonia YMCA
Rockford
Rockford High School Pool
Royal Oak
South Oakland Family YMCA

MINNESOTA
Duluth
Center for Personal Fitness
Lakeville
Kenwood Trail Junior High
School
McGuire Junior High School
LeRoy
LeRoy Ostrander Community
Pool
Minneapolis
YWCA of Minneapolis (#3)
Uptown YWCA (#5)
University of Minnesota
Aquatic Center (#8)
Red Wing
Red Wing YMCA
Rochester
Rochester / Olmsted
Recreation Center
Saint Louis Park
The St. Louis Park Masters
Swim

Shoreview
Shoreview Community Center
White Bear Lake
White Bear Racquet & Swim
Woodbury
Woodbury Junior High School
Pool
Woodbury Senior High School
Pool

MISSISSIPPI
Biloxi
Biloxi Natatorium
Hattiesburg
Institute For Wellness & Sports
Medicine
Jackson
Mississippi Baptist Fitness
Center Masters
Downtown YMCA
Tupelo
Tupelo Aquatic Club

MISSOURI
Blue Springs
Centennial Pool-Plex
Chesterfield
West County YMCA
St. Louis Masters
Kansas City
* Clay-Platte YMCA
Kirksville
Northeast Missouri State
University Natatorium
Saint Louis
Webster YMCA (#9)

MONTANA
Billings
Billings YMCA
Bozeman
Bozeman Swim Center
Missoula
Missoula Family YMCA
* Grizzly Pool

NEBRASKA
Lincoln
Northeast YMCA
Lincoln Racquet Club
Omaha
Maverick Adult Swim Program

NEVADA
Minden
Carson Valley Swim Center
Reno
Sierra Nevada Masters
YMCA of the Sierra - Reno
Family Branch

NEW HAMPSHIRE
Concord
Concord YMCA
Dover
Dover Indoor Pool

Exeter
  Results Swim & Fitness
Hanover
  * Karl B. Michael Pool
Milford
  Hampshire Hills Sports &
    Fitness

NEW JERSEY
Basking Ridge
  Somerset Hills YMCA
Berkeley Heights
  Berkeley Aquatic Club Masters
Bridgewater
  Somerset Valley YMCA
Madison
  Madison Area YMCA
Montclair
  Montclair YMCA
Mount Laurel
  Jersey Wahoos Swim Club
Piscataway
  Sonny Werblin Recreation
    Center
Red Bank
  Red Bank YMCA
Toms River
  Ocean County YMCA Masters
Trenton
  Aquatics Center
Voorhees
  Echelon YMCA
West Orange
  Jewish Community Center
    Metro West

NEW MEXICO
Albuquerque
  Valley High Pool
  Highland Swimming Pool
  Sandia Pool
Farmington
  Farmington Aquatic Center
Los Alamos
  Larry R. Walkup Aquatics Center
Santa Fe
  Fort Marcy Complex
  * Salvador Perez Swimming
    Pool

NEW YORK
Albany
  * Albany YMCA
  Albany Jewish Community
    Center
  The Albany Academy
Annandale-on-Hudson
  Bard Tidal Waves
Canandaigua
  Canandaigua Master Swim Club
Clifton Park
  Southern Saratoga YMCA
East Islip
  Belfran Health & Fitness Center

Freeport
  Freeport Wrecks
Glens Falls
  Glens Falls YMCA Masters
Hempstead
  Jackson Express Masters
Holtsville
  Brookhaven-Roe YMCA
Huntington
  Huntington YMCA Masters
    Swim Club
Jamestown
  Jamestown YMCA
Johnson City
  West Branch YMCA
Kenmore
  Kenton Family YMCA
Kingston
  Kingston Masters Swim Club
Mount Kisco
  Saw Mill Ace Masters
New Windsor
  New Windsor ≈ New Wave
    Masters
N.Y.C. - Brooklyn
  Bay Ridge Masters (#5)
N.Y.C. - Manhattan
  Red Tide of NYC (#26 & 34)
  * New York City YWCA (#29)
  MPHC Masters (After #38)
  Asphalt Green Aquacenter (#41)
N.Y.C. - Queens
  Cross Island Masters (After #45)
N.Y.C. - Staten Island
  Staten Island YMCA
    Psyquatics (After #48)
  Staten Island Aquatics Masters
    (#49)
Oneida
  Tri-Valley Y Masters
Oneonta
  * Binder Gymnasium Pool
Poughkeepsie
  Dutchess County YMCA
Rochester
  MCC Masters (#60)
Schenectady
  * Schenectady YWCA
  Union College Masters
Syracuse
  Syracuse Masters Swim Club
Troy
  RPI Masters
Utica
  * Utica College
West Point
  West Point Masters Swim Club
White Plains
  White Plains YWCA

NORTH CAROLINA
Asheboro
  Randolph-Asheboro YMCA

Asheville
  Blue Ridge Masters
Chapel Hill
  Chapel Hill Community Center
    Pool
  North Carolina Aquatic Masters
Charlotte
  Mecklenburg County Aquatic
    Center (#3)
  Mecklenburg Aquatic Club (#10)
Durham
  *Rock Quarry Indoor Pool
  Irwin R. Holmes Indoor Pool
Greensboro
  Triad Masters Swimming
Greenville
  Greenville Athletic Club
Kannapolis
  Cannon Memorial YMCA &
    Community Center
Lumberton
  Lifestyle Fitness Center
Morehead City
  Sports Center 'Undertoads'
Raleigh
  Pullen Aquatic Center
  Optimist Park Pool
Salisbury
  Rowan County YMCA
Winston-Salem
  Central YMCA of Winston-
    Salem
  Winston-Salem Y Masters

NORTH DAKOTA
Grand Forks
  Hyslop Sports Center

OHIO
Ashland
  Ashland YMCA
Beavercreek
  Beavercreek YMCA
Canton
  * Canton Downtown YMCA
Centerville
  Washington Township
    Recreation Center
Cincinnati
  Keating Natatorium (#8)
  Cincinnati Sports Club (#9)
Cleveland
  Athletic Club at One Cleveland
    Center (#31)
Cuyahoga Falls
  The Natatorium in Cuyahoga
    Falls
Dayton
  Lohrey Center
Fairview Park
  O*H*I*O* Masters Swim Club
Findlay
  Findlay YMCA

Hamilton
  Hamilton West YMCA
Kettering
  South Community Family YMCA
Louisville
  Louisville YMCA
Orange
  O*H*I*O* Masters Swim Club
Parma
  Ridgewood YMCA
Sandusky
  Sandusky Area YMCA
Toledo
  Toledo YWCA
Westlake
  Bally's Scandinavian Health Spa
Wooster
  Wooster YMCA Pool
Youngstown
  Central Branch YMCA

OREGON
Beaverton
  Recreation Swim Center
Bend
  Juniper Aquatic Center
Corvallis
  Osborn Aquatic Center
Eugene
  Sheldon Pool
  Eugene Family YMCA
Grants Pass
  Grants Pass Family YMCA
Lincoln City
  Lincoln City Community Center
    Pool
Newberg
  Chehalem Pool
North Bend
  North Bend Municipal
    Swimming Pool
Portland
  Metro Family YMCA (#2)
  * Princeton Athletic Club (#5)
  Dishman Pool (#8)
Roseburg
  Douglas County Family YMCA

PENNSYLVANIA
Bellefonte
  Bellefonte Family YMCA
Berwyn
  Upper Main Line YMCA
Camp Hill
  West Shore YMCA
Carlisle
  Carlisle YMCA
Clearfield
  Clearfield YMCA
Dunmore
  Greater Scranton YMCA
Greensburg
  Greensburg YMCA

Hatboro
  Hatboro Area YMCA
Indiana
  Indiana County YMCA
Lancaster
  Lancaster Family YMCA
Lansdale
  North Penn YMCA
Lansdowne
  Community YMCA of Eastern
    Delaware County
Lebanon
  Lebanon Valley Family YMCA
Meadville
  YWCA of Meadville
Nazareth
  * Nazareth YMCA
Philadelphia
  Pennypack Aquatic & Fitness
    Center (#3)
  St. Joseph's University
    Masters/Triathlon Club (#7)
Phoenixville
  Phoenixville Area YMCA
Pittsburgh
  Downtown Pittsburgh YMCA
    (#23)
Sewickley
  Sewickley Valley YMCA
Wilkes-Barre
  Wilkes-Barre YMCA

RHODE ISLAND
Barrington
  Barrington YMCA Masters
    Swimming
Cranston
  Cranston Branch YMCA
Peace Dale
  South County Branch YMCA

SOUTH CAROLINA
Anderson
  Anderson Masters
Charleston
  Palmetto Masters Swimming
Columbia
  Columbia YMCA
Greenville
  Westside Aquatic Center
  * Cleveland Street YMCA
Mount Pleasant
  R.L. Jones Recreation Center

SOUTH DAKOTA
Sioux Falls
  Sioux Falls YWCA
  Sioux Falls YMCA
  Sioux Valley Hospital Wellness
    Center
Sturgis
  Sturgis Community Center
    Pool

TENNESSEE
Brentwood
  Athletic Club Maryland Farms
Bristol
  Bristol Family YMCA
Germantown
  Germantown Centre
Memphis
  Mason YMCA
Nashville
  Downtown YMCA
Oak Ridge
  Oak Ridge Masters Swim
    ClubSevierville
  Community Center Pool

TEXAS
Austin
  The Hills Fitness Center
Bryan
  Aerofit Health & Fitness Center
College Station
  Masters of Brazos
The Colony
  The Colony Aquatic Park
Dallas
  YWCA of Metropolitan Dallas
    (#8)
  The Verandah Club (#12)
  The Cooper Fitness Center
    (#18)
  Baylor/Lone Star Masters
    (After #24)
El Paso
  Northeast Family YMCA
Fort Worth
  The Ft. Worth-Arlington Swim
    Team (#28)
Houston
  The Texas Club (#37)
  H₂Ouston Swims (#39 & after
    #s 45 & 49)
  Rice University Pool (#41)
  Westside Family YMCA (#50)
Kingwood
  Kingwood Athletic Club
Lufkin
  Live Well Athletic Club
Plano
  Plano Aquatic Center
Richardson
  Richardson YWCA Natatorium
San Antonio
  Blossom Aquatic Center (#66)
Webster
  Williams Indoor Pool &
    Recreation Center
The Woodlands
  Woodlands Athletic Center

UTAH
Logan
  HPER Building - Campus
    Recreation

MASTERS LISTINGS _____ **CONTINUED**

VERMONT
Essex Junction
  Racquet's Edge Health &
    Fitness Center
Rutland
  Pico Sports Center
South Burlington
  Twin Oaks Sports & Fitness

VIRGINIA
Arlington
  Washington-Lee Swimming Pool
  Wakefield Swimming Pool
Ashburn
  Ashburn Village Sports Pavilion
Burke
  Burke Racquet & Swim Club
Chester
  Chester YMCA
Falls Church
  The Skyline Club
Harrisonburg
  Valley Wellness Center
Herndon
  * Herndon Community Center
Leesburg
  Ida Lee Park Recreation Center
Lexington
  Warner Center
Midlothian
  Virginia Masters Swim Team
Newport News
  Riverside Wellness & Fitness
    Center
Norfolk
  Norfolk YMCA
Prince William
  Chinn Aquatics & Fitness Center
Reston
  Reston Community Center

Richmond
  Tuckahoe Family YMCA
Staunton
  Staunton Racquet Club

WASHINGTON
Anacortes
  Fidalgo Pool & Fitness Center
Bellevue
  The Seattle Club Bellevue
  Newport Hills Swim & Tennis
    Club Masters
  Bellevue Pool
  Eastside Family YMCA
Bellingham
  Whatcom Family YMCA
Des Moines
  Mt. Rainier Pool
Enumclaw
  Enumclaw Pool
Federal Way
  King County Aquatic Center
Issaquah
  Issaquah Pool
Kennewick
  Tri-City Court Club
Mercer Island
  Mercer Island Pool
  Stroum Jewish Community
    Center
Oak Harbor
  Vanderzaicht Pool
Port Townsend
  Mountain View Elementary
    School Swimming Pool
Poulsbo
  North Kitsap School District
    Community Pool
Pullman
  Washington State University
    Swim Club

Renton
  Renton Pool
Seattle
  Evans Pool (#4)
  Helene Madison Pool (#15)
  Shoreline Pool (#18)
Sequim
  Sequim Aquatic Recreation
    Center
Spokane
  Shadle Park Swimming Pool
Tumwater
  Valley Athletic Club Pool

WEST VIRGINIA
Charleston
  University of Charleston
Clarksburg
  Harrison County YMCA

WISCONSIN
Appleton
  Appleton Family YMCA
La Crosse
  La Crosse Family YMCA
Madison
  Madison East YMCA
Monroe
  * Green County Family YMCA
Neenah
  * Neenah-Menasha YMCA
Sheboygan
  Sheboygan YMCA
Stevens Point
  Stevens Point Area YMCA

WYOMING
Cheyenne
  City of Cheyenne Municipal Pool

RECIPROCAL IHRSA CLUBS

The following are all of the facilities listed in the main directory which have indicated that they admit members of International Health and Racquet Sportsclub Association (IHRSA) affiliated clubs on a preferred basis. To take advantage of reciprocal access privileges at an affiliated club, a member should purchase a copy of the current IHRSA *Passport* at the home club and present it with the home club membership card on check-in. Reciprocal access privileges may not be available within 50 miles of the home club.

ALABAMA
Birmingham
  Sportslife - Vestavia
  Sporstlife - Birmingham
Hoover
  Sportsplex Hoover
Mobile
  Sportsplex Mobile

ALASKA
Anchorage
  The Alaska Club (#3)
Fairbanks
  Fairbanks Athletic Club

ARIZONA
Flagstaff
  Flagstaff Athletic Club West
Mesa
  Golden's Health & Racquet Club
Phoenix
  Central Park Square Athletic
    Club (#2)
  City Square Athletic Club (#3)
  Fitness West (#4)
  The Village Racquet & Health
    Club (#7)
Scottsdale
  Club Ultra Sport (#19)
Sedona
  Sedona Health Spa at Los
    Abrigados Resort
Tempe
  Western Reserve Club Family
    Sports Center
Tucson
  Lakeside Sportsclub (#40)
  El Conquistador Racquet Club
    (#41)

ARKANSAS
Fort Smith
  Fort Smith Racquet Club
Little Rock
  Little Rock Athletic Club

CALIFORNIA-NORTHERN
Alameda
  Harbor Bay Club
Antioch
  Delta Park Athletic Club
Aptos
  Seascape Sports Club
Auburn
  Auburn Court House & Athletic
    Club
Burlingame
  Prime Time Athletic Club

Carmichael
  Sports Courts
Chico
  Chico Sports Club
  Kangaroo Kourts
Citrus Heights
  Willow Creek Racquet Club
Concord
  Big 'C' Athletic Club
  Clayton Valley Athletic Club
Cotati
  24 Hour Club
Daly City
  What A Racquet Athletic Club
  24-Hour Nautilus
El Sobrante
  Lakeridge Athletic Club
Elk Grove
  Laguna Creek Racquet Club
Fair Oaks
  Rollingwood Racquet Club
Fremont
  Schoeber's Athletic Club
  Clubsport
Fresno
  Fig Garden Swim & Racquet
    Club
Gilroy
  Parkside Athletic Club
Gold River
  Gold River Racquet Club
Livermore
  Livermore Valley Tennis Club
Lodi
  Twin Arbors Athletic ClubS (2)
Los Gatos
  Courtside Tennis Club
  Los Gatos Swim & Racquet Club
Madera
  Madera Athletic Club
Merced
  Merced Sports Club
Milpitas
  South Bay Athletic Club
Modesto
  S.O.S. Club
Moraga
  Moraga Tennis & Swim Club
Napa
  Exertec Fitness Center
Novato
  Rolling Hills Club
Oakland
  Courthouse Athletic Club (#2)
  The Hills Swim & Tennis Club
    (#5)

  Sports Club at City Center
    Oakland (#7)
  Oakland Hills Tennis Club (#9)
Paradise
  Sporthaven Health Club
Petaluma
  Rancho Arroyo Racquet Club
Pleasanton
  Schoeber's Athletic Club
Redwood City
  Peninsula Covenant
    Community Center
  Pacific Athletic Club
Roseville
  Johnson Ranch Racquet Club
Sacramento
  Capital Athletic Club (#12)
  Alhambra Athletic Club (#13)
  Del Norte Swimming & Tennis
    Club (#16)
  Rio del Oro Racquet Club (#17)
  24 Hour Workout (#18)
  Natomas Racquet Club (#20)
Salinas
  Chamisal Tennis & Fitness Club
San Francisco
  CLUB ONE at Museum Parc
    (#25)
  San Francisco Athletic Club
    (#35)
San Jose
  Schoeber's Athletic Club
  24-Hour Nautilus
San Ramon
  Clubsport
Santa Clara
  Decathlon Club
Santa Rosa
  The Parkpoint Club
  Montecito Heights Health &
    Racquet Club
  La Cantera Racquet & Swim
    Club
Sonoma
  The Parkpoint Club
Stockton
  West Lane Racquet Club
Sunnyvale
  24-Hour Nautilus
Tracy
  Tracy Sports Club
Ukiah
  Redwood Health Club
Vallejo
  Lakeridge Athletic Club

RECIPROCAL IHRSA CLUBS   CONTINUED

Walnut Creek
  Walnut Creek Sports & Fitness
    Club
  Valley Vista Tennis Club
Woodland
  Country Oaks Racquet Club
Yuba City
  Yuba City Racquet & Health
    Club

CALIFORNIA-SOUTHERN
Atascadero
  Kennedy Nautilus Center
Claremont
  The Claremont Club
El Segundo
  Spectrum Club - Manhattan
    Beach
Fullerton
  Sequoia Athletic Club /
    Racquetball World
Irvine
  The Sporting Club
  Racquet Club of Irvine
Laguna Niguel
  Laguna Niguel Racquet Club
Long Beach
  Bally's Sports Connection
Los Angeles
  Marina Athletic Club (#16)
Montclair
  L.A. Fitness
Newport Beach
  University Athletic Club
Ojai
  Ojai Valley Racquet Club
Palm Desert
  Palm Valley Spa & Racquet
    Club
Redlands
  Redlands Swim & Tennis Club
Santa Ana
  Sequoia Athletic Club /
    Racquetball World
Santa Barbara
  Santa Barbara Athletic Club
Santa Monica
  The Club at MGM Plaza
Simi Valley
  Oakridge Athletic Club
Torrance
  South End Racquet & Health
    Club, Inc.
West Hollywood
  Bally's Sports Connection
Woodland Hills
  Warner Center Club

COLORADO
Aurora
  Heartwood Athletic Club
  International Athletic Club

Boulder
  Rally Sport
  Flatiron Athletic Club
Copper Mountain
  Copper Mountain Racquet &
    Athletic Club
Denver
  Athletic Club at Denver Place
    (#3)
  Athletic Club at Monaco (#15)
  Aerobic & Sports Conditioning
    Center (#16)
Englewood
  Greenwood Athletic Club
  Athletic Club at Inverness
  The Sporting Club
Fort Collins
  Fort Collins Pulse Aerobic &
    Fitness Center
Glendale
  Cherry Creek Sporting Club
Greeley
  Greeley Work Out West
Lakewood
  Lakewood Athletic Club
Longmont
  Longmont Athletic Club
Vail
  Vail Athletic Club

CONNECTICUT
Bristol
  New England Health &
    Racquet Club
Cromwell
  Tri-Town Sports
Enfield
  New England Health &
    Racquet Club
  The Club at Bigelow Commons
Farmington
  Farmington Farms Racquet Club
Granby
  Swim Center One
Newington
  New England Health &
    Racquet Club
Stamford
  Sportsplex
  The Stamford Athletic Club
Stratford
  Stratford Club
Wallingford
  Healthworks
West Hartford
  Cornerstone Aquatics Center

DELAWARE
New Castle
  Delaware Swim & Fitness
    Center
Wilmington
  Pike Creek Fitness Club

DISTRICT OF COLUMBIA
Washington
  Tenley Sport & Health Club (#7)
  ANA Hotel, Washington, D.C.
    (#13)

FLORIDA
Boca Raton
  Athletic Club of Boca Raton
Fort Lauderdale
  The Athletic Club at Weston
Gainesville
  Gainesville Health & Fitness
    Center
Miami Beach
  The Spa at the Fontainebleau
    Hilton Resort
Orange Park
  'Q' the Sports Club
Palm Coast
  Belle Terre Swim & Racquet
    Club
Saint Augustine
  Anastasia Athletic Club

GEORGIA
Atlanta
  Peachtree Center Athletic Club
    (#3)
  Sportslife Buckhead (#14)
  Concourse Atheltic Club (#18)
  Sportslife Cobb (#21)
Duluth
  Sportslife Gwinnett
Marietta
  Main Event Fitness

HAWAII
Kohala Coast
  Mauna Lani Racquet Club

IDAHO
Boise
  Park Center Health & Racquet
    Club
  The Court House
Sandpoint
  Sandpoint West Athletic Club

ILLINOIS
Alton
  Nautilus Fitness/Racquet Center
Chicago
  The Randolph Athletic Club (#1)
  Athletic Club at Illinois Center
    (#2)
  East Bank Club (#13)
  Downtown Sports Club (#15)
  Lakeshore Athletic Club (#18)
  President's Fitness Center (#33)
Deerfield
  Multiplex
Downers Grove
  The Esplanade Fitness Center

RECIPROCAL IHRSA CLUBS   CONTINUED

Highland Park
  Forty-One Sports Club
Joliet
  Charlie Fitness Club
Libertyville
  Centre Club
Lisle
  Central Park Athletic Club
Melrose Park
  Gottlieb Health & Fitness Center
Palatine
  Forest Grove Athletic Club
Palos Hills
  Palos Olympic Health &
     Racquet Club
Rosemont
  Rosemont's Willow Creek Club
Springfield
  Club West
Wheaton
  Wheaton Sports Center
Willowbrook
  Willowbrook Athletic Club

INDIANA
Schererville
  Omni 41 Sports & Fitness
    Center

IOWA
West Des Moines
  Fitness World West

KANSAS
Overland Park
  Dales Athletic Club

KENTUCKY
Crestview Hills
  Four Seasons Sports Country
    Club
Lexington
  Lexington Athletic Club
  Lexington Sports Club
Louisville
  American Fitness Centers (#7)
  Blairwood Club (#8)

LOUISIANA
Mandeville
  Franco's Athletic Club
New Orleans
  New Orleans Athletic Club

MAINE
Rockport
  Samoset Resort on the Ocean

MARYLAND
Baltimore
  Downtown Athletic Club (#3)
  Harbor View Health Club (#14)
Bethesda
  Bethesda Sports & Health

Gaithersburg
  Athletic Express Racquet &
    Health Club
  Rio Sports & Health Club
Silver Spring
  The Aspen Hill Club

MASSACHUSETTS
Auburn
  Auburn Racquet & Health Club
Beverly
  New England Health &
    Racquet Club
Boston
  Boston Athletic Club (#31)
Concord
  The Thoreau Club
Dedham
  Dedham Racquetime Athletic
    Club
Framingham
  Suburban Athletic Club
  The Framingham Club
Franklin
  Silver's Health & Fitness Center
Hanover
  New England Health &
    Racquet Club
Haverhill
  Cedardale Athletic Club
Hyannis
  The Tara Club
Lancaster
  Orchard Hills Athletic Club
Lexington
  The Lexington Club
Lynnfield
  The Colonial Club
Manchester
  Manchester Athletic Club
Marlboro
  Wayside Racquet & Swim Club
Nantic
  Longfellow Sports Club
North Dartmouth
  New England Health &
    Racquet Club
North Eastham
  Norseman Athletic Club
Norwood
  Mad Maggie's Health &
    Racquetball Club
Pittsfield
  Berkshire West Athletic Club
Plymouth
  Plymouth Athletic Club
Revere
  North Shore Athletic Club
Watertown
  The Mount Auburn Club
Wayland
  Longfellow Tennis & Fitness
    Club

Wellesley
  Babson Recreation Center
Westboro
  Westboro Tennis & Swim Club
Westford
  Westford Racquet & Fitness
    Club
Weymouth
  Weymouth Club
Worcester
  Worcester Athletic Club

MICHIGAN
Birmingham
  Beverly Hills Racquet & Health
    Club
Davison
  Davison Athletic Club
East Lansing
  Michigan Athletic Club
Flint
  Hurley Health & Fitness Center
Grand Rapids
  East Hills Athletic Club
  Michigan Athletic Club
Livonia
  Park Place Athletic Club
Okemos
  Court One Athletic Clubs
Port Huron
  Birchwood Athletic Club
Roseville
  Rose Shores Fitness &
    Racquet Club
Southfield
  Franklin Fitness & Racquet Club
  CMI-Health & Tennis Club Inc.

MINNESOTA
Brooklyn Center
  Highway 100 North France
    Racquet, Swim & Health
    Club
Eden Prairie
  Flagship Athletic Club
  Crosstown Racquet, Swim &
    Health Club
Fridley
  Moore Lake Northwest
    Racquet, Swim & Health
    Club
Minneapolis
  Arena Club (#2)
  Calhoun Beach Club (#7)
Minnetonka
  Ruth Stricker's The Marsh
Ramsey
  HealthQuest Athletic Club
Rochester
  Rochester Athletic Club
Saint Louis Park
  Northwest Racquet, Swim &
    Health Club

White Bear Lake
  White Bear Racquet & Swim

MISSISSIPPI
Jackson
  The Courthouse Racquet Club
  Courthouse Racquet Club
    Northeast

MONTANA
Billings
  Billings Athletic Club
Helena
  Crossroads Sports & Fitness
    Center
  Broadwater Athletic Club & Hot
    Springs
Kalispell
  Second Wind Sport & Fitness
    Center
Missoula
  Western Montana Sports
    Medicine & Fitness Center

NEBRASKA
Lincoln
  Lincoln Racquet Club
  Cottonwood Club
Omaha
  The Westroads Club

NEVADA
Henderson
  Green Valley Athletic Club
Las Vegas
  Sporting House of Las Vegas
Reno
  Sports West Athletic Club
  Lakeridge Tennis Club

NEW HAMPSHIRE
Exeter
  Results Swim & Fitness
Laconia
  Laconia Athletic & Swim Club
Manchester
  Executive Health & Sports
    Center - Airport
Milford
  Hampshire Hills Sports &
    Fitness
Nashua
  The Royal Ridge Club
Salem
  Salem Athletic Club
Somersworth
  The Works Athletic Club

NEW JERSEY
Allenwood
  The Atlantic Club
Atlantic City
  The Spa at Bally's Park Place
Cherry Hill
  Fitquest

Deptford
  Haddonwood Tennis / Swim &
    Health Club
Egg Harbor Township
  Tilton Athletic Club
Medford
  Eastern Athletic Club
Morristown
  Headquarters Health &
    Racquetball Club
Paramus
  The Health Spa 2
Pompton Plains
  Spa 23 & Racquet Club
Short Hills
  The Hilton at Short Hills
Somers Point
  Eastern Athletic Club

NEW MEXICO
Albuquerque
  Midtown Sports & Wellness
  River Point Swim & Racquet
    Club, Inc.
Farmington
  Royal Spa & Court Club
Santa Fe
  The Club El Gancho
  Quail Run Club

NEW YORK
Briarcliff Manor
  Club Fit
East Islip
  Belfran Health & Fitness Center
East Northport
  The Fitness Club
Fishkill
  All Sport Fitness & Racquet Club
Jefferson Valley
  Club Fit
Loudonville
  Colonie Athletic Club, Inc.
Mount Kisco
  Saw Mill River Club
New Windsor
  Hudson Valley Club
N.Y.C. - Brooklyn
  Paerdegat Athletic Club (#12)
  Starrett at Spring Creek Pool,
    Fitness & Tennis (#14)
N.Y.C. - Manhattan
  Sheraton Manhattan Health
    Club (#28)
  Manhattan Plaza Health Club
    (#38)
Newburgh
  Golds Gym & Athletic Club
White Plains
  Club Fit

NORTH CAROLINA
Fayetteville
  The Sports Center
Greensboro
  Sportime Racquet & Athletic
    Club
Greenville
  Greenville Athletic Club
Morehead City
  Sports Center
Raleigh
  Raleigh Athletic Club
Research Triangle Park
  Imperial Athletic Club
Roanoke Rapids
  Roanoke Athletic Club
Sanford
  Sanford Nautilus & Racquet
    Club

OHIO
Akron
  CitiCenter Athletic Club
Celina
  Lake Front Racquet & Health
    Club
Cincinnati
  Cincinnati Sports Club (#9)
Cleveland
  Athletic Club at One Cleveland
    Center (#31)
Columbus
  Continental Athletic Club
  Sawmill Athletic Club
East Liverpool
  Skylight Health Spa
Toledo
  Aquarius Athletic Club
  St. James Club
  Aquarius Athletic Club South
Westerville
  Westerville Athletic Club

OREGON
Beaverton
  Griffith Park Athletic Club
Bend
  Athletic Club of Bend
Eugene
  Downtown Athletic Club
  Courtsports Athletic Club
Gresham
  Cascade Athletic Club
Keizer
  Courthouse Athletic Club
Milwaukie
  East Side Athletic Club
Pendleton
  Roundup Athletic Club
Portland
  Willamette Athletic Club (#1)
  Cascade Athletic Club (#10)
Salem
  Courthouse Athletic Club (2)

RECIPROCAL IHRSA CLUBS

PENNSYLVANIA
Altoona
  The Summit Athletic Club
Broomall
  Sussex Fitness Center
Chalfont
  Highpoint Athletic Club
Erie
  The Pennbriar Athletic Club
Feasterville
  B & R Full Health & Fitness Club
Monroeville
  The Racquet Club of Pittsburgh
Philadelphia
  The Sporting Club at the
    Bellevue Hotel (#2)
Pittsburgh
  Club One (#18)
  Executive Fitness Center (#22)
Wilkes-Barre
  Odyssey Total Fitness Center

RHODE ISLAND
East Providence
  New England Health &
    Racquet Club
Warwick
  New England Health &
    Racquet Club

SOUTH CAROLINA
Spartanburg
  Spartanburg Athletic Club

TENNESSEE
Brentwood
  Athletic Club Maryland Farms
Memphis
  'Q' The Sports Club
  Wimbleton Sportsplex
Nashville
  Westside Athletic Club

TEXAS
Amarillo
  Gold's Gym
Austin
  The Hills Fitness Center
  'Q' The Sports Club
Corpus Christi
  Corpus Christi Athletic Club
Dallas
  Texas Club (#6)
  The Premier Athletic Club (#10)
  Centrum Sports Club (#15)
  North Dallas Athletic Club (#21)
  Signature Athletic Club (#22)
  Lincoln City Club (#23)
  Tom Landry Sports Medicine &
    Research Center (#24)

Garland
  Northstar Athletic Club
Houston
  The Houstonian Hotel & Club
    (#45)
  Fit Inn / Charlie Club Hotel (#59)
Kingwood
  Kingwood Athletic Club
League City
  The Fitness Center at South
    Shore Harbour
McAllen
  Summit Sports Club
San Antonio
  Concord Athletic Club (#65)
  World Gym (#67, 68, 69, & 73)
Westlake
  The Solana Club
The Woodlands
  Woodlands Athletic Center

UTAH
Park City
  Prospector Athletic Club
Salt Lake City
  Sports Mall (#9)

VERMONT
Essex Junction
  Racquet's Edge Health &
    Fitness Center

VIRGINIA
Alexandria
  The Center Club
Arlington
  Fitness Center at the
    Doubletree Hotel
  Skyline Club at Crystal Park
Ashburn
  Ashburn Village Sports Pavilion
Burke
  Burke Racquet & Swim Club
Chantilly
  The Club at Westfields
Fairfax
  The Fitness Club of Fairfax
Gloucester
  Riverside Wellness & Fitness
    Center - Middle Peninsula
Hampton
  Sentara Hampton Health &
    Fitness Center
Herndon
  Worldgate Athletic Club
McLean
  McLean Racquet & Health Club
  McLean Hilton
  Regency Sport & Health Club
  Sporting Club at Tysons
    Corner

Midlothian
  Woodlake Swim & Racquet Club
  Riverside Wellness & Fitness
    Center - Briarwood
Newport News
  Riverside Wellness & Fitness
    Center
Richmond
  Robious Sports & Fitness Center
Woodbridge
  Devil's Reach Sport & Health
    Club

WASHINGTON
Bellevue
  The Seattle Club Bellevue
  PRO Sports Club
Edmonds
  Harbor Square Athletic Club
Kennewick
  Tri-City Court Club
Puyallup
  Bally's Pacific West
Richland
  Columbia Basin Racquet Club
Seattle
  Gateway Athletic Club (#2)
  Seattle Athletic Club (#5)
  The Seattle Club (#10)
  Highline Athletic Club (#17)
Spokane
  Sta-Fit East
  Sta-Fit North
Tumwater
  Valley Athletic Club Pool
Yakima
  Yakima Athletic Club

WISCONSIN
Brookfield
  Highlander Elite Fitness &
    Racquet Club
Eau Claire
  Eau Claire Athletic Club
Greenfield
  Club Universe
Kohler
  Sports Core

WYOMING
Casper
  Wyoming Athletic Club

RECIPROCAL BALLY'S CLUBS

The following listings are all of the facilities included in the main directory which are operated by the Bally's Health and Tennis Corporation or its subsidiaries, or which have indicated they will admit members of Bally's clubs on a preferred basis. Bally's clubs are shown with the word 'Bally's' included in the club name, although some of them may not use it in their signage, advertising or telephone listings. Most Bally's clubs offer a variety of membership options, some of which may not include reciprocal access to other Bally's facilities.

ARIZONA
Glendale
  Bally's U.S. Swim & Fitness
Phoenix
  Bally's U.S. Swim & Fitness
    (#10 & 11)
Tucson
  Bally's U.S. Swim & Fitness
    (#28)

CALIFORNIA-NORTHERN
Sacramento
  Alhambra Athletic Club (#13)

CALIFORNIA-SOUTHERN
Anaheim
  Bally's Holiday Spa
Cerritos
  Bally's Holiday Spa
Chatsworth
  Bally's Holiday Spa
Costa Mesa
  Bally's Sports Connection
Fullerton
  Bally's Holiday Spa
Hollywood
  Bally's Holiday Spa
Huntington Beach
  Bally's Holiday Spa
Long Beach
  Bally's Holiday Spa
  Bally's Sports Connection
Montclair
  Bally's Holiday Spa
Montebello
  Bally's Holiday Spa
North Hollywood
  Bally's Holiday Spa
Riverside
  Bally's Holiday Spa
San Diego
  Bally's Holiday Spa (#23)
Santa Monica
  Bally's Sports Connection
Torrance
  Bally's Sports Connection
West Covina
  Bally's Holiday Health Spa
West Hollywood
  Bally's Sports Connection
West Los Angeles
  Bally's Holiday Spa

COLORADO
Arvada
  Bally's Holiday Health &
    Fitness Center

Aurora
  Bally's Holiday Health &
    Fitness Center
Colorado Springs
  Bally's U.S. Swim & Fitness
Copper Mountain
  Copper Mountain Racquet &
    Athletic Club
Littleton
  Bally's Southwest

CONNECTICUT
Middlebury
  Bally's Holiday Matrix Fitness

FLORIDA
Altamonte Springs
  Bally's Health & Racquet Club
Boca Raton
  Bally's Scandianvian Health &
    Fitness Center
Clearwater
  Bally's Health & Racquet
    Center
  Bally's Total Fitness
Davie
  Bally's Scandinavian Health &
    Fitness Center
Fort Lauderdale
  Bally's Scandinavian Health &
    Fitness Center
Miami
  Bally's Scandinavian Health &
    Fitness Center
North Miami Beach - Aventura
  Bally's Scandinavian Health &
    Fitness Center
Orlando
  Bally's Bay Hill (#7)
  Bally's South Orlando (#13)
Seminole
  Bally's Total Fitness
Tampa
  Bally's Total Fitness (#20 & 23)
West Palm Beach
  Bally's Scandinavian Health &
    Fitness Center
Winter Park
  Bally's Health & Racquet

GEORGIA
Norcross
  Bally's Holiday Health Club
Roswell
  Bally's Holiday Health Club
Smyrna
  Bally's Holiday Health Club

Tucker
  Bally's Northlake

ILLINOIS
Aurora
  Bally's Chicago Health Club
Calumet City
  Bally's Chicago Health Club
Chicago
  Bally's Chicago Health Club
    (#3, 5, 11, 52, & 54)
  Bally's Health Club (#8)
Countryside
  Bally's Chicago Health Club
Deerfield
  Bally's Chicago Health Club
Fairview Heights
  Bally's Vic Tanny
Glendale Heights
  Bally's Chicago Health Club
Lombard
  Bally's Chicago Health Club
Matteson
  Bally's Chicago Health Club
Melrose Park
  Bally's Chicago Health Club
Morton Grove
  Bally's North Shore Health
    Club
Mount Prospect
  Bally's Chicago Health Club
Oak Lawn
  Bally's Chicago Health Club
Oak Park
  Bally's Chicago Health Club
Orland Park
  Bally's Chicago Health Club
Rockford
  Bally's Rockford Health Club
Vernon Hills
  Bally's Chicago Health Club

INDIANA
Greenwood
  Bally's Scandinavian Health
    Spa
Indianapolis
  Bally's Scandinavian Health
    Spa (#10 & 12)

KANSAS
Overland Park
  Bally's Health & Racquet

MARYLAND
Greenbelt
  Bally's Holiday Health Spa

RECIPROCAL BALLY'S CLUBS   CONTINUED

Rockville
Bally's Holiday Health Spa
White Marsh
Bally's Holiday Health Spa

MASSACHUSETTS
Cambridge
Bally's Holiday Health Club
Lowell
Bally's Holiday Health Club
Peabody
Bally's Holiday Health Club
Revere
Bally's Holiday Health Club
Worcester
Bally's Holiday Health Club

MICHIGAN
Ann Arbor
Bally's Vic Tanny (2)
Bloomfield Hills
Bally's Vic Tanny
Dearborn
Bally's Vic Tanny
Novi
Bally's Vic Tanny
Plymouth
Bally's Vic Tanny
Redford
Bally's Vic Tanny
Saint Clair Shores
Bally's Vic Tanny
Southfield
Bally's Vic Tanny
Sterling Heights
Bally's Vic Tanny
Troy
Bally's Vic Tanny
Waterford
Bally's Vic Tanny

MINNESOTA
Bloomington
Bally's U.S. Swim & Fitness
Eagan
Bally's U.S Swim & Fitness
Fridley
Bally's U.S. Swim & Fitness
Little Canada
Bally's U.S. Swim & Fitness
New Hope
Bally's U.S. Swim & Fitness
Richfield
Bally's U.S. Swim & Fitness
Saint Paul
Bally's U.S. Swim & Fitness
(#13)

MISSOURI
Clayton
Bally's Vic Tanny
Crestwood
Bally's Vic Tanny
Independence
Bally's Health & Racquet

Manchester
Bally's Vic Tanny
Maryland Heights
Bally's Vic Tanny
Saint Ann
Bally's Vic Tanny
Saint Charles
Bally's Vic Tanny

NEW JERSEY
Brick
Bally's Jack LaLanne
East Brunswick
Bally's Jack LaLanne
Englewood Cliffs
Bally's Jack LaLanne
Springfield
Bally's Jack LaLanne
Voorhees
Bally's Holiday Fitness Center

NEW YORK
Amherst
Bally Matrix Fitness Center
Bay Shore
Bally's Jack LaLanne
Copaigue
Bally's Jack LaLanne
De Witt
Bally Matrix Fitness Center
Lake Grove
Bally's Jack LaLanne Fitness
Center
Levittown
Bally's Jack LaLanne Fitness
Center
N.Y.C. - The Bronx
Bally's Jack LaLanne (#2)
N.Y.C. - Brooklyn
Bally's Jack LaLanne (#11)
N.Y.C. - Manhattan
Bally's Jack LaLanne Health
Spa (#19)
Bally's The Vertical Club (#23,
27, & 31)
Rochester
Bally's Holiday Health &
Fitness Center (#59)

NORTH CAROLINA
Charlotte
Bally's Holiday Health Club
(#8)

OHIO
Akron
Bally's Scandinavian Health
Spa
Beachwood
Bally's Scandinavian Health
Spa
Brook Park
Bally's Scandinavian Health
Spa
Canton

Bally's Scandinavian Health
Spa
Centerville
Bally's Vic Tanny
Cincinnati
Bally's Scandinavian (#13)
Columbus
Bally's Scandinavian Holiday
Spa
Kettering
Bally's Vic Tanny
Maple Heights
Bally's Scandinavian Health
Spa
Sylvania
Bally's Vic Tanny
Toledo
Bally's Vic Tanny
Westlake
Bally's Scandinavian Health
Spa
Willoughby
Bally's Scandinavian Health
Spa

OKLAHOMA
Tulsa
Bally's Health Club

PENNSYLVANIA
Bethel Park
Bally's Scandinavian Health
Spa
King of Prussia
Bally's Holiday Spa
Penn Hills
Bally's Scandinavian Health
Spa
Philadelphia
Bally's Holiday Fitness Center
(#17)
Willow Grove
Bally's Holiday Spa

RHODE ISLAND
East Providence
Bally's Holiday Health Center

TENNESSEE
Knoxville
Bally's Holiday Fitness Center

TEXAS
Arlington
Bally's President's Health Club
(#4)
Dallas
Bally's President's Health Club
(#7, 16, &19)
Fort Worth
Bally's President's Health Club
(#26)
Garland
Bally's President's Health Club

RECIPROCAL BALLY'S CLUBS CONTINUED

Houston
  Bally's President & First Lady
    Health Club (#40, 46, 48,
    51, 53, 54, 55, 58, 60, &
    61)
Hurst
  Bally's President's Health Club
Plano
  Bally's President's Health Club
San Antonio
  Bally's President's Health Club
    (#74)
Webster
  Bally's President & First Lady
    Health Club

VIRGINIA
Alexandria
  Bally's Holiday

Chesapeake
  Bally's Holiday Health Club
Newport News
  Bally's Health & Fitness
Virginia Beach
  Bally's Health Club

WASHINGTON
Bellevue
  Bally's Pacific West
Federal Way
  Bally's Pacific West
Kent
  Bally's Pacific West
Kirkland
  Bally's Pacific West
Lynnwood
  Bally's Pacific West

Olympia
  Bally's Pacific West
Puyallup
  Bally's Pacific West
Tacoma
  Bally's Pacific West

WISCONSIN
Brookfield
  Bally's Vic Tanny
Cudahy
  Bally's Vic Tanny
Madison
  Bally's Vic Tanny
Milwaukee
  Bally's Downtown Club
West Allis
  Bally's Vic Tanny

CITIES WITH YWCAS

Below are listed all of the cities where we located YWCAs with year-round swimming pools and the names of non-YWCA facilities which honor YWCA membership. In the interest of conserving space, the individual YWCA names are not listed. Most YWCAs are called 'The YWCA of [city name]' and are easy to locate within the main directory. The names of non-YWCA facilities which honor YWCA membership are included after the name of the cities in which they are listed.

We believe that most YWCAs permit visiting YWCA members to swim on the same basis as local members, but we were unable to verify reciprocity policies for the facilities we contacted by telephone.

ARKANSAS
El Dorado
Little Rock

CALIFORNIA-NORTHERN
San Francisco - Swimming &
  Fitness at the Sheehan
  Hotel (#21)

CALIFORNIA-SOUTHERN
Glendale
San Bernardino

CONNECTICUT
Greenwich
Hartford
New Britain
New Haven
Waterbury

DISTRICT OF COLUMBIA
Washington (#1)

FLORIDA
West Palm Beach

GEORGIA
Brunswick
Macon
Marietta

HAWAII
Honolulu (#2)

ILLINOIS
Alton

Bloomington
Danville
Decatur
Evanston
Freeport
Pekin
Peoria
Rock Island
Rockford
Springfield

INDIANA
Anderson
Evansville
Fort Wayne
Greensburg - Decatur County
  YMCA
Hammond
Kokomo
Lafayette
Muncie
Terre Haute

IOWA
Burlington
Clinton
Des Moines
Dubuque
Muscatine
Ottumwa
Sioux City - Siouxland Y
Waterloo

KANSAS
Salina
Topeka

KENTUCKY
Lexington

MAINE
Bangor
Lewiston
Portland

MASSACHUSETTS
Boston
  YWCA of Boston (#6)
  Hyde Park Family Branch
    YMCA (#29)
Cambridge - Cambridge Family
  YMCA
New Bedford
Newburyport
Worcester

MICHIGAN
Bay City
Flint
Grand Rapids
Lansing
Monroe - Monroe Family YMCA
Redford

MINNESOTA
Brainerd - Brainerd Family
  YMCA
Minneapolis (2) (#3 & #5)

CITIES WITH YWCAS — CONTINUED

Saint Paul (#10)
Winona

MISSOURI
Kansas City
Raytown
Saint Louis (#4)

NEBRASKA
Lincoln

NEVADA
Reno

NEW HAMPSHIRE
Nashua

NEW JERSEY
Jersey City
New Brunswick
Newark
Orange
Princeton
Ridgewood
Summit
Trenton

NEW YORK
Buffalo
Cortland
Elmira
New Windsor
N.Y.C. - Brooklyn (#10)
N.Y.C. - Manhattan (#29)
Poughkeepsie
Schenectady
Troy
Utica
White Plains

NORTH CAROLINA
Asheville
Charlotte (#5)
Greensboro
High Point
Raleigh
Winston-Salem

OHIO
Bryan
Cincinnati (#1)
Cleveland (#28)
Columbus
Lakewood - Lakewood Y
Lima
Massillon
Middleburg Heights
Newark
Tallmadge
Toledo
Warren
Youngstown

OKLAHOMA
Oklahoma City
Tulsa (2)

OREGON
Portland (#4)
Salem

PENNSYLVANIA
Allentown
Burnham - Juniata Valley YMCA
Chester
Erie
Gettysburg
Hazleton
Johnstown
Lancaster
Meadville

Philadelphia (#16)
Pittsburgh (#25)
Washington
Williamsport
York

SOUTH CAROLINA
Greenville
  YWCA of Greenville
  Cleveland Street YMCA

SOUTH DAKOTA
Sioux Falls

TENNESSEE
Knoxville

TEXAS
Beaumont
Corpus Christi
Dallas (#8)
El Paso
Houston (#42)
Lubbock
Richardson
Waco
Wichita Falls

UTAH
Salt Lake City (#7)

VIRGINIA
Danville
Dunn Loring
Roanoke

WEST VIRGINIA
Charleston

WISCONSIN
Green Bay
Racine
Waukesha

RECIPROCAL IPFA CLUBS

The following are all of the listings in the main directory which have indicated that they will admit members of International Physical Fitness Association (IPFA) affiliated clubs on a preferred basis. Unless otherwise noted, reciprocal privileges are available at no charge at IPFA affiliated clubs more than 25 miles from the home club, for up to 30 consecutive days.

ARIZONA
Chandler
  L.A. Fitness & Sports Club

CALIFORNIA-NORTHERN
Capitola
  Spa Fitness Center
Sacramento
  Alhambra Athletic Club (#13)

CALIFORNIA-SOUTHERN
Downey
  Imperial Spa, Inc.

San Diego
  Family Fitness Center (#30)
  California Health Spas (#32)
COLORADO
Copper Mountain
  Copper Mountain Racquet &
    Athletic Club
Englewood
  American Fitness, Inc.

GEORGIA
Duluth
  Workout America

Kennesaw
  Workout America
Riverdale
  Workout America

ILLINOIS
Belleville
  Belleville Fitness Center

INDIANA
Greenwood
  Bally's Scandinavian Health
    Spa

RECIPROCAL IPFA CLUBS   **CONTINUED**

Indianapolis
  Super Spa Fitness Center (#7)
  Bally's Scandinavian Health
    Spa (#10 & 12)

KENTUCKY
Louisville
  American Fitness Centers (#7
    & 10)

MARYLAND
Baltimore
  The Baltimore Sports Club
    (#11)

MICHIGAN
Ann Arbor
  Bally's Vic Tanny
Dearborn
  Bally's Vic Tanny
Grandville
  Premier Athletic Center
Novi
  Bally's Vic Tanny
Plymouth
  Bally's Vic Tanny
Redford
  Bally's Vic Tanny
Saint Clair Shores
  Bally's Vic Tanny
Southfield
  Bally's Vic Tanny
Sterling Heights
  Bally's Vic Tanny
Troy
  Bally's Vic Tanny
Waterford
  Bally's Vic Tanny

MINNESOTA
Bloomington
  Bally's U.S. Swim & Fitness

MISSOURI
Kansas City
  Gold's Gym
Lees Summit
  Summit Fitness
Springfield
  Northpark Fitness Center

NEW JERSEY
Manahawkin
  Stafford Pool & Fitness Center

NEW YORK
Binghamton
  Sneakers Fitness Center
East Islip
  Belfran Health & Fitness Center
Johnson City
  Court Jester Athletic Club
N.Y.C - The Bronx
  Bally's Jack LaLanne (#2)
Rochester
  Bally's Holiday Health &
    Fitness Center (#59)

NORTH CAROLINA
Asheville
  Gold's Gym & Athletic Club
  Spa Health Club
Gastonia
  GAC Fitness Today
West End
  Forever Fit Nautilus

OHIO
Akron
  Bally's Scandinavian Health Spa
Beachwood
  Bally's Scandinavian Health Spa
Brook Park
  Bally's Scandinavian Health Spa
Canton
  Bally's Scandinavian Health Spa
Cincinnati
  Bally's Scandinavian (#13)
Columbus
  Bally's Scandinavian Holiday
    Spa
Kettering
  Bally's Vic Tanny
Milford
  Royal Health & Fitness
Sylvania
  Bally's Vic Tanny
Toledo
  Aquarius Athletic Club
  St. James Club
  Bally's Vic Tanny
  Aquarius Athletic Club South
Westlake
  Bally's Scandinavian Health Spa
Willoughby
  Bally's Scandinavian Health Spa

OKLAHOMA
Oklahoma City
  All American Fitness Center

OREGON
Portland
  USA Oregon Athletic Club (#13)

PENNSYLVANIA
Bethel Park
  Bally's Scandinavian Health
    Spa
Philadelphia
  Pennypack Aquatic & Fitness
    Center (#3)
  Nirvana (#4)
  Bally's Holiday Fitness Center
    (#17)

RHODE ISLAND
West Warwick
  American Health Fitness
    Center

TEXAS
Austin
  HQ Fitness
Houston
  Olympia Fitness & Racquetball
    Club (#56)
San Antonio
  World Gym (#67, 68, 69, & 73)
Weatherford
  Health Forum

VIRGINIA
Alexandria
  Bally's Holiday
Chesapeake
  Bally's Holiday Health Club
Newport News
  Bally's Health & Fitness
Virginia Beach
  Bally's Health Club

WASHINGTON
Tumwater
  Valley Athletic Club Pool

WISCONSIN
Madison
  Princeton Club

U.S. MILITARY LISTINGS

The facilities listed below are located on U.S. Military installations and are accessible to U.S. Armed Forces personnel and their families and to authorized employees of the Department of Defense; or they are non-military facilities which have indicated that members of the U.S. Military are admitted on a preferential basis.

ALASKA
Fort Richardson
  Buckner Physical Fitness
    Center Swimming Pool
Ketchikan
  Kayhi Pool

ARKANSAS
Little Rock
  Downtown YMCA

CALIFORNIA-SOUTHERN
San Diego
  The Field House Pool (#40)
  Naval Station Indoor Pool (#41)
  Base Pool (#42)

CONNECTICUT
New Britain
  New Britain-Berlin YMCA
Stamford
  Stamford YMCA
Wilton
  Wilton Family Y

FLORIDA
Jacksonville
  Jacksonville Naval Air Station
    Pool

INDIANA
Anderson
  Anderson YMCA
Elkhart
  Elkhart YMCA
Evansville
  YMCA of Southwestern Indiana
Greensburg
  Decatur County YMCA
La Porte
  La Porte Family YMCA
Muncie
  Muncie Family YMCA
South Bend
  YMCA of Michiana

IOWA
Cedar Rapids
  Central YMCA

Clinton
  Clinton Family YMCA
Mason City
  Mason City Family YMCA

LOUISIANA
Harvey
  Manhattan Athletic Club

MARYLAND
Easton
  Talbot YMCA

MASSACHUSETTS
Middleboro
  Old Colony YMCA

MICHIGAN
Birmingham
  Metro Detroit YMCA
Monroe
  Monroe Family YMCA

MINNESOTA
Austin
  Austin YMCA
Red Wing
  Red Wing YMCA
Rochester
  Rochester Area Family YMCA

NEW YORK
Cortland
  Cortland County Family YMCA
Huntington
  Huntington YMCA
N.Y.C. - Manhattan
  1199 Plaza Rec. Center (#35)

NORTH CAROLINA
Gastonia
  Gaston County Family YMCA

OHIO
Ashland
  Ashland YMCA
Cambridge
  Cambridge Area YMCA
Canton
  Canton Downtown YMCA

Lancaster
  Lancaster Family YMCA
Lebanon
  Countryside YMCA
Lorain
  Lorain Family YMCA
Sandusky
  Sandusky Area YMCA
Youngstown
  Youngstown Area Jewish
    Federation (JCC)

OREGON
Portland
  Princeton Athletic Club (#5)

PENNSYLVANIA
Carlisle
  Carlisle YMCA
Corry
  Corry YMCA
Kittanning
  Armstrong County YMCA
New Kensington
  YMCA of New Kensington

VIRGINIA
Fort Belvoir
  Benyaurd Indoor Pool
Petersburg
  YMCA of Southside Virginia

WASHINGTON
NSB Bangor
  Bangor Pool
Seattle
  Sandpoint Naval Station Pool
    (#6)

WISCONSIN
Stevens Point
  Stevens Point Area YMCA

JCC & YM-YWHA LISTINGS

The following are all of the listings in the main directory which are Jewish Community Centers (JCCs) or YM-YWHAs. At the time we were conducting our research we were not aware that the two organizations are affiliated, so we did not ask JCCs whether they honor YM-YWCA memberships, and *vice versa*. We subsequently found out about the affiliation and have combined them in one list for this Appendix. Most JCCs and YM-YWHAs do offer some form of reciprocal access privileges. If you belong to one or the other, you'll probably get a break at most of the facilities listed below.

For those who do not belong to either, please note that most JCC and YM-YWHA facilities are closed on Friday evenings and Saturday mornings in observance of the Jewish Sabbath. Additionally, some may offer male-only or female-only pool sessions. Jewish faith or heritage is not necessarily a requirement for membership in a JCC or YM-YWHA.

CALIFORNIA-NORTHERN
Los Gatos
  Addison Penzac Jewish
    Community Center
Palo Alto
  Albert L. Schultz Jewish
    Community Center
San Francisco
  San Francisco Jewish
    Community Center (#41)
San Rafael
  Marin Jewish Community
    Center

CALIFORNIA-SOUTHERN
La Jolla
  Lawrence Family Jewish
    Community Center of San
    Diego County
Los Angeles
  Westside Jewish Community
    Center (#6)

CONNECTICUT
Stamford
  Stamford JCC
West Hartford
  Greater Hartford Jewish
    Community Center

FLORIDA
Boca Raton
  Levis Jewish Community
    Center
Davie
  Jewish Community Center
Miami
  Jewish Community Center
North Miami Beach - Aventura
  Michael Ann Russell Jewish
    Community Center
West Palm Beach
  Jewish Community Center of
    the Palm Beaches

GEORGIA
Atlanta
  Jewish Community Center (#6)

INDIANA
Indianapolis
  Jewish Community Center
    (#13)

MARYLAND
Rockville
  Jewish Community Center

MASSACHUSETTS
Worcester
  Worcester JCC

MICHIGAN
Monroe
  Monroe Family YMCA
West Bloomfield
  Jewish Community Center

MISSOURI
Saint Louis
  Jewish Community Centers
    Association (#13)

NEW JERSEY
Cherry Hill
  Jewish Community Center of
    Southern New Jersey
Margate
  Jewish Community Center
Tenafly
  Jewish Community Center
West Orange
  Jewish Community Center
    Metro West

NEW YORK
Albany
  Albany Jewish Community
    Center

Buffalo
  Jewish Center
Getzville
  Jewish Center of Greater
    Buffalo, Inc.
N.Y.C. - Bronx
  Riverdale YM-YWHA (#3)
N.Y.C. - Manhattan
  Educational Alliance Emanu-El
    Midtown Y (#15)
  Center For Health, Fitness &
    Sport (#40)
Plainview
  Mid Island Y JCC
Scarsdale
  YM YWHA of Mid-Westchester
Schenectady
  Jewish Community Center of
    Schenectady

OHIO
Youngstown
  Youngstown Area Jewish
    Federation (JCC)

PENNSYLVANIA
Philadelphia
  Gershman YM/YWHA (#15)
Pittsburgh
  Jewish Community Center
    (#21)

TENNESSEE
Memphis
  Jewish Community Center

WASHINGTON
Mercer Island
  Stroum Jewish Community
    Center

RECIPROCAL NACA CLUBS

Members of clubs affiliated with the Northwest Athletic Club Association (NACA) are admitted to the following listed clubs on a preferential basis:

CALIFORNIA-NORTHERN
Chico
  Kangaroo Kourts
Sacramento
  Alhambra Athletic Club (#13)

COLORADO
Copper Mountain
  Copper Mountain Racquet &
    Athletic Club

IDAHO
Boise
  The Court House
Sandpoint
  Sandpoint West Athletic Club

OREGON
Bend
  Athletic Club of Bend
Clackamas
  East Side Athletic Club

Coos Bay
  Bay Area Athletic Club
The Dalles
  The Dalles Fitness & Court Club
Eugene
  Downtown Athletic Club
Hood River
  Hood River Sports Club
Keizer
  Courthouse Athletic Club
Lake Oswego
  River's Edge Athletic Club
Milwaukie
  East Side Athletic Club
Pendleton
  Roundup Athletic Club
Portland
  Willamette Athletic Club (#1)
Salem
  Courthouse Athletic Clubs (2)

WASHINGTON
Arlington
  Stillaguamish Athletic Club
Bellevue
  The Seattle Club Bellevue
Edmonds
  Harbor Square Athletic Club
Kennewick
  Tri-City Court Club
Richland
  Columbia Basin Racquet Club
Spokane
  North Park Racquet/Athletic
    Club
Yakima
  Yakima Athletic Club

GOLD'S GYMS

The following listings are all of the facilities included in the main directory which are affiliated with Gold's Gyms or which have indicated they will admit members of clubs affiliated with Gold's Gyms on a preferred basis. Members of affiliated clubs should obtain a 'Gold's Gym Travel Card', which will entitle them to a limited number of free visits to other Gold's Gyms.

CALIFORNIA-NORTHERN
Sacramento
  Alhambra Athletic Club (#13)

CALIFORNIA-SOUTHERN
Redondo Beach
  Executive Gold's Gym

COLORADO
Copper Mountain
  Copper Mountain Racquet &
    Athletic Club

MISSOURI
Kansas City
  Gold's Gym

NEW HAMPSHIRE
Portsmouth
  Gold's Gym & Athletic Club

NEW YORK
De Witt
  Gold's Gym at Sundown
Liverpool
  Gold's Gym at Sundown

Newburgh
  Gold's Gym & Athletic Club

NORTH CAROLINA
Asheville
  Gold's Gym & Athletic Club

TEXAS
Amarillo
  Gold's Gym
Denton
  Gold's Gym

CSI CLUBS

The following listings are all of the facilities included in the main directory which have indicated that they will admit members of clubs affiliated with Club Sports International ('CSI') on a preferred basis:

CALIFORNIA-NORTHERN
Sacramento
  Alhambra Athletic Club (#13)

COLORADO
Copper Mountain
  Copper Mountain Racquet &
    Athletic Club

Denver
  Aerobic & Sports Conditioning
    Center (#16)

OHIO
Cleveland
  Athletic Club at One Cleveland
    Center (#31)

TENNESSEE
Brentwood
  Athletic Club Maryland Farms

TEXAS
Dallas
  Signature Athletic Club (#22)
Kingwood
  Kingwood Athletic Club

SWIMMERS GUIDE DISCOUNTS

The following clubs offer visiting owners of the current edition of *Swimmers Guide* preferential access to their facilities. To take advantage of the offer, you must call the club in advance and show your copy of *Swimmers Guide* to the reception desk when you check in.

CALIFORNIA-NORTHERN
Citrus Heights
  Willow Creek Racquet Club
Fair Oaks
  Rollingwood Racquet Club

MARYLAND
Baltimore
  Downtown Athletic Club (#3)

MASSACHUSETTS
Lexington
  The Lexington Club

NEW JERSEY
Deptford
  Haddonwood Tennis / Swim &
    Health Club

NORTH CAROLINA
Asheville
  Gold's Gym & Athletic Club

SWIMMING SUPPLY MAIL ORDER COMPANIES

Few sporting goods stores offer much variety in swim suits, goggles or other swimming accessories. Mail order suppliers offer a wider selection of products and styles, often at very good prices. Swimmers will want to be on the mailing list of one or more of the following companies:

Companies which sell swim suits and other swimming supplies manufactured by several companies:

World Wide Aquatics
Toll-free: 800-726-1530
International: 813-972-0818
Fax: 813-972-0905

USA Aquatics
Toll free: 800-445-8721
International: 702-831-8326
Fax: 702-831-1826

Adolph Kiefer & Associates
Toll-free: 800-323-4071
In Illinois and International: 708-872-8866
Fax: 708-746-8888

Companies which specialize in products of one manufacturer, but may include some products from others.

ISHOF Mail Order Company
(The Finals® brand swim suits.)
Toll-free: 800-431-9111
Fax: 305-525-4031

The Victor
(The Victor™ brand swim suits.)
Toll-free: 800-356-5132
International: 305-821-7067
Fax: 305-828-3628

Aardvark Swim & Sport
(TYR® brand swim suits.)
Toll-free: 800-729-1577
International: 703-631-6045
Fax: 703-968-3293

Rothhammer International Inc.
(Sprint® brand water fitness equipment, swimming aids, pool games, etc.)
Toll-free: 800-235-2156
International: 805-481-2744
Fax: 805-489-0360

Other mail order retailers whose advertisements we have seen, but whose catalogs we have not received:

Action Accents
Toll-free: 800-338-0231
Fax: 515-279-4136

Competitive Aquatic Supply
Toll-free: 800-421-5192

Kast-A-Way Swimwear
Toll-free: 800-543-2763

NorCal Swim Shop
Toll-free: 800-752-7946

Sportwide
Toll-free: 800-631-9684

Swim Zone
Toll-free: 800-329-0013
International: 813-822-7946

TruWest
Toll-free: 800-322-3669

Triathletetes will be especially interested in:

Road Runner Sports
Toll free: 800-551-5558
International: 619-622-0439

ORDERING INFORMATION
If you can't find *Swimmers Guide* at your local bookstore, you can order a copy directly from the publisher. Send a check or money order for $16.95 to:

ALSA Publishing, Inc.
P.O. Box 1064
Stuart, FL 34995

Your book will be sent via U.S. Postal Service 'Book Rate', please allow three to four weeks for delivery. For delivery to Florida addresses, add $1.02 for state sales tax. We're sorry, C.O.D. and credit card orders cannot be accepted.